Enhancing Commu
& Collaboration in
Interdisciplinary Research

To the students whose resolve to transcend disciplinary thinking and insight into how to do so have inspired and informed this volume.

Enhancing Communication & Collaboration in Interdisciplinary Research

Michael O'Rourke
Michigan State University

Stephen Crowley
Boise State University

Sanford D. Eigenbrode
University of Idaho

J. D. Wulfhorst
University of Idaho

Editors

Los Angeles | London | New Delhi
Singapore | Washington DC

Los Angeles | London | New Delhi
Singapore | Washington DC

FOR INFORMATION:

SAGE Publications, Inc.
2455 Teller Road
Thousand Oaks, California 91320
E-mail: order@sagepub.com

SAGE Publications Ltd.
1 Oliver's Yard
55 City Road
London EC1Y 1SP
United Kingdom

SAGE Publications India Pvt. Ltd.
B 1/I 1 Mohan Cooperative Industrial Area
Mathura Road, New Delhi 110 044
India

SAGE Publications Asia-Pacific Pte. Ltd.
3 Church Street
#10-04 Samsung Hub
Singapore 049483

Acquisitions Editor: Vicki Knight
Editorial Assistant: Jessica Young
Production Editor: Laura Barrett
Copy Editor: Megan Granger
Typesetter: C&M Digitals (P) Ltd.
Proofreader: Laura Webb
Indexer: Terri Corry
Cover Designer: Candice Harman
Marketing Manager: Nicole Elliott
Permissions Editor: Adele Hutchinson

Copyright © 2014 by SAGE Publications, Inc.

Printed in the United States of America

Library of Congress Cataloging-in-Publication Data

Enhancing communication & collaboration in interdisciplinary research / [edited by] Michael O'Rourke, Michigan State University, Stephen Crowley, Boise State University, Sanford D. Eigenbrode, University of Idaho, J. D. Wulfhorst, University of Idaho.

pages cm
Includes bibliographical references and index.

ISBN 978-1-4522-5566-8 (pbk. : alk. paper)

1. Interdisciplinary research. I. O'Rourke, Michael, 1963-II. Title: Enhancing communication and collaboration in interdisciplinary research.

Q180.55.I48E54 2013
001.4—dc23   2013012626

This book is printed on acid-free paper.

13 14 15 16 17 10 9 8 7 6 5 4 3 2 1

Brief Table of Contents

Detailed Table
of Contents

Preface

Hofstadter's Law famously states: "It always takes longer than you expect, even when you take into account Hofstadter's Law."[1] Where the study of interdisciplinarity is concerned, one must acknowledge the corollary that not only does it take longer than you expect—it will be far harder and much more puzzling as well.

The editors of this volume initially came together as a result of an attempt to solve a small although not insignificant issue in interdisciplinary pedagogy at the University of Idaho. The issue: What is the best way to facilitate communication and collaboration between members of interdisciplinary research teams participating in the university's National Science Foundation–sponsored Integrative Graduate Education and Research Traineeship (IGERT) project? Seven years of hard work have generated insights and enlightenment, but much remains to be done with the issues that arose out of that initial "small" problem.

Our work on the nature of interdisciplinary communication and collaboration led us to organize an international conference on that topic that met in Coeur d'Alene, Idaho, from September 30 to October 2 of 2010. That conference, "Enhancing Communication in Cross-Disciplinary Research" (ECCDR), brought together experts in cross-disciplinary research, both practitioners and theorists, to discuss solutions to the communication challenges that confront collaborative research. The goal was to generate new ideas and useful insights about cross-disciplinary communication through robust conversation among cross-disciplinary research practitioners, specialists in the interdisciplinary process, and philosophers and sociologists of integrated science.

---

[1]Hofstadter, D. (1999). *Gödel, Escher, Bach: An eternal golden braid* (20th anniversary ed.). Cambridge, MA: Basic Books, p. 152.

The essays in this volume began life as presentations at ECCDR. All presenters at the conference were encouraged to submit proposals for chapters that could be included in this collection, and after a process of peer evaluation, only a few were selected. We regret that we had to turn down numerous quality proposals, due to space limitations.

Acknowledgments

This volume is based on work supported by the National Science Foundation under Grant No. SES-0823058 and IGERT Grant No. 0114304. Any opinions, findings, and conclusions or recommendations expressed in this material are those of the authors and do not necessarily reflect the views of the National Science Foundation. We are also grateful to the Interdisciplinary Activities Grant program (College of Graduate Studies, University of Idaho) and the Fund for Interdisciplinary Teams (Environmental Science Program, University of Idaho) for project support that led to the production of this book.

As noted in the Preface, this volume originated in the ECCDR conference held September 30 to October 2, 2010, in Coeur d'Alene, Idaho. We are grateful to the University of Idaho, Boise State University, and the Coeur d'Alene Resort Hotel for assistance in planning and funding ECCDR. At the University of Idaho, we were supported by President M. Duane Nellis and his office, Katherine Aiken, Douglas D. Baker and his office, Kjelda Berg, Steven B. Daley-Laursen, Teresa Dillon, Barbara Ham, Melissa Erwin Jones, Douglas Lind, John K. McIver, Nathan Myatt, Virginia Pellegrini, Tania Thompson, and Kathleen Zillinger. Mark Rudin, the vice president for research at Boise State University, provided financial support for ECCDR. Scott Shellman at Framework Meetings was a critical part of making the meeting run smoothly. We are also grateful to Christoph Bellardi, Tricia Krisher, Kathy Larson, and the staff at The Coeur d'Alene Resort.

The members of the Toolbox Project have provided substantial assistance to us in preparing this volume: Nilsa Bosque-Pérez, Brian Crist, Ruth Dahlquist, Shannon Donovan, Troy E. Hall, Renée Hill, Justin Horn, Chris Looney, Ian O'Loughlin, Sara Pepper, Liela Rotschy, Brianne Tice Suldovsky, and our advisers Frank Davis, Paul E. Griffiths, and Julie Thompson Klein.

Our Advisory Board contributed significantly to determining the approach to communication and collaboration that we have adopted. They also reviewed all the chapter proposals we received and advised us concerning which should become chapters in the volume. Once received, each chapter was evaluated in a blind process by several referees. We are grateful to those who contributed very useful critical commentary: Betsy Wackernagel Bach, University of Montana; Gabriele Bammer, The Australian National University; Jan Boll, University of Idaho; Nilsa Bosque-Pérez, University of Idaho; Ingo Brigandt, University of Alberta; Adam Briggle, University of North Texas; Frank Davis, University of California, Santa Barbara; Bruce Glymour, Kansas State University; Michael E. Gorman, University of Virginia; Troy E. Hall, University of Idaho; Graham Hubbs, University of Idaho; Joann Keyton, North Carolina State University; Julie Thompson Klein, Wayne State University; Tim A. Kohler, Washington State University; Holly Falk-Krzesinski, Elsevier; William Newell, Miami University; Christian Pohl, ETH Zurich; Thomas P. Seager, Arizona State University; Matthew Slater, Bucknell University; Daniel Stokols, University of California, Irvine; David Stone, Northern Illinois University; Paul B. Thompson, Michigan State University; and Kyle Powys Whyte, Michigan State University.

We also received valuable assistance from several reviewers for SAGE Publications: Jennifer J. Henderson, Virginia Tech University; Dave Conz, Arizona State University; Richard Castellana, Fairleigh Dickinson University; Julie Borkin, Oakland University; Walter C. Metz, Southern Illinois University–Carbondale; Betsy Greenleaf Yarrison, University of Baltimore; Karen G. Bell, Delta State University; Marcia Hines-Colvin, Saint Mary's University of Minnesota; Khadijah O. Miller, Norfolk State University; Jill LeRoy-Frazier, East Tennessee State University; James Welch IV, University of Texas–Arlington; Barbara J. Holtzclaw, University of Oklahoma; Tinola Mayfield-Guerrero, Owens Community College; and Angela Hunter, University of Arkansas at Little Rock.

Finally, we are very grateful to our publisher at SAGE, Vicki Knight, and her staff for sharing our excitement about this project and for making it happen as painlessly as possible!

Advisory Board

Betsy Wackernagel Bach, *University of Montana*

Gabriele Bammer, *The Australian National University*

Frank Davis, *University of California, Santa Barbara*

Holly Falk-Krzesinski, *Elsevier*

Steve Fiore, *University of Central Florida*

Paul E. Griffiths, *University of Sydney*

Troy E. Hall, *University of Idaho*

Joann Keyton, *North Carolina State University*

Julie Thompson Klein, *Wayne State University*

William Newell, *Miami University*

Gary Olson, *University of California, Irvine*

Eduardo Salas, *University of Central Florida*

Daniel Stokols, *University of California, Irvine*

About the Editors

Michael O'Rourke is professor of philosophy and faculty in AgBioResearch at Michigan State University. His research interests include environmental philosophy; the nature of epistemic integration and communication in collaborative, cross-disciplinary research; and the nature of linguistic communication between intelligent agents. He is director of the Toolbox Project, a NSF-sponsored research initiative that investigates philosophical approaches to facilitating interdisciplinary research. He was principal investigator on the NSF-funded project "Improving Communication in Cross-Disciplinary Collaboration" (SES-0823058), which extended the development and application of the "Toolbox" method designed to improve communication and understanding among members of cross-disciplinary research teams. He has published extensively on the topics of communication, interdisciplinary theory and practice, and robotic agent design. He has been a coprincipal investigator or collaborator on funded projects involving autonomous underwater vehicles, biodiversity conservation, sustainable agriculture, and resilience in environmental systems. He cofounded and served as codirector of the Inland Northwest Philosophy Conference, an interdisciplinary conference on philosophical themes, and as coeditor of the Topics in Contemporary Philosophy series published by MIT Press.

Stephen Crowley is associate professor of philosophy at Boise State University. He is a graduate of Indiana University (Bloomington), where he was part of a rich interdisciplinary community (philosophers, computer scientists, psychologists, and biologists) working on issues in animal cognition. He was also a founding member of the Indiana University Philosophy Department's Empirical Epistemology Laboratory—a group focused on applying methods from the social sciences to issues within the theory of knowledge in particular as well as philosophy more generally. Since arriving at Boise State, Stephen, while continuing to work on providing a coherent intellectual framework for empirical philosophy, has focused his research on developing an understanding of the barriers to and mechanisms for conducting interdisciplinary collaborative research. Some of this work involves agent-based modeling, but the major focus has been on empirically informed investigation with the Toolbox Project (http://www.cals.uidaho.edu/toolbox/) at the University of Idaho. As a side project, Steve spends time wondering why things are so much easier in theory than in practice when it comes to interdisciplinary collaboration!

Sanford D. Eigenbrode is University Distinguished Professor and chair of entomology at the University of Idaho. He received a BS in biology, an MS in natural resources, and a PhD in entomology from Cornell University. Sanford conducts research on chemical ecology of insect–plant and multitrophic interactions. He has expertise in host plant resistance, natural products chemistry, scanning electron microscopy, and integration of host plant resistance into insect pest management. Recently, he has focused on the chemical ecology, landscape ecology, and management of insect-vectored viruses of wheat, potatoes, and legumes. He is director of a NIFA-funded Risk Avoidance and Mitigation Program project on legume virus risk mitigation. His landscape ecology research has included study of insect pests affecting coffee agroforestry systems in Costa Rica. He is coprincipal investigator on a renewed NSF-IGERT project on Resilience of Ecological and Social Systems in Changing Landscapes and coordinator of the Joint Doctoral Program between the University of Idaho and CATIE (Tropical Agricultural Research and Higher Education Center) in Turrialba, Costa Rica. He is project director for a $20-million NIFA Coordinated Agricultural Project on Regional Approaches to Climate Change in Pacific Northwest Agriculture. As an outgrowth of these broadly interdisciplinary, collaborative projects, Sanford is engaged in research and education focused on improving the process of collaborative science, which continues to thrive through his engagement with the ECCIR volume and the project that has produced it.

J. D. Wulfhorst is professor of rural sociology and chair of the board of advisors for the Social Science Research Unit at the University of Idaho. He received a BA in interdisciplinary studies from Appalachian State University, an MS in sociology from the University of Kentucky, and a PhD in rural sociology from Utah State University. He has expertise in risk perceptions, constraints to adoption of technology in farm systems, conflict in rangeland management, and the negotiated order(s) of natural resource management. Recently, he has begun work in the area of climate science related to agricultural systems, societal adaptation, and community resilience. He has developed a niche as a social scientist collaborating with interdisciplinary teams addressing natural resource and agricultural challenges within the western United States. As a member of this editorial team, J. D. has developed an interest in team-based research processes, especially with respect to how social dynamics affect groups with turnover and institutional change.

About the Contributors

Gabriele Bammer is a professor at The Australian National University (ANU). She is developing the new discipline of Integration and Implementation Sciences (I2S) to improve research strengths for tackling complex real-world problems through synthesis of disciplinary and stakeholder knowledge, understanding and managing diverse unknowns, and providing integrated research support for policy and practice change (see http://i2s.anu.edu.au). This is described in her latest book, *Disciplining Interdisciplinarity: Integration and Implementation Sciences for Researching Complex Real-World Problems* (ANU E Press, 2013). She is director of the Research School of Population Health and of the National Centre for Epidemiology and Population Health, ANU College of Medicine, Biology and Environment. She is also an ANU public policy fellow, a research fellow at the Program in Criminal Justice Policy and Management at Harvard University's John F. Kennedy School of Government, and the convenor of the ARC Centre of Excellence in Policing and Security's Integration and Implementation research program.

L. Michelle Bennett is the deputy scientific director for the National Heart Lung and Blood Institute (NHLBI), National Institutes of Health. The NHLBI Intramural Research Program comprises intramural scientists and clinicians working in basic, translational, and clinical research. Dr. Bennett is responsible for scientific programmatic oversight, strategic planning, and implementing strategies to support the research mission. Previously, she was a deputy director at the CCR, NCI, where she developed and implemented projects and activities that cut across a broad range of scientific areas to accelerate research progress. She has been engaged in the practical aspects of facilitating collaboration, has extensive practical experience in promoting team-based approaches by bringing together research scientists with diverse backgrounds and expertise to solve complex scientific problems. She has published works highlighting the fundamental characteristics that contribute to successful scientific team functioning, including a workbook, *Collaboration and Team Science: A Field Guide,* that serves as a primer for investigators who are building or participating on a research team. She has been invited to give numerous presentations, conduct workshops, and work with groups interested in learning to better implement successful strategies for building and sustaining scientific collaborations and research teams. She has experience working with people one-on-one and in teams to meet their individual objectives, overcome challenges, and improve their group dynamics for successful team functioning.

Stuart Blythe is an associate professor of rhetoric and writing at Michigan State University. His research interests include technical communication and the intersections of public and expert discourse on environmental policy.

Daniel Boden is a doctoral candidate at the Center for Public Administration and Policy at Virginia Tech. He holds a master's degree in public administration from Virginia Tech and a bachelor's degree in history from Brigham Young University. His current research interests are higher education policy, organization theory, and collaborative management.

Richard D. Boone is professor of ecosystem ecology in the Department of Biology and Wildlife and the Institute of Arctic Biology at the University of Alaska Fairbanks. He received his BA in biology from Oberlin College, MS in forest ecology from Oregon State University, and PhD in forest soils from the University of Massachusetts, Amherst. Boone served as chair of the Department of Biology & Wildlife from 2006 to 2010 and as associate dean of undergraduate studies in the College of Natural Science and Mathematics from 2010 to 2011. During his tenure as chair he promoted and facilitated a shift in instruction from lecturing to a blended approach with active learning. He also served as the principal investigator of an NSF-funded GK–12 project that pairs STEM graduate students (fellows) with K–12 teachers and their students over a full academic year; the fellows gain teaching and communication skills and bring their research and inquiry-based approaches to the K–12 classroom. Currently, Boone is serving as a program director in the Integrative Graduate Education and Research Traineeship program at the U.S. National Science Foundation. Professional interests include stimulating a shift in STEM graduate student education from an apprenticeship model to a traineeship model that emphasizes the broader professional development of graduate students. Boone was appointed as an Aldo Leopold Leadership Fellow in 2001 and a National Academies Education Fellow in the Life Sciences in 2007.

Maura Borrego is an associate professor and former director of the Graduate Program in the Department of Engineering Education at Virginia Tech, and is currently serving as a program director in the Division of Undergraduate Education at the National Science Foundation. She recently held a 2010–2011 AAAS Science & Technology Policy Fellowship at the National Science Foundation. Dr. Borrego's research interests focus on interdisciplinary faculty members and graduate students in engineering and science. Dr. Borrego holds a U.S. NSF CAREER Award and Presidential Early Career Award for Scientists and Engineers for this research. She is an editorial board member for *Journal of Engineering Education* and chair of the American Society for Engineering Education's Educational Research and Methods Division. All Dr. Borrego's degrees are in materials science and engineering. Her MS and PhD are from Stanford University, and her BS is from University of Wisconsin–Madison.

Nilsa A. Bosque-Pérez is a professor of entomology and 16-year member of the University of Idaho College of Agricultural and Life Sciences faculty. She directs the university's National Science Foundation–funded Interdisciplinary Graduate Education and Research Traineeship program, which funds interdisciplinary teams of students and faculty working on resilience of social–ecological systems in Idaho and Costa Rica. The program has created a unique team-based interdisciplinary graduate educational model that has received recognition across the country. She is also a member of the Toolbox Project and has been engaged in interdisciplinary research and graduate education throughout her career. She additionally conducts research on plant-virus-vector interactions, host plant resistance to insects, and the impact of diverse land uses and management practices on insect pollinators of plants.

Steven L. Bosserman is the founder of Bosserman & Associates, Inc., a management consulting firm specializing in strategic framing and organizational design. Steve enables clients to tap emerging trends in markets, technologies, and work and to develop business initiatives that increase stakeholder participation, rate of innovation/adaptation, and commercialization of products/services. His deliverables include convening and moderating networks, communities, and teams to be more responsive in the face of opportunities; coaching leaders on how to improve their decision making in conjunction with organizational culture and performance metrics; and guiding members to be more consequent and intentional with their communications both within and outside the organization. During the 1994 to 2001 period, Steve cofounded WorkSpan, Inc.—a consulting firm specializing in systems change strategies for land-grant universities, foundations, government agencies, and professional societies. Services included delivery of leadership for institutional change workshops; development of internal strategies for change predicated on convening and facilitating conversations that would not occur otherwise; and coaching of individuals/teams dedicated to influencing organizational performance. Many of these concepts are outlined in the book he coauthored, *Together We Can: Pathways to Collective Leadership in Agriculture at Texas A&M*. Steve's recent focus is in sustainable local economic development and community self-reliance through the introduction of value network structures, value accounting systems, and complementary currencies.

Sarah E. Cornell is an environmental scientist with a research background in global environmental dynamics and a strong interest in improving ways to integrate different discipline-based knowledges about the world we live in. She currently coordinates the steadily expanding Planetary Boundaries Research Network, an international collaboration initiative for global sustainability led by the Stockholm Resilience Centre. In her previous role, she was the science manager and synthesis leader for the UK Natural Environment Research Council's £23-million program *Quantifying and Understanding the Earth System*. She established the United Kingdom's first master's programme in earth system science at the University of Bristol, which aimed explicitly at providing transdisciplinary training and learning. Sarah has also worked in environmental consultancy and policy roles, including as sustainability advisor to a UK government cabinet member and as a contributor to the United Kingdom's Foresight projects. These experiences underpin her view that there is no substitute for deep and gritty dialogue in building good interdisciplinary understandings.

Michael M. Crow became the 16th president of Arizona State University (ASU) on July 1, 2002. He is guiding the transformation of ASU into one of the nation's leading public metropolitan research universities, an institution that combines the highest levels of academic excellence, inclusiveness to a broad demographic, and maximum societal impact—a model he designed, known as the "New American University." Under his leadership, ASU has established major interdisciplinary research initiatives such as the Biodesign Institute, Global Institute of Sustainability, and more than a dozen new transdisciplinary schools, and witnessed an unprecedented academic infrastructure expansion, tripling of research expenditures, and attainment of record levels of diversity in the student body. Crow was previously executive vice provost of Columbia University, where he served as chief strategist of Columbia's research enterprise and technology transfer operations. He has been an advisor to the U.S. Departments of State, Commerce, and Energy, as well as defense and intelligence agencies, on matters of science and technology policy in areas related to intelligence and national security. He is a fellow of the American Association for the Advancement of Science and National Academy of Public Administration, and a member of the Council on Foreign Relations and U.S. Department of Commerce National Advisory Council on Innovation and Entrepreneurship. He is the author of books and articles analyzing science and technology policy and the design of knowledge enterprises. Crow received his PhD in public administration (science and technology policy) from the Maxwell School of Citizenship and Public Affairs, Syracuse University.

William B. Dabars is Research Fellow for University Design in the Office of the President, Arizona State University. He has served in various research capacities for the University of Southern California, University of California, Santa Barbara, and Getty Research Institute, where he participated in editorial projects focused on aesthetic and architectural theory. He has also served as an editorial consultant for the Getty Conservation Institute and University of Colorado, Boulder. He received a PhD in history from the University of California, Los Angeles. His dissertation, publications, and current research focus on the American research university.

Shannon Donovan received her BS in wildlife management from the University of New Hampshire, her MS in recreation, parks and tourism resources from West Virginia University, and her PhD in environmental science from the University of Idaho (UI). At UI, she served as a National Science Foundation Integrative Graduate Education and Traineeship fellow working on two interdisciplinary projects designed to craft conservation strategies for the Volcánica Central de Talamanca Biological Corridor of Costa Rica and the Palouse region of the Inland Northwest. Shannon has served as both a post-doc and affiliate researcher for the Toolbox Project. She is currently an assistant professor of environmental studies at the University of Alaska. She is working on the forest plan revision process with the Chugach National Forest and researches food security issues and needs within the state of Alaska. Outside of work, Shannon can be found playing outdoors with her son and husband.

Robert Frodeman (PhD, philosophy; MS, geology) is professor of philosophy and former chair of the Department of Philosophy and Religious Studies at the University of North Texas (UNT), where he specializes in environmental philosophy, the philosophy of science policy, and the philosophy of interdisciplinarity. He served as a consultant for the U.S. Geological Survey for 8 years, was the 2001–2002 Hennebach Professor of the Humanities at the Colorado School of Mines, and was an ESRC fellow at Lancaster University in England in the spring of 2005. In addition to more than 80 published articles and $1.8 million in federal grants, Frodeman is the author and/or editor of nine books, including *Geo-Logic: Breaking Ground Between Philosophy and the Earth Sciences* (SUNY, 2003), the *Encyclopedia of Environmental Ethics and Philosophy* (MacMillan, 2008), and the *Oxford Handbook of Interdisciplinarity* (OUP, 2010). Frodeman is the founding director of the Center for the Study of Interdisciplinarity at UNT (www.csid.unt.edu).

Howard Gadlin has been ombudsman and director of the Center for Cooperative Resolution at the National Institutes of Health since the beginning of 1999. From 1992 through 1998 he was university ombudsperson at UCLA. He was also director of the UCLA Conflict Mediation Program and codirector of the Center for the Study and Resolution of Interethnic/Interracial Conflict. While in Los Angeles, Dr. Gadlin served as consulting ombudsman to the Los Angeles County Museum of Art. Prior to coming to UCLA, Dr. Gadlin was ombudsperson and professor of psychology at the University of Massachusetts, Amherst. At present, Dr. Gadlin is studying the dynamics of scientific teams and collaborations. An experienced mediator, trainer, and consultant, Dr. Gadlin has years of experience working with conflicts related to race, ethnicity, and gender, including sexual harassment. Currently, he is developing new approaches to addressing conflicts among scientists. He is often called in as a consultant/mediator in "intractable" disputes. Dr. Gadlin has designed and conducted training programs internationally in dispute resolution, sexual harassment, and multicultural conflict. Dr. Gadlin is the author of, among other writings, "Bargaining in the Shadow of Management: Integrated Conflict Management Systems," "Conflict, Cultural Differences, and the Culture of Racism," and "Mediating Sexual Harassment." He is the coauthor of "Neutrality: What an Organizational Ombudsperson Might Want to Know" and "Conflict Resolution and Systemic Change." Most recently, he has coauthored "Collaboration and Team Science: A Field Guide."

Ardyth H. Gillespie is an associate professor in the Division of Nutritional Sciences at Cornell University, where she coleads the Family and Community Food Decision-Making Program with community-based partners. Along with her research on the processes and pathways of family and community food decision making, she has focused on developing methodology for advancing transdisciplinary research on the complex relationships and dynamics of changing both food systems and food and eating practices and for integrating research with campus education and community-based practice. Developers and practitioners of this evolving methodology, called collaborative engaged research (CER), seek to improve health and well-being of children, youth, and their families by fostering thoughtful, collective food decision making in families and communities. Through CER, Gillespie and her collaborators engage families and community change agents, students, and scholars in building local capacity for collective decision making and for generating and applying new knowledge about family and community food decision-making systems. Gillespie is a past president of the Society for Nutrition Education and Behavior and currently a faculty fellow in the David R. Atkinson Center for a Sustainable Future at Cornell University. Gillespie is also a collaborator faculty member at Iowa State University and coleader of the Harrisdale Homestead CER Leadership Institute.

Paul E. Griffiths was educated at University of Cambridge and Australian National University (ANU), receiving his doctorate from ANU in 1989. After teaching in Australia and New Zealand, he moved to the University of Pittsburgh in 2000, returning to Australia in 2004 as an Australian Research Council Federation fellow. Currently, he is based at the University of Sydney, where he is university professorial research fellow in the Department of Philosophy and associate academic director for humanities and social sciences at the Charles Perkins Centre, a multidisciplinary research institute focused on obesity, diabetes, and cardiovascular disease. He is also a visiting professor in the ESRC Centre for Genomics in Society at the University of Exeter, United Kingdom. He is a fellow of the American Association for the

Advancement of Science; fellow of the Australian Academy of the Humanities; president of the International Society for History, Philosophy and Social Studies of Biology; and from 2006 to 2012 was a member of the Australian Health Ethics Committee of NHMRC.

Casey Hoy is a professor and former associate chairman of the Ohio State University Department of Entomology and has held the Kellogg Endowed Chair in Agricultural Ecosystems Management since 2006, providing leadership to the interdisciplinary Agroecosystems Management Program. He received both BS and PhD degrees in entomology from Cornell University. Casey's past research has included systems analysis and its application to integrated pest management and applied ecology. His current work is developing the theoretical and applied knowledge base essential to advancements in agroecosystem health and sustainable agricultural communities. Casey also leads development of sustainable agriculture degree programs in Ohio and outreach focused on building social networks that promote entrepreneurship in diverse agricultural enterprises. His recent service includes various federal grant review panels, the Ohio Food Policy Advisory Council, the Cuyahoga Valley Countryside Conservancy Board of Trustees and the executive committee for the Inter-institutional Network for Food and Agricultural Sustainability, a Kellogg-endowed national network of agriculture and food system leaders. Together with his coauthors, Casey hopes to continue developing practical approaches for pursuing interdisciplinary as well as intercultural communication challenges and opportunities.

Julie Thompson Klein is professor of humanities in the English Department and faculty fellow for Interdisciplinary Development in the Division of Research at Wayne State University. She has also held appointments as visiting foreign professor in Japan, Fulbright lecturer in Nepal, foundation visitor at the University of Auckland, New Zealand, and Mellon fellow and visiting professor of digital humanities at the University of Michigan. In addition, she was senior fellow at the Association of American Colleges and Universities and the Center for the Study of Interdisciplinarity. Holder of a PhD in English from the University of Oregon, Klein is past president of the Association for Interdisciplinary Studies (AIS) and former editor of the AIS journal. Her books include *Interdisciplinarity: History, Theory, and Practice* (1990); *Interdisciplinary Studies Today* (coedited, 1994); *Crossing Boundaries: Knowledge, Disciplinarities, and Interdisciplinarities* (1996); *Transdisciplinarity* (coedited, 2001); *Interdisciplinary Education in K–12 and College* (edited, 2002); the monograph *Mapping Interdisciplinary Studies* (1999); *Humanities, Culture, and Interdisciplinarity* (2005); and *Creating Interdisciplinary Campus Cultures* (2010). She was also associate editor of the *Oxford Handbook on Interdisciplinarity* (2010). Klein has received awards at Wayne State University and was honored with the Kenneth Boulding Award for outstanding scholarship on interdisciplinarity, Yamamoorthy & Yeh Distinguished Transdisciplinary Achievement Award, and Joseph Katz Award for Distinguished Contributions to General and Liberal Education. She is currently coeditor of the University of Michigan Press series Digital Humanities@digitalculturebooks and is completing a new book on mapping digital humanities.

Benson P. Lee is the founding CEO of Technology Management, Inc., which is commercializing energy solutions based on a proprietary, kilowatt-scale solid oxide fuel cell technology developed by Standard Oil of Ohio and acquired from British Petroleum. He received his BEE and master's certificate in engineering from Cornell University and completed all coursework for his MBA and PhD at the NYU Graduate School of Business. After working in industry for IBM and Westinghouse, he founded Biolectron, which successfully commercialized a medical device to heal broken bones using electricity. As a practicing social entrepreneur, he is experienced using private-sector solutions to solve public-sector problems at the formative stages, where entrepreneurial championship, innovation, and invention have the greatest impact. His interdisciplinary approach evolved from decades of problem solving on nonprofit boards, including Cornell University, where he is an Emeritus Trustee, The Cleveland Foundation, the world's first community foundation with assets of more than $2 billion, and on visiting and advisory committees for technology commercialization, engineering, business, and sustainability for Cornell, University of Pennsylvania, Case Western Reserve, Cleveland State and Baldwin Wallace universities. He is currently committed to the commercialization of fuel cells for distributed generation as a new U.S. industry and for distributed infrastructure in developing countries where fuel cells, embedded in a business framework and converting indigenous renewable biofuels into electricity, can sustain economic development, improved public health, and affordable local services for 1.3 billion people now living without electricity. His goal is to demonstrate for replication by other social entrepreneurs how a social enterprise business model can manage an energy technology as an asset and generate the economic returns required to attract continuing investments from public, private, and philanthropic sources.

Arika Ligmann-Zielinska is an assistant professor in the Department of Geography and Environmental Science and Policy Program at Michigan State University. She is a PhD graduate from a Joint Doctoral Program in Geography at San Diego State University and University of California Santa Barbara. She got her MS in geography from Adam Mickiewicz University in Poznan, Poland. Her research activities encompass a broad range of modeling approaches that capture the dynamic relationships within coupled human and natural systems. To date, her core research has focused on agent-based modeling of land use change and water quality in various exurban areas across the United States. She has also pioneered spatiotemporal sensitivity analysis of model output. This exploratory technique allows for partition model outcome variability such that the underlying causes of the simulated emerging phenomena (like urban land development, water pollution, and deforestation) can be identified and adequately addressed. As part of her teaching agenda, Arika has contributed to the development of a modeling curriculum at Michigan State University. She has also coauthored a modeling workbook titled "Agent Analyst: Agent-Based Modeling in ArcGIS," which exposes students to the theoretical as well as practical challenges in integrative agent-based model building.

Chris Looney is an entomologist with the Washington State Department of Agriculture. Dr. Looney's research has focused on the diversity and conservation of epigeal beetles, gall-inducing wasps, and native bees in eastern Washington State. He has also participated in interdisciplinary research exploring social and biophysical dimensions of conservation in fragmented, working landscapes and approaches to improving communication within interdisciplinary research teams. His current projects include documenting the spread of exotic Lepidoptera pests in Washington State and building an online information and resource center for Pacific Northwest sawflies.

Ross B. MacDonald is a research scientist in the Ohio State University Department of Entomology, providing leadership in curricular and program development. He holds a BA degree in English literature from the University of California at Berkeley, an MA degree also in English literature from California State University at Chico, and an individual major PhD in instructional communication from the University of California at Davis. He is the former director of the Program in Science and Society in the College of Agricultural and Environmental Sciences at UC Davis and has also worked with several nonprofit organizations on peace and justice issues in Haiti, Iran, and the Basque Region of Spain. His specialty is issue-based learning and action achieved through collaborations with diverse partners across cultures and disciplines. He is also known for his extensive work on behalf of postsecondary tutoring programs. Ross continues to work with creative individuals to develop innovative curricular approaches to address important contemporary issues at the intersection of science and society.

Sandra Marquart-Pyatt is an associate professor of sociology and environmental science and policy at Michigan State University. Her research interests are in the areas of comparative social change, environmental sociology, political sociology, and quantitative methods. Her current work focuses on identifying cross-national patterns on an array of environmental attitudes, beliefs, behavioral intentions, and behaviors that include climate change, general concern for the environment, and sustainability. She has published numerous articles on the application of advanced quantitative techniques to pressing global social issues related to the environment and politics, including environmental concern, democratic values, and views of the state. She is coauthor of the monograph *Nonrecursive Models: Endogeneity, Reciprocal Relationships and Feedback Loops* in the SAGE series Quantitative Applications in the Social Sciences. She has also been an instructor in the InterUniversity Consortium for Political and Social Research's Summer Program in Quantitative Methods at the University of Michigan for a graduate seminar on simultaneous equation models.

Wayde C. Morse is an assistant professor in the School of Forestry and Wildlife Sciences at Auburn University. He received his PhD in 2007 from the University of Idaho, Department of Conservation Social Sciences and from the Center for Tropical Agricultural Research and Higher Education in Costa Rica. The combined degree is the result of an innovative multi-institutional program funded by the National Science Foundation's Integrative Graduate Education and Research Traineeship program. Morse's research interests include linked social–ecological systems, conservation decision making and behavior, ecosystem services, issues of scale, volunteer tourism, and outdoor recreation in the United States and Latin America. He has research projects in Costa Rica, Guatemala, and Ecuador, and throughout the southern United States. Morse has been a guest editor for a special issue in the journal *Urban Ecosystems* and has been an associate editor for the journal *Society and Natural Resources*. He currently serves on the Alabama Trails Commission.

M. Duane Nellis was the president of the University of Idaho and is the new president of Texas Tech University. As the chief executive officer of Idaho's nationally recognized research and land-grant university, he was responsible for nearly 14,000 employees and students as well as a budget in excess of $453 million. That responsibility extended to more than 70 education, research, and extension facilities. He also served as a commissioner for the Northwest Commission of Colleges and Universities and the Western Interstate Commission for Higher Education. At Texas Tech University, Nellis will oversee a comprehensive national research university with 32,500 students and an overall budget approaching $800 million. He has also held other leadership positions and continues to be active in other national and international bodies, including the Association of Public and Land-Grant Universities; the Association of American Geographers; the National Council for Geographic Education; and Gamma Theta Upsilon, the international geographic honor society. Previously, he served as provost and senior vice president at Kansas State University. He also served as dean of the Eberly College of Arts and Sciences, West Virginia University's largest academic college. He also has been recognized for his research and teaching by the Association of American Geographers and the Institute of British Geographers. In addition, he is a fellow of the American Association for the Advancement of Science.

Laura Schmitt Olabisi is an assistant professor at Michigan State University, jointly appointed in the Environmental Science & Policy Program and the Department of Community, Agriculture, Recreation, and Resource Studies. She is a systems ecologist and modeler, often working directly with stakeholders using participatory model-building techniques. Laura's past and present research has addressed soil erosion, population growth, greenhouse gas emissions, water sustainability, energy use, deforestation, adoption of organic/sustainable agricultural techniques, climate change and human migration, and climate change and human health. Laura holds a BS in environmental science from Brown University and a PhD from the State University of New York College of Environmental Science and Forestry.

Prior to her appointment at Michigan State, she worked as a postdoctoral researcher with the Ecosystem Science and Sustainability Initiative, housed at the University of Minnesota. Together with coauthors Arika Ligmann-Zielinska and Sandra Marquart-Pyatt, Laura is helping create a master's level environmental modeling certificate at Michigan State, which will be offered beginning in fall semester 2013.

Jenneth Parker, PhD (Sussex), Msc (LSE), BA (Cardiff), Cert Ed, is a research director at the Schumacher Institute, dedicated to 'putting people at the heart of a sustainable economy'. She has a background in philosophies of science, social science, and ethics, which underpins her approach to transdisciplinary research on sustainability. She has undertaken policy work for UNESCO and the European Union. She is currently working on the transdisciplinary critique and synthesis aspects of the EU Framework Programme 7–funded CONVERGE project. In addition to her academic qualifications, she is a qualified adult and community educator and experienced facilitator in participatory planning events.

David Pietrocola is a robotics and software engineer with a variety of experiences in research, government, and industry. During his 18-month appointment at the National Science Foundation, David served as the analyst for the IGERT program in the Division of Graduate Education. His contributions spanned a variety of projects and initiatives, a portfolio analysis of the IGERT program, a report to Congress on communication of science training for IGERT trainees, and a forthcoming NSF report on recent trends and outcomes from IGERT awards. David earned an MS in systems engineering from the University of Pennsylvania and a BS in electrical engineering with honors and Phi Beta Kappa from Trinity College in Hartford, Connecticut. He has published and presented peer-reviewed research in several areas, including autonomous mobile robots, agent-based modeling, virtual agents, human behavior modeling, serious games, digital copyright laws, and graduate education. He has helped develop several award-winning autonomous robots for outdoor navigation in uncertain environments and has been an organizer for the Trinity College Fire-Fighting Home Robot Contest since 2006. He is a member of IEEE, the IEEE-USA Intellectual Property Committee, and the IEEE-USA Research and Development Committee.

Melur K. Ramasubramanian is D. W. Reynolds Professor of Mechanical Engineering and department chair at Clemson University, South Carolina. He also holds a joint faculty position in bioengineering. Prior to that, he was most recently program director for the Integrative Graduate Education and Research Traineeship program at the National Science Foundation from July 2009 to 2012 and a professor of mechanical and aerospace engineering, North Carolina State University, Raleigh, from 1994. In addition, he held an associate appointment with the Joint UNC-NC State Biomedical Engineering Department. He was the director of the Mechatronics Program in Mechanical Engineering, jointly administered with Electrical and Computer Engineering, an interdisciplinary graduate program. He received his PhD in mechanical engineering from Syracuse University in 1987 and worked in Research and Development, Georgia Pacific Corporation, as a research associate from 1987 to 1994, when he joined NC State University as an assistant professor. He has a vibrant externally funded research program and currently advises two PhD students. His current research interests are in the area of biomimetics, microfluidics and tissue engineering, biomechatronics, and computational mechanics. Current research projects include mosquito biting mechanics and applications to painless microneedle design, microencapsulation of islets for xenotransplantation using 3-D microfluidics, implantable sensors (passive MEMS intraocular pressure sensor), near-bedside opto-fluidic sensors for blood agglutination detection, and computational mechanics. He is a fellow of ASME and TAPPI, and a senior member of IEEE and EMBS.

Liela Rotschy is a graduate student in linguistics at The Ohio State University, focusing on formal semantics and pragmatics. She has an MA in teaching English as a second language from the University of Idaho, where she became involved with the Toolbox Project in 2010. As a member of the project she has contributed to development of the translational health science and climate science applications of the Toolbox approach.

Carol F. Stoel is a program officer for the Interdisciplinary Graduate Education Research Traineeships program, the Science Master's Program, and for evaluation activities in the Division of Graduate Education in the Education and Human Resources Directorate of the National Science Foundation (NSF). She has been in the Graduate Division since 2004 and was the acting division director from June 2007 through February 2009. Prior to joining NSF in 2004, Ms. Stoel worked in the nonprofit and higher education sectors. She served as vice president of the Council for Basic Education and director of its Schools Around the World program, comparing student work and teacher development practices across nine industrialized countries; principal partner of the Education Trust at the American Association for Higher Education, developing K–16 partnerships; and director of the American Association for University Women's Foundation, funding graduate dissertation fellowships for U.S. and international women and developing the Eleanor Roosevelt Fund to attract more young women into science and engineering studies. At the University of Maryland's University College she served as vice chancellor and at Hood College as the associate provost and executive assistant to the president. From 1973 to 1984, Ms. Stoel served as deputy director and program officer for the Fund for Improvement of Postsecondary Education in the Department of Education. Her BA is from Connecticut College for Women and her MAT from Harvard Graduate School of Education.

Daniel Stokols is Research Professor and Chancellor's Professor Emeritus in psychology and social behavior and planning, policy, and design at the University of California, Irvine (UCI). He holds courtesy appointments in public health, epidemiology, and nursing sciences at UCI. Dr. Stokols served as director and founding dean of the School of Social Ecology at UCI between 1988 and 1998. He is coauthor of *Behavior, Health, and Environmental Stress* (1986) and coeditor of the *Handbook of Environmental Psychology* (1987), *Environmental Simulation* (1993), and *Promoting Human Wellness* (2002). Dr. Stokols is recipient of the Career Award from the Environmental Design Research Association and UCI's Lauds & Laurels Faculty Achievement Award. Stokols served as scientific consultant to the National Cancer Institute (NCI), Division of Cancer Control and Population Sciences, and as a member of NCI's Science of Team Science (SciTS) team between 2005 and 2011. He is currently a team science consultant for the National Academies Keck Futures Initiative. Stokols's research interests include (1) SciTS and factors that influence the success of transdisciplinary research and training programs; (2) the environmental psychology of the Internet, especially the ways qualities of virtual life affect people's behavior and well-being; (3) the health and behavioral impacts of environmental stressors such as traffic congestion, crowding, and information overload; (4) the application of environmental design research to urban planning and facilities design; and (5) the design and evaluation of community health promotion programs.

David A. Stone is the associate vice president for research and an associate professor of public health at Northern Illinois University. He holds two interdisciplinary degrees (MA and PhD) from the University Professors Program at Boston University, the former combining studies in law, psychiatry, and phenomenological philosophy, and the latter combining philosophy of science, philosophy of technology, substantivist economics, sociology of work, organizational behavior, cognitive science, and expert systems. Over the past 20 years, Dr. Stone has served as an academic research scientist (public policy, health services research, public health, and clinical medicine research) at the Harvard School of Medicine, the Harvard School of Public Health, the Tufts University School of Medicine, and Sheffield University (UK). He has also served as founding director of the South East European Research Center (Greece), director of the Boston Violence Prevention Project at the Harvard School of Public Health, cofounder of the Pediatric and Adolescent Research Center at Tufts University, and director of the Fenway Health Center Research Department in Boston. As an interdisciplinary researcher and team scientist, Dr. Stone has published and taught in clinical medicine, public health, health services research, health policy, philosophy, political science, research administration and management. His most recent work seeks to provide a transdisciplinary hermeneutic basis for our understanding of interdisciplinarity.

Karola Stotz is an Australian research fellow in the Department of Philosophy at the University of Sydney. Her research contributes to a reconciliation of nature and nurture, a dualism that stands in the way of a full understanding of development, evolution, and heredity. She has been instrumental in importing this debate into cognitive science and psychology (http://nanu.dynalias. org). Together with Paul E. Griffiths, she pioneered the use of "experimental philosophy" methods in the field of philosophy of science, analyzing the diversification of the gene concept in different research communities within contemporary biology (http://representinggenes.org). This work has received significant attention from biologists and was discussed in *Nature* (441: 398–401). More recently, she and her collaborators have turned their attention to the concepts of innateness and human nature. With Griffiths, she coauthored *Genetics and Philosophy* (Cambridge University Press, April 2013), which combines enthusiasm for the revolutionary impacts of molecular biology with a rejection of "genocentrism" and "reductionism". By examining the molecular biology of the "environment", it situates genetics in the developmental biology of whole organisms and reveals how the molecular biosciences have undermined the nature/nurture distinction. Other research areas that inform her approach are embodied, distributed, and extended cognition, and animal minds.

Guan-Jen Sung is a PhD candidate in the Family and Community Food Decision-Making Program in the Division of Nutritional Sciences at Cornell University. During and after her undergraduate study in plant sciences at National Taiwan University, she was a research assistant in plant biotechnological studies at the Development Center for Biotechnology and in plant mitochondria origination research at the Academia Sinica of Taiwan. She connects her plant sciences background across disciplines with human nutrition and Taiwanese Chinese medicine for her advanced degrees. She studied antioxidants in lotus embryotic germination for her master's training at Cornell and investigated food decision making about medicinal food use for her doctoral research. She has engaged in various fields of practice. She was an education assistant at the Cornell Plantations and trained as a counselor at Cornell's EARS (Empathy, Assistance & Referral Service). She is a certified registered dietitian of Taiwan. Her interests in developing cross-cultural communication methods as well as methodology in collaborative engaged research led her to the Toolbox Project and coauthoring of a chapter in this book, with Professor Ardyth H. Gillespie. She is currently writing her dissertation about perceptions on medicinal and medicated food use among Taiwanese immigrant families in the United States.

Rick Szostak is professor of economics at the University of Alberta, where he has taught since receiving his PhD in economics from Northwestern in 1985. He is also president of the Association for Interdisciplinary Studies. He is the author of 10 books and more than 30 articles, all interdisciplinary in nature. For decades, his research has focused on how to facilitate quality interdisciplinary research and teaching. Most recently, he has worked on developing a non–discipline-based universal classification system. This would not only help interdisciplinary researchers find relevant works and ideas in other fields but would clarify the meaning of key concepts. Toward this end, he has published several articles in information science journals and elsewhere that justify and develop such a classification in general, and his Basic Concepts Classification in particular. He is coauthoring a book on interdisciplinary knowledge organization. His paper in this volume draws on his research in interdisciplinary classification to suggest guidelines for facilitating interdisciplinary communication.

1

Introduction

◆ Stephen Crowley, Sanford D. Eigenbrode,
Michael O'Rourke, and J. D. Wulfhorst

Research is a process of using existing information to generate new, whether by reinterpretation and synthesis or by acquiring new data in light of what is known. When we collaborate in research, this process will be distributed among collaborators who must share information. Information sharing in a collaborative research context is both a communication challenge and a collaboration challenge, especially when the research involves multiple intellectual disciplines. These aspects of information sharing are entangled in interdisciplinary contexts and yet central to the success of interdisciplinary research. It is their enhancement that constitutes the thematic focus of this volume. In this introduction, we first explain why this is a compelling and timely topic and then describe the contents of the volume. We conclude with a few suggestions for uses and applications.

Communication, Collaboration, and the _____Landscape of Interdisciplinary Research

Successful discovery through research requires creativity by individuals and increasingly by groups of collaborators. To *create collaboratively*, researchers must combine their individual and sometimes distinct creative processes. This type of collaboration, which is a key attribute of *interdisciplinary* research, can be both challenging and enormously rewarding.

1

Interdisciplinary research is a powerful mode of discovery, combining different epistemic perspectives in a synergistic, integrated whole that goes well beyond what each part can accomplish on its own (Klein, 1996). In the first lines of their sweeping examination of interdisciplinary research, the National Academies trumpet this point:

> Interdisciplinary research . . . can be one of the most productive and inspiring of human pursuits—one that provides a format for conversations and connections that lead to new knowledge. As a mode of discovery and education, it has delivered much already and promises more. (National Academy of Sciences [NAS], 2004, p. 1)

By combining differences in research orientation, interdisciplinarity can reveal new dimensions of a problem space and spark innovative responses (Miller et al., 2008). Multiple intellectual and disciplinary cultures can and often must be combined to address multifaceted problems, such as climate change and agricultural sustainability (Eaglesham & Hardy, 2009; Robertson et al., 2008).

Nonetheless, interdisciplinary research can be difficult and demanding. The combination of different perspectives and the complexity of implementation generate challenges that can make success an infrequent achievement. Principal among these are *communication challenges* that are manifest at the professional and interpersonal levels (Burbules & Bruce, 2001). Researchers trained in different disciplines often use different vernaculars and belong to different disciplinary cultures, creating the need for translation on multiple levels (Galison, 1997; Schoenberger, 2001; Strober, 2011). Linguistic differences can lead collaborators to use the same term for different concepts, such as *dynamic* or *triangulation*, impairing communication by creating both false disagreement and false agreement (Bracken & Oughton, 2006; Eigenbrode et al., 2007; O'Rourke & Crowley, 2012). Cultural differences can undermine trust and respect, leading to disciplinary chauvinism (Bennett, Gadlin, & Levine-Finley, 2010; Giri, 2002; Maglaughlin & Sonnenwald, 2005). Manifestations of communication failure can be severe when research styles diverge widely—for example, when integrating the social sciences with the physical sciences (Sievanen, Campbell, & Leslie, 2011). And communication challenges multiply in the context of the group's relationship with its institution (Bennett & Gadlin, Chap. 17 this volume; Klein, 2010).

Complex problems such as those involving climate change, bioregional sustainability planning, and public health involve nonlinear causal interactions among a multitude of different elements, resisting uniform solutions from isolated perspectives (Klein, 2004); these problems are "wicked" and sui generis, resisting a "single correct formation," lacking a regular causal structure, and admitting only of "solutions" that are more or less acceptable to stakeholders (Rittel & Webber, 1973). Such problems cry out for interdisciplinary investigation for two reasons.[1] First, successful interdisciplinary research respects the complexity of problems and seeks solutions that reflect that complexity (NAS, 2004, p. 40). Second, attending to the many elements that constitute these problems requires different types of expertise, as does the ability to determine which of these elements might be safely ignored for the purposes of a given project. Even if the solution to some complex problem were as "simple" as finding the right string to pull to untangle a knot, identifying that solution would typically require examination from multiple perspectives. While the need for multiple perspectives does not *necessarily* entail collaboration, the highly specialized nature of modern disciplines and the resulting scarcity of "Renaissance" persons call for cross-disciplinary collaboration (Qin, 1994).

Thus, the increasing interconnectedness and complexity of contemporary problems recommends collaboration. Furthermore, some evidence suggests that collaboration inherently improves the quality of scientific work (Andrade, López, & Martín, 2009). For this improvement to occur, collaborators must speak in a unified voice that harmonizes the variety of viewpoints informing the collaboration, whether crafting grant proposals, manuscripts, or policy recommendations.[2] This, in turn, requires achieving "collective communication competence," which depends on "numerous interrelationships among communicators, contexts, goals, and the participants' abilities to simultaneously be appropriate and effective" (Thompson, 2009, p. 281). All this entails effective communication, consonant with the National Academy's observation that "at the heart of interdisciplinarity is communication—the conversations, connections, and combinations that bring new insights to virtually every kind of scientist and engineer" (NAS, 2004, p. 19).

Concepts Fundamental to the Volume

Enhancing Communication and Collaboration in Interdisciplinary Research offers new insights about interdisciplinary communication and collaboration for students, researchers, practitioners, and administrators. The title of this volume contains the main concepts that frame its contents: *interdisciplinary research*, *collaboration*, *communication*, and *enhancement*. While

---

[1]One might question whether interdisciplinary investigation is up to the task of addressing wicked problems. After all, Rittel and Webber (1973) are keen to point out that the "systems-approach" to wicked problems, which typically involves multiple disciplinary orientations, is inadequate because it assumes that their solution can be planned and "organized into distinct phases" (p. 162). While interdisciplinary approaches can be programmatic in this way, they can also be responsive to the manifold, contextual characteristics that are the hallmark of wicked problems.

[2]See Cornell and Parker (Chap. 7 this volume), who focus on the notion of synthesis that may be thought of as a form of "unified speaking."

interdisciplinary research has been scrutinized for decades (Klein, 1996), contemporary thinking about its main dimensions remains in flux. Fittingly then, each of our four main concepts is used in various ways in this volume, reflecting the vibrant and exciting state of this field of inquiry. Given this variation, proper appreciation of the subsequent chapters requires that we canvass the range of interpretations of the concepts on which they rely.

Interdisciplinary Research

Most of the chapters concern integrative research involving input from different disciplines.[3] To say more requires resolving the concept into its two parts, *interdisciplinarity* and *research*. With respect to the first of these, we follow standard practice and contrast this with strict disciplinarity, involving perspectives, methodologies, and techniques drawn from a single disciplinary source, as well as with *multidisciplinarity*, which involves more than one discipline but with little or no integration (Morse, Chap. 12 this volume; Morse, Nielsen-Pincus, Force, & Wulfhorst, 2007). All the chapters in this volume discuss interdisciplinarity, with some providing more specific and constrained interpretations than others (e.g., Chaps. 4, 5, 6, and 12). Interdisciplinarity is also different from but closely related to *transdisciplinarity*, another concept that refers to integrated activity that typically involves input from more than one disciplinary source. Transdisciplinarity comprises several forms of integrated activity, three of which are evident in this volume. First, transdisciplinarity can be understood as interdisciplinarity that results in a transformed perspective (e.g., a new discipline—see Eigenbrode et al., 2007); this form receives attention in Chapters 2, 7, 12, and 14, and especially in Chapter 4. Second, transdisciplinarity can imply participatory interaction involving stakeholders (Roux, Stirzaker, Breen, Lefroy, & Cresswell, 2010), a European conceptualization discussed in Chapters 2, 6, 9, 12, and 15. Finally, the term can be used in a broader sense to imply going "beyond" the disciplinary, as employed by David A. Stone in Chapter 5.

With respect to the second part of the concept, *research*, our authors are primarily interested in scholarly and creative discovery that aims to *produce* new knowledge. In this way, we contrast it with education, or the *transmission* of knowledge. It is difficult to separate these two fully—researchers cannot do what they do without remaining students of their subject matter, and they are often themselves teachers who transmit knowledge to future researchers. This blurry-edged duality is embodied in interdisciplinary

---

[3]Discussions of the epistemic integration that figures into interdisciplinarity tend to be metaphorical, couched in terms of, for example, *combination, blending, synthesis,* and *trading zones* (Boix Mansilla, 2010). The key idea is that integration involves bringing together different elements under a single relation that is important for one's interests and purposes. For more on the notion of integration, see the chapters in Repko, Newell, & Szostak (2012), especially Klein (2012).

research educators, who approach both research and education tasks with an orientation that prepares them for the translational complexity of disciplinary integration. As Daniel Stokols observes, this orientation (or "intellectual outlook") includes "the core values, attitudes, beliefs, knowledge, and behaviors" that prepare the research educator to contribute to interdisciplinary efforts (Chap. 4 this volume, p. 56). Several chapters in this volume address the challenges confronting research educators who will train future generations of integrative researchers, including Chapters 2, 4, 6, 14, 15, 16, and 18.

Collaboration

Interdisciplinary research often must be collaborative, especially when problems addressed are complex and impacts widespread (e.g., climate change, hunger, poverty). Collaboration varies along a number of dimensions, including *number of participants*, from pairs (e.g., several coauthor groups in this volume) to very large teams (e.g., the Manhattan Project); *location*, from local to globally distributed; and *mode*, from face-to-face to fully virtual. The essence of collaboration is that individuals *work together* in pursuit of collective goals. Successful collaborations achieve a degree of "collective intentionality," marked by joint planning and interlocking execution of group activities, with collaborators distributing labor across the collective and relying on one another to contribute to the joint effort. Instead of a collection of "I"s, the group members think in "we" mode, even if integration is not deep or consistent across the effort (Tuomela, 2007). But understanding how collaborative success occurs or can be facilitated is nascent. Much of what is written in this volume aims to contribute to that understanding, with collaboration receiving special emphasis in the chapters in Part II, along with Chapters 2, 11, 12, 14, and 17.

Communication

We agree with L. Michelle Bennett and Howard Gadlin (Chap. 17 this volume) that it has become clichéd to classify problems in collaborative research as "problems in communication" (cf. Frodeman, Chap. 6 this volume), but we take the appeal of this cliché as evidence for the claim made by NAS, quoted above, that *communication* lies at the "heart of interdisciplinarity." To guard against reliance on this cliché, the authors in this volume adopted a more sophisticated model of communication, involving both *affective* and *instrumental* communication (Keyton, 1999). Affective communication challenges include building a collective identity and managing conflict, while instrumental challenges involve such tricky issues as the transfer of information when the information is couched in different vernaculars and the transfer involves people at different career stages (Bennett, Gadlin, & Levine-Finley,

2010). Both of these dimensions relate directly to the problem of information sharing that we used to open this introduction: Successful information sharing requires that collaborators be willing to share with one another and that information be formulated to facilitate sharing. The linguistic, relational, and cultural challenges that make successful communication difficult will be met only if they are conceptualized within this more sophisticated model.[4] So understood, communication ties interdisciplinary collaborators to one another but also to those on whom they depend for support (e.g., universities and funding agencies; see the chapters in Part IV in this volume) and to those who depend on them for research solutions (e.g., managers and stakeholders; see the chapters in Part II in this volume).

Enhancement

The point of this volume is to provide anyone undertaking interdisciplinary research with perspectives and results that help them improve the efficiency and effectiveness of their work. In other words, this collection is not meant merely to theorize or comment on communication and collaboration in interdisciplinary research but to offer *enhancements* for them. Specifically, each chapter aims to inform understanding and/or practice in ways that are conducive to more effective interdisciplinary communication and collaboration, and through those, to more productive interdisciplinary research. Together, the chapters can contribute to the development of an interdisciplinary research group's "collective communication competence" (Thompson, 2009). Our commitment to enhancement is especially evident in Part III, which is devoted to tools for investigators, but contributions in the form of theoretical models (Part I), case studies (Part II), and contextual reflections (Part IV) all provide additional ways of thinking about enhancement.

The Structure of the Volume

The volume begins and ends with chapters that take expansive views of communication and collaboration in interdisciplinary research—the first, by Julie Thompson Klein, frames the volume as a whole, while the closing chapter, by Gabriele Bammer, describes where we might go from here. The intervening 15 chapters are divided into four parts, each addressing different dimensions of the volume's theme.

---

[4]It should be acknowledged that this is only a necessary condition on success. Like collaboration, our understanding of communication across disciplinary lines is still emerging; for example, how the affective and instrumental dimensions interrelate and whether they stand alone in framing the relevant phenomena remain two open questions that lie at the edge of this exciting frontier.

In her opening chapter (Chap. 2), Klein provides a framework for thinking about communication and collaboration in interdisciplinary research. In a wide-ranging review of literatures associated with these topics, Klein documents the "growing interest in interdisciplinary research" (p. 000). She begins by discussing the perspectives on communication and collaboration in interdisciplinary research supplied by philosophy, linguistics, communication studies, and management. She then turns to perspectives rooted in integration and learning, two themes of critical importance to interdisciplinary research. Klein argues that "communicative actions" performed by interdisciplinary collaborators produce expertise in interdisciplinary research, understood as "a form of boundary work that bridges cognitive and social dynamics of knowledge production in integrative research cultures" (p. 000).

Chapters 3 through 17 are organized into four parts: *Theory, Case Studies, Tools,* and *Contexts.* Each part opens with an introduction that (a) motivates its specific angle on communication and collaboration in interdisciplinary research and (b) provides thumbnail sketches of the arguments made by each of the chapters. Part I addresses the theoretical character of interdisciplinary research as seen through the lens of communication and collaboration. Parts II through IV concern the practice of interdisciplinary research in one form or another. This volume assumes that interdisciplinary practitioners will confront communication and collaboration challenges stemming from their team-based interaction and the fact that their work does not take place in a vacuum. Three important ways of enhancing the practice of interdisciplinarity serve as the focus of the remaining parts: learning from complex, multidimensional case studies that focus on examples of collaborative, interdisciplinary research and the communication challenges they confront (Part II); adopting tools that could be used to address various communication and collaboration challenges that arise (Part III); and appreciating the communication and collaboration challenges that arise out of the various contexts that influence and constrain interdisciplinary research (Part IV).

The volume closes with a chapter that describes a way forward for those engaged in interdisciplinary research. In "From Toolbox to Big Science Project: A Bold Proposal," Bammer argues that communication and collaboration in interdisciplinary research contexts would benefit from the development of a new discipline that could, among other things, organize the ideas and insights presented in this book. This discipline, which she calls "Integration and Implementation Sciences," or "I2S," would aim to bring structure to the flux mentioned above, enhancing interdisciplinary communication by enabling theorists and practitioners to organize the diversity of interdisciplinary teaching and research innovations and thereby bring together the fragmented insights currently scattered across a wide variety of locations and literatures. Bammer recognizes the immensity of the task she calls for, urging the community of interdisciplinary educators and researchers to launch a "Big Science project" capable of "construct[ing] a new discipline and populat[ing] it with the extensive array of concepts, methods, and case studies that interdisciplinary research, education, and community have produced and continue to provide" (p. 000).

How to Use This Book

This is a book about how to conceptualize and conduct interdisciplinary research that focuses on the dual aspects of information sharing—communication and collaboration—that constitute the "heart of interdisciplinarity" (NAS, 2004, p. 19). This book is for anyone interested in the rewarding yet difficult activity that is interdisciplinary work—including educators, administrators, researchers, practitioners, and students. As such, we intend the volume to have value for anyone working under the banner of interdisciplinarity. Educators who seek to impart understanding of the challenges and methods for improving interdisciplinary communication and collaboration can use the volume in graduate and undergraduate courses. Administrators can use it to inform the motivation and development of interdisciplinary research capacity. Researchers can use it to broaden their understanding of the theory and application of collaborative, interdisciplinary science. Practitioners interested in bridging research and practice can use it as a resource, sampling it as necessary given the demands of their own projects.

The chapters in Part I provide a foundation for evaluating the case studies in Part II and the recommendations made about interdisciplinary research in context in Part IV. For those engaged in pursuing or supporting interdisciplinary research, Part III offers ideas about how to facilitate its successful completion. Each part of the book stands independently, and they can be read out of order or sampled—although it would be best to begin by reading the framing chapter by Klein. The chapters in each part also stand independently, although together they constitute constellations that reveal important aspects of the communicative and collaborative aspects of interdisciplinary research.

References

Andrade, H. B., López, E. R., & Martín, T. B. (2009). Dimensions of scientific collaboration and its contribution to the academic research groups' scientific quality. *Research Evaluation, 18*, 301–311.

Bennett, L. M., Gadlin, H., & Levine-Finley, S. (2010). *Collaboration and team science: A field guide*. Washington, DC: National Institutes for Health.

Boix Mansilla, V. (2010). Learning to synthesize: The development of interdisciplinary understanding. In R. Frodeman, J. T. Klein, & C. Mitcham (Eds.), *The Oxford handbook of interdisciplinarity*. Oxford, UK: Oxford University Press.

Bracken, L. J., & Oughton, E. A. (2006). 'What do you mean?' The importance of language in developing interdisciplinary research. *Transactions of the Institute of British Geographers, 31*, 371–382.

Burbules, N. C., & Bruce, B. C. (2001). Theory and research on teaching as dialogue. In V. Richardson (Ed.), *Handbook of research on teaching* (4th ed.). Washington, DC: American Educational Resarch Association.

Eaglesham, A., & Hardy, R. W. F. (Eds.). (2009). *Adapting agriculture to climate change* (Report No. 21). Ithaca, NY: National Agricultural Biotechnology Council.

Eigenbrode, S. D., O'Rourke, M., Wulfhorst, J. D., Althoff, D. M., Goldberg, C. S., Merrill, K., et al. (2007). Employing philosophical dialogue in collaborative science. *BioScience, 57,* 55–64.

Galison, P. (1997). *Image and logic.* Chicago: University of Chicago Press.

Giri, A. K. (2002). The calling of a creative transdisciplinarity. *Futures, 34,* 103–115.

Keyton, J. (1999). Relational communication in groups. In L. R. Frey, D. S. Gouran, & M. S. Poole (Eds.), *The handbook of group communication theory and research* (pp. 192–222). Thousand Oaks, CA: Sage.

Klein, J. T. (1996). *Crossing boundaries: Knowledge, disciplinarities, and interdisciplinarities.* Charlottesville: University Press of Virginia.

Klein, J. T. (2004). Interdisciplinarity and complexity: An evolving relationship. *E:CO, 6,* 2–10.

Klein, J. T. (2010). *Creating interdisciplinary campus cultures: A model for strength and sustainability.* San Francisco: Jossey-Bass.

Klein, J. T. (2012). Research integration: A comparative knowledge base. In A. F. Repko, W. H. Newell, & R. Szostak (Eds.), *Case studies in interdisciplinary research* (pp. 283–298). Thousand Oaks, CA: Sage.

Maglaughlin, K. L., & Sonnenwald, D. H. (2005). Factors that impact interdisciplinary natural science research collaboration in academia. In P. Ingwersen & B. Larsen (Eds.), *Proceedings of ISSI 2005.* Stockholm: Karolinska University Press.

Miller, T. R., Baird, T. D., Littlefield, C. M., Kofinas, G., Chapin, F. S., III, & Redman, C. L. (2008). Epistemological pluralism: Reorganizing interdisciplinary research. *Ecology and Society, 13*(2), 46. Retrieved from http://www.ecologyandsociety.org/vol13/iss2/art46/

Morse, W. C., Nielsen-Pincus, M., Force, J. E., & Wulfhorst, J. D. (2007). Bridges and barriers to developing and conducting interdisciplinary graduate-student team research. *Ecology and Society, 12*(2), 8. Retrieved from http://www.ecologyandsociety.org/vol12/iss2/art8/

National Academy of Sciences, Committee on Facilitating Interdisciplinary Research and Committee on Science Engineering and Public Policy. (2004). *Facilitating interdisciplinary research.* Washington, DC: National Academies Press.

O'Rourke, M., & Crowley, S. (2012). Philosophical intervention and cross-disciplinary science: The story of the Toolbox Project. *Synthese.* doi:10.1007/s11229-012-0175-y

Qin, J. (1994). An investigation of research collaboration in the sciences through the philosophical transactions 1901–1991. *Scientometrics, 29*(2), 291–238.

Repko, A. F., Newell, W. H., & Szostak, R. (Eds.). (2012). *Case studies in interdisciplinary research.* Thousand Oaks, CA: Sage.

Rittel, H. W. J., & Webber, M. M. (1973). Dilemmas in a general theory of planning. *Policy Sciences, 4,* 155–169.

Robertson, G. P., Dale, V. H., Doering, O. C., Hamburg, S. P., Melillo, J. M., Wander, M. M., et al. (2008, October 3). Sustainable biofuels redux. *Science, 322,* 49–50.

Roux, D. J., Stirzaker, R. J., Breen, C. M., Lefroy, E. C., & Cresswell, H. P. (2010). Framework for participative reflection on the accomplishment of transdisciplinary research programs. *Environmental Science & Policy, 13*, 733–741.

Schoenberger, E. (2001). Interdisciplinarity and social power. *Progress in Human Geography, 25*, 365–382.

Sievanen, L., Campbell, L. M., & Leslie, H. M. (2011). Challenges to interdisciplinary research in ecosystem-based management. *Conservation Biology, 26*(2), 315–323.

Strober, M. (2011). *Interdisciplinary conversations: Challenging habits of thought.* Palo Alto, CA: Stanford University Press.

Thompson, J. L. (2009). Building collective communication competence in interdisciplinary research teams. *Journal of Applied Communication Research, 37*(3), 278–297.

Tuomela, R. (2007). *The philosophy of sociality: The shared point of view.* Oxford, UK: Oxford University Press.

2

Communication and Collaboration in Interdisciplinary Research

◆ Julie Thompson Klein

This chapter addresses the core question of this book: "What constitutes interdisciplinary communication in teams?" After situating the topic in current contexts and definitions, it investigates the interrelationship of communication and collaboration (C^2) within interdisciplinary research (IDR) from two sets of perspectives. The first set brings together insights from the specialties of philosophy, language studies, communication studies, and management. The second set situates those findings in the literature on interdisciplinarity through discourse analysis of the intersecting thematics of integration and learning. The underlying premise is that IDR is a form of boundary work that bridges cognitive and social dynamics of knowledge production in integrative research cultures. Expert praxis does not lie in generic formulas. It emerges from communicative actions in an iterative process that requires collaborative readiness, robust platforms, negotiation of differences, management of conflict, collective communication competence (CCC), mutual learning, interactions in trading zones of language communities, and construction of common ground. The chapter concludes with take-home lessons in the form of questions for teams to ask throughout the research process, encapsulating the wisdom of theory and practice for interdisciplinary C^2.

Introduction

The 2010 conference that gave rise to this book—Enhancing Communication in Cross-Disciplinary Research (ECCDR)—is one of many events that document growing interest in IDR. It is fitting that this conference emanated from a project funded by the U.S. National Science Foundation (NSF), since the earliest substantive literature on IDR emanated from conferences cosponsored by NSF in the late 1970s and 1980s (Klein, 1990a). In 2010, Lance Haworth of NSF's Office of Integrative Activities framed the ECCDR meeting within the context of the agency's new internal and disciplinary cross-cutting programs and activities. And, in late 2011, NSF's Directorate for Social, Behavioral, and Economic Sciences took a step further in a new report on the future of research that places increased priority on interdisciplinary training, integration, and synthesis.

Other organizations have also heightened the profile of interdisciplinarity. At the National Institutes of Health (NIH), interest accelerated after the 2003 launch of a new Roadmap for Medical Research that included a targeted focus on "Research Teams of the Future." Interest deepened with a multiyear initiative in transdisciplinary research (TDR) aimed at building new paradigms in health and wellness. By 2006, the NIH Tenure Review Committee had revised its internal criteria to include credit for team science. The Clinical and Translational Science Awards Consortium was also established to promote interdisciplinary collaboration, the NIH Guide for Intramural Research was revised to include a fuller description of teams, and the Science of Team Science network partnered with NIH in the study of collaborative research. Outside the United States, the European-based Network for Transdisciplinary Research, known as td-net, is a major forum for TDR, involving stakeholders in society in real-world problem solving (Bennett, Gadlin, & Levine-Finley, 2010, p. 2; http://www.scienceofteamscience.org/; http://www.transdisciplinarity.ch/d/index.php).

Not all forms of collaborative research are interdisciplinary, so preliminary definitions are in order. Interdisciplinary teams, Mitchell McCorcle (1982) explains, operate in a more complex environment than other teams. They are open, not closed, systems that have a heterogeneous though interconnected membership. In tackling the core question of this chapter—"What constitutes interdisciplinary communication in teams?"—Britt Holbrook (2012) cautions that the answer is not straightforward, because views of interdisciplinary communication have a normative relationship with views of interdisciplinarity. Nevertheless, a recognized baseline vocabulary provides a framework for thinking about C^2 in IDR and TDR (Klein, 2010b; Scholz, 2011, pp. 373–378).

> *Multidisciplinarity* juxtaposes two or more disciplines or bodies of knowledge focused on a common problem, question, topic, or theme. From the standpoint of C^2, communication occurs typically at the level of coordinating information, not collaborating.

Interdisciplinarity integrates information, data, methods, tools, concepts, or theories from two or more disciplines or bodies of knowledge to address a complex question, problem, topic, or theme. Work may occur individually or in teams, though in the latter case, communication is essential to successful collaboration.

Transdisciplinarity transcends disciplinary worldviews through (1) more comprehensive frameworks and/or (2) problem-oriented research that crosses boundaries of academic disciplines and the public and private spheres. Major examples of the first connotation—new synthetic frameworks—include general systems theory, feminist theory, sustainability, new paradigms for health and wellness, and new principles of unity informed by the worldview of complexity in science. In the second connotation, mutual learning, joint work, and knowledge integration are key to solving "real-world" problems.

The first step in investigating the role of C^2 across types of cross-disciplinarity (i.e., multi-, inter-, and trans-) is to inform understanding with the baseline vocabulary of major forms and insights from the specialties of philosophy, language studies, communication studies, and management.

Philosophy

Philosophers would contend that their discipline is the logical starting point for this investigation. It is, after all, the oldest discipline and has long been concerned with communication. The subdiscipline of epistemology studies how we know what we know, and the subdiscipline of philosophy of language examines the nature, origins, and use of language. Philosophy is also an appropriate starting point because the NSF-funded Toolbox Project that gave rise to the ECCDR conference and this volume is a philosophically informed framework for understanding and improving cross-disciplinary communication (Chap. 11 this volume; see also http://www.cals.uidaho.edu/toolbox/). The project is based on the premise that differences in disciplinary worldviews must be identified and clarified to develop effective communication and minimize interference with collaboration.

In an in-depth exploration of the core question of what constitutes interdisciplinary communication, Holbrook argues that three alternative answers appear in philosophy of science and social/political philosophy. The answers are framed by Donald Davidson's (1974) contention that different disciplines constitute different conceptual schemes and, hence, different ways of organizing or being tested by facts. Each discipline has its own language, but Davidson believed they ought to be translatable. It is useful to think of these three alternatives as differing views about the possibility and nature of translating between disciplinary languages. The three views correspond, very roughly, to the claims that (1) translation is possible (Habermas–Klein);

(2) translation is impossible—communication requires adopting the other's language (Kuhn–MacIntyre); and (3) translation is impossible—communication requires creating a new language.

Dominant view of translatability: The Habermas–Klein thesis. The first thesis is prominent in the work of philosopher and critical theorist Jürgen Habermas (1976/1998) and interdisciplinary scholar Julie Thompson Klein (1990b, 1996, 2005, 2010b, 2012). The dominant view in the literature, this thesis asserts that integrating two or more disciplinary languages can generate a new common understanding through reciprocal comprehension and consensus. From the standpoint of C^2, consensus is a social–psychological construct requiring individual commitments to bring about intersubjective mutuality. The keys are common vocabulary, shared knowledge, reciprocal comprehension, mutual trust, and social accord.

Rival view: The Kuhn–MacIntyre thesis. Based on philosopher Thomas Kuhn's ideas about knowledge paradigms and philosopher Alasdair MacIntyre's (1988, 1990) ideas about traditions of moral enquiry, the second thesis holds that disciplinary languages are in principle and often in fact incommensurable. Communication can occur only by learning the language of another discipline. Although Davidson treated this act as one of translation, Kuhn (2000) preferred to use the notion of interpretation. According to MacIntyre, two notions are relevant: a weak notion of translatability and a strong notion of linguistic competence that comes from a process akin to learning a second first language, a form of linguistic competence that entails the capacity to improvise and innovate. For MacIntyre, it is the second of these processes that is central to interdisciplinary communication. By highlighting incommensurability, the Kuhn–MacIntyre thesis opposes the idea of interdisciplinarity as integration and consensus between disciplines. But, Holbrook stresses, it is through focus on their interactions.

Rival view: The Bataille–Lyotard thesis. Based on the work of French writer Georges Bataille (1988, 1992, 1993) and philosopher Jean-François Lyotard (1988), the third thesis holds that incommensurability reveals itself when attempts at communication fail. At that point, further communication is possible only by inventing a new language. Bataille opposed the notion of a strong and powerful sense of communication to a weak or feeble sense. Communication within particular disciplines is usually of the weak variety, with disputes settled under the banner of litigation more than under Lyotard's concept of *differend*. By litigation, Lyotard means the kind of disagreement that can be resolved by appeal to rules acceptable to all parties in the disagreement. In contrast, the concept of *differend* highlights a type of communication breakdown, signaled by a feeling of not being able to find words, that occurs within disciplines but, Holbrook emphasizes, is more likely to occur between disciplines, propelling a "first moment of strong interdisciplinary communication." The second moment emerges from invention of a new genre of discourse. More than a simple integration of previously existing genres, it is a novel cocreation that entails risk and relinquishing disciplinary identities. The important question, Holbrook adds, is not whether different disciplines are integrated but whether participants can move forward as though they understand each other (Bataille's notion of weak communication) or not (Lyotard's notion of *differend*).

Taken as a composite framework on the core question (What constitutes interdisciplinary communication?), the three theses raise related questions that now need to be considered through the comparative lenses of other specialties. Two questions arise. What role does language play in interdisciplinary communication? And how can differences in worldviews be overcome? Language studies are central to answering both questions.

Language Studies

The study of language is not confined to one specialty. It lies at the heart of the ancient discipline of rhetoric vested in the arts of persuasion, and it is central to the modern discipline of linguistics, which explores the structure, meaning, and contexts of language in subspecialties such as psycholinguistics, sociolinguistics, and discourse analysis. The concept of linguistic relativity is central to understanding interdisciplinary communication. (For a fuller definition, see the work of Benjamin Whorf in Carroll, 1956.) The core premise is that language shapes the ways speakers conceptualize their worldviews, including the ways they think (cognition) and act (behavior). One of the most prominent related topics in studies of collaborative IDR is the meaning of words. In a case study of an urban development project in the Swiss Lowlands, Baccini and Oswald (2008) identified two crucial communication tasks: learning each other's specialized language and understanding perceptions hidden in words. The project began in 1993 when Baccini and Oswald, a scientist and an architect, realized they had a common interest in sustainable urban development. It expanded when other collaborators joined them. One group (morphologists) was rooted in the academic culture of architecture and urban planning, while the other group (physiologists) was composed of natural scientists, engineers, and an economist. Participants found that even such basic words as *landscape*, *urban*, *project*, and *process* were understood differently.

In an early study of interdisciplinary communication, Gerhard Frey (1973) reported that interdisciplinary discussions normally take place on a level similar to a "popular scientific presentation." Discussions become more precise as individuals combine everyday and specialist languages. When another major initiative, the Austrian Landscape Research program, engaged stakeholders in society in the research process, organizers expected participants to use everyday language. However, everyday language is ambiguous. Teams might adopt formal languages, such as metamathematics or general systems theory, for greater precision. Yet Bergmann and colleagues (2010) advise, formal languages must be adapted to the "concrete occasions" and "constellations of disciplines and stakeholder views" within particular projects. Successful collaboration, they add, requires getting past nonspecialist understandings of common colloquialisms and trying out terms that foster "interdisciplinary connectivity" through bridge words. Recalling the Swiss project, earlier 2 years of mutual learning resulted in a shared definition of the underlying concept of "urbanity" and the bridge concept of "net city" (*Netzstadt*) as an agglomeration of lowlands with connected knots or nodes, rather than a fixed center. In another sustainability project, the bridge word *mobility* functioned as a boundary object, a focal point enabling individuals to work together on a common interest while retaining separate identities and interpretations. It fostered cooperation and coordination around the common objective of "sustainable renovation" of housing units (Bergmann & Jahn, 2008).

In the second philosophical thesis Holbrook identified, MacIntyre likened interdisciplinary communication to learning a second language. Bilingualism is a popular metaphor of interdisciplinary work. However, mastery of two disciplinary languages rarely occurs. Holbrook likens the invention of a new language described in the third philosophical thesis to two concepts in science studies: pidgin and creole. A pidgin is an interim tongue, providing a trade language between groups with different primary languages. A creole is a first language among members of a new social and cognitive community. These concepts are also familiar to linguists, though in science studies they are associated with anthropology because Peter Galison (1997), who introduced the terms to science studies, borrowed them from anthropology to explain interactions in physics as part of the concept of "trading zones." The core idea is that dissimilar subcultures can find common ground through exchanges, such as bartering fish for baskets. In physics, exchanges occurred between scientific subcultures of theory and experiment, and across different traditions of making instruments and subcultures of theorizing.

Ultimately, Wilhelm Vosskamp (1994) suggests, the quality of collaborative outcomes cannot be separated from the development and richness of a shared language culture, whether the trading zones are small teams or large-scale programs. Achieving that goal, Myra Strober (2011) advises, requires understanding that styles of communication derive from disciplinary cultures and the habits of mind they instill. Individuals need to become "ethnographers" of their own disciplines (Strober, 2011, pp. 57, 161–162). They also need some understanding of insights developed in the field of communication studies. In a guide to conducting IDR, Catherine Lyall, Ann Bruce, Joyce Tait, and Laura Meagher (2011, p. 59) identify difficulty of communication as one of the key challenges. The underlying notion of "communication," though, is ambiguous because the term is used widely across popular, academic, and professional contexts.

Communication Studies

Academic studies of communication range across a wide variety of interests, from conversation analysis and the dynamics of small-group communication to social networks, computer-mediated communication, and training for the communication industries. Specialties and schools of thought, Robert Craig (1999) also reports, operate separately in rhetorical, semiotic, phenomenological, cybernetic, sociopsychological, sociocultural, and critical traditions. Few of these studies have focused directly on IDR, although the closest links have been drawn in studies of group communication.

In defining the underlying concept of "communication," Burtis and Turman (2006) highlight two processes: "transfer of information from one source to another" and "making and sharing meaning" (pp. 10, 53–54). All group communication, they add, engages in "boundary spanning," necessitating "boundary negotiations" in both internal and external communication. Transferring information, sharing meaning, boundary spanning, and boundary negotiation take on greater importance in collaborative IDR. It is a joint effort, Defila, Di Giulio, and Scheuermann (2006) emphasize. Awareness of the diversity of disciplinary languages is prerequisite to achieving a common language and theoretical basis for research (Defila et al., 2006, pp. 128, 131, 133). Communication studies scholar Jessica Leigh Thompson (2009) takes a step further in placing the concept of CCC at the heart of IDR collaboration. CCC is based on the premise that there are interrelationships among communicators, goals, participants' abilities to integrate knowledge and expertise from different sources, and a range of interpersonal, relational, organizational, and pedagogical contexts. Many communication scholars, Thompson adds, use systems theory to explain the complexity of small-group interactions in dynamically changing environments.

Thompson's ethnographic study of an academic team as a participant-observer looked closely at processes that facilitated and hindered communication. The team was focused on human behaviors related to the production of greenhouse gas emissions in urban areas. Her findings led Thompson to make four suggestions for team members and managers: (1) build in trust-building time, (2) host explicit discussions about language differences, (3) schedule social time, and (4) confront communication challenges early. She also recommends using a facilitator to reflect on and navigate challenges that require team members to continually negotiate their standards for CCC. The key points of connection between the literature on IDR collaboration and Thompson's synthesis of communication studies include openness, willingness to learn from each other, and early negotiation of language differences.

Her concepts of "presence" in the form of engagement and "deep listening" are also crucial, requiring self-consciousness and awareness of the impact of individual behavior and assertions of personal status on group dynamics. Reflexive communication, Thompson adds, helps members reinforce mutual trust and gain confidence about sharing individual perspectives and insights.

Combined insights from philosophy, language studies, and communication studies indicate that collaborative IDR is a form of boundary work that bridges cognitive and social dynamics of knowledge production in integrative research cultures. Expert praxis in the form of authoritative knowledge and actions does not lie in generic formulas. It emerges from actions that also require management, the fourth source of pertinent insights into interdisciplinary C^2.

Management

Studies of IDR in the management literature tend to focus on organizing teams and facilitating interactions. The formal study of teams, James Davis (1995) recalled in his book on interdisciplinary team teaching, started in employment settings. Early studies of group behavior, Davis added, evolved into more specialized studies of human communication and the social psychology of groups. Interdisciplinary task force management has also been a feature of military operations, civilian affairs, engineering projects, feasibility studies, and industrial research and development. World War II was a watershed in collaborative IDR, highlighted by major interdisciplinary initiatives, including the Manhattan Project and problem-focused operations research. Communication researchers also cite the World War II era as a heyday for small group communications, preceded by studies in the 1920s that adapted John Dewey's work on democratic group decision making. By the 1970s and 1980s, international competition in science-based industries heightened the demand for collaborative IDR, especially in manufacturing, computer sciences, biomedicine and pharmaceuticals, and high technology. This development, in turn, prompted new studies of large-scale complex projects, including the Human Genome Initiative (Klein, 1996, pp. 173–208; 2010a, pp. 16–21).

The early literature tended to apply management and organizational theories of the day to studies of IDR collaboration, with emphasis on organizational structures, leadership strategies, and types of teams. Over time, the focus expanded from managing teams and organizational units to creating institutional research cultures and the behavioral dynamics of collaboration. In a study of leadership in TDR, Barbara Gray (2008) identified three general categories of tasks for enhancing collaboration: cognitive, structural, and processual. The success of C^2 depends in no small part on management of structural components that require coordinating tasks, internal linkages, and information flows. The organizational chart and task distribution must allow time for interaction, joint activities, coordinated use of common research facilities and instruments, consensus building, shared decision making, and networking across subprojects. Thompson (2009) came to a similar conclusion in urging regular attention to CCC, and Hindenlang, Heeb, and Roux (2008) highlight the role of platforms for handling structural tasks. Operating as loosely structured social networks, platforms create a space for communication, fostering mutual understanding, shared goals, concrete ideas and measures, and common assessment.

Even with strong platforms in place, conflicts arise. Status conflicts are especially tenacious. They arise for many reasons, including disciplinary and professional pecking orders as well as differences between quantitative versus qualitative approaches, academic rank, and gender, race, and cultural background. The theory of "status concordance" holds that success is linked to matched and equal factors. Rarely, though, do perfect matches occur (Klein, 1990b, pp. 127–128). Members of IDR teams also exhibit many of the same fighting and thwarting behaviors as other groups, echoing Bruce Tuckman's (1965) model of group development in stages of forming, storming, norming, performing, and (a fifth stage added later) advocating or transforming (see also Tuckman & Jensen, 1977). Conflict is associated with both technical issues (definition of a problem, methodologies, and scheduling) and interpersonal issues (leadership style and disciplinary ethnocentrism). Interdisciplinary teams must also overcome "boundaries of reticence" that disciplinary socialization creates, to avoid defaulting to disciplinary worldviews. Individuals must also grant power to others and surrender some degree of control (Caudill & Roberts, 1951; Stone, 1969).

Difference, though, can be an asset. The consent/dissent (*Alteritaet*) structure necessary for all communication, Vosskamp (1994) advises, shapes the possibility of interdisciplinary dialogue. Misunderstandings, animosities, and competitions must be taken seriously, not mitigated or glossed over. Moreover, even if differences are negotiated and mediated, they do not go away. They recur as participants work through their differences and attempt to resolve them in the interest of a common goal. In her pioneering study of working relationships among specialists in mental-health projects, Margaret Barron Luszki (1958) reported that members of interdisciplinary teams paid a price for congeniality in the short run. By not dealing with conflicts in definitions of core terms, such as *aggression*, they reduced the number of creative problem-solving conflicts that would have promoted high-level shared concepts in the long run. Certain ideal characteristics of interdisciplinary individuals have been identified, including flexibility, patience, willingness to learn, sensitivity toward and tolerance of others, reliability, and openness to diversity, new roles, and risk. These are ideals, however (Klein, 1990b, p. 183; Strober, 2011, p. 121). Participants are usually unwilling to abstain from approaching a topic from their own worldviews. Yet, Bruce Thiessen (1998, pp. 49–50) admonishes, adaptive behavior is required to achieve common ground in both language and goal directedness.

The *Collaboration and Team Science* field guide from the Office of the Ombudsman at NIH (Bennett & Gadlin, Chap. 17 this volume) emphasizes the importance of managing tensions. One of the recommendations for communicating about science is to establish ground rules for how participants will be expected to communicate in meetings. The distinction between dialogue and debate lies at the heart of the ground rules. Dialogue is a collaborative act of working together toward common understanding, rather than being oppositional. Common ground is the goal, not being close-minded, winning individual points, or defending one's position as the "best." An open-minded attitude and openness to being wrong and to change are needed. Listening to others provides a basis for agreement or consensus, along with seeing strengths in others' positions rather than flaws and weaknesses (Bennett et al., 2010, pp. 29–30).

The insights gained from findings in pertinent literatures come together in the overriding thematics of integration and learning in interdisciplinary C^2.

Integration

Integration is often regarded as the leading candidate for a distinguishing characteristic of collaborative IDR and its baseline vocabulary (see Holbrook, 2012; Repko, 2010). However, there is no universal theory or model of integration because the scope, degree of coordination of perspectives, nature of interactions, and goals of projects and programs vary too widely to allow a single coherent theoretical perspective. For example, teams operate in many institutional contexts: academic, industrial, governmental, and community organizations and nongovernmental organizations. Yet Pohl, van Kerkhoff, Hirsch, and Bammer (2008) identified four primary classes of "tools" for integration: (1) mutual understanding through communication, (2) theoretical concepts, (3) models, and (4) methods. This last category includes some well-known methods that have been widely applied, such as systems theory and modeling, Delphi and scenario building, simulation, concept mapping, computer synthesis of data and information flow, and integrated environmental assessment and risk management. Other methods target communication processes, including facilitating common understanding, mental mapping of stakeholder views, consensus conferences, and collaborative learning.

Yet, integration in collaborative IDR is a social process that requires coconstruction of common ground, even when using well-known approaches. Optimal integration, Davis (1995) exhorts, requires high levels of collaboration: "The greater the level of integration desired, the higher the level of collaboration required" (p. 20). Joint definition of a project is required, along with the core research problem, questions, and goals. Role clarification and negotiation help members assess what they need and expect from each other while clarifying differences in disciplinary language and approaches. And, ongoing communication and interaction foster mutual learning and interdependence, expanding individual identities into group identity. Young teams, Stone (1969) found, exhibit secondary-group relations. Members are self-protective, thinking in terms of "I." Primary-group relations are characterized by dedication to a common task, thinking in terms of "we." When the singularity of individual disciplinary identity is called into question, Holbrook suggests, Bataille's notion of strong interdisciplinary communication is operative.

In an analogy that will ring true for veterans of collaborative research, Koepp-Baker (1979) likens an interdisciplinary health care team to a polygamous marriage. The team is launched by announcement of intentions, engagement, publicity, a honeymoon, and finally the long haul (Koepp-Baker, 1979, p. 54). The Collaborators Pre-Nup, adapted from NIH, highlights the importance of early discussion of goals, roles, coauthorship, ownership of intellectual property, and obligations of teamwork (Ledford, 2008). From the outset, contextual factors also influence "collaborative readiness." In their studies of TDR centers, Stokols et al. (2010; Stokols, Misra, Moser, Hall, & Taylor, 2008) concluded, the more contextual factors in place at the outset, the greater the chances of success. Antecedents span interpersonal, environmental, and organizational parameters of research:

- Institutional supports for collaboration
- Breadth of disciplines, departments, and institutions at a center
- Prior experience working as team members on projects
- Spatial proximity or distance of offices and laboratories
- Electronic linkages (Stokols et al., 2008, 2010)

Making it through the "long haul" requires ongoing management of integrative process. Processual tasks, Gray (2008) stipulates, ensure constructive and productive interactions, with subtasks devoted to designing meetings, determining ground rules, identifying tasks that move partners toward common objectives, building trust, and ensuring effective communication. Defila et al.'s (2006) literature review of case studies identified more than 500 tips. And, McDonald, Bammer, and Deane's (2009) repertoire of dialogue methods includes hypothesis and model building, integrative assessment procedures, boundary objects and concepts, heuristics, research questions, artifacts and products, mutual learning, and stakeholder participation. Defila et al. (2006) also consider recursive procedure to be a general design principle of TDR. Iterative peer editing is one of the most common methods, fostering coassessment of individual contributions, collective reconciliation of differences, and greater likelihood of moving beyond multidisciplinary juxtaposition to interdisciplinary integration. Ideal models, Maurice DeWachter (1982) counsels, start with the assumption that individuals will suspend their disciplinary/professional worldviews. Yet his experience in bioethical decision making indicates the best chance of success lies in starting by translating a global question into the specific language of each discipline then working back and forth in iterative fashion. By constantly checking the relevance of each answer to a core question, no single answer is privileged. This process clearly entails the second overriding theme—learning.

Learning

Even with the current heightened profile of IDR, educational needs are underserved. The top recommendations for students in the National Academy of Sciences report on *Facilitating Interdisciplinarity Research* include taking a broad range of courses while developing a solid background in one discipline (Committee on Facilitating Interdisciplinary Research, 2004). Undergraduates in particular are urged to seek courses at the interfaces of traditional disciplines that address basic research problems, courses studying social problems, research experiences spanning more than one discipline, and opportunities to work with faculty with expertise in both their disciplines and interdisciplinary process. Graduate students are encouraged to gain knowledge and skills in one or more fields beyond their primary area: by doing theses or dissertations with advisers from different disciplines, participating in conferences outside their primary fields, and, for all students, working with mentors from more than one discipline. The top recommendations for educators are to develop curricula incorporating interdisciplinary concepts, offer more interdisciplinary studies courses, take teacher-development courses on interdisciplinary topics and methods of teaching nonmajors, and provide opportunities that relate foundation courses, data gathering and analysis, and research activities to other fields of study and to society at large. The report also urged more training across the board in interdisciplinary research techniques, team management skills, and summer immersion experiences for learning new disciplinary languages and cultures (Committee on Facilitating Interdisciplinary Research, 2004).

Professional organizations have also called for greater attention to the need for interdisciplinary education. Pellmar and Eisenberg's (2000) *Bridging Disciplines in the Brain, Behavioral, and Clinical Sciences* presents models for training at all levels, from undergraduate curricula through postdoctoral fellowships, predoctoral and postdoctoral training programs, and career-long opportunities. The targeted areas for improving communication in particular are jargon, intellectual turf, team building, leadership, and interactions within physical spaces. *BIO 2010* (National Research Council, 2003) presents a blueprint for aligning undergraduate education in biology with contemporary research in a curriculum that integrates physical sciences with information technology and mathematics with life sciences. Both reports also expand the locus of learning from traditional academic curricula to open spaces of faculty development programs and training modules *in situ*. Training for IDR and TDR shares many features with traditional programs, but its distinct emphasis, Justin Nash (2008) points out, is developing researchers who can synthesize theoretical and methodological approaches from multiple disciplines. The most common form of training is a multimentor apprenticeship model, with mentors in separate disciplines in addition to multiple faculty advisors and time in residence in centers (Nash, 2008, p. S133).

The principle of mutual learning also repeats across levels, from the pragmatics of daily work to theory and epistemology. "Mutual learning" requires knowing how to recognize ignorance of a particular area, then soliciting and gathering new information and knowledge. In defining transdisciplinarity in domains of environmental literacy, Roland Scholz (2011) stresses processes of capacity/competence building, consensus building, analytic mediation, and legitimation of public policy. Generating "socially robust knowledge" when working with stakeholders in public and private sectors goes beyond listening to their inputs to actually engaging them in the research process in a manner that provides feedback to the generation of scientific knowledge and theory building (Scholz, 2011, pp. 373–374). Knowledge is not simply exchanged. It is constructed as individuals with differing views and stakes work together.

In defining the three major forms of collaboration in TDR—common group learning, deliberation among experts, and integration by a subgroup or individual—Pohl et al. (2008) capture the principle of mutual learning at the heart of the first form. "Common group learning," they admonish, "means that integration takes place as a learning process of the whole group" (p. 415). Management is still crucial, however. Leaders need to coach the process by promoting joint learning activities. Adopting a conscious, targeted approach to communication, Schmithals and Berhenhage also urge, is crucial for integrating knowledge and methods when working across cognitive cultures (cited in Bergmann et al., 2010). A project-specific "cooperation and communication culture" must be established, with attention paid to interfaces: to points where the work of one participant is necessary for the work of another and to points where participants must coordinate effectively (Schmithals & Berhenhage, cited in Bergmann et al., 2010). For leaders, creating a common culture also entails the third of Gray's (2008) general categories of tasks for enhancing collaboration—cognition. The cognitive task requires managing sensemaking by creating a mental model, map, or mind-set of goals and ways of achieving them through visioning and framing (Gray, 2008, pp. S125–S126).

In a case study of an interdisciplinary team focused on STEM education (science, technology, engineering, and mathematics), DuRussel and Derry (2011) integrate conceptual understandings of mental models with the concept of *situation awareness* in organizational literature. Social and cognitive integration, DuRussel and Derry affirm, are tightly interwoven in situation awareness. An individual's prior knowledge helps shape his or her mental model (i.e., cognitive representation) of a particular situation. Yet models are dynamic and changing. As situational learning occurs, new models influence and change the content and structure of permanent schemas. The key insight is *alignment* of mental models. Common features correlate positively with productivity, but, akin to the Toolbox Project, models must be made explicit if common understanding is to be achieved. Contexts range from *goals* and *objectives* of projects to the variety of *tools* that mediate between individual work and team objectives. They also include *norms* and *rules* that influence communication patterns, as well as distribution of tasks and patterns of interactions, including regular participation in meetings and common criteria of evaluation. Visioning and (re)framing models stimulate ideas about how disciplines might overlap in constructive ways that generate new understandings and encourage collaborative work modes.

In a project that brings together learning theory, epistemology, and sociology of knowledge, Boix Mansilla, Lamont, and Sato (forthcoming-a, forthcoming-b) posit an emerging model of *sociocognitive platforms for interdisciplinary collaboration*. The team studied experts working in nine established research programs and networks. Their case studies yield an empirically based picture of the *social-interactive* ways participants construct group membership and collective norms, and the ways norms contribute to or hinder creation of common platforms. They also considered the *cognitive-epistemic ways* experts define their enterprise and platforms for integration. Preliminary data from five networks affirm the need for early investments of time and effort to define a problem space and approach. The group climate of networks differs, though, influencing problem definition, intellectual agendas, degrees of exchange and integration, and patterns of dominance in particular disciplinary mixes. One network, for instance, had a just-in-time approach. Its "agile" and "opportunistic" work style contrasted with the prescriptive style of another group. Contrasts in emotional intensity also appeared, and products that function as boundary objects varied. Products provide "concrete space" for interaction, coproduction, and disciplinary translation in the form, for example, of graphics, concept maps, and constructs. Platforms also change over time. Gains in communicative and collaborative capacity in particular include greater clarity about disciplinary languages, increased comfort with unknown terrains, and recalibrated beliefs about another discipline. Microsocial networks realign, too, with growing "deliberative competency" at the group level and individual-level sociocognitive gains, such as the ability to provide "honest and constructive feedback" (Boix Mansilla et al., forthcoming-a, forthcoming-b).

Conclusion

A final example bridges the two core concepts engaged in this investigation— communication and collaboration. Vosskamp (1994) and Klein (1996) treat interdisciplinarity as communicative action, and in a major study of an urban planning project, Després and colleagues (2008) extended this idea. Scientific and academic knowledge alone, they argue, cannot deal adequately with the complexity of subjects and problem domains such as revitalization of neighborhoods, including their case study of retrofitting older residential neighborhoods on the outskirts of Quebec City. Following Habermas's (1987) *Theory of Communicative Action,* instrumental, ethical, and aesthetic forms of knowledge are all needed. Moreover, rational knowledge comes out of not only "what we know" but "how we communicate" it, generating a form of "communicative rationality." Stakeholders entering into negotiation confront the four kinds of knowledge in a series of encounters that allow representatives of each type to express their views and proposals. In the process, a fifth type of knowledge progressively emerges. It is a hybrid product, the result of "making sense together." Fostering "intersubjectivity," the fifth type of knowledge requires ongoing efforts to achieve mutual understanding, aided in this case by a mediator who helped extract individual interests or views. As progressively shared meanings, diagnoses, and objectives emerge, individual interests and views are seen in different perspectives.

The underlying premises of this case study—communicative action, communicative rationality, negotiation, intersubjectivity, and mutual understanding—bring us full circle back to philosophy. Anne Balsamo (2011, p. 163; see also Balsamo & Mitcham, 2010, p. 270) frames that return in ethical principles of collaboration. The first two principles accentuate requirements for individuals:

Intellectual confidence: The understanding that one has something important to contribute to the collaborative process. This is the commitment that makes one accountable for the quality of an individual's contribution to the collaboration. Everyone's contribution to the collaboration must be reliable. It must be thorough and full of integrity; it must refuse shortcuts and guard against intellectual laziness.

Intellectual humility: The understanding that one's knowledge is always partial and incomplete and can always be extended and revised by insights from others. This is the quality that allows people to admit they don't know something without suffering loss of confidence or a blow to their self-esteem.

The second two principles move from individuality to group responsibility:

Intellectual generosity: The sincere acknowledgment of the work of others. This acknowledgment must be explicitly expressed to collaborators as well as through citation practices. Showing appreciation for other ideas in face-to-face dialogue and throughout the process of collaborative process sows the seeds for intellectual risk taking and courageous acts of creativity.

Intellectual flexibility: The ability to change one's perspective based on new insights that come from other people. This is the capacity both for play and reimagining the rules of reality: to suspend judgment and to imagine other ways of being in the world, and other worlds to be within.

An overriding principle of integrity emerges from the move to group responsibility:

Intellectual integrity: The habit of responsible participation that serves as a basis for the development of trust among collaborators. This is a quality that compels colleagues to bring their best work and contribute their best thinking to collaborative efforts.

Skills of research integration, McDonald et al. (2009) assert, have become as essential today as disciplinary skills. These skills are all the more important when disciplines are undergoing changes characterized by greater boundary crossing, openness to interdisciplinary developments, prioritizing of real-world problems, and grappling with the complexities of contingency, contextualization, and diversity. However, much of the wisdom of practice is not captured for future use. Handbooks and networks are vital forums for disseminating wisdom of practice, highlighted recently by a new online suite of team science learning modules on the Team Science website (http://teamscience.net/) and the NIH Team Science Toolkit (http://www.teamsciencetoolkit.cancer.gov/public/Home.aspx). However, "expert praxis" does not lie simply in formulas, well-honed guidelines, or tested models. It is emergent from communicative actions among the participants. O'Donnell and Derry (2005) liken the challenge that interdisciplinary teams face to Krauss and Fussell's (1990) concept of the "'mutual knowledge' problem." Experts within a discipline typically share a "common referential base," aiding communication. Participants in collaborative IDR must develop "a shared knowledge base" that constitutes "group intelligence" (O'Donnell & Derry, 2005, pp. 73, 76–77).

Take-Home Messages

A number of lessons emerge from comparative exploration of interdisciplinary C^2. They can be thought of as aims for teams to be striving toward throughout the research process. Only by keeping these aims steadily in view will the prospect of success increase:

- C^2 should be understood as an interdisciplinary construct, not viewed through the lens of a single disciplinary framework.
- Explicit moments and actions for reflection on integration and collaboration should be built into the research process, starting with assessment of collaborative readiness.
- CCC should be achieved through mutual learning and the social process of establishing trust, common vocabulary, and shared knowledge.
- Differences should be negotiated through management of conflict.
- Explicit attention should be paid to the boundary work of connectivity and integration while drawing on the accumulated wisdom of practice and theory in pertinent literatures.

Acknowledgments

I thank Britt Holbrook, Veronica Boix Mansilla, Michael O'Rourke, Stephen Crowley, and anonymous external reviewers for feedback on an earlier draft of this chapter.

References

Baccini, P., & Oswald, F. (2008). Designing the urban: Linking physiology and morphology. In G. Hirsch Hadorn, H. Hoffmann-Riem, S. Biber-Klemm, W. Grossenbacher-Mansuy, D. Joye, C. Pohl, et al. (Eds.), *Handbook of transdisciplinary research* (pp. 79–88). Dordrecht, Switzerland: Springer.

Balsamo, A. (2011). *Designing culture: The technological imagination at work.* Durham, NC: Duke University Press.

Balsamo, A., & Mitcham, C. (2010). Interdisciplinarity in ethics and the ethics of interdisciplinarity. In R. Frodeman, J. T. Klein, & C. Mitcham (Eds.), *The Oxford handbook of interdisciplinarity* (pp. 206–219). New York: Oxford University Press.

Bataille, G. (1988). *Inner experience* (L. A. Boldt, Trans.). Albany: SUNY Press.

Bataille, G. (1992). *On Nietzsche* (B. Boone, Trans.). New York: Paragon House.

Bataille, G. (1993). *Literature and evil* (A. Hamilton, Trans.). New York: Marion Boyers.

Bennett, L., Gadlin, H., & Levine-Finley, S. (2010). *Collaboration and team science: A field guide.* Bethesda, MD: National Institutes of Health. Retrieved from http://ombudsman.nih.gov/collaborationTS.html

Bergmann, M., & Jahn, T. (2008). CITY:mobil: A model for integration in sustainability research. In G. Hirsch Hadorn, H. Hoffmann-Riem, S. Biber-Klemm, W. Grossenbacher-Mansuy, D. Joye, C. Pohl, et al. (Eds.), *Handbook of transdisciplinary research* (pp. 89–102). Dordrecht, Switzerland: Springer.

Bergmann, M., Jahn, T., Knobloch, T., Krohn, W., Pohl, C., & Schramm, E. (2010). *Methoden transdisziplinärer forschung: Ein uberblick mit anwendungsbeispielen* [Transdisciplinary research methods]. Frankfurt/Main: Campus Verlag.

Boix Mansilla, V., Lamont, M., & Sato, K. (Forthcoming-a). Cognitive-emotional interactional platforms: Markers and conditions for successful interdisciplinary collaborations.

Boix Mansilla, V., Lamont, M., & Sato, K. (Forthcoming-b). Successful interdisciplinary collaborations: Toward a socio-emotional-cognitive platform for interdisciplinary collaborations. Canadian Institute for Advanced Research.

Burtis, J. O., & Turman, P. D. (2006). *Group communication pitfalls: Overcoming barriers to an effective group experience.* Thousand Oaks, CA: Sage.

Carroll, J. B. (Ed.). (1956). *Language, thought, and reality: Selected writings of Benjamin Lee Whorf.* Cambridge: MIT Press.

Caudill, W., & Roberts, B. H. (1951). Pitfalls in the organization of interdisciplinary research. *Human Organization, 10*(4), 12–15.

Committee on Facilitating Interdisciplinary Research. (2004). *Facilitating interdisciplinary research.* Washington, DC: National Academies Press.

Craig, R. T. (1999). Communication theory as a field. *Communication Theory, 9*(2), 119–161.

Davidson, D. (1974). On the very idea of a conceptual scheme. *Proceedings and Addresses of the American Philosophical Association, 47,* 5–20.

Davis, J. (1995). *Interdisciplinary courses and team teaching: New arrangements for learning.* Phoenix, AZ: American Council on Education, Oryx.

Defila, R., Di Giulio, A., & Scheuermann, M. (2006). *Forschungsverbundmanagement: Handbuch für die gestaltung inter-und transdisziplinärer projekte.* Zurich: vdf Hochschulverlag AG.

Després, C., Fortin, A., Joerin, F., Vachon, G., Gatti, E., & Moretti, G. (2008). Retrofitting postwar suburbs: A collaborative design process. In G. Hirsch Hadorn, H. Hoffmann-Riem, S. Biber-Klemm, W. Grossenbacher-Mansuy, D. Joye, C. Pohl, et al. (Eds.), *Handbook of transdisciplinary research* (pp. 327–341). Dordrecht, Switzerland: Springer.

DeWachter, M. (1982). Interdisciplinary bioethics: But where do we start? A reflection on epochè as method. *Journal of Medicine and Philosophy, 7*(3), 275–287.

DuRussel, L. A., & Derry, S. J. (2011). Schema (mis)alignment in interdisciplinary teamwork. In S. Derry, C. D. Schunn, & M. A. Gernsbacher (Eds.), *Interdisciplinary collaboration: An emerging cognitive science* (pp. 187–220). Mahwah, NJ: Lawrence Erlbaum.

Frey, G. (1973). Methodological problems of interdisciplinary discussions. *RATIO, 15*(2), 161–182.

Galison, P. (1997). *Image and logic: A material culture of microphysics.* Chicago: University of Chicago Press.

Gray, B. (2008). Enhancing transdisciplinary research through collaborative leadership. *American Journal of Preventive Medicine, 35*(2), S124–S132.

Habermas, J. (1987). *The theory of communicative action, Vol. 2: Lifeworld and system: A critique of functionalist reason* (T. McCarthy, Trans.). Boston: Beacon.

Habermas, J. (1998). What is universal pragmatics? In M. Cooke (Ed.), *On the pragmatics of communication* (pp. 21–104). Boston: MIT Press. (Original work published in 1976)

Hindenlang, K. E., Heeb, J., & Roux, M. (2008). Sustainable coexistence of ungulates and trees: A stakeholder platform for resource use negotiations. In G. Hirsch Hadorn, H. Hoffmann-Riem, S. Biber-Klemm, W. Grossenbacher-Mansuy, D. Joye, C. Pohl, et al. (Eds.), *Handbook of transdisciplinary research* (pp. 315–326). Dordrecht, Switzerland: Springer.

Holbrook, J. B. (2012). What is interdisciplinary communication? Reflections on the very idea of disciplinary integration. *Synthese, 177*(2). doi:10.1007/s11229-012-0179-7

Klein, J. T. (1990a). Innovation and change in organizational relationships: Interdisciplinary contexts. *R&D Management, 20*(2), 97–102.

Klein, J. T. (1990b). *Interdisciplinarity: History, theory, and practice.* Detroit, MI: Wayne State University Press.

Klein, J. T. (1996). *Crossing boundaries: Knowledge, disciplinarities, and interdisciplinarities.* Charlottesville: University Press of Virginia.

Klein, J. T. (2005). Interdisciplinary teamwork: The dynamics of collaboration and integration. In S. J. Derry, C. D. Schunn, & M. A. Gernsbacher (Eds.), *Interdisciplinary collaboration: An emerging cognitive science* (pp. 23–50). Mahwah, NJ: Lawrence Erlbaum.

Klein, J. T. (2010a). *Creating interdisciplinary campus cultures.* San Francisco: Jossey Bass.

Klein, J. T. (2010b). A taxonomy of interdisciplinarity. In R. Frodeman, J. T. Klein, & C. Mitcham (Eds.), *The Oxford handbook of interdisciplinarity* (pp. 15–30). New York: Oxford University Press.

Klein, J. T. (2012). Research integration: A comparative knowledge base. In A. F. Repko, W. H. Newell, & R. Szostak (Eds.), *Interdisciplinary research: Case studies of integrative understandings of complex problems* (pp. 283–298). Thousand Oaks, CA: Sage.

Koepp-Baker, H. (1979). The craniofacial team. In K. R. Bzoch (Ed.), *Communicative disorders related to cleft lip and palate*. Boston: Little, Brown.

Krauss, R. M., & Fussell, S. R. (1990). Mutual knowledge and communicative reflectiveness. In J. Galegher, R. E. Kraut, & C. Egido (Eds.), *Intellectual teamwork: Social and technological foundations of cooperative work* (pp. 111–145). Hillsdale, NJ: Lawrence Erlbaum.

Kuhn, T. S. (2000). *The road since structure*. Chicago: University of Chicago Press.

Ledford, H. (2008, April). Collaborations: With all good intentions. *Nature, 452,* 682–684.

Luszki, M. B. (1958). *Interdisciplinary team research methods and problems*. Washington, DC: National Training Laboratories.

Lyall, C., Bruce, A., Tait, J., & Meagher, L. (2011). *Interdisciplinary research journeys: Practical strategies for capturing creativity*. London: Bloomsbury Academic.

Lyotard, J.-F. (1988). *The differend: Phrases in dispute*. Minneapolis: University of Minnesota Press.

MacIntyre, A. (1988). *Whose justice? Which rationality?* Notre Dame, IN: Notre Dame University Press.

MacIntyre, A. (1990). *Three rival versions of moral enquiry*. Notre Dame, IN: Notre Dame University Press.

McCorcle, M. (1982, August). Critical issues in the functioning of interdisciplinary groups. *Small Group Behavior, 13,* 291-310.

McDonald, D., Bammer, G., & Deane, P. (2009). *Research integration using dialogue methods*. Canberra: Australian National University. Retrieved from http://epress.anu.edu.au/dialogue_methods_citation.html

Nash, J. (2008). Transdisciplinary training: Key components and prerequisites for success. *American Journal of Preventive Medicine, 35*(2S): S133–S140.

National Research Council. (2003). *BIO 2010: Transforming undergraduate education for future research biologists*. Washington, DC: National Academies Press.

National Science Foundation, Directorate for Social, Behavioral, and Economic Sciences. (2011). *Rebuilding the mosaic: Fostering research in the social, behavioral, and economic sciences at the National Science Foundation in the next decade*. Arlington, VA: Author.

O'Donnell, A. N., & Derry, S. J. (2005). Cognitive processes in interdisciplinary groups: Problems and possibilities. In S. Derry, C. D. Schunn, & M. A. Gernsbacher (Eds.), *Interdisciplinary collaboration: An emerging cognitive science* (pp. 51–82). Mahwah, NJ: Lawrence Erlbaum.

Pellmar, R., & Eisenberg, L. (Eds.). (2000). *Bridging disciplines in the brain, behavioral, and clinical sciences*. Washington, DC: National Academies Press.

Pohl, C., van Kerkhoff, L., Hirsch, G. H., & Bammer, G. (2008). Integration. In G. Hirsch Hadorn, H. Hoffmann-Riem, S. Biber-Klemm, W. Grossenbacher-Mansuy, D. Joye, C. Pohl, et al. (Eds.), *Handbook of transdisciplinary research* (pp. 411–426). Dordrecht, Switzerland: Springer.

Scholz, R. W. (2011). *Environmental literacy in science and society: From knowledge to decisions.* New York: Cambridge University Press.

Stokols, D., Hall, K. L., Moser, R. P., Feng, A. X., Misra, S., & Taylor, B. K. (2010). Cross-disciplinary team science initiatives: Research, training, and translation. In R. Frodeman, J. T. Klein, & C. Mitcham (Eds.), *The Oxford handbook of interdisciplinarity* (pp. 471–493). New York: Oxford University Press.

Stokols, D., Misra, S., Moser, R. P., Hall, K. L., & Taylor, B. K. (2008). The ecology of team science: Understanding contextual influences on transdisciplinary collaboration. *American Journal of Preventive Medicine, 35*(2), S96–S115.

Stone, A. R. (1969). The interdisciplinary research team. *Journal of Applied Behavioral Science, 5*(3), 351–365.

Strober, M. (2011). *Interdisciplinary conversations: Challenging habits of thought.* Palo Alto, CA: Stanford University Press.

Thiessen, B. L. (1998). Shedding the stagnant slough syndrome: Interdisciplinary integration. *Creativity Research Journal, 11*(1), 47–53.

Thompson, J. L. (2009). Building collective communication competence in interdisciplinary research teams. *Journal of Applied Communication Research, 37*(3), 278–297.

Tuckman, B. W. (1965). Developmental sequence in small groups. *Psychological Bulletin, 63,* 384–399.

Tuckman, B. W., & Jensen, M. A. (1977). Stages of small-group development revisited. *Group and Organization Studies, 2,* 419–427.

Vosskamp, W. (1994). Crossing of boundaries: Interdisciplinarity as an opportunity for universities in the 1990s. *Issues in Integrative Studies, 12,* 43–54.

PART I

Theory

Theory is critical to understanding natural and social phenomena, and understanding is critical to successful intervention in these phenomena. In this volume, the phenomena that concern us are communication and collaboration in interdisciplinary research, and the type of influence we seek to foster is enhancement. We therefore begin this volume with four chapters that examine theoretical aspects of communication in interdisciplinary collaboration. The purpose of this part is to map out key topics of theoretical interest and modes of theorizing about them.

Think of successful collaborative, interdisciplinary research as involving an ability to "play well with others." You might theorize that ability by thinking about *who* gets to play (Chap. 6) or what sorts of persons make good playmates (Chap. 4) or what sorts of "toys" (e.g., concepts) are easiest to play with (Chap. 3); alternatively, you might describe in general what it is like to play the game (Chap. 5). As will become clear, these differences in focus lead to different kinds of theories and different modes of theorizing. To focus on just one dimension of difference, two of the chapters (Chaps. 3 and 5) present abstract accounts of interdisciplinary activity in general, while the other two focus more squarely on interdisciplinary practice. Taken together, these chapters provide the reader with an introduction to state-of-the-art theoretical engagement with collaborative interdisciplinary research.

In the opening chapter of Part I, "Communicating Complex Concepts," Rick Szostak presents a framework for thinking about the communication challenges involved in collaborative interdisciplinary research. The key component of this framework and the focus of the chapter's discussion is the notion of *ambiguity*. For Szostak, ambiguity is the result of "complex" concepts—that is, concepts whose meanings shift from discipline to discipline. Ambiguity results from the use of such concepts because claims expressed using them invite misunderstanding by collaborators from disciplines that understand the concepts differently. Szostak's analysis focuses on the management of ambiguity. In Szostak's view, there are appropriate amounts and kinds of ambiguity for any research project as well as ways to move the total ambiguity involved in the project toward desirable levels. Szostak provides general guidelines for (1) identifying appropriate levels and forms of ambiguity and (2) reducing ambiguity by replacing "complex" concepts with "basic" concepts (i.e., concepts whose meanings are relatively stable across disciplines).

In Chapter 4, Daniel Stokols reflects on the nature of transdisciplinarity with an eye to improving the training of transdisciplinary scholars. In "Training the Next Generation of Transdisciplinarians," he develops an account of the "transdisciplinary intellectual orientation," which is a perspective on research problems and activities that emphasizes a maximal degree of "cross-disciplinary dialogue, integration, and innovation" (p. 60). Examining the transdisciplinary orientation as an individual-level construct, he discusses "the developmental phases and core attitudes, beliefs, values, cognitive skills, and behaviors" that underlie its "cultivation" (p. 56). Deeper appreciation for what enables the individual to engage successfully in transdisciplinary research and practice, Stokols argues, should guide one in developing curricula to instill a transdisciplinary orientation in undergraduate and graduate students. He concludes his chapter by illustrating these longer-term training modalities in the context of courses taught in the School of Social Ecology at the University of California, Irvine.

In Chapter 5, "Beyond Common Ground: A Transdisciplinary Approach to Interdisciplinary Communication and Collaboration," David A. Stone develops and defends a "transdisciplinary" approach to interdisciplinarity that contrasts with what he takes to be the dominant, "disciplinary" approach. This dominant approach is disciplinary for two reasons: (1) It is usually developed from the perspective of a discipline, such as cognitive psychology or intellectual history, and (2) it presupposes the disciplinary division of human knowledge about the world. In contrast with this approach, which privileges the theory of knowledge (i.e., epistemology) and the search for common ground, Stone recommends an approach rooted in a prior concern for ontology and a desire to get *beyond* epistemological common ground. Drawing from Heidegger, he develops a "hermeneutic–phenomenological" account that emphasizes the world under investigation as meaningful and held in common by investigators ahead of any disciplinary divisions. Stone then mobilizes this approach "to show how it may be possible to move *beyond* the epistemologically framed common ground aspired to by the dominant approach to develop transdisciplinary practices that improve interdisciplinary communication" (p. 82).

Part I concludes with "Interdisciplinarity, Communication, and the Limits of Knowledge," by Robert Frodeman. In this chapter, Frodeman looks back on what he calls the "age of disciplinarity" and ahead to the "age of interdisciplinarity." The age of disciplinarity has been marked by academics writing for other academics, governing themselves through systems of peer review, and striving for knowledge in a way that recognizes no limits. By contrast, the age of interdisciplinarity finds the nonacademic world involved as partner and evaluator in the production of knowledge. "Academics become more accountable," Frodeman writes, "which complicates traditional notions of academic autonomy" (p. 103). One consequence of the coproduction of knowledge is the possibility that limits will be imposed, constraining our search for knowledge in various, nonepistemic ways. Communication is central to this argument: In the age of disciplinarity, academics communicate with and for other academics, but in the coming age of interdisciplinarity, participation in the conversation will be much broader and more diverse, a fact that underlies changes in what counts as knowledge, how it is produced, and how far it should go.

3

Communicating Complex Concepts

◆ Rick Szostak

Complex concepts—those that are understood differently across disciplines—can be broken into basic concepts that lend themselves to broadly shared understandings across disciplines. This enhances interdisciplinary communication directly but also aids in exposing differences in disciplinary assumptions of various sorts. Though reducing ambiguity completely is neither possible nor desirable, we can generally reduce ambiguity enough to facilitate cross-disciplinary conversation without impeding scholarly creativity. Several guidelines are proposed regarding how, when, and why to reduce ambiguity.

Introduction_____

Why is interdisciplinary conversation so difficult? One reason is that disciplinary researchers absorb a host of disciplinary assumptions in the course of their education: epistemological, ethical, ideological, theoretical, and methodological. They often may not be conscious of these buried assumptions. Yet they interpret what others say through the lens of these assumptions. Since scholars from other disciplines will not have grounded their utterances in the same set of assumptions, misunderstanding is common. Sometimes the misunderstanding is clear at the time. Commonly, in such situations the hearer wonders how on earth the speaker could have said something so at odds with the hearer's view of how the real and/or scholarly worlds should or do work. More insidiously, the misunderstanding may not be obvious at first, and erstwhile collaborators carry on for some time under a mistaken impression of shared understanding. The solution for this sort of misunderstanding pursued in many chapters in this book is to have collaborators share, compare, and discuss their assumption sets.

Yet there is a second source of barriers to interdisciplinary communication, related to but much simpler than the first. Scholars from different disciplines may quite simply attach different meanings to the same words. When economists speak of "investment," they mean only expenditures on buildings or machines that are used to produce goods or services. An accountant may use "investment" in a manner more in line with common parlance to refer to any expenditure intended to earn a financial return through time. Buying a bond is investment to one but not the other. Such instances of differing definition are common. Yet the expert in one discipline may not feel any need to define words that he or she uses all the time.

The solution to this second type of communication problem must involve reducing differences in meaning—in other words, the degree of ambiguity—across disciplines. But how? And how much? The next section of this chapter will argue that the key lies in breaking complex concepts—those that lend themselves to different interpretations across disciplines (or cultures)—into basic concepts that can be understood similarly across disciplines. Globalization means many things to different people, but its constituent parts—expanded world trade, migration, an increased tendency to watch the same movies—are much less ambiguous.

Addressing the "how" question involves thinking about the nature of concepts. Philosophers have debated the nature of concepts for millennia. They have developed a handful of competing theoretical approaches. We will attempt to integrate these theories. It seems fitting to apply the interdisciplinary strategy of integration to identify the attitude toward concepts best suited to interdisciplinary research. With regard to the "how much" question, one insight of the next section is that interdisciplinary researchers need not pursue the degree of precision generally sought by philosophers: A little ambiguity is acceptable. Indeed, we will find that certain minimal types of ambiguity can actually stimulate discovery.

If the two types of communication problem are related, it follows that solutions to one type may also reduce the other. And, indeed, it will be argued in the third section that breaking complex concepts into basic concepts will often (though not always) expose the sorts of assumptions that generate the first type of communication challenge. Identifying "globalization" or "patriarchy" in terms of basic concepts is not possible without exposing such assumptions.

Succeeding sections of the paper return to questions regarding the ideal amount and type of ambiguity to be sought in interdisciplinary research. The fourth section of the chapter derives several general guidelines regarding ambiguity in interdisciplinary communication. The fifth section discusses how these guidelines inform particular communicative tasks of importance in interdisciplinary research.

The sixth section relates the perspectives developed in earlier sections to literatures in several fields beyond philosophy that have also investigated conceptual ambiguity. This chapter eschews in general the usual practice of referencing these related literatures along the way in favor of summarizing their approaches in a single section (the sixth) and showing in each case how the analysis of this chapter is supported by those literatures. This treatment allows us to show that the approach to ambiguity taken in this chapter can be seen as an interdisciplinary common ground among these various scholarly literatures.

Breaking Complex Concepts Into Basic Concepts

Current philosophical work on the nature of concepts falls into five main schools, along with several less popular lines of argument.[1] Philosophers tend most of the time to argue for the superiority of one of these points of view. But what attitude should the interdisciplinary scholar take toward the philosophical literature? Interdisciplinary researchers are generally counseled away from the sort of "either/or" thinking exemplified in much of the philosophical literature—which suggests that only one theory must be correct—in favor of a "both/and" attitude toward conflicting arguments that urges us to integrate (the best parts of) competing insights into one holistic insight (see Repko, 2011).

It turns out that the major area of disagreement in concept theory revolves around the question of whether complex concepts can be broken into more basic concepts. While these terms—*complex concept, basic concept*, and, indeed, *concept*—are highly contested (Durbin, 1988, p. 51), we can reasonably define them for our purposes. Complex concepts can be defined as those that lend themselves to different interpretations across groups (whether disciplines or cultural groups). Basic concepts can be defined as those for which broadly similar understandings across groups are possible (but not inevitable). These definitions are functional: They focus on the role that concepts play in communication. The titles of the two terms imply that the difference in degree of ambiguity (i.e., variation across groups) rests on "complexity" versus "simplicity"—that the difference in function rests on a difference in essence—but we need not include these

---

[1]The discussion here is necessarily far from exhaustive. Nor is concept theory the only philosophical investigation of ambiguity. Some philosophies, including phenomenology and epistemology, argue that ambiguity is unavoidable. This does not mean that reducing it is not still feasible and desirable. And again, the interdisciplinary scholar should be careful of adopting the most pessimistic among diverse philosophical perspectives.

terms in our definitions. Thus, our test of whether a concept is "basic" lies not in some philosophical evaluation of its simplicity but in a pragmatic evaluation of its potential for limited ambiguity. The fact that the bulk of philosophical work on concepts over the past two millennia has involved attempting to render complex concepts such as freedom in terms of more basic concepts that everyone could agree on indicates that these definitions are at least broadly consistent with the main thrust of philosophical speculation.

If it turns out that complex concepts can be broken into basic concepts—defined as those that lend themselves to shared understandings across groups—then the path to enhancing interdisciplinary communication is clear. We can seek a translation into basic concepts for any complex concepts implicated in interdisciplinary communication. Note that basic concepts need not be understood in an identical fashion across groups. We will discuss in the next section how ambiguous they could and should be. We are seeking here broadly shared understandings.

In what follows, I will briefly sketch the five main types of concept theory (see Margolis & Laurence, 2011, for a survey), key objections made to each within the philosophical literature, and how the interdisciplinary scholar might salvage from each a consistent (but nuanced) attitude toward the possibility of breaking complex concepts into basic concepts. (A lengthier treatment of each from the point of view of information science can be found in Szostak, 2011.)[2]

The classical concept theory. The classical theory was dominant in Western philosophy until well into the late 20th century. It is still commonly pursued. It argues that complex concepts are indeed logical combinations of more basic concepts.

Objections: The primary objection is empirical. Despite millennia of effort, philosophers have been unable to satisfactorily render complex concepts such as "freedom" into basic concepts that all agree on.

Interdisciplinary analysis: Philosophers seek a degree of precision far greater than is required by interdisciplinary research. We need not insist on a precise definition but just a broadly shared understanding. After all, does interdisciplinary communication often stumble over misunderstandings regarding the meaning of "freedom"? Moreover, philosophers have naturally devoted most of their attention to the

---

[2]This article establishes the feasibility of developing a universal classification grounded not in disciplines but in the things we study and the relationships among them. Interdisciplinary researchers would then be better able to find relevant documents *and* understand the concepts used in those documents. (That is, improving communication is not the only benefit of the approach advocated here.) If this were not possible, then information scientists might wish to focus on domain-specific classifications and translations across pairs of documents. And interdisciplinary researchers would continue to painfully master the literature and jargon of other disciplines and/or develop pidgins at the interface of disciplines.

most intractable concepts. We could reasonably expect that there are other complex concepts that are much more readily translated into basic concepts. *Globalization* is a good example, for one could provide a fairly concise list of the economic, political, and cultural processes and outcomes generally associated with that term.

The prototype theory. This theory argues that concepts are not defined logically but, rather, probabilistically. Individuals will be more likely to say "a is an X" if *a* carries certain characteristics they associate with X. Advocates of the theory note that individuals are more likely to associate apples than plums with the concept "fruit," even though both equally fit most scientific definitions of fruit.[3]

Objections: This is clearly not true for at least some concepts, such as "chairs bought on Wednesday," which can be comprehended only logically. Individuals also indicate that they are more likely to associate 3 than 7 with the concept "prime number," even though "prime number" is comprehensible (only?) as a logical combination of "integer" and "nondivisible by another integer." So experimental results need not imply a lack of logical content in concepts.

Interdisciplinary analysis: We can still strive to break complex concepts into basic ones while appreciating that different people/groups may emphasize different elements. Note that interdisciplinary communication can proceed as long as we identify the source of different interpretations of complex concepts. Imagine that some cultural group objects to plums as fruit. As long as we can identify the source of this disagreement, members of that group can communicate without difficulty with others.

The theory theory. This concept theory has become very popular in recent decades. It argues that concepts can be understood only within an individual's web of theories and beliefs. That is, each individual defines concepts to fit within his or her belief set. It is thus not possible for any two individuals to share an identical meaning of a concept or, indeed, to readily comprehend the source of their differences.

Objections: If this theory were entirely correct, then conversation between individuals would be much more difficult than it is. In practice, we are generally able to comprehend others. Moreover, there is good reason to think that concepts precede theories, rather than the reverse—that Newton had clear ideas of "force" and "mass" in place before hypothesizing $F = ma$, rather than developing his theory and seeking concepts to fit. If so, people who support different theories

---

[3]This result holds for societies in which apples are common, but different prototypes may dominate in societies where apples are rare. In cognitive science, prototypes are viewed as the core mental model for a concept.

might either share similar concepts (creationists can understand what evolution of species means) or at least be able to identify the source of such differences (economists and accountants can readily appreciate each other's definitions of investment without needing to master each other's theories).

Interdisciplinary analysis: While the theory theory need not deter us from the pursuit of basic concept translations, we are well advised to appreciate that (at least for many concepts) the meaning an individual/ group attaches to a particular complex concept will be influenced by a host of beliefs. In this way, the approach pursued in this paper can be seen as symbiotic with the approach taken elsewhere in this volume of encouraging collaborators to identify their key beliefs on a host of issues.

Conceptual atomism. This theory argues that concepts are grounded in our perceptions of the real world. Our understanding of dogs comes from perceiving dogs.

Objections: As with prototype theory, it has been noted that some sort of logical analysis must be important for at least some concepts. For our purposes, one key objection has been to the assumption that all concepts have clear external referents. It has been suggested that one might conceive of some concepts as being built up from those with external referents.

Interdisciplinary analysis: Conceptual atomism provides hope that individuals can share understandings of concepts if they share broadly similar perceptions (though of course our perceptions may to some extent be shaped by our beliefs). It also suggests that shared understandings are most likely for things (and relationships, such as "hitting" or "paying") that we readily perceive. But interdisciplinary scholars are likely to join those who have suggested that some concepts may be combinations of other concepts that have external referents. If so, these latter could be what we have termed *complex concepts*, and we could be confident that they can be broken into the basic concepts from which they were generated.

Pluralism. Despite the tendency of philosophers to argue for one philosophical approach, there is an increasing tendency to appreciate that each of the above approaches, and perhaps others, provides useful insight. It could be that some theories are more appropriate for some concepts than others.

Objections: The main objection is implicit in the arguments of those philosophers who believe that only one approach is meritorious. If it is argued that only one theory is correct, then it cannot be accepted that multiple theories have value.

Interdisciplinary analysis: The pluralist approach is clearly supportive of the interdisciplinary "both/and" orientation. The interdisciplinary scholar can be comfortable in concluding that at least some complex concepts—likely most, maybe all—can indeed be broken into basic concepts that can be understood across groups. We are guided to look in particular toward grounding basic concepts in shared perceptions and, thus, in the things and relationships we observe in the real world. Yet we are guided to appreciate that people's understandings of concepts may differ because of different beliefs or different senses of the key characteristics of a concept. In such a situation, we should strive to identify the source of disagreement. It is in this sort of endeavor that the interdisciplinary scholar could inform and be informed by the sort of inquiry regarding beliefs and preferences advocated elsewhere in this volume.

It was noted above that philosophers tend to pursue a degree of precision greater than is required by the interdisciplinary researcher. It should be stressed that whereas the philosopher asks, "Is there ambiguity?" the interdisciplinarian asks, "Is there too much ambiguity?" This—in concert with the more positive message that can be derived from other theories of concepts—should guide us away from the claims of more pessimistic versions of the theory theory regarding the possibilities of interdisciplinary communication. It should also guide us to add an empirical element to the theoretical considerations of philosophers. As we address particular concepts, we can ask how easy it is to break these into basic concepts and also which concept theory(ies) seems most relevant.[4]

Concepts and Assumptions

It is useful at this point to expand on how the approach of breaking complex concepts into basic concepts is symbiotic with the task of identifying researchers' philosophical and methodological assumptions. Let us imagine that a research group is studying some aspects of "globalization." In breaking this complex concept into basic concepts, it would be noted that it involves how economic and political integration, and the spread of cultural elements through mass media, affects political sovereignty, local economies, and local cultures. It would clearly be useful for the researchers in the group to appreciate which of the causal forces and which of the effects is stressed

---

[4]Szostak (2011) recommends a similar empirical approach within information science. This paper provides empirical support for the type of argument made here by summarizing how a lengthy section of the Dewey Decimal Classification (300 through 399.9) can be translated into basic concepts. See also my outline of the Basic Concepts Classification and the detailed results of the translation exercise at http://www.economics.ualberta.ca/en/FacultyandStaff/~/media/economics/FacultyAndStaff/Szostak/Szostak-Basic-Concept-Classification2.pdf and http://www.economics.ualberta.ca/en/FacultyandStaff/~/media/economics/FacultyAndStaff/Szostak/Szostak-Dewey-Conversion-Table.pdf.

by each researcher (prototype theory would guide us to appreciate that some see globalization as primarily economic while others see it as primarily cultural). While "globalization" lends itself to considerable ambiguity, we could anticipate a much greater degree of shared understanding of elements of globalization such as "increased trade flows as a share of GDP," "increased flows of foreign investment" (though, as seen previously, we need then to clearly define investment), "increased international access to songs via the Internet" and so on.[5] Yet the research group would benefit from a further probing of assumptions of various types that each researcher may carry into the research project:

> **Ethical, ideological:** "Globalization" is often employed by scholars who suspect that it is largely or even entirely a negative process. Yet others hail certain aspects of globalization: the spread of democratic ideals, technological innovations, and/or cultural attitudes toward the role of women. While, arguably, a scientific concept should be defined in a value-free manner, in practice these attitudes will have an important impact on what "globalization" truly means to individual researchers. Note that it will be possible to get much more precise answers to this question if one has first identified the range of effects commonly associated with globalization.

> **Epistemological, methodological:** Is it a good research strategy to investigate the effects of a vaguely defined "globalization" itself, or does research best focus at the level of particular causal relationships: How do the particular economic, political, and cultural elements of globalization interact, and how do they generate particular effects? (The author confesses to a strong preference for the latter.) The research group is much more likely to agree on specific research strategies if there is some shared understanding of how best to study globalization. Note that it is much easier to ask and interpret the answers to this sort of inquiry if one has first broken the concept of globalization into its constituent parts (both causes and effects).

At the risk of digressing a bit, the author would argue here that one of the key benefits of breaking complex concepts into basic concepts is precisely that it will encourage research in terms of concepts with broadly shared understandings. Simply put, research involving concepts whose meanings are fairly clear is usually much more useful than research involving vaguely defined terminology (we try to clarify what is meant by "fairly

---

[5]One reader of this chapter wondered what the value of the broad ambiguous term *globalization* then is. Its value may well depend on the degree to which the cultural, economic, and political aspects of globalization interact. This degree of interaction needs to be determined empirically, not casually assumed.

clear" in the next section). Arguing that "globalization causes X" without clearly defining what is meant by "globalization" not only means that one's results are unnecessarily ambiguous but also may generate skeptical responses to one's research: How can one accurately study what is not even defined? Moreover, if the purpose of the research is to inform public policy or political attitudes, how can we know how to reduce the deleterious effects (or enhance the positive effects) of globalization without clearly identifying the precise causal mechanisms at work? An argument that increased flows of certain types of foreign investment increase economic instability is easier to understand, easier to evaluate, and lends itself to the identification of specific policies that might ameliorate the difficulty identified.

> **Theoretical:** It is useful for members of research teams to understand the theoretical preferences of team members. Yet, as the theory theory argues, it can be difficult to fully appreciate another's theoretical outlook. One very useful practice here would be to ask all team members to "map" their theoretical assumptions onto the basic concepts identified. That is, they would identify the causal forces and effects they pay most attention to and draw arrows among these to indicate what affects what. They would then briefly describe the nature of the effect(s) posited along each arrow (the advantages of mapping causal arguments for interdisciplinary research are stressed in Repko, 2011). Note that such effects should ideally be included within the translation of "globalization" into basic concepts. As noted above, these effects include not just the things we perceive but the relationships among them. Yet in practice it may be hard to list all the causal relationships posited within the vast literature on globalization (especially those that may be only vaguely described). So, while this would be useful, interdisciplinary research teams may often find that they need to focus on the theories posited by (and perhaps those disdained by) team members.

In sum, then, the practice of interrogating researcher assumptions can serve (for at least some concepts) as an invaluable extension of the process of breaking complex concepts into basic concepts. In turn, the process of breaking complex concepts into basic concepts can aid in the process of interrogating assumptions because it allows for questions regarding assumptions of various types to be targeted to the precise needs of the research team. It is useful to tease out the general epistemological attitudes of team members, but asking a precise question regarding the value of posing research questions in terms of a complex concept such as globalization or a basic concept such as foreign investment may serve both to clarify the epistemological outlook of team members and to highlight the challenges for the overall research project of epistemological differences.

How Much and What Kind of Ambiguity?

One critical insight from the second section is that we need not and should not seek perfection: It is not necessary that scholars share the exact same understanding of a concept (that is, that the concept be "univocal") but only that they share a broadly similar understanding. This insight allows us to appreciate the philosophical conclusion that some ambiguity is inevitable without interpreting this as an absolute barrier to interdisciplinary conversation. Only by backing away from the search for perfection are we able to salvage hope of shared understanding. But how much ambiguity should we accept?

Indeed, we should be clear that the second section has established only the *possibility* of shared cross-disciplinary understandings. It established that some degree of ambiguity is acceptable. But it did not, and indeed could not, establish that an acceptable degree of ambiguity is attainable. This can be established only in practice. Since the philosophical literature hardly embraces the question of "how much," it cannot by its nature tell us if we can reduce ambiguity enough. Yet the simple fact that we do manage to converse across cultural and disciplinary boundaries suggests that this must often be the case.

This point deserves emphasis. It was noted earlier that philosophers focus on the most intractable of definitional challenges. The interdisciplinary researcher will often confront concepts less challenging than "freedom" or "justice." The following should thus be stressed before moving on:

> *There are "boring" concepts out there with shared definitions.* We should thus be clear that for some concepts (which may be much less boring to the interdisciplinary researcher than to the philosopher of concept theory), a high degree of definitional clarity is both readily achievable and desirable.

But there are also many complex concepts out there that are interpreted quite differently by different individuals or groups. These will be our focus in the rest of this section. An important additional wrinkle here comes from the observation that ambiguity is not always a bad thing. Poetry exerts much of its attraction precisely because words are employed in a way that simultaneously evokes different meanings. It is thus not surprising that humanists, such as Bal, have been some of the staunchest advocates of the value of conceptual ambiguity in stimulating intellectual curiosity (see especially Bal, 2002). Yet Bal also appreciates that ambiguity imposes costs and, thus, that concepts "need to be clear, explicit, and defined" (p. 22). Interdisciplinary analysis will be incoherent unless scholars can agree on what particular concepts mean (p. 28). This suggests that there may be some ideal degree and kind of ambiguity that somehow maximizes the benefit-to-cost ratio.[6]

Paul E. Griffiths and Karola Stotz (see Chap. 10 this volume) also argue that ambiguity in our understanding of concepts can sometimes stimulate research. Notably, their examples are from natural science. Griffiths and Stotz argue that the "gene" concept worked despite ambiguity because it guided research and because there were sufficient similarities across three broad types of definition that they have identified (though they doubt there is one definition that covers all three). That is, differing definitions were broadly complementary but emphasized elements of interest to researchers in different fields, and as a result the research produced was also largely complementary. In contrast, debate regarding "innateness" has been a disaster because there are eight key constituents and the concept derives from a folk biology belief in inherent characteristics. As a result, at present, researchers emphasize quite independent aspects of innateness and thus talk past each other. Griffiths and Stotz conclude that ambiguity is like cholesterol: There are good and bad kinds.

Our discussion in the second section allows us to draw some important inferences from the analyses provided by Griffiths, Stotz, and Bal. These can be proposed as guidelines for coping with ambiguity in interdisciplinary research. We begin with some general reflections on ambiguity and definition and proceed toward more detailed discussion of how decomposition into basic concepts affects both good and bad kinds of ambiguity.

- *Ambiguity stimulates curiosity and thus diversity.* One major advantage of ambiguity is that it means the curiosity of different researchers can be stimulated in different ways. They each may be attracted to different and often conflicting characterizations of a concept. Gene researchers could find aspects of interest in complementary definitions of "gene," some of which focused on how genes were generated, others on how they were constituted, and still others on their function. And many researchers will be enticed to clarify meaning, while others will thrill to the very multifaceted nature of a concept. Scholarly understanding advances through scholarly conversation, and scholars of interdisciplinarity are disposed to believe that this conversation will be most fruitful if scholars with different backgrounds are involved. Some degree of ambiguity encourages a richer scholarly conversation.

- *In cases where decreasing ambiguity does decrease curiosity, this will often be a good thing.* We need to ask whether the sort of curiosity being encouraged is likely to result in productive research. For example, breaking a concept such as "innateness" into its constituent basic concepts

---

[6]For example, though ambiguity may be essential to literature, it need not be essential to the study of literature. While it may at times be useful to employ ambiguity in illustrating the ambiguities within a particular text, there should still be scope for (striving to) unambiguously identifying ambiguities.

will illustrate that the idea of "innateness" abstracts away from the fact that genetic inheritance and environmental circumstances interact in generating behaviors and personality. If one draws a map that contains the many hypothesized interactions between genes and environment in generating personality traits, then it should be obvious that "innateness"—at least as understood by some groups of researchers as involving direct influences of genes on behavior—makes sense only if these interactions are relatively unimportant. An appreciation of this might guide researchers away from analysis in terms of "innateness" toward more carefully specified research into how particular aspects of genetic inheritance exert their effects within a (well-mapped) set of interactions.[7]

• *It may not be necessary (at first) for everyone in the conversation to share the same understanding, as long as these understandings are potentially consistent.* Imagine that one group of scholars conceives of genes primarily in terms of their chemical makeup and pursues research designed to further clarify this, another group conceives of genes primarily in terms of the role they play in organisms and focuses on researching that aspect of genes, and a third group identifies genes in terms of how they evolve and studies that. In such a situation, we could well imagine that the three groups are able to achieve much. They will even be able to usefully borrow insights from one another as long as their definitions are consistent. But if one group's conception of the chemical composition of genes is inconsistent with another group's conception of how they evolve or how they work, then it may prove impossible to resolve (and perhaps even comprehend) this inconsistency without first achieving some shared understanding of "gene" itself.[8]

• *It is useful to ask whether different definitions conflict or merely focus on different aspects of a problem.* Once the working definitions employed by different researchers have been broken into basic concepts, the interdisciplinary researcher can usefully ask if they are in conflict or not. If they are in conflict, then strategies for overcoming that conflict (see above) can be employed. If they are not in conflict, one need do no more than clarify how different interpretations are related. There is likely a middle ground where there is a large core of shared understanding but disagreements around the edges. Definitions of particular subatomic particles might fall into this category: Physicists agree on a lot, but theories disagree about important elements. In such a case it is still useful for scholars to understand the source of disagreements, but attempting to overcome disputes may be premature. In other words, the remaining ambiguity is likely the good kind of ambiguity:

---

[7]Griffiths and Stotz (Chap. 10 this volume) suggest that researchers would be better off if they organized research around what was "in DNA."

[8]Note that it may be much more important to have consensus regarding *what* a concept is than *why* it exists or *how* it operates. (Asking *what*, *how*, *why*, and maybe *where* and *when* can be a good strategy for clarifying definitions.)

Scientists can test different theories and ideally achieve consensus over time on a less ambiguous definition. And note that theories can best be tested against each other if the subtle differences in definition underpinning different theories are appreciated.

- *Direct conflicts in definition likely create more of a challenge than potentially consistent differences but may be addressed more quickly.* This may seem obvious but deserves emphasis. Researchers that have different but consistent understandings of a concept should generally be able to converse more readily than those who have incompatible definitions. Yet there is an important caveat: Those who disagree may soon come to appreciate that they have different starting points, whereas it may take some time for those who are taking on different aspects of a shared concept to appreciate that their starting points are different (albeit not in conflict). Thus, while the first situation is more troubling, it may be addressed more quickly than the second.

- *Breaking complex concepts into basic concepts can reduce the costs of ambiguity with limited or no effects on the benefits.* In a case like gene research, outlining how each of the three groups conceives of genes in terms of more basic concepts—and likely mapping these overlapping understandings[9]— would allow researchers to better appreciate how they might learn from others. But it would not at all prevent members of each group from continuing research as they had before.

- *Ambiguity can be decreased without all researchers sharing the same definition.* If different definitions are consistent, then this result is straightforward. But even if definitions conflict, researchers can potentially come to understand the source of this conflict. They can then understand what another researcher is saying (and why) even though they continue to disagree regarding definitions. The literature on interdisciplinary research suggests various strategies for overcoming such conflicts: It may be possible to adjust the conflicting definitions so the conflict is resolved, or it may be better to appreciate that the two concepts are in fact referring to different things and/ or processes in the world. Either strategy depends on first identifying the source of the conflict (Repko, 2011). East Germany claimed to be a "democracy" because its definition of democracy did not insist on "free elections" among "self-selected candidates." If we had a general definition of democracy that included these elements, it would be straightforward to identify how the East German definition was different. By identifying the source of conflicts, interdisciplinary communication can be enhanced directly.

- *One bad kind of ambiguity is one in which vagueness about the meaning of a concept serves to hide logical or theoretical inconsistencies at its heart.* Ambiguity of this sort is the most harmful, for scholars investigating

---

[9]A diagram might show how genes evolve to have certain characteristics and how these generate certain outcomes.

such a concept are unlikely to advance human understanding. Breaking such a concept into basic concepts is likely to expose these inherent inconsistencies (as in the "innateness" example).

• *One good kind of ambiguity is one associated (temporarily) with cutting-edge research.* In the earliest days of gene research, researchers could not know many key details of what a gene was and how it worked. Different definitions of "gene" might then be associated with different theories, and it would be hard to define gene such that advocates of different theories would understand it in the same way. Advocates of theory theory might argue that such definitions are clearly theory dependent. Nevertheless, interdisciplinary scholars could strive to define/map these competing definitions in a way that would contribute to the all-important task of deciding which definition accords best with empirical analysis. Note here that while the example is drawn from natural science, this beneficial sort of ambiguity might be even more common in the social sciences and humanities.

• *The key to the right kind of clarity is inclusiveness.* In developing a definition, one should not casually ignore the interpretation of a concept pursued by any group. One will be able at times to show that different understandings are consistent and at other times to overcome inconsistencies. In other instances, it may turn out that different groups are in fact talking about different things. In none of these cases does the act of clarification deter research (unless some group studying hamsters recoils at the insight that they are not studying the more popular "dog"). The only case where research is deterred is when some inconsistency at the very heart of a concept is uncovered, and presumably this is not the sort of ambiguity that anyone wishes to celebrate. We want enough ambiguity to stimulate curiosity but not enough to cause confusion and certainly not so much as to render research unintelligible.

Addressing Particular Research Communication Tasks

The above comments have been focused at the general level of interdisciplinary communication. Further clarification can be provided with respect to some of the more focused concerns that motivate this volume.

Negotiation and Compromise

Negotiation and compromise will proceed best in general when researchers understand what they are talking about. Political negotiation may seem to present a counter-example to this claim. For example, compromise in Canadian constitutional negotiations has often been achieved only by different parties attaching different meanings to key concepts such as "nation."

However, this sort of ambiguous compromise generates huge potential head-aches in legal interpretation. For a research team, a compromise grounded in ignorance of what the other believes or intends seems ill advised. The potential for the research process to derail as this misunderstanding unfolds is huge. The research team is thus strongly encouraged to, at the very least, understand how team members define key concepts and, ideally, to strive for shared or consistent understandings.[10]

In agreeing on a shared research enterprise, researchers will necessarily grapple with the meanings of multiple concepts. Halperin (1997) argues that scientists must grapple with six types of relationship among concepts.[11] The first of these, "X causes Y," was addressed by the mapping exercise outlined earlier. Three more, "X is a part of Y," "X is an example of Y," and "X is a characteristic of Y," should be addressed as each complex concept is broken into basic concepts. A fifth, "X is like Y (or not)," would be addressed as it was determined whether different researchers were talking about the same thing or not. The last, "X is evidence of Y," would be dealt with only through a combination of clarity in definition and agreement on matters epistemological and methodological. The Halperin categorization may not be exhaustive—relationships themselves may be concepts—but the analysis here suggests that the procedures advocated above would allow a research team to negotiate not just the meaning of concepts but the place of each concept in the research program.[12]

Identity

Likewise, it is useful for differences in identity to be reasonably transparent. If you are going to collaborate with another, you will want to know whom you are dealing with. The process outlined above, in which interrogation of assumptions is integrated with clarification of definitions in terms of basic concepts, will elucidate key elements of researcher identity.

---

[10]This chapter has not directly addressed the power imbalances that can afflict inter-disciplinary team research. The guidelines provided above may be of little use to an arrogant team leader who simply ignores what more junior colleagues have to say. But if team members are disposed in principle to try to understand one another, then the guidelines suggested here should serve as an antidote to the human tendency to ignore those who are hard to understand or have less social status.

[11]Linguists distinguish between ambiguity associated with a particular concept and ambiguity associated with a particular phrase. The latter often revolves around what a subordinate clause refers to (as in the famous "I shot an elephant in my pajamas"). For our purposes, we can focus on being explicit about relationships rather than worrying about sentence structure.

[12]Meltzoff (1998) argues that research will be weak unless research questions are framed clearly. He stresses in particular the importance of establishing (1) whether X exists, (2) the characteristics and classification of X, and (3) the components of X.

It is worth noting here that the concept "identity" itself yields two related but distinct understandings: one focused on an individual's view of self and the other on one's sense of group identification. Since interdisciplinary researchers are often somewhat atypical of disciplines in which they may have been trained, it may be useful for them to reflect on both their disciplinary identity and personal identity.

Communicating With the Public or Granting Agencies or Administrators

Translation of complex concepts into basic concepts is often straightforward. The exercise pursued in Szostak (2011) suggests that the vast majority of complex social science concepts employed as subject headings in the Dewey Decimal Classification can be comprehended in terms of between two and five basic concepts. We can thus imagine a classification system for scholarly understandings that is grounded in basic concepts; such a classification could be comprehended and navigated by both scholars and the public. Nevertheless, in some cases—and especially when related understandings need to be mapped in order for complex concepts to be clarified—the sort of definition that is recommended above may prove too complex for purposes of outside communication. It may be best in such circumstances to use the most relevant part of a definition for a particular external audience, perhaps with a link to the complete definition. While this solution is not ideal, it is still generally preferable to not having a precise (if complex) definition to communicate in the first place.

The compromise just suggested reflects important facts about the nature of language. While Noam Chomsky and other linguists have suggested that the ubiquity of ambiguity must mean that language has not been evolutionarily selected for communication, other scholars of linguistic evolution have argued that evolution must grapple with a trade-off between precision and simplicity (in both memory and utterances).[13] We must extend our utterances significantly to achieve precision (and absolute precision is generally unattainable). In everyday conversation, context (plus the fact that there are often dominant meanings of particular concepts) usually allows a fair degree of shared understanding of utterances couched in ambiguous concepts and clausal structures. When precision is particularly important, as in legal documents, we sacrifice simplicity in its pursuit. The recommendation here—that we use different degrees of precision in different contexts—is, thus, simply a recognition of this evolutionarily important trade-off.

---

[13]See the article by Piantadosi, S. T., Tily, H., and Gibson, E. at http://web.mit.edu/piantado/www/papers/PiantadosiTilyGibson2010-submitted.pdf (accessed September 6, 2011).

Relating Our Discussion to Many Relevant Literatures _____

The above analysis is broadly consistent with many scholarly literatures. Rather than interrupt the flow of the preceding analysis with frequent references to diverse literatures, these are reviewed here. In briefly surveying these literatures, I follow the stricture, invoked with respect to concept theory earlier, that we should seek to respect competing views rather than select only one.

Semiotics

Semiotics stresses that the words used to signify the things in the world never perfectly capture what they signify. There is thus inevitable ambiguity in human communication. The semiotician should aid in the process of interpretation (e.g., Barthes, 1957/2000). That is, while ambiguity is inevitable, we can pursue strategies to lessen the degree of ambiguity. The strategies outlined in this paper are thus consistent with a long tradition of attempts to reduce the inevitable ambiguity in human communication.

Communications Theory

Communications theory generally addresses "thought units" rather than "concepts." A single sentence may contain several thought units, or several sentences may form one thought unit. Theorists study how one thought unit provides context for others (Keyton & Beck, 2010). A critical insight here is that the context in which a particular concept is uttered *may* serve to clarify its meaning. Sentences are thus usually less ambiguous than words, and paragraphs less ambiguous than sentences. Nevertheless, politicians and others can still produce ambiguous statements of great length. While placing concepts in context does not guarantee clarity, this analysis does reinforce our belief that it is possible to reduce conceptual ambiguity through discussion and analysis.

This leads to an even more central implication of communications theory: that meaning is developed intersubjectively through communication. It is appreciated that team members bring different expectations and understandings. Team members then work toward shared understandings conversationally. They can be trained in (imperfect) strategies for reducing the ambiguity that necessarily results. Success in reducing ambiguity will depend critically on the development of compatible "mental models" among participants. That is, they need not see the world in the same way but must come to see it in compatible ways (Keyton, Beck, & Asbury, 2010). Breaking complex concepts into basic concepts and mapping the differences in meaning that group members may attach to complex concepts is a practice (one that can be trained) that should indeed lead to compatible mental models.

Linguistics and Anthropology

The debates regarding the Sapir-Whorf hypothesis—that the structures of different languages severely constrain cognitive processes in quite different ways and thus cause different groups to perceive the world quite differently— seem to have resulted in a fair degree of consensus that these effects exist but are limited in scope: that, for the most part, human cognitive capabilities are universal. Still, linguists appreciate that one source of cross-cultural misunderstanding may be that different languages exert some effect on thought patterns (e.g., Cook & Bassetti, 2010). Though one must be careful in extrapolating from cross-language communication to within-language communication, it seems likely that the difficulties experienced by those who speak the same language but define concepts differently should be manageable. Linguists work to reduce cross-cultural misunderstanding by more fully documenting the structures of different languages. We can work to reduce misunderstanding rooted in different conceptual understandings by outlining the different sets of basic concepts that ground different understandings of particular concepts.

Metaphor

Paul Ricoeur (1978) is perhaps the most famous of those who have argued that a novel metaphor provides a new insight into the concepts to which it refers. The value of metaphor in generating interdisciplinary understanding has been celebrated by (among others) Bill Newell and Allen Repko (see Repko, 2011). But metaphors are never perfect, and scholarly understanding must eventually advance to appreciate in what precise ways A is like B and in what ways it is not. Think here of how evolutionary theory is applied to a host of different phenomena. To say that "culture evolves" is a highly useful way of capturing much that is important about how cultures change. But, arguably, the source of mutations, transmission mechanisms, and selection environment are qualitatively different in important ways from biological evolution (the type of evolution with which most people are most familiar), and these differences need to be carefully articulated to avoid misunderstanding. The process of breaking complex concepts into basic concepts allows us to retain the benefits of metaphor while avoiding misunderstanding. Note that in some cases it may take a considerable amount of scholarly reflection to clarify why a particular metaphor seems so powerful—indeed, especially in the humanities, this sort of pursuit may never achieve closure. It is nevertheless the direction in which we should strive to move.

Ricoeur (and many others) also stressed the importance of narrative in making sense of people's lives. That is, we all construct a narrative of how we are affected by others and in turn act in the world. It follows that an individual's understanding of a concept may be embedded in narrative. As a result, the best way of uncovering the meaning they attach to a concept is to map how they see that concept acting and being acted on in the world. These are often important aspects of the definition of a concept and also inform our understanding of a concept's internal composition or essence.

Trading Zones and Pidgins

Galison (1997) argues that interdisciplinary research collaboration often requires the development of trading zones or pidgins that allow researchers from different fields to understand enough of what the other is talking about to be able to collaborate. Physicists and engineers working together on radar developed the concept of "equivalent circuits," which was defined in complementary but different fashions by the two groups: to accord with field theory by physicists and with radio technology by engineers. Julie Thomson Klein has in various works (e.g., Klein, 1996) also discussed the value of such trading zones or pidgins. The key messages that one might draw from this literature are that, even in natural science, ambiguity is a major barrier to interdisciplinary collaboration, collaborators need not understand all aspects of the other's discipline, and collaborators do need to understand how the objects of interest in a research collaboration fit within the other's broader understandings. To place these insights within the terminology employed in this paper, we need not define every concept employed in source disciplines but only those involved in the research exercise and, indeed, only the shared elements of these complex concepts. Particular care should be taken in understanding relationships in which concepts are involved. Surgeons evaluating MRI results need not comprehend every detail of the workings of that device but do need to learn which markings represent real lesions rather than merely artifacts of how the machine operates; this lesson could first be learned only by someone familiar with both MRI technology and the needs of surgeons (Baird & Cohen, 1999). Thus, breaking complex concepts into basic concepts (understanding the necessary details of how the MRI works) and mapping relationships among these (this mark signifies a lesion) seems like a good strategy.

Information Science

The author of this chapter has advocated many of the ideas in this chapter within the field of information science (see Szostak, 2011, in particular). Information scientists struggle with issues of ambiguity. Notably, their awareness of the philosophical literature on ambiguity has not deterred them from treating complex concepts within classification systems. Yet most general classification systems in use today are grounded in disciplines. Is this a historical artifact or a reflection of the nature of ambiguity? I have argued for the former and in particular for the development of a universal classification system grounded not in disciplines but in basic concepts.[14]

The task of breaking all complex concepts into basic concepts segues into the development of a universal hierarchical classification of the things we study and the relationships that might exist among these. While a particular research team may be concerned with only a handful of complex concepts, it is worth noting here that the task of clarifying the constituent components of a complex concept can be aided by also speaking to what a concept is not. We understand a quark better, not just by identifying its characteristics as a type of subatomic particle but also by identifying the characteristics of other subatomic particles. And further clarity comes from appreciating different types of quark. There is, thus, a huge complementarity both across the efforts of different scholars to break particular complex concepts into basic concepts and between such efforts and those proceeding within information science to develop a hierarchical classification of basic concepts (see Szostak, 2011).

Take-Home Messages

While we cannot pinpoint the ideal degree of ambiguity in any sort of measureable fashion (short of somewhat tautologically deciding that the degree is good if research is proceeding well)—though we could strive to identify good and bad ambiguity—we have achieved a more important pragmatic conclusion:

• Breaking complex concepts into basic concepts, coupled with interrogation of the assumptions of researchers, as advocated in the second section of this chapter, can be expected to move us toward the ideal form of ambiguity. That is, the fact that ambiguity may sometimes be useful is not a rationale for discouraging the pursuit of some considerable degree of clarity.

• The bulleted points in the fourth section can be seen as clarifications of this conclusion. They provide guidance on how, when, and why to reduce ambiguity.

• One critical question is whether "good" ambiguity is always temporary. If one hopes that scholarly conversation generates a narrowing of the range of plausible understandings, then it might be expected that ambiguity in definition should fade as the range of plausible understandings of what

---

[14]This would, among other things, allow us to identify different definitions of complex concepts precisely with reference to a common set of basic concepts.

a thing is or how a certain process operates diminishes. Of course, this process may be slow and uneven, and ambiguity may necessarily increase at times as new understandings are suggested. Recall the discussion of "middle ground" earlier: Should we expect that the core of shared understanding expands (albeit unsteadily) through time while areas of disagreement erode?

- A positive answer to the preceding point—and, indeed, our confidence that breaking complex concepts into basic concepts will be a positive process—depends on ambiguity not exerting positive effects not addressed earlier. Does ambiguity sometimes cause researchers to draw valid connections among things or processes that were mistakenly thought at first to be parts of the same concept? Perhaps. But do we urge laboratory scientists to be sloppy because sloppiness helped Fleming discover penicillin? The process of mapping relationships that was advocated above seems a much more straightforward and powerful strategy for identifying new relationships than relying on happy surprises grounded in confusion. We can hope instead that resolving the source of ambiguity will generate concepts that inspire constructive curiosity.

Acknowledgments

The author thanks participants at the "Enhancing Communication in Cross-Disciplinary Research" conference for helpful advice. He thanks anonymous referees and especially the editors for useful guidance in revising the paper.

References

Baird, D., & Cohen, M. S. (1999). Why trade? *Perspectives on Science, 7*(2), 231–254.

Bal, M. (2002). *Travelling concepts in the humanities: A rough guide.* Toronto: University of Toronto Press.

Barthes, R. (2000). *Mythologies* (A. Lavers, Trans.). New York: Hill & Wang. (Original work published in 1957)

Cook, V., & Bassetti, B. (2010). *Language and bilingual cognition.* New York: Psychology Press.

Durbin, P. T. (1988). *Dictionary of concepts in the philosophy of science.* New York: Greenwood Press.

Galison, P. (1997). *Image and logic: A material culture of microphysics.* Chicago: University of Chicago Press.

Halperin, D. F. (1997). *Critical thinking across the humanities.* Mahwah, NJ: Lawrence Erlbaum.

Keyton, J., & Beck, S. J. (2010). Perspective: Examining communication as macro-cognition in STS. *Human Factors, 52*(2), 335–339.

Keyton, J., Beck, S. J., & Asbury, M. B. (2010). Macrocognition: A communication perspective. *Theoretical Issues in Ergonomics Science, 11*(4), 272–286.

Klein, J. T. (1996). *Crossing boundaries: Knowledge, disciplinarities, and interdisciplinarities*. Charlottesville: University of Virginia Press.

Margolis, E., & Laurence, S. (2011). Concepts. In *Stanford encyclopedia of philosophy*. Retrieved from http://plato.stanford.edu/entries/concepts/

Meltzoff, J. (1998). *Critical thinking about research*. Washington, DC: American Psychological Association.

Repko, A. (2011). *Interdisciplinary research: Process and theory* (2nd ed.). Thousand Oaks, CA: Sage.

Ricoeur, P. (1978). The rule of metaphor: Multi-disciplinary studies in the creation of meaning in language (R. Czerny, Trans.). Toronto: University of Toronto Press.

Szostak, R. (2011). Complex concepts into basic concepts. *Journal of the American Society for Information Society and Technology, 62*(11), 2247–2265.

4

Training the Next Generation of Transdisciplinarians

◆ Daniel Stokols*

Team members' capacity for cross-disciplinary communication and collaboration can be enhanced through a variety of training strategies, ranging from short-term, project-specific approaches (e.g., team science training workshops, collaborative readiness audits) to longer term modalities (e.g., college curricula, experiential learning, graduate and postgraduate internships incorporating multiple mentors from different fields) that are designed to cultivate an enduring transdisciplinary (TD) intellectual orientation that occurs over the course of an individual's career development. This chapter addresses the developmental phases and core attitudes, beliefs, values, cognitive skills, and behaviors underlying the cultivation of a scholar's TD orientation. Differences between the proposed conceptualization of a TD orientation and related theoretical constructs are considered. Examples are presented of curricular strategies designed to promote a TD orientation among undergraduate and graduate students within the School of Social Ecology at University of California, Irvine, and to enable them to communicate and collaborate more effectively as members of TD research teams. Efforts to evaluate the effectiveness of these training strategies also are discussed.

*The author thanks Julie Thompson-Klein and the editors of this volume for their helpful comments on earlier versions of the manuscript.

Introduction

The chapters in this volume reflect the surge of interest in cross-disciplinary approaches to a wide range of scientific and community problems that have emerged over the past few decades (cf., Frodeman, Klein, & Mitcham, 2010; Hirsch Hadorn et al., 2008; Kessel, Rosenfield, & Anderson, 2008; Klein, 1996; Repko, 2008; td-net, 2010; Whitfield, 2008). Cross-disciplinary teams have become increasingly prevalent across many research domains, owing to the growing recognition in academia and society at large that the world's most complex and intractable problems—including global climate change, poverty, war, famine, and disease—can be better understood and ameliorated from a broad interdisciplinary perspective than from the narrower vantage points of separate fields (Berkes, Colding, & Folke, 2003; Crow, 2010; Esparza & Yamada, 2007; Fry, 2001; Laszlo, 2001; Wuchty, Jones, & Uzzi, 2007).

The presumed benefits of cross-disciplinary approaches to scientific and community problems are widely touted, especially the potential for achieving a more comprehensive understanding of those problems when viewed from multiple rather than singular conceptual and methodological perspectives (Abrams, 2006; Higginbotham, Albrecht, & Connor, 2001; Naveh, 2001; Rosenfield, 1992; Weingart & Stehr, 2000). Yet it is also apparent that cross-disciplinary research programs and teams are not uniformly successful and occasionally falter due to the linguistic divides and interpersonal tensions that may arise among proponents of divergent scientific worldviews, and the labor intensity of collaborative ventures (Fiore, 2008; Morse, Nielsen-Pincus, Force, & Wulfhorst, 2007; Pickett, Burch, & Grove, 1999; Stokols, Misra, Hall, Taylor, & Moser, 2008). Confronted by the conceptual, logistical, and interpersonal challenges inherent in cross-disciplinary projects, research teams that successfully compete for large interdisciplinary grants (e.g., to support interdisciplinary centers) often shift toward a more "silo-ed" and less integrative work style once their collaborative grant application has been funded (cf., Cummings & Kiesler, 2007; Eigenbrode et al., 2007; Stokols, Harvey, Gress, Fuqua, & Phillips, 2005).

The burgeoning interest and investment in cross-disciplinary research, as well as the need to better understand the circumstances that facilitate or constrain collaborative success, have given rise to a rapidly growing field— the *science of team science,* or SciTS (Börner et al., 2010; Croyle, 2008; Stokols, Hall, Taylor, & Moser, 2008). One goal of SciTS scholarship is to evaluate the scientific and societal returns on investments in team-based research. Another important goal of the SciTS field is to translate lessons learned from prior cross-disciplinary research projects into practical tools and guidelines for improving the effectiveness of future collaborations among academicians, government officials, corporate leaders, and community stakeholders (Falk-Krzesinski et al., 2010; Hall, Feng, Moser, Stokols, & Taylor, 2008; Shen, 2008).

Examples of translational team science innovations include the Toolbox for Philosophical Dialogue described in Chapter 11 in this volume (cf., Eigenbrode et al., 2007) and the training modules, "prenuptial agreements," and guidebooks for facilitating successful cross-disciplinary collaborations that are available online (COALESCE, 2012; National Cancer Institute [NCI], 2008, 2011; National Institutes of Health, 2010; NUCATS, 2010; ResearchToolkit.org, 2010; Science of Collaboratories, 2011). A key assumption underlying the development of these tools is that they can enhance communication and collaborative processes in team research. Preliminary efforts to evaluate the impacts of some of these resources (e.g., the Toolbox workshops) suggest that they do, in fact, facilitate more effective collaboration among team members (Eigenbrode et al., 2007; Schnapp, Rotschy, O'Rourke, & Crowley, 2012).

A common feature of the training resources cited above is that they are usually implemented on a project-specific, short-term basis—for example, when a research team is first funded to establish a cross-disciplinary center and during the early stages of participant collaboration. Whereas these short-term tools and strategies can be used effectively in many settings to improve cross-disciplinary communication, they cannot be relied on in all situations to ensure collaborative success. In some settings, certain individuals may persist in expressing unfavorable attitudes toward the disciplinary perspectives of their partners, thereby undermining interpersonal trust and the team's effectiveness in meeting its goals (cf., Sonnenwald, 2003). In other situations, a leader's inexperience may unnecessarily complicate collaborative processes (Gray, 2008). Also, some members may decide that they prefer to work individually, anchored in their own theoretical perspectives, rather than invest substantial time in cross-disciplinary exchanges with colleagues even after they've begun working as part of a research team or center (Austin, Park, & Goble, 2008; Campbell, 2005; Paletz & Schunn, 2010; Stokols et al., 2003). These examples of circumstances (including personal values, attitudes, and interpersonal styles) that can undermine cross-disciplinary collaboration highlight the importance of supplementing short-term, project-specific training strategies for improving team communication with longer term modalities (e.g., college curricula, experiential learning programs, and graduate or postgraduate internships incorporating multiple mentors from different fields) designed to cultivate an enduring intellectual orientation among students and scholars—one that is conducive to and supportive of their engagement in cross-disciplinary collaborative research.

A scholar's intellectual orientation and inclination to engage in cross-disciplinary research are cumulatively influenced by the educational environments, multiple mentors, and collaborative opportunities she or he encounters over the course of his or her career (Bammer, 2005; Barker, 1979; Callahan, 2010; Kessel et al., 2008; Klein, 2010a; National Academy of Sciences [NAS], 2005; Rhoten & Parker, 2004). Yet, to be most effective, educational efforts to instill a TD intellectual outlook among students and scholars (and to assess its influence on the processes and outcomes of cross-disciplinary collaboration) must be guided by a clear conception of what this orientation entails (Borrego & Newswander, 2010).

The ensuing discussion identifies distinctive facets of a TD intellectual orientation, including the core values, attitudes, beliefs, knowledge, and behaviors encompassed by this scholarly perspective (Fuqua, Stokols, Gress, Phillips, & Harvey, 2004; Hall, Stokols, et al., 2008; Klein, 2008; Stokols, 1998). Alternative approaches for nurturing a TD intellectual orientation also are discussed, including training programs that promote disciplinary specialization as a prerequisite for engaging in cross-disciplinary research as well as those that emphasize cross-disciplinary education and curricula at the outset of a student's career (Campbell, 1969; Heemskerk, Wilson, & Pavao-Zuckerman, 2003; Nash, 2008). Finally, examples of curricular strategies aimed at promoting a TD orientation among undergraduate, graduate, and postdoctoral trainees within an interdisciplinary academic program (the School of Social Ecology at the University of California, Irvine) will be presented, including a graduate seminar on Strategies of Theory Development that encourages students to develop their conceptual skills as cross-disciplinary theorists (Stokols, 2012).

Cultivating a TD Intellectual Orientation

Before discussing the core facets of a TD intellectual orientation, it is useful to consider different forms of cross-disciplinary research, including *multidisciplinarity*, *interdisciplinarity*, and *transdisciplinarity*, and their implications for designing training strategies that nurture student and scholar predilection for engaging in cross-disciplinary inquiry. Rosenfield (1992) and Kessel et al. (2008) define three forms of cross-disciplinary collaboration in contrast to *unidisciplinarity* (UD), whereby scholars from a single field work together to address a common research problem. In *multidisciplinary* (MD) collaborations, scholars from different fields work independently or sequentially, each from his or her disciplinary perspective, with the goal of eventually combining their perspectives to address a common research question. In *interdisciplinary* (ID) collaborations, team members work jointly, each drawing on his or her discipline-specific perspective, to address a common research problem. In TD teams, partners work jointly to develop shared conceptual frameworks and novel methodologies that ultimately synthesize and extend research on a particular topic across the boundaries of two or more fields.[1]

---

[1]Transdisciplinarity is conceptualized by some scholars as always involving, by definition, close collaboration between researchers and community stakeholders who work together to understand and ultimately resolve societal problems (td-net, 2010). In this chapter, TD research that bridges both academic and nonacademic perspectives as a basis for redressing societal problems is referred to as *transdisciplinary action research* (Stokols, 2006). At the same time, it is recognized that TD collaborations can occur among partners who represent primarily academic (discipline-based) rather than nonacademic epistemologies, and whose collaborative goals focus more on intellectual discovery rather than on the development of translational solutions to community problems.

These alternative forms of collaborative research reflect a continuum extending from the least amount of interchange among team members from different fields (UD) to the greatest degree of cross-disciplinary dialogue, integration, and innovation (TD).

As noted by Nash (2008), the distinctions between MD, ID, and TD research suggest corresponding approaches for training cross-disciplinary students and scholars. In MD training programs, students are taught a single disciplinary approach but also learn to work collaboratively with researchers from other fields. In ID settings, trainees are provided a working knowledge of the conceptual and methodological approaches of different disciplines. In TD programs, the major goal is to produce scholars capable of synthesizing concepts and methods from different fields that pertain to a particular research topic. Each of these approaches can be implemented to strengthen student receptiveness to and capacity for engaging in cross-disciplinary research. It seems reasonable to assume, however, that owing to their particular emphasis on conceptual synthesis, TD training programs have the greatest capacity to foster student abilities to frame research questions broadly and to integrate theoretical, philosophical, and methodological perspectives drawn from diverse fields.

It is important to note that the definitions and practice of UD, MD, ID, and TD research and training strategies are not mutually exclusive. In fact, many research and training programs involve mixtures of these orientations, whereby scholars and students emphasize different orientations over the course of their time in the program (cf., Klein, 2010b). Moreover, certain values, attitudes, and behaviors associated with a TD intellectual orientation are shared by and overlap with other collaborative perspectives, such as MD and ID research. Nonetheless, the conceptualization of a TD intellectual orientation proposed in this chapter is based on the assumption that it is the particular combination and synergy among certain collaborative values, beliefs, attitudes, and behaviors, in combination with certain conceptual strategies that emphasize multilevel theorizing and contextual analyses of research and societal problems, that distinguish a TD orientation from UD, MD, and ID perspectives.

Several scholars (cf., Bunderson & Sutcliffe, 2003; Cannella, Park, & Lee, 2008; Fiore et al., 2010; Keyton, Beck, & Asbury, 2010; Van der Vegt & Bunderson, 2005) have suggested that collaborative orientations are emergent states of teams learned by their members over the course of their working together. A team's collaborative orientation can be fostered either by recruiting a diversity of members, each of whom brings unique disciplinary expertise to the team, or by recruiting individuals who are each familiar with multiple fields and predisposed toward cross-disciplinary integration prior to joining the team. Presumably, a team collaborative orientation can emerge from either of these team composition strategies, though the relative effectiveness of these approaches likely depends on the particular types of research and societal problems addressed by the team.

Recognizing that *collaborative orientations can be defined either as individual- or group-level constructs*, the present chapter focuses on the intrapersonal rather than the emergent team-based qualities of a TD orientation for the following reasons. First, organizational scholars have given considerable attention to the development of team-based collaborative orientations, yet the personal qualities that constitute an individual's TD orientation have received relatively little attention in prior research. Second, because the communicative and collaborative success of cross-disciplinary teams depends at least in part on their members and the intellectual styles that each brings to the group, it seems plausible that identifying core attributes associated with a TD orientation and developing educational programs to nurture those personal qualities may improve the prospects for effective cross-disciplinary communication and collaboration. More specifically, cultivating an individual's TD orientation may enable him or her to communicate more effectively with fellow team members who represent diverse disciplinary and philosophical perspectives, and to identify more readily with the collaborative and integrative goals of the team—activities that are crucial for effective team cognition and interpersonal coordination (cf., Fiore et al., 2010; Keyton et al., 2010).

Considering the unique features of MD, ID, and TD forms of cross-disciplinarity and acknowledging that these orientations are at least partly overlapping in regard to their identifying characteristics, the ensuing discussion focuses primarily on the distinctive qualities and developmental trajectory of a TD orientation among students and scholars. Clearly, significant and innovative discoveries can be achieved through UD, MD, and ID research, as well as through TD scholarship (cf., Klein, 2010b). At the same time, multiple lines of earlier research suggest that scholars who possess diverse knowledge sets drawn from multiple fields, as well as the inclination to integrate multiple analytic levels in their work, are more likely to generate highly radical innovations as compared with those whose knowledge and conceptual strategies are more narrowly circumscribed (Cohen & Levinthal, 1990; Leung, Maddux, Galinsky, & Chiu, 2008; Root-Bernstein, Bernstein, & Garnier, 1995; Simonton, 2009). Accordingly, a TD orientation may be more conducive to achieving highly novel scientific and societal advances at the boundaries of multiple fields than may those associated with MD or ID approaches. The present analysis suggests that to the extent scholars aspire to study and help mitigate complex societal problems that are inherently multifaceted and (often) seemingly intractable, they will be more likely to arrive at a comprehensive and novel understanding of those problems when they approach them from a broadly integrative, TD perspective than if they approach from the narrower vantage points of particular fields (Association of American Colleges and Universities [AACU], 2007; Bammer, 2005; Brown, Harris, & Russell, 2010; Fuller, 2003; Holley, 2009; Laszlo, 2001; Naveh, 2001).

Finally, it is useful to note that all four research orientations (UD, ID, MD, TD) can be pursued either by a single scholar working independently or by members of a research team who decide to work collaboratively (Abrams,

2006; Stokols et al., 2003). Thus, a TD intellectual orientation can be expressed both through independent as well as collaborative scholarship. To the extent that students and established scholars prefer to work collaboratively as members of a TD research team, their training should foster the development of interpersonal skills conducive to effective collaboration. We turn now to a consideration of the core facets of a TD intellectual orientation, which is the intended outcome of TD training.

Core Facets of an Individual's TD Orientation

An individual's *TD orientation* is a constellation of personal attributes that emerges developmentally over the course of a scholar's career and is shaped through exposure to multiple learning environments, mentors, and research settings. Whereas each stage of an individual's development (including kindergarten through high school, college, graduate school, and continuing education later in one's career) contributes to his or her overall intellectual orientation, the present discussion highlights the formative impact of university and postgraduate training experiences. For most individuals, it is during these life stages that one's intellectual orientation emerges most clearly (cf., Bammer, 2005; Chang, Hursting, Perkins, Dores, & Weed, 2005; Golde & Gallagher, 1999; IGERT, 2010; Jantsch, 1970; Klein, 2010a; Misra, Stokols, Hall, & Feng, 2010; NAS, 2005).

The TD intellectual orientation as conceptualized here encompasses at least five categories of personal attributes: (1) *TD values* that predispose one toward acquiring a broad understanding of complex research and societal problems and translating integrative insights about them into practical solutions; these values are closely linked to (2) a set of *attitudes* favorable toward engaging in integrative scholarship bridging multiple disciplines; (3) *beliefs* that integrating concepts and methods from diverse fields is essential for achieving important scientific and societal advances; (4) *conceptual skills and knowledge* that enable scholars to traverse multiple levels of analysis, synthesize disparate disciplinary and philosophical perspectives, and develop novel conceptualizations that transcend preexisting constructs and theories; and (5) *TD behaviors* that are conducive to learning about and synthesizing concepts and methods from disparate fields and collaborating effectively as a research team member.

TD Values

Certain values are highly consistent with participation in collaborative research spanning multiple fields. Human values are the guiding principles that a person aspires or adheres to across the various spheres of his or her life (cf., Rokeach, 2000; Schwartz & Bilsky, 1990). Examples of these are *integrity* and *fairness*, which motivate individuals to behave honestly and equitably in their interactions with others. Values especially conducive to a scholar's participation in TD research include *open-mindedness, tolerance, and respect* toward other points of view; an *inclusive rather than exclusionary stance* toward perspectives that are unfamiliar or different from one's own; and an emphasis on *pluralism rather than determinism* when considering the causal structure of scientific and societal problems. As well, individual desire to promote *social justice* and *environmental sustainability* may fuel their efforts to engage with community partners in translational TD action research aimed at ameliorating societal and ecological problems (AACU, 2007; Brown & Jennings, 2003; Schor, 1992; Stokols, 2006). The principles and ideals mentioned earlier are a representative but not exhaustive set of the value commitments associated with a TD orientation. These values enable members of cross-disciplinary teams to resist certain constraints, such as in-group versus out-group biases, parochialism, and the tendency to associate with and feel attracted to similar others (cf., Byrne, 1971; Lau & Murningham, 2005; Raskas & Hambrick, 1992; Tajfel, 1982), that commonly arise among collaborators who have been trained in different fields and have inculcated discipline-centric worldviews. TD value commitments are the *motivational* core that supports and sustains a variety of attitudes, beliefs, conceptual approaches, and behaviors that are mutually consistent with one another and jointly constitute the TD intellectual orientation.

TD Attitudes

A person's attitudes reflect his or her positive, negative, or neutral feelings toward particular topics, ideas, people, or things (cf., Rosenberg, 1956). Individuals who embrace values of openness to new ideas and plural perspectives on science and society are likely to be more favorable toward opportunities to collaborate with others in cross-disciplinary research than are those who are less receptive to unfamiliar points of view. Similarly, they may be more willing to invest additional time in learning the subject matter of diverse fields because they regard cross-disciplinary studies and the societal outcomes of such research as highly valuable. At a more general level, positive attitudes toward persisting on complex tasks, even when confronted by logistical, interpersonal, or conceptual challenges, may be a prerequisite for achieving successful outcomes in collaborative research. Favorable attitudes toward the processes and outcomes of cross-disciplinary inquiry may be rooted in more general and enduring personal dispositions, such as psychological hardiness, optimism, perseverance, stamina, adaptability, intellectual curiosity, tolerance for uncertainty, and willingness to take risks (cf., Kruglanski, Pierro, Manetti, & Grada, 2006; Maddi, 2001; Nash, 2008).

TD Beliefs

Beliefs reflect an individual's cognitions about the relationships between two or more attitude objects, such as beliefs about the causes of a particular phenomenon or opinions about another person's distinctive qualities (Fishbein & Ajzen, 1975). In studies of cross-disciplinary scientific collaboration, scholars' beliefs about the favorable and/or negative outcomes of participating as members of research centers and teams have been identified and measured. For example, the NCI Research Orientation Scale measures the degree to which individuals believe that the benefits of collaborating with other scientists outweigh the costs of such work or that they tend to be more productive working on their own rather than as members of a collaborative research team (Hall, Stokols, et al., 2008). The Toolbox research project queries participants about their *philosophical beliefs* (including their ontological and epistemological assumptions) concerning the kinds of evidentiary support required for validating scientific measurements and findings and the extent to which the value of research stems from its applicability to community problem solving or its potential for producing basic discoveries (Eigenbrode et al., 2007). Other studies of scientific teams have assessed participants' beliefs that their efforts to work collaboratively with fellow scholars across disciplinary and geographic boundaries will result in *innovative theoretical insights, significant empirical discoveries,* and *translations of research findings into societal improvements* (Olson et al., 2008). Interestingly, an *individual's belief in his or her ability to be creative* as a theorist and researcher may be one of the most important prerequisites for scholarly success (Sternberg, 2002), especially in the context of cross-disciplinary studies where innovative efforts to forge new linkages across the boundaries of multiple fields are essential. These examples, though limited in number and scope, reflect the kinds of beliefs that are central to an individual's initial engagement and sustained participation in TD research.

TD Conceptual Skills and Knowledge

An individual's capacity to participate effectively in TD research projects depends in part on his or her acquisition of certain conceptual skills and types of knowledge. The ability to view research and societal problems reflexively and critically from multiple levels of analysis and to achieve an integrative and holistic understanding of their causes and consequences are essential ingredients of a TD orientation (Boix Mansilla, 2010; Pohl & Hirsch Hadorn, 2008; Wickson, Carew, & Russell, 2006). One's capacity to create novel conceptual frameworks that transcend the constructs and methods of particular fields is greater to the extent that she or he is able to think broadly and contextually about the multiple underpinnings of complex problems (Klein, 2008; Stokols, 1987; Suedfeld & Tetlock, 1977).

Graduate and undergraduate students increasingly are being taught skills that align with these attributes in a growing number of university programs that focus on the integration of diverse disciplinary perspectives and strategies of creative theorizing spanning multiple levels of analysis (Bammer, 2005; Borrego & Newswander, 2010; Klein, 2010a; Misra et al., 2009,

2010; Nash, 2008). For instance, Bammer (2005) developed a university program focusing on *integration and implementation sciences*. Bammer contends that certain categories of knowledge are required to facilitate a scholar's ability to learn and implement these conceptual skills, especially *systems thinking, participatory methods*, and *knowledge management* strategies. Additional knowledge sets emphasized in other TD training programs include methods and tools (e.g., stakeholder analysis, anticipatory governance, and conflict resolution strategies) that can enable students to prepare for community-based TD research (Bergmann et al., 2012; Pohl & Hirsch Hadorn, 2008; Wiek, Withycombe, & Redman, 2011).

In the Strategies of Theory Development course described in a later section (Stokols, 2012), students also are introduced to principles of *human and social ecology, contextual and transformational theorizing*, and ways of *incorporating diverse analytic perspectives* into their conceptual frameworks (e.g., objectivism and subjectivism, determinism and pluralism, individual and aggregate analysis, grand and middle-range theorizing, inductive-grounded and deductive-a priori modeling, analogical and visual reasoning). Scholars possessing these kinds of conceptual skills and knowledge sets should be better prepared to comprehend and manage the integrative complexities inherent in multilevel, cross-disciplinary research projects.

TD Behaviors

Several behaviors are reflective and supportive of a TD intellectual orientation. Some personal practices and routines increase a scholar's exposure to diverse disciplinary perspectives and knowledge—for instance, reading articles and books, taking courses, attending conferences and presentations outside of one's primary field, and engaging in frequent meetings with colleagues from different disciplines to share and integrate ideas (Hall, Stokols, et al., 2008; Klein, 2010b; NAS, 2005; Stokols et al., 2005). Other behaviors facilitate effective communication and collaboration in team settings, such as communicating with colleagues respectfully, maintaining proper etiquette when sending electronic messages, and gaining extensive experience working collaboratively in TD research projects and centers, initially as a student and later as an established scholar. The more collaborative experience one acquires in TD research settings, the better prepared she or he will be to lead and manage future team-based projects. Thus, certain behaviors enable a scholar to facilitate TD collaboration with and among one's colleagues—especially, acting in ways that enable them to cooperatively develop and openly share their ideas, as well as negotiate and resolve intellectual or interpersonal disagreements (Gray, 2008; Klein, 2010b; Morgan et al., 2003; Obstfeld, 2005).

The TD values, attitudes, beliefs, conceptual skills, and behaviors mentioned above constitute a partial but illustrative sample of the personal attributes associated with a TD orientation. As mentioned earlier, each of these values, attitudes, beliefs, behaviors, and conceptual orientations may share some commonality with other collaborative styles, such as MD and ID perspectives. However, it is *composite synergy* among TD attitudes, beliefs, and values, in combination with highly integrative conceptual and behavioral skills, that accounts for the distinctive capacity of the TD intellectual orientation (even as compared with ID research) to generate exceptionally novel scientific and societal innovations. Having identified certain core facets of this intellectual perspective, we next consider the structure of educational programs designed to cultivate a TD orientation among undergraduate, graduate, and postdoctoral students, as well as among scholars previously trained in specific fields.

Educational Strategies for Nurturing a TD Intellectual Orientation

The interrelated facets of a TD outlook suggest specific criteria for designing and evaluating educational programs aimed at nurturing this orientation among students and scholars. Ideally, these programs should be organized to include curricular and didactic elements that foster TD attributes and skills. Accordingly, the efficacy of a TD program can be evaluated by measuring the extent to which it promotes intended developmental changes in student value commitments, attitudes, beliefs, conceptual skills, and behavior both during and after training.

Whereas many ID and TD proponents would agree on the broad goals and intended consequences of cross-disciplinary training (e.g., the development of an individual's ability to synthesize concepts and methods from diverse fields), there has been some divergence of opinion about the best curricular strategies and institutional designs for achieving those goals. Scholars have expressed contrasting views about various pedagogical issues, such as whether or not specialized disciplinary training is an essential prerequisite for, and should always precede, one's efforts to cultivate TD competencies. For instance, Campbell (1969) asserts that students should be encouraged to engage in problem-focused cross-disciplinary inquiry during the earliest stages of their educational careers. As an alternative to trying to master the subject matter of one or more fields before engaging in cross-disciplinary scholarship, Campbell exhorts students to pursue "fish-scale" research topics that overlap the boundaries of two or more fields. With sufficient encouragement from mentors to acquire and synthesize information from multiple disciplines pertinent to topics lying at the interface of those fields, students become proficient in conducting cross-disciplinary research. Also, by embracing problem-focused rather than discipline-centric research at the outset of their careers, they are better able to avoid the conceptual biases associated with *disciplinary chauvinism* and the *ethnocentrism* of traditional academic departments (cf., Heemskerk et al., 2003).

Klein (2010a) offers an alternative and more sanguine view of the educational benefits that students derive through their exposure, often concurrently, to UD, MD, ID, and TD training cultures and programs. She observes that these diverse forms of scholarship, rather than being antithetical to one another, often coexist comfortably and constructively within the same educational settings—and within the same scholars, who may shift between UD, MD, ID, and TD modes of inquiry depending on the particular research project (or phase of research) in which they are engaged at a given time. Klein (2008) specifically emphasizes the educational benefits that derive from a "quadrangulation" of UD *depth*, MD *breadth*, ID *integration*, and development of TD *competencies* within baccalaureate, doctoral, and post-graduate training programs.

A related concern is whether or not entire universities and educational systems should be restructured to facilitate TD training and problem-oriented rather than discipline-centric education (cf., Jantsch, 1970). At many universities, cross-disciplinary training is provided by research institutes and degree-granting programs that exist alongside (yet often peripheral and marginal to) the more traditional and prevalent disciplinary departments on campus. Some suggest that university students be encouraged to participate in these adjunct cross-disciplinary programs to supplement their discipline-based training (Klein, 2008; Lattuca, 2001; NAS, 2005; Weingart & Stehr, 2000), and to apply for postdoctoral fellowships that afford opportunities to work with multiple mentors representing diverse fields (Chang et al., 2005; Robert Wood Johnson Foundation, 2008).

On the other hand, Michael Crow (2010), president of Arizona State University, offers a radically different vision of higher education—one that emphasizes TD training, community engagement, and problem-focused research at all levels of the institution. According to Crow, TD scholarship and solutions to the epochal problems of our time (e.g., planetary sustainability, human rights, poverty alleviation) can best be advanced through a comprehensive redesign of the New American University that replaces traditional academic departments organized around arbitrary (and increasingly "ossified") disciplinary boundaries with problem-oriented, TD schools and institutes focusing on broad topics such as global sustainability and human evolution and social change. A fundamental restructuring of American universities around core themes such as integrative learning, community engagement, and societal relevance also is envisioned by the AACU (2007), though it often works within existing university structures while supporting efforts to promote more enduring institutional changes.

Whereas some university-based programs emphasize TD training at the outset of a student's undergraduate or graduate studies as envisioned by Campbell and Crow, most efforts to promote cross-disciplinary training incorporate a blend of UD, MD, ID, and TD experiences as described by Klein. In many of these programs, students are required to specialize within a particular field and then supplement their disciplinary coursework with cross-disciplinary fellowships and apprenticeships supervised by multiple mentors. Excellent examples of these programs are the National Science Foundation–funded Integrative Graduate Education and Research Traineeships (IGERTs) offered at many U.S. universities (Borrego & Newswander, 2010; IGERT, 2010) and NCI's Cancer Prevention Fellowship Program (Chang et al., 2005).

An extensive review of curricular innovations and training programs that cultivate a TD intellectual perspective is beyond the scope of this chapter. A comprehensive, internationally oriented review of educational programs designed to instill ID and TD competencies is provided by Klein (2010a). The ensuing discussion focuses instead on an academic unit at the University of California, Irvine (UCI)—namely, the School of Social Ecology (UCI, 2012)—and its predecessor, the Program in Social Ecology (hereafter, "the School" and "the Program"). The Program was established at UCI in 1970 with the explicit mission of training students to analyze research and policy questions from a broad ecological perspective that integrates multiple disciplines and links basic theory and research with community problem solving. Social Ecology evolved from a program for a school on the Irvine campus in 1992, following a 3-year review by the UC Regents, Administration, and Academic Senate. Social Ecology at UCI is one of the longest standing, cross-disciplinary degree-granting units within a major research university.

UCI's School of Social Ecology

From its inception, the Program incorporated certain innovative features, including (1) required core courses for the BA, MA, and PhD degrees in social ecology that introduce students to the integrative conceptual and methodological themes (e.g., the ecological paradigm, systems theory, problem-oriented research and practice, principles of TD inquiry) bridging the multiple disciplines represented within the Program; (2) an undergraduate field study curriculum that requires all Social Ecology BA students to complete internships at local government agencies, NGOs, or private firms for the purpose of encouraging experiential learning and community-engaged scholarship; (3) recruitment of faculty members and graduate students trained in a variety of different fields, such as urban and regional planning, psychology and social behavior, criminology and law, demography, environmental sciences, and public health; (4) cultivation of several problem-oriented action research programs focusing on complex social and environmental problems; and (5) participation of Social Ecology faculty members in local community decision-making groups, such as the Irvine City Council and Planning Commission.

The Program grew rapidly during the 1970s and 1980s, attracting scores of doctoral students and more than 1,500 BA majors by 1985. Student enrollments and faculty recruitments continued to climb during the 1990s, fueling additional expansion of the School's degree programs and facilities.

With more than 3,500 BA students by 1998, social ecology became the second largest undergraduate major on the Irvine campus. Not surprisingly, the rapid growth of the School and its occupancy of additional space in multiple buildings precipitated certain tensions between the original cross-disciplinary mission and organization of the School, on the one hand, and its increasingly departmentalized and decentralized structure by the late 1990s, on the other. For instance, the number of schoolwide required core courses was reduced over the years to accommodate the curricular requirements of newly established, department-based graduate and undergraduate degree programs. These organizational developments are described in greater detail elsewhere (cf., Binder, 1972; Stokols, 1998).

Despite the inevitable tensions prompted by the School's rapid growth and departmentalization, it has continued over four decades to offer a series of core courses that introduce its annual cohorts of incoming students to the integrative themes associated with ecologically oriented TD action research. The School's faculty members also offer elective courses and serve as mentors in fellowship programs that afford graduate and undergraduate students opportunities to participate in team-based TD research teams. Moreover, they have established several institutes and centers to engage faculty and students from across the entire campus in problem-focused TD research (UCI, 2012).

Social Ecology Curricula Designed to Nurture a TD Intellectual Orientation

In this section, three specific courses designed to foster a TD intellectual stance among UCI students are described. The results of evaluative studies to assess the educational outcomes associated with two of these courses also are noted. First, the Interdisciplinary Summer Undergraduate Research Experience (ID-SURE) was established in 2004 with funding from the National Institutes of Health to provide junior and senior students with training in the principles and strategies of team-based TD research. ID-SURE fellows complete a one-quarter course in the Social Ecology of Health Promotion that focuses on multilevel systems analyses of public health problems and disease prevention strategies (UCI, 2004). One of the course requirements is that participants work on team-based research projects with fellow students representing two or more BA majors at UCI.

A 3-year study undertaken to assess the educational processes and outcomes generated by the ID-SURE curriculum found that the components of this program bolstered students' TD orientation in terms of the extent to which they gained appreciation for the value of collaborative scholarship and became more knowledgeable about TD research concepts and methods. Moreover, the extent to which students engaged in behaviors associated with a TD orientation (e.g., reading journal articles and attending lectures outside of their primary academic major) was found to increase over the course of the training program (Misra et al., 2009).

At the doctoral level, the Seminar in Social Ecology (SE200) is a core course taken by all first-year PhD students in the School during their initial quarter of graduate studies. This foundational seminar, established in 1973, introduces graduate students to principles of human and social ecology, systems theory, multilevel contextual analyses of scientific and societal problems, and strategies of community-engaged action research. The course readings and lectures examine the history of the ecological paradigm and the challenges posed by efforts to translate research findings into evidence-based community interventions and public policies (cf., Altman, 1995; Catalano, 1979; Stokols, 2013). These issues are addressed from the perspectives of the School's diverse academic departments and research centers.

An evaluation of the educational outcomes of the schoolwide TD doctoral training program in social ecology, including the introductory SE200 seminar, was conducted by Mitrany and Stokols (2005). Based on a content analysis of each dissertation written by PhD candidates from the various doctoral training programs in the School, independent reviewers rated the TD qualities of the dissertations, including the degree to which they reflected broad gauged integration of concepts and methods from different fields and incorporated multiple levels of analysis and diverse research methods. On the whole, Mitrany and Stokols's data suggested that the School's core training program has been moderately successful in nurturing a cross-disciplinary orientation among its graduates. Although relatively few dissertations presented conceptual frameworks transcending the boundaries of multiple fields, many of them demonstrated strong ID attributes, such as the establishment of links between concepts and methods from different disciplines and multilevel contextual analyses of research questions and societal problems. These results offer encouraging evidence for the short-term impacts of ID and TD training programs, but the longer term educational outcomes of these curricula (including graduates' career trajectories and cumulative scholarly accomplishments) remain to be evaluated in future studies.

One other course in the School designed to promote a strong TD orientation in students' current and future work is the graduate seminar on Strategies of Theory Development, SE261 (Stokols, 2012). This seminar is not required for all PhD students in the School but is typically taken by all social ecology degree candidates and by many enrolled in other doctoral programs at UCI. A fundamental purpose of the course is to encourage students to develop their skills as creative theorists. Another goal of the seminar is to introduce them to key issues and controversies facing the development of multilevel TD theories—for example, the conceptual challenges that arise when scholars attempt to integrate the contrasting epistemologies and worldviews associated with distinctly different disciplines. Because the ability to creatively synthesize conceptual and methodological perspectives from diverse fields is so fundamental to the cultivation of a TD intellectual orientation, the remaining discussion focuses on the principal assumptions and didactic approaches emphasized in Social Ecology's Strategies of Theory Development seminar as it has been taught over the past 30 years.

Cultivating a TD Orientation Through Strategies of Cross-Disciplinary Theorizing

Graduate curricula in the behavioral and natural sciences typically emphasize the development of methodological skills for testing hypotheses. All too often, however, graduate training gives short shrift to the hypothesis-formation phase of research. A key assumption of the Strategies of Theory Development seminar is that TD theorizing can be enhanced by encouraging students and scholars to develop their skills as creative theoreticians. The development of novel hypotheses is essential for progress in any type of scholarship, including UD, MD, ID, and TD research. Yet the capacity to create novel conceptual frameworks bridging multiple levels of analysis is absolutely fundamental to TD inquiry. Moreover, the challenges inherent in TD theorizing are especially daunting when formulating new theories that integrate the perspectives of highly divergent fields—for instance, creating broad gauged frameworks spanning environmental, biomedical, psychological, organizational, and sociological levels of analysis, as compared with narrower models linking disciplines whose analytic levels and conceptual/methodological perspectives are relatively similar, such as molecular biology, pharmacology, and neuroscience (cf., Klein, 2010b; Misra et al., 2010; Stokols et al., 2003).

As noted earlier in this chapter and in Chapter 11 in this volume, the Toolbox Project is designed to promote communication and understanding among team members about their disciplinary vantage points and dissimilar theoretical, philosophical, and methodological assumptions as they initiate and continue to work together on a cross-disciplinary research project (Eigenbrode et al., 2007). Similarly, Heemskerk et al. (2003) emphasize the value of conceptual discussions and efforts among research partners to create shared graphical models as strategies for bridging their disciplinary perspectives and enhancing collaborative success. The Strategies of Theory Development seminar at UCI is intended to introduce graduate students to the contrasting epistemologies and worldviews of multiple fields *at the outset of their careers* so that as they participate in subsequent TD projects they will be better prepared to understand, appreciate, and assimilate the alternative philosophical assumptions, constructs, and methods associated with disparate fields and levels of analysis.

Efforts to cultivate the conceptual skills and knowledge base needed for creative TD theorizing often confront major challenges. First, graduate students usually are advised to focus on their empirical research projects and postpone efforts to develop novel theories until they have completed their graduate studies and in some instances until they have achieved tenure at a university. Creative theorizing is regarded by many faculty mentors as an ill-advised goal for PhD candidates, especially those who are just beginning their graduate careers. The Strategies of Theory Development seminar aims to disabuse students of these typical biases against encouraging theory development efforts among doctoral candidates. Efforts are made early in the course to demystify the processes of informal theorizing and formal theory development (Marx, 1976). Seminar participants are encouraged at the outset to make a staunch commitment to developing their skills as creative theorists (cf., Levy, 1968; Sternberg, 2002) and to draw on their personal experiences and intuitions as a basis for developing new theoretical insights (Mills, 1959).

Several features of the Theory Development Seminar are designed to bolster student motivation and capacity to generate novel ideas and provide ample opportunity for them to share their conceptual work with fellow students trained in a variety of different fields. First, course readings introduce strategies for enhancing creative problem solving and developing new ideas through techniques such as visual and analogical reasoning for avoiding "conceptual ruts" and analytical approaches that help alleviate conceptual, emotional, psychological, and interpersonal barriers to creative thinking (cf., Adams, 2001; Crovitz, 1970; Gordon, 1974; McKim, 1980; Weick, 1974; Wicker, 1985). Second, seminar participants prepare three short "idea papers" over the course of the 10-week quarter, in which they propose new concepts, gradually define and differentiate their constructs into a set of interrelated subtypes, and eventually articulate hypothesized relationships among subcategories in the form of a more structured theoretical statement. Third, students share and comment on one another's idea papers during three group tutorial sessions (each lasting 2–3 hours) that occur outside of the 10 weekly, 3-hour class sessions. Fourth, participants compile a journal of their own ideas and personal reactions to the assigned readings each week, which they turn in at the end of the quarter (cf., Mills, 1959).

Whereas these strategies afford class members opportunities to develop and communicate novel ideas and obtain constructive feedback from the instructor and fellow students, they do not directly confront another fundamental challenge associated with nurturing student capacity for creative TD theorizing—namely, the disciplinary biases and worldviews that they have accumulated as BA majors in various fields during their college years, which are often reinforced by faculty mentors who themselves are strongly aligned with scholarly paradigms endorsed by particular fields (cf., Kuhn, 1970). To counter these biases against synthetic cross-paradigm theorizing, the Theory Development Seminar exposes participants to widely different epistemological assumptions, many of which are arrayed along bipolar continua such as rationalism versus empiricism, objectivist versus subjectivist representations of reality, reductionist versus contextualist analyses of research topics, qualitative and/or quantitative research methods, grand versus middle-range theorizing, and aggregate versus individual (or macro, meso, and micro) levels of analysis adopted when investigating particular phenomena. Seminar students are explicitly encouraged to learn about the contrasting assumptions inherent in these metatheoretical continua and to become adept at transversing and integrating different points along each continuum rather than getting "stuck" at the extreme ends of the continua and thereby locked into a particular *disciplinary orthodoxy* (for instance, by embracing exclusively microlevel analyses of the biomedical or psychological antecedents of disease while neglecting macroeconomic or sociological facets of the problem; cf., Becker, 1993).

The seminar readings assigned each week are selected to highlight contrasting epistemological perspectives. For instance, Platt's (1964) essay on "strong inference" and Gergen's (1978) article on "generative theory" illustrate the divergent perspectives of positivist and relativist philosophies of science. Park, Burgess, and McKenzie's (1925) objectivist "Chicago School" perspective on human ecology is contrasted with Firey's (1945) subjectivist analysis of "sentiment and symbolism as ecological variables." Also, students read Marx and Engels's (1968) *Communist Manifesto* and Weber's (1958) *Protestant Ethic and the Spirit of Capitalism* as exemplars of materialist/ deterministic versus rationalist/pluralistic interpretations of history; they compare Merton's (1968) writings on deductive middle-range and grand theories with Glaser and Strauss's (1967) inductive approach to creating grounded theories; and they discuss Lewin's (1936) microlevel analysis of psychological facts with Durkheim's (1938) macrosocietal conceptualization of social facts. Moreover, they are assigned readings that highlight the differences between reductionism and contextualism as metatheoretical approaches to theory development (Jessor, 1958; Stokols, 1987).

To date, no studies have been conducted to directly assess the effectiveness of the School's graduate seminar on Strategies of Theory Development in cultivating the core values, attitudes, beliefs, conceptual skills, and behaviors associated with a TD intellectual orientation. However, several students who participated in the seminar over the years developed doctoral dissertations based on the theoretical ideas initially outlined in their seminar papers and quarterly journal. And in some cases, seminar participants went on to publish elaborated versions of their theory development course papers as solo-authored theoretical articles in peer-reviewed scholarly journals (e.g., Alfonzo, 2005; Campbell, 1983).

Conclusion

The initial sections of this chapter traced the growing interest and investment in TD approaches to research, teaching, and community problem solving. As well, the core facets of a *TD intellectual orientation* were described, and alternative educational approaches for nurturing TD values, attitudes, beliefs, knowledge, and behaviors were discussed. The latter portions of the chapter summarized curricular strategies implemented in the School of Social Ecology at UCI for the purpose of cultivating a TD orientation among baccalaureate, graduate, and postgraduate trainees.

Take-Home Messages

- Intrapersonal facets of a TD intellectual orientation were emphasized, rather than viewing this orientation as a group-level construct that emerges through ongoing collaborations among team members.
- A key assumption underlying this chapter is that the cultivation of an intrapersonal TD orientation and scholarly identity can add substantial value to team science collaborations—especially by preparing team members representing diverse disciplinary backgrounds and scientific worldviews to communicate and coordinate with one another more effectively in both basic research and translational (i.e., practice-oriented) settings.
- Not all scholars will be equally amenable toward engaging in cross-disciplinary collaborative projects with others—even after exposure to TD training programs and curricula. Some individuals, because of their particular research interests, talents, and/or dispositional styles, will be more comfortable and productive by choosing to study discipline-centric problems in an individualized rather than collaborative fashion. One size or type of intellectual orientation does not fit all scholars and research topics equally well.
- Thus, it is important not to force broadly integrative TD values, attitudes, beliefs, behaviors, and cognitive styles on all students and scholars, and to recognize that after being introduced to alternative intellectual orientations (e.g., ranging from UD to MD, ID, and TD), some individuals will opt for UD and noncollaborative approaches in their future research.
- Developing educational strategies that identify students' unique intellectual talents and encouraging them to pursue the research settings and careers that are best suited to them (whether those be UD or TD, collaborative or noncollaborative) warrant further consideration in future studies of team science, training, and practice.
- Future expansion of educational programs designed to strengthen scholars' capacity for creative, multilevel theorizing is needed since most college and graduate training programs give insufficient attention to strategies of theory development and typically do little to encourage students' efforts to create novel ideas and conceptual frameworks—especially those that are of broad scope and integrate the diverse perspectives of multiple fields.
- It is now more important than ever to find ways of encouraging and supporting scholars' efforts to create broadly integrative TD theories and conceptual frameworks. The present analysis of curricular strategies for nurturing a TD orientation is intended to provide a useful starting point for designing new and improved educational initiatives to advance the goals of collaborative TD scholarship, teaching, and the translation of research findings into community-based practices and policies.

References

Abrams, D. B. (2006). Applying transdisciplinary research strategies to understanding and eliminating health disparities. *Health Education & Behavior, 33*(4), 515–531.

Adams, J. L. (2001). *Conceptual blockbusting: A guide to better ideas* (4th ed.). Cambridge, MA: Basic Books, Perseus.

Alfonzo, M. (2005). To walk or not to walk: The hierarchy of walking needs. *Environment and Behavior, 37*(6), 808–836.

Altman, D. G. (1995). Sustaining interventions in community systems: On the relationship between researchers and communities. *Health Psychology, 14,* 526–536.

Association of American Colleges and Universities. (2007). *College learning for the new global century.* Washington, DC: Author.

Austin, W., Park, C., & Goble, E. (2008). From interdisciplinary to transdisciplinary research: A case study. *Qualitative Health Research, 18*(4), 557–564. doi:10.1177/1049732307308514

Bammer, G. (2005). Integration and implementation sciences: Building a new specialization. *Ecology and Society, 10*(2), 6. Retrieved from http://www.ecologyandsociety.org/vol10/iss2/art6/

Barker, R. G. (1979). Settings of a professional lifetime. *Journal of Personality and Social Psychology, 37*(12), 2137–2157.

Becker, M. H. (1993). A medical sociologist looks at health promotion. *Journal of Health and Social Behavior, 34,* 1–6.

Bergmann, M., Jahn, T., Knobloch, T., Krohn, W., Pohl, C., & Schramm, E. (2012). *Methods for transdisciplinary research: A primer for practice.* Frankfurt/Main, Germany: Campus Verlag.

Berkes, F., Colding, J., & Folke, C. (2003). *Navigating social-ecological systems: Building resilience for complexity and change.* New York: Cambridge University Press.

Binder, A. (1972). A new context for psychology: Social ecology. *American Psychologist, 27,* 903–908.

Boix Mansilla, V. (2010). Learning to synthesize: The development of interdisciplinary understanding. In R. Frodeman, J. T. Klein, & C. Mitcham (Eds.), *The Oxford handbook on interdisciplinarity* (pp. 288–306). New York: Oxford University Press.

Börner, K., Contractor, N., Falk-Krzesinski, H. J., Fiore, S. M., Hall, K. L., Keyton, J., et al. (2010). A multi-level systems perspective for the science of team science. *Science Translational Medicine, 2*(49).

Borrego, M., & Newswander, L. K. (2010). Definitions of interdisciplinary research: Toward graduate-level interdisciplinary learning outcomes. *Review of Higher Education, 34*(1), 61–84.

Brown, K. D., & Jennings, T. (2003). Social consciousness in landscape architecture education: Toward a conceptual framework. *Landscape Journal, 22*(2), 99–112.

Brown, V. A., Harris, J. A., & Russell, J. Y. (Eds.). (2010). *Tackling wicked problems through the transdisciplinary imagination.* London: Earthscan.

Bunderson, J. S., & Sutcliffe, K. M. (2003). Management team learning orientation and business unit performance. *Journal of Applied Psychology, 88*(3), 552–560.

Byrne, D. (1971). *The attraction paradigm.* New York: Academic Press.

Callahan, D. (2010). A memoir of an interdisciplinary career. In R. Frodeman, J. T. Klein, & C. Mitcham (Eds.), *The Oxford handbook on interdisciplinarity* (pp. 419–428). New York: Oxford University Press.

Campbell, D. T. (1969). Ethnocentrism of disciplines and the fish-scale model of omniscience. In M. Sherif & C. W. Sherif (Eds.), *Interdisciplinary relationships in the social sciences* (pp. 328–348). Chicago: Aldine.

Campbell, J. M. (1983). Ambient stressors. *Environment and Behavior, 15*(3), 355–380.

Campbell, L. M. (2005). Overcoming obstacles to interdisciplinary research. *Conservation Biology, 19*(2), 574–577.

Cannella, A. A., Park, J. H., & Lee, H. U. (2008). Top management team functional background diversity and firm performance: Examining the roles of team member colocation and environmental uncertainty. *Academy of Management Journal, 51*(4), 768–784.

Catalano, R. (1979). *Health, behavior and the community: An ecological perspective.* New York: Pergamon Press.

Chang, S., Hursting, S. D., Perkins, S. N., Dores, G. M., & Weed, D. L. (2005). Adapting postdoctoral training to interdisciplinary science in the 21st century: The Cancer Prevention Fellowship Program at the National Cancer Institute. *Academic Medicine, 80*(3).

COALESCE. (2012). CTSA online assistance for leveraging the science of collaborative effort (COALESCE). Department of Preventive Medicine, Feinberg School of Medicine, Northwestern University. Retrieved February 24, 2013, from http://www.preventivemedicine.northwestern.edu/research/coalesce.html?t=vC2

Cohen, W. M., & Levinthal, D. A. (1990). Absorptive capacity: A new perspective on learning and innovation. *Administrative Science Quarterly, 35*(1), 128–152.

Crovitz, H. F. (1970). Recurrence and memory. In H. F. Crovitz (Ed.), *Galton's walk: Methods for the analysis of thinking, intelligence, and creativity* (pp. 23–52). New York: Harper & Row.

Crow, M. M. (2010). Organizing teaching and research to address the grand challenges of sustainable development. *BioScience, 60*(7), 488–489.

Croyle, R. T. (2008). The National Cancer Institute's transdisciplinary centers and the need for building a science of team science. *American Journal of Preventive Medicine, 35*(2S), S90–S93.

Cummings, J. N., & Kiesler, S. (2007). Coordination costs and project outcomes in multi-university collaborations. *Research Policy, 36*(10), 1620–1634. doi:10.1016/j.respol.2007.09.001

Durkheim, E. (1938). *The rules of sociological method.* New York: Free Press.

Eigenbrode, S. D., O'Rourke, M., Wulfhorst, J. D., Althoff, D. M., Goldberg, C. S., Merrill, K., et al. (2007). Employing philosophical dialogue in collaborative science. *BioScience, 57*(1), 55–64.

Esparza, J., & Yamada, T. (2007, April 16). The discovery value of "Big Science." *Journal of Experimental Medicine, 204*, 701–704. doi:10.1084/jem.20070073

Falk-Krzesinski, H. J., Borner, K., Contractor, N., Cummings, J. N., Fiore, S. M., Hall, K. L., et al. (2010). Advancing the science of team science. *Clinical and Translational Science, 3*(5), 263–266.

Fiore, S. M. (2008). Interdisciplinarity as teamwork: How the science of teams can inform team science. *Small Group Research, 39*(3), 251–277. doi:10.1177/1046497w8317797

Fiore, S. M., Rosen, M. A., Smith-Jentsch, K. A., Salas, E., Letsky, M., & Warner, N. (2010). Toward an understanding of macrocognition in teams: Predicting processes in complex collaborative contexts. *Human Factors: Journal of the Human Factors and Ergonomics Society, 52*(2), 203–224. doi:10.1177/0018720810369807

Firey, W. (1945). Sentiment and symbolism as ecological variables. *American Sociological Review, 10,* 140–148.

Fishbein, M., & Ajzen, I. (1975). *Belief, attitudes, intention, and behavior: An introduction to theory and research.* Reading, MA: Addison-Wesley.

Frodeman, R., Klein, J. T., & Mitcham, C. (Eds.). (2010). *The Oxford handbook of interdisciplinarity.* New York: Oxford University Press.

Fry, G. L. A. (2001). Multifunctional landscapes—towards transdisciplinary research. *Landscape and Urban Planning, 57*(3–4), 159–168.

Fuller, S. (2003). *Interdisciplinarity: The loss of the heroic vision in the marketplace of ideas.* Retrieved August 8, 2010, from http://www.interdisciplines.org/interdisciplinarity/papers/3/printable/paper

Fuqua, J., Stokols, D., Gress, J., Phillips, K., & Harvey, R. (2004). Transdisciplinary scientific collaboration as a basis for enhancing the science and prevention of substance use and abuse. *Substance Use and Misuse, 39*(10–12), 1457–1514.

Gergen, K. J. (1978). Toward generative theory. *Journal of Personality and Social Psychology, 36,* 1344–1360.

Glaser, B. G., & Strauss, A. L. (1967). *The discovery of grounded theory: Strategies for qualitative research.* New York: Aldine.

Golde, C. M., & Gallagher, H. A. (1999). The challenges of conducting interdisciplinary research in traditional doctoral programs. *Ecosystems, 2*(4), 281–285.

Gordon, W. J. J. (1974). Some source material in discovery-by-analogy. *Journal of Creative Beahvior, 8,* 239–257.

Gray, B. (2008). Enhancing transdisciplinary research through collaborative leadership. *American Journal of Preventive Medicine, 35*(2), S124–S132. doi:10.1016/j.amepre.2008.03.037

Hall, K., Feng, A., Moser, R., Stokols, D., & Taylor, B. (2008). Moving the science of team science forward: Collaboration and creativity. *American Journal of Preventive Medicine, 35*(2S), S243–S249.

Hall, K. L., Stokols, D., Moser, R. P., Taylor, B. K., Thornquist, M., Nebeling, L., et al. (2008). The collaboration readiness of transdisciplinary research teams and centers: Findings from the National Cancer Institute TREC year-one evaluation study. *American Journal of Preventive Medicine, 35*(2S), 161–172.

Heemskerk, M., Wilson, K., & Pavao-Zuckerman, M. (2003). Conceptual models as tools for communication across disciplines. *Conservation Ecology, 7*(3), 8.

Higginbotham, N., Albrecht, G., & Connor, L. (Eds.). (2001). *Health social science: A transdisciplinary and complexity perspective.* Melbourne, Australia: Oxford University Press.

Hirsch Hadorn, G., Hoffman-Riem, H., Biber-Klemm, S., Grossenbacher-Mansuy, W., Joye, D., Pohl, C., et al. (Eds.). (2008). *Handbook of transdisciplinary research.* Dordrecht, Switzerland: Springer.

Holley, K. A. (2009). Understanding interdisciplinary challenges and opportunities in higher education [Special issue]. *ASHE Higher Education Report, 35*(2).

IGERT. (2010). Integrative Graduate Education and Research Traineeship (IGERT) program: Mission and history. Retrieved August 8, 2010, from http://www.igert.org/public/about/history-and-mission

Jantsch, E. (1970). Inter- and transdisciplinary university: A systems approach to education and innovation. *Policy Sciences, 1*(4), 403–428.

Jessor, R. (1958). The problem of reductionism in psychology. *Psychological Review, 65*, 170–178.

Kessel, F. S., Rosenfield, P. L., & Anderson, N. B. (Eds.). (2008). *Interdisciplinary research: Case studies from health and social science.* New York: Oxford University Press.

Keyton, J., Beck, S. J., & Asbury, M. B. (2010). Macrocognition: A communication perspective. *Theoretical Issues in Ergonomics Science, 11*(4), 272–286. doi:10.1080/14639221003729136

Klein, J. T. (1996). *Crossing boundaries: Knowledge, disciplines, and interdisciplinarities.* Charlottesville: University of Virginia Press.

Klein, J. T. (2008). Education. In G. Hirsch Hadorn, H. Hoffman-Riem, S. Biber-Klemm, W. Grossenbacher-Mansuy, D. Joye, C. Pohl, et al. (Eds.), *Handbook of transdisciplinary research* (pp. 399–410). Dordrecht, Switzerland: Springer.

Klein, J. T. (2010a). *Creating interdisciplinary campus cultures: A model for strength and sustainability.* San Francisco: Jossey-Bass.

Klein, J. T. (2010b). A taxonomy of interdisciplinarity. In R. Frodeman, J. T. Klein, & C. Mitcham (Eds.), *The Oxford handbook of interdisciplinarity* (pp. 15–30). New York: Oxford University Press.

Kruglanski, A., Pierro, A., Manetti, L., & Grada, E. (2006). Groups as epistemic providers: Need for closure and the unfolding of group-centrism. *Psychological Review, 113*(1), 84–100.

Kuhn, T. (1970). *The structure of scientific revolutions.* Chicago: University of Chicago Press.

Laszlo, E. (2001). *Macroshift: Navigating the transformation to a sustainable world.* San Francisco: Berrett-Koehler.

Lattuca, L. R. (2001). *Creating interdisciplinarity: Interdisciplinary research and teaching among college and university faculty.* Nashville, TN: Vanderbilt University Press.

Lau, D. C., & Murningham, J. K. (2005). Interactions within groups and subgroups: The effects of demographic faultlines. *Academy of Management Journal, 48*(4), 645–659.

Leung, A. K., Maddux, W. W., Galinsky, A. D., & Chiu, C. Y. (2008). Multicultural experience enhances creativity: The when and how. *The American Psychologist, 63*(3), 169–181. doi:10.1037/0003-066X.63.3.169

Levy, L. H. (1968). Originality as role-defined behavior. *Journal of Personality and Social Psychology, 9*, 72–78.

Lewin, K. (1936). *Principles of topological psychology.* New York: McGraw-Hill.

Maddi, S. R. (2001). *Personality theories: A comparative analysis* (6th ed.). Long Grove, IL: Waveland Press.

Marx, K., & Engels, F. (1968). *Selected works.* New York: International Publishers.

Marx, M. H. (1976). Theorizing. In M. H. Marx & F. E. Goodson (Eds.), *Theories in contemporary psychology* (2nd ed., pp. 261–286). New York: Macmillan.

McKim, R. H. (1980). *Thinking visually: A strategy manual for problem solving.* Belmont, CA: Wadsworth.

Merton, R. K. (1968). On sociological theories of the middle range. In R. K. Merton (Ed.), *Social theory and social structure* (pp. 39–71). New York: Free Press.

Mills, C. W. (1959). Appendix: On intellectual craftsmanship. In *The sociological imagination* (pp. 195–226). New York: Oxford University Press.

Misra, S., Harvey, R., Stokols, D., Pine, K., Fuqua, J., Shokair, S., et al. (2009). Evaluating an interdisciplinary undergraduate training program in health promotion research. *American Journal of Preventive Medicine, 36*(4), 358–365.

Misra, S., Stokols, D., Hall, K. L., & Feng, A. (2010). Transdisciplinary training in health research: Distinctive features and future directions. In M. Kirst, N. Schaefer-McDaniel, S. Huang, & P. O'Campo (Eds.), *Converging disciplines: A transdisciplinary research approach to urban health problems* (pp. 133–147). New York: Springer.

Mitrany, M., & Stokols, D. (2005). Gauging the transdisciplinary qualities and outcomes of doctoral training programs. *Journal of Planning Education and Research, 24*, 437–449.

Morgan, G., Kobus, K., Gerlach, K. K., Neighbors, C., Lerman, C., Abrams, D. B., et al. (2003). Facilitating transdisciplinary research: The experience of the transdisciplinary tobacco use research centers. *Nicotine & Tobacco Research, 5*(Suppl. 1), S11–S19.

Morse, W. C., Nielsen-Pincus, M., Force, J. E., & Wulfhorst, J. D. (2007). Bridges and barriers to developing and conducting interdisciplinary graduate-student team research. *Ecology and Society, 12*(2), 8. Retrieved from http://www.ecologyand society.org/vol12/iss2/art8/

Nash, J. M. (2008). Transdisciplinary training: Key components and prerequisites for success. *American Journal of Preventive Medicine, 35*(2S), S133–S140. doi:10.1016/j.amepre.2008.05.004

National Academy of Sciences. (2005). *Facilitating interdisciplinary research.* Washington, DC: National Academies Press.

National Cancer Institute. (2008). Science of team science. Retrieved August 9, 2010, from http://cancercontrol.cancer.gov/brp/scienceteam/index.html

National Cancer Institute. (2011). NCI Team Science Toolkit. Retrieved February 24, 2013, from https://www.teamsciencetoolkit.cancer.gov/public/home.aspx?js=1

National Institutes of Health. (2010). Collaboration and team science. Retrieved May 28, 2010, from https://ccrod.cancer.gov/confluence/display/NIHOMBUD/Home

Naveh, Z. (2001). Ten major premises for a holistic conception of multifunctional landscapes. *Landscape and Urban Planning, 57*(3–4), 269–284.

NUCATS. (2010). SciTS and team science resources. Northwestern University Clinical and Translational Science Institute. Retrieved August 8, 2010, from http://scienceofteamscience.northwestern.edu/team-science-resources

Obstfeld, D. (2005). Social networks, the Tertius lungens orientation, and involvement in innovation. *Administrative Science Quarterly, 50*, 100–130.

Olson, J. S., Hofer, E. C., Bos, N., Zimmerman, A., Olson, G. M., Cooney, D., et al. (2008). A theory of remote scientific collaboration (TORSC). In G. M. Olson, A. Zimmerman, & N. Bos (Eds.), *Scientific collaboration on the Internet* (pp. 73–98). Cambridge: MIT Press.

Paletz, S. B. F., & Schunn, C. D. (2010). A social-cognitive framework of multidisciplinary team innovation. *Topics in Cognitive Science, 2*, 73–95.

Park, R., Burgess, E., & McKenzie, R. D. (Eds.). (1925). *The city.* Chicago: University of Chicago Press.

Pickett, S. T. A., Burch, W. R., Jr., & Grove, J. M. (1999). Interdisciplinary research: Maintaining the constructive impulse in a culture of criticism. *Ecosystems, 2*, 302–307.

Platt, J. (1964). Strong inference. *Science, 146*, 347–353.

Pohl, C., & Hirsch Hadorn, G. (2008). Methodological challenges of transdisciplinary research. *Natures Sciences Societies, 16*, 111–121.

Raskas, D., & Hambrick, D. (1992). Multifunctional managerial development: A framework for evaluating the options. *Organizational Dynamics, 21*(2), 5–17.

Repko, A. F. (2008). *Interdisciplinary research: Process and theory.* Los Angeles: Sage.

ResearchToolkit.org. (2010). PRIMER: A toolkit for health research in partnership with practices and communities. University of Washington Institute for Translational Health Sciences, CTSA Award. Retrieved February 24, 2013, from http://www.researchtoolkit.org/

Rhoten, D., & Parker, A. (2004). Risks and rewards of an interdisciplinary research path. *Science, 306*, 2046.

Robert Wood Johnson Foundation. (2008). Robert Wood Johnson Foundation Health and Society Scholars. Retrieved August 15, 2010, from http://www.healthandsocietyscholars.org/

Rokeach, M. (2000). *Understanding human values.* New York: Free Press.

Root-Bernstein, R., Bernstein, M., & Garnier, H. (1995). Correlations between avocations, scientific style, work habits, and professional impacts of scientists. *Creativity Research Journal, 8*(2), 115–137.

Rosenberg, M. (1956). Cognitive structure and attitudinal affect. *Journal of Abnormal and Social Psychology, 53*, 367–372.

Rosenfield, P. L. (1992). The potential of transdisciplinary research for sustaining and extending linkages between the health and social sciences. *Social Science and Medicine, 35*, 1343–1357.

Schnapp, L. M., Rotschy, L., O'Rourke, M., & Crowley, S. (2012). How to talk to strangers: Facilitating knowledge sharing within translational health teams with the Toolbox dialogue method. *Translational Behavioral Medicine.* doi:10.1007/s13142-012-0171-2

Schor, I. (1992). *Empowering education.* Chicago: University of Chicago Press.

Schwartz, S. H., & Bilsky, W. (1990). Toward a theory of the universal content and structure of values: Extensions and cross-cultural replications. *Journal of Personality and Social Psychology, 58*(5), 878–891.

Science of Collaboratories. (2011). Science of collaboratories. Retrieved February 23, 2013, from http://soc.ics.uci.edu/

Shen, B. (2008). Toward cross-sectoral team science. *American Journal of Preventive Medicine, 35*(2S), S240–S242.

Simonton, D. K. (2009). Varieties of (scientific) creativity: A hierarchical model of domain-specific disposition, development, and achievement. *Perspectives on Psychological Science, 4*(5), 441–452. doi:10.1111/j.1745-6924.2009.01152.x

Sonnenwald, D. H. (2003). Managing cognitive and affective trust in the conceptual R&D organization. In M.-L. Huotari & M. Iivonen (Eds.), *Trust in knowledge management and systems in organizations* (pp. 82–106). Hershey, PA: Idea.

Sternberg, R. J. (2002). Creativity as a decision. *American Psychologist, 57*, 376.

Stokols, D. (1987). Conceptual strategies of environmental psychology. In D. Stokols & I. Altman (Eds.), *Handbook of environmental psychology* (pp. 41–70). New York: John Wiley & Sons.

Stokols, D. (1998, May 21). *The future of interdisciplinarity in the School of Social Ecology.* Paper presented at the Social Ecology Associates Annual Awards Reception, School of Social Ecology, University of California, Irvine. Retrieved August 1, 2010, from https://eee.uci.edu/98f/50990/Readings/stokols.html

Stokols, D. (2006). Toward a science of transdisciplinary action research. *American Journal of Community Psychology, 38*(1), 63–77.

Stokols, D. (2013). *Graduate Seminar on Social Ecology (SE200), School of Social Ecology, University of California, Irvine.* Retrieved April 14, 2013, from https://eee.uci.edu/12f/50880.

Stokols, D. (2012). Graduate seminar on strategies of theory development (SE261), School of Social Ecology, University of California, Irvine. Retrieved February 15, 2012, from https://eee.uci.edu/12w/50890

Stokols, D., Fuqua, J., Gress, J., Harvey, R., Phillips, K., Baezconde-Garbanati, L., et al. (2003). Evaluating transdisciplinary science. *Nicotine & Tobacco Research, 5*(Suppl. 1), S21–S39.

Stokols, D., Hall, K. L., Taylor, B., & Moser, R. P. (2008). The science of team science: Overview of the field and introduction to the supplement. *American Journal of Preventive Medicine, 35*(2S), S77–S89.

Stokols, D., Harvey, R., Gress, J., Fuqua, J., & Phillips, K. (2005). In vivo studies of transdisciplinary scientific collaboration: Lessons learned and implications for active living research. *American Journal of Preventive Medicine, 28*(2S2), 202–213.

Stokols, D., Misra, S., Hall, K., Taylor, B., & Moser, R. (2008). The ecology of team science: Understanding contextual influences on transdisciplinary collaboration. *American Journal of Preventive Medicine, 35*(2S), 96–115.

Suedfeld, P., & Tetlock, P. (1977). Integrative complexity of communications in international crises. *Journal of Conflict Resolution, 21*(1), 169–184.

Tajfel, H. (1982). *Social identity and intergroup behavior.* Cambrige, UK: Cambridge University Press.

td-net. (2010). Transdisciplinary research. Retrieved November 30, 2012, from http://www.transdisciplinarity.ch/e/Transdisciplinarity/

University of California, Irvine. (2004). About ID-SURE. Retrieved February 23, 2013, from http://www.urop.uci.edu/id-sure.html

University of California, Irvine. (2012). The School of Social Ecology. Retrieved February 23, 2013, from http://socialecology.uci.edu/

Van der Vegt, G. S., & Bunderson, J. S. (2005). Learning and performance in multidisciplinary teams: The importance of collective team identification. *Academy of Management Journal, 48*(3), 532–547.

Weber, M. (1958). *The Protestant Ethic and the spirit of capitalism.* New York: Charles Scribner's Sons.

Weick, K. E. (1974). Middle range theories of social systems. *Behavioral Science, 19,* 357–367.

Weingart, P., & Stehr, N. (Eds.). (2000). *Practising interdisciplinarity.* Toronto: University of Toronto Press.

Whitfield, J. (2008, October). Group theory. *Nature, 455,* 720–723.

Wicker, A. W. (1985). Getting out of our conceptual ruts. *American Psychologist, 40,* 1094–1103.

Wickson, F., Carew, A., & Russell, A. (2006). Transdisciplinary research: Characteristics, quandaries and quality. *Futures, 38*(9), 1046–1059. doi:10.1016/j.futures.2006.02.011

Wiek, A., Withycombe, L., & Redman, C. L. (2011). Key competencies in sustainability: A reference framework for academic program development. *Sustainability Science, 6,* 203–218.

Wuchty, S., Jones, B. F., & Uzzi, B. (2007). The increasing dominance of teams in production of knowledge. *Science, 316,* 1036–1038.

5

Beyond Common Ground

*A Transdisciplinary Approach to
Interdisciplinary Communication
and Collaboration*

◆ David A. Stone

This chapter introduces the reader to a transdisciplinary, onto-logical approach to the understanding of interdisciplinarity and the problem of interdisciplinary communication, offering it as complementary to the dominant, epistemologically oriented approach. The dominant approach to the study of interdisciplinarity is disciplinary in the sense that most research on the subject is rooted in one or another disciplinary perspective. These efforts all share in common a focus on epistemological-level integration of theories, methodologies, and concepts as the key to interdisciplinarity. This chapter questions the naturalistic ontological position that underwrites the dominant epistemological approach and offers, instead, a transdisciplinary approach rooted in a hermeneutic–phenomenological ontology. This transdisciplinary approach is then mobilized to show how it may be possible to move *beyond* the epistemologically framed common ground aspired to by the dominant approach to develop transdisciplinary practices that improve interdisciplinary communication and collaboration.

_____ **Introduction**

The dominant discourse on interdisciplinarity is disciplinary. By this I mean that when the subjects of interdisciplinarity, interdisciplinary communication, or interdisciplinary collaboration are approached, they are approached from the perspective of one or another specific discipline—for example, cognitive psychology (Repko, 2011), intellectual and institutional history (Klein, 1990, 1996, 2005, 2008, 2010) or literary criticism (Moran, 2002). And while disciplinary approaches to interdisciplinarity do not exhaust the discourse, they do dominate it, including the way efforts at understanding interdisciplinarity are evaluated in the literature and peer reviewed for funding (Klein, 2008). These approaches all share a standpoint and a set of assumptions, which I will discuss further below, that belong to their being disciplinary *as such*. From this shared standpoint, they provide us with the dominant understanding of what "interdisciplinarity" is, what the barriers to its successful implementation are, and what proposed solutions to overcome those barriers might look like. The premise of this chapter is that this disciplinary approach to interdisciplinarity limits our understanding of the phenomenon; in doing so, it mischaracterizes, and so limits, our ability to address specific barriers to it (e.g., communicating effectively across disciplines), and it limits our ability to imagine how interdisciplinary collaboration can be done and what we can do with it.

The purpose of this chapter is not to do away with our disciplinary understanding of interdisciplinarity but to allow us to better see its limits and to supplement discipline-based understanding of interdisciplinarity with what I will call a "transdisciplinary" understanding. By *transdisciplinary*, for now, let us simply mean "beyond disciplinary." [1] In moving beyond a discipline-based understanding, we may find that we can come to a different sense of what "interdisciplinary" means and thereby identify different barriers to the successful implementation of interdisciplinarity and find solutions to overcoming those barriers. Along the way, I will also uncover a number of classic

_____

[1]In using the term *transdisciplinary* in this way, I am returning to one of its original definitions—that is, as an approach that spans more than a single discipline. Other examples include phenomenology, Marxism, and systems thinking. Thus, when I say that our approach is "beyond disciplinary," I mean that it operates outside of the standard disciplinary framework for understanding objects. This meaning will be fleshed out further below. I will note here that the meaning I am using differs from two more common uses. The first, which can be seen in the work of Stokols and others (Stokols, Hall, Taylor, & Moser, 2008; Stokols, Misra, Moser, Hall, & Taylor, 2008), takes transdisciplinarity to involve collaborations across the range of inputs in the action research cycle and is focused on how such collaborations can be sustained. The second, which I will come back to near the end of the chapter, is the European use of the term that denotes approaches to problem solving involving community stakeholders from the problem definition stage through the process of research and policy development (see Hirsch Hadorn et al., 2008).

black boxes (e.g., tacit knowledge, paradigm, and habits of mind) that serve as conceptual placeholders for extra-rational elements of disciplinary and interdisciplinary practice. By employing a transdisciplinary approach, I hope to "open up" these black boxes in ways that allow us to use their contents, rather than being restricted to pointing at them from the "outside."

I will call the transdisciplinary standpoint from which we will be exploring interdisciplinarity and the prevailing approaches to its understanding "ontological."[2] By using the term *ontological*, I am forcing a distinction with the term *epistemological*. Epistemology asks, "How we know what we know?" It explores the nature and value of knowledge and guides us in determining whether what is known is reliable and/or valid. In the context of the discipline-based approach to interdisciplinarity, it serves as the foundational level of understanding of and for the disciplines. In concrete terms, for disciplinary studies of interdisciplinarity, the epistemological level of inquiry characterizes disciplines and interdisciplinary approaches in terms of theories, methods, concepts, and assumptions (Boden, 1990; Huutoniemi, Klein, Bruun, & Hukkinen, 2010; Klein, 1990, 2008; Mansilla, 2010; Repko, 2011). It is at this level that the need for common ground and common language is said to arise. To work across disciplines, it is said that we need to identify or work toward common theoretical or conceptual elements, because it is these shared elements that allow collaborators to begin to work together by speaking a shared language. (See, for example, Repko, 2011.)

But as we will see, our transdisciplinary, ontological approach will suggest that we can ask a question prior to asking "how we know what we know"—that is, "How are we such that we can know?" In doing so, our approach will allow us to go beneath the level of theories, methods, concepts, and assumptions, to the shared ontological understanding that makes the disciplinary, epistemologically driven reliance on these categories possible. In so doing, I will not be suggesting that finding common ground at these levels is not important but that there is a *beyond common ground*—a place beyond the epistemological ground that we tend to take as bedrock—which, as we shall see in our final section, may lead to improvement in our capacity to communicate and cooperate across disciplines. Finally, it should be said that, for most readers, this chapter represents at best only an introduction to a transdisciplinary, ontological approach and that, as such, it can

---

[2]Bhaskar, Frank, Høyer, Næss, and Parker (2010) also use the term *ontology* in the context of their understanding of interdisciplinarity. However, their use derives from Bhaskar's critical realist approach and should not be confused or conflated with the phenomenological sense of the term employed here. This latter sense, which informs the approach to this chapter, is drawn from the ways of thought offered by Martin Heidegger (1927/2008). Briefly, for Heidegger, the term *ontology* refers to the problem of how things can show up for us (i.e., be) at all, so before we get to epistemological questions about how we can know things or how we can form justified true beliefs about them, we must first address how it is that the world and our relation to it exist such that intelligibility itself is possible at all.

only point toward new ways of operating in collaborative, interdisciplinary settings. Further work will be needed to bring this approach into practice.

Discipline-Based Understanding of Interdisciplinarity

What does it mean to take a disciplinary approach to interdisciplinarity? To begin with, it means that authors and researchers who take up the question of interdisciplinarity do so from some given discipline, say cognitive psychology or intellectual history. Adopting a transdisciplinary approach reveals that these discipline-based approaches all share a number of starting points or basic assumptions in common, which, as I noted earlier, result from their shared understanding of ontology. Our goal in this section is to identify these key assumptions and so provide a basic outline of this epistemological approach.

To begin, it will be helpful to better define the terms *discipline* and *interdisciplinary* but to do so in full recognition that while there are many roughly similar definitions in this literature, there is not universal agreement on the meaning of these key terms.[3] I will begin with definitions commonly found in the literature; later in the chapter, I will revisit some of them in the context of our transdisciplinary understanding. In her literature review on interdisciplinarity for the Higher Education Academy, Chettiparamb (2007) notes that there are three standpoints generally taken in the definition of the term *discipline* and in assigning attributes to it. "The first of these standpoints emanates from a scientific-epistemological approach and clarifies analytical features of what might constitute a discipline. The second emphasizes and relates the discipline to society, while the third stresses the institutional/organisational aspect of disciplines" (Chettiparamb, 2007, p. 3). Klein takes up the first of these, which fits my purposes, and defines disciplines as the "tools, methods, procedures, exempla, concepts and theories that account coherently for a set of objects or subjects" (as quoted in Strober, 2011, p. 13).

Though there is much debate and discussion around the edges, interdisciplinarity[4] or interdisciplinary studies tend to be defined as a process that

---

[3]While there is, in fact, less than total agreement on the definition of these and related terms, as exhibited by the chapters in this volume, all the proffered definitions remain within the shared ontological understanding that we attribute to the disciplinary approach to interdisciplinarity. It is this ontological understanding that I will discuss in Section III.

[4]Much ink has been spilled on the distinctions among multi-, cross-, inter-, trans-, and other varieties of disciplinarity. I will not here lay out these distinctions in any detail but simply note that they tend to follow the logic of integration; that is, multi- and cross-disciplinarity are held to involve less, if any, integration, while transdisciplinarity is held to involve the integration of disciplinary and interdisciplinary perspectives. As indicated above, I think of transdisciplinarity differently and will provide my own definition of it later in the chapter.

brings together "separate bodies of specialized data, methods, tools, concepts, and theories in order to create a synthetic view" (Huutoniemi et al., 2010, p. 83). As such, interdisciplinary activities are seen as arising from— or even as parasitic on—the disciplines (Hansson, 1999). Interdisciplinary research fills gaps in disciplinary knowledge or extends the research beyond the cognitive limits of existing disciplines with the oft-expressed ultimate goal of unity (Chettiparamb, 2007) or at least a proximal goal of greater comprehensiveness of knowledge and understanding (Klein, 1990; Repko, 2011). The implied metaphor is that the natural, social, and psychological phenomena of the world lie at the center of the collective gaze of the disciplines, which encircle the world, each taking up their own perspective with interdisciplinary approaches filling the gaps.[5]

From these two definitions, it can be seen in a practical sense what I mean by the epistemological level inherent in the discipline-based approach to interdisciplinarity. What is at play are understood to be epistemological categories: theories, concepts, assumptions, methods, etc. This is made more explicit in the descriptions of what constitutes interdisciplinary activity. As Boix Mansilla states it, "the principal work of interdisciplinary studies is the integration of knowledge and modes of thinking from two or more disciplines" (as quoted in Repko, 2011, p. 23). Indeed, Allen Repko (2011) makes the concept of integration the centerpiece of his influential textbook, *Interdisciplinary Research*. In that work, Repko distills themes from the vast literature on interdisciplinarity to describe a precise method for conducting interdisciplinary studies. In summary thereof, he states, "Interdisciplinary integration, then, is the cognitive process of critically evaluating disciplinary insights and creating common ground among them to construct more comprehensive understanding. The understanding is the product or result of the integrative process" (p. 263). In Repko's method, the key is learning how to modify theories, concepts, methods, and assumptions in one discipline so they are similar enough to structures in another discipline that they can be jointly worked with. This process is termed the search for "common ground." Without common ground in the use of key epistemic terms, communication across disciplinary boundaries is prone to misunderstanding and interdisciplinary collaboration is compromised.

One result of this approach, which is evident in the literature cited above, is that from this discipline-based, epistemological perspective, the central

---

[5]In the past, I have used the metaphor of the bicycle wheel, wherein each of the disciplines sits on the rim and is connected to the hub (the world and all its phenomena) by the spokes. The spokes represent each discipline's approach to the world—that is, their unique collection of theories, methods, assumptions, and concepts. In this metaphor, interdisciplinarity thus means somehow yoking together elements (theories, methods, insights, etc.) of two or more spokes (disciplines). In this metaphor, new interdisciplines thus take their place between existing spokes, thereby enhancing the comprehensiveness of our knowledge of reality (the hub), with the ultimate goal of filling in each and every space, resulting in a unity of knowledge.

barrier to effective interdisciplinary collaboration boils down to language, to our inability to communicate concepts, theories, and methods across disciplines in interdisciplinary contexts. Disciplinary languages are frequently said to be incommensurable (Lattuca, 2003). Capacities and techniques to address this linguistic barrier to interdisciplinary communication are commonly cited in both theoretical and empirical literature on interdisciplinary collaboration in terms such as *communicative competence* (Klein, 1990, 1996), *trading zones* (Daston & Galison, 1992; Gorman, 2002), and *boundary objects* (Gorman, 2002).

A final facet of the disciplinary approach, used to account for the inability of scientists to speak across their disciplinary boundaries, is a number of what might be called "black boxes."[6] These include, for example, tacit knowledge[7] (Polanyi, 1964), paradigms[8] (Kuhn, 1996), and habits of mind[9] (Strober, 2011). As black boxes (i.e., opaque intermediaries between inputs and outputs), these and similar concepts[10] are frequently deployed to account for extra-rational elements of how scientists think. That is, beyond the formal, empirical elements of theories and methods, these concepts represent the outcomes of various forms of informal socialization. It is this socialization process that informs how scientists respond in specific instances in ways they do not consciously attend to and are generally incapable of rationally reconstructing. As such, they also affect how scientists talk—that is, not just the terms they use, with their particular meanings and the assumptions that inform them, but also how they marshal evidence, make arguments, present findings, and articulate distinctions, and how all those are received by listeners within the discipline.

---

[6]For prior work on this issue of black boxes, see Stone (2011).

[7]*Tacit knowledge* is a term introduced by Michael Polanyi in the 1950s to refer to the fact that there are things we know that we cannot say. As such, they differ from explicit knowledge, that which we can say and so organize and formalize. Polanyi's point was that science includes both kinds of knowledge, and so it is impossible to account entirely for how science works because the tacit elements cannot be fully explicated.

[8]Kuhn coined the modern use of this term in the 1960s to refer to the idea that when we are trained to become scientists we are given more than information and methods for applying that information; what happens is more akin to becoming socialized or acculturated in the ways of thinking, speaking, and doing that are involved in science, and that process is often driven by being taught or apprenticed in canonical or "paradigmatic" ways of doing things. Here, again, the idea is that what it is to become and operate as a scientist cannot be fully accounted for or explicated; it is more than the following of a set of rules or procedures.

[9]*Habits of mind* is a term coined by Dewey (1916) around the turn of the 20th century and used to refer to a manner of thinking that we fall into out of repetition and so come to employ without consciously thinking about it.

[10]Stober (2011, p. 37), citing Amey and Brown (2004), includes lenses, frames, orientations, cultural filters, habits of expectation, mental models, and cognitive maps.

These black boxes point to an aspect of disciplinary practice that produces barriers to interdisciplinary communication that the disciplinary approach to interdisciplinarity cannot adequately account for and so has no way of working with.

So the logic of the disciplinary understanding of interdisciplinarity goes like this: Disciplines are collections of theories, methods, and concepts that create languages, practices, and worldviews that foster unique modes of thought. As a result, they cannot easily communicate with one another because they are built on different epistemological scaffolding and so use different terminologies. Therefore, to work across disciplines in a truly interdisciplinary fashion, the key is to establish common epistemological ground by integrating insights and assumptions across disciplines, thereby creating integration or synthesis. Once this is accomplished, gaps in our understanding of real-world problems will be filled and knowledge will move in the direction of unity.

Clearly, if one accepts this logic, identifying ways of improving our "communicative capacity"—our ability to speak and listen across disciplinary boundaries—will, perforce, enhance our ability to conduct successful interdisciplinary collaborations. The remainder of this chapter challenges this logic. It suggests that the self-evidence of this logic blinds us to alternative approaches to these issues, and it offers one such approach.

A Transdisciplinary Approach to Interdisciplinarity

To take a transdisciplinary approach to interdisciplinarity and interdisciplinary communication, we begin where we find ourselves: invested in an epistemological, discipline-based approach to our understanding of the world around us. Epistemology asks "how we know what we know," but modern epistemology is predicated on an understanding of ontology wherein we are subjects and relate to the world primarily, if not exclusively, as the object of our knowledge. Whatever their epistemological differences, all disciplines share this ontological presupposition, that the natural world around us comprises "objects" (i.e., material stuff and its analogues) because of the fact that, and only insofar as, they are amenable to certain forms of empirical investigation. The technical term for this ontological position is *empirical naturalism*, and it is the ontological understanding that undergirds the dominant, disciplinary view of interdisciplinarity.[11]

---

[11]Within this ontology, as the New Philosophy of Science (Feyerabend [e.g., Lakatos, Feyerabend, & Motterlini, 1999]; Fleck, 1981; Hanson, 1958; Kuhn, 1996; Polanyi, 1964; and others) has shown, the world reveals itself differently based on epistemological differences among the sciences—for example, differing paradigms or different ways social forces impact the science (i.e., social constructivism). Nevertheless, ontologically (i.e., what there is in the world) remains the same.

Reorienting to a Transdisciplinary Ontological Approach

But if we are going to take a transdisciplinary ontological approach, we cannot presuppose this world of natural objects; we must begin otherwise. In other words, we must ask, what is it like to make sense of the world when we do not assume ourselves to be thinking subjects operating in a world of material objects? If we begin from an examination of our own experience, and if we can steadfastly abstain from the presumption that we exist in a world of objects available to us only through our senses and our rational capacities, a different understanding emerges. But accomplishing this is no simple task. The dominant, default understanding of our relation to the world is one in which our most basic relation is one of knowing the world through conscious, cognitive, conceptual reckoning of our perceptions of it, and setting this aside requires constant attention to our assumptions to ensure that we do not lose sight of what our experience shows us. If, however, we can accomplish this, disciplinary understanding will reveal itself in a new light.

In experience, the world does not reveal itself to us primarily as a stream of sense perceptions acted on by memory and logic. What passes behind the shuttered window is not a low rumbling sound accompanied by a subtle Doppler effect that reminds us of similar sounds. What passes by the window is a motorcycle. In experience, the world presents itself to us as meaningful, as making sense to us *as* this or that, or at worst, as something we cannot quite make sense of or that is unclear in its meaning to us (which then becomes how we make sense of it). In our experience, we dwell in a world of meaning—meaning already given to us by our history, language, culture, and our own past experiences and meaning made by us in response to our purposes, goals, and intentions. For the most part, things in the world come already packaged with meaning, and that is how we encounter them.

In addition, though, in specific instances, we can make sense of something in specific response to our needs or goals. I can make sense of the rock I find near the campsite *as* a hammer if I am camping in the woods and need to drive a tent stake. Taken more broadly, this means that in everyday experience, we have the capacity to make things *be* (i.e., *mean*) this or that. The rock I find at the campsite can *be* a hammer for me in this instance; that is, it can mean "something useable for driving stakes" or it can be (i.e., mean) "something beautiful and fashionable that I make jewelry with."

Indeed, we dwell in a meaningful world even before we perceive. Return again to experience. Every moment of every day, from the time we wake up, we find ourselves in a mood, some mood or other. And in that mood, certain things show up for us as mattering—as meaningful for us now—and some things do not. Some things take on meaning that is out of all proportion to their actual importance, and some things that should matter to us do not. Our mood also affects our purposes, our goals, and our intentions and so alters the meaning we make of our circumstances and our surroundings.

As an example of how intentions can affect meaning, consider the following: If your intention is to grab a sip of milk from the refrigerator in the middle of the night but because the refrigerator light is out you accidentally grab the water bottle instead of the milk bottle, your reaction will be to instantly spit out what tastes like curdled milk. Taste is not a hardwired, molecular, neural process directly linking taste buds to brain centers for taste. The taste of milk is meaningful; it tastes nourishing, comforting, familiar, and wholesome, and it comes with contexts that allow it to taste those ways. We project those meanings in advance of our actions, and when our experience does not match the meaning we expected to find there, we cannot make sense of our experience, and water, which is usually tasteless, suddenly tastes like spoiled milk—like what we expected gone wrong.

We also dwell before we conceptualize—that is, before we would say we have knowledge of something or before we are able to put that knowledge into words, we first live with that thing. Again, if we do not begin with Descartes' presupposition that our encounters with the world must begin with clear and distinct ideas and develop deductively from there, we see that in experience we do not just encounter things and then name and conceptualize them cognitively.[12] Much of what we encounter daily, we don't cognize at all (e.g., door handles, stop signs, the words we use when we're shooting the breeze). Most of the time, our attention is running well ahead of the doorknob or the stop sign to where we are going and what we're going to do when we get there. More basically, even when we do encounter something with intention, we do not just encounter it; we bring both ourselves (e.g., our purposes for the encounter, our past encounters with similar things) and a sense (or range of senses) of what we are about to encounter that allow us to encounter it at all.

The experiential fact is that we always encounter things as existing within a web of involvements, relations, and significances, and it is these that provide them with their intelligibility. We never encounter an entity alone; we always encounter it in the context of the ways we are approaching it and the purpose for which we are approaching it. Further, we encounter it through the ways it is involved with and related to other things we encounter, through the ways we are involved with and related to these things, and through the kinds of significances that these things have for us. Significances are the ways things arise for us in terms of our understanding of who we are and of how what we are doing fits in to that understanding. Significances can, in this sense, be thought of as how and in what ways things and their involvements and relations matter to us.

---

[12]René Descartes was a 17th-century French philosopher who is widely credited with establishing the philosophical basis for modernity. In his *Meditations*, Descartes presents a framework for modern thought that requires that thinking proceed only on the basis of so-called "clear and distinct" ideas and proceed systematically from there.

Central to these contextual relations is the role of temporality. To exist as a human being is always to be on the way to becoming who we already are. We exist as existentially thrown; that is, the fact that we live in time means that we have no choice but to live out into our futures that person whom we already understand ourselves to be. This means that in every instance we are projecting ourselves ahead of ourselves. For the sake of being who I already know myself to be (i.e., that person I carry forward from my past), and to do the things I need to do to be that person, I project myself ahead of myself in terms of plans, goals, expectations, and next steps, and I exist as that thrown projection. And in the context of that thrown projection, the world arises for me with its historical and other meanings already attached in such a manner that I create the present meaning of the things I engage with to meet my goals and expectations.

Now, within that broader, temporally driven context lies a set of additional contexts through which we make meaning. This process, which we can recognize from our own experience, has a tripartite structure that the philosopher Martin Heidegger termed "the fore-structure of understanding." That is, before we have a cognitive, conceptual grasp of something (e.g., an object, an idea, an event, an action, a situation) that allows us to make assertions about it or place it in logical or causal relations, we already have a preunderstanding of it that arises from our existing relation to it as dwelling in an already meaningful world (Heidegger, 1927/2008).[13]

Heidegger's (1927/2008) "fore-structure" delineates a very definite sense we have of things before we grasp them cognitively, conceptually, and through language. To begin with, we always already "have" the thing in a certain way in advance, in the sense that everything we encounter exists for us within a broader contextual web of involvements and significances (i.e., other things, meanings, purposes, feelings) within which the thing arises. Heidegger calls this structural moment "fore-having." Second, we approach that which we understand (1) from a past that in some definite way locates us in relation to it (i.e., brings us to it from a definite direction) and (2) on the basis of the plans, purposes, and goals that are already there, prestructuring our involvement with it. That is, our understanding of anything is prefigured, in part, by what we are going to do with it and by what that understanding is for (i.e., "fore-sight"). In these two ways, before we engage with anything, our understanding of it already comes from some definite perspective. And third, we already have a preconceptual grasp of it; that is, we have some sense of the conceptual space the thing occupies either on the basis of our own sense of the thing or by having an outside conceptual sense already attached to it (i.e., "fore-conception").

All meaning making has this same threefold structure that comes before—and informs, prefigures, and prestructures—how we conceptualize, make assertions about, and operate with things (e.g., others, ideas, events,

---

[13]What follows here is drawn largely from Division 1 of Heidegger's (1927/2008) *Being and Time*.

actions) we encounter in the world. And together, these three elements of the fore-structure of understanding constitute what is missing from and, in fact, unavailable to the disciplinary accounts of understanding. It is what they are unknowingly trying to point to as hidden inside the black boxes of "habits of mind," "intellectual cultures," and "paradigms." It is, in essence, what we think of as the *tacit*—that is, a sense of things or an orientation we have that allows us to understand and do things but that we do not cognitively grasp and cannot put into words. However, to develop an appreciation for this difficult-to-discern dimension, it will be helpful to approach it in relation to assertion, a dimension we more readily understand. And for my purposes, it will be helpful to think of assertion as "a pointing-out which gives something a definite character and which communicates" (Heidegger, 1927/2008, p. 199). In seeing how assertion is arrived at and what happens to our relation to the world when we talk about things, we will see all the more clearly how assertion differs from and yet relies on the *tacit*.

Once we have understood and interpreted an entity in the course of our everyday dealings with it, we can move to that mode of interpretation that Heidegger (1927/2008, pp. 195–203) terms *derivative*—namely, assertion. For Heidegger, assertions and knowing are derivative forms of interpretation because they arise only upon the understanding and interpretation provided through our active, more practical, and not yet cognitive engagement with the world. In the shift from using something to making an assertion about it, its mode of being changes such that the entity we held in our fore-having as something handy now presents itself to us as something objectively present.[14] In this shift, "something *at hand with which* we have to do or perform something, turns into something 'about which' the statement that points it out is made" (Heidegger, 1927/1996, p. 147; emphasis in original). In this shift, our fore-sight now directs itself to the objectively present nature of the entity—that is, to the "what" of it and its look. In so doing, the original nature of the thing as handy, as there for us in its utility, function, and purpose, is transmogrified as the fore-sight of the assertion provides the thing with its definite character. In this shift, the entity no longer reaches out to the totality of involvements, referents, and relations that the entity did as handy. This new fore-having and fore-sight focus our attention on its attributes, properties, and characteristics, disconnecting us from "that significance which, as such, constitutes environmentality" (Heidegger, 1927/2008, p. 200), leaving us

---

[14]For Heidegger, entities in the world can show up for us in two distinct modes of intelligibility, or modes of being. They can arise in the course of our everyday dealings with them—that is, in a handy way—and their meanings can arise for us from the assignments and references that attach to their involvements, relations, and significances (e.g., the usability or serviceability of a tool). Or we can step back from our everyday dealings and things can arise in the mode that Heidegger called "present-at-hand," wherein we find the intelligibility of the object in what arises when we just stare at it and consider it in terms of its "look" and its properties (Heidegger, 1927/2008, pp. 102–107).

with an object that is "exhibited . . . in such a way that we just look at it" (p. 201). Finally, the fore-conception of the entity, now "had" and "seen" only in its objective presence, foregrounds its conceptual, lexical, logical connections to other terms and concepts along the narrow plane of its properties, attributes, and characteristics. In this way, even when we attempt to interrogate the conception of something known or asserted, our tendency is to do so only on the basis of those lexical and logical connections, or in terms of properties and attributes, rather than having the meaning arise from our experience of involvements, relations, and significances.[15]

Taking a Transdisciplinary Approach to Disciplines

It is here that we will locate the nature of the *tacit*. The *tacit*—that sense we have of how to handle something, what it may be good (or wrong) for, or what to say in a certain situation and how to say it—is fore-structured interpretive understanding. It is also here that we see the origin of the black box problem of the dominant approach. Because the dominant ontology takes the level of knowledge and assertion to be our foundational relation to the world, it cannot go beneath that level. It cannot, therefore, access the level of the tacit, the level of our connection to the world as experienced in terms of relations, involvements, and significances. We will come back to this issue of the tacit in the last section of the chapter. First, we must explore one final element of the dominant ontology—namely, what makes disciplines disciplines?

As everyday understanding of the world is fore-structured by moods and preunderstandings, in a related way, so is disciplinary understanding. First, as a way of encountering the world as meaningful, disciplinary understanding brings with it the same structure of preunderstanding that everyday experience brings. But in addition—and here we begin to come back to our central concerns with common ground and interdisciplinary communication—in the same way that

---

[15]As we experience it, the world is not "over there" or "out there," separate from us and the meaning it has for us. We do not attach meaning and value to naked entities. As our experience shows us, we live in a world already imbued with meaning; as human beings, we respond to that world by making sense of it in and through *all* our encounters, engagements, and actions in the world, not just through those that require thematic, cognitive attention, conceptual thought, or articulation through assertions, propositions, and sentences. This ontological position I am sketching is not any kind of idealism; I am not saying that if we were not here the world and all the things in it would cease to exist. I am saying that the world, as it exists for us, exists as meaningful and, as such, exists as the interplay—the intentional relation—between us and the world. Nor is this an argument for social construction. Social construction argues that the specific meanings that subjects give to objects arise out of a set of social relations and practices. Ontology in this sense reveals how it is that things have meaning at all—that is, before they have a derivative meaning for us as objects of knowledge. Thus, before specific meanings are attached to things through definitions and contexts of concepts and theories, we are already oriented to them as something and so are prepared to react to or address them even before we may be able to say what they are.

all understanding shares a common structure of preunderstanding, all *disciplinary* understanding shares a common structure, one that lies beyond, or beneath, the much-sought-after epistemological possibilities for common ground.

The shift from everyday understanding to scientific understanding begins with an effort to leave behind our everyday level of concerned involvement for a level of thematic, cognitive, focused engagement on some specific aspect of the world. That effort unfolds as a set of specific moves that are shared by all disciplines, no matter what the subject. They all begin by staking out a specific ontological region—that is, a specified region of "objects." But as we have said, this is a specific form of demarcation; it sets out in advance of itself (another form of projection) a sense of what counts as "really real" for it and so also the context within which things in that region can be understood and explained. For example, biology defines its "object" as the region of living things.

In shifting our relation to something from our ready-to-hand engagement with it (i.e., working with it in a practical, handy way) to an objectifying scientific standpoint, the process Heidegger calls "thematization," three moves are required. To thematize something—that is, to turn it from an entity we encounter in everyday experience into a scientific object—we must mathematize it. This means it must become the kind of thing that is measureable in specifiable, measurable, quantifiable units. Mathematization allows for comparison, mathematical manipulation, and representation (e.g., extension into space in units, location in space on a uniform grid). Thematization also requires functionalization. Functionalizing locates the object in an if–then relation, such as a cause-effect relation that makes each object either a cause, an effect, or both (or schedules of reinforcement in behavior psychology or initial-state/end-state relations). Functionalization accounts for movement and change by specifying how an object got to its present location and where it is when it is at rest. The final element in the thematization process is formalization. Formalizing is the process of abstracting the object in terms of material, context-free aspects; this in turn permits modeling, theorizing, and generating laws pertaining to the object. Such theories and models can then be refined and validated with respect to the "facts" generated with regard to the thematized object.

So what our transdisciplinary approach reveals is three levels of interpretation at play. Conscious, conceptual understanding and assertion arise out of our fore-structure of involvements and significances. Assertions and propositions arise within an already structured world of meanings (i.e., linguistic, cultural, historical, and logical relations) and are prestructured by those relations. And scientific and disciplinary theories, methods, assumptions, and concepts arise out of both those preunderstandings and the particular ways a given discipline thematizes its objects within its regional ontology.

The question now is, so what? In the words of our introduction, what does this transdisciplinary approach tell us about what "interdisciplinary" means, what the barriers are to the successful implementation of interdisciplinarity, what the proposed solutions to overcoming those barriers might look like, and how opening up the black boxes we have identified is related to addressing these questions?

First, we can address the disciplinary explanation for the barriers to communication across disciplines. And here we come back to the issue of black boxes. The dominant approach needs concepts such as "habits of mind" and "paradigms," which rely on the existence of tacit knowledge to explain why we cannot simply translate scientific languages from one discipline to another. That is, two disciplines cannot simply translate one set of terms into another, because those terms are embedded in habits of mind or paradigms— that is, ways of thinking and operating—that dictate how those terms function in each discipline. The disciplines can see these phenomena from the outside, but they can only label what goes on inside them as extra-rational (i.e., neither explicitly identifiable nor amenable to rational reconstruction). But as we can now see, the concept of tacit knowledge as it has been deployed in the dominant, disciplinary approach to interdisciplinarity is a misinterpretation that treats the tacit as a species of knowledge rather than, as we have shown, the fore-structure of understanding that precedes and prefigures what we think and talk about anything *as being*.

The disciplinary approach also could not see the role played by the thematization process in prefiguring how the process of objectification is differentially operationalized by different disciplines, or that the steps in the process are shared by all disciplines. The thematization process also plays into how habits of mind and paradigms operate in creating the meanings at play within disciplines. Now that we can see that these three processes (tacit fore-structure, the interpretation of assertions, and thematization) are at play in the ways disciplines make meaning, we are still confronted with the disciplinary understanding of these phenomena as extra-rational—as phenomena we can see but that, because they are tacit, cannot be worked with to help us address how interdisciplinarity works or how to improve our capacity to engage in it. In our last section, we will refute this understanding and demonstrate how we can use the fruits of our transdisciplinary understanding to improve interdisciplinary communication.

Active Speaking and Active Listening[16]

In Plato's analogy of the cave,[17] the prisoner's soul is turned around when he finally sees the light of the sun. In terms of the dominant philosophical traditions that have followed from Plato (including modern science and the

---

[16]While these terms have a history in psychological, self-help, and gender and language literatures, they are suitably descriptive for the purposes they will be put to here, despite their use in other fields.

[17]Plato was a classical Greek philosopher and student of Socrates. In his work *The Republic*, he uses the metaphor of prisoners bound in a cave who mistake shadows cast on the wall by a fire behind them for reality because that is all they can see. Plato analogizes the process of education to freeing the slaves and leading them out into the sunlight, which is the source of truth.

disciplines), this turn is represented metaphysically as the turn from sensually perceiving changeable matter (i.e., things we encounter in experience) to thinking about unchanging forms—and, thus, from mere existence to essences, from the real to the ideal, from mere entities to their being. In Heidegger's terms, in distinction from Plato, an instance of this moment is represented in our shift from operating within the ready-to-hand mode of being to recognizing ready-to-handedness as such as a way things show up for us in the world. In the shift, it is the turn from fluid, engaged involvement with something (e.g., a tool, an idea, a process) to a recognition of the being (i.e., the how-it-is-to-be) of fluid engaged involvement itself.

Following Plato, however, the dominant approach assumes that this shift is not from handy things to a consideration of their handiness but from handy things to a theoretical explanation of their "essential nature." Hence, for science and the disciplines, this means turning from handy use to the measurement and explanation of the material makeup and expected behavior of handy "objects" when they are considered just as perceived objects regardless of their use status. For the disciplines, the tacit-level understanding embedded in their black boxes are embedded in skills, practices, and ways of operating that are inculcated in apprenticeship, individual training, socialization, and experiences of success and failure. As such, this tacit dimension is ineffable and cannot be separated from these experiences and objectified and made explicit so that the experiences can be used. Indeed, in coining the term *tacit knowledge*, Michael Polanyi (1964) specifically argued that objectifying the tacit knowledge gained in these experiences by trying to make it explicit would change its meaning (Stone, 2011). But Heidegger shows us that this need not be so at all. It is perfectly possible, for example, to consider practical activities with handy things as the kind of activities they are, and unless one insists on adopting the thinking of the dominant approach, what changes is not the meaning of the practice but our experiential awareness of what it is like. In moving from just using a tool in a handy way to recognizing that I am engaging in a kind of practice[18] that allows this entity to arise for me as a tool that is handy (i.e., as having this and that operability and a certain serviceability for such-and-such an activity), the meaning of the tool does not change, but the whole way I am able to function with the meaning does. In this turn, I move from an atmosphere wherein things show up for me only as "what" they are to an atmosphere wherein they show up for me as "how" they are what they are, even before I make any attempt to conceptualize objectively "what" they are.

As in Plato's cave analogy, turning the soul around is temporarily disorienting, as one struggles to understand what one is seeing and how to work

---

[18]Note that I am using the term *practice* here to denote a specific constellation of involvements, relations, and significances. That is, as I take up the practice of hammering a nail, a whole fore-structure of understanding comes into play that allows everything to show up for me in ways that make sense and that I can work with in a fluid way.

with it. In this, Plato is right, making this shift in understanding is very difficult, and it will take more than reading this chapter to be able to accomplish it. It is also transformational; this means that as helpful as it would be to provide an example of what turning the soul around is like, any such attempt would be insufficient. In this, turning the soul around is akin to other transformational activities such as learning phenomenological seeing (Casey, 1997; Papadimitriou, 2008) or Gene Gendlin's (1997) focusing and thinking at the edge, where real understanding comes from having had the experience and there is no simple analogue that can serve as a sufficient example for it. It is like the Gestalt[19] situation wherein we tell you there is a duck here but all you can see is a rabbit. But what turning the soul around amounts to is, eventually, the ability to work directly with the tacit as our everyday preunderstandings. I can attune myself to my fore-structure of understanding, which underlies the world of objects, properties, concepts, and theories I encounter, and I can see how the tacit (i.e., my practices and my fore-structure of understanding) is at work prestructuring those objects. This gives rise to three further possibilities: First, with this awareness, I can work out and modify the tacit in my own approach to the world. Second, I can attune myself to "how it is" for others, such that I can listen and speak in ways that attend to the tacit that fore-structures their understanding. And third, I can begin to build practices that account not only for the use of tools and concepts but also for the way my practices themselves structure what is available for me in terms of tools and concepts and how they are available.

In this same manner, I can also reflect (in this experiential way) on my thematization process. I can reflect on how I modify the phenomenon I study when I mathematize it, functionalize it, and formalize it. I can then see how each of these moves sets up the object (1) to be addressed by the methodologies my discipline brings to it, (2) to be specified theoretically and understood conceptually, and (3) to be grounded in my key disciplinary assumptions along the way. Pushing still further, turning the soul around allows me to relate my preunderstandings (i.e., my tacit fore-structures) to my interpretations of existing meanings and to my disciplinary thematization process and so have a sense of the full atmosphere in which I operate as a scientist.

From this point forward, we get to the real payoff; that is, we get *beyond* common ground. *Beyond* common ground means that there is a common starting point from which we can develop shared understanding. But in this instance, common ground is not sought at the epistemological level by

---

[19]Gestalt is a school of psychology developed in Germany at the beginning of the 20th century. The central tenet of Gestalt is that people (through their eyes and brains) see things holistically first and only thereafter are able to distinguish their parts. Gestalts are exemplified by a series of classic images, such as the duck-rabbit, wherein the observer sees a drawn image as either the head of a duck or that of a rabbit but never both simultaneously.

attempting to integrate disciplinary understandings by way of theories, insights, methodologies, assumptions, and concepts. Going *beyond* this level of common ground means, first, learning to turn one's soul around—that is, learning to see how the meanings of key entities, terms, and concepts arise for us out of our practices and the fore-structures of understanding that those practices gather our involvements, relations, and significances in the ways they do.

Second, it means coming to understand how one[20] objectifies one's object of study through the thematization process. In this way, we move beyond the common ground established at the level of theories and methodologies to arrive at the insight that all sciences share the fact that they mathematize, functionalize, and formalize their areas of interest into objects to which their theories, methodologies, and concepts apply.

Next, on the basis of this understanding, one can engage in interdisciplinary collaborative activities in a new way. First, one can employ what I want to call "active speaking." In active speaking, one speaks intentionally from (and to) the atmosphere that one's fore-structure of understanding and thematization process generate. One does this by including in one's own dialogue a sense of where meanings, conceptualizations, and thematizations come from and how they operate in one's approach. In the simplest possible terms, for example, this would mean beginning one's statement by saying, "First, let me say something about where I am coming from."

Second, one can also engage in what I want to call "active listening." By active listening, I mean learning to listen for the fore-structures of understanding and thematizations that one's collaborator brings to the collaborative discussion. In this way, a new kind of interdisciplinary dialogue ensues, one that operates *beyond* the traditional level of common ground and gives rise to a space for meaning that is less constrained by the collaborators' disciplinary starting points. In this type of interdisciplinary collaboration, habits of mind, paradigms, and tacit knowledge are not insuperable barriers to interdisciplinary communication; rather, each person's tacit understandings are available for use, modification, and joint development within the course of the collaboration.

One way of understanding this is seeing what happens to the "object" on the table in a collaborative conversation. In the dominant understanding, participants from various disciplines recognize the object on the table as "the same thing" seen from each of the disciplinary perspectives and approaches represented at the table. But in a collaborative conversation employing the

---

[20]The pronoun *one* is employed here and below as a reminder that when human beings act in socially, culturally, or practice-based ways that are understandable to others, they are acting "as one does" in such situations. That is, we are not so much the authors of our own choices as we are actors in behaving "as one does" in given contexts or situations.

transdisciplinary approach offered here, engaging in active speaking and listening, the collaborators are aware that there is not one object on the table seen from different perspectives but, rather, that each participant brings his or her own version of "the same" object, which arises for each of them from their individual preunderstandings and thematizations (cf., Mol, 2002). The first thing this realization does is free the participant from the need to hang on at all costs to his or her own version or understanding of the object as though failing to do so will mean letting go of reality. In the transdisciplinary approach, reality in this traditional ontological sense is not in play. The other thing this realization does is remind each of the participants that in this transdisciplinary collaboration their goal is to develop an understanding of the "object" (e.g., problem, entity, process, action) of interest in a manner that is responsive to their relational involvement with it (i.e., their involvements and significances that constitute their preunderstandings) rather than their preestablished, disciplinary involvement. (Of course, they can still bring into the discussion insights about the object from their disciplinary understanding.) This process can allow them to carry forward newly formed (and shared) objectifications on which they can work collectively. And in cases where the phenomena or the problem spaces are new, they can work together to develop "interdisciplines." This process, however, is not simply filling gaps between existing disciplines, thereby creating more "comprehensive" understanding on the way to the unity of knowledge. Rather, the result of this process would be a new kind of transdisciplinary understanding that allows collaborators to come at problems in a wholly new way arising directly out of their experiences with them and into a shared atmosphere of discovery and understanding.

Like phenomenological seeing, Gendlin's "focusing" and "thinking at the edge" (see, for example, Gendlin, 1961, 1992, 1995, 1997), and Mol's (2002) "multiple ontologies," turning the soul around, active speaking, and active listening can be taught. In this process, nothing is lost; practitioners of existing disciplines can retain their disciplinary understandings, approaches, and insights. They are free to use these in interdisciplinary settings. The tools offered here simply allow them experiential access to where those understandings and approaches come from, how they have arrived at them, and how they might modify them if they so choose. In addition, these tools offer access to a common ground that is *beyond* that which can be constructed across disciplinary frameworks, one that shows the common processes they share as scientists and that, perhaps more important, shows the common processes they share as human beings—that is, not just as scientists but as citizens, soldiers, producers, consumers, mothers and fathers, sons and daughters. It is this latter possibility that links our approach to transdisciplinarity with the promising European approach to transdisciplinarity, which asks science to work collaboratively with affected community stakeholders through the full arc of problem identification, definition, and solution. The ability for scientists to share common ground with lay stakeholders at the level of involvements and significances would surely take us *beyond* common ground as we know it.

Take-Home Messages

- The predominant approach to the study of interdisciplinarity is disciplinary. That is, interdisciplinarity is almost always studied from the perspective of one or another specific discipline. It is important to recognize the limitations inherent in approaching interdisciplinarity from any single disciplinary perspective.

- Disciplinary approaches all share a common framework; they explore interdisciplinary communication at the epistemological level and focus on the integration of theories, methodologies, and concepts. It is important to recognize the limitations of epistemological construals of phenomena.

- Hermeneutic phenomenology offers a transdisciplinary approach, in the classical sense that it transcends approaches that are methodologically focused on a given regional ontology of "objects." Working with a hermeneutic phenomenological approach means eschewing the ontological separation of knowing subjects from known objects and working iteratively to interpret how we engage the world as meaningful.

- Working transdisciplinarily, we can identify three moments of meaning making that give rise to disciplinary understanding: (1) our fore-structure of understanding (i.e., the web of involvements, relations, significances that prestructure meaning making); (2) our interpretative engagement with language that structures how we understand assertions; and (3) the unique ways disciplines establish their regional ontologies and thematize (or objectify) their objects of study through mathematization, functionalization, and formalization.

- By learning to recognize these three moments in ourselves and others (what we have called "turning the soul around"), one can, through active speaking and active listening, push beyond the common ground that may be available at the epistemological level and engage with collaborators from other disciplines at the deeper level of the ways they make the phenomena they are investigating meaningful in the first place. This same process could then be used to collaboratively explore new phenomena to develop new kinds of interdisciplines.

Acknowledgments

This chapter grew out of an NSF workshop (#1024477) "Acquiring and Using Interactional Expertise: Psychological, Sociological, and Philosophical Perspectives" which I co-directed with Evan Selinger and Gregory Feist in 2010 and subsequent presentations at the NSF-sponsored Enhancing Communication in Cross-Disciplinary Research Conference and the 2012 Science of Team Science Conference. Thanks to all those who attended those meetings and who helped shape my thinking on these issues. Special thanks to Bob Scharff and Christina Papadimitriou for multiple readings of the drafts and countless helpful suggestions, as well as to the reviewers and editors for this volume.

References

Amey, M. J., & Brown, D. F. (2004). *Breaking out of the box: Interdisciplinary collaboration and faculty work.* Greenwich, CT: Information Age.

Bhaskar, R., Frank, C., Høyer, K. G., Næss, P., & Parker, J. (Eds.). *Interdisciplinarity and climate change: Transforming knowledge and practice for our global future.* London: Routledge.

Boden, M. A. (1990). Interdisciplinary epistemology. *Synthese, 85*(2), 185–197.

Casey, E. S. (1997). Sym-phenomenologizing: Talking shop. *Human Studies, 20*(2), 169–180.

Chettiparamb, A. (2007). *Interdisciplinarity: A literature review.* Southampton, UK: Interdisciplinary Teaching and Learning Group, Subject Centre for Languages, Linguistics and Area Studies, School of Humanities, University of Southampton. Retrieved from http://www.heacademy.ac.uk/assets/documents/sustainability/interdisciplinarity_literature_review.pdf

Daston, L., & Galison, P. (1992). The image of objectivity. *Representations,* (40), 81–128.

Dewey, J. (1916). *Democracy and education: An introduction to the philosophy of education.* New York: Macmillan.

Fleck, L. (1981). *Genesis and development of a scientific fact.* Chicago: University of Chicago Press.

Gendlin, E. T. (1961). Experiencing: A variable in the process of therapeutic change. *American Journal of Psychotherapy, 15*(2), 233–245.

Gendlin, E. T. (1992). The primacy of the body, not the primacy of perception. *Man and World, 25*(3), 341–353.

Gendlin, E. T. (1995). Crossing and dipping: Some terms for approaching the interface between natural understanding and logical formulation. *Minds and machines, 5*(4), 547–560.

Gendlin, E. T. (1997). *Experiencing and the creation of meaning: A philosophical and psychological approach to the subjective.* Evanston, IL: Northwestern University Press.

Gorman, M. E. (2002). Levels of expertise and trading zones: A framework for multidisciplinary collaboration. *Social Studies of Science, 32*(5–6), 933–938.

Hanson, N. R. (1958). *Patterns of discovery: An inquiry into the conceptual foundations of science.* Cambridge, UK: Cambridge University Press.

Hansson, B. (1999). Interdisciplinarity: For what purpose? *Policy Sciences, 32*(4), 339–343.

Heidegger, M. (1996). *Being and time: A translation of* Sein und Zeit (J. Stambaugh, Trans.). Albany: State University of New York Press. (Original work published in 1927)

Heidegger, M. (2008). *Being and time.* New York: Harper Perennial. (Original work published in 1927)

Hirsch Hadorn, G., Hoffmann-Riem, H., Biber-Klemm, S., Grossenbacher-Mansuy, W., Joye, D., Pohl, C., et al. (2008). *Handbook of transdisciplinary research.* Dordrecht, Switzerland: Springer. Retrieved from http://books.google.com/books?hl=en&lr=&id=FzM5FtqBHxoC&oi=fnd&pg=PA2&dq=Pohl+transdisciplinarity&ots=w00dJ32vqk&sig=NLgMT9CXL09qVz_H9xHCrhjDeTc

Huutoniemi, K., Klein, J. T., Bruun, H., & Hukkinen, J. (2010). Analyzing interdisciplinarity: Typology and indicators. *Research Policy, 39*(1), 79–88. doi:10.1016/j.respol.2009.09.011

Klein, J. T. (1990). *Interdisciplinarity: History, theory, and practice*. Detroit, MI: Wayne State University.

Klein, J. T. (1996). *Crossing boundaries: Knowledge, disciplinarities, and interdisciplinarities*. Charlottesville: University Press of Virginia.

Klein, J. T. (2005). *Humanities, culture, and interdisciplinarity: The changing American academy*. Albany: State University of New York Press.

Klein, J. T. (2008). Evaluation of interdisciplinary and transdisciplinary research. *American Journal of Preventive Medicine*, *35*(2), S116–S123. doi:10.1016/j.amepre.2008.05.010

Klein, J. T. (2010). *Creating interdisciplinary campus cultures: A model for strength and sustainability*. San Francisco: Jossey-Bass.

Kuhn, T. S. (1996). *The structure of scientific revolutions*. Chicago: University of Chicago Press.

Lakatos, I., Feyerabend, P., & Motterlini, M. (1999). *For and against method: Including Lakatos's lectures on scientific method and the Lakatos-Feyerabend correspondence*. Chicago: University of Chicago Press.

Lattuca, L. R. (2003). Creating interdisciplinarity: Grounded definitions from college and university faculty. *History of Intellectual Culture*, *3*(1), 1–20.

Mansilla, V. B. (2010). Learning to synthesize: The development of interdisciplinary understanding. In R. Frodeman, J. T. Klein, & C. Mitcham (Eds.), *The Oxford handbook of interdisciplinarity* (p. 288). New York: Oxford University Press.

Mol, A. (2002). *The body multiple: Ontology in medical practice*. Durham, NC: Duke University Press Books.

Moran, J. (2002). *Interdisciplinarity*. London: Routledge.

Papadimitriou, C. (2008). The "I" of the beholder: Phenomenological seeing in disability research. *Sports Ethics and Philosophy*, *2*(2), 216–233.

Polanyi, M. (1964). *Personal knowledge: Towards a post-critical philosophy*. New York: Harper Torchbooks.

Repko, A. F. (2011). *Interdisciplinary research: Process and theory* (2nd ed.). Thousand Oaks, CA: Sage.

Stokols, D., Hall, K. L., Taylor, B. K., & Moser, R. P. (2008). The science of team science: Overview of the field and introduction to the supplement. *American Journal of Preventive Medicine*, *35*(2), S77–S89.

Stokols, D., Misra, S., Moser, R. P., Hall, K. L., & Taylor, B. K. (2008). The ecology of team science: Understanding contextual influences on transdisciplinary collaboration. *American Journal of Preventive Medicine*, *35*(2S), S96–S115.

Stone, D. A. (2011, November). The experience of the tacit in multi- and interdisciplinary collaboration. *Phenomenology and the Cognitive Sciences*, 1–20.

Strober, M. H. (2011). *Interdisciplinary conversations challenging habits of thought*. Stanford, CA: Stanford University Press.

6

Interdisciplinarity, Communication, and the Limits of Knowledge

◆ Robert Frodeman

This chapter argues that differences in communication and audience are the key features distinguishing disciplinary knowledge from the emerging era of inter- and transdisciplinary knowledge production. In disciplinary knowledge production, nonacademics are marginal players in the process of knowledge creation. Disciplinary knowledge production is governed by the process of peer review: Academics rule themselves in ways that harken back to Plato. In contrast, under an inter- and transdisciplinary regime, communication with nonacademics becomes central to the process of knowledge production. As coproduced, knowledge becomes subject to the judgment of nonacademics. Academics become more accountable, which complicates traditional notions of academic autonomy. Moreover, the coproduction of knowledge raises questions concerning limits to the production of knowledge, in that users have limited need and capacity for knowledge. The age of interdisciplinary knowledge production is likely to be defined by a struggle between competing urges for infinite and restricted knowledge production.

Introduction

We stand at the edge of a new era in knowledge production. The regime of knowledge creation and dissemination dating from the end of the 19th century—the age of disciplinarity—is in the midst of disruption. The disciplinary academy awaits its coup de grace, likely to be delivered via the development of an academic version of Napster.

We are at the end of the age of disciplinarity. This essay lays down some markers for understanding its implications. The situation within the United States provides focus for these remarks, but the points made here should have wider salience.

Disciplinarity Disrupted

The sources of disruption are well known:

1. Over the past 2 years, the cost of higher education has risen faster than health care costs (Weissmann, 2012). At the same time, new web-based technologies raise the possibility of radically reducing the cost of providing an education. This sets the stage for a "disruptive innovation"—a thorough restructuring of the knowledge system (Christensen & Eyring, 2011). Indicative of the future, 160,000 students worldwide took a computer science course online with a professor at Stanford in the fall of 2011, and in the spring of 2012, MIT and Harvard announced plans for creating an online platform to offer free courses from both universities. This platform will include both engineering and humanities courses; for the latter, "essays might be graded through crowd-sourcing, or assessed with natural-language software" (Lewin, 2012). Today, only one quarter of the faculty in American universities have tenure stream appointments (Thornton, 2011, p. 7, Fig. 1). What will happen to this last quarter when courses can be delivered online to tens of thousands? There are perhaps 20,000 individuals with PhDs in philosophy in the United States today; will we videotape the 50 or 100 most renowned—or telegenic—and let the rest go?

2. These economic and technological facts have been compounded by the rise of an individualistic, neoliberal political philosophy fatal to publicly funded education. In the aftermath of World War II, higher education was conceived as having larger social and political as well as economic purposes. Conservatives made the noneconomic argument for higher education: Students should go to college not only to get trained for a job but also to become educated in democratic virtues as a bulwark against communism (Schrum, 2007). But in the 1980s, as the fear of communism faded, state governments no longer saw higher education as a public good. Rather, the individuals who reap the benefits of education should bear the costs. Public

funding for universities has been in decline for 40 years, to the point where state universities are becoming "state" in name only. (The Ohio State University receives 7% of its budget from the State of Ohio [Martin, 2012]; the University of Colorado, 5.7% [University of Colorado, 2012].) One consequence is that student debt in the United States has now passed the trillion-dollar mark (FinAid, 2013).

3. Just as consequent, however, is the fact that universities no longer control the creation and dissemination of knowledge. Corporations now spend nearly triple the amount on research compared with public sources such as the National Science Foundation (American Association for the Advancement of Science, 2008). Of even greater portent is the growth of Web 2.0: Content is generated everywhere today, through billions of blogs, tweets, texts, pictures, and videos. The infosphere has become a cloud of data, a smog of information that we "surf," cherry-pick, or simply ignore. One ironic result is that, with so much information, we now lack the time to think. Academics race to and fro, giving talks at conferences to other distracted academics who sit in the audience checking their e-mail. They then return home to write papers that no one has time to read. Heidegger (1954/1976) described our predicament: "Most thought-provoking in our thought-provoking time is that we are still not thinking" (p. 6).

There are currently some 2,400 four-year-or-more colleges and universities in the United States.[1] We may be looking at a massive consolidation of the academic market as economies of scale and advancing technology make it possible to deliver education worldwide. Elite institutions will survive, but nonname brand colleges and universities may be priced out of the market as higher education becomes both more (Harvard) and less (online courses and degrees) expensive.

These are some of the signs of the end of the age of disciplinarity. Of course, it is also possible that the disciplines will adapt. Perhaps marginal changes will suffice: the status quo continuing with only a few online courses here and an applied philosophy course there. But I would not bank on it. Universities are the second oldest institution in Western civilization (the University of Bologna dates from 1088; only the Catholic Church is older). As University of California President Clark Kerr once noted, 85 human institutions have survived for the past 500 years. These include the Catholic Church, the Parliaments of Iceland and the Isle of Man, some of the Swiss cantons—and some 70 universities (Carey, 2012). The system is ripe for privatization and economies of scale.

---

[1]The number varies by how one counts. According to the U.S. Department of Education, the total number of 4-year degree-granting institutions is 2,364; public 4-year institutions, 612; private 4-year colleges, 1,752 (see http://nces.ed.gov//programs/digest/d02/dt244.asp). The US News & World Report ranking lists some 1,400 four-year colleges.

We need to understand the age that is passing away. Disciplinarity may be ending, but disciplines will continue. Disciplines will always serve a crucial function. Even if we lose half or two thirds of our current institutions of higher learning, disciplines will remain a powerful way to organize knowledge. One cannot study everything at once, and disciplines train us to do one thing well. We will still need to be able to handle a fair number of problems in a discrete (i.e., disciplinary) fashion. And society will continue to look for experts who can speak authoritatively and act skillfully in a wide range of subjects. Whether in the classroom or online, students will still major in a field, and the highest level of academic achievement—the PhD—will still largely (but one hopes, no longer *entirely*) mark the mastery of a recondite area of knowledge.

But disciplines will no longer be the *end*—that is, the be-all and end-all—of knowledge. They will form part of a larger whole and will be framed in terms of a different set of goals. And this suggests that portentous changes may be in the offing.

If we seek a name for this larger whole, we can call it the "age of interdisciplinarity." The term is not without its problems. *Interdisciplinarity* contains significant conceptual deficits, the biggest of which is that the term implies that the main challenge consists of integrating disciplinary knowledge across the academy. Such integration *is* hard, but that should not be our central concern. The central issue academics face is responding to the growing interpenetration of knowledge production and use across the academy and society. Indeed, the very idea that there are two classes, one consisting of knowledge producers, the other of the recipients of such knowledge, is a disciplinary notion in the process of disappearing. Web 2.0 means that ours is the age of user-produced content.

Other terms make up for some of the inadequacies of *interdisciplinarity*. *Transdisciplinarity* has cachet across Europe and does a better job of emphasizing that knowledge today needs to be coproduced, the combined creation of producer and user. But even this term does not get at the underlying phenomenon we face, which is not something "disciplinary" at all. Knowledge now comes in all shapes and sizes, sites and directions, in streams, fountains, and fire hoses. In contrast to the stately and relatively stable processes of disciplinary knowledge, knowledge now is surfed—a phrase that emphasizes the speedy, slippery nature of our knowledge acts. It's a piquant irony that the massive increase of knowledge that has penetrated every corner of our daily lives has also made our knowing more insecure and difficult to parse. Disciplined knowledge will continue to exist, at least at points. But disciplinary knowledge now functions more as a raft or lifebuoy that we cling to in the hope that we can make it safely to shore.

Eventually we will come up with a better descriptor for the new world of knowledge. In the meantime, let *interdisciplinarity* function as the marker for the changes under way. Rather than coining a (another) new word, I will offer some color to a term that has hitherto functioned as something of an empty vessel.

Assumptions and Antecedents

The disciplinary age—dating roughly from the end of the 19th century to the beginning of the 21st century—has been characterized by a number of assumptions about knowledge. Not knowledge in the sense of epistemological debates over positivism, élan vital, or justified true belief but, rather, knowledge in another, largely implicit, institutional sense—the tacit principles and articles of faith that constitute the academic regime of knowledge production. These include the view that knowledge is essentially benign; the idea that every discipline has basically the same task of pursuing knowledge within one or another discrete regional domain; a one-dimensional understanding of intellectual rigor; and the belief that the pursuit of knowledge is an infinite cultural project. Note, however, that all these points fit within the larger theme of the academic era of knowledge production. The disciplinary age is chiefly defined as the time when academic institutions controlled the levers of knowledge production and certification.

To put the point differently, disciplinarity turns on the question of communication. The crucial element of disciplinary knowledge production consists in keeping the production and certification of academic knowledge as separate as possible from societal influence. Knowledge is always tied to power and, thus, always political in nature; disciplinary knowledge production offers a distinctive position on the question of *qui loqui*: Who gets to speak?

Academic knowledge has always made its way beyond the ivory tower. But in the disciplinary age, knowledge was first defined and certified through an internal market, only later making it into the hands of other disciplines and finally the public. The initial and primary audience for products of knowledge consisted of one's disciplinary colleagues. Chemists reviewed the research of chemists, and decisions of whether a biologist received tenure were largely made by other biologists. Outsiders—nonacademics—received academic knowledge only after it had been internally certified (Turner, 2000). The modern, disciplinary university was a closed epistemological circle. Knowledge circulated among disciplinary-based researchers, then to researchers in other disciplines and to students. It reached the larger world only through indirect means and as a finished product.

The flow of information was patterned as a one-way process, from the disciplines outward and downward. The transmission of knowledge was understood as mainly automatic in nature and little theorized as a sociopolitical act. Communication with those outside one's discipline, and especially with the public, was described in terms of "dissemination," "outreach," and "dumbing down"—hardly the language for groups viewed as equal partners in the production of knowledge. Rhetoric, in the sense of completing the act of truth by shaping one's message for a particular audience, was a marginal art. Rhetorical efforts by academics to speak to nondisciplinary audiences were—and remain—suspect, dismissed as "arm-waving" or "bullshitting."

And it is true that rhetorical power is largely irrelevant when one's main conversational partners are those who share your disciplinary language.

As for communication beyond the university, academic knowledge was conceived as forming a reservoir for society to draw on. Academics fill the reservoir but have not been responsible for how knowledge is used. The public could use knowledge whenever and however they wanted (Pielke & Byerly, 1998). In effect, academics embraced a claim concerning knowledge similar to the bumper-sticker philosophy, "Guns don't kill people; people kill people." New knowledge was a good and useful thing; academics could concentrate on its production confident that it would pass down to society through a natural and benign process similar to trickle-down economics. The uses of knowledge were not a concern for academics; their research was "curiosity driven" in nature.

These assumptions prompted the development of a distinctive method for self-governance within the academy. Knowledge produced for one's disciplinary colleagues, as well as the process of evaluating these same colleagues, was controlled by a process known as "peer review." Whether for tenure and promotion, the review of grants, or the evaluation of programs and universities, peer review became the means for managing academic life—disciplinary experts judging the work of other disciplinary experts. The result was, and remains, a kind of academic Platonism that ensures the autonomy of academic knowledge production.

In the *Republic,* Socrates seeks to design the ideal city. In Book 3, after describing the need for a guardian class as rulers of the city, the question of "who will guard the guardians" arises. How will a community keep its leaders focused on the good of the whole, rather than turning governance into an exercise in self-interest? Socrates argues that philosophic training will temper the souls of the guardians so they will choose the welfare of the whole over their own self-interests.

In modern democracies the people rule, at least intermittently, through processes such as voting, recalls, and referenda. The innovation of the American constitutional experiment is that everyone guards everyone else through a system of "checks and balances"; power is distributed across multiple institutions, at multiple levels—executive, legislative, and judicial; local, state, and federal. The modern (again: that is, disciplinary) academy is one major social institution that followed Socrates's lead, remaining nondemocratic and elitist. Academics claimed they had a special justification for self-rule: Their activities were both so specialized and so important that ordinary people could not properly judge their work. Instead, academics would evaluate themselves through the process of peer review and report out to the larger community in the aftermath.

Peer review is the guarantor of the disciplinary regime. Claims of expertise depend on the existence of domains of knowledge that are essentially separable from one another. There are no "experts of everything"—unless one wants to nominate philosophers for this role, a claim inconsistent with the Socratic tradition of philosophy—and so claims of epistemological privilege turn on the ability to treat issues as consisting of discrete problems. In contrast, on the account offered here, it *is* possible to become adept at interdisciplinary work, but such skill is as much a matter of character (e.g., being flexible and open-minded) as it is of knowledge and is not reducible to the claim to possessing a special kind of interdisciplinary expertise. That would be a contradiction in terms. Expertise depends on disciplinarity, disciplinarity requires the existence (or stipulation) of a discrete domain cut off from the larger world, and the evaluation of disciplinary expertise is governed by the process of peer review.[2]

The decay of this process of academic self-rule is one of the clearest indications of the end of the disciplinary age. Academics now face a wide variety of demands for which they must demonstrate a greater degree of accountability. At the National Science Foundation, grant proposals are no longer judged simply in terms of their disciplinary merit. Since 1997, proposers have also had to address the "broader impacts" of their research (Frodeman & Parker, 2009). Extra- and nondisciplinary criteria (e.g., the design of an outreach program or the prospect of marketable discoveries) are now weighed alongside disciplinary criteria. The net result is the dedisciplining of the peer-review process. Nor is this only an American phenomenon. Similar demands for greater accountability for academic research are now required at science agencies across Europe and within the European Commission's Seventh Framework Programme and Horizon 2020 (Holbrook & Frodeman, 2011).

Similar developments affect the professorate as universities move toward a greater reliance on metrics for evaluating professors. Indices such as the H Index, which counts how often a researcher's work is cited, and journal impact factors, which calculate the average number of citations an article within a given journal receives, are seen as more "objective" than peer review. They provide a number that makes comparisons between researchers, even those across disciplines, easier—thus legitimating the evaluation of disciplinarians by nonspecialists. (The argument is often made that metrics are unfair to the social sciences and the humanities—because many of the journals in these disciplines are not included in citation indices or because books are not included, *not* because of a basic, underlying problem with the idea of such metrics.)

The irony is that metrics themselves rely on the process of peer review—the papers tabulated in terms of their citations were themselves vetted through peer review, as were the reviewers themselves (e.g., by their own universities). But this does not change the fact that such metrics now allow nondisciplinary experts such as deans, boards of regents, and state legislators to make their own judgments about quality and funding. Nor are metrics limited to bibliometrics. At Texas A&M, for instance, professors are

---

[2]For a thoughtful account of expertise, see Harry Collins and Robert Evans's (2007) *Rethinking Expertise.*

now given a bottom-line value where their salaries are compared against how much research money they generate and how much revenue they bring in from teaching (Patel, 2010).

The rise of broader impacts criteria and the increasing reliance on various types of metrics underscore the breakdown of the disciplinary consensus. Communication with and evaluation by nonacademics is becoming central to the process of knowledge production. So is the rise of various types of "crowd sourcing." The result is not the simple loss of academic autonomy but, rather, a blending and redefinition of the relationship between autonomy and accountability. Academics decry these developments as implying the loss of academic freedom. But these changes also represent an opportunity for new institutional structures leading to new theoretical possibilities. Academics stand at the edge of a new age of knowledge production and should avoid one-dimensional models where more accountability necessarily means less autonomy.

The Future of Knowledge Production

An era of coproduced and coevaluated knowledge is likely to be characterized by a vibrant pluralism. Knowledge will come from a dizzying variety of sources and approaches. Academic knowledge, once the gold standard, will give way to an epistemological terrain in constant contestation—a process that is already well advanced (think of the climate change debate or the rise of alternatives to mainstream media). Evaluation schemes will run the gamut from discipline-based peer review to automated systems of metrics to crowd-sourced review. The university, while likely to remain prominent, will continue to lose its status as the central place for knowledge production. Even the "place" of the university will change in ways difficult to anticipate. Traditionally consisting of bricks and mortar, already the university library is a virtual presence, accessed anywhere with a wireless device. Similarly, the speed of publishing is increasing as the lengthy process of peer review gives way to various types of peerless publishing and self-publishing.

Tremendous computing power and public access via the web will put knowledge production and dissemination at everyone's disposal—a phenomenon already quite visible on Facebook, YouTube, and millions of blogs and twitter feeds. In terms of evaluation, complaints that nondisciplinary knowledge is not properly vetted (e.g., Wikipedia) are already becoming anachronistic. The disciplinary concept of a peer may become irrelevant as knowledge becomes more inter- and transdisciplinary in nature. Peer review will increasingly be supplemented and supplanted by evaluation by a variety of stakeholders, perhaps widening, perhaps destroying the concept of "peer."

To take one example, consider the process of grant review currently in place at the Dutch Technology Foundation (STW). Every proposal submitted must be accompanied by a "statement of attention" from an actual or potential user group. Representatives of these users sit on user committees that supervise the research, in a process that includes regular meetings between researchers and users across the period of research (STW, 2013). Consider another example: Researchers at the website Altmetrics have developed a tool for evaluating scholarly productivity that they call Total Impact. Total Impact supplements the current system of peer review, H Index, and Journal Impact Factors with information about "blog posts, articles, data sets, and software they've written" (Altmetrics, 2012). Total Impact allows researchers to track the effects of their research in real time while also giving them insight into how nondisciplinary users have taken up their research.

But another issue surrounding disciplinary knowledge may dwarf these changes: The coproduction of knowledge raises questions about whether we will be facing limits to the production of knowledge.

There is perhaps no idea more foreign to academic culture than the suggestion that there should be limits to knowledge production. The academy has long operated until the sign of infinity. Academics are trained to assume that every result raises additional questions, ad infinitum. More research is always needed, whether in subatomic physics or Milton studies. In a bizarre act of mental gymnastics, additional knowledge is thought of as being at once inherently useful—indeed, beneficial—while the negative results of that knowledge are not the fault of the producers of that knowledge.

Nevertheless, there are several reasons why the question of infinite knowledge production is likely to become an issue. Most immediate, perhaps, are the budget concerns spoken of earlier, about which I will say nothing more here. But there are also prudential concerns of the type voiced by Bill Joy. In his 2000 article "Why the Future Doesn't Need Us," Joy argues that the technologies now coming onboard—what he calls GNR (genetics, nanotechnology, and robotics)—raise the possibility that by accident or intentionality we may destroy ourselves. These technologies are so powerful that they can spawn whole new classes of accidents and abuses. Most dangerous, for the first time these accidents and abuses are widely within the reach of individuals or small groups. They will not require large facilities or rare raw materials. Knowledge alone will enable their use (Joy, 2000).

Joy's radical response to this situation was to call for "relinquishment"—the voluntary cessation of dangerous types of research. While his call has been ignored, continuing controversies such as those surrounding the development of a manmade strain of H5N1 avian influenza virus show that questions about the malign uses of knowledge will continue to surface (Enserink, 2011). We may be one major incident away from a societal debate about whether we should be producing such knowledge at all.

A second factor may also contribute to the limits of knowledge production: People have a limited need and capacity for knowledge. Disciplinary knowledge production assumes that the knowledge being produced will eventually be utilized in one way or another; it is not the role of the knowledge producer to coordinate discoveries with a particular "user group." I heard this view repeatedly expressed during my years with the U.S. Geological Survey (USGS). Research scientists at the USGS would speak of "throwing the science over the wall"—the wall thought to separate science and society. Honoring this separation was considered to be part of the ethical responsibility of the scientist: This distance was thought to help ensure the "objectivity" of research results. Researchers had no recognition that scientific research always has values embedded within it—in even the simple choice of what is worth researching—or that for scientists not to get involved in public debates was itself a value-laden decision.

For thousands of years it was a given within Western culture that there were, and should be, limits to knowledge. From the time of the Greeks (think Oedipus) and the Old Testament (e.g., the snake) to popular myths and fables (e.g., *Frankenstein*, "The Sorcerer's Apprentice"), the dangers of excessive knowledge were amply recognized. Knowledge was limited for a variety of prudential, religious, technological, and political reasons (Shattuck, 1997).

This moral proscription was linked to a technical inadequacy. Before Johannes Gutenberg's invention in 1439, written communication was limited to the handwritten manuscript. Even after the invention of the printing press, books were heavy, bulky, and expensive. Information was difficult to access and usually secluded in places such as universities and libraries. With the creation of the telegraph in 1844—electronic bits of information sent at the speed of light—information began its transition from atoms (i.e., physical things) to bits (electronic pulses). The transition is not yet complete—people still buy physical magazines and books—but the rise of Kindles, Nooks, and iPads portends the end of an era. The dusty, romantic stacks of books at iconic bookstores such as City Lights and Powell's Books and represented in movies such as *Hugo* are destined to become a thing of the past.

The Enlightenment changed our assumption concerning limits to knowledge; limits were now treated as something to be overcome. Descartes (1701) claimed in the *Rules for the Direction of the Mind* that if one follows his method, "there is no need for minds to be confined at all within limits." And in Goethe's *Faust*, Faust is willing to sell his soul to gain access to all the knowledge and experiences he desires. Today, however, this commitment to epistemological infinity is no longer constrained by technology. Knowledge acquisition, storage, and dissemination are for practical purposes infinite—creating their own distinctive problem, known as "big data" (Manyika et al., 2011).

Questions of limits thus are reasserting themselves in a variety of ways. For instance, Sustainability Studies touch constantly on the question of limits, whether in terms of pollution, climate change, population, or resource exploitation (or not, as in the minds of the followers of Julian Simon [1981], "cornucopians" who see human intelligence and creativity as the "ultimate resource" that can overcome any scarcity of material resources). But seldom raised is the question of whether we face a type of limit tied to the development of inter- and transdisciplinary communication.

Consider, by way of example, an account from the early 2000s. In those days, I spent my time as a philosopher who worked with scientists and engineers on the ethics and values aspects of societal problems. I also had two daughters in grade school. One day I fell into conversation with our principal about how the district could do a better job of integrating ethics into the science curriculum. We ended up submitting a $40,000 National Science Foundation grant that called for training fifteen K–12 teachers across a 2-week period in the summer in how to integrate ethics and policy in the science curriculum.

In due time, the grant was awarded. This is where we ran into problems. We had no difficulty attracting applicants, who were happy to discuss these issues across the summer for a little extra pay. But actually integrating new materials in the classroom? Our teachers balked. The curriculum was so stuffed with information already—much of it state mandated—that the idea of squeezing in extra lesson material was absurd. Teachers were inundated with resources of all types; the problem they faced was one of selection and elimination. The last thing they needed was additional information.

This is not a problem limited to K–12 teachers. As anyone who has worked with policymakers knows, one-page memos are the norm and presentations of 5 minutes are common. The idea of a policymaker reading an entire book on a subject, much less studying the literature on a point, is far-fetched. Of course, this is what staffers are for, but even their time is constrained, as are their opportunities to transmit what they have learned to their bosses.

To date, this issue—what might be called, with a nod to Heidegger, "communication and time"—has had little effect on the production of knowledge. But I suspect that this is about to change.

Conclusion

To be clear, I am not claiming that knowledge production will inevitably be controlled or limited. On the contrary, any talk of limits to knowledge will certainly elicit a great deal of pushback, and many will argue that it is impossible to stop the production of knowledge. Our current system of knowledge production, like our economic system generally, is built on constant growth. Humanity+ enthusiasts such as Ray Kurzweil celebrate the steady acceleration of knowledge leading to technological change and dismiss the purported dangers (moral or prudential) of continued knowledge production that concern people such as Bill Joy (e.g., Kurzweil, 2000).

I do believe, however, that the question of the possible limits to knowledge is likely to become part of our social and political conversation. At what point, for instance, will Evangelicals start asking questions about knowledge production in medical research, given that upcoming advances may double or triple our life span beyond the Bible's "three score and ten"?

For that matter, do we really want to know who the winners and losers will be in an era of decisively changed climate?

The age of interdisciplinary knowledge production is likely to be defined by a struggle between competing urges for infinite and restricted knowledge production. The conversation could take many forms: We might, for instance, hear calls for limiting the production of PhDs in the humanities or questioning the purpose of dissertations on what strike nonacademics as arcane and useless topics of research. And we are one accident away from a serious conversation about restricting lab work on dangerous topics such as H5N1.

Take-Home Messages

In Socratic fashion, the take-home message here consists of a series of questions:

- What happens to knowledge production when it is no longer considered an end in itself and when its impacts are considered to be neutral or negative as well as benign?
- How does knowledge production change when we take seriously the limitations (in terms of time, money, and attention span) that knowledge consumers live within?
- How should our notions of academic rigor change when we do inter- and transdisciplinary work—that is, with an eye toward the perspectives of nondisciplinary users of this knowledge?
- Does asking such questions imply the merchandizing of the academy, where academic work loses its freedom and critical dimension under the rubric of "the customer is always right"? Or is it a sign that knowledge producers are (finally) becoming more responsible for their work?
- Does academia need to recognize its own question of sustainability—that knowledge production itself needs to be sustainable (Frodeman, 2011)?

These are questions likely to preoccupy the next generation of thinkers.

References

Altmetrics. (2012). *Altmetrics*. Available at http://altmetrics.org/manifesto/

American Association for the Advancement of Science. (2008). *Guide to R&D funding data—total U.S. R&D (1953–)*. Retrieved from http://www.aaas.org/spp/rd/guitotal.shtml

Carey, K. (2012, March 13). The higher education monopoly is crumbling as we speak. *New Republic*. Retrieved from http://www.newrepublic.com/article/politics/101620/higher-education-accreditation-MIT-university#

Christensen, C. M., & Eyring, H. J. (2011). *The innovative university: Changing the DNA of higher education from the inside out.* San Francisco: Jossey-Bass.

Collins, H., & Evans, R. (2007). *Rethinking expertise.* Chicago: University of Chicago Press.

Descartes, R. (1701). Rule 1. In *Rules for the direction of the mind.* Retrieved from http://www.surftofind.com/descartes

Enserink, M. (2011, November 23). Scientists brace for media storm around controversial flu studies. *Science Insider.* Retrieved from http://news.sciencemag.org/scienceinsider/2011/11/scientists-brace-for-media-storm.html

FinAid. (2013). Student loan debt clock. Retrieved from http://www.finaid.org/loans/studentloandebtclock.phtml

Frodeman, R. (2011). Interdisciplinary thinking and academic sustainability: Managing knowledge in an age of accountability. *Environmental Conservation, 38*(2), 105–112.

Frodeman, R., & Parker, J. (2009, Fall). Intellectual merit and broader impact: NSF's broader impacts criterion and the question of peer review [Special issue]. *Social Epistemology, 23* (3–4) 337–345.

Heidegger, M. (1976). *What is called thinking?* (J. G. Grey, Trans.). New York: Harper & Row. (Original work published in 1954)

Holbrook, J. B., & Frodeman, R. (2011). Peer review and the *ex ante* assessment of societal impacts. *Research Evaluation, 20*(3), 239–246.

Joy, B. (2000, April). Why the future doesn't need us. *Wired, 8.04.* Retrieved from http://www.wired.com/wired/archive/8.04/joy.html

Kurzweil, R. (2000). *The age of spiritual machines: When computers exceed human intelligence.* New York: Penguin Books.

Lewin, T. (2012, May 2). Harvard and M.I.T. team up to offer free online courses. *New York Times.* Retrieved from http://www.nytimes.com/2012/05/03/education/harvard-and-mit-team-up-to-offer-free-online-courses.html

Manyika, J., Chui, M., Brown, B., Bughin, J., Dobbs, R., Roxburgh, C., et al. (2011, May). *Big data: The next frontier for innovation, competition, and productivity.* McKinsey Global Institute. Retrieved from http://www.mckinsey.com/insights/mgi/research/technology_and_innovation/big_data_the_next_frontier_for_innovation

Martin, A. (2012, May 14). Slowly, as student debt rises, colleges confront cost. *New York Times.* Retrieved from http://www.nytimes.com/2012/05/15/business/colleges-begin-to-confront-higher-costs-and-students-debt.html?pagewanted=all

Patel, V. (2010, September 1). A&M system grades faculty—by bottom line. *The Eagle.* Retrieved from http://www.ncpa.org/sub/dpd/index.php?Article_ID=19797

Pielke, R. A., Jr., & Byerly, R. (1998). Beyond basic and applied. *Physics Today, 51*(2), 42–46.

Schrum, E. (2007). Establishing a democratic religion: Metaphysics and democracy in the debates over the president's Commission on Higher Education. *History of Education Quarterly, 47*(3), 277–301.

Shattuck, R. (1997). *Forbidden knowledge: From Prometheus to pornography.* New York: Mariner Books.

STW. (2013). *STW: Nieuwe technologie mogelijk maken* [Dutch Technology Foundation]. Available at http://www.stw.nl/en/

Simon, J. (1981). *The ultimate resource.* Princeton, NJ: Princeton University Press.

Thornton, S. (2011, March–April). *It's not over yet: The annual report on the economic status of the profession, 2010–11*. Washington, DC: American Association of University Professors. Retrieved from http://www.aaup.org/AAUP/comm/rep/Z/ecstatreport10-11/

Turner, S. (2000). What are disciplines? And how is interdisciplinarity different? In N. Stehr & P. Weingart (Eds.), *Practising interdisciplinarity* (pp. 46–65). Toronto: University of Toronto Press.

University of Colorado. (2012). CU budgets. Retrieved from https://www.cu.edu/cubudgets

Weissmann, J. (2012, June 13). How in the world did college costs rise 15% in only two years? *The Atlantic*. Retrieved from http://www.theatlantic.com/business/archive/2012/06/how-in-the-world-did-college-costs-rise-15-in-only-2-years/258463/

PART II

Case Studies

As we noted earlier, understanding something is requisite to enhancing it, and so generating an improved understanding of collaborative, interdisciplinary research is a key goal of this volume. While theory promotes understanding (see Part I), it must be coupled with observation and reflection on carefully chosen examples (i.e., case studies). This is not just because case studies provide a means for corroborating or refining theory but also because they reveal particular, local aspects of collaborative, interdisciplinary research that are of use to both students and practitioners in their work. How the case studies do this varies, depending on the methodologies employed.

The chapters in Part II cover a broad swath of collaborative, interdisciplinary research projects—from large multinational, multi-institutional projects to local food systems networks. They also employ a range of methods, from ethnographic, participant-observer methods to those that are more historical and conceptual. Among the central aspects of collaborative, interdisciplinary research they examine are issues as diverse as technology, character, conceptual resources, and the ability to reflect on one's own practice. Although four chapters can provide only a sample,[1] these have been selected to reveal a variety of collaborative, interdisciplinary projects involving scientific partners. They can be viewed as a "constellation" that reveals, via the connections among the four chapters, the space of

---

[1]For a slightly larger tip of the iceberg, see Repko, A. F., Newell, W. H., & Szostak, R. (Eds.). (2011). *Case studies in interdisciplinary research*. Thousand Oaks, CA: Sage.

117

options for interdisciplinary work. Finally, these chapters do not merely "display" their cases; the authors direct our attention to features that illuminate interdisciplinary research and the role of communication in executing and applying it.

In their contribution to Part II—Chapter 7, "Rising to the Synthesis Challenge in Large-Program Interdisciplinary Science: The QUEST Experience"—Sarah E. Cornell and Jenneth Parker present a detailed account of their experience as part of QUEST (Quantifying and Understanding the Earth System), a large scientific project that was collaborative, interdisciplinary, multi-institutional, and international. The focus of the case study is the attempt by QUEST participants, toward the end of their project, to *synthesize* the results. In this case, the process of synthesis involves connecting distinct sets of results and then framing the resultant, more holistic perspective for stakeholder consumption. QUEST participants undertook this reflection because they believed it would improve the quality of project outputs. In addition to a rich account of interdisciplinary research, Cornell and Parker give us an account of interdisciplinary scientists reflecting explicitly on their own practice to better understand the nature of their work. Thus, this chapter gives us an interesting and detailed example of how the study of interdisciplinarity can inform its practice.

In Chapter 8, "Enhancing Interdisciplinary Communication: Collaborative Engaged Research on Food Systems for Health and Well-Being," Ardyth H. Gillespie and Guan-Jen Sung present two rich examples of the challenges and rewards of community engaged collaborative research. To frame their case studies, Gillespie and Sung provide a clear and concise account of the theoretical framework (collaborative engaged research, or CER) within which they do their work. CER draws on a number of perspectives to generate a democratic and engaged program whose five phases can interact in a variety of ways. The first case study, "Cooking Together for Family Meals," involves the application of CER to changing food-system habits (e.g., meal planning, food acquisition, preparation, consumption), in part to address issues with child obesity in upstate New York. The second case study, "Leveraging the Locavore Movement," is a description of an even more ambitious project. In this case, the CER team works with hunters and fishers as well as food preparers/consumers to identify ways wild-caught fish and game can be more fully integrated into the local food system. Between their theoretical perspective and case studies, Gillespie and Sung provide a wealth of material about communication and collaboration in interdisciplinary settings.

Casey Hoy, Ross B. MacDonald, Benson P. Lee, and Steve Bosserman present a set of four linked case studies in Chapter 9, "Discourse Communities, Disconnects, and Digital Media: The Case of Relocalizing Economies for Sustainable Agriculture and Energy Systems," that highlight the need for collaborative, transdisciplinary communication to facilitate systems change. The first case study presented in this chapter concerns "agroecosystems," which are the complex systems that generate our food, fiber, and, increasingly, energy. These systems have a wide variety of stakeholders, each with their own perspectives and styles of communication. As a result, organizing for change must be transdisciplinary. The second case study discusses how best to introduce a new technology (i.e., fuel cells) into parts of the world that would most benefit from it—specifically, those with very low household income and no electrical grid. In the case of this complex system, the means for focusing communication and action was not technological but social. To advance the fuel cell project, a demonstration project was needed to clarify its value. The third case study focuses on the experience of multicultural community members in the United States, which is often not positive and requires them to adapt by developing skills such as those that are crucial to transdisciplinary work. Just what those skills are and how they are developed in the multicultural context is the focus of the case study. The final case study presents a unique approach to economic development that concerns creating a local food economy in northern Ohio. This example adds a rich discussion of the role of social networking technology in this sort of community organizing. This chapter makes clear not just the great challenges and rewards of collaborative, transdisciplinary work but also the variety of ways (e.g., theoretical, social, and technological) that exist to communicate across the boundaries of the groups involved.

In Chapter 10, "Conceptual Barriers to Interdisciplinary Communication: When Does Ambiguity Matter?" Paul E. Griffiths and Karola Stotz present a series of linked case studies that explore the conditions under which conceptual ambiguity can play either a creative or destructive role in scientific research. Their three studies examine how different research traditions communicate in situations where they share a key term but understand that term differently. The first case study examines Mendelian and molecular conceptualizations of the gene. Griffiths and Stotz describe these as the "identities" that the gene takes on in two different theoretical contexts. The two identities exist alongside one another in genetics and play complementary roles. In this case, ambiguity has not led to misunderstanding but has promoted a productive slippage of meaning. Griffiths and Stotz argue that this is because there are many "boundary objects" shared between these different research traditions.[2] Boundary objects are entities, either concrete or abstract, that are available to two or more research traditions. They have different meanings in each tradition, but enough is shared across the traditions to allow these objects to act as sites of intellectual exchange. The second case study examines two ways of thinking about genes that characterize two different fields studying the genetic basis of

---

[2]See Star, S. L., & Griesemer, J. R. (1989). Institutional ecology, 'translations' and boundary objects: Amateurs and professionals in Berkeley's Museum of Vertebrate Zoology, 1907–39. *Social Studies of Science, 19,* 387–420 (specifically, p. 393).

behavior: quantitative behavior genetics and developmental psychobiology. These conceptual differences have historically been a barrier to communication between those fields, but recent technical developments have promoted better communication. Griffiths and Stotz argue that those developments have made available boundary objects that facilitate communication between the two traditions. The final case study examines some debates between nativists and antinativists about the mind. Here, misunderstanding and miscommunication predominate. Griffiths and Stotz suggest that this is the result of a lack of boundary objects. The overall thrust of their chapter is that *boundary objects* shared between different traditions are an important facilitator of interdisciplinarity.

Rising to the Synthesis Challenge in Large-Program Interdisciplinary Science

The QUEST Experience

◆ Sarah E. Cornell and Jenneth Parker

Much sustainability science is now carried out in large, multiproject, multi-institutional interdisciplinary programs. While this recognizes that addressing complex social–environmental problems requires diverse knowledge inputs, it presents new and underappreciated challenges for internal and external communications about research progress and outcomes. We propose that challenges of community integration can usefully be seen through a sociological lens, while knowledge integration requires philosophical and methodological attention. Both these areas of research integration and synthesis require the development of skills, capabilities, and new knowledge. Using a recently completed U.K. research program as a case study, we use an interdisciplinary frame with sociological, philosophical, and learning dimensions to analyze interdisciplinary working. Our purpose is to explore the character of communication issues in synthesis phases of major interdisciplinary programs. We note that dynamic processes of leadership, collaborative learning, and "interdisciplinary acculturation" shape the evolving priorities and different phases of a program, and we argue that these phases should be better anticipated, planned for, and managed in large programs, by funders, science coordinators, and researchers alike, to support the effective identification and communication of new shared scientific insights.

The Challenge: Knowing What Is Known in Interdisciplinary Research Programs

Recent years have seen growing calls for academia to develop "Sustainability Science(s)" capable of supporting decision making for all our futures (Earth System Science Partnership, 2001; International Council for Science, 2012). Oriented toward practice and policy, this research is necessarily interdisciplinary (Clark & Dickson, 2003). In global environmental change research, it increasingly involves very large multipartner initiatives. Considerable attention has been paid to the creation, management, and evaluation of such interdisciplinary programs (e.g., Bruce, Lyall, Tait, & Williams, 2004; Committee on Science, Engineering, and Public Policy [COSEPUP], 2004; Lyall, Bruce, Marsden, & Meagher, 2011), but much less is given to the processes by means of which they promise to provide new "integrated" knowledge.

We reflect on issues in interdisciplinary communication that emerged in a major multiconsortium environmental research program, drawing insights for sustainability-related research. QUEST (Quantifying and Understanding the Earth System, 2003–2011; see Section II) was a national flagship program funded by the U.K. Natural Environmental Research Council (NERC). QUEST aimed to improve understanding of large-scale processes in the Earth system and their implications for human activities. Interdisciplinary communication and integration explicitly informed its organizational structure and processes (described in Section III), yet toward the end of the program, the need for more systematic and comprehensive synthesis of the research advances into coherent shared outputs became evident. Our focus in Sections IV and V is on the synthesis process convened at the request of QUEST's funders.

By synthesis, we mean the processes involved in reflection on research achievements, reviewing the state of the art, contextualizing new insights, and exploring how best to present this expanded field of knowledge to the program's diverse stakeholders.[3]

---

[3]In some interdisciplinary funding calls "synthesis" is demanded, but this is often ambiguous between *thematic synthesis* of knowledge across disciplinary areas to apply to a particular context and *synthesis across disciplinary "fundamentals."* The former may be achievable in a project, but the latter may either be impossible in principle or be a lengthy undertaking that would be impossible within the lifetime of a specific project.

Perhaps surprisingly, explicit interdisciplinary research synthesis of this nature is still an unusual process in mainstream research programs. Although there is extensive experience in "synthesis research" and integrative assessments in environmental and sustainability science (e.g., Carpenter et al., 2009; Hackett et al., 2008; Hampton & Parker, 2011; Pickett, 1999), this is often channeled through specialist institutions and initiatives (e.g., the U.S. National Science Foundation's National Centre for Ecosystem Analysis and Synthesis, the European Science Foundation's Forward Looks and position papers, and global assessments such as the U.N. Environment Programme's periodic Global Environmental Outlooks). The crossover of experience from these recognized synthesis activities to the day-to-day working of most academics is limited. Some argue that synthesis should be a specialist capability in its own right (Bammer, 2005; COSEPUP, 2004), while others have highlighted the career risks that researchers may experience through engagement in interdisciplinary knowledge production (Rhoten & Parker, 2004). Indeed, scholars have tended to emphasize the many difficulties of interdisciplinary work (e.g., Aboelela et al., 2007; Glied, Bakken, Formicola, Gebbie, & Larson, 2007; Griffin, Medhurst, & Green, 2006; Heckhausen, 1972; Hulme, 2008; Schneider, 1992); Nissani (1997) stands almost alone in highlighting the potential joys and rewards.

Of course "synthesis" as we have defined it happens in day-to-day research, but while single-discipline programs predominated, there was arguably less need for a concerted effort to assess and collate the outcomes through a synthesis "lens." The research findings of such programs tend to be incrementally and progressively entrained into the disciplinary field; specialist review papers often perform an adequate synthetic function. Within disciplines, judgments about the extent and quality of research progress are also relatively uncontentious and well benchmarked. For programs as large and transdisciplinary as QUEST, identifying and communicating research advances requires more than discipline-based peer judgments, raising issues of how we might judge the "success" or otherwise of such collaborations. We present the QUEST experience as a case study of learning from interdisciplinary research that bears out the value of collective reflection and analysis of the interactions, and (often intuitive) working procedures of experienced discipline-based scholars. Ultimately, this collaborative learning should be regarded and valued as a key research output in itself (see also Tuinstra, Jäger, & Weaver, 2008).

Our take on interdisciplinary research is itself an interdisciplinary collaborative venture. We come to sustainability science with different disciplinary backgrounds (Cornell's in environmental sciences and Parker's in education and philosophy). Together, we coordinated QUEST's synthesis phase. We studied the synthesis phase as it unfolded, with particular attention to a 2-day workshop convened as an inclusive opportunity for cross-program reflection and planning for specific synthesis outputs. We were pivotal in planning, facilitating, recording, and participating in the event, so we engaged as participant-observers (a social sciences methodology), aware that this approach was novel—and itself a learning experience—for the mainly biophysical scientists taking part.

We focus on the synthesis challenges faced by research that seeks to bridge the biophysical and social sciences, with particular attention to communication issues arising with large research initiatives. Our data provide reflections on QUEST as a whole and on the development, positioning, and purpose of the synthesis phase itself. We inquire into the philosophical, sociological, and learning dimensions of interdisciplinary research, aiming to provide useful understanding to practitioner communities. We challenge the (default) position that good and effective interdisciplinary research can take place without specific and explicit attention to its problems, preconditions, and characteristic processes.

QUEST and Its Communication Challenges in a Global Context

QUEST's conceptualization and organization were informed by the prior experience of the scientists involved and the funders; so from the outset, those involved in the program design and coordination knew they faced the following communication and integration challenges:

- **Communication across the sciences:** Bringing together the best available understanding of Earth's natural dynamics requires much improved understanding of physical, chemical, and biological processes—and their interrelationships.
- **Communication across different methods and techniques:** Even within a given environmental field, scientists (modelers, data analysts, and field and laboratory experimentalists) have highly specialized knowledge, skills, and tool kits, and often work in comparative isolation.
- **Communication across time scales of interest:** An integrated picture of global environmental change involves piecing together many strands of evidence, and very different research approaches apply to the study of past, present, and potential future states of the world.
- **Communication between the natural and social sciences:** Many "environmental issues" (e.g., pollution, overexploitation of natural resources) are now recognized as social–environmental issues, requiring improved conceptualizations of the interactions and interdependencies of humans and their environment.
- **Deeper, more responsive interaction between science and policy communities:** Earth system science developed within a context of awareness of the societal importance of its findings. The desire for more effective engagement with policy is driving a new focus on the codevelopment and communication of research.

- **The public communication of science:** In the highly charged societal and policy context of global change research, meanings and motivations both influence and are influenced by the ways research results are formulated and presented. In the face of the risk of miscommunication and the opportunity for informing social learning and transformation, communication needs ongoing reassessment.

Appreciating the nature and magnitude of these challenges requires some background to Earth system science and its links to sustainability science.

Interdisciplinary Research in the "Sustainability Sciences"

Interdisciplinary research is required in response to many important challenges and is increasingly demanded by diverse public and private research funders in Europe, the United States, and elsewhere (e.g., COSEPUP, 2004; Economic and Social Research Council [ESRC], 2007; Ecosystem Services for Poverty Alleviation, 2012; International Council for Science, 2006; Jäger et al., 2011; Living With Environmental Change, 2011; Strathern, 2006). Furthermore, research councils and government bodies are increasingly issuing joint calls for *solution-oriented* transdisciplinary research.

The need for interdisciplinary research is most pressing (and profoundly embedded) in research relating to the development of a sustainable global future: The Brundtland report (U.N. World Commission on Environment and Development, 1987) describes sustainability as "harmony among humans and between humans and nature." The insights needed for maintaining a sustainable balance between human society and the natural environment need to be drawn from all of today's disciplines (Inter Academies Panel, 2010), making sustainability perhaps the ultimate interdisciplinary knowledge challenge (Cronin, 2008; Keen, Brown, & Dyball, 2006). Holm et al. (2009) note that "this requires 'deep' forms of interdisciplinarity that are achieved rather than given, and require significant efforts from researchers" (p. 35). In this context, the synthesis phase of research deserves particular attention: Communication or translation of results is a key task, taking place at disciplinary interfaces and also at the boundary of expert and user groups.

The Interdisciplinary Field of Earth System Science

One of the great scientific challenges of the 21st century is to forecast the future of planet Earth. . . . We find ourselves, literally, in uncharted territory, performing an uncontrolled experiment with planet Earth that is terrifying in its scale and complexity.

—Lawton (2001, p. 1965)

In recent decades, the concept of the "Earth system" has been very fruitful in the study of environmental change, including its human-induced causes and social consequences. This field aims to develop dynamic studies of the living and nonliving "components" of Earth, giving a more integrated and predictive understanding of global environmental change (Cornell, Prentice, House, & Downy, 2012). Currently, four international collaborative global change programs address different dimensions of Earth system research (see http://www.essp.org):

- The World Climate Research Program deals with the physical climate system.
- The International Geosphere-Biosphere Program (IGBP) addresses global biogeochemical change.
- Diversitas supports biodiversity research.
- The International Human Dimensions Program on Global Environmental Change (IHDP) focuses on the social sciences.

These programs not only reflect current discipline-based understanding, but they have also institutionalized strategic research efforts along separate broadly disciplinary lines. Over time, it has become evident that these structural divides present obstacles to the further development of global change research that meets society's needs for joined-up, big-picture evidence to inform action toward global sustainability.

QUEST[4] was developed as the United Kingdom's response to this problem. Informed by an extensive international consultative process (e.g., Mayer & Marks, 2003), the £23-million (almost $35 million U.S.), 8-year initiative began in 2003 with the establishment of a small core team of scientists whose role was to focus on crosscutting research and to nurture the program's science-policy relationships. The program was structured around three scientific themes (see Figure 7.1; Cornell, Downy, House, & Prentice, 2011), each consisting of several projects with inputs from multiple disciplines and using a broad tool kit of research methods. Making investigation of planetary behaviors possible involves the construction of dynamic global models of ecological and biogeochemical processes, linked to existing physical climate models. QUEST also invested in developing statistical methods to evaluate these complex models against observational data. Its studies of past environments required the compilation and statistical analysis of globally representative data sets from many disparate records, such as ice cores, ocean sediments, and fossil records. The program also assessed the potential impact of climate change on key socioeconomic sectors.

---

[4]See http://quest.bris.ac.uk.

Figure 7.1	QUEST: A Large, Multiconsortium Interdisciplinary Research Program (Cornell et al., 2011)

Theme 1
How important are biotic feedbacks to 21st century climate change?
Mar QUEST
Marine biogeochemistry and ecosystem initiative in QUEST
QUAAC
Quantifying Ecosystem Roles in the Carbon Cycle
Advanced Fellowship
High precision CO_2 and O_2 measurements
CCMAP
Climate–carbon modelling, assimilation and prediction
Feedbacks QUEST
Quantifying biogeochemical climate feedbacks

Theme 2
How are climate and atmospheric composition regulated on time scale up to a million years?
Quaternary QUEST
Data synthesis and modelling for a full glacial cycle
PalaeoQUMP
Using palaeodata to reduce uncertainties in climate prediction
QUEST Deglaciation
Change in the climate and biogeochemical cycles during the last deglaciation
DESIRE
Anglo-French collaboration on atmospheric ice core records
Dynamics of the PETM
Relevance of the Paleocene-Eocene thermal maximum to future global change

Theme 3
How much climate change a) is dangerous b) can be avoided by managing the biosphere?
QUEST GSI
An assessment of global scale impacts of climate change
QUATERMASS
Quantifying the potential of terrestrial biomass to mitigate climate change
JIFor
Providing a scientific basis for a JI forestry demonstrator climate mitigation project
QUEST_Fish
Impacts and consequences of climate change on fisheries
FireMAFS
Fire modelling and forecasting system

QUEST Earth System Model
A new fully coupled Earth System Model of intermediate resolution

Crosscutting and Integrative Activities
Over 20 working groups; Annual Science Meetings; International outreach; Interaction with policy makers; QUEST Earth System Data Initiative

Interdisciplinarity Project
Examining interdisciplinarity and learning lessons from QUEST's experiences

Recognizing QUEST's Knowledge Communities and Building New Ones

We, the authors, noted recurrent tropes in our conceptualization of interdisciplinary working, which influenced the way we communicated with project scientists to address the integrative challenges and supported our choice of frame and methodology for our analysis of the synthesis process (discussed more fully in Section V). These tropes were evident in our science planning documents, meeting plans and study notes, and formal reports to the funder. We often referred to interdisciplinarity as a *relationship* that can in principle be brokered and managed (by attention to praxis and the learning of skills and techniques). We referred to disciplines as *different approaches*, perhaps even incommensurable ones, for describing the same world (essentially a philosophical and epistemological angle). We also talked of *different knowledge communities*, maybe with profoundly different worldviews and certainly with different cultural norms and ethics (a sociological perspective).

Our experience has made it clear that interdisciplinary research requires attention to both "community integration" and "knowledge integration." Figure 7.2 provides an account of known issues with interdisciplinarity that often yield self-reinforcing virtuous (or vicious) cycles. Our main focus is on understanding issues on the right-hand side to inform decisions relating to research capacity and institutional aspects on the left-hand side. These considerations remind us that communication is always "from" a certain place and set of commitments and motivations; so here we briefly outline QUEST's position at the start of the synthesis phase.

Figure 7.2   Issues Affecting Interdisciplinary Knowledge Communities (adapted from Parker, 2011)

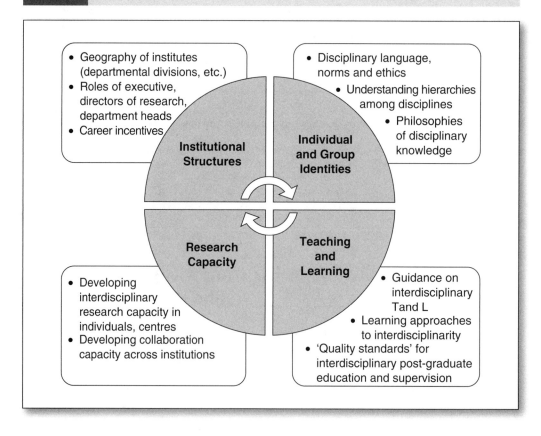

QUEST's Shared Framings

Cronin (2008) has argued that in research for sustainability, "a [transdisciplinary research] orientation would ask these questions: (1) In which way do processes constitute a problem field and where are the needs for change? (2) What are more sustainable practices? (3) How can existing practices be transformed?" (p. 15).

QUEST's research problem field was defined primarily in terms of limitations of knowledge about the links between biogeochemical processes and the climate system. Although global sustainability concerns motivated the research and its emphasis on ultimately policy-relevant outcomes, the links between this process knowledge and action toward sustainability were only sketchily articulated at the outset of the program.

Essentially, the unifying task was the development of the United Kingdom's next-generation climate model, containing state-of-the-art scientific representations of many Earth system components. The United Kingdom has long been a key player in international climate science and policy. Institutionally, physical climate modeling and model development have been primarily the domain of the U.K. Met Office, while in-depth inquiry into the other components now being incorporated into Earth system models, together with research into societal impacts and responses to climate change, has been the domain of universities and research centers.

A core goal of QUEST was to broker effective research relationships between these different groups, generating new "communities of practice." As a scientific endeavor, this was ambitious—and successful by many measures (Cornell et al., 2011). By the synthesis phase, notable progress had been made on integration across the sciences, across the time scales of global change, and across techniques and methods (the first three of the main communication challenges identified earlier). The most impregnable communication barriers remained between the human and biophysical sciences, reflecting the limited engagement of the social sciences in identifying QUEST's problem field at the outset (an unavoidable consequence of the funder's remit at the time).[5]

Modeling was the "first language" for cross-QUEST communication. Collaborative development and use of model code linked the three themes, even when there was limited shared understanding of the underlying specialist science addressed within the themes. Furthermore, the model was the most visible external marker of QUEST's activity; having the new model as

---

[5]The U.K. research and policy communities have recently created a partnership, Living With Environmental Change, to improve the codevelopment and delivery of research that bridges and integrates across disciplines. Living With Environmental Change (http://www.lwec.org.uk) comprises several organizations with an interest in environmental change and its impacts, including the U.K. research councils, government departments and agencies, and private-sector and civil-society organizations.

a goal proved to be a powerful common reference point for all program participants, including the nonmodelers. However, the language of numerical modeling in fact applies significant constraints to the generation of useful and usable knowledge about the real world. We echo Strathern's (2006) recognition that while a shared simplified "pidgin" language allows for some epistemic transfer—and in QUEST's case, the abstraction and simplification in model development did exactly that—it is ill equipped for critical deliberation and evaluation of the interdisciplinary knowledge being developed. A technical common language cannot provide an account of the wider common purposes of a collaborative program.

With regard to the transformation of practices in the "real world," QUEST's approach was to inform policy recommendations for climate adaptation and mitigation strategies, on the basis of the improved insights from its modeling and related research. Whilst stakeholder engagement capacity was built into program management, the potential relevance of the research to actual policy requirements tended to be considered toward the end of the research process. The need for theories and perspectives on the human dimensions of the research thus also tended to be retrofitted.

Developing and Managing Relationships in Complex Research Communities

QUEST's starting point for community integration could be regarded as something of a shotgun wedding: As a flagship program, it had an unusually high degree of top-down direction, in an area where self-organization is the norm. Most projects involved contractual commitments to new multipartner consortia, in which participating academics were selected because their science fitted this new research agenda. At the same time, some long-established research relationships that existed prior to QUEST were not supported. Thus, some new project partnerships faced conflict, internally and externally, that needed to be resolved.

Managing the range of relationships needed for the breadth and ambition of QUEST demanded creativity in crafting different groupings for the intended research, and in identifying and enabling more opportunistic initiatives unforeseen at the inception of the program. In addition to conventional project structures, the core team explored flexible models for supporting interdisciplinary working, with opportunities for self-organization and emerging synergies. The hope was that new relationships created in the program would be mutually beneficial and evolve into enduring communities. A significant budget was allocated to support crosscutting working groups (Cornell & Prentice, 2010), designed to generate novel high-impact outputs that would incentivize the participants for working together in these perhaps unfamiliar ways.

The external relationships of major programs are equally important, characteristically involving a wider network of stakeholders and a more complex set of intended messages and outcomes than do single-discipline research initiatives. Communicating interdisciplinary outcomes to this broader network proved to be a contested issue. Questions raised included the degree of interpretation or translation that *project* scientists should undertake to communicate with *program* stakeholders, who might primarily be interested in synthesis outcomes rather than specialist project results. People also expressed discomfort about having to represent someone else's expertise, hinting also of misgivings about sharing a platform and diluting the impact of one's own expertise. A further concern was the assessment of the success of a major program—not least in terms of follow-on funding and the legacy of the collective work embodied in such programs. Measures of success devised for the evaluation of single-discipline programs are equipped to capture only parts of the success of interdisciplinary programs (e.g., COSEPUP, 2004, Chap. 8; Lamont, Mallard, & Guetzkow, 2006).

Integration of Different Knowledge Communities

The metaphor of disciplinary knowledge communities as different cultures proved useful in reflections on scientific coordination and in operational communications with project teams. Enough time has elapsed since QUEST's first science meetings to note in print that they held many hallmarks of a first encounter between different cultures (despite all participants being environmental scientists), including mutual curiosity, tentative information exchanges, and ebbs and flows of unease and reassurance as discussions moved from one area of science or policy to another. At times, discussions were tense and frustratingly unproductive—in early events, some individuals disengaged conspicuously when discussion moved away from their particular specialism. Stark differences were evident in people's routine customs for research resource prioritization and their capacity and willingness to engage beyond their own specialist fields. They often fell back on their own discipline-based research priorities even when substantial resources were available for new crosscutting explorations (e.g., the working groups).

In this initial phase, the core team reverted to the less mutually beneficial but more familiar approach of centralized, top-down decision making about priorities for crosscutting research, drawing as much as possible on input from scientists who engaged actively in the deliberations. Gradually, a recognizable and more harmonious "QUEST community" developed, with later science meetings becoming dynamic, constructive, policy-engaged international events. As projects began yielding results, attention shifted toward attempts to synthesize and communicate program insights, introducing new shared framings and goals. In synthesis-focused events in late stages of the program (described next), many participating scientists alluded to their "acculturation" through the life of QUEST, speaking positively about both the transformative research relationships that developed and the broadened intellectual horizons enabled by the program.

The QUEST Synthesis Phase: A Closer Look _____

> When you have an interdisciplinary project, it's much less clear what the outcomes are or even how you should manage the process of sustained inquiry between the team. And I think one of the important things is to keep re-negotiating what everyone wants from the project . . . you talk and you share and you work in each other's cultures almost.
>
> —Participant quote in Griffin et al. (2006, p. 39)

Why Have an Explicit Synthesis Phase?

By spring 2009, when projects were poised to deliver their planned outputs, QUEST had 18 research projects, more than 250 scientists working in more than 30 institutions, and strong international connections. Through much of the program, the three research themes and the joint goal of the QUEST model formed the communication focus and program identity. The themes "knew their place" in the program, so to speak, which tended to mean that communication, learning, and stakeholder engagement remained within the themes' largely preexisting knowledge communities.

In the run-up to the synthesis phase, QUEST's communication focus shifted across projects and outward. At the final annual science meeting in 2009, it became obvious that there were significant opportunities—and, given the scale of investment, a responsibility—to draw together the main findings in an interdisciplinary synthesis clearly setting out the new state of the art in QUEST's areas of global change research. The normal way for NERC's research programs to communicate their outcomes has been via scientific conferences and "finale events" targeted at policy stakeholders. QUEST's discussions about appropriate end-of-program dissemination led to a shared recognition of extra challenges arising from its international connectivity and much broader interdisciplinary scope. The discussions revealed previously obscured differences in perspective about the nature of collective integrative research outcomes. Some people regarded synthesis as outside their "pure science" remit and thus someone else's responsibility, while others looked ahead with trepidation at the (limited) opportunities for future funding, seeing that synthesis was vital for the recognition of their new fields of collaborative research.

On the recommendation of the international Scientific Advisory Board, the funders agreed that a specific cross-program synthesis phase was needed. (As the culmination of this phase, QUEST convened an open science conference in April 2010,[6] its policy finale was held in November 2010,[7] and a

---

[6]Earth System Science 2010, the QUEST/AIMES Open Science Conference, was held in Edinburgh (see http://quest.bris.ac.uk/workshops/AIMES-OSC/index.html).

[7]See http://www.nerc.ac.uk/research/programmes/quest/events/101104/.

book coauthored by 45 program scientists was published in 2012 [Cornell et al., 2012].) Here, we highlight features of QUEST's experience that have a bearing on our later discussion:

- The *need for a strategic synthesis* emerged through the project process. By working together, scientists recognized the challenges of building and presenting an *interdisciplinary* understanding of global change. In particular, a year from the program end, they recognized that funding prospects largely depended on a collective expression of research progress and value. Without synthesis, their work would lie at the peripheries of discipline-defined funding streams.

- Synthesis was *retrofitted*. QUEST's Advisory Board argued strongly that the major new insights needed to be identified, described, and communicated more widely than originally envisaged. The program needed to do much more than present key messages from the three research themes to their three distinct stakeholder networks, and the program's earlier crosscutting activities (Figure 7.1) did not adequately fill the "synthesis gap." Some successfully generated new outputs, but they were "interdisciplinary clusters" (Parker, 2012) rather than a fully representative transdisciplinary effort.

- It was *resource constrained*. Because synthesis on this scale was not usual for national programs, it had not been planned from the outset. It represented additional effort by project scientists, and although the funders covered core staff costs for a further year, the working budget was tight. The Advisory Board cochairs had previously directed two of the international global change programs (IGBP and IHDP), for which periodic research synthesis was a core activity, and were thus able to provide invaluable authoritative "steering" and well-targeted advice on the required processes.

- It was *process oriented*, which has both positive and negative aspects. It focused on designing and facilitating ways to maximize interdisciplinary outputs but was not specifically identified as comprising philosophical and other kinds of reflection. We address this issue later.

Convening and Studying the Synthesis Workshop

We convened a synthesis workshop in September 2009 in order to

- collectively review the progress, findings, and outputs of projects and working groups;
- reflect on program processes and achievements, informing follow-on issues such as maintaining the research community built up by the program;
- agree on content and processes for communicating outcomes effectively to stakeholders; and
- encourage deeper interdisciplinary discussion toward identifying and ultimately delivering additional integrative, cross-program outputs.

We needed to accommodate instrumental (information-gathering), reflective, creative, and practical planning aspects, so the event was designed around the following activities:

- Using learning and mapping techniques to describe and synthesize multiple strands of information from the projects, including their international and institutional contexts
- Giving time for groups to self-organize according to interests
- Recording discussions and giving feedback for further development and cross-fertilization of synthesis product ideas
- Providing periodic overviews, including a final action plan for the remainder of the synthesis phase

We also asked some participants to share their personal analysis of specific elements for the benefit of the core team and to prompt deeper reflection. These were

- an overview of QUEST's success points and achievements,
- perceptions of QUEST in the peer science communities,
- reflections on the success of QUEST's interdisciplinary working, and
- reflections on the synthesis phase and the workshop itself.

The rationale for the event was provided in advance to participants, along with the core team's preliminary list of possible synthesis products. Participation was open to all project scientists. Project leaders were particularly encouraged to attend and invited to contribute short presentations on their work, but despite our active efforts to entrain their input, not all attended. We did not study the nonattendees, so we can only speculate about their views.

When this workshop was proposed, there was broad agreement that some form of facilitation was needed, but it was unclear exactly what kind. The Advisory Board noted QUEST's considerable "social capital" in teams skilled at carrying out good integrative science, but given the program's breadth and the time and resource pressures, they argued for expert neutral facilitation. The event was consciously breaking new ground, linking the backward-looking task of critically assessing and learning from people's experiences with forward-facing proactive planning for the future of QUEST-style research. While both authors are experienced facilitators, Parker was new to the program and did not have prior "ownership" of the research being discussed. She led the planning and facilitation of the event, enabling Cornell and her core team colleagues to engage actively in the deliberations.

Participants were informed that our documentation of the meeting would also be part of our ongoing inquiry into "enabling interdisciplinary research." Participants received an explanatory note outlining the purposes and methods of our study and assuring them of their anonymity in the write-up of data, and all gave written permission for us to document the meeting for research purposes. As participant-observers, our approach could be described as "philosophical field research"—we were guided by a model that includes philosophy as *part* of the analysis needed, which we now describe.

_____Analyzing and Understanding the Synthesis Process

An Interdisciplinary Frame for Discussion of Interdisciplinary Research

Several recent U.K. studies of interdisciplinarity set the foundations for our work. Griffin et al. (2006) reviewed the effectiveness of interdisciplinarity in joint programs of the ESRC and the Arts and Humanities Research Council. Another ESRC-funded project addressed society and interdisciplinarity (Barry, Born, & Weszkalnys, 2008; Weszkalnys, 2006). The leadership of the NERC/ESRC program "Rural Economy and Land Use" viewed it as a radical experiment in capacity building for "deep" interdisciplinarity, and they documented their activities accordingly (Marzano, Carss, & Bell, 2006; Phillipson, Lowe, & Liddon, 2011; Rural Economy and Land Use Programme, 2013). QUEST itself invested in research on leadership and management of interdisciplinarity (Lyall et al., 2011), which also tracked and informed the synthesis phase.

Commenting on an ESRC/Leverhulme Trust program[8] exploring disciplinary contributions to "scientific evidence," Davies (2008) suggested that *sociologically*, disciplinarity should be seen as "a mode of choosing and examining material that is widely recognized" and *philosophically* a "recognition of the incommensurability of disciplines." At a meta-level, this dual framing resonated with our incipient approach. The emergence of shared knowledge cultures supported by the development of philosophically robust foundations is an important element in ensuring that communication practices really are effective (see Figure 7.3).

However, we wanted to go beyond the analytic understanding of interdisciplinarity to a much more reflexive application. In this context, we were keen to participate in discussions around the Toolbox approach, which seeks to "surmount the difficulties created by different research languages and assumptions" (Enhancing Communication in Cross-Disciplinary Research, 2010). But we also wanted to go deeper than the praxis level of communication, drawing effectively from and making sense of the many different approaches to interdisciplinary research. In our

---

[8]See http://128.40.111.250/evidence/projects/integrated/index.asp.

Figure 7.3   Elements in Effective Interdisciplinary Communication

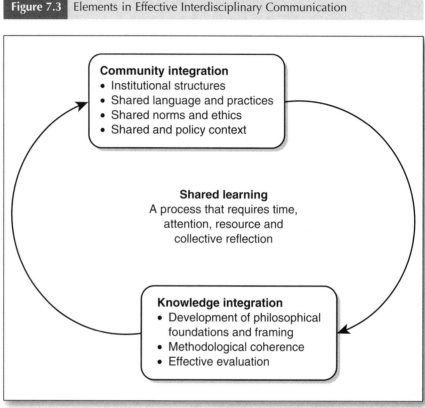

Figure 7.3   Elements in Effective Interdisciplinary Communication

approach (see Figure 7.3), we combine aspects from philosophy, sociology, and learning theory for the analysis and understanding of interdisciplinary research. Here, we explain why:

• **Philosophy and methodology:** Different models of how we can come to know about reality (and perspectives on the extent to which this is possible) present stumbling blocks at all points in interdisciplinary research processes. Epistemological presumptions condition the crucial tasks of setting and unpacking research questions, and fundamentally determine what counts as success in answering these questions. Ensuring the adequacy of the knowledge foundations for interdisciplinary collaboration means that methodological questions should be of prime importance, especially in rapidly developing areas of "deep" interdisciplinary research crossing the biophysical and social sciences and humanities. However, the success of "the scientific method," with its emphasis on "objectivity" independent of the experimenter-scientist, has led to a long-standing norm of downplaying methodology in the physical sciences to the point that often it is not articulated at all, beyond mere description of the process followed. We agree with Brown (2009) that for knowledge integration, particularly when knowledge is to be applied in the real world, this lack must be addressed.

- **The sociology of interdisciplinary working:** Viewing interdisciplinarity as engagement across different knowledge communities highlights issues of language, power, politics, and identity. Different norms on working relationships, hierarchies, and ownership of knowledge outputs often emerge through the research process, and research ethics vary greatly across disciplines, causing unforeseen difficulties in agreeing on collaborative approaches. Because professional research identities are linked to norms and ethics (Strathern, 2005), interpersonal conflict can arise in interdisciplinary teams; such a possibility becomes more likely when there are tendencies for disciplinary triumphalism (e.g., Gibson, 2003; Liverman & Roman-Cuesta, 2008). The perceived or actual power of different research groups can hinder interdisciplinary research, especially when there is a perception that interdisciplinary "synthesis" actually means reduction to the terms of the most powerful discipline. Furthermore, the pressure for interdisciplinary research to deliver on policy objectives can be extreme, making honest meta-reflection (arguably an area where social science has much experience to offer) a tricky enterprise. In this context, we find approaches such as "communities of inquiry" useful in developing a group ethos of collaboration and respect, recognizing that different disciplines bring different things to the table.

- **Learning theory:** Learning is acknowledged to be a frequently unsettling and challenging process (Kerdeman, 2003), and experienced researchers can find it especially hard to be placed in a position of relative ignorance. Research on the personality requirements of interdisciplinary research stresses confident dispositions and openness to new challenges (Griffin et al., 2006). Not all participants in interdisciplinary research teams have these characteristics (nor is it desirable that they should), so some extra degree of understanding and management of teams as mutual learning groups is usually needed. Learning across conceptual and discursive boundaries has been theorized to some extent in Education for Sustainability, and different approaches to group learning have been proposed (Barth, Godemann, Rieckmann, & Stoltenberg, 2007; Maternal and Child Health, 2009; Parker, 2010). These kinds of activities require participant protocols of respect and mutual learning similar to those proposed in the "communities of inquiry" literatures.

Insights From the Synthesis Workshop

This section outlines findings from our study of the synthesis workshop, drawing on the scientists' discussions and our observations of the event. The latter are necessarily colored by our participation, understandings, and preoccupations, but the discussion shows how our combined approach can help diagnose issues that lead to obstacles to interdisciplinary progress.

Philosophy: W(h)ither Methodology

QUEST's primary focus was to achieve agreement on the details of a shared method: quantitative modeling. Setting clear research goals and situating them in the wider landscape of scientific progress is a key leadership task. Comments from scientists confirmed that the core team focus on this common goal had a unifying effect:

> The big questions . . . put people off initially—but people bought into it because QUEST has had a big view and because it was going somewhere.

It is of course possible to engage in collaborative mapping of research goals and outcomes across transdisciplinary terrain at the outset of a project. However, goal setting often seems to take place by default or to be an unacknowledged aspect of effective research leadership. Equally, the methodology for such research is rarely spelled out in ways that allow others to trace it and engage with it critically and constructively.

The difficulty of agreeing on methodology (or failing to) becomes evident occasionally. An Earth system research priority gives an example. QUEST contributed to a major international effort (Analysis, Integration and Modelling of the Earth System, 2010) for coupling economic models (based on statistical patterns in past economic data) to climate models (based on the physical, immutable laws of radiative balance, fluid dynamics, and so on). The former are explanatory; the latter are (scientifically speaking) predictive. It is far from clear what the coupled product is, but the growing deployment of such integrated global models to inform policy about the state of the world in 2100 and beyond suggests that Earth system scientists assume they fall on the positivist predictive side (or *prophetic*, to use Popper's term). This motivates Earth system science's push for "better engagement with the social sciences," but as Demeritt (2001) notes, "The objective of comprehensive Earth-system modeling leaves the physical reductionism of the [climate models] unchallenged" (p. 316). At the synthesis workshop, this looming challenge was frequently acknowledged but left entirely unexplored:

> It's not that difficult to be interdisciplinary between physics and chemistry . . . but more difficult with social science.

A related topic of concern discussed at the workshop was the growing challenge of "benchmarking" complex models (Zaehle, Prentice, & Cornell, 2011)—models such as QUEST's presumed cause-and-effect behaviors. They draw on empirical observational data to define processes and parameters ("control variables") within the model and also to "validate" the models (ensuring that they accurately represent the system being modeled). However, despite the fundamental importance of explicit methodological communication in elucidating the meanings of purported "realistic outputs" of complex models, all these discussions lapsed back to questions of method rather than methodology:

> We need to think about ways that different models weight certain background or consistent elements.

Can it [a semi-automated data assimilation system] distinguish between criteria of weighting—in other words, is it a probability weighting?

Sociology, Language, and Identities

Effective transdisciplinary synthesis depends in part on the expectations and collaborative working habits of participating scientists. These factors in turn are affected by perceptions of their host institutions' priorities and modes of operating, including their reputation for interdisciplinary and/or disciplinary excellence. Participants indicated that the QUEST experience had changed their institutional "identities."

QUEST has changed the way they work—made us more interinstitutional.

Interdisciplinarity is an issue—one of the things that people do is go back to their individual priorities, my little bit of data.

The active engagement of researchers in QUEST's synthesis phase nevertheless depended on a clear hint from the program's senior scientists, prominently signaled through their participation in the workshop, that they themselves were committed to delivering shared outputs and that those outputs were valuable. In a sense, the synthesis event provided an extended kind of collective peer review, a particularly tricky issue for interdisciplinary research (Holbrook, 2010; Parker, 2012). It highlighted the extent to which cross-program interdisciplinary communication related to the conceptualization and achievement of planned program goals and outcomes. QUEST's senior scientists needed to show sensitivity to participants' other institutional commitments and recognize that synthesis efforts needed to build their profile in their own host institutions. Such active leadership plays a key part in setting the frame for communication and is required for interdisciplinary programs to achieve their potential (Cronin, 2008; Parker, 2011).

During the course of QUEST, recognizing "cultural differences" among different groups, we had already developed working policies on operational and functional matters, such as authorship, data sharing, and policy engagement. These guidelines and protocols were shared well before the synthesis event and proved useful in developing common norms and enabling the relatively uncontentious participation of a broad range of project scientists.

Interdisciplinary communication takes place within social and political contexts, where global change science is particularly politicized, with strong drivers for "policy relevance" (e.g., Demeritt, 2001; McCright & Dunlap, 2010; Sarewitz & Pielke, 2007). The synthesis phase raised anew the acknowledged difficulties with the concept of "policy-relevant science." The climate-science mantra, originating from the Intergovernmental Panel for Climate Change, is that research should be "policy-relevant but not policy prescriptive." However, this distinction is not always easy to maintain. Participants noted that many statements required from scientists by policymakers are in the form,

> If you want to achieve X (e.g., no more than 2 degrees of global warming), do Y.

Such analyses are already framed in terms of policy options. Scientists are also often asked to spell out the consequences of action and inaction in terms that can be understood by policymakers and, sometimes, by the wider public. In these cases, a considerable degree of interpretation of science has to take place. Getting these boundary cases right can be a fraught business, especially when discussing controversial claims that are politically resisted by certain interests. The expectations and situation of funding bodies— themselves not immune to political and media scrutiny—also need to be taken into account. These kinds of cases require a degree of leadership and debate that is informed by the current consensus on acceptable levels of interpretation and the media politics of representation of scientific results.

Even for groups of scientists experienced in collective working, language matters. QUEST was not unusual in experiencing the phenomenon of apparently shared terms dissolving into very different meanings on inspection, confounding interdisciplinary conversations.

> Synthesis requires us to talk the same language—we need more time to do it.

> We need to take extra care when we are talking about developing slippery concepts (like "uncertainty").

"Slippery" concepts causing pause for debate at the workshop included *uncertainty* (which often conflates physical indeterminacy, numerical error analysis, and agency or choice), as well as the terms *tipping points, thresholds,* and *feedbacks* (which have very specific definitions in systems science and more flexible meanings in lay use). Participants recognized the need to reach a common understanding of concepts, but we noted the tendency for academics to want to avoid "those pointless semantic discussions" (especially about terminology from the social sciences), which means there is a recurrent risk of talking at cross purposes.

A further problematic interdisciplinary construct is that of *ecosystem services* (which in the policy context now embeds economic valuation; see Cornell, 2010b) and even *impacts*. Climate impact scientists talk about both biophysical and social impacts. This enables them to treat climatic causalities "objectively" and consistently in their modeling. However, it becomes problematic in aggregating the impacts (e.g., in the economic terms that policymakers are taken to require) and engaging with other (social) drivers of change. In contrast, socioeconomists often apply the "driver-pressure-state-impact-response" framework (e.g., Organisation for

Economic Co-operation and Development, 1993; Turner, Georgiou, Clark, Brouwer, & Burke, 2004), which makes a pragmatically anthropocentric distinction between the change in state of the environment and the impact as experienced by society. This issue surfaced in the following comment about different frames of reference:

> For instance, different economic scenarios talk about millions at risk, or money.

Learning in and From the QUEST Experience

"Learning from experience" is recognized good practice at the end of large programs. Normally, the project leadership documents outputs and achievements, often with a formal external review. QUEST's synthesis workshop was explicitly part of the learning process, but it sought views from a wide range of participants and provided the (still unusual) opportunity for collective reflection on processes and issues. Several scientists at the workshop saw the QUEST experience as one of mutual learning and valued this opportunity:[9]

> It provided a chance to widen my field.

However, the extent to which fields widened beyond the program's own academic context was limited, despite its strong remit for external policy engagement. An example of this limited engagement was observed at the meeting, when QUEST's task was described in terms of a widely applied popular policy analysis of the climate challenge, framing different mitigation options as incremental "wedges" (Pacala & Socolow, 2004). Some of those present did not know this concept, with one participant observing,

> If you're a scientist you don't read overviews.

Given that the wedges analysis was published in *Science*, one of the world's highest impact journals in the field of Earth system science, it appears possible that "if you're a scientist, you don't read anything but your own science."

In several similar instances, knowledge and skills gaps emerged in the discussion. Gassett (1932) noted the phenomenon of the "learned ignoramus," "formally ignorant of all that does not enter into his specialty"

---

[9]For QUEST's policy-oriented finale event (see http://quest.bris.ac.uk/meetings/finale.html), nearly 50 of the researchers involved in the program submitted short reflections on their experience, many of which expressed positive enthusiasm for the opportunity to learn about interdisciplinary working.

(p. 79). When the task is to develop shared interdisciplinary knowledge, especially knowledge intended for ultimate application to real-world action, this implies that a common framing of the task needs to be much more explicit.

The 2-day workshop was not long enough for developing skills and capabilities for in-depth engagement with the meta-questions of interdisciplinary working among participants who had mostly operated—and are comfortable operating—only on the pragmatic level of the research process, even at that advanced stage in the program. From our own perspective, the limitations of the participant-observer method were profoundly felt when transported into the unfamiliar terrain of the biophysical sciences. Participants noted that facilitated meetings are unusual in climate research, which holds an ideal of collegiality (blended with a complex hierarchy of discipline-linked intellectual competition). The idea of reflexive cocreation of the meta-understanding of interdisciplinarity was alien to participants, although it could provide key underpinning for the development of good synthesis outcomes, in the sense of advanced transdisciplinary knowledge of the world and mutually valuable research products.

Conclusion

In QUEST, "research synthesis" was viewed both as a point reached in the interdisciplinary research process and a further point that could be reached by deliberately focusing on gaining more shared "synthesis products" toward the end of the component projects. It was also intrinsically linked to maintaining the recently formed working communities beyond the program life span. A synthesis phase is essential to all major interdisciplinary projects. We argue that deeper thinking about ways to support this phase would yield dividends in terms of research processes, outputs, and communication to stakeholders.

Cornell (2010a), Stirling (2009), and others have called for a three-way fix for addressing the philosophical, cultural, and operational challenges of sustainability research, all borne out by the insights from QUEST's synthesis phase. Interdisciplinary working is necessarily provisional—disciplines can only provide a partial perspective on a wholly complex real world. This means that the transactions among the different perspectives need ontological and epistemological attention. "Joining the pieces" thus also implies broadened participation in knowledge creation and a focus on relational and "cultural" aspects of communication. And given that all processes of inquiry differ from each other in the way that problems are defined and framed by these participants (and other ways, too), the process must embed habits, awareness, and skills that we clump into the multipurpose term *reflexivity* (Macnaghten, Kearnes, & Wynne, 2005; Romm, 1998; Scoones et al., 2007).

Take-Home Messages

Keeping the general context just specified in mind, the following are the key messages from our synthesis study:

- There is still a pressing need to assemble an interdisciplinary understanding of how to develop and lead interdisciplinary research programs, especially those with an explicit mission to engage with policy or wider society.
- Developing an overall team vision of research goals in terms of the wider landscape of current knowledge and key problem areas is a vital leadership function in interdisciplinary research.
- The management, evaluation, and overarching synthesis of interdisciplinary research need to be built in at the outset in all project proposals. Too often, as in our case, these are an underresourced afterthought.
- It is useful to identify at the outset that the communications focus will develop and change throughout the program—and that by the time synthesis is attempted, the more highly charged questions of "translation" of scientific results for communication with stakeholders will be an issue requiring adequate time, particular skills, and collective attention.

Were these elements set out in funding requirements, scientists who are not currently motivated to engage might take synthesis more seriously.

- If the practice of analytical reporting on meta-aspects of interdisciplinarity is to become more widespread, much of the work is likely to rely on the participant-observer model, despite its limitations.
- We strongly recommend that good practice include scientists in this work from the outset, as cocreators of this meta-knowledge about the processes and issues of interdisciplinary research.
- The focus on practical societal concerns means that theoretical and meta-analytic engagement has often been bypassed in sustainability research. Identifying key differences in perspective at the outset through deliberative diagnostic process could help fast-track development of common understanding of the task in hand.
- Within a research domain, setting out clearly the operational and functional terms for engagement and consolidation is tremendously powerful. This (arguably pragmatic) approach can define the commonalities of loosely orbiting communities and entrain them into a shared orbit. It is no guarantee of synergy, but it is a precondition.

Acknowledgments

We thank all QUEST scientists, especially those who engaged actively in the synthesis phase, and even more especially those who took an interest in our research into interdisciplinarity. We also acknowledge the U.K. Natural

Environment Research Council, which funded QUEST and continues to support innovating interdisciplinary environmental research. We also thank the University of Bristol Institute for Advanced Studies for providing important forums for our wider discussions of interdisciplinarity and sustainability from 2005 to 2010.

References

Aboelela, S. W., Larson, E., Bakken, S., Carrasquillo, O., Formicola, A., Glied, S. A., et al. (2007). Defining interdisciplinary research: Conclusions from a critical review of the literature. *Health Services Research*, 42, 329–346.

Analysis, Integration and Modelling of the Earth System. (2010). *Science plan and implementation strategy* (IGBP Report No. 58). Stockholm: International Geosphere-Biosphere Program Secretariat.

Bammer, G. (2005). Integration and implementation sciences: Building a new specialization. *Ecology and Society, 10*(2), 6.

Barry, A., Born, G., & Weszkalnys, G. (2008). Logics of interdisciplinarity. *Economy and Society*, 37(1), 20–49.

Barth, M., Godemann, J., Rieckmann, M., & Stoltenberg, U. (2007). Developing key competencies for sustainable development in higher education. *International Journal of Sustainability in Higher Education, 8*(4), 416–430.

Brown, S. F. (2009). *Naivety in systems engineering research: Are we putting the methodological cart before the philosophical horse?* Presented at the Seventh Annual Conference on Systems Engineering Research, Loughborough, UK.

Bruce, A., Lyall, C., Tait, J., & Williams, R. (2004). Interdisciplinary integration in Europe. *Futures, 36*(4), 457–470.

Carpenter, S. R., Armbrust, E. V., Arzberger, P. W., Chapin, F. S., III, Elser, J. J., Hackett, E. J., et al. (2009). Accelerate synthesis in ecology and environmental sciences. *BioScience, 59*(8), 699–701.

Clark, W. C., & Dickson, N. M. (2003). Sustainability science: The emerging research program. *PNAS, 100*(14), 8059–8061.

Committee on Science, Engineering, and Public Policy. (2004). *Facilitating interdisciplinary research*. Washington, DC: National Academies Press. Retrieved from http://books.nap.edu/catalog/11153.html

Cornell, S. (2010a). Climate change: Brokering interdisciplinarity across the physical and social sciences. In R. Bhaskar, C. Frank, K. G. Høyer, P. Næss, & J. Parker (Eds.), *Interdisciplinarity and climate change: Transforming knowledge and practice for our global future* (pp. 116–134). London: Routledge.

Cornell, S. (2010b). Valuing ecosystem benefits in a dynamic world. *Climate Research, 45*, 261–262.

Cornell, S. E., Downy, C. J., House, J. I., & Prentice, I. C. (2011). *QUEST final programme report*. Swindon, UK: Natural Environmental Research Council.

Cornell, S., & Prentice, C. (2010, November 26). *Making working groups that work* (QUEST Report to Programme Board). Swindon, UK: Natural Environmental Research Council.

Cornell, S. E., Prentice, I. C., House, J. I., & Downy, C. J. (Eds.). (2012). *Understanding the Earth system: Global change science for action*. Cambridge, UK: Cambridge University Press.

Cronin, K. (2008, September). *Transdisciplinary research (TDR) and sustainability.* Report prepared for the Ministry of Research, Science and Technology, New Zealand. Retrieved October 12, 2012, from http://learningforsustainability.net/pubs/Transdisciplinary_Research_and_Sustainability.pdf

Davies, J. (2008, April). *Interdisciplinarity and teaching: After the Leverhulme Evidence Project.* Contribution to the Teaching and Learning Conference, University College London.

Demeritt, D. (2001). The construction of global warming and the politics of science. *Annals of the Association of American Geographers, 91*(2), 307–337.

Earth System Science Partnership. (2001). *The Amsterdam Declaration on global change.* Retrieved June 1, 2012, from www.essp.org/index.php?id=41

Economic and Social Research Council. (2007). *ESRC delivery plan 2007–2008.* Retrieved June 1, 2012, from www.esrc.ac.uk/_images/ESRC_Delivery_Plan_07-08_tcm8-13458.pdf

Ecosystem Services for Poverty Alleviation. (2012, January 13). *Ecosystem Services for Poverty Alleviation (ESPA): Announcement of opportunity.* Retrieved from http://www.rcuk.ac.uk/international/Offices/India/Funding/prev/Pages/PovertyAlleviationESPA.aspx

Enhancing Communication in Cross-Disciplinary Research: 2010 conference. (2010). *Toolbox.* Retrieved June 6, 2012, from www.cals.uidaho.edu/toolbox/ECCDR_Conference.html

Gassett, J. O. (1932). *The revolt of the masses.* New York: New American Library.

Gibson, J. M. (2003, February). Arrogance—a dangerous weapon of the physics trade? *Physics Today,* 54–55.

Glied, S., Bakken, S., Formicola, A., Gebbie, K., & Larson, E. L. (2007). Institutional challenges of interdisciplinary research centers. *Journal of Research Administration, 38*(2), 28–36.

Griffin, G., Medhurst, P., & Green, T. (2006, May). *Interdisciplinarity in Interdisciplinary Research Programmes in the UK.* University of Hull. Retrieved from http://www.york.ac.uk/res/researchintegration/Interdisciplinarity_UK.pdf

Hackett, E. J., Amsterdamska, O., Lynch, M. E., & Wajcman, J. (Eds.). (2008). *The handbook of science and technology studies* (3rd ed.). Cambridge: MIT Press.

Hampton, S. E., & Parker, J. N. (2011). Collaboration and productivity in scientific synthesis. *Bioscience, 61*(11), 900–910.

Heckhausen, H. (1972). Discipline and interdisciplinarity. In *Interdisciplinarity: Problems of teaching and research in universities* (pp. 83–89). Paris: Organisation for Economic Co-operation and Development.

Holbrook, J. B. (2010). Peer review. In R. Frodeman, J. T. Klein, & C. Mitcham, (Eds.), *The Oxford handbook of interdisciplinarity* (pp. 321–332). New York: Oxford University Press.

Holm, P., Guilhot, N., Dumitrescu, D., Griffin, G., Jarrick, A., Rév, I., et al. (2009). *METRIS report: Emerging trends in research in social sciences and humanities.* Luxembourg: European Commission.

Hulme, M. (2008). Geographical work at the boundaries of climate change. *Transactions of the Institute of British Geographers, 33*(1), 5–11.

Inter Academies Panel. (2010, January). *Biodiversity and ecosystem services.* Conference communique, Royal Society, London.

International Council for Science. (2012). *Future Earth.* Retrieved June 1, 2012, from www.icsu.org/future-earth

Jäger, J., Pálsson, G., Goodsite, M., Pahl-Wostl, C., O'Brien, K., Hordijk, L., et al. (2011, December). *Responses to environmental and societal challenges for our unstable earth (RESCUE)*. Strasbourg, France: European Science Foundation, European Cooperation in Science and Technology. Retrieved from http://www .esf.org/uploads/media/rescue.pdf

Keen, M., Brown, V. A., & Dyball, R. (Eds.). (2006). *Social learning in environmental management: Towards a sustainable future*. London: Earthscan.

Kerdeman, D. (2003). Pulled up short: Challenging self-understanding as a focus of teaching and learning. *Journal of Philosophy of Education, 37*, 2.

Lamont, M., Mallard, G., & Guetzkow, J. (2006). Beyond blind faith: Overcoming the obstacles to interdisciplinary evaluation. *Research Evaluation, 15*(1), 43–55.

Lawton J. (2001). Earth system science. *Science, 292*(5524), 1965.

Liverman, D. M., & Roman-Cuesta, R. M. (2008). Human interactions with the Earth system: People and pixels revisited. *Earth Surface Processes and Landforms, 33*, 1458–1471.

Living With Environmental Change. (2011, September 6). *Living With Environmental Change: A major interdisciplinary partnership to tackle living with environmental change, Strategy 2008–2013*. Retrieved from http://www.lwec.org.uk/sites/ default/files/LWEC%20Strategy%202008~2013.pdf

Lyall, C., Bruce, A., Marsden, W., & Meagher, L. (2011). *Key success factors in the quest for interdisciplinary knowledge*. Edinburgh, UK: ESRC Innogen Centre.

Macnaghten, P., Kearnes, M. B., & Wynne, B. (2005). Nanotechnology, governance and public deliberation: What role for the social sciences? *Science Communication, 27*, 268–291.

Marzano, M., Carss, D. N., & Bell, B. (2006). Working to make interdisciplinarity work: Investing in communication and interpersonal relationships. *Journal of Agricultural Economics, 57*(2), 185–198.

Maternal and Child Health. (2009, June). *Maternal and Child Health leadership competencies* (version 3.0). Retrieved from http://devleadership.mchtraining. net/mchlc_docs/mch_leadership_comp_3-0.pdf

Mayer, T., & Marks, J. (Eds.). (2003, May). *Global problems, global science: Europe's contribution to global change research* (ESF Forward Look Report 1). Strasbourg, France: European Science Foundation. Retrieved June 1, 2012, from www.esf.org/publications/forward-looks.html

McCright, A. M., & Dunlap, R. E. (2010). Anti-reflexivity: The American conservative movement's success in undermining climate science and policy. *Theory, Culture and Society, 27*, 100–133.

Nissani, M. (1997). Ten cheers for interdisciplinarity: The case for interdisciplinary knowledge and research. *Social Sciences Journal, 34*, 201–216.

Organisation for Economic Co-operation and Development. (1993). *OECD core set of indicators for environmental performance reviews* (OECD Environment Monograph 83). Paris: Author.

Pacala, S., & Socolow, R. (2004). Stabilization wedges: Solving the climate problem for the next 50 years with current technologies. *Science, 305*, 968–972.

Parker, J. (2010). Competencies for interdisciplinarity in higher education. *International Journal of Sustainability in Higher Education, 11*(4), 325–338. Retrieved from www.emeraldinsight.com/10.1108/14676371011077559

Parker, J. (2011). *Strategic leadership for interdisciplinarity.* Paper presented at the UNESCO Higher Education for Sustainable Development Conference, Leuphana University, Lüneberg, Germany.

Parker, J. (2012). *Degrees of interdisciplinarity and the difference they make* (CONVERGE Working Paper).

Phillipson, J., Lowe, P., & Liddon, A. (2011, November). *Adventures in science: Interdisciplinarity and knowledge exchange in the RELU programme* (RELU Briefing No. 16). Newcastle upon Tyne: Rural Economy and Land Use Programme. Retrieved from www.relu.ac.uk/news/briefings.htm

Pickett, S. T. A. (1999). The culture of synthesis: Habits of mind in novel ecological integration. *Oikos, 87,* 479–487.

Rhoten, D., & Parker, A. (2004, December). Risks and rewards of an interdisciplinary research path. *Science, 306,* 2046.

Romm, N. R. A. (1998). Interdisciplinarity practice as reflexivity. *Systemic Practice and Action Research, 11,* 63–77.

Rural Economy and Land Use Programme. (2013). Interdisciplinarity. Retrieved from http://www.relu.ac.uk/research/Interdisciplinarity/Interdisciplinarity.html

Sarewitz, D., & Pielke, R. A., Jr. (2007). The neglected heart of science policy: Reconciling supply of and demand for science. *Environmental Science and Policy, 10*(1), 5–16.

Schneider, S. H. (1992). The role of the university in interdisciplinary global change research: Structural constraints and the potential for change. An editorial. *Climatic Change, 20*(1), vii–x.

Scoones, I., Leach, M., Smith, A., Stagl, S., Stirling, A., & Thompson, J. (2007). *Dynamic systems and the challenge of sustainability* (STEPS Working Paper 1). Brighton: STEPS Centre.

Stirling, A. (2009). Participation, precaution and reflexive governance for sustainable development. In W. N. Adger & A. Jordan (Eds.), *Governing sustainability* (pp. 193–225). Cambridge, UK: Cambridge University Press.

Strathern, M. (2005). *Anthropology and interdisciplinarity.* London: Sage.

Strathern, M. (2006). A community of critics? Thoughts on new knowledge. *Journal of the Royal Anthropological Institute, 12,* 191–209.

Tuinstra, W., Jäger, J., & Weaver, P. M. (2008). Learning and evaluation in integrated sustainability assessment. *International Journal of Innovation and Sustainable Development, 3*(1–2), 128–152.

Turner, K., Georgiou, S., Clark, R., Brouwer, R., & Burke, J. (2004). *Economic valuation of water resources in agriculture* (FAO Water Reports 27). Rome: Food and Agriculture Organization of the United Nations. Retrieved October 2, 2012, from www.fao.org/docrep/007/y5582e/y5582e00.htm

U.N. World Commission on Environment and Development. (1987). *Our common future* [The Brundtland report]. Oxford, UK: Oxford University Press. Retrieved from http://www.un-documents.net/wced-ocf.htm

Weszkalnys, G. (2006, December). *Mapping interdisciplinarity: Report of the survey element of the project 'Interdisciplinarity and Society: A Critical Comparative Study' (ESRC Science in Society, 2004–06).* Retrieved from http://www.geog.ox.ac.uk/research/technologies/projects/mapping-interdisciplinarity.pdf

Zaehle, S., Prentice, I. C., & Cornell, S. E. (2011). The evaluation of Earth system models. *Procedia Environmental Sciences, 4,* 210–215.

8

Enhancing Interdisciplinary Communication

Collaborative Engaged Research on Food Systems for Health and Well-Being

◆ Ardyth H. Gillespie and Guan-Jen Sung

Collaborative engaged research (CER) depends on and enhances communication with decision makers across disciplines. CER for sustainability of food systems to enhance health and well-being is conducted by interdisciplinary team members, including family and community food systems stakeholders, practitioners, and academic researchers. The CER members are leaders in food decision making. Complex and multifaceted, CER facilitates dynamic communication patterns and develops interactions among the members, with external stakeholders, and within families and communities for collective decision making. This chapter discusses CER as applied in food systems and health research and practice, and describes two cases—one focused on family food decision making, and the other on community food decision making. It concludes with an analysis of challenges, guidelines for applying CER methodology, and opportunities for further development.

_____ **Introduction**

It is well established that communication across academic disciplines is complex and time-consuming. In the context of the emerging field of food systems for health, achieving productive communication is further complicated by the need to incorporate multiple community stakeholders in the process. For the theory and practice of community-based food systems to grow, new strategies must evolve that address these inherent communication challenges and opportunities. Development of the CER approach has begun to tackle this challenge. CER is an asset-based approach (i.e., it identifies and builds on strengths and resources rather than focusing on problem solving) that engages food systems stakeholders, local practitioners, and researchers in a collective decision-making process. It requires a high level of communication competence to support that process. CER addresses the roles of both information flow and food decision making in mediating the impact of community food systems on health and well-being. After introducing food decision-making research and cross-perspective communication for CER, we describe the CER methodology and two CER case studies. We discuss findings, from these and other CER cases, and opportunities for continued development of CER methodology. Finally, we conclude with guidelines for fostering communication competence and summarize CER as an alternative approach to understanding and facilitating systems and behavioral change to improve public health and family and community well-being.

Food Systems for Health and Well-Being

Food is essential for survival; it is not only the key source of our nutrition but also a source of pleasure and recreation. It is often a part of building and maintaining relationships—creating a context for socialization and interpersonal communication. Food consumption, including acquisition, preparation, eating, and disposal, can be a major topic in daily communication, as can debate at all scales up to national and international food or natural resources policy. Food systems are inherently complex, embedded in social and biophysical ecosystems with related cause-and-effect relationships (Gillespie & Gillespie, 2007). Food production, for example, can both contribute to and be impacted by climate change. Thus, food systems are best understood from multidisciplinary and multisectoral[1] perspectives.

Considered the primary food decision-making unit, a family is defined as any configuration of people who regularly eat together or eat from the same household food resources and who mutually influence decisions about their

_____

[1]Sectors include community private, nonprofit, citizen groups or individuals who view issues and opportunities through a particular set of presuppositions.

food. Families typically collaborate to make decisions about purchasing and preparing food and may also discuss issues related to nutrition and diet. Families interact at the community level with institutions that offer food, health care, education, and transportation. Community food systems, made up of farmers, consumer markets, retailers, distributors, processors, and other institutions and businesses, are collaborations with communication patterns that have evolved over centuries in North America. Community food decision makers, such as school nutritionists, planners, emergency food assistance program staff, and even supermarket managers, determine what foods are "practically available" to families (Gillespie & Gillespie, 2007). Thus, beyond the family and within the community context, the discourse around food becomes even more complex.

Community food systems, in turn, are shaped by national and global food systems, which are themselves shaped in large measure by national government and trade policy. Researchers from a broad range of disciplines and perspectives are contributing to understanding (1) the societal and natural impacts on food systems and (2) the potential for food systems research to contribute to community development, sustainability, biodiversity, land use, climate change, and more. More and more, these two perspectives must come together to create systems change and, thus, decision-making processes that engage or at least influence multiple stakeholders in communities.

Communication for collective decision making is complex, in part because of the complexity of food systems, eating behaviors, and variations in stakeholders' perspectives or worldviews. CER learning teams reflect this complexity. In addition to researchers, they include *change agents* and *connectors* who can represent a wide range of perspectives. Change agents may be educators but also include a broad spectrum of individuals and organizations working to change individual behavior as well as social and biophysical systems (family, community, and beyond). Connectors are people who bring together team members with common interests and facilitate communication to integrate multiple perspectives. Contrary to popular practice, participants in a learning team are not expected to "represent" their organization or "kind" but, rather, to bring their own perspectives—shared in part with their organization or kind—into genuine dialogue.

Cross-Perspective Communication and CER

"Cross-perspectives refers to the notion that individual 'frames of reference,' and perspective[s], are inevitable and lead to different 'stories' and different 'social realities' about what would on the surface appear to be the same thing" (G. Gillespie, personal communication, July 12, 2012). Starting from this position, we focus on cross-perspective communication, which includes communication across disciplines, sectors, and dimensions of food systems.

The CER approach integrates principles and practices of appreciative inquiry (AI; Watkins, Mohr, & Kelly, 2011) and open space technology

(OST; Owen, 1997) to create a context for transparent communication, transformative learning (Taylor, 2000), and establishing communication competence (Thompson, 2009). A pattern of egalitarian communication, the dyadic dialogue method (DDM),[2] which involves two individuals taking turns as leader and respondent, is introduced. Together with AI, DDM can build and strengthen trusting relationships among CER members and further advance the CER approach.

CER methodology not only opens doors inviting those from various disciplines to (re)consider their expectations on "the same thing" but also facilitates achieving "the same thing" effectively. The CER methodology guides the generation of change initiatives and the formation of CER learning teams as change initiatives are generated. In the Food Decision-Making (FDM) Program, initiatives for change include those for engaging in community improvement; for being supported by sustainable, just, and equitable community food systems; for developing healthy attitudes toward food and eating; for making thoughtful food decisions; and for helping each individual align his or her behaviors with personal understandings, goals, and current scientific knowledge.[3]

The following sections offer a window into the evolution of CER communication for food systems research and practice by the FDM Program. The two cases discussed give a sense of both how the CER methodology has been applied and how it is evolving.

Collaborative Engaged Research

Adding practitioners and community stakeholders to multidisciplinary research teams multiplies the challenges but also the opportunities of such research. In particular, it creates opportunities for changing communication processes that help build community capacity. The CER approach connects community food decision makers with external resources to create a vision and accompanying strategies that build on community assets. CER helps cultivate thoughtful food decision making and create a culture of cooperation and communication competence. The methodology is based on findings from CER projects led by FDM teams, communication with informants, and innovative communication and education approaches.

---

[2]DDM was introduced in "Dialogue Method for Collaborative Communication: Adapting Qualitative Analysis Techniques for Enhancing Understanding," by Guan-Jen Sung, Holly D. Archer, and Ardyth MH Gillespie, at the conference "Enhancing Communication in Cross-Disciplinary Research," held at The Coeur d'Alene Resort in Coeur d'Alene, Idaho, September 30 through October 2, 2010.

[3]CER furthers the vision of the FDM Program for the health and well-being of all, where children and their families benefit from these initiatives for change (see http://familyfood.human.cornell.edu).

The Cross-Disciplinary Communication Perspective in Nutrition

The initial application of communication theory to community nutrition and nutrition education[4] was built on the work of communication scholars at Iowa State University, notably Paul Yarbrough (1981) and associates. Developers of the nutrition communication model (Gillespie & Yarbrough, 1984) recognized that, although mass media were more cost-effective information channels, interpersonal or relational communication was superior for changing behavior in food and nutrition education. Although the communication approach for CER has shifted from persuasive communication (Gillespie & Yarbrough, 1984) to communicative exchange, where each participant is a communicator as well as a receiver, the same theoretical underpinnings remain, including the following:

1. *Individual differences:* Different people respond differently to the same message, and a person responds differently to different messages (Hovland & Janis, 1959; Katz & Lazarsfeld, 1964; Lazarsfeld, 1949). Such predispositions are based on relationships with others, understanding, knowledge, and attitudes about what is considered food, acquiring food, its preparation, the way it is served and consumed, and eating contexts.

2. *Social status–based roles:* These influence responses by affecting predispositions and situations. For example, the role "mother" suggests certain food-preparation responsibilities.

3. *Social relations:* The social relations perspective (Katz & Lazarsfeld, 1964; Rogers, 1983) sees people as socially organized and membership in groups as influencing their responses to mass communications and adoption and diffusion of innovative approaches.

4. *Metacommunication:* Watzlawick, Bavelas, and Jackson (1967) introduced the notion of metacommunication, "communication *about* communication." They proposed that "communication dysfunction is more likely to occur because of the disagreement over the rules than over the manifest content" (p. 10). For example, when a program attempts to include fathers in considering food and eating practices, it may break down if the father does not believe that this is part of his parental role. For a description of these theories and the nutrition communication model, see Gillespie and Yarbrough (1984). Watzlawick and colleagues' work has been developed by other scholars and informs the current work in relational communication

---

[4]Nutrition education emerged as a research area as well as a mode of practice and became a major strategy in community nutrition (see Gillespie, 2012).

(Keyton, 1999). The CER process presented in the following pages embraces relational communication in groups.[5]

Influenced by these communication perspectives, CER presupposes that (1) humans are inherently good and seek community; (2) as members of society, people jointly construct a shared understanding of "reality" (social constructionism); (3) people actively interact with their environment in making decisions based on their understandings of reality (agency and free will); and (4) in addition to increasing the scientific understanding of change, research can and should facilitate social change.

Cross-Perspective Communication for CER: Dynamics and Challenges

Engagement in CER means developing communication competence for colearning, collective decision making, and cocreating a sustainable world in which people are nourished and nurtured. While the CER approach shares some processes and perspectives with intervention science, community-based participatory research, participatory action research, and other participatory methods (Greenwood & Levin, 1998; Israel et al., 2003), it is characterized by a family and community development perspective that builds on assets and aspirations and identifies opportunities, in contrast to approaches that address problems to be solved.

Part of identifying opportunities and collaborators is assessing whether the CER approach or an alternative approach best fits the particular situation. Each initiative is unique, and thus each team should seek an appropriate balance in priorities and processes that engage team members' and participating organizations' strengths and assets to create a context in which innovation thrives. The CER approach requires a considerable commitment of time and energy for engagement from all participants. The guidelines for engagement are that

1. the primary goal is to build family and community capacity for thoughtful food decision making, resulting in sustained change;

2. research, education, and action are integrated, and the CER team shares responsibility for integration, decision making, and communicative exchange across perspectives;

---

[5]"Relational communication in groups refers to the verbal and nonverbal messages that create the social fabric of a group by promoting relationships between and among group members. It is the affect or expressive dimension of group communication, as opposed to the instrumental, or task-oriented dimension. . . . Thus, relational communication in groups encompasses both the structures and processes of a group social reality—that is, the connections, relations, and communication *among* members of the group" (Scheerhorn & Geist, as cited in Keyton, 1999, p. 192).

3. emerging research findings influence practice and change initiatives; and

4. the CER approach is self-renewing through ongoing analysis, reflection, and evaluation.

By focusing on opportunities when considering individual and collective strengths and family and community assets and aspirations, the group moves in a positive direction. The CER methodology as summarized next serves as a guide for cross-perspective teams as they consider a CER approach.

The CER Methodology

Figure 8.1 depicts the CER methodology as a continuous loop. The components of the process are identifying opportunities and collaborators, organizing CER learning teams, creating communicative exchange strategies, inquiring and analyzing, and reflecting and innovating. As the process continues cycling, findings from a particular initiative are not the end but rather the beginning of another cycle of inquiry and innovation. Reflection, on an individual and collective basis, about changing meanings and mind-sets and thinking creatively about *what could be* moves the process toward realizing individual and

Figure 8.1   CER Process

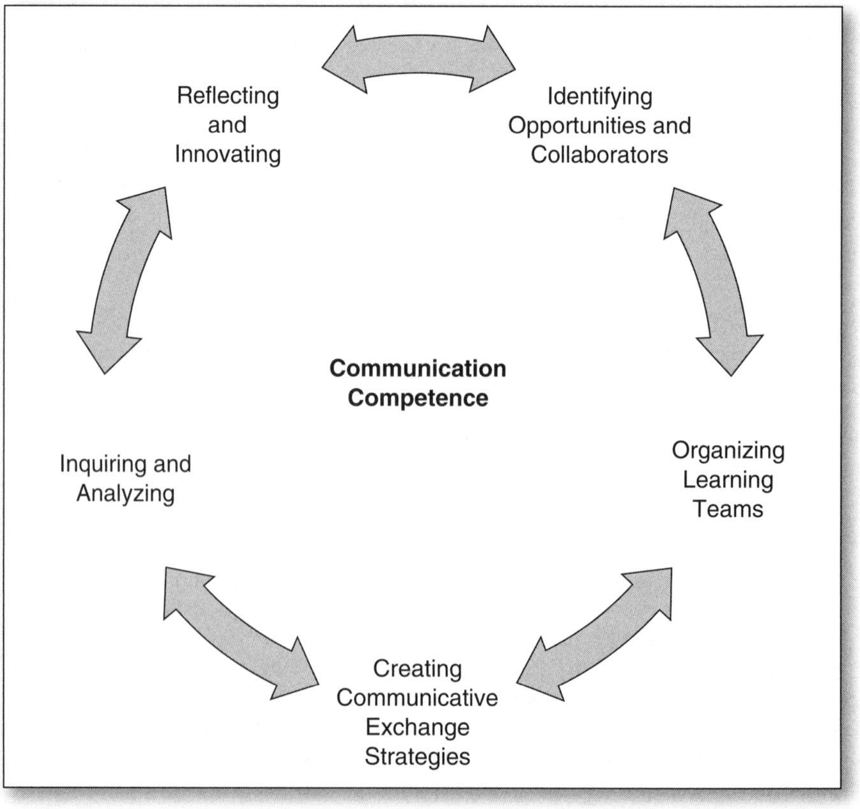

collective aspirations. This process is bidirectional, as sometimes it is useful to go back to previous stages within a cycle. Furthermore, as the process continues cycling, the outcomes expand by building on the previous cycle.

Identifying Opportunities and Collaborators

Opportunities to collaborate may come out of strategic planning in which common and/or complementary goals are identified. Opportunities may also be identified as an outcome of previous projects, through existing collaborations, or from identified needs. Initiators may come from stakeholder groups, researchers, or practitioners. Part of identifying opportunities is garnering existing resources or acquiring new resources. Things to keep in mind when making decisions about proposed projects, members of the CER team, and funding sources include (1) compatibility among potential collaborators' values and principles of collaboration and about change strategies; (2) the relative priority of building capacity for sustainability and achieving shorter term, project-specific outcomes; and (3) the level of dependency on external funding and associated constraints.

These considerations often involve trade-offs—either among project priorities or among collaborating organizations' and/or funders' priorities. Differences in approaches and/or principles need to be resolved to reduce the risk of conflict as the project unfolds.

Organizing CER Learning Teams

CER teams form around common and complementary goals. Their aims are to (1) explore opportunities for improving the sustainability of food systems for health and well-being; (2) develop integrated research and practice agendas based on family and community priorities as well as research and intervention agendas; and (3) collaborate in data collection, analysis, interpretation, and application (Gillespie & Gillespie, 2006).

A foundational element of CER is engaging in genuine dialogue for colearning and cocreating. "The discipline of team learning starts with 'dialogue,' the capacity of members of the team to suspend assumptions and enter into a genuine 'thinking together.'. . . The discipline of dialogue also involves learning how to recognize the patterns of interaction in teams that undermine learning" (Senge, 1990, p. 10). Genuine dialogue fosters colearning, improves relational communication competence, and enhances collaborative practice for cocreating a sustainable world. Learning teams practice new techniques in a safe environment while sharing credit and risk, expanding human potential, and challenging each other on the road to discovery.

Through colearning, CER teams can construct their reality and create a preferred future within the limits imposed by social and biophysical system constraints. This strategy enhances opportunities for developing integrated research and practice agendas based on community priorities as well as external research and intervention agendas.

Creating Communicative Exchange Strategies

Communicative exchange strategies emphasize the role of relational as well as instrumental components of communication for creating a culture in which CER participants can engage in collaborative communication.

CER draws on work about relational communication in groups (Keyton, 1999) and metacommunication (Watzlawick et al., 1967) to facilitate collaboration and development of a shared vision and to foster communication competence. The communication process involves creating trusting interpersonal and interorganizational relationships and balancing and blending ways of thinking (mind-sets and perspectives; Gillespie, Ganter, Craig, Dischner, & Lansing, 2003). This relational component of communication complements the instrumental component of communication that focuses on issues such as developing protocols, the committing of necessary internal resources, identification of external funding sources as needed, and developing the CER plan.

Inquiring and Analyzing

CER employs an asset-based approach to inquire about aspirations. That is, it asks what features are in place to support movement toward these aspirations and what underutilized resources might be invested to speed this movement. Gillespie (2010) articulated three questions to be addressed in collective decision making about community food systems: *What do we want? What are our options? How do we decide among these?* Since CER teams can construct their own forward-looking reality, not just identify problems to be solved, these three questions are addressed by beginning with an *inquiry about what is*—what is in place that is working to advance sustainability of the food system and to support health and well-being—and then *analyzing what could be*.

By focusing on opportunities when considering individual and collective strengths and assets, the CER teams can move in a positive direction. This asset/strength-based inquiry identifies underutilized resources that could be invested to create community capital. Each of the seven types of community capital—human, social, cultural, natural, built, financial, and political—is relevant to food decision making (Flora & Gillespie, 2009). The community capital framework provides a way of assessing assets and the interchange among the types of capital. Through this interchange, multiple capitals may be increased, leading to a spiraling-up effect (Emery & Flora, 2006). This assessment provides a basis for collective decision making about priorities, trade-offs, and interrelationships within food systems.

Reflecting and Innovating

Senge, Kleiner, Roberts, Ross, and Smith (1994) suggest that individual and group reflection offers the opportunity for engaging in genuine dialogue, "the capacity of members of a team to suspend assumptions and enter into a genuine thinking together" (p. 10). Team members often bring different perspectives to the dialogue. When these perspectives bump up against each other and/or overlap at the edges *and* minds are open to rethinking and gaining new perspectives, the context is ripe for innovation. Barker (2008) describes this as "innovation at the verge of differences" (p. 155). He posits that thinking on the verge occurs more commonly at the fringes of established disciplines and organizational cultures in the work of those less constrained by these traditions. The innovative communication generated by CER reflects and fosters the cogeneration of theory and advances methodology.

Discovering Effective Cross-Perspective Communication Methods and Strategies

The two case studies presented here illustrate the application of the CER methodology to a family food decision-making project and a community food decision-making project. We describe the projects according to each element of the CER methodology as described earlier, followed by a discussion of the projects' communication dynamics and challenges. The CER teams in both cases included members from multiple perspectives (henceforth referred to as cross-perspective CER teams), and so these cases further our understanding of cross-perspective communication.

Case Study #1: Cooking Together for Family Meals

Cooking Together for Family Meals (CTFM) is an innovative childhood obesity prevention project for children and their families based on CER. It is a series of six weekly classes designed to help middle-school children and their parents work together to prepare quick, healthy, and low-cost vegetable-rich meals and enjoy eating them together. These hands-on classes focus on adding a variety of vegetables such as dark leafy greens, winter squashes, cruciferous vegetables, and beans to family meals. All participants develop cooking and food safety skills, and parents gain confidence in their children's abilities to help with food preparation. These classes enable children to take on new roles in family food decision making and preparation and help families develop more positive child–parent relationships involving food-related activities as the family also improves its communication competence.

The long-term goals for the program developed by a cross-perspective CER learning team were to (1) reduce the risk of childhood obesity by increasing appreciation, accessibility, and consumption of vegetables typically underused in family diets, and (2) experiment with and advance CER methodology and food decision-making communication competence.[6] Cornell Cooperative Extension (CCE) educators and Cornell University Division of Nutritional Sciences faculty and dietetic interns worked with children and their families to develop this pilot nutrition education and cooking program and inquire about family food decision making. Concurrently, the project leaders applied CER principles and strategies as they advanced the food decision-making CER communication process and methodology.

Identifying Opportunities and Collaborators

CTFM was initiated by CCE community nutritionists in the Finger Lakes region of New York to address the needs of children and their families. Through their experiences with nutrition education for families, they made the following observations:

1. Nutrition program participants lacked knowledge and skills in vegetable preparation.

2. Parents' food decision-making behaviors could affect their child's dietary risk factors for obesity.

3. There were no CCE nutrition programs targeting parents and their children together.

These observations suggested an opportunity for a new initiative that supported families in learning together with fewer constraints than the current CCE nutrition education models presented.

The CCE nutrition educators who initiated the program invited university faculty members leading the youth nutrition program and the food decision-making program to partner in a CER initiative to reduce the risk of childhood obesity by increasing vegetable consumption. This expanded team developed a proposal based on these presuppositions:

- Parents want to increase consumption of vegetables by their children but are constrained by limited availability (practically available in convenient retail markets), accessibility (cost, transportation, food preparation skills), and appreciation (preferences based on flavors, familiarity, and cultural meanings).
- Knowledge about vegetables and recipes will lead to healthier and more varied food choices.

---

[6]Drawing from Thompson's description of collective communication competence and Senge et al.'s (1994) definition of dialogue, communication competence for CER is the extent to which team members are able to (1) reflect on and communicate their own presuppositions, (2) engage in productive dialogue by temporarily suspending assumptions to engage in "genuine thinking together," and (3) develop effective communication programs that support collective food decision making.

- Understanding and responding to individual differences among participants will improve program effectiveness.
- Replacing caloric-dense foods in family meals and encouraging eating routines with vegetables would contribute to healthy weights of children and their families.
- Improved food decision making about both processes and outcomes would nourish and nurture children now and for succeeding generations.

Organizing the CER Learning Team

The initiators[7] invited other extension nutritionists to join the team to develop a project proposal for classes for children and their parents learning together, including cooking and food safety skills, preparation methods for vegetables and dried beans, and ways to include vegetables in family meals. Because of the long-term goal of improving availability and accessibility of vegetables within the community food system, the proposal explicitly included families across the income spectrum.

A grant proposal for internal funding from the institution was developed by the county extension nutritionists in collaboration with faculty members on the team. The 3-year pilot project was funded by CCE administration and included staff from five counties in upstate New York: Kathleen Dischner and Cheryl Neal (Onondaga); Christine Gutelius and Rebecca Crawford (Cayuga); Helen Howard and Tina Foster (Tompkins); Loree Symonds and Jonathan Sterlace (Steuben); Paddy Redihan and Melissa Clary (Schuyler); and Holly Gump (Food and Nutrition Education in Communities, Finger Lakes Nutrition Region). Over the course of the 3 years, there was some turnover of staff, which changed the composition of the CER team and resulted in an increase in the number of perspectives and insights generated by the team and provided fertile ground for adopting CER perspectives and applying CER principles. The CER team members all contributed to CTFM program development, evaluation, and research. Additionally, learning team members created alliances with community organizations and agencies within each of their communities.

The team agreed on a systems approach with thoughtful reflection about collaboration and communication. They also created an atmosphere of trust using humor and an appreciation of others' contributions to learning and cocreation. The group developed protocols for communication at face-to-face meetings and by e-mail and telephone. The team members acknowledged the potential for conflict among team members with different goals. This diversity of approach was accepted, and team members worked together to develop a self-sustaining, family-responsive program. The learning team met periodically over the 3 years of development and testing of the curriculum and CER communication methodology.

---

[7]The initiators were Kathleen Dischner, Holly Gump, and Helen Howard.

The communication processes for food decision making of interest in this project were interactions among family members, between family members and change agents, and among CER team members. Primary theoretical perspectives involved individual differences, social roles and categories, and the notion of metacommunication as described above.

The CER team engaged in collaborative communication and decision making to develop an approach that would balance the multiple goals and priorities of families, practitioners, evaluators, and researchers. Based on relationships of trust, respect, and camaraderie developed in previous collective decision-making experiences, the initiators advanced their communication competence for collective decision making and expanded this colearning to new members of the CER team.

Figure 8.2 provides an overview of the communication events during the program development and testing.

| **Figure 8.2** | Project Timeline of Communication Events for the CTFM Project |

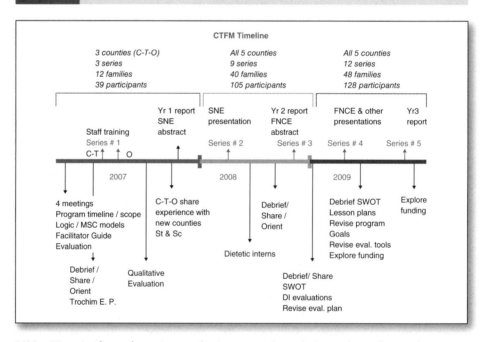

MSC = *Most significant change* is an evaluation approach in which significant changes that may or may not have been planned are identified and followed throughout the program. In CTFM, this was only minimally useful for the overall evaluation.

C = Cayuga County, T = Tompkins County, O = Onondaga County, New York

Trochim = Bill Trochim, professor, Cornell University, and evaluation consultant for this project

SNE = Society for Nutrition Education; later added *behavior*, so currently SNEB

SWOT = Strengths, weaknesses, opportunities, threats identified by the CER team

FNCE = Food and Nutrition Conference and Expo 2011 of the American Dietetics Association (since renamed Academy of Nutrition and Dietetics)

Some aspects of the CER approach emerging from the application of these theoretical perspectives and associated worldviews challenged the culture and approaches of the CCE system and its gatekeepers.

Inquiring and Analyzing

The team proposed the following questions for consideration using the CER methodology: What is happening? Why is it happening? How can we share it? What are we learning? And, as the project progressed, Why is everyone involved (children, parents, facilitators, CER team, volunteers, collaborating organizations) so enthusiastic about the program process? Multiple methods involving multiple team members were used to address these questions: a survey of participants, follow-up phone interviews, participant observation, and strategies to identify most significant change. At the completion of the program, families reflected on and reported changes in a post–pre–evaluation questionnaire that asked first what they were doing or thinking at the end of the program and then what they remembered doing or thinking before participating in the program. Although this approach is considered by some researchers as less rigorous than a pre-post design, it is advantageous for engaging participants in reflection about their own family's changes and intentions. It is also less burdensome on participants than completing surveys twice, as with pre-post designs (see "challenges" below for a discussion of the impact of research and evaluation designs on program effectiveness).

Following the completion of the 3-year project and follow-up, CER learning team members were interviewed for their perspectives on the CER methodology. Participating families who had completed the program at various times over the previous 4 years were gathered to reflect on their experiences; parents and children reported that memorable parts of the program included working with their family members, interacting with other families, and the good food. The children were now actively involved in family food decision making and food acquisition and preparation. Some families began eating meals together, which provided another context for family communication.

The team discovered that the structured yet flexible class routine was welcome in the chaotic lives of most families (particularly as it related to food and eating practices). The informal communication between children and their parents, with other families, and with class facilitators provided time and safe space for discussing parental concerns such as the weight of their child or eating issues.

The classes fostered teamwork and colearning within and among families and between families and change agents. There was also evidence that colearning and increased communication competence for thoughtful food decision making carried over to the home environment. For example, one mom reported: "Grocery shopping has become more interesting (and takes longer!), since we are reading more labels and discovering new veggies!" Another mother reported, "I enjoy cooking with my child now—I can't believe I am saying this!" and another, "My kids are helping more in the kitchen." Two children who had been part of the CTFM classes demonstrated "how to prepare fruits and vegetables to children in a Head Start class." One participant wrote: "What I enjoyed most was our instructor. She helped us out so much and she was a great teacher for someone like me to understand who never cooks. The whole class was great!"

Reflecting and Innovating

By means of periodic meetings during the program development and evaluation process, the learning team reflected on what they were learning about CER, family communication with program leaders, and communication with each other. Facilitators/educators appreciated the flexibility of implementation and evolution of the curriculum as the pilot testing progressed. The CER team discussed ways the curriculum, including the leaders guide, could provide guidance for adapting lesson plans to respond to participant needs, or the particular group dynamics, and the setting for the class. The team decided that since the program is complex and interactive, rather than organizing the curriculum linearly, they would include a set of elements to assist program leaders and facilitators in designing, educating, and communicating strategies for a particular group of families and class-specific dynamics. Finally, the "flexible routine" of the classes was appreciated by facilitators as well as participants; some families reported that they carried this approach into their family food and eating routines.

Case Study #2: Leveraging the Locavore Movement: Exploring Family and Community Food Decision Making

The second case study illustrates community food decision making and its interaction with family food decision making in the context of increasing the availability, accessibility, and appreciation of locally harvested wild fish and game. This project provides an example of bringing together multiple perspectives on community food systems from within the community as well as from multiple disciplines. The first year of the 3-year project has been completed.

Identifying Opportunities

The idea for a project to connect hunters and fishers with local food advocates and families struggling to feed their children came out of a conversation over breakfast between a county-based extension nutritionist (Moira Tidball) and her husband (Keith Tidball), a senior extension associate in natural resources at the university. They identified potential for improving food security by increasing wild fish and game consumption, in turn influencing the recruitment and retention of hunters and anglers, and increasing the appreciation of fish and game as sources of protein in the local diet. Both K. and M. Tidball hunt and fish themselves and are well connected to the local hunting and fishing scene in Seneca County, New York, the site of the project. M. Tidball also teaches classes on safe preparation of wild fish and game, manages the Wild Harvest Table website (http://senecawildharvest. blogspot.com/), and teaches nutrition to low-income audiences. Thus, each represented community stakeholders and lived and worked in the county.

The working hypothesis is that consumption of wild fish and game plays a limited role in the diets of New Yorkers due to a number of "barriers to consumption." The potential barriers identified by previous research and practice include cultural norms of what is considered "food," lack of available official information concerning nutritional content of relevant species, negative stereotypes regarding fish and game taste and quality, and limited information about, experience with, and access to fish and game procurement, processing, and preparation.

Three methods designed to assess barriers and opportunities include

1. interviews with extension community nutritionists engaged with families,

2. an open community workshop with the three stakeholder groups (fishers and hunters, "locavores,"[8] and low-income families), and

3. interviews with the three stakeholder groups.

Organizing the CER Learning Team

To develop a CER team to improve the availability, accessibility, and appreciation of fish and game as sources of protein in the local diet, the Tidballs connected with Cornell researchers in natural resources (Paul Curtis) and the food decision-making program (Ardyth Gillespie), who were selected based on their work with natural resource and food system stakeholders in New York counties. The project leaders framed their project within the context of family and community food decision making and proposed a pilot project to engage individuals and families from the three stakeholder groups in a community workshop to discuss perspectives and opportunities to expand hunting and fishing as a recreational activity as well as the potential for making it more accessible to others in the local community. With the exception of Gillespie, the learning team had worked together on previous projects to further the goals of the Wild Harvest Table extension program and associated research projects.

Connections were made with faculty from other institutions (Iowa State University and the Pennsylvania State University) and state and federal agencies (New York Department of Natural Resources and the U.S. Department of Agriculture) interested in expanding fishing and hunting and the use of wild fish and game, and/or decision-making processes within families and communities. As the project has progressed, others who learned about the project through various communication networks have

---

[8]*Locavores* is the term for people who seek locally produced foods.

offered ideas and/or assistance, for example adding specific expertise and perspectives to the workshop.

Developing Communication Processes

Members of the CER learning team were experienced with cross-disciplinary and cross-sector research and its application in extension programming. The team held several face-to-face sessions to discuss CER, their perspectives on research and practice, and their integration. A high level of communication competence for collective decision making facilitated moving through the elements in the CER framework. It also provided a basis for developing a workshop for members of the three targeted food system stakeholders (fishers and hunters, locavores, and low-income families) as part of the second phase of the project. Based on these discussions, the objectives of the project, integrating natural resource education goals and food decision-making project goals, were identified. They are as follows:

1. Determine the importance of wild fish and game consumption to food security in rural local New York State communities

2. Evaluate why people are motivated to eat, or not eat, wild fish and game

3. Examine the importance of nutritional analysis for wild fish and game, and the way this information influences consumer choices

4. Determine how people acquire and adopt information about processing and preparing wild fish and game

To meet these objectives, during the first year of this 3-year project, three major tasks were undertaken:

- The team assisted M. Tidball in developing questions for semistructured interviews with 10 community nutrition practitioners to determine from their experience with families the contribution of fish and game to food security (Phase 1).
- M. Tidball orchestrated a time-sensitive collaboration among fishers and hunters to obtain, prepare, and transfer samples to the USDA and Penn State laboratories for nutritional analysis. Three wild species commonly harvested and consumed in the eastern United States (Canada goose, ruffed grouse, and brook trout) were analyzed to create a standard nutrition label for each species (Phase 2).
- The team developed and implemented an open space workshop using findings from Phase 1 to guide a discussion among workshop participants, facilitated by Gillespie and Flora (Phase 2).

Inquiring and Analyzing

The interviews conducted by M. Tidball (objectives 1 and 2) formed the first part of the inquiry into the contribution of fish and game to food security for the stakeholder group of low-income families. The rest of the team assisted with developing the interview questions and analyzing the interviews.

Building on what we learned from these interviews, the specific objectives for the workshop were to begin to discover the goals and aspirations for each stakeholder group, identify resources that might be invested by the community to promote these goals, and consider next steps.

The leaders recognized the importance of creating safe space for conversation among these diverse groups in the workshop setting. The initial idea was to hold it at a local hunting club with a chef who could prepare wild fish and game. However, it was decided that this location might be intimidating for the other two target groups, and so a local firehouse was secured. A chef new to preparing game and wild fish was secured. He shared his positive experience (as well as delicious food) with the workshop participants and acknowledged the expert assistance and coaching of M. Tidball. Some participants expressed interest in attending the next workshop that M. Tidball was offering. Additionally, the project leaders were called into service to help with the food preparation and so got some hands-on experience as well.

Careful consideration was given to what might enhance or constrain open communication. For example, although state representatives of fish and wildlife agencies were an essential part of the conversation, they were asked to represent themselves as hunters and downplay their government role by wearing their hunting clothes rather than their uniforms. This worked well, as they blended into the workshop activities and then posed "what if" questions about making wild fish and game available in retail outlets for the group to consider. This issue was based on themes that had just been reported by the small groups and sparked an open discussion that revealed differing perspectives on the potential sale of wild fish and game—whether it is a good idea to make it more accessible or whether it would cause hunting for profit and destroy the rich wildlife in the community. One result of this conversation on challenges and opportunities was an initial proposal by K. Tidball to consider a state-managed program for the sale of venison, logistically similar to venison donation programs but steering some venison to the high-end meat market, the proceeds of which would be returned to habitat management rather than hunters' pockets. This proposal is currently under discussion by game management professionals in the state. The participant evaluations also indicated an interest in volunteering to help the community move these ideas into action.

Reflecting and Innovating

Individual and team reflection throughout the proposal development and first year of the project has led to an innovative integration of the two disciplinary perspectives and between extension education and academic research. The team successfully navigated a serious challenge to the concept of integration of research with practice when the funding decision makers required that the original CER proposal be split into two proposals (with no additional funding)—one for research and one for extension education. Although they were funded separately, the CER methodology has maintained the integration of the shared and complementary objectives of the two parts of the project.

In the development of the workshop, the team brought together their multiple perspectives, approaches, and expertise to create a program that integrated the principles of AI, OST, communication competence, and facilitated transformative learning. Team members each reflected on the workshop and will engage in group reflection and dialogue in the next phase of the project. M. Tidball noted, "The atmosphere of the workshop was very comfortable and welcoming, with all participants sharing in small group discussions. In this setting, people were willing to try new foods." The next step will be the team's analysis of and reflections on the workshop and a discussion of future directions and opportunities for advancing and utilizing this emerging CER method.

Findings and Opportunities for Continued Development of CER Methodology

Findings from the two case studies described above highlight communication dynamics and challenges discovered in previous CER applications as well. While these studies represent important advances in CER methodology, challenges remain and there is more to learn about CER communication dynamics. At the systems level, embedded cultures, mind-sets, approaches to change, and philosophies make it difficult to introduce innovations—especially those generated in collaboration with family and community food system stakeholders. Within university cooperative extension systems, blending and balancing priorities and addressing trade-offs among multiple stakeholders is an ongoing challenge. Perhaps the most common tension university faculty experience involves engaging in ways that honor community priorities while at the same time meeting the publication and fundraising requirements for tenure and promotion. This issue goes beyond the academy—local leaders as well as scholars are increasingly pressed to raise money and produce high-profile outputs. These requirements often compete with the promotion of significant and sustainable systems as well as individual behavior changes.

In the CTFM case, as indicated earlier, communication between the CER team and nutrition program gatekeepers was a challenge because of the differing perspectives on research design and curriculum requirements and their impact on program effectiveness. The tension between system requirements and the findings regarding the importance of flexibility in the curriculum and its application is an example. The system required a traditional curriculum, which in this case had to receive approval from the academic institution before county or state program resources could be invested in the innovative family cooking program. Another constraint was that system resources could be used only for low-income families, whereas an important aspect of the cooking program was that it did not discriminate amongst participants based on their income.

Related to systems dynamics and constraints, collaborators in most CER initiatives as well as the families and food system stakeholders involved express concern about competition among multiple priorities for their time and other resources. They are stressed by the lack of time for basic food and eating activities along with reflection and renewal.

Conclusions and Opportunities for Further Development of CER

The communication framework described here combines theoretical insights and methodology from communication, human sciences, and our findings from food decision making CER. The basic communication process for CER is characterized by simultaneous sending and receiving, where every team member is a communicator. The relational component as well as the instrumental component of communication is emphasized. This dynamic cycle expands outward to connect other community members, professionals, practitioners, and/or researchers to enrich the ideas and information exchange beyond team members and to inspire innovative thinking.

Both of the case studies described, as well as previous CER, have shown us that effective food decision making CER communication requires sufficient time and safe space for developing communication competence for collective decision making rooted in trusting relationships. It also requires an approach to dialogue in which each participant is valued and a commitment to setting aside one's own perspectives and mind-sets to explore new ways of thinking and acting. These findings have suggested additional opportunities for further development of CER for FDM and other community development research and practice. CER offers an alternative approach to understanding and facilitating systems and behavioral change to improve public health and family and community well-being by

- improving external validity,
- building family and community capacity for self-sustained improvements,
- guiding local team adaptations and specific applications that fit their particular situation,
- creating flexible research designs with minimal interference in program goals and strategies, and

- continually improving and expanding methods for the CER process, such as DDM, to build relationships within CER learning teams, families, and communities and with external stakeholders, which helps create contexts for community-initiated inquiry and innovation.

Some would argue that CER is a less rigorous approach to building evidence for changing food systems and improving diets. On the other hand, CER may be more externally valid, and in most cases, CER designs are less dependent on external resources (financial, human, social) and, thus, potentially more sustainable. CER teams have also found that this engaged approach inspires participants to share responsibility for their own change and for improving the systems that constrain them. CER methodology can more fully engage family and community members to build capacity and thus provide a better chance for sustainable change in family and community food decision-making processes and outcomes. These are some of the trade-offs to consider when deciding whether to use CER methodology. As our case studies have shown, this path toward a better future will require passion, commitment, and patience sustained by hope and belief in the goodness of mankind.

Take-Home Messages

CER communication competence for creating sustainable food systems that support health and well-being is fostered by the following activities:

- Committing sufficient time for face-to-face and distance communication to foster communication competence for collective decision making and for shifting mind-sets and cultures from competition toward collaboration, from dependency toward healthy interdependence
- Valuing each participant's perspective and understanding of the phenomenon and the local context
- Recognizing that CER is a long-term investment in health and well-being for children, families, and communities
- Facilitating communication competence for collective decision making by engaging in open dialogue aimed at colearning, changing mind-sets, ways of thinking, and innovation "on the verge"
- Building systems that foster collaboration, caring, and shared responsibility for making a difference
- Creating learning environments that expand human potential

Acknowledgments

We would like to acknowledge the important role of campus and community collaborators during the evolution of CER methodology. These include many scholars (students, staff, and faculty) and community partners for the two projects described here and for other CER projects.

References

Barker, J. A. (2008). Innovation at the verge of differences. In D. Kennedy (Ed.), *Putting our differences to work: The fastest way to innovation, leadership, and high performance* (pp. 155–162). San Francisco: Berrett-Koehler.

Emery, M., & Flora, C. (2006). Spiraling-up: Mapping community transformation with community capitals framework. *Journal of the Community Development Society, 37*(1), 19–35.

Flora, C. B., & Gillespie, A. H. (2009). Making healthy choices to reduce childhood obesity: Community capitals and food and fitness. *Community Development, 40*(2), 114–122.

Gillespie, A. H. (2012). Nutrition education. In J. M. Rippe (Ed.), *Encyclopedia of lifestyle medicine and health*. Thousand Oaks, CA: Sage.

Gillespie, A. H., Ganter, L., Craig, S., Dischner, K., & Lansing, D. (2003). Productive partnerships for food: Principles and strategies. *Journal of Extension, 41*(2). Retrieved from http://www.joe.org/joe/2003april/a8.php

Gillespie, A. H., & Gillespie, G. W. (2006). Generating grounded theory with community partners. *Journal of Community Nutrition, 8*(1), 16–23.

Gillespie, A. H., & Gillespie, G. W. (2007). Family food decision-making: An ecological systems framework. *Journal of Family and Consumer Sciences, 99*(2), 22–28.

Gillespie, A. H., & Yarbrough, P. (1984). A conceptual model for communicating nutrition. *Journal of Nutrition Education, 16*(4), 168–172.

Gillespie, G. W. (2010). 2009 AFHVS presidential address: The steering question: Challenges to achieving food system sustainability. *Agriculture and Human Values, 27*(1), 3–12.

Greenwood, D. J., & Levin, M. (1998). *Introduction to action research: Social research for social change*. Thousand Oaks, CA: Sage.

Hovland, C., & Janis, I. (Eds.). (1959). *Personality and persuasibility*. New Haven, CT: Yale University Press.

Israel, B. A., Schulz, A. J., Parker, E. A., Becker, A. B., Allen, A. J., III, & Guzman, J. R. (2003). Critical issues in developing and following community-based participatory research principles. In M. Minkler & N. Wallerstein (Eds.), *Community-based participatory research for health* (pp. 53–76). San Francisco: Jossey-Bass.

Katz, E., & Lazarsfeld, P. F. (Eds.). (1964). *Personal influence: The part played by people in the flow of mass communications* (Vol. 2). New York: Columbia University.

Keyton, J. (1999). Relational communication in groups. In L. R. Frey, D. Gouran, & M. S. Poole (Eds.), *The handbook of group communication theory and research* (pp. 192–222). Thousand Oaks, CA: Sage.

Lazarsfeld, P. (1949). Communication research. In W. Dennis, R. Lippitt, & K. T. Behanan (Eds.), *Current trends in social psychology* (pp. 218–273). Pittsburgh, PA: University of Pittsburgh Press.

Owen, H. (1997). *Open space technology: A user's guide* (2nd ed.). San Francisco: Berrett-Koehler.

Rogers, E. M. (1983). *Diffusion of innovations* (3rd ed.). New York: Free Press.

Senge, P. M. (1990). *The Fifth discipline: The art and practice of the learning organization.* New York: Currency/Doubleday.

Senge, P. M., Kleiner, A., Roberts, C., Ross, R. B., & Smith, B. J. (1994). *The fifth discipline fieldbook: Strategies and tools for building a learning organization.* New York: Currency/Doubleday.

Taylor, E. W. (2000). Analyzing research on transformative learning theory. In J. Mezirow & Associates (Eds.), *Learning as transformation* (pp. 285–328). San Francisco: Jossey-Bass.

Thompson, J. L. (2009). Building collective communication competence in interdisciplinary research teams. *Journal of Applied Communication Research, 37*(3), 278–297.

Watkins, J. M., Mohr, B., & Kelly, R. (2011). *Appreciative inquiry: Change at the speed of imagination.* San Francisco: Pfeiffer.

Watzlawick, P., Bavelas, J. B., & Jackson, D. D. (1967). *Pragmatics of human communication: A study of interactional patterns, pathologies, and paradoxes.* New York: W. W. Norton.

Yarbrough, P. (1981). Communication theory and nutrition education research. *Journal of Nutrition Education, 13*(1), S16–S27.

9

Discourse Communities, Disconnects, and Digital Media

The Case of Relocalizing Economies for Sustainable Agriculture and Energy Systems

◆ Casey Hoy, Ross B. MacDonald, Benson P. Lee, and Steve Bosserman

This chapter describes four interwoven case studies that highlight the challenges of cross-disciplinary communication as research is extended into action for systemic change in the world. Case studies include agroecosystems management as a very cross-disciplinary endeavor with diverse stakeholders, commercializing fuel cell technology in the developing world, appreciating and promoting the cross-disciplinary communication skills of multicultural students, and catalyzing local economies centered on food and agriculture. Conclusions from the combined experience in these real-world examples are that cross-disciplinary communication can be improved (1) when it is focused on meeting basic human needs such as food and energy, (2) by methodology and technology that are applicable across disciplines and disparate forms of data to improve understanding of complex systems, and (3) when it recognizes interpersonal stories and individual skills and capacities to position diversity as a guiding intellectual and moral force in cross-disciplinary and cross-cultural discourse.

Introduction

Our food and energy systems are composed of highly evolved and quite complex global supply chains. We predict, however, that they will not be well adapted to conditions that may result from climate change and increasing oil prices. Energy systems will need to shift to new, innovative sources of renewable fuels, and food systems will need to become more decentralized again. As a result, opportunities for enhancing understanding and innovation abound in these systems. But to seize any of these opportunities requires an ability to collaborate.

This chapter describes our combined practical experience with promoting local economies based on food and energy to counterbalance and complement global systems in pursuit of a more resilient food and energy future. The communication challenges and potential solutions that arise in these real-world applications are both cross-disciplinary and cross-cultural.

Several discourse communities necessarily interact in our work. For our purposes, *discourse community* refers to any social group (Pogner, 2003) of people who share a complex set of conventions for communicating with one another and common frameworks for approaching problems and opportunities of mutual interest (Bizzell, 1994). Because we are focused on communication dynamics, we use the term *discourse community* as opposed to the broader concept *community of practice* (for a comparison, see Pogner, 2005). However, we believe that discourse communities share important characteristics with the broader concept of communities of practice. These include dynamic and disputable boundaries and memberships, and uneven power dynamics (Roberts, 2006). In these dynamic, overlapping, figurative borderlands, differences among discourse communities, the fluidity of ideas and circumstances within and across discourse communities, and unequal distributions of power can confuse, disadvantage, and frustrate broad-based collaboration and support for systems change. Therefore, a bridging of semiotic and sociocultural traditions of communication theory (Craig, 1999) is needed to progress in the face of these communication challenges.

We will review four areas in which we are working, individually or together, on systemic change. First, agroecosystems include both people and the land and function on a very large scale, so research in agroecosystems management requires effective communication among social, biological, and physical science disciplines, and the management itself requires the concerted action of entire farming communities. Second, introducing solid-state fuel cells as electricity infrastructure in remote rural areas worldwide requires communication among private-, philanthropic-, and independent-sector communities and disciplines as diverse as engineering, finance, philanthropy, agricultural systems, cultural anthropology, and rural sociology. Third, multicultural communities in the United States occupy a "borderland" because they are marginalized by dominant cultures. As a result, community members seeking a place in the U.S. economy must develop unique abilities to communicate across cultures. Fourth, in many places, localization of business ecosystems (consisting of a set of business entities such as competitors, customers, financial institutions, suppliers, etc., that interact with each other and with their business environment) through import substitution is an effective counterbalance to wholesale globalization, but it requires connecting many diverse contributors, with their equally diverse ways of viewing and engaging with the world and communicating with others.

Our overall goal is to draw parallels between the communication challenges in working to improve economies, agriculture, and societal well-being, and the communication challenges faced in communicating across scientific disciplines. Systemic change requires communication across sciences, professions, sectors, economies, and cultures. The breadth of communication necessary is as great as any addressed in this volume. Our examples, and lessons gained from working toward system change, may inform and help improve scientific discourse across disciplines. As noted above, we focus on concepts, practices, and technologies that assist with bridging discourse-community semiotic and sociocultural perspectives on the challenges we describe (Craig, 1999). Our experience suggests that a combination of known communication techniques, new technologies that increase common ground, and focus on basic needs common to all offers the best chance of achieving effective communication for systems change.

Agroecosystems Management

Agroecosystems and agroecosystems management are not a part of the common dialogue in most communities. We define agroecosystems broadly to include both people and the land and the interactions between them. Although most people experience the agroecosystem of which they are a part in terms of the multifunctional benefits of agriculture (Boody et al., 2005), such as pastoral scenery, open space, and possibly local farm products, few people spend the time and effort to understand them as a complex system of interactions between people and the land. Therefore, communicating the functioning of such a complex system to all the people interacting within it is very challenging.

Agroecosystems function over areas large enough to include not just individual farms but many farms and surrounding habitats and human communities. Management, in this context, is not what individuals do to manage their land but what multiple communities of people do to influence the entire landscape. Included are farmers and farms but also residential and commercial landholders and their properties. Their experience varies, and their values and goals for an agroecosystem may depend on the role they play within it.

The complexity inherent in agroecosystems becomes evident when one considers the challenge of teaching university students how agroecosystems function and how they are managed. To a student interested in agriculture, agroecosystems are the framework for all coursework, with the more advanced and focused courses in agricultural topics building on basic courses in the social sciences and economics as well as biology, particularly ecology, and physical sciences such as geology and chemistry. For a university student, synthesizing all the individual topics they experience into a larger framework to provide context for their future livelihood is a central feature of their education. However, such a framework does not emerge and crystallize easily when their focus is on a few of the individual topics within this broad framework at any given time, as might be encouraged by their coursework. Furthermore, real-world experience connected with their formal education may be needed before a larger systems view emerges. The real-world experience gives specific examples of and incorporates the variation among people, points of view, and places, allowing a more complete understanding of how they all interrelate.

Examples of roles, values, and goals will illustrate the kind of variation among discourse communities in the way people think about agroecosystems and the resulting lack of a common framework for thinking about them. To farmers, agroecosystem management means finding a style of farming that pays the bills, that the neighbors and community want to support and protect, and that their sons and daughters want to continue. In other words, their point of view may be very personal, focusing on their experience with their own farm and family and how it relates to surrounding communities and landscape. An agricultural scientist, on the other hand, would consider agroecosystems management to be the basis of scientific inquiry at the intersection of the agricultural disciplines, both social/behavioral and biological/physical. Agriculture would need to be viewed as a complex system, encompassing all production and much more, to describe how subsystems interact and how potentially competing goals such as productivity, environmental quality, and social responsibility can be addressed. And, in contrast to how agroecosystems have been traditionally viewed—as a set of production challenges that must be solved—researchers will need to understand both problems and opportunities as properties that emerge from the entire system rather than a specific attribute of one of its parts.

Others with an interest in agroecosystems include environmentalists who focus on qualities such as biodiversity and water quality, businesses focusing on entrepreneurial opportunities and supply chains, consumers with a primary interest in food and other agricultural products, and policymakers who may focus on either short- or long-term objectives. The goals of environmentalists and business people are different enough that they may sometimes conflict in their view of how agroecosystems should be managed, and finding opportunities to enhance social and environmental bottom lines while giving equal importance to the economic bottom line is the real challenge for both. Consumers expect continuous improvement from an agriculture that can be trusted to provide healthy and affordable food from a healthy ecosystem, and increasing numbers of consumers expect both a fair return to the farmer and affordable food for all. Policymakers, on the other hand, may need to focus on long-term simultaneous gains in environmental, social, and economic dimensions that outweigh short-term gains in any one area, perhaps resisting political pressure from consumers or special interests to do so.

Each of the groups described above has been engaged in the work of agroecosystem management over the history of the Agroecosystems Management Program at The Ohio State University. This cross-disciplinary research, teaching, and outreach program aims to balance the social, economic, and environmental dimensions of agriculture, promoting sustainable agroecosystems. The diversity of its stakeholders, however, greatly increases the challenge of communication across many discourse communities. The concept of collaborative learning (Daniels & Walker, 1996), which combines soft-systems methodology to address semiotic challenges with some form of dispute resolution and an adaptive management process, describes the approach taken over time in the Agroecosystems Management Program. However, learning tools that improve communication remain a particular challenge.

One means of responding to the multiple-stakeholder and multiple-discourse-community challenge in agroecosystems management has been to seek research methodologies that can analyze and combine the diverse kinds of data that are relevant to the system, and the many discourse communities. Relatively simple examples of such methodology are within the experience of stakeholders. For example, the Current Agricultural Use Value (CAUV) of farmland is an Ohio tax calculation that values farmland in economic terms based on its estimated production capacity based on soils data. The CAUV methodology, therefore, creates a bridge between financial and natural capital. Agroecosystems, however, require even more kinds of data, including social, economic, biological, and physical, to describe the ways they function.

A challenge posed by stakeholders was to develop a means of assessing the state, at a particular time, of an agroecosystem in combined social, economic, and environmental terms. The idea that assessing an agroecosystem needed this many parameters was grasped easily enough, but it was not at all obvious to most how to combine these parameters to determine how well the system was functioning. A common question was, "How do you get your arms around it?" This question of assessing the status or health of an agroecosystem has been a topic of considerable discussion in the literature, with many views on whether it was achievable and, if so, how to accomplish it.

A number of studies had suggested that health was a useful metaphor for the state of agroecosystems, given the many services that society expects from them and the importance of human behavior in how they function (Conway, 1987; Okey, 1996). Both criteria (Waltner-Toews, 1996) and properties (Conway, 1985, 1987) had been proposed to elaborate on this metaphor. Potential indicators of agroecosystem health include a wide range of possibilities (Okey, 1996; Suter, 1993; Waltner-Toews, 1994, 1996; Wicklum & Davies, 1995; Xu & Mage, 2001; Yiridoe & Weersink, 1997), which vary from the farm to the landscape level (Parkes & Panelli, 2001; Patil, Brooks, Myers, Rapport, & Taillie, 2001; Spiegel et al., 2001; Wilcox, 2001). Overall, the goal of this work was to develop a conceptual framework for the assessment of agricultural sustainability as a result of driving forces (e.g., Rao & Rogers, 2006), but no quantitative methodology had been proposed for implementing the conceptual framework.

We developed an approach to combine data in each of these areas into an index that could be mapped spatially. Our rationale was that an overlay of the various data layers could identify spatial variation in the drivers of agroecosystem health and provide a map of where conditions were relatively healthy, because all the drivers were in a supportive state, and where agroecosystem health was more challenged, because one or more of the drivers was in a less supportive state. We presented the idea of such an index to a group of about 25 of our stakeholder partners, using acetate overlays to illustrate the concept of layering data to map agroecosystem health, and they enthusiastically endorsed the idea. Our resulting study identified key variables that describe agroecosystems in various social, economic, and environmental dimensions; combined them using analytical hierarchy process (Saaty, 1992, 1994; Saaty & Sodenkamp, 2010); and mapped the resulting index to describe variation in the current state of agroecosystem health across a landscape (Vadrevu et al., 2008). Although work continues on this methodology—in particular, mapping agroecosystem health over larger areas, and using more readily available data and validating the index with independent indicator variables—the work did demonstrate the opportunity to address a complex combination of variables in a way that allows multiple discourse communities to gain a common view.

Additional emerging methodologies that could provide a similar means of communicating about complex systems across multiple discourse communities include network analysis and agent-based modeling. Agent-based modeling is a flexible systems simulation tool in which the agents can be either people whose values and decision-making behavior may vary (e.g., Garcia-Barrios, Speelman, & Pimm, 2008), firms with particular business practices and preferences (e.g., Kempener, Beck, & Petrie, 2009; Valente, 2010), or ecological entities such as plant or animal populations or habitat patches (e.g., McLane, Semeniuk, McDermid, & Marceau, 2011; Topping, 2011). Agent-based modeling is also being used to examine management decisions made by people, along with ecosystem responses (e.g., An, 2012;

Gevers, Hoye, Topping, Glemnitz, & Schroeder, 2011; Kurz et al., 2000). In a fashion similar to the spread of agent-based modeling across disciplines, network analysis arose in the social sciences as a means of analyzing social interactions, including those related to natural resource management (e.g., Ernstson, Sörlin, & Elmqvist, 2008), and then expanded to other applications. For example, we are using network analysis techniques to analyze agricultural supply networks, and others have used social network analysis to examine similar questions regarding business ecosystems (e.g., Ashton, 2008; Kempener et al., 2009; Liu, Yang, Chen, & Zhang, 2011). Network analysis is also being used by ecologists to evaluate the structure of such biological networks as food webs (Johnson, Luczkovich, Borgatti, & Snijders, 2009) and animal dispersal routes (Bode, Wood, & Franks, 2011). Some connection is recognized between these areas of research; for example, social networks are recognized as being a key contributor to the growth of business and entrepreneurial ecosystems (Cohen, 2006; Neck, Meyer, Cohen, & Corbett, 2004). But linking networks across social, economic, and ecological dimensions is a current scientific frontier. The methodologies described above provide an opportunity to generate a more holistic picture of agroecosystems that includes "foreign" concepts as well as those familiar to most scientists, and perhaps to communicate that picture to a much wider community in intuitively appealing forms such as maps.

Technology Management, Inc.

Deploying modular fuel cell systems for a village-based electricity infrastructure running on fuels grown and hand-pressed by local farmers in the most rural and impoverished regions of the world presents practical challenges in spanning discourse communities. Particularly difficult is explaining how the combination of social returns on social capital and financial returns on financial capital can stimulate economic development that can be scaled easily to meet local needs, and how it can become financially self-sustaining as a result. This vision of layering an energy infrastructure onto an agroecosystem to achieve economic development is very different from typical investments in energy projects, which focus on generating power, not on translating the power into high-value benefits such as clean water and sanitation to boost public health or affordable power for small farmers and businesses to increase income, or into a new form of currency for economic development from customers such as nongovernmental organizations and multinational corporations. Communicating these potential impacts on a local economic system to a diverse audience is critical when building the business case for financing. The following is our vision of how a social enterprise commercializing an emerging technology can do better for its shareholders by doing better for humanity.

Today, nearly 1.3 billion people live in developing nations with no access to electricity, clean water, or clean heat for cooking. Eight-hundred million live in areas too poor, too remote, or too sparsely settled for grid-based electricity to be economically justified and depend on women and children fetching water and gathering wood and dung for cooking and comfort heat (United Nations Foundation, 2012, p. 13). After dark, any light for reading or studying comes from flames—for example, from kerosene lamps or fires, which can produce harmful byproducts such as soot and smoke. Such communities often consist largely of farms of less than an acre yielding a family income of about $2 to $3 per day. However, an emerging technology called a fuel cell can convert raw oils locally grown and hand-pressed by farmers (e.g., jatropha, palm, croton nut) into electricity with clean heat as a byproduct. In contrast to engine-driven generators, which are noisy, smelly, and produce lethal carbon monoxide, fuel cell systems use an electrochemical process to generate power at the point of use that is clean enough to use safely indoors. Fuel cells are modular, meaning the capacity they offer can expand and contract easily to match local needs, can be highly efficient, and can operate continuously and quietly on a range of fuels, both fossil and bio-based, including locally produced vegetable oil. According to a recent U.N. report, the power generated by a 1-kilowatt system the size of a two-drawer file cabinet is enough to impact the quality of life for 20 families (U.N. Advisory Group on Energy and Climate Change, 2010).

Demand is likely to grow as the value of services enabled by electricity is realized by local families and word spreads, probably through social media and cell phones. The speed of this self-scaling will depend on the quality of social returns and the social capital available through the social enterprise. Like social media and associated technology such as cellular communications, which have become a widely used technology that is contributing to profound social change in the developing world (Howard & Parks, 2012), a distributed electrical infrastructure, one that does not require wires for distribution from a central power plant or need to be oversized to accommodate growth, would bypass a huge capital investment barrier now keeping electricity from those who need it the most.

The above vision of an energy future for developing countries was presented by Benson Lee (2006), social entrepreneur and CEO of Technology Management, Inc. (TMI), at a symposium titled "Finding Philanthropy's New Sweet Spot." Lee's audience was made up of about 200 philanthropists, foundations, and friends invited by the Rockefeller Philanthropy Advisors (RPA) and its founder, Eileen Rockefeller Growald (Lee, 2006). Many shared a common interest in alleviating poverty in developing countries. A social entrepreneur herself, Growald wanted to illuminate the emerging role of social entrepreneurship by highlighting the untapped intersection of business and philanthropy, encouraging the audience to intentionally push the traditional grantmaking boundaries of the philanthropic community toward investing for desired impacts while staying within the mission of their foundations.

This case study is based on our retrospective analysis of the progression from initial enthusiasm about this vision to a widespread lack of interest, a result caused by the difficulties of grappling with cross-disciplinary complexity. After the loss of interest, discussions between Lee and senior RPA staff concluded that the holistic vision involved too many disciplines and interdependent mechanisms or "moving parts." Using the right brain–left brain metaphor, initial positive "gut responses" from the right brain were eventually overwhelmed by the tedious communications required as the analytical left brain began engaging. We later realized that most funding recommendations in philanthropy are from staff trained in the behavioral and social sciences and not experienced with the quantitative analyses common in engineering, physical science, or business. RPA's recommendation was to defer discussion of details until after an actual system was put in place, thus showing the feasibility of performing the tasks promised in the vision and deferring detailed discussion until after a concrete goal had been established. Features of the "demonstration" model of the system would include fuel cell technology, how it supports local infrastructure, the social enterprise and its social impact, and the use of program-related investments (PRIs)[1] or their equivalent as a source of "patient" social capital.

This experience in 2006, although discouraging at the time, helped guide TMI, the product developer of fuel cells and systems, toward markets with known demand first. Today, very few investors, whether groups or individuals, make financial commitments without performing due diligence, an investigative task that requires analyzing a business proposal, its sources of revenues, and its expenses, and then calculating the net returns on investment (ROI) over time to rank risk profiles. Recognizing that demand for electricity in (virgin, greenfield) markets can take extra time, patient capital is required to finance the original fuel cell systems, the same way long-term "mortgages" leverage the buying power of young professionals. TMI has calculated that the ROI for fuel cells will become competitive for market-based capital if 5 years of social returns can be substituted for financial returns. This financing strategy is different from blended returns.[2] By separating financial and social returns, TMI can compete for investments from two capital sources, traditional financial investors as well as social capitalists.

In retrospect, Lee's vision assumed that the due diligence process would show the philanthropic community how early social capital investments (rather than grants) could offset the high risks and potentially longer payback period, result in large and high-impact social returns, and, over time,

---

[1]PRIs, defined in Section 4944 of the Internal Revenue Code, are investments designed to further a private foundation's exempt purposes and made primarily to accomplish one or more charitable purposes, and no significant purpose of the investment is the production of income or the appreciation of property (Internal Revenue Service, 2012).

[2]*Blended value investing*, a term first coined by Jed Emerson (http://www.blended value.org), is an approach that recognizes that value is nondivisible and naturally incorporates social, ethical, environmental, or charitable elements.

generate financial returns attractive to traditional financial capital. Specifically, the perceived risks would include (1) commercializing a disruptive technology, one that can displace an existing and well-established technology (in this case, fuel cell systems as an alternative to the traditional central power and distribution network model as infrastructure for economic development); (2) funding an energy infrastructure, albeit distributed, despite the strong preference among foundations to fund operations or activities; (3) producing social returns (e.g., production of clean water, refrigeration of vaccines, clean heat for cooking, lights after dark, and recharging battery-dependent devices) only indirectly because they are "enabled" by the infrastructure; (4) using a PRI, an IRS-approved investment instrument for foundations that was unfamiliar to many in the audience; and (5) integrating social and financial capital to capitalize a for-profit social enterprise, which could become self-sustaining over time.

The key lesson learned is that the systems approach may be necessary but not sufficient when communicating complex systems concepts in which the pieces are interdependent and cannot stand alone. Using fuel cells for infrastructure has no intrinsic value unless services are enabled that local farmers and stakeholders value and are willing to buy or work for. Even then, it may take a system that services many users and applications, purchasing electricity based on time of day and demand (similar to large centralized utilities in developed countries), to ensure the rates charged to local farmers and entrepreneurs are affordable.

The lessons from this case study, which have been substantiated in the years since, are (1) disruptive technologies require working demonstrations to be credible to potential investors; (2) PRI from the philanthropic sector is an ideal source of patient capital, which allows time for social enterprises to begin generating financial returns; and (3) early stage investment decisions will be made based on subjective reactions to a vision, rather than quantitative analysis of the business plan. Summarized differently, (early stage) investors don't read, and readers don't invest.

Multicultural Experience, the Borderlands

Both interdisciplinary research and building local and regional economies necessarily involve a variety of discourse communities and their respective communicative conventions, reflecting a range of experiences, backgrounds, expertise, and interests within and across communities. The presence of such diversity is inherently problematic for effective communication, not just because words and phrases and constructions vary but because behind the communication are social and psychological processes by which we define difference and exercise power. This section of the chapter briefly describes these dynamics, the marginalization of those perceived as different by the dominant culture, the special capacities of the marginalized for working with the dynamics of diversity, and the potential value of those capacities for those engaged in transdisciplinary efforts and systems change.

In addition to discourse community literature, the content of this section has been influenced by Craig's (1999) contention that "all communication theories are mutually relevant when addressed to a practical life world" (p. 119). In particular, for the complex problems with which this chapter is concerned, Craig's three categories of sociopsychological, sociocultural, and critical theories of communication are the most immediately relevant sources of "tools to think with" (Harding, 1996) in the analysis of communication strategies among diverse participants within and across discourse communities.

At the sociocultural level, the term *diversity* has many meanings, few explicit. *Diversity* can at once refer to a value, a description of broad membership or participation, or the satisfaction of a social goal. For the purposes of this discussion, diversity is defined as a continually expanding awareness of the dynamics of difference in regard to social power, personal perceptions, and judgments about others. A dynamic definition moves the concept of diversity beyond its typical "head-count typology" often based on superficial features of skin tone, gender, and so forth. Because head counts offer a static set of definitive concepts (Blumer, 1986), they are at once compelling and limiting. They support the comforting illusion that thinking about diversity is both powerful and meaningful by virtue of simply counting the number of people in a set of ethnic or racial or other fixed categories, which mark them as somehow different. The presence of those perceived as different then simplistically equates to success or progress in addressing the value, goal, or inclusion dimensions of diversity. Yet such framing means that we "lock in" to a narrow definition of diversity based on superficial or simplistic distinctions such as language, discourse patterns, ethnicity, gender, or religion and, thus, comfortingly blind ourselves to the power dynamics that swirl around diversity.

The consequence of this kind of thinking is that individuals may become data points, to be understood in terms of a set of fixed characteristics, which are then used to sort them irretrievably into mutually exclusive categories. Then these categories are essentialized: considered as properties (essences) that define the characteristics of that category and remain unchanged (Steinberg & Kincheloe, 2001). When any group measures progress toward diversity based on changes in relative numbers of minorities present, they equate the tally of minorities to the fundamental nature of diversity. Such applications of definitive concepts of diversity and an accompanying essentialization of people into static and simplistic categories blinds group members to the less visible, more complex interactional dynamics of difference, to people's participation in that dynamic, and to the range of positive and negative consequences of the dynamic for the group and its individual members (Delpit, 1995, hooks, 1990, 2003). At work is a quality of "otherness" (hooks, 1990, 2003). Otherness refers to processes of marginalization in which those with more social power make inclusion/exclusion decisions about others with less power, or are unable or unwilling to even acknowledge them (hooks, 1990). In these decisions, perceived differences in communication conventions, experiences, capacities, appearances, preferences, and/or behaviors are devalued because the nature of those differences is unfamiliar or misunderstood (Delpit, 1995). Ironically, therefore, when a group measures progress toward a diversity goal by head counts alone, they actually avoid dealing with critical and more substantive issues of marginalization and privilege in their interactive dynamics.

One recent example in our experience involved a well-intentioned but misguided attempt to improve food safety in a very low-income urban neighborhood. To be sure that residents heated meat to proper temperatures, educators from outside the community widely distributed refrigerator magnets listing acceptable temperature ranges for various kinds of meats. The magnet contained few words and instead offered attractively designed images of a pork crown roast, a whole turkey, a leg of lamb, a large beef roast of some type, and a fish. The problem is that these attractive, full color images showed cuts of meat that few residents could afford. One resident's comment was, "Why would they do that? On a good day, we eat tuna helper—with tuna." Another's sarcastic comment was, "And they give us pictures because they don't think we know how to read." Clearly, the originators of the materials and the intended audience came from different discourse communities. As a result, the effort to educate not only lacked relevance for the daily lives of the audience but falsely presumed their low literacy levels.

At the sociopsychological level, in the process of developing local and regional economies, minority, low-income, and/or inner-city participants are likely to be affected by inclusion/exclusion decisions that restrict access to the social benefits of food and energy or devalue their contributions to creating economic opportunities. Therefore, groups of people building local and regional economies need skills for working across differences, for understanding multiple perspectives.

The development of such skills begins with the combination of the struggle to be oneself (identity), to be part of a community (belonging), and to affect a larger economic or social effort (agency). When this struggle is compounded by the psychological duress that accompanies marginalization, individuals and their discourse communities experience extraordinary additional stress. Ironically, stress experienced by the marginalized can compel the development of a creative set of strategies by which to work with diversity and the accompanying power dynamics (MacDonald & Bernardo, 2005). They share common skills for communicating and approaching problems and opportunities in the face of power exercised against them. Unfortunately, a consequence of otherness is a failure to recognize these strategies and people's skills in deploying them, which, if recognized and supported, could be of broad societal benefit (Astin, 1991; Bowen & Bok, 1998; Delpit, 1995; Freire, 1970; Giroux, 1995, 1997, 2001; Giroux & Giroux, 2004; hooks, 1990, 2000, 2003; Hytche, 1992; Wilson, 1992).

What are these strategies? Recent unpublished research by Ross MacDonald describes the sociopsychological consequences of the sociocultural challenges to identity, belonging, and agency experienced by undergraduate minority students. Based on reports of minority students who were just out of high school and in their first year at university, MacDonald traces these students' progress in developing creative adaptive strategies for working in and across social, communicative, and disciplinary boundaries. This study provides some guidance for other multicultural and transdisciplinary efforts. Discourse analysis of minority students' stories of crossing cultural worlds in their daily lives, and follow-up interviews with those students, revealed three fluid stages of development, each with its own epistemology and discourse markers. The third and most sophisticated stage, hybridity, is depicted in Table 9.1.

Table 9.1	Hybridity as a competence, derived from the unpublished table depicting "borderlands challenges and competencies"

Hybridity: A dynamic state in which multiple identities are creatively organized in a dynamic self, both unified and fluid, characterized by the expansion and transcendence of boundaries in the continual development of self

Discourse markers:

1. Assertions are contextualized, impermanent (e.g., "What we know at this point . . ." or "Our best understanding is . . .").

2. Statements of relationships among seemingly competing truths ("I realized that all three identities were within me").

3. Statements signaling expansive, mutable knowledge ("Seeing culture from [other] points of view will make your view more diverse and enhance your perspective"; "The experiences including different people, cultures, and people's views each shape me as the time passes. Because culture is constantly changing and intertwining, there will never be a finished product and it will never be perfect"; "My parents tried to change the tradition of how a child should be raised but did not succeed; they did in fact improve it").

4. Statements assembling disparate parts ("You yourself cannot comprehend the world, but those around you can help you find those pieces that are missing from your own perspective"; "My Mexican traditions, celebrations, and beliefs are part of what make me who I am. However, there is another culture which I belong to and that is the American culture").

5. Metaphors of change, transformation, adaptability, growth ("I am a chameleon"; "I am a mutt"; "My identity is like a collage. Yes, it has parts and it is also an artistic whole").

(Continued)

Table 9.1	(Continued)

Nature of truth and knowledge:

1. Varies by context, by person, by group.

2. Is an ongoing pursuit of the most complete understanding possible while recognizing uncertainty of truth claims and the ongoing impacts of social power.

3. Seeming contradictions among multiple truths (ambiguities, paradoxes, competing claims) are of great interest but do not necessarily require resolution.

4. Array of knowledge forms are increasingly seen as resources from which one can draw.

5. Power influences claims of truth, but one's experiences with power and the accompanying learning that results may be used to benefit one's inquiry.

6. Recognition that some truths have more discrete boundaries than others.

Inquiry processes:

1. Truth and objectivity are pursuits netting imperfect but useful outcomes.

2. Inquiry is in part a creative process based on consideration of multiple perspectives and multiple levels of meaning.

3. Knowledge of power dynamics advantages inquiry.

Worldview:

1. Characterized by increasing levels of comfort with uncertainty, variability, hybridization, and change.

2. Multiple realities coexist, and complex relationships are possible among them.

3. Emerging belief in ingenuity (the creative power of the human imagination) to address complex problems and develop effective approaches and solutions.

4. One has choices and recognizes that there are limitations to those choices, but one also can create other choices or hybridize existing ones.

SOURCE: © 2004 by Ross B. MacDonald.

Hybridity is a label for a dynamic state of organizing and adapting multiple identities into a coherent sense of self. Hybridity emerges after students struggle with other, ultimately inadequate constructions of self. First, they attempt a singularity, a desire to be definitively one thing by isolating one part of self as one's entire identity; second, they attempt a plural identity, a desire to acknowledge multiple selves while avoiding confusion by isolating each from the other. Both create considerable psychological tension according to students' reports.

Hybridity is an ongoing process and a creative adaptive outcome of the struggle to claim self and be effective in one's world. Hybridity is reflected in one's discourse, one's conceptions of truth and knowledge, inquiry processes, and ultimately one's worldview. In Table 9.1, representative examples of the kinds of student statements that characterized hybridity are shown first, followed by qualities of the student inferred from the analysis, clustered under three additional headings: worldview, nature of truth and knowledge, and inquiry processes.

The concept of hybridity brings to light ways of talking about and organizing transdisciplinary efforts. Imagine, for example, if those seeking systemic change in local economies could adopt practices suggested in Table 9.1. Inflexible assertions can be replaced by summaries of current best understandings. Individual businesses can also be a part of a cluster of businesses. Multiple businesses can both compete and collaborate in the same way as sports teams in an organized league.

If entrepreneurs or transdisciplinary teams were employing discourse structures that promote hybrid thinking, reframing truth and knowledge in less hegemonic terms, and working together based on processes of creating rather than debating who is right and who is wrong, then any transdisciplinary effort, including the creation of local and regional economies, can be characterized by

1. increasing levels of comfort with uncertainty, variability, hybridization, and change;

2. acceptance of the coexistence of multiple realities and of complex relationships among them;

3. support for ingenuity, the creative capacity of the human imagination, to solve problems and create opportunity; and

4. recognition of choices and their consequences.

The research reported in this section of the chapter, in aggregate, suggests that there are those living in the margins who are already skilled at processes for working across personal, discourse community, and disciplinary boundaries. Their capacities and skills can be both a critical part of the process and a valuable resource for finding ways to work effectively together to create business collaborations and transdisciplinary understandings.

Localizing Economies

Community sustainability rests in the capability of its members to meet their basic needs, as in the fuel cell example described above. To secure relevant resources, members participate in economic or other exchanges within business ecosystems extending from their local community to the whole world. The more distant the sources of these resources, the more dependent members are on others for the sustainability of their community. Localization shifts sources of essential resources closer to home and can increase community self-reliance. However, such shifts can disturb prevailing patterns of economic exchange among participants in existing national and global business ecosystems. Application of a localization infrastructure becomes an effective approach to facilitating communications among multiple discourse communities so that participants can successfully repattern these exchanges. Localization opens up significant opportunities for the start-up and scale-up of community-based businesses focused on water, food, energy, waste, clothing, housing, security and safety, health care, education and training, and so on. This opportunity to build business ecosystems that make the gaps between the points of consumption and production as short as possible, however, can disrupt prevailing delivery patterns as communities shift from dependence on global sources for their needs toward increased self-reliance.

How to act on the opportunities that come from localization presents a formidable challenge, because such action requires substantial business development across entire supply chains simultaneously to replace well-established national or global supply chains. Through grants by USDA-Specialty Crop Research Initiative/Regional Partnerships for Innovation and the Fund for Our Economic Future, a coalition of foundations in Northeast Ohio, a project team associated with The Ohio State University began to address this challenge as a way to catalyze economic development in agriculture and related biosciences as an industry cluster in Northeast Ohio. We found that the challenge created a compelling agenda around which to convene multiple discourse communities and offer a framework for action. Furthermore, the exchanges generated creative energy toward import substitution for food, renewable energy and renewable materials associated with agriculture, and entrepreneurship through the emergence of many small but replicable businesses throughout the region.

Our localization infrastructure design centered on three fundamental principles: (1) Participation is open to all, (2) participation matters, and (3) participation starts with consumption. We will consider each in more detail, starting with the first principle—participation is open to all. Within any given community, members have several roles they can play that contribute to the localization of their business ecosystems: (1) At a minimum, they can choose to buy from local sources rather than a global alternative; (2) they can justify their choices to buy local on the basis of value measures other than price alone (e.g., supporting people they know, improved personal health, reduced environmental impact, better safety controls, etc.); (3) they can offer personal testimony about the benefits derived from sourcing products and services from local businesses so as to attract other community members to also buy from those businesses; (4) they can exercise political advocacy to reverse layers of laws, codes, and regulations enacted in support of globalization over previous decades so they are in favor of faster and more pervasive localization; and (5) they can invest a wide range of capitals at their disposal, such as human, built, natural, or financial, in local businesses. These five "portals" provide access for local community members to participate in building the local economy.

The second principle is that participation matters. Much like the earlier examples of complex new technologies or agroecosystems, local economies in their entirety can be difficult for community members to grasp, and so to understand how their day-to-day efforts on the ground make a difference. This challenge can reduce willingness to get involved. Community members will be more forthcoming in their conversations and more committed to translate words into positive action if they know how they fit into the over-all system, see measurable results, and have a satisfying experience in the process. The challenge in a business ecosystem localization process is for community members to find a productive role, defined in ways that make sense to them and their discourse communities but connected well enough across these discourse communities to develop a shared agenda. If successful, the results of their shared agenda could satisfy conventional metrics of business growth, job creation, and increased income, as well as self-reliance metrics unique to a localization infrastructure such as profitable import substitution and the generation, retention, and reinvestment of local wealth.

The challenge to making widespread participation matter is twofold: first, how to make the developing localization infrastructure more tangible and less abstract and, second, how to facilitate ongoing communications across discourse communities that identify opportunities—business ideas and business cases—to start, scale, and sustain local businesses. A virtual landscape, on which plans can be shared online, may provide a guide for action. We have developed a social networking site with a number of views of what is being planned, including (1) a form for members to fill out that documents their business ideas and cases with information that includes business type and location; (2) an online interactive network diagram that illustrates the potential interconnections along supply chains that include documented business ideas and cases in a localized business ecosystem; and (3) a means of contacting individual entrepreneurs who could share the same supply chain.

The project team convened a series of face-to-face stakeholder sessions for entrepreneurs and localization advocates. Sessions discussed ways of participating in a localized business ecosystem and facilitated conversations about the opportunities for business growth that participants saw in their communities. Each session resulted in a wide array of ideas for new and expanded businesses as well as ways to support the launch of these possibilities. Ideas addressed all stages of a localized supply chain such as year-round food production, cottage food processing and street-side food preparation, composting for waste management and heat generation, and logistics, as well as a wide variety of information and decision support services. Participants generated more than 250 business ideas during the course of 11 stakeholder sessions. Discussion groups were set up on the social networking site where participants could easily continue conversations started at the face-to-face sessions, position their business ideas with respect to others, note the geographic proximity of supply chain businesses to each other and the potential for their interconnections, and communicate with those behind the business ideas and cases. The combination of the face-to-face sessions and an online networking infrastructure provided a commons in which community members could experiment with alternative scenarios to localize their business ecosystem and sustain clusters of networked businesses within it.

The third principle is that participation starts with consumption. The prime motivator for community members to participate in building local food systems is a reasonable answer to the question, "How do we increase our self-reliance?" A common agenda of increased self-sufficiency can lead to shared metrics for the degree of self-sufficiency, by which community members can gauge their progress toward localization. From a design perspective, localization means starting with points of consumption to register demand from local markets and working back to points of production at minimum distances. Doing so compresses a number of supply-chain steps, such as preparation, storage, and processing, so they are much closer to the point of consumption. The combination of known demand and higher added value provides a rationale for a flow of local assets and multiple types of capital into business ideas, cases, and plans. Members, representing the full complexity of multiple discourse communities, have the opportunity to become both customers and investors in the localized business ecosystem.

Promoting local economies based on food and energy involves communication strategies that promote and protect the participation of all in processes of open-ended inquiry (as described in approaches to agroecosystems management), nonprescriptive brainstorming, creative (even playful) generation of new ideas, alternative perspectives, questions, and challenges. To do so is not to diverge endlessly but to prevent the preemptive and creativity-stifling convergence of dialogue on ideas brought about by those who have the power to do so. If we instead rely on those who can most easily work across boundaries and understand power dynamics, then they can help crystallize key moments where synergistic insights and suggestions emerge from the open-ended inquiry just described. In that space between preemptive "resolution" on the one hand and the emergence of new ways of thinking and problem solving on the other, we support the full expression of human ingenuity. In this way, communities attempting to organize broad-based collaboration and support for systems change—where the differences among discourse communities and the fluidity of ideas and circumstances threaten to complicate, confuse, and often frustrate participants—can instead generate the creativity and collaboration needed to build local economies based on food and energy and so counterbalance and complement global systems. At stake is nothing less than a more resilient food and energy future for all members of society.

Technology That Improves Communication

We are experimenting with the use of social networking platforms to integrate the business ideas of entrepreneurs into localized business ecosystems along global supply chains. Our goal is to create an adaptive communication infrastructure that attracts, engages, and connects those willing to self-organize and advance such opportunities. Communication researchers are beginning to address how social media influences systems change, particularly the recent impact of social media on widespread political change (Howard & Parks, 2012). At least in opinion pieces, the scientific community is embracing the opportunities for resolving differences among discourse communities provided by social media, which reinforces our commitment to experimentation with social networking technology to accelerate this progress. We use it because it is a means of reaching across communities in a relatively new and common form, used both by scientists and the masses (Van Eperen & Marincola, 2011). The relatively open and egalitarian form of communication that takes place through social media can open new opportunities for engaging in open discourse, including between scientists, academics, or engineers and the general public (Regenberg, 2010).

Asset inventory mapping provides one common framework for connecting the capacities of multiple communities around opportunities. Because open-source online tools provide more equitable access, we are designing a set of steps toward collaboration that works for a diverse range of discourse communities. As part of this development, we are working with minority entrepreneurs and their unique experience in working outside of the dominant capital and market structures. A measure of success for the online infrastructure we are developing would be whether it is useful regardless of the existing capacity, available capital, or norms of social organization in communities.

The same principles of connection and spanning of discourse communities may be applicable in the development and commercialization of new technology, such as the solid-state fuel cells being commercialized by TMI.[3] Fuel cells have the capacity to meet demands for primary power beyond the physical and economic limitations of the existing utility grid. Thus, particularly in remote rural areas worldwide where electrical needs are modest and fuels such as vegetable oil or bio-gas are locally available, this technology has the potential to greatly improve the livelihoods of rural people by enabling high-impact services such as pumping and purification of water for drinking and sanitation, LED lights for reading, support of health care teams, and power-dependent instruments, and, perhaps most important, to support growing communications infrastructure. The key to

---

[3]See http://www.AnywherEnergy.com.

successfully introducing and sustaining such technology, however, is to fit it within the social norms of the people using it, creating a sense of ownership and a commitment to care for, use, adapt, and replicate. Even if funding for capital equipment is provided by philanthropic organizations to make the technology quickly available, responsibility for its installation, ongoing operation, maintenance, and replacement must rest locally. Participation of people like village elders and leaders of nongovernmental organizations is absolutely critical. Such participation helps avoid the problem of misaligning response with community realities, as described in the refrigerator magnet story, and instead aligns innovations and how they are framed with the stated needs and concerns of the community the innovation is intended to benefit. Similarly, getting an energy infrastructure to scale requires widespread communication of the value of on-site energy for the individual family (e.g., improved productivity in the field or a better quality of life in the household). The tipping point is when measureable market demands are large enough to replace patient money from philanthropic sources with private investments. We believe that, despite the superficial differences between these off-grid experiences and the use of social media described earlier, there are common conceptual constructs, principles of communication, and evolutions of collaboration that can be extracted from both case studies.

Where the Opportunities Lie

Some of the challenges we are working on can be resolved by known communication techniques, such as the use of stories, common experience, and concrete examples as a starting point for communication. We have discovered three additional areas of opportunity for meeting the challenges of these cross-disciplinary and cross-cultural efforts as a result of our common experience. First, common language can sometimes be found in the form of methodologies that describe and mechanistically explain various systems and scenarios. For example, techniques of social network analysis can be applied to business ecosystems, supply chain networks, and ecological food webs, thus providing a unique set of common analytical techniques across a wide range of disciplines and phenomena related to a complex system. A second opportunity for uniting discourse communities is through a focus on basic common needs such as food and energy, with practical examples that are common elements of everyday life for everyone. Finally, by recognizing that different communities tend to have specific capacities and skills that allow them to lead in particular ways, such as multicultural experience leading to interdisciplinary inquiry and collaborative leadership, we can position the presence of diversity as a guiding intellectual and moral force for cross-disciplinary and cross-cultural discourse.

Take-Home Messages

- Interpersonal stories and examples that focus on common experiences can communicate across discourse communities more effectively than detailed logical arguments.
- One instance of such examples is live demonstrations of innovations, such as stand-alone fuel cells, that allow communities to see what the innovation is and decide for themselves what its benefits are and how it can be described favorably to others.
- Focusing on basic human needs at the level of individual families, such as food, health, and energy, helps various discourse communities understand a system context, see that they are included in that system, and relate it to their own lives.
- Technology that can be applied in a wide range of social, economic, biological, and physical fields can be an effective tool for bridging discourse communities and levels of expertise from the general public to disciplinary specialists. For example, geographic information systems can layer multiple kinds of data from many fields in intuitively understandable maps.
- Social networking technology can increase open and equitable discourse that empowers a wider range of participants to share both the benefits and challenges of systems change—for example, in building local economies that meet basic human needs.

References

An, L. (2012). Modeling human decisions in coupled human and natural systems: Review of agent-based models. *Ecological Modelling, 229*, 25–36.

Ashton, W. (2008). Understanding the organization of industrial ecosystems: A social network approach. *Journal of Industrial Ecology, 12*(1), 34–51.

Astin, A. W. (1991). *Assessment for excellence: The philosophy and practice of assessment and evaluation in higher education.* New York: MacMillan.

Bizzell, P. (1994). Discourse community. In A. Purves (Ed.), *Encyclopedia of English studies and language arts* (pp. 395–397). New York: Scholastic.

Blumer, H. (1986). Symbolic interactionism: Perspective and method. Berkeley: University of California Press.

Bode, N. W. F., Wood, A. J., & Franks, D. W. (2011). Social networks and models for collective motion in animals. *Behavioral Ecology and Sociobiology, 65*(2), 117–130.

Boody, G., Vondracek, B., Andow, D. A., Krinke, M., Westra, J., Zimmerman, J., et al. (2005). Multifunctional agriculture in the United States. *Bioscience, 55*(1), 27–38.

Bowen, W. G., & Bok, D. (1998). *The shape of the river: Long-term consequences of considering race in college and university admissions.* Princeton, NJ: Princeton University Press.

Cohen, B. (2006). Sustainable valley entrepreneurial ecosystems. *Business Strategy and the Environment, 15*(1), 1–14. doi:10.1002/bse.428

Conway, G. R. (1985). Agroecosystem analysis. *Agricultural Administration, 20*(1), 31–55.

Conway, G. R. (1987). The properties of agroecosystems. *Agricultural Systems, 24*(2), 95–117.

Craig, R. T. (1999). Communication theory as a field. *Communication Theory, 9*(2), 119–161.

Daniels, S. E., & Walker, G. B. (1996). Collaborative learning: Improving public deliberation in ecosystem-based management. *Environmental Impact Assessment Review, 16*, 71–102.

Delpit, L. (1995). *Other people's children: Cultural conflict in the classroom.* New York: New Press.

Ernstson, H., Sörlin, S., & Elmqvist, T. (2008). Social movements and ecosystem services: The role of social network structure in protecting and managing urban green areas in Stockholm. *Ecology & Society, 13*(2), 1–27.

Freire, P. (1970). *Pedagogy of the oppressed.* New York: Continuum.

Garcia-Barrios, L. E., Speelman, E. N., & Pimm, M. S. (2008). An educational simulation tool for negotiating sustainable natural resource management strategies among stakeholders with conflicting interests. *Ecological Modelling, 210*(1–2), 115–126.

Gevers, J., Hoye, T. T., Topping, C. J., Glemnitz, M., & Schroeder, B. (2011). Biodiversity and the mitigation of climate change through bioenergy: Impacts of increased maize cultivation on farmland wildlife. *Global Change Biology Bioenergy, 3*(6), 472–482.

Giroux, H. A. (1995). *Border crossings: Cultural workers and the politics of education.* New York: Routledge.

Giroux, H. A. (1997). *Pedagogy and politics of hope: Theory, culture, and schooling: A critical reader.* Boulder, CO: Westview Press.

Giroux, H. A. (2001). *Theory and resistance in education: Towards a pedagogy for the opposition* (Rev. & Exp. ed.). Westport, CT: Greenwood.

Giroux, H. A., & Giroux, S. S. (2004). *Take back higher education: Race, youth, and the crisis of democracy in the post-civil rights era.* New York: Palgrave Macmillan.

Harding, S. (1996). Science is "good to think with." In A. Ross (Ed.), *Science wars* (pp. 16–28). Durham, NC: Duke University Press.

hooks, b. (1990). *Yearning: Race, gender, and cultural politics.* Boston: South End Press.

hooks, b. (2000). *Where we stand: Class matters.* New York: Routledge.

hooks, b. (2003). *Teaching community: A pedagogy of hope.* New York: Routledge.

Howard, P. N., & Parks, M. R. (2012). Social media and political change: Capacity, constraint, and consequence. *Journal of Communication, 62*(2), 359–362.

Hytche, W. P. (1992). Educating a culturally diverse professional work force for the agricultural, food, and natural resource system. In *Agriculture and the undergraduate: Proceedings* (sponsored by the Agricultural Research Council; pp. 86–94). Washington, DC: National Academy Press.

Internal Revenue Service. (2012, May 21). *Notice of proposed rulemaking examples of program-related investments.* Retrieved from http://www.irs.gov/irb/2012-21_IRB/ar11.html

Johnson, J. C., Luczkovich, J. J., Borgatti, S. P., & Snijders, T. A. B. (2009). Using social network analysis tools in ecology: Markov process transition models applied to the seasonal trophic network dynamics of the Chesapeake Bay. *Ecological Modelling, 220*(22), 3133–3140.

Kempener, R., Beck, J., & Petrie, J. (2009). Design and analysis of bioenergy networks. *Journal of Industrial Ecology, 13*(2), 284–305.

Kurz, W. A., Beukema, S. J., Klenner, W., Greenough, J. A., Robinson, D. C. E., Sharpe, A. D., et al. (2000). TELSA: The tool for exploratory landscape scenario analyses. *Computers and Electronics in Agriculture, 27*(1–3), 227–242.

Lee, B. P. (2006). Fuel cell technology and for-profit business solutions serving public health problems: Unlikely partners? In D. A. Barroso (Ed.), *Finding philanthropy's new sweet spot: Powerful and innovative ideas for grantmakers, investors, and nonprofits* (pp. 34–44). Stanford, CA: Stanford Social Innovation Review.

Liu, G. Y., Yang, Z. F., Chen, B., & Zhang, Y. (2011). Ecological network determination of sectoral linkages, utility relations and structural characteristics on urban ecological economic system. *Ecological Modelling, 222*(15), 2825–2834.

MacDonald, R., & Bernardo, M. (2005). Reconceptualizing diversity in higher education: The borderlands research program. *Journal of Developmental Education, 29*(1), 22–31.

McLane, A. J., Semeniuk, C., McDermid, G. J., & Marceau, D. J. (2011). The role of agent-based models in wildlife ecology and management. *Ecological Modelling, 222*(8), 1544–1556.

Neck, H. M., Meyer, G. D., Cohen, B., & Corbett, A. C. (2004). An entrepreneurial system view of new venture creation. *Journal of Small Business Management, 42*(2), 190–208.

Okey, B. W. (1996). Systems approaches and properties, and agroecosystem health. *Journal of Environmental Management, 48*(2), 187–199.

Parkes, M., & Panelli, R. (2001). Integrating catchment, ecosystems and community health: The value of participatory action research. *Ecosystem Health, 7*(2), 85–106.

Patil, G. P., Brooks, R. P., Myers, W. L., Rapport, D. J., & Taillie, C. (2001). Ecosystem health and its measurement at landscape scale: Toward the next generation of quantitative assessments. *Ecosystem Health, 7*(4), 307–316.

Pogner, K. H. (2003). Writing in the discourse theory of engineering. *Journal of Pragmatics, 35*(6), 855–867.

Pogner, K. H. (2005). *Discourse communities and communities of practice: On the social context of text and knowledge production in the workplace.* Paper presented at the 21st EGOS Colloquium, Freie Universität Berlin. Retrieved September 14, 2012, from http://openarchive.cbs.dk/bitstream/handle/10398/7320/discourse%20communities.pdf?sequence=1

Rao, N. H., & Rogers, P. P. (2006). Assessment of agricultural sustainability. *Current Science, 91*(4), 438–448.

Regenberg, A. C. (2010). Tweeting science and ethics: Social media as a tool for constructive public engagement. *American Journal of Bioethics, 10*(5), 30–31.

Roberts, J. (2006). Limits to communities of practice. *Journal of Management Studies, 43*(3), 623–639.

Saaty, T. L. (1992). A natural way to make momentous decisions. *Journal of Scientific & Industrial Research, 51*(8–9), 561–571.

Saaty, T. L. (1994). Highlights and critical-points in the theory and application of the analytic hierarchy process. *European Journal of Operational Research, 74*(3), 426–447.

Saaty, T. L., & Sodenkamp, M. (2010). The analytic hierarchy and analytic network measurement processes: The measurement of intangibles decision making under benefits, opportunities, costs and risks. *Handbook of Multicriteria Analysis, 103,* 91–166.

Spiegel, J. M., Bonet, M., Yassi, A., Molina, E., Concepcion, M., & Mas, P. (2001). Developing ecosystem health indicators in Centro Habana: A community-based approach. *Ecosystem Health, 7*(1), 15–26.

Steinberg, S. R., & Kincheloe, J. L. (2001). Setting the context for critical multi/ interculturalism: The power blogs of class elitism, white supremacy, and patriarchy. In S. R. Steinberg (Ed.), *Multi/intercultural conversations: A reader.* New York: Peter Lang.

Suter, G. W. (1993). A critique of ecosystem health concepts and indexes. *Environmental Toxicology and Chemistry, 12*(9), 1533–1539.

Topping, C. J. (2011). Evaluation of wildlife management through organic farming. *Ecological Engineering, 37*(12), 2009–2017.

U.N. Advisory Group on Energy and Climate Change. (2010, April 28). *Energy for a sustainable future: The secretary-general's Advisory Group on Energy and Climate Change (AGECC) summary report and recommendations.* Retrieved September 30, 2012, from http://www.un.org/wcm/webdav/site/climatechange/ shared/Documents/AGECC%20summary%20report%5B1%5D.pdf

United Nations Foundation. (2012, June). Energy access practitioner network: Towards achieving universal energy access by 2030. Washington, DC: Author. Retrieved from http://www.sustainableenergyforall.org/images/content/ FINAL%20ESG%20ALL.pdf

Vadrevu, K. P., Cardina, J., Hitzhusen, F., Bayoh, I., Moore, R., Parker, J., et al. (2008). Case study of an integrated framework for quantifying agroecosystem health. *Ecosystems, 11*(2), 283–306.

Valente, M. (2010). Demystifying the struggles of private sector paradigmatic change: Business as an agent in a complex adaptive system. *Business & Society, 49*(3), 439–476.

Van Eperen, L., & Marincola, F. M. (2011). How scientists use social media to communicate their research. *Journal of Translational Medicine, 9,* 199.

Waltner-Toews, D. (1994). The impact of agriculture on ecosystem health [Special issue]. *Medecine Veterinaire du Quebec, 53*–55.

Waltner-Toews, D. (1996). Ecosystem health: A framework for implementing sustainability in agriculture. *Bioscience, 46*(9), 686–689.

Wicklum, D., & Davies, R. W. (1995). Ecosystem health and integrity. *Canadian Journal of Botany, 73*(7), 997–1000.

Wilcox, B. A. (2001). Ecosystem health in practice: Emerging areas of application in environment and human health. *Ecosystem Health, 7*(4), 317–325.

Wilson, E. P. (1992). Striving toward cultural diversity. In *Agriculture and the undergraduate: Proceedings* (Sponsored by the Agricultural Research Council; pp. 165–172). Washington, DC: National Academy Press.

Xu, W., & Mage, J. A. (2001). A review of concepts and criteria for assessing agroecosystem health including a preliminary case study of southern Ontario. *Agriculture Ecosystems & Environment, 83*(3), 215–233.

Yiridoe, E. K., & Weersink, A. (1997). A review and evaluation of agroecosystem health analysis: The role of economics. *Agricultural Systems, 55*(4), 601–626.

Conceptual Barriers to Interdisciplinary Communication

When Does Ambiguity Matter?[1]

◆ Paul E. Griffiths and Karola Stotz

We examine three cases in which different conceptualizations of the same object of research have existed alongside one another. The first of these cases features the Mendelian and molecular identities of the gene. We show that these identities exist alongside one another in genetics and play complementary roles. In this case, ambiguity in a key theoretical construct has not led to misunderstanding but has promoted a productive slippage of meaning. We argue that is because of the creation of "boundary objects" (Star & Griesemer, 1989) shared between these different research traditions. Boundary objects, such as genetic loci and specific sequences of DNA nucleotides, contain features that play roles in two different scientific contexts and therefore facilitate the communication

[1]This research was supported under Australian Research Council's Discovery Projects funding scheme (project number DP0878650). Portions of the text are based on a forthcoming book (Griffiths & Stotz, 2013).

between them, despite them having different, or at least only partially over-lapping, meanings in both fields. In our second case, we contrast two ways of thinking about genes found in different fields studying the genetic basis of behavior. We show that this has historically been a barrier to communication between those fields but that recent technical developments have promoted better communication. We argue that those developments have done so by creating boundary objects that facilitate this communication. Our third case looks at some disputes about behavioral development centered on the ambiguous and contested concept of innateness. We offer some tentative thoughts on how the intractability of these debates may reflect a paucity of functional boundary objects. In the first two of the three case studies, we draw extensively on arguments developed in our forthcoming book *Genetics and Philosophy* (Griffiths & Stotz, 2013), arguments that we can reproduce only in a much abbreviated form. We use the conclusions drawn there to reflect on the question of interdisciplinary communication. For those interested in the full arguments for these conclusions, we recommend consulting the book.

Mendelian and Molecular Genetics

In this section, we outline the Mendelian and molecular conceptions of the gene and show that they coexist in biology even today. The term *gene* is understood in two different ways by investigators, sometimes even by the same investigator at different points in a single research project. The flexibility of the gene concept, which allowed the coexistence of multiple conceptualisations of the gene, has generally been productive rather than problematic, as many authors have noted (Beurton, Falk, & Rheinberger, 2000; Falk, 1984, 1986; Griffiths & Stotz, 2013; Stanford & Kitcher, 2000; Waters, 1994). Our discussion illuminates how such slippage of meaning plays a productive role.

The Mendelian Gene and the Molecular Gene

The gene of classical Mendelian genetics—the research tradition that flourished in the first half of the 20th century, before the advent of molecular biology—had a very distinctive status. It was not an observable entity, but it was more than an unobservable entity postulated to explain the data. The gene was a tool for predicting and explaining the outcome of breeding one organism with another. Mendelian genetics calculates the results of breeding organisms using their genotypes, not merely their phenotypes. The relationship between parent and offspring phenotypes is mediated by relationships between genotypes. So the gene was not merely postulated to explain the success of Mendelian genetics; it played a key role in that successful scientific activity.

Geneticists naturally hoped that the gene would be shown to exist as a physical reality within the cells of the organism. But the special role of the gene in the practice of Mendelian genetics meant that the gene would remain an important and legitimate idea even if this did not work out. The leading classical geneticist T. H. Morgan remarked in his Nobel Prize acceptance speech, "At the level at which the genetic experiments lie, it does not make the slightest difference whether the gene is a hypothetical unit, or whether the gene is a material particle" (Morgan, 1934). One could interpret Morgan this way: If genes are not material particles, then they must be something like centres of mass in physics. When two bodies act on one another, for example by being at the two ends of a lever, their masses are distributed throughout each body. But when we calculate how the bodies will affect one another, the whole mass is assigned to a single, infinitesimal point—the centre of mass. The centre of mass is not a material particle, but every object nevertheless has a centre of mass. In the same way, even if there were no straightforward physical particles corresponding to genes, they would still exist in the calculus of heredity.

The historian of genetics Raphael Falk (1984, 2009) has summed up this situation by saying that the gene of classical Mendelian genetics had two separate "identities." One identity was as a hypothetical material entity, and some genetic research was directed to confirming the existence of these entities and finding out more about them. But the gene had a second, and more important, identity as an instrument used to do biology. The future development of genetics was the result of the interplay between these two identities.

The practice of classical genetics eventually led to the emergence of a new, molecular conception of the gene. This occurred because in the decades after the discovery of DNA the material identity of the gene became the most prominent, not because of dissatisfaction with the Mendelian paradigm. Rather, the Mendelian paradigm—the core ideas of Mendelian genetics and the practice of genetic analysis—was not overthrown but persists even today.

The rise of molecular biology was associated with a new conception of the gene as a distinctive molecular structure in the DNA sequence. This is the gene presented in biology textbooks today. Each gene has a "promoter region" that acts as a signal to the machinery that transcribes the DNA into RNA. This is followed by an "open reading frame," a series of nucleotides that correspond to the series of RNA codons that specify the amino acids in a protein, plus a "start codon" and a "stop codon" that act as signals to the respective machinery that transcribes the DNA into RNA and translates the RNA into protein. The gene of molecular biology is the linear image of a gene product in the DNA.[2] The linear correspondence between DNA and its products was at the heart of the vision of the gene advanced by Francis Crick as early as 1958, but its epistemological significance was brought to philosophical attention by C. Kenneth Waters (1994). Linear correspondences between nucleic acid sequences and other molecules are fundamental to

---

[2] We owe this expression to Rob D. Knight.

biologists' ability to identify and manipulate those molecules. That molecular genes are sequences that have a linear correspondence to their products (via DNA replication, DNA transcription, and RNA translation) is the key to the practical utility of the molecular gene concept in research and in biotechnology. This is true despite the extent to which transcriptional and posttranscriptional processes can distort this relationship in multicellular organisms (Djebali, Davis, et al., 2012; Djebali, Lagarde, et al., 2012; Gerstein et al., 2007; Griffiths & Stotz, 2013).

The Explanatory Roles of Genes in the Two Research Traditions

The emergence of the classical molecular gene appears to be a successful example of the research strategy of identifying a causal role and seeking the concrete occupant of that role. In this case, the role was that of the Mendelian gene, something whose distinctive pattern of transmission from one generation to the next explains the phenomena of heredity. We might suppose that the occupant of that role is the molecular gene—an open reading frame with an adjacent promoter region. But this turns out to be too simple.

The role-occupant framework (Lewis, 1966) starts from the observation that some concepts can be analysed in terms of the causes and effects of the thing being conceptualised, or its "causal role." Lightning was originally known only as something that causes bright flashes in the sky during thunderstorms and whose destructive effects we see as lightning strikes. When it was shown that the flashes and destructive strikes are the effects of atmospheric electrostatic discharges, it followed necessarily that lightning is atmospheric electrostatic discharge. Now, the gene was certainly originally identified by the causal role it played—it was the cause of Mendelian patterns of inheritance. Later, it was discovered that this causal role was played by pieces of DNA passing from parent to offspring. So it follows necessarily that these pieces of DNA are Mendelian genes.

This framework seems at first glance to provide a good model of what happened in the transition from Mendelian to molecular genetics: With the unravelling of the genetic code and of the basic processes of transcription and translation in the 1960s, the two identities of the gene in classical genetics, the instrumental Mendelian and the hypothetical material, converged on a single identity—the molecular gene. Looked at more closely, however, the theoretical role of the gene had been significantly revised so as to take account of findings about the material gene.

In classical Mendelian genetics, the gene played three theoretical roles. It was the unit of mutation—changes in genes give rise to new, mutant alleles[3]

---

[3]The "alleles" of a gene are the different forms of a single gene. In diploid organisms such as humans, each individual has two copies of each gene. These may be the same allele or different alleles.

of the same gene. It was also the unit of recombination. Crossover between chromosomes either separates genes that were previously linked or links genes that were previously inherited independently. Finally, the gene was the unit of function. The genotype that interacts with the environment to produce the phenotype is a collection of genes, and any effect of genotype on phenotype can be traced back to some gene or combination of genes. It was natural to project these ideas from Mendelian genetics onto the gene as a hypothetical material entity and to expect that the material gene would be a unit of mutation, of recombination, and of genetic function. But the new, molecular concept of the gene that emerged in the 1960s did not live up to that expectation.

A mutation is something that can happen to any stretch of the DNA molecule, not only to genetically meaningful units such as molecular genes. Recombination is a highly regulated process involving chromosomes and an accompanying cast of enzymes. In analysing this process, there is no need to divide the DNA itself into "units of recombination": Recombination can occur within a molecular gene so that one part of one allele is recombined with the complementary part from its sister allele, as well as occurring between whole alleles, and it can occur between segments of DNA that are not molecular genes at all. So the new conception of the molecular gene was one in which the gene is only the unit of function and not the unit of mutation or recombination, and with a slightly changed function at that.

The concept of the molecular gene applies only to sequences that have a structure something like that described above and that act as the template for making a gene product. But in humans, for example, only 1% to 2% of the DNA consists of structures used to make proteins. There are many segments of chromosome that have some effect on the phenotype and hence behave as Mendelian alleles but do not count as genes under the new molecular conception. Any difference in the sequence of DNA that causes a difference in phenotype will function as a Mendelian allele, but it need not be an allele of any molecular gene.

It would be foolish to redefine *allele* so as to restrict the term to alleles of molecular genes, because the fact that these other sequences are behaving as Mendelian alleles is not something to gloss over. If there is an inherited cause of phenotypic differences, we want to know about it! Conversely, the molecular gene cannot be redefined as any piece of DNA that can act as a Mendelian gene, because this would render it unsuitable for the purpose for which it is used in molecular biology—namely, to identify sequences that have a linear correspondence to the biomolecules made from the DNA.

These observations would be a mere quibble if as a matter of fact the pieces of DNA picked out by the instrumental, Mendelian conception of the gene were always sequences that are also genes according to the molecular conception of the gene. But this is not the case. There are now known to be many other ways DNA sequences can play a role in the development of phenotypes besides acting as linear templates for the synthesis of biomolecules. When one of these other pieces of DNA comes in two or more forms with different phenotypic effects, they will behave as Mendelian alleles and can be investigated via genetic analysis. Even if they are not called genes, they are treated as (Mendelian) genes, and sometimes they *are* called genes but only when speaking in an appropriate context. Such is the flexibility of scientific language. For example, when a medical geneticist is seeking the "genes for" a disorder, she is looking for Mendelian alleles: sections of chromosome whose inheritance explains the phenotypic differences observed in patients. Translated into molecular terms, these sequences may turn out not to be molecular genes but segments of DNA that fulfil other, regulatory functions.

A clear example of the continuing coexistence of the Mendelian and molecular identities of the gene comes from studies of the gene *Lmbr1* in the mouse and its homologue[4] on human chromosome seven (Lettice et al., 2002). This locus is known to house an allele that produces abnormal limb development in both mice and humans. But further molecular analysis of that locus shows that the molecular gene within which the mutation is located is not a molecular gene that plays a role in the development of these abnormalities. Instead, there is a sequence embedded in a noncoding stretch within that gene that acts to regulate the gene "*sonic hedgehog*" (*shh*). The gene *shh* is located around a million DNA nucleotides away on the same chromosome and is known to be important in limb development. The regulatory sequence at the original locus is called an "enhancer" in molecular genetics, not a gene, since it does not code for a product. It is not a functional component of the molecular gene within which it is physically located, since this mutation doesn't affect the product of that gene or the posttranscriptional processing of that product. But this regulatory sequence is the Mendelian allele for the abnormal limb development. Conversely, *shh* is a paradigmatic molecular gene, but there exists no allele of *shh* that causes (is the Mendelian allele for) this kind of abnormal limb development. Instead, in one experimental context—that of hunting for the mutation responsible for the phenotype—the idea of gene assumes its Mendelian identity, while in the other context—that of analysing the DNA sequence— the idea of gene assumes its molecular identity. In many cases, these two identities of the gene converge on the same sequence of DNA, but sometimes they do not (for a more extended analysis of this issue, see Weber, 2005, pp. 215–233).

So the relationship between Mendelian and molecular conceptions of the gene defies at least the simplest form of role-occupant analysis (for a more adequate treatment, see Stanford & Kitcher, 2000). Biologists were looking for the physical occupant of the role of the Mendelian gene. But what they found, and what molecular geneticists call a gene, occupies only part of that role, and the original role remains important, too. This complex situation helps explain the long-running controversy in philosophy of science about

---

[4]The two genes are derived from a common ancestor, rather than evolved independently.

whether Mendelian genetics has been reduced to molecular biology (for a summary of this debate, see Schaffner, 1993; and for a similar diagnosis, Weber, 2005). One clear sense in which Mendelian genetics does not reduce to molecular genetics is that it continues to exist alongside molecular genetics as another, complementary way of thinking about DNA. Molecular biology enriched genetics with a new way of thinking about genes, and biologists today have two valid ways of thinking about genes. They move smoothly between these two contextually activated representations of genes as they move from one research context to another (Griffiths & Stotz, 2013).

The Boundary Objects Shared by Mendelian and Molecular Genetics

Biologists seem able to move smoothly between these two representations according to the context in which they find themselves. We suggest that this is possible because of the rich variety of "boundary objects" (Star & Griesemer, 1989) that exist in both contexts. Star and Griesemer introduce the idea of boundary objects as follows:

> Boundary objects are objects which are both plastic enough to adapt to local needs and constraints of the several parties employing them, yet robust enough to maintain a common identity across sites. They are weakly structured in common use, and become strongly structured in individual-site use. They may be abstract or concrete. They have different meanings in different social worlds but their structure is common enough to more than one world to make them recognizable, a means of translation. The creation and management of boundary objects is key in developing and maintaining coherence across intersecting social worlds. (p. 393)

Star and Griesemer's (1989) paper outlines an approach to case studies in history of science that explains how scientists manage to cooperate despite heterogeneity in their scientific and social fields. In their original case study, they analysed the collaboration between professionals, administrators, patrons, and amateurs connected to a research natural history museum. Here, we are interested in communication between different areas of genetics (in the next two sections, we will look at two further examples of communication between scientists from different research traditions). The boundary objects that feature in genetics may be abstract, such as genetic loci, or concrete, such as a specific mutant strain of *Drosophila* that can pass from one lab to another. In either case, these boundary objects exist in both research contexts and therefore allow the integration of research conducted with different conceptualizations of the object of that research.

A good example of boundary objects in genetics is the "loci" that genes occupy on chromosomes. Genetic loci are like the latitude and longitude system used in terrestrial navigation, a highly stable practice of identifying location supported by widely agreed-on procedures that are updated as better methods become available. The investigations into limb abnormalities described previously involved the locus 7q36, the 36th band from the centromere on the long arm (q) of chromosome 7. The staining procedures needed to make such bands on the chromosome visible were historically important, but the regions named in this way can now be accessed via genome databases containing a standardized representation of the actual DNA sequence. Loci are thus not tied to any one experimental technique. The same loci are used in both Mendelian and molecular genetics. In an instructive exercise, Marcel Weber (2005, pp. 215–233) compared descriptions of certain loci in *Drosophila* made using classical genetic methods and later descriptions of the same loci made using molecular methods. These descriptions often agree in the number of genes at the locus and their roles, but sometimes they do not, something we have already shown in our example of limb abnormalities. But, however complex the relationship between the genes identified by Mendelian methods and those identified by molecular methods, the shared loci that both disciplines recognise provide common ground—almost literally—on which to explore and resolve those differences.

In this section, we have described two conceptions of the gene that play a role in contemporary biology. A third will be described in the next section, and we have described yet others elsewhere (Griffiths & Stotz, 2007, 2013). We suggest that the availability of well-characterized lines of organisms, well-characterized mutations, practices of chromosome mapping, and, later on, the availability of DNA sequence data—all of which can act as "boundary objects" between different research contexts—explains how genetics has been so successful with such a multifaceted and contextual concept as that of the gene at its heart.

Genes and Behavior

In this section, we will introduce another ambiguity in the concept of the gene but one that has given rise to greater problems for interdisciplinary communication. We will suggest that this was due to an inability to create boundary objects that would have allowed communication without a shared conceptualisation of the gene, a situation that is now changing.

The Mendelian and the Abstract Developmental Gene

There are two very different ways responsibility for a behavioral difference can be sheeted home to a genetic difference. These involve two identities of the gene, the familiar Mendelian allele and another identity that we call the "abstract developmental gene." The ambiguities introduced by these different ways of thinking about genes, and the different conceptions of gene action that accompany them, have led to severe miscommunication between scientists from different disciplines that study the genetic basis of behavior.

Traditional behavioral genetics was the application of Mendelian genetic analysis and quantitative genetics to behavioral phenotypes. In human behavioral genetics, quantitative genetic methods predominated. Quantitative genetics was developed to integrate Mendelian genetics with statistical methods for studying heredity. The most familiar result of quantitative genetics is a figure for the *heritability* of a phenotypic trait. The heritability of a trait is used to estimate the extent to which the phenotypic differences between individuals in a population can be explained by genetic differences between those individuals. In human behavioral genetics, where it is not possible to conduct controlled breeding experiments, heritabilities are inferred from observations of the correlations between relatives. For example, one kind of "twin study" uses the correlations between monozygotic twin pairs, who share all their genes (meaning all their Mendelian alleles), and dizygotic twin pairs, who share only half their genes. If the monozygotic twins resemble each other more closely than do the dizygotic twins, then, all other things being equal, this can be attributed to their greater proportion of shared genes.

Behavior genetics has always been controversial because of concerns about its social and political implications. This has tended to draw attention away from more substantial scientific criticisms, but in fact there have been many of these. Some of the strongest criticism of behavioral genetics has come from scientists who study the development of behavior, a field known as developmental psychobiology. Developmental psychobiologists have historically been scathing about quantitative genetic approaches, arguing that they do not yield any genuine scientific insight into the genetic basis of behavior (Griffiths & Tabery, 2008; Tabery & Griffiths, 2010).

Behavior geneticists, and quantitative geneticists more generally, conceptualize genes as Mendelian alleles. While they have not typically identified specific Mendelian alleles for complex human behaviors, their study designs and statistical models deal with the consequences of differences in the proportion of shared Mendelian alleles between individuals. In contrast, developmental psychobiologists conceptualize genes as determinants of the value of a developmental variable in the context of a larger system (we will refer to these as "abstract developmental genes"). In many instances, we think that both sides would pick out the same specific DNA sequence elements if they had sufficient information about the molecular basis of a trait. But until very recently, that information has not been available. Genes have existed for both communities only in the conceptual foundations of their methods, rather than being grounded in specific sequences of DNA that could have functioned as boundary objects that would have allowed the two communities to transcend their different ways of thinking about "genes."

Traditional work in developmental psychobiology investigates how normal development at each stage of the life cycle depends on the interaction of the organism with specific features of the environment. This work typically involved experimentation under controlled conditions rather than the observational analysis of natural populations. Recent work in developmental psychobiology has begun to link factors in these models to the expression of specific sequences in the genome. However, for most of the history of this research tradition, it has not been possible to experimentally manipulate genetic factors of a developmental system in the same way as environmental factors. Although developmental psychobiologists conceived of genes as mechanistic causes of development, the lack of direct access to these causes led them to appear in an extremely abstract form, as the hypothesized determinants of the value of certain parameters or variables in the model.

This "abstract developmental" conception of the gene can be traced back to the attempts of embryologists to integrate genetics into their discipline in the 1930s. If it is assumed that the biochemical processes that construct phenotypes are the result of gene action, then some or all of the factors in a developmental model can be labelled as "genes." Julian Huxley (1932/1972) speaks of "rate genes" determining the value of variables in his models of relative growth. These hypothetical genes have no empirical foundation besides the model itself. The same abstract conception of the gene features in the famous models of "developmental canalization" due to C. H. Waddington (1940, 1957).

The Explanatory Roles of Genes in the Two Research Traditions

Mendelian alleles and abstract developmental genes are two legitimate ways to think about DNA sequences in two very different research contexts. But the explanatory roles the "gene" plays in those two contexts are very different. An abstract developmental gene can explain a phenotype only via the mediation of many other developmental factors. In contrast, the Mendelian allele for a phenotypic difference explains that difference without the need for explicit reference to other developmental factors. The abstract developmental gene has no identity apart from its role in a developmental model. In a model intended as an actual characterization of a developmental process, the introduction of specific "genes" is justified by reference to the ability of the model as a whole to explain the effects of manipulations of its variables. So explaining the presence of a phenotype by reference to the presence of a gene means drawing attention to how that genetic factor interacts with the other factors. The same is true of phenotypic differences, which are explained by reference to how a genetic difference ramifies through the system (Griffiths & Tabery, 2008; Tabery & Griffiths, 2010). Developmental psychobiologists seek to "explain" phenotypes in the sense characterised by mechanist theories of explanation in the philosophy of science (Griffiths & Stotz, 2013): The fact that development produces an outcome is explained by showing that the specific ways the parts of that system are arranged, and the behavior of those parts in accordance with standard physical laws, lead to the phenotypic outcome.

Explanations of phenotypes in terms of the presence of Mendelian alleles do not share these features. The presence of an allele (or of different alleles) explains the presence of the associated phenotype (or a phenotypic difference) because of a statistical association between alleles and phenotypes in a pedigree or a population.[5] The epistemological value of this relationship derives precisely from the fact that it applies robustly across the actual distributions of developmental factors in the population from which it is derived and in which it can be legitimately extrapolated, or that it applies often enough for the average effect produced to be useful knowledge. Thus, the abstract developmental gene explains by reference to the causal structure of the developmental system, whilst the Mendelian allele explains by importing statistical information about specific alleles and phenotypes from some reference class. Explanation in this context is best understood not as providing a mechanism but as causal explanation in James Woodward's sense (Waters, 2007; Woodward, 2010): The cause is a variable that can be used to manipulate another variable, the effect, and this relationship is robust across a certain range of values of other variables.

Thus, from the perspective of the abstract developmental gene, it makes no sense to explain the presence of a phenotype (or difference) by alluding to the presence of a particular gene in the absence of any understanding of its role in a broader developmental system. From this perspective, the fact that a gene has a specific phenotypic effect raises the question of why it has had that effect rather than another effect it might have had if other factors had been different. The frequent claim by developmental psychobiologists that the mere presence of a gene cannot in itself explain the presence of a phenotype reflects this conception of how genes explain phenotypes.

Conversely, if genes are Mendelian alleles, then it seems unreasonable to demand knowledge about how a gene interacts with other genes and with the environment before accepting an explanation that cites the presence of this allele as the "actual difference maker" between one phenotype and another (Waters, 2007). If the organism or organisms whose phenotypes are to be explained have been drawn from a suitable reference class, then those other factors will not make a difference (Griffiths & Tabery, 2008; Tabery & Griffiths, 2010).

Hence, an important aspect of the disagreement between behavioral geneticists and developmental psychobiologists is over the scientific relevance of factors that do not vary in nature. Behavioral geneticists argued that developmental factors that do not account for any of the actual variance seen in populations are irrelevant to the explanation of *phenotypic differences* seen in those populations. In contrast, the causal–mechanistic study of

---

[5]Note that we have switched back from considering quantitative genetic models to considering a simple Mendelian model in which a single genetic difference makes a phenotypic difference. But the same point applies when many genetic differences make small contributions to a phenotypic difference.

behavioral development has traditionally been concerned with the development of *species-typical phenotypes*, a feature it shares with most traditional developmental biology. The factors that do not vary are relevant because they are part of the developmental process in virtue of which those that do vary exert an influence on the phenotype. Because developmental psychobiology aims to characterize the mechanisms of development, it has no reason to privilege *actual* causes over *potential* causes (Waters, 2007).

One of the most dramatic misunderstandings that has arisen from these conceptual differences concerns "gene–environment interaction." In behavioral genetics, gene–environment interaction is understood as a statistical phenomenon that requires the introduction of an additional term into the analysis of variance. Part of the variance is a "main effect" of genetics (G); another part is a main effect of environment (E), but a further part is an "interaction effect" (G×E). In contrast, for developmental psychobiologists, interaction is not primarily a statistical phenomenon. It is the fact that genetic and environmental factors physically interact in the causal processes that give rise to phenotypes—that a single developmental mechanism has components that are genetic and components that are environmental.

James Tabery (2007) has labelled these two concepts of gene–environment interaction the "biometric" concept ($G×E_B$) and the "developmental" concept ($G×E_D$). The long-standing dispute between behavioral geneticists and their critics over gene–environment interaction is to a significant extent the result of their using these two different concepts of interaction, corresponding to the two different conceptions of the gene outlined above. Behavioral geneticists regularly detect large main effects for genes and fail to identify a high level of statistical interaction ($G×E_B$) between genes and environment. For a behavioral geneticist, this translates, by definition, into low interaction. But for developmental psychobiologists, interaction is fundamentally a property of causal networks and $G×E_B$ is only the statistical manifestation of actual causal relationships. Developmental psychobiologists claim that gene–environment interaction is ubiquitous despite the failure of behavioral geneticists to detect large statistical interactions (Gottlieb, 2003, p. 343). Michael Meaney (2001) writes that "phenotype emerges only from the interaction of gene and environment. The search for main effects is a fool's errand. In the context of modern molecular biology, it is a quest that is without credibility" (p. 51). Meaney is undoubtedly aware that substantial main effects *are* found in this context, so to understand what he means, we need to recognise that two different senses of interaction are in play. Behavioral geneticists have recognized this, but they have typically argued that the statistical sense is the important one and that the other sense amounts to little more than complexity worship:

> Unfortunately, discussions of genotype–environment interaction have often confused the population concept with that of individual

development. It is important at the outset to distinguish genotype–
environment interaction from what we shall call *interactionism*, the
view that environmental and genetic threads in the fabric of behavior are so tightly interwoven that they are indistinguishable. (Plomin,
DeFries, & Loehlin, 1977, p. 309)

But a far more sympathetic reading of "interactionism" is possible. Developmental psychobiologists think they have conclusive evidence for the
highly interactive (GxE_D) nature of development: "From such systems will
we derive main effects? I think not" (Meaney, 2001, p. 54). But, as we have
noted, behavioral geneticists do extract substantial main effects from such
systems. Scientists such as Meaney respond to this absence of statistical
interaction (GxE_B) by looking for experimental interventions that will create
statistical interaction corresponding to the causal interaction (GxE_D). This
can often be done by exposing the organism to environments outside the
normal range. In other cases, the lack of statistical interaction under normal
conditions indicates that development is structured so as to render some
outcomes insensitive to some range of environmental variation mechanisms
such as redundancy, canalization, and feedback. In that case, experimentation on modified versions of the system itself may be required to disentangle
these details of the mechanism.

It is sometimes argued that, while the developmental sense of interaction is
relevant to understanding how each individual develops, it is not relevant to
understanding development at the population level—to explaining differences
between individuals. But Tabery has argued convincingly that the developmental, causal sense of interaction *can* be coherently applied to individual
differences in a population, and in recent years scientists have started to
describe how differences arise from what Tabery (2009) calls "difference
mechanisms."

Finding Boundary Objects for the Two
Research Traditions

Traditional quantitative genetic methods in behavioral genetics are
rapidly giving way to molecular methods. This seems to have created the
grounds for a rapprochement between the two sides in this dispute. It has
led to a greater appreciation by behavioral geneticists that the value of
"gene hunting" is not to identify *the* cause of a behavioral difference but
to find an entry point to the molecular pathways involved in the production of that difference (Hamer, 2002). Conversely, the effects of environmental interventions in developmental science are increasingly being
analysed at the level of gene expression (Meaney & Szyf, 2005; Suomi,
2004). The ground on which the disputants are meeting is the actual
sequence of DNA nucleotides. The ability to investigate actual DNA

sequences produces shared boundary objects that simultaneously make concrete both abstract developmental genes and the Mendelian alleles whose existence was inferred from quantitative genetic studies.[6] This is not to say that the two disciplines have converged on the molecular concept of the gene. Both abstract developmental genes and Mendelian alleles may be made concrete as DNA sequences that are not molecular genes, for the reasons described in the previous section. The critical convergence between the two approaches is less in their concept of the gene than in their methods of investigation and in the nature of the objects investigated—namely, DNA sequences and their expression levels. We suggest that this is another example of the scientific role of boundary objects (Star & Griesemer, 1989). DNA sequences and their expression levels are objects of investigation that can mediate between different intellectual contexts.

In the previous section, we encountered two alternative, contextually activated representations of the gene that coexist in biology, corresponding to two different ways of thinking about DNA grounded in two different kinds of scientific activity. We suggested that this led to productive slippage of meaning that facilitated scientific progress, rather than unproductive miscommunication, because of the abundance of boundary objects shared between the different contexts. In this section, we have seen two different representations of the gene built into the foundations of two very different research approaches to the genetic basis of behavior. The result was several decades of unproductive miscommunication. We have suggested that this situation will be—and is being—resolved by the construction of shared boundary objects due to the introduction of molecular methods in both disciplines. We do not suggest that students of the genetics of behavior will all come to conceptualize genes in the same ways but, rather, that disagreements will increasingly be perceived as empirical or conceptual, rather than as the result of sloppy thinking by one's opponents.

The Contested Concept of Innateness

Here we introduce a third and final example, one that is widely agreed to have led to long-standing debates that are "semantic" in the worst sense of the word. This is the concept of innateness, which lies at the heart of much of the debate over nature and nurture.

---

[6]Searching for these alleles has created the so-called "missing heritability" problem. Current methods typically reveal a large number of loci, each of which accounts for a very small amount of variance and which collectively account for much less of the variance than is believed to be genetic on the basis of traditional quantitative genetic studies (see, e.g., Manolio et al., 2009).

Between Nativism and Anti-Nativism

It is a truism that the term *innate* is multiply ambiguous:

> At least six meanings are attached to the term: present at birth; a behavioral difference caused by a genetic difference; adapted over the course of evolution; unchanging throughout development; shared by all members of a species; and not learned. . . . Say what you mean (even if it uses a bit more space) rather than unintentionally confuse your readers by employing a word such as innate that carries so many different connotations. (Bateson, 1991, pp. 21–22)

In later work, Matteo Mameli and Patrick Bateson (2006) identified no fewer than 26 proposed definitions of *innate* from the scientific literature and judged 8 of these to be both genuinely independent definitions and separate, potentially valuable scientific constructs.

We and our collaborators have presented evidence that the idea of an innate trait is one expression of an implicit theory of the "natures" of living things shared by scientists and nonscientists alike (Griffiths, 2002; Griffiths, Machery, & Linquist, 2009; Linquist, Machery, Griffiths, & Stotz, 2011). Just as there are common-sense ideas about physical objects and the forces acting on them ("folk physics"; see, e.g., Clement, 1983), so there are common-sense ideas about biology. It is part of "folkbiology" (Atran, 1999) that some traits are expressions of the inner nature of animals and plants whilst other traits result from the influence of the environment. Echoing older critiques of the innateness concept in animal behavior research, we argue that folkbiology conflates the three issues of whether a trait is typical of the species, whether it is part of the design of the species (an adaptation), and whether its development is insensitive to the environment. Attempts to redefine innateness in a way that stresses just one of its aspects have been and will continue to be stymied by the fact that this multiply ambiguous concept of innateness is entrenched in the common-sense way of looking at the world.

The view that the ambiguity of the term *innate* obstructs scientific understanding has a long history in animal behavior research. At the heart of this critique is the claim that innateness conflates different biological questions and leads researchers to commit fallacies of ambiguity. For example, evidence that a trait is an adaptation is used to reach the conclusion that it is species typical, or vice versa. Evidence that a trait is an adaptation is used to infer that it is insensitive to environmental variation, or vice versa (for some recent examples, see Linquist et al., 2011, p. 445). When such inferences are laid out explicitly, it is clear that they do not follow without further evidence. However, if the discussion is conducted in terms of whether the trait is "innate"— a term that is used on different occasions to refer to each of these distinct, biological properties—it is easy to slide from one to the other.

The ambiguity of the innateness concept has not proved productive for the study of behavioral development. The study of innate behavior is not known for mutually supportive communication between different fields, each of which conceptualises the innate/acquired distinction somewhat differently. Instead, nativists[7] and anti-nativists are both convinced that they have a sophisticated vision of development that does justice to the complementary roles of gene and environment, and regard their opponents as confused (compare, for example, the diametrically opposed visions of how the nature/nurture dispute has been resolved in two very well-informed popular books, Gary Marcus's [2004] *The Birth of the Mind: How a Tiny Number of Genes Creates the Complexities of Human Thought* and David S. Moore's [2001] *The Dependent Gene: The Fallacy of "Nature vs. Nurture")*.

The Absence of Boundary Objects

Can this situation be explained by an absence of boundary objects that would allow the opponents' differing understandings to be reframed by some wider collective activity, such as shared investigative strategies? We tentatively suggest that this diagnosis may, indeed, be applicable here as well. Some of the fields in which nativism and anti-nativism are popular certainly use very different methods to investigate behavioral development. There is a strong strain of nativism in contemporary cognitive developmental psychology. Noam Chomsky's (1965) "language acquisition device" has served as an exemplar for research on the innate contributions to other psychological domains. Like the language acquisition device, other putatively innate features of the mind are thought to embody innate "knowledge" or innate "theories" about specific cognitive domains. For example, the eminent cognitive developmental psychologists Susan Carey and Elizabeth Spelke (1996) argue that children possess four domains of innate "core knowledge" that underlie much of their later cognitive development. These domains are "objects, agents, numbers and space" (p. 517; see also Carey, 2011). In theory, nativist developmental psychologists put a great deal of weight on "poverty of the stimulus arguments": The environment of the child does not contain the right stimuli for the child to acquire certain things, which must therefore be innate. However, collecting evidence for a poverty of the stimulus argument is demanding, and there is little evidence of poverty of the stimulus for many aspects of human psychology that have been labelled innate (Sterelny, 2003). Instead, many nativist claims rest on evidence that the putatively innate features are specific to one cognitive domain rather than another, that they emerge in a characteristic sequence in the development of the child, or that the same features are found in many human cultures. The last of these features speaks to the issue of whether the

---

[7]Nativism is the view that some aspect of mind or behavior is innate.

feature is species typical. The first two, and especially domain specificity, speak to the issue of whether the putatively innate feature serves a specific function and is plausibly a result of evolutionary design.

Anti-nativists are a more diverse group. Here we want to emphasize the opposition to nativism from the research tradition discussed in the previous section, developmental psychobiology. These researchers stress the dependence of all aspects of development on specific interactions with the environment.[8] A classic research exemplar is Celia Moore's (1984) work on penile reflexes in rats (see also Moore, 1992). She showed that the spinal cord nuclei of male rats differ from those of female rats in ways that allow the male to use his penis during copulation. These neural differences result from differences in gene expression in the developing spinal cord of the rat pup, which in turn result from differences in the licking of the genital area by the mother, which in turn result from the different composition of the urine of male pups. The ability of the male rat to use his penis during copulation is a species-typical trait and surely an adaptation, but the fact that it depends on very specific interaction with the environment is taken by developmental psychobiologists to show that it is not innate. This concern with dependence on the environment speaks to the aspect of the innateness concept according to which innate traits are insensitive to the developmental environment.[9] This is a contrast to the nativist research foci described earlier, which speak to the aspects of the innateness concept according to which innate traits are typical of the species and part of the design of the species.

Our argument at this point is tentative and exploratory. Our sketch of these two research traditions has been very brief, and more evidence and argument are needed to document the contrast we have suggested between them. If such a contrast does exist, however, there may be few shared boundary objects for these two traditions that would help them translate their differences into cooperation. There may be few concrete boundary objects because the two work on very different experimental systems. Nativist cognitive developmental psychology has a strong human focus. Developmental psychobiology has traditionally relied on experimental interventions that perturb the normal course of development, something that leads to an inevitable focus on animal models.[10] There may also be few

---

[8]Good popular introductions to this research tradition, with a plethora of examples, are Bateson and Martin (1999) and Moore (2001). For a textbook treatment, see Michel and Moore (1995), and for a handbook approach, Hood, Halpern, Greenberg, and Lerner (2010).

[9]The same might be said of another major strand of anti-nativist thought, so-called "neural constructivism" (Elman et al., 1996).

[10]A notable exception to this generalization is Esther Thelen and collaborators' "microgenesis" paradigm for the study of infant development (Thelen & Smith, 1994; Thelen & Ulrich, 1991).

abstract boundary objects. For example, the idea of a cognitive domain is important in nativist work on cognitive development, but cognitive domains do not constitute a shared ground in the way genetic loci do for different conceptions of the gene, since they cannot be anchored to a shared map of the brain in the same way genetic loci are anchored in shared representations of chromosomes.

Take-Home Messages

- In our first example of Mendelian and molecular genetics, we described how two alternative, contextually activated representations of the gene coexist in biology, corresponding to two different ways of thinking about DNA grounded in two different kinds of scientific activity. We suggested that this led to productive slippage of meaning rather than unproductive miscommunication because of the abundance of boundary objects shared between the different contexts.
- In our second example—research on the genetic basis of behavior in traditional, quantitative behavioral genetics and in developmental psychobiology—we described two different representations of the gene built into the foundations of these different forms of research regarding the genetic basis of behavior. The result was several decades of unproductive miscommunication. We suggested that this situation has been improved by the introduction of molecular methods in both disciplines, resulting in a sharing of boundary objects.
- In our third example, we examined disputes about behavioral development focused on the concept of innateness. We tentatively sketched some ways the inability to resolve these disputes might reflect an absence of boundary objects.
- The take-home message of these examples is a form of empiricism— although we hope not a naïve one. Scientists and science commentators frequently decry the vagueness or ambiguity of key theoretical constructs and suggest that disputes about such constructs are more semantic than empirical.[11] We would argue that the way forward in such cases is not, as is usually supposed, to seek a precise, stable conceptualisation of the subject matter. If we are correct, then the way to achieve mutual understanding, and to convert semantic disputes to empirical ones, is not to construct a conceptual straitjacket but to seek materials that can act as boundary objects and around which a thousand conceptual flowers may bloom.

---

[11]Another such dispute, to which one of us has contributed, concerns the concept of emotion in psychology (Griffiths, 2007).

_____**References**

Atran, S. (1999). Itzaj Maya folkbiological taxonomy: Cognitive universals and cultural particulars. In D. L. Medin & S. Atran (Eds.), *Folkbiology* (pp. 119–203). Cambridge: MIT Press.

Bateson, P. (1991). Are there principles of behavioural development? In P. Bateson (Ed.), *The development and integration of behaviour* (pp. 19–39). Cambridge, UK: Cambridge University Press.

Bateson, P., & Martin, P. (1999). *Design for a life: How behavior and personality develop*. London: Jonathan Cape.

Beurton, P., Falk, R., & Rheinberger, H.-J. (Eds.). (2000). *The concept of the gene in development and evolution: Historical and epistemological perspectives*. Cambridge, UK: Cambridge University Press.

Carey, S. (2011). *The origin of concepts*. New York: Oxford University Press.

Carey, S., & Spelke, E. (1996). Science and core knowledge. *Philosophy of Science, 63*(4), 515–533.

Chomsky, N. (1965). *Aspects of the theory of syntax*. Cambridge: MIT Press.

Clement, J. (1983). A conceptual model discussed by Galileo and used intuitively by physics student. In D. Gentner & A. L. Stevens (Eds.), *Mental models* (pp. 325–340). Hillsdale, NJ: Lawrence Erlbaum.

Djebali, S., Davis, C. A., Merkel, A., Dobin, A., Lassmann, T., Mortazavi, A., et al. (2012). Landscape of transcription in human cells. *Nature, 489*(7414), 101–108.

Djebali, S., Lagarde, J., Kapranov, P., Lacroix, V., Borel, C., Mudge, J. M., et al. (2012). Evidence for transcript networks composed of chimeric RNAs in human cells. *PLoS ONE, 7*(1), e28213. doi:10.1371/journal.pone.0028213

Elman, J. L., Bates, E. A., Johnson, M. A., Karmiloff-Smith, A., Parisi, D., & Plunkett, K. (1996). *Rethinking innateness: A connectionist perspective on development*. Cambridge: MIT Press.

Falk, R. (1984). The gene in search of an identity. *Human Genetics, 68*, 195–204.

Falk, R. (1986). What is a gene? *Studies in the History and Philosophy of Science, 17*, 133–173.

Falk, R. (2009). *Genetic analysis: A history of genetic thinking*. Cambridge, UK: Cambridge University Press.

Gerstein, M. B., Bruce, C., Rozowsky, J. S., Zheng, D., Du, J., Korbel, J. O., et al. (2007). What is a gene, post-ENCODE? History and updated definition. *Genome Research, 17*, 669–681.

Gottlieb, G. (2003). On making behavioral genetics truly developmental. *Human Development, 45*(6), 337–355.

Griffiths, P. E. (2002). What is innateness? *The Monist, 85*(1), 70–85.

Griffiths, P. E. (2007). Precision, stability and scientific progress (commentary on Scherer). *Social Sciences Information, 46*(3), 391–395.

Griffiths, P. E., Machery, E., & Linquist, S. (2009). The vernacular concept of innateness. *Mind and Language, 24*(5), 605–630.

Griffiths, P. E., & Stotz, K. (2007). Gene. In M. Ruse & D. Hull (Eds.), *Cambridge companion to philosophy of biology* (pp. 85–102). Cambridge, UK: Cambridge University Press.

Griffiths, P. E., & Stotz, K. (2013). *Genetics and philosophy: An introduction*. New York: Cambridge University Press.

Griffiths, P. E., & Tabery, J. (2008). Behavioral genetics and development: Historical and conceptual causes of controversy. *New Ideas in Psychology, 26*, 332–352.

Hamer, D. (2002). Rethinking behavior genetics. *Science, 298*, 71–72.

Hood, K. E., Halpern, C. T., Greenberg, G., & Lerner, R. M. (2010). *Handbook of developmental science, behavior and genetics.* Chichester, NY: Wiley-Blackwell.

Huxley, J. (1972). *Problems of relative growth.* New York: Dover. (Original work published in 1932)

Lettice, L. A., Horikoshi, T., Heaney, S. J. H., van Baren, M. J., van der Linde, H. C., Breedveld, G. J., et al. (2002). Disruption of a long-range cis-acting regulator for *Shh* causes preaxial polydactyly. *Proceedings of the National Academy of Sciences, 99*(11), 7548–7553.

Lewis, D. K. (1966). An argument for the identity theory. *Journal of Philosophy, 63*(1), 17–25.

Linquist, S., Machery, E., Griffiths, P. E., & Stotz, K. (2011). Exploring the folkbiological conception of human nature. *Philosophical Transactions of the Royal Society B, 366*(1563), 444–453.

Mameli, M., & Bateson, P. (2006). Innateness and the sciences. *Biology and Philosophy, 22*, 155–188.

Manolio, T. A., Collins, F. S., Cox, N. J., Goldstein, D. B., Hindorff, L. A., Hunter, D. J., et al. (2009). Finding the missing heritability of complex diseases. *Nature, 461*(7265), 747–753.

Marcus, G. (2004). *The birth of the mind: How a tiny number of genes creates the complexities of human thought.* New York: Basic Books.

Meaney, M. J. (2001). Nature, nurture, and the disunity of knowledge. *Annals of the New York Academy of Sciences, 935*(1), 50–61.

Meaney, M. J., & Szyf, M. (2005). Environmental programming of stress responses through DNA methylation: Life at the interface between a dynamic environment and a fixed genome. *Dialogues in Clinical Neuroscience, 7*(2), 103–123.

Michel, G. F., & Moore, C. L. (1995). *Developmental psychobiology: An interdisciplinary science.* Cambridge: MIT Press.

Moore, C. L. (1984). Maternal contributions to the development of masculine sexual behavior in laboratory rats. *Developmental Psychobiology, 17*(4), 347–356.

Moore, C. L. (1992). The role of maternal stimulation in the development of sexual behavior and its neural basis. *Annals of the New York Academy of Sciences, 662*, 160–177.

Moore, D. S. (2001). *The dependent gene: The fallacy of "nature vs. nurture."* New York: Henry Holt.

Morgan, T. H. (1934). *Nobel lecture: The relation of genetics to physiology and medicine.* Retrieved from http://nobelprize.org/nobel_prizes/medicine/laureates/1933/morgan-lecture.html

Plomin, R., DeFries, J. C., & Loehlin, J. (1977). Genotype–environment interaction and correlation in the analysis of human behavior. *Psychological Bulletin, 84*, 309–322.

Schaffner, K. F. (1993). *Discovery and explanation in biology and medicine.* Chicago: University of Chicago Press.

Stanford, P. K., & Kitcher, P. (2000). Refining the causal theory of reference for natural kind terms. *Philosophical Studies, 97*, 99–129.

Star, S. L., & Griesemer, J. R. (1989). Institutional ecology, "translations," and boundary objects: Amateurs and professionals in Berkeley's Museum of Vertebrate Zoology, 1907–39. *Social Studies of Science, 19*(3), 387–420.

Sterelny, K. (2003). *Thought in a hostile world: The evolution of human cognition.* Oxford, UK: Blackwell.

Suomi, S. J. (2004). How gene–environment interactions can influence emotional development in rhesus monkeys. In C. Garcia-Coll, E. L. Bearer, & R. M. Lerner (Eds.), *Nature and nurture: The complex interplay of genetic and environmental influences on human behavior and development* (pp. 35–52). Mahwah, NJ: Lawrence Erlbaum.

Tabery, J. (2007). Biometric and developmental genotype–environment interactions: Looking back, moving forward. *Development and Psychopathology, 19,* 961–976.

Tabery, J. (2009). Difference mechanisms: Explaining variations with mechanisms. *Biology & Philosophy, 24*(5), 711–723.

Tabery, J., & Griffiths, P. E. (2010). Historical and philosophical perspectives on behavioral genetics and developmental science. In K. E. Hood, C. T. Halpern, G. Greenberg, & R. M. Lehrer (Eds.), *Handbook of developmental science, behavior, and genetics* (pp. 41–60). Malden, MA: Wiley-Blackwell.

Thelen, E., & Smith, L. (1994). *A dynamic systems approach to the development of cognition and action.* Cambridge: MIT Press.

Thelen, E., & Ulrich, B. D. (1991). Hidden skills: A dynamic systems analysis of treadmill stepping during the first year. *Monographs of the Society for Research in Child Development, 56*(1), 1–104.

Waddington, C. H. (1940). *Organisers and genes.* Cambridge, UK: Cambridge University Press.

Waddington, C. H. (1957). *The strategy of the genes: A discussion of some aspects of theoretical biology.* London: Ruskin House/Allen & Unwin.

Waters, C. K. (1994). Genes made molecular. *Philosophy of Science, 61,* 163–185.

Waters, C. K. (2007). Causes that make a difference. *Journal of Philosophy, 104*(11), 551–579.

Weber, M. (2005). *Philosophy of experimental biology.* Cambridge, MA: Cambridge University Press.

Woodward, J. (2010). Causation in biology: Stability, specificity, and the choice of levels of explanation. *Biology & Philosophy, 25*(3), 287–318.

PART III

Tools

Given the challenges of communication in collaborative, interdisciplinary research highlighted in previous parts of this volume, difficulty in communication can seem an unavoidable cost of "doing business" in such a context. Project leaders and senior personnel can be resistant to available approaches to improving communication, which might seem irrelevant, a waste of time, or worse. At the same time, project participants can feel that they are on their own in their effort to function effectively within their team. Fortunately, communication among collaborators can be enhanced by reflection on the *process* of collaborative, interdisciplinary research and specifically on how the team understands and approaches this type of research. This attention to process can have the greatest impact if undertaken early in a team's life, before unproductive patterns become established.

This part of the volume presents specific tools that can be utilized by collaborators to illuminate their research process and improve their communicative efficiency. Each of the approaches in this part rests on proven techniques for enhancing collaborative communication: dialogue methods in Chapters 11 and 12, concept maps in Chapter 12, and models in Chapter 13. In each case, the tool supplied can be understood either as a *boundary object*—that is, an object held in common by collaborators from different disciplines that can be used as a "means of translation" between them—or a means of discovering boundary objects.[1] These boundary objects can structure a team's reflection on its own processes, enabling it to transcend habits that undermine effective team communication.

The first chapter in Part III is a contribution from the Toolbox Project, a U.S. National Science Foundation–sponsored initiative that uses philosophical concepts to enhance communication in collaborative, cross-disciplinary scientific teams. The Toolbox Project has developed a dialogue method that involves use of a survey instrument, the "Toolbox," in workshop settings. In "Seeing Through the Eyes of Collaborators: Using Toolbox Workshops to Enhance Cross-Disciplinary Communication," members of the Toolbox Project provide a detailed, step-by-step description of the Toolbox method that is designed to enable readers to conduct their own Toolbox workshop. After articulating the leading idea and providing evidence of effectiveness, the chapter supplies a protocol that covers workshop preparation, facilitation, and follow-up.

In Chapter 12, "Integration of Frameworks and Theories Across Disciplines for Effective Cross-Disciplinary Communication," Wayde C. Morse develops a method based on concept mapping and dialogue for generating an "interdisciplinary metatheoretical framework to guide research" (p. 245). Morse characterizes disciplinary research with the nested concepts of *framework* and *theory*—many theories about aspects of a domain can be contained within a broader conceptual framework. Frameworks and theories "conceptualize taxonomies of components and fundamental underlying assumptions about the nature of the world regarding their subject matter" (p. 244). When researchers collaborate across disciplines, as they must to address complex problems, their frameworks and theories can be incommensurable in various ways. As has been argued elsewhere in this volume, these differences create communication challenges that must be surmounted or at least addressed if effective, integrative responses to these problems are to be produced. Morse offers an iterative dialogue method based on a systematic approach to concept mapping that can guide an interdisciplinary research team from interdisciplinary theme development and problem formulation through to the creation of a "team systems concept map" or "metatheoretical framework." This map guides collaborative research effort by systematically demonstrating ways of integrating disciplinary frameworks and theories.

Laura Schmitt Olabisi, Stuart Blythe, Arika Ligmann-Zielinska, and Sandra Marquart-Pyatt present quantitative computer models as tools for enhancing interdisciplinary communication and collaboration in Chapter 13,

---

[1] See Star, S. L., & Griesemer, J. R. (1989). Institutional ecology, 'translations' and boundary objects: Amateurs and professionals in Berkeley's Museum of Vertebrate Zoology, 1907–39. *Social Studies of Science, 19,* 387–420 (especially p. 393). For additional discussion of boundary objects, see Griffiths and Stotz, Chapter 10, this volume.

"Modeling as a Tool for Cross-Disciplinary Communication in Solving Environmental Problems." The central role of models in contemporary science is undeniable, and as the authors note, "easy access to high-speed computing power and sophisticated model-building software have made quantitative, data-intensive computer models central to research that informs policy or management outcomes" (p. 271). They are especially valuable in interdisciplinary scientific efforts that address complex systems, such as climate change and environmental sustainability. But the authors argue that while the role of models as "scientific tools" is clear, they are not often seen as "communicative tools." In this chapter, they argue that quantitative models "have the potential to be powerful communicative tools for facilitating communication within research teams and between these teams and other scientists and decision makers" (p. 272). Specifically, they detail the communicative benefits and challenges that can arise for a team when it uses models. The authors conclude the chapter by outlining "best practices" associated with the communicative application of quantitative computer-based models, aimed at modelers who work with interdisciplinary research teams and the academic institutions that train them.

11

Seeing Through the Eyes of Collaborators

Using Toolbox Workshops to Enhance Cross-Disciplinary Communication

◆ Chris Looney, Shannon Donovan, Michael O'Rourke, Stephen Crowley, Sanford D. Eigenbrode, Liela Rotschy, Nilsa A. Bosque-Pérez, and J. D. Wulfhorst

The emerging literature on the challenges of cross-disciplinary research emphasizes the critical importance of effective communication to project success, but mechanisms for developing such communication remain scarce. This chapter presents one approach to improving communication in cross-disciplinary research teams—the Toolbox method, a dialogue method rooted in the philosophy of science. Disparate views about the nature of phenomena studied and methods of inquiry can make research communication challenging for cross-disciplinary teams of scientific collaborators. The Toolbox method uses a philosophically based questionnaire in a workshop setting to guide dialogue about the nature and practice of science. This dialogue promotes understanding of diverse research worldviews within a team and helps participants identify potential conflict as well as common ground. The workshop can also reveal communication dynamics while helping build trust and mutual respect. This chapter provides background information on the nature and usefulness of the Toolbox, offers instructions for preparing and running a Toolbox workshop, outlines the necessary personnel and their roles, and provides examples of how to conduct a successful session. Follow-up activities and suggestions for using workshop results to improve team function and dynamics are also provided.

Introduction

Differences between scientific cultures make collaborative, cross-disciplinary research both powerful and perplexing—powerful because the combination of different orientations enables scientists to respond to complex problems in complex ways typically unavailable to investigators working from single perspectives, and perplexing because these responses require scientists to communicate effectively with representatives of different intellectual cultures (Jakobsen, Hels, & McLaughlin, 2004; Stokols et al., 2003).[2]

To help unleash the full potential of collaborative, cross-disciplinary research, we describe an approach to enhancing communication across disciplines that emphasizes dialogue about the fundamental assumptions and scientific approaches that typify those disciplines (cf., McDonald, Bammer, & Deane, 2009). Specifically, we supply a dialogue method—the Toolbox method—centered on a semistructured, philosophical conversation about research assumptions that takes place in a workshop setting, bringing collaborators together around a common, jointly constructed understanding of their specific combination of disciplines (Eigenbrode et al., 2007). Toolbox Project members have conducted 90 of these workshops (2006–2012) around the United States and provided feedback to participating teams about their communication dynamic. Post-workshop evaluations indicate that participants are overwhelmingly positive about the method as a way to improve awareness of disciplinary assumptions and group communication.

In this chapter, we develop the rationale and motivation for the Toolbox method—namely, that philosophical dialogue enhances the collaborative practice of teams conducting cross-disciplinary research and similar efforts. We present a detailed account of the Toolbox method to use as a guideline for those who wish to conduct a workshop of their own, highlighting what

---

[2]We use the term *cross-disciplinary* to denote the range of efforts that involve integrating different disciplines to various degrees, including *multidisciplinary, interdisciplinary,* and *transdisciplinary* efforts (cf., Morse, Nielsen-Pincus, Force, & Wulfhorst, 2007). We also intend it to accommodate *translational* efforts that involve the integration of disciplinary research with various professions (e.g., natural resource management, medicine) and stakeholders. This type of research is known as *transdisciplinary* in some circles, adding to the potential confusion that we seek to avoid by using a more generic term (see Klein, 2008).

should occur, how to make it occur, and how to interpret what transpires during the workshop. Finally, we provide a synopsis of our ongoing efforts to improve the Toolbox method, fine-tune it for specific kinds of collaboration, and integrate the exercise into the broader context of improving communication within collaborative teams.

Framing

The Toolbox Idea

One well-established way of enhancing collaborative communication is with dialogue, understood as the joint creation of "'meaning and shared understanding' through conversation" (McDonald et al., 2009, p. 2, quoting Franco, 2006, p. 814). Dialogue happens organically, of course, but it can also be structured through *dialogue methods* employed by groups as they work to develop their "collective communication competence" (Thompson, 2009). Among these methods are scenario planning, mind mapping, nominal group technique, and the Delphi technique (McDonald et al., 2009; Winowiecki et al., 2011). We offer the Toolbox method as a novel yet tested dialogue method that complements other available methods. While other dialogue methods support the performance of critical functions, such as conceptualizing problems and rapidly and inclusively making decisions, the Toolbox method is concerned more generally with cross-disciplinary research readiness. This method prepares teams to perform research functions by revealing and clarifying fundamental assumptions made by team members about the nature, conduct, and application of research. We propose that improved clarity at this deeper level allows teams to function more effectively by identifying and illuminating fundamental differences among their constituent disciplines (cf., Bammer, 2013). To achieve this, a conversation must be structured in a way that meets two requirements:

1. It makes the disciplinary assumptions of each participant salient to both the individual and the rest of the team.

2. It clarifies genuine differences and similarities among the assumptions in the team (e.g., disagreements about research practices of team members) and distinguishes them from superficial differences and similarities (e.g., merely verbal disagreements).

As Klein (Chap. 2, this volume) argues, there are a number of theoretical domains available that could provide structure for a conversation that aims to meet these two requirements—for example, applied linguistics, management, and philosophy. Each of these addresses a level of genuine difference. Linguistics focuses on the character of the languages used to talk about research, while management theory highlights organizational structures and dynamics. Philosophy, though, is best positioned to foreground conceptual assumptions that frame the research practices of the participants. The Toolbox approach to these requirements exploits this advantage of philosophy and frames conversation in terms of the philosophy of science. The philosophy of science and its subdisciplines address the breadth of scientific practice, seeking common principles of this practice that constitute a conceptual framework inclusive of all scientific disciplines. Genuine differences about research assumptions across a team can be described as differences with respect to specific "common principles." For example, one common principle is that the credibility of empirical claims depends on their evidentiary support. However, what counts as evidence, what form it takes, and how much is required to substantiate claims varies significantly across—and within—disciplines. Recognition that different attitudes toward evidence are each responses to a common principle makes them salient (Requirement 1) and establishes them as genuine and commensurable (Requirement 2). The framework of common principles supports discovery and comparison of different research assumptions, supplying common ground that collaborators can use to develop greater mutual understanding about their research practices. In addition, philosophical common ground can be neutral territory supporting vigorous dialogue that is relevant to the success of the project but abstracted from the potentially more contentious project-specific details in which collaborators may be personally invested (Black & Anderson, 2012).

The Toolbox method is based on the proposition that philosophical discussion concerning the practice of science and the nature of the world under investigation can engender mutual understanding about issues within and between disciplines that are rarely discussed among collaborators. These topics are addressed by the following questions: What methods are appropriate for answering scientific questions, and why? Must effective science employ hypotheses, and how should hypotheses be used? Does validation require replication? Is value-neutral scientific research possible? What is the inherent value of science to humankind? These and other questions related to the philosophical nature of research are assembled in the Toolbox instrument, a questionnaire designed to elicit and structure conversation in a workshop setting. The Toolbox instrument is described in detail in Section III of this chapter.

Does It Work?

It is an assumption of our effort, and indeed the efforts of the contributors to this volume and other works on team science (e.g., Falk-Krzesinski et al., 2011; National Academy of Sciences, 2004; Pohl & Hirsch Hadorn, 2007), that improved communication leads to improved collaboration. The Toolbox method is unique in addressing the need for improved cross-disciplinary communication by inviting collaborators to examine their disciplinary assumptions about science and identify fundamental similarities and differences. The leading idea behind the Toolbox method is that enhanced understanding across a team will improve the efficiency and effectiveness of team communication. Specifically, development of mutual understanding should make it easier to integrate different disciplinary vocabularies and conceptual schemes, enabling more efficient information transfer; further, enhanced mutual understanding should positively impact team cohesion (Casey-Campbell & Martens, 2009). The literature suggests that understanding at this level supports collaborators as they grapple with a pressing research problem (e.g., Bracken & Oughton, 2006; McDonald et al., 2009; Ramadier, 2004), and we have gathered empirical evidence indicating that the Toolbox method is beneficial for team members. Specifically, we have collected and analyzed post-workshop questionnaire surveys from 35 of the 90 participating teams over the past 6 years. Of the 147 (of 285) participants who returned surveys, 84.9% indicated that the workshop had a positive impact on awareness of the knowledge, opinions, or scientific approach of teammates, and 77.4% reported a positive impact on their professional development (Schnapp, Rotschy, Hall, Crowley, & O'Rourke, 2012).

Who Can Benefit and How?

While any participant in a Toolbox workshop can benefit from greater awareness of fundamental assumptions about scientific work, the intent of the Toolbox workshop is to improve understanding and communication within actively collaborating cross-disciplinary teams.[3] The teams that have participated in Toolbox workshops have varied significantly in character. They have been constituted by collaborating researchers, graduate students in team-based courses, undergraduate researchers in summer research experience programs, research-center leaders, experienced researchers newly interested in collaborative cross-disciplinary research, and otherwise unconnected individuals simply interested in the Toolbox method. Participating teams have also been engaged in a variety of efforts, including academic research, interdisciplinary teaching or mentoring, transdisciplinary or transprofessional work on complex problems, and outreach.

An important dimension of workshop variety is disciplinary composition, since this has implications for the diversity of research assumptions. Some of the teams have had broad disciplinary representation (e.g., a team comprising social scientists, economists, biologists, engineers, and educators) and others have been more narrow (e.g., one comprising computer scientists and evolutionary biologists); however, we have found that diversity of views on philosophical issues is not necessarily dependent on disciplinary breadth, as even people within the same discipline can differ significantly in their scientific assumptions. The key point, however, is that teams with

---

[3]We distinguish between *groups* and *teams*, taking the latter to be groups that exhibit greater cohesion and a common identity (Fiore, 2008).

different compositions, purposes, and levels of experience can engage with the Toolbox and learn from the activity.[4]

The Toolbox method is designed to enhance self- and mutual understanding of research assumptions within cross-disciplinary research teams. Participants report in their post-workshop questionnaires that the workshop has given them a heightened awareness of genuine differences among their professional and research perspectives, a better appreciation of the cross-disciplinary dimensions of their projects, and a reduction in conflict stemming from the erroneous belief that the team shares fundamental assumptions about research and its application.

When Should a Research Team Employ the Toolbox Workshop?

The Toolbox workshop was originally conceived as a method best suited to research teams just beginning their work together, but we have conducted workshops for teams at all stages of collaboration. The Toolbox workshop can function to establish mutual understanding at the outset of a collaboration so communication about research decisions will go more smoothly. For this reason, it also has value early in a graduate or undergraduate course that emphasizes team-based, interdisciplinary interaction or research. Other teams have reported that the exercise can be valuable if conducted after a team's research focus has matured, with the Toolbox serving to stimulate project-relevant dialogue needed for data integration, synthesis, or other cross-disciplinary goals. A few teams have also found repeated interventions with the Toolbox to be helpful (e.g., following membership turnover or team expansion). In other words, just as there are many ways to collaborate successfully (Klein, 1996), there are many stages in a collaboration where the Toolbox method can add value.

Toolbox Do-It-Yourself

In addition to the Toolbox workshops we have facilitated, some research teams have conducted wokshops independently, based on a reading of Eigenbrode et al. (2007). To facilitate such "do-it-yourself" workshops we have developed

---

[4]In principle, the idea of enhancing cross-disciplinary communication through philosophical dialogue is not limited in application to *scientific* collaborations; however, the structured intervention we have designed is based on an instrument created with scientific collaborations in mind. We have used this instrument with nonscientific teams and found it to be less effective at creating common ground among participants. The Toolbox Project is working on extending the intervention into these directions through the development of new instruments that relate more effectively to less research-focused teams.

an updated guide to conducting and interpreting a Toolbox workshop that employs the latest version of the instrument and draws on our experience delivering workshops for diverse teams. The method has five primary elements: (1) preparing for a workshop, (2) the Toolbox instrument, (3) conducting the workshop, (4) post-workshop analysis, and (5) follow-up activities.

Preparing for a Workshop

It is important for one of the members of a team that plans to conduct a Toolbox workshop to assume the role of workshop organizer. Four important tasks for the organizer prior to the workshop are as follows:

- *Compile information about the team.* The organizer should seek answers to several questions about the team, including, Why is the team participating in the Toolbox workshop—is it to improve their functionality or merely to learn about the Toolbox approach? How many participants will there be? Who are they (e.g., students, administrators, researchers, practitioners)? What is the team's history (e.g., is the team just assembling, or have they worked together for a long time)? What is the nature and focus of the collaboration (e.g., fundamental or applied research, addressing a particular stakeholder-driven issue, classroom project)? This information will guide judgments about the nature of the workshop and the instrument employed. For example, newly formed teams may require more time for members to introduce themselves to one another before feeling comfortable enough to speak openly about their research assumptions. Also, we have found that the opportunity for engaged dialogue seems to be greatest in workshops with fewer than 10 participants (cf., Krueger & Casey, 2000); larger teams may wish to divide into two or more workshop groups, which could entail additional planning and resources.

- *Secure a venue.* Sessions require a comfortable space that can accommodate the team and allow audiorecording if desired. Participation by some team members via video-link has been successful, but high-quality connections are desirable.

- *Distribute preparatory reading.* This should include literature providing information about the purpose and nature of the Toolbox workshop, explanation of its focus on philosophical themes, and discussion of its potential benefits for cross-disciplinary research teams. Eigenbrode et al. (2007); Crowley, Eigenbrode, O'Rourke, and Wulfhorst (2010); or O'Rourke and Crowley (2012) can function in this role.

- *Obtain Institutional Review Board approval (if required).* If the information obtained from the team before, during, or after the workshop will be used for research purposes, it is important to obtain Institutional Review Board approval and participant consent prior to collecting data. (See http://grants.nih.gov/grants/policy/hs/ for more information.)

- *Notify participants about data collection.* If data about the participants or the workshop are to be collected for research purposes, the participants should be apprised of this fact before they gather for the workshop.

Two additional tasks, to be described in the next two subsections, are determining the specific character of the Toolbox instrument to be used in the workshop and determining the personnel to run it.

Understanding and Building Your Toolbox Instrument

The Toolbox instrument is a set of modules, each comprising a core question and probing statements that concern philosophical aspects of science. Each probing statement is associated with a 5-point Likert-type scale, along with selections for "don't know" and "not applicable," that participants are asked to score prior to the dialogue. For "do-it-yourself" purposes, the Likert-type scale encourages participants to take a position as a springboard for discussion. The instrument also comes with a demographic table that gathers various pieces of participant information (e.g., gender, discipline(s), years of experience in cross-disciplinary work). Three Toolbox instruments have been developed, targeting different audiences: cross-disciplinary research involving STEM[5] disciplines, research in the translational health science domain (Schnapp et al., 2012), and research in the translational climate science domain.[6] This chapter focuses on the STEM Toolbox instrument, which comprises six modules, three of which are built around core questions exploring epistemic dimensions of science (i.e., how scientific knowledge is created) and three around core questions exploring metaphysical dimensions of science (i.e., the nature of the world under study).[7] The module areas and core questions for this Toolbox instrument are as follows:

Epistemological questions:

- *Motivation*: Does the principal value of research stem from its applicability for solving problems?

---

[5]The STEM fields are science (including social science), technology, engineering, and mathematics.

[6]"Translational" refers to the transfer of research knowledge from its point of origin (e.g., a laboratory) out into the world. In the health sciences, translational research is popularly known as "bench-to-bedside" research and typically involves nonresearch partners such as doctors, nurses, K–12 educators, and patients (National Institutes of Health, 2011). We extend the translation metaphor to climate science and other research that involves participation of nonacademic partners, such as natural resource managers and growers (Greenland & Leach, 2008; Musacchio, 2008).

[7]See Eigenbrode et al. (2007) for further elaboration.

- *Methodology*: What methods do you employ in your disciplinary research (e.g., experimental, case study, observational, modeling)?
- *Confirmation*: What types of evidentiary support are required for knowledge?

Metaphysical questions:

- *Reality*: Do the products of scientific research more closely reflect the nature of the world or the researcher's perspective?
- *Values*: Do values negatively influence scientific research?
- *Reductionism*: Can the world under investigation be reduced to independent elements for study?

In the Toolbox instrument, each core question in a module is followed by five to seven statements designed to probe specific aspects of the core question and stimulate discussion. There are 34 probing statements in all. As an example, the Motivation Module (Figure 11.1) demonstrates the general layout and nature of the probing statements; the full Toolbox instrument can be accessed at www.sagepub.com/orourke.

Although the complete Toolbox instrument addresses philosophical concepts that are relevant to most projects, not all teams will have the time to explore the full instrument. The modular nature of the Toolbox allows teams to select a subset of modules for their workshop, tailoring their experience to the areas most pressing or interesting for them. Consider two examples: A policy-oriented team may wish to conduct a short session on the Values Module; a team that is struggling to reconcile qualitative methods with quantitative methods may wish to focus on the Methodology and Confirmation Modules. This tailored approach enables teams to select modules highlighting conceptual aspects of scientific research that they find especially interesting or relevant.

The Toolbox Workshop

We now focus on conducting a Toolbox workshop, emphasizing the roles of the facilitator and other personnel who are not members of the dialogue team. We describe the workshop experience in detail, emphasizing how typical workshops unfold, some of the team interactions a facilitator might expect, and examples of effective facilitator responses.

Workshop Personnel

Workshop personnel are involved in the session but are not members of the dialogue group. The facilitator is the most important nonparticipant and

Figure 11.1 The Motivation Module, Part of the Epistemology Section of the Toolbox

I. Motivation

Core Question: *Does the principal value of research stem from its applicability for solving problems?*

1. The principal value of research stems from the potential application of the knowledge gained.

   Disagree   *Agree*

   1   2   3   4   5   I don't know   N/A

2. Cross-disciplinary research is better suited to addressing applied questions than basic questions.

   Disagree   *Agree*

   1   2   3   4   5   I don't know   N/A

3. My disciplinary research primarily addresses basic questions.

   Disagree   *Agree*

   1   2   3   4   5   I don't know   N/A

4. The importance of our project stems from its applied aspects.

   Disagree   *Agree*

   1   2   3   4   5   I don't know   N/A

5. The members of this team have similar views concerning the motivation core question.

   Disagree   *Agree*

   1   2   3   4   5   I don't know   N/A

is indispensable to a successful Toolbox experience. The facilitator must effectively execute five primary functions:

- Introduce the session
- Answer questions from the participants about the Toolbox concept, the Toolbox instrument, and the workshop structure prior to the dialogue
- Help the team find connections between dialogue topics in the Toolbox instrument *without becoming part of the dialogue*
- Ensure that the team has the opportunity to address all the toolbox modules
- Prompt participants to clarify their statements or provide further details

In executing these functions, the facilitator should be careful to encourage the participants to explore on their own the issues raised in the instrument and should avoid trying to direct or control the discussion. Specific examples of approaches a facilitator might use effectively are presented in the following section. For several reasons, someone outside the team should serve as facilitator. A team member who serves as facilitator will necessarily abstain from participating in the dialogue, thereby compromising the value of the workshop for the team. Open and frank discussion may be inhibited if the facilitator is a team member with a leadership role (e.g., a faculty team leader facilitating a workshop that includes student research associates). The impartiality of a facilitator is critical to ensuring a balanced exploration of the Toolbox instrument. Perception of the facilitator as external to the team tends to promote a more formal attitude among participants, which can encourage more conscientious participation.

If a team wishes to record and transcribe or further analyze their workshop dialogue, a recorder should also be present. The primary task of the recorder is to create a record that enables a transcriber to assign speakers to each statement within the transcript. One way to do this is by associating each new speaking turn with a speaker (using participant codes—see below) and a distinctive word or phrase to make it clear to the transcriber which comment is associated with that turn (see Figure 11.2). The recorder may also note nonverbal cues or other incidents. Some teams may also wish to include a third nonparticipant who functions as an observer, focusing on communication process elements such as energy dynamics, body language, and other nonverbal forms of communication. The facilitator, recorder, and observer can later share their impressions of the activity during debriefing with the team (see p. 236) but should not speak with one another during the session. It is important to consider the size of the team and the space where the workshop will be held when determining whether to include an observer. For small teams (three to four participants), three nonparticipants in the room can inhibit dialogue.

Running a Workshop

The typical structure of the workshop is as follows: (a) collection of participant information, (b) facilitator introduction, (c) participant introductions, (d) pre-dialogue instrument distribution and completion, (e) dialogue, (f) post-dialogue instrument distribution and completion, and (g) debriefing. Full workshops can be completed in 2 to 3 hours. In what follows, we will describe each of these stages in turn.

Collection of Participant Information. If there is a desire to keep track of the participants for any reason (e.g., to contact them after the workshop), they should be asked to sign in at the beginning of a workshop and provide their names and contact information. If data will be collected, they should also be

Figure 11.2 Excerpt of Recorder Notes From a Typical Toolbox Workshop

Speaker	Question	Keywords/ Observations	Speaker	Question	Keywords/ Observations
4	general		5	motivation	... how define interests ...
1	"	N/A's	1	"	... how we define applied ..."
4 }			laughter . .		-
1 }			1	"	you're the lead....
5	demographic	who am I	3		the students we will attract ...
8		reply	10		impediments to Inter-D Sci
" general .		- -	1	defn x-discip	trans - D .
5	.	who am I . .	3,1,10,9, . .		general - defn of x-discip
4		wrong lover?			
5		odd duck?	3	"	
1		bristle?	10	"	1st [illegible] play
4			JD	"	clarify
general	team Q's	don't know	7	"	Ideal is when get lots of stimulation ..
8	'		chuckles		
general			5	"	Kinds of x-disciplinary "those disciplines need to work . ."
7			chuckles		
4	team Q's	reporting scores.	10	"	"..a Q that can only be answered . . . "

assigned participant codes and be asked to indicate their consent to be research subjects. The participant code should be assigned in a straightforward way (e.g., beginning with one person and continuing in sequence around the room) and is used by the recorder to keep track of participant speaking turns anonymously. It is also copied by the participants into the demographic form on the Toolbox instrument so Likert-scale reactions can be associated with workshop comments. If signed consent forms are required per an organization's Institutional Review Board, this is also an appropriate time to distribute and collect those.

Facilitator Introduction. Workshops begin with a preamble by the facilitator, addressing the following points:

- *The structure of the session.* After a self-introduction, the facilitator will describe how the workshop is organized and what participants will do.
- *The purpose of the session.* Based on the character of the team as revealed by the preliminary information collected, speak to the opportunities that exist to develop their communicative and collaborative capacities in the workshop. Emphasize the importance of understanding the research assumptions of one's collaborators and the power of philosophical dialogue to enable collaborators to see the research landscape through each other's eyes, thereby enhancing mutual understanding and scientific communication.

- *The organization of the Toolbox instrument.* Note the modules to be discussed by the team and why they were selected. Indicate that each module comprises a core question and probing statements, each of which is accompanied by a numeric scale of agreement. Remind participants that the "don't know" and "not applicable" categories are acceptable choices.

- *The nature of the statements.* Explain that the probing statements are intended to promote dialogue. Some of the terms used in the statements may seem vague or ambiguous. Participants should be encouraged to address this as part of their discussion—coming to a mutual understanding of the different interpretations of these terms is part of the exercise. Some of the statements contain absolute terms (e.g., *must, never, always*). This is intentional and designed to elicit distinct reactions on the Likert scale but, more important, to motivate discussion that seeks more precise or measured understanding of the issue raised by the prompts.

- *The nature of the dialogue.* Explain that the dialogue will begin once the Toolbox instruments have been completed. There is no one starting point within the Toolbox—where a team begins will depend on what issues are of greatest interest to participants. Explain that the facilitator will not participate in the dialogue but will encourage movement around the instrument to ensure coverage. Indicate that the participants should discuss the core questions and probing statements rather than engage in an abstract discussion of the instrument or workshop, as the debrief will afford opportunity for that discussion.

- *Detail about data collection.* As indicated above, participants should be notified in advance if data will be collected from them for research purposes; further, they should be asked to provide consent to be research subjects prior to delivery of the preamble. Even so, the preamble should be used to ensure that participants fully understand the planned uses of these data. If the session will be audiorecorded, explain why and how the recording will be handled and archived. Remind participants that all data collected will remain confidential.

- *Follow-up activities.* If data will be collected, what will be done with them? At the very least, the workshop will generate Likert reactions as recorded on the instruments used by the participants, and these could be collected and stored as data. Any follow-up analysis or conversation about data collected during the workshop should be described.

Participant Introductions. Although not necessary if the participants know one another, a brief introduction by each participant sets the tone for a session. In particular, setting aside time for participants to describe themselves (e.g., what discipline(s) they represent and how much research experience they have) can contribute to the formation of a temporary community that supports a candid exchange of assumptions. The goal is to help generate the

comfort and trust necessary for an engaged and honest dialogue (Bracken &
Oughton, 2006; Lewicki, McAllister, & Bies, 1998).

Pre-Dialogue Instrument Distribution and Completion. After the introductory remarks and participant introductions, the facilitator distributes the
Toolbox instrument and instructs the participants to respond to each of the
34 statements using the Likert scales. This will take about 15 minutes.
Participants should be encouraged to make notes on the instruments about
their scoring decisions or other thoughts they might have about the prompts.
This can be useful during the dialogue to help participants remember the
reasons they selected a certain score. Participants will likely change their
minds about various prompts but should be encouraged not to change their
Likert scores during the discussion if the organizer has planned to collect a
second Toolbox instrument after the dialogue.

Dialogue. After each participant has completed the Toolbox, the facilitator will
invite anyone in the team to initiate the discussion by commenting on a core
question or probing statement that intrigues them. The dialogue can continue
for up to 2 hours. For some teams, 2 hours may feel inadequate, while other
teams will have covered the material in a shorter time. The facilitator must judge
when to close the dialogue based on available time and group energy level.

There will be concerns about the specific language used in some of the
prompts. As noted above, not all the terms used in the instrument have precise,
unambiguous meanings, and we intentionally do not provide a glossary of the
terms used. By leaving the terms undefined, the Toolbox instrument makes
room for participants to articulate during the dialogue how they understand
these terms and the scientific or philosophical concepts they denote and to move
toward common ground even in the short time of one session. This is valuable
because it requires participants to articulate tacit commitments they may not
have considered clearly before, and it can enable negotiation among collaborators about how the terms should be understood in the context of their project.
Note, for example, the following exchange, which likely would not have happened if the instrument came with definitions for key terms such as *science*:

Participant 9:   Well, I put a "one" [strongly disagree] because I don't
believe the world is independent of the investigators. But if
I were focusing on the first part of the thing, "scientific
research aims" [to identify facts about a world independent
of the investigators], then I probably would have said,
"Yeah, I agree with that."

Participant 1:   I think it depends on how you define science. The conventional definition of science, which equates almost to experimentation, you would put "yes." But science is being
reinterpreted through Habermas and different philosophers about research.

Leaving key terms undefined frees participants to think more broadly about different aspects of the research process, such as this exchange about basic and applied research:

Participant 7:   I would like us to think about our definitions of basic and applied research. . . . I think of some of the social-science type research I do as basic, because I'm trying to understand human behavior. But to me, applied research has taken on sort of an unrealistic definition, and is often considered less valued than basic research.

The above statement was shortly followed by this one:

Participant 3:   One of the challenges is that there's a vocabulary thing, and what I find actually quite funny in a lot of peer-reviewed papers is people will do an absolutely, perfectly good piece of work. But then because they feel this tension about being applied, they try to show how they've also done something basic, and they start—to put it bluntly—bullshitting their way around.

There is no single formula for successful workshop facilitation because teams differ widely in engagement, composition, and group dynamics. Ideally, facilitator involvement in the dialogue will be minimal, but some involvement can be necessary, including responses to direct questions or concerns about the workshop process and suggestions to break a silence and move the team along. These responses require tact and restraint to avoid disrupting the flow of the discussion. Generally, the facilitator should interrupt active discussion only when a participant directly asks a question. Procedural questions should be answered as succinctly as possible. If participants ask about the meaning of a word, the facilitator should remind them that group discussion of vague or ambiguous words is a valuable part of the Toolbox process by saying something like this:

Facilitator: "Values" is one of those words that we use to get participants to think about their meaning. So becoming clear on what that term means in different contexts is a goal of this particular set of statements.

If necessary, the facilitator can draw out details about participant views when they are important to the unfolding dialogue, particularly when the conversation becomes stalled. Sometimes this can involve simply asking a participant to explain his or her Likert score:

Facilitator: So what *did* cause you to circle four there?

At other times, a direct appeal for expanded discussion will be helpful:

Facilitator: So I'll just ask, as facilitator—did others find selecting a score impossible or difficult?

The facilitator should also ensure that each module of the Toolbox is discussed, although the importance of this will be based on the team's goals and the available time. In our experience, it is more important to spend time on each of the modules than on each of the prompts, not all of which may speak to a given team. Comprehensive coverage of the modules can be accomplished by encouraging participants to discuss other areas of the Toolbox when the conversation becomes excessively focused on a single prompt or module:

Facilitator: I'm curious, in light of this conversation about social construction, what your responses were to the preceding statements in that section?

On the other hand, a long discussion about a particular prompt may reveal important differences in research approach among team members, and further discussion—perhaps even after the Toolbox—might be warranted.

Near the end of the dialogue, the facilitator may invite conversation about undiscussed parts of the Toolbox to ensure participants consider, however briefly, other concepts that interest them:

Facilitator: You did discuss a lot that pertains to [prompts] 22 and 27 with respect to values, so I'm going to ask in the last 10 minutes if there are questions in [the Values Module] or anywhere else in the Toolbox where you felt that we didn't cover something that was intriguing to you.

The facilitator should take note of prompts that generate pronounced philosophical difference. These can be revisited by the team after the workshop, either in team meetings or subsequent Toolbox discussions. (See the section on p. 237, "How to Build on the Toolbox Workshop.") How the team addresses these differences—which may not be problematic—will depend on team goals and the context of their project.

Post-Dialogue Instrument Distribution and Completion. It is an important part of the Toolbox method to complete a post-dialogue instrument. This helps participants lock in awareness of how their perspectives have been influenced by the Toolbox dialogue. When we conduct Toolbox workshops, we do this immediately after the dialogue; however, it is also an option to e-mail the instrument to the participants for completion after the session. This may be necessary given time or logistical constraints in the workshop session, and it may be desirable because it allows time for ideas to percolate—although it should be sent within a few days to minimize the impact of non-workshop-related influences.

Debriefing. The final part of the workshop should be a debrief conducted by the facilitator. The debrief provides an opportunity for the team to reflect on the experience. Participants are often eager to offer personal reactions and suggest ways to improve the activity, and it is important that they have an opportunity to do so as part of the workshop. The debrief can be centered on questions such as these:

- What are the most interesting things you learned during the workshop?
- Are there aspects of scientific research that you would have liked to talk about but were not included in the Toolbox?
- Do you think the team would benefit from additional time with the Toolbox?
- Do you have additional comments or questions?

These questions provide an opportunity for teams to summarize the experience for themselves and identify issues for further discussion by the team. The facilitator should close the workshop by explaining any post-workshop activities and products that will be produced, such as transcripts or Likert-score analyses, as described in the next section. If follow-up reactions from the participants will be collected via a survey instrument, this should also be mentioned at the end of the workshop.

Analyzing Toolbox Data

The workshop can generate two types of data available for subsequent analysis: a transcribable audio file and the pre- and post-dialogue Likert-scale reactions to the probing statements. Analysis and reflection on these data are important parts of the method, helping the team make sense of the experience and improve its communication and collaboration. Data of both sorts can reveal important characteristics of individual teams that can help them work more effectively together. For example, careful review of the transcript or audio file can support reflection on the research assumptions discussed during the dialogue, revealing for the team areas of potential conflict.

Transcripts can be examined for the number, distribution, and order of speaking turns and total time speaking by participants, which can reveal structure and relationships within the team (Woolley, Chabris, Pentland, Hashmi, & Malone, 2010). The length of discussion and number of participants contributing to discussion of a particular core question or probing statement can help identify issues important to the team.

A summary of pre- and post-dialogue Likert scoring can reveal patterns in the views held by the team. For example, team members may agree on issues such as the importance of applied science and the role of stakeholders but disagree on the validity of reductionist methods. Examination of pre- and post-dialogue scores can show whether these views were stable or changed during the workshop. Many of the prompts in the Toolbox instrument are intended to engender discussion rather than serve as the basis for rigorous analysis.[8] Nonetheless, the scores can be used by the team to reflect on their experience. The scores can be visualized by using standard graphing programs to display pre- and post-dialogue reactions in a variety of ways, such as displaying the reactions of all participants to each prompt (see Figure 11.3).

The Likert reaction summaries, the transcripts, and transcript analyses can help teams identify areas that warrant further attention as they continue their collaborative work. These areas could include problematic conceptual differences or more project-specific issues. The Likert score summaries and transcript or audio file can also be shared with new team members, easing their transition into the collaboration.[9]

How to Build on the Toolbox Workshop

As a stand-alone exercise, a Toolbox workshop can help a team understand the diversity of views among its members about fundamental aspects of science and collaboration. These insights can inform a team's approach to formulating research questions, structuring collaborative effort, and generating products consistent with its goals. The Toolbox Project has also developed follow-up activities to capitalize on workshop insights. Such activities are part of a more comprehensive set of practices designed to enhance group

---

[8]This is so for two reasons. First, as we have noted, many of the statements contain terms that are vague or ambiguous, giving rise to conflicting initial interpretations that are occasionally revealed to be terminological in character; thus, wide variation in initial scoring need not signify wide cognitive variation. Likewise, similarities in scores may not signal agreement. Second, the Likert scales are intended at least in part to spur dialogue by presenting the appearance of difference, motivating participants to talk about the statements.

[9]The Toolbox Project team is available as a partner in data analysis and other aspects of the Toolbox experience. After Toolbox Project–facilitated workshops, we can provide a complete analytic report that includes the perceptions of the session facilitator and recorder, a synopsis of a post-workshop questionnaire, summaries of Likert-score and transcript statistics, a complete copy of the transcript, and suggested next steps for the participating teams. The Toolbox Project maintains a database developed from the workshops we have conducted, including transcripts, Likert scores, and demographic data. Partnership with the Toolbox Project makes possible comparative analysis across other teams selected on the basis of variables important to the participating team. In addition, the Toolbox Project team (see http://www.cals .uidaho.edu/toolbox/) can assist with the creation of project-specific modules, suggest new tools for team development, and provide "Train the Trainers" workshops for teams interested in developing the Toolbox idea further.

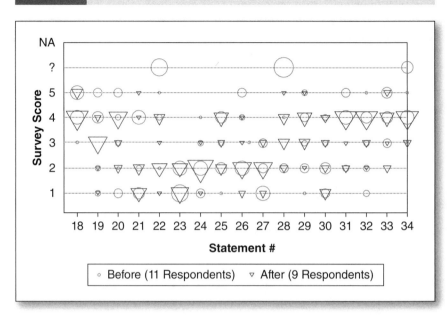

Figure 11.3   Pre- and Post-Workshop Likert Scores

NOTE: The magnitude of each symbol indicates how many respondents chose that score for that question. For questions 22 and 28, the change of many participants' answers from "?" to a numeric scale suggests that discussion relevant to this question may have clarified team members' views on the probing statement.

communication and collaboration skills, which are interdependent and necessary for cross-disciplinary success (see Klein, Chap. 2, this volume). Below we describe a few follow-up activities that the Toolbox Project has used with collaborating teams.

Reflection

Several teams have indicated that they continue to discuss their Toolbox experience during their ongoing work together. Some have dedicated post-workshop meetings to reflecting on the experience and digesting summary documents when these have been generated. In the Toolbox Project, we distribute a post-workshop survey and use this when developing our response to the participating team. Self-administered workshops could employ a similar survey to guide follow-up discussion. Useful prompts include the following:

- Describe the key discovery for you as an individual scientist during the dialogue.
- Explain why you think (or do not think) participating in the Toolbox workshop helped your professional development.
- From your experience with this team, explain whether you think mutual understanding of one another's philosophical orientations and disciplines is important for interdisciplinary team function.

- How have your individual views on the philosophical basis of your disciplinary science shifted since completing the workshop? Explain whether the Toolbox workshop contributed to that shift.
- What philosophical aspects of scientific research were not well covered through the Toolbox?

Follow-Up Workshops

Several teams have requested a second workshop, in some cases involving new members. A few of these have been conducted at one of the team member's homes in the evening in a relaxed atmosphere. In this setting, exploration of the Toolbox prompts can become deeply personal, contributing in diverse ways to group coherence and understanding. Follow-up workshops need not cover the entire scope of the Toolbox instrument, instead focusing on modules or prompts that have emerged as important for the team.

Customized Toolbox Instruments

The Toolbox in its current form is modular, which facilitates the creation of specialized core questions and prompts that pertain specifically to the team. As indicated earlier, we have created two new instruments for translational health science and climate science, developing modules that are appropriate to teams working in those contexts. These contexts put in play different philosophical issues, such as the challenge of harmonizing evidential standards between the bench and the clinic and cultivating trust between natural resource managers and academic scientists.[10] Both instruments were designed collaboratively with teams who ultimately used them in pilot workshops. Another approach is to insert into the relevant modules customized prompts submitted by team members that target specific issues of concern for the team. To retain the texture of Toolbox prompts, these should focus on abstract or conceptual dimensions of the team's collaborative work. In the principal case where we employed this method, the team spent most of their follow-up workshop discussing these customized prompts, which included, "It is possible to combine qualitative and quantitative approaches from different disciplines to answer interdisciplinary questions," and "Verbal communication (e.g., phone, Skype, face-to-face) with all team members present is critical for team success."

Other

Additional follow-up activities include concept mapping and specialized case analysis. Cross-disciplinary projects can benefit from concept mapping

---

[10]For more details about the translational health science instrument, see Schnapp et al. (2012).

to delineate the systems under investigation and identify research questions and integration opportunities (Heemskerk, Wilson, & Pavao-Zuckerman, 2003; Morse, Chap. 12, this volume). These exercises can be enriched using the insights gained from a Toolbox workshop, indicating on the map the concepts and activities related to important philosophical dimensions within the team. Maintaining and adjusting these maps as the project progresses can be a helpful way to revisit these aspects of the research effort.[11] Specialized case-study analysis involves developing focused, detailed vignettes that emphasize conceptual issues that arose for the team in the workshop. For example, a team of biologists and engineers might identify *hypothesis* as a concept that divides them; armed with this information, they could then describe situations in which these differences could threaten the success of their collaborative project. The vignettes then could be distributed among team members and discussed in a follow-up meeting. Also available are exercises designed to promote collaborative decision making, aid in the formulation of research questions, illuminate group dynamics, and enhance mutual understanding and awareness (e.g., McDonald et al., 2009; Repko, 2008; Winowiecki et al., 2011).

Conclusion

The Toolbox workshop can be thought of as an "epistemological intervention"—that is, an interruption of day-to-day research business designed to highlight the styles of knowledge making distributed across a collaborating team (O'Rourke & Crowley, 2012). This intervention can be extremely valuable in addressing complex problems for teams that work across disciplines. Teams of this type can devote significant effort to determining how to collaborate successfully and may struggle if differences in research approaches used by different members go unidentified. Such differences, especially if not uncovered early in a team's life, can complicate the work of the team and even make it dysfunctional, resulting in a degraded effort.

Having a group conversation about underlying assumptions can engender mutual understanding and improve communication about science that continues throughout the life of the project. The Toolbox method is designed to generate just such a discussion, making these assumptions salient by exposing the philosophical "landscape" of a team during a single workshop. Prospective

---

[11]We have employed concept maps extensively in the National Science Foundation Integrative Graduate Education and Research Traineeship (IGERT) projects at the University of Idaho. The six IGERT teams in the current project have explored this approach, and it has contributed to their thinking about research design, integrative research questions, and available integration opportunities; our impression is that it has promise if conducted iteratively as a project concept is developed.

participants may balk at the idea of spending 3 hours "talking philosophy," even if it is philosophy of science. However, we like to think that this type of conversation is analogous to turning on a desk lamp before sitting down to work—a small investment of time, energy, and attention that can pay big dividends down the road.

Take-Home Messages

- Effective communication across disciplines is important to the success of cross-disciplinary research teams.
- Guided discussion about philosophical aspects of research (e.g., epistemology, metaphysics) provides an opportunity to illuminate team dynamics and research worldviews in an abstract landscape while avoiding project-specific baggage.
- The Toolbox workshop provides cross-disciplinary research teams with a framework for engaging in discussion about concepts fundamental to scientific practice, promoting mutual understanding among team members about their disciplinary perspectives and practices.
- The do-it-yourself instructions identify the essential aspects of running a Toolbox workshop and provide suggestions for post-workshop activities to enhance the experience for participants.

Acknowledgments

This material is based on work supported by the National Science Foundation under Grant No. SES-0823058 and IGERT Grant No. 0114304. Any opinions, findings, conclusions, and/or recommendations expressed in this material are those of the authors and do not necessarily reflect the views of the National Science Foundation.

This chapter is much improved thanks to comments received from Gabriele Bammer, Troy E. Hall, Graham Hubbs, Julie Thompson Klein, and David Stone.

We thank all additional members of the Toolbox Project and Toolbox collaborators who have contributed to the approach presented in this essay: Carolyn Hovde Bohach, Brian Crist, Ruth Dahlquist, Troy E. Hall, Renée Hill, Justin Horn, Graham Hubbs, Ian O'Loughlin, Sara Pepper, Dan Schmidt, Lynn Schnapp, Lori Stinson, David Stone, Brianne Tice Suldovsky, Andrew Turner, Chris Williams, and our project advisers Frank Davis, Paul Griffiths, and Julie Thompson Klein. We are grateful to the participants of the "Enhancing Communication in Cross-Disciplinary Research" conference held in Coeur d'Alene, Idaho, in October 2010 for stimulating discussion of these issues.

We are also grateful to the more than 700 participants in 91 workshops conducted in the United States and Canada since 2006.

References

Bammer, G. (2013). *Disciplining interdisciplinarity: Integration and Implementation Sciences for researching complex real-world problems*. Canberra: Australian National University E Press. Retrieved from http://epress.anu.edu.au/titles/disciplining-interdisciplinarity

Black, L. J., & Anderson, D. F. (2012). Using visual representations as boundary objects to resolve conflict in collaborative model-building approaches. *Systems Research and Behavioral Science, 29*(2), 194–208.

Bracken, L. J., & Oughton, E. A. (2006). 'What do you mean?' The importance of language in developing interdisciplinary research. *Transactions of the Institute of British Geographers, 31*, 371–382.

Casey-Campbell, M., & Martens, M. L. (2009). Sticking it all together: A critical assessment of the group cohesion-performance literature. *International Journal of Management Reviews, 11*(2), 223–246.

Crowley, S., Eigenbrode, S. D., O'Rourke, M. R., & Wulfhorst, J. D. (2010). Localization in cross-disciplinary research: A philosophical approach. *Multilingual, 114*. Retrieved from http://www.multilingual.com/downloads/114LCDR.pdf

Eigenbrode, S. D., O'Rourke, M., Wulfhorst, J. D., Althoff, D. M., Goldberg, C. S., Merrill, K., et al. (2007). Employing philosophical dialogue in collaborative science. *BioScience, 57*, 55–64.

Falk-Krzesinski, H. J., Contractor, N., Fiore, S. M., Hall, K. L., Kane, C., Keyton, J., et al. (2011). Mapping a research agenda for the science of team science. *Research Evaluation, 20*(2), 145–158.

Fiore, S. M. (2008). Interdisciplinarity as teamwork: How the science of teams can inform team science. *Small Group Research, 39*, 251–277.

Franco, L. A. (2006). Forms of conversation and problem structuring methods: A conceptual development. *Journal of the Operational Research Society, 57*, 813–821.

Greenland, A., & Leach, J. E. (2008). Translational research for developing and sustainable agriculture. *Current Opinion in Plant Biology, 11*(2), 163–165.

Heemskerk, M., Wilson, K., & Pavao-Zuckerman, M. (2003). Conceptual models as tools for communication across disciplines. *Conservation Ecology, 7*, 8. Retrieved May 21, 2012, from www.consecol.org/vol7/iss3/art8/

Jakobsen, C. H., Hels, T., & McLaughlin, W. J. (2004). Barriers and facilitators to integration among scientists in transdisciplinary landscape analyses: A cross-country comparison. *Forest Policy and Economics, 6*, 15–31.

Klein, J. T. (1996). *Crossing boundaries: Knowledge, disciplinarities, and interdisciplinarities*. Charlottesville: University Press of Virginia.

Klein, J. T. (2008). Evaluation of interdisciplinary and transdisciplinary research: A literature review. *American Journal of Preventive Medicine, 35*(2S), S116–S123.

Krueger, R. A., & Casey, M. A. (2000). *Focus groups: A practical guide for applied research* (3rd ed.). Newbury Park, CA: Sage.

Lewicki, R. J., McAllister, D. J., & Bies, R. J. (1998). Trust and distrust: New relationships and realities. *Academy of Management Review, 23*(3), 438–458.

McDonald, D., Bammer, G., & Deane, P. (2009). *Research integration using dialogue methods*. Canberra: Australian National University E Press.

Morse, W. C., Nielsen-Pincus, M., Force, J. E., & Wulfhorst, J. D. (2007). Bridges and barriers to developing and conducting interdisciplinary graduate-student team research. *Ecology and Society, 12,* 8. Retrieved January 12, 2008, from http://www.ecologyandsociety.org/vol12/iss2/art8/

Musacchio, L. R. (2008). Metropolitan landscape ecology: Using translational research to increase sustainability, resilience, and regeneration. *Landscape Journal, 27,* 1–8.

National Academy of Sciences. (2004). *Facilitating interdisciplinary research.* Washington, DC: National Academies Press.

National Institutes of Health. (2011). *Restructuring the National Institutes of Health to advance translational science* (Submission to the Department of Health and Human Services). Bethesda, MD: Department of Health and Human Services. Retrieved from http://www.nih.gov/about/director/ncats/NCATSbudget.pdf

O'Rourke, M., & Crowley, S. (2012, September). Philosophical intervention and cross-disciplinary science: The story of the Toolbox Project. *Synthese.* doi:10.1007/s11229-012-0175-y

Pohl, C., & Hirsch Hadorn, G. (2007). *Principles for designing transdisciplinary research* (A. B. Zimmerman, Trans.). Munich: oekom Verlag.

Ramadier, T. (2004). Transdisciplinarity and its challenges: The case of urban studies. *Futures, 36,* 423–439.

Repko, A. (2008). *Interdisciplinary research: Process and theory.* Thousand Oaks, CA: Sage.

Schnapp, L. M., Rotschy, L., Hall, T. E., Crowley, S., & O'Rourke, M. (2012, December). How to talk to strangers: Facilitating knowledge sharing within translational health teams with the Toolbox dialogue method. *Translational Behavioral Medicine, 2,* 469–479. doi:10.1007/s13142-012-0171-2

Stokols, D., Fuqua, J., Gress, J., Harvey, R., Phillips, K., Baezconde-Garbanati, L., et al. (2003). Evaluating transdisciplinary science. *Nicotine and Tobacco Research, 5,* S21–S39.

Thompson, J. L. (2009). Building collective communication competence in interdisciplinary research teams. *Journal of Applied Communication Research, 37*(3), 278–297.

Winowiecki, L., Smukler, S., Shirley, K., Remans, R., Peltier, G., Lothes, E., et al. (2011). Tools for enhancing interdisciplinary communication. *Sustainability: Science, Practice, & Policy, 7*(1), 74–80.

Woolley A. W., Chabris, C. F., Pentland, A., Hashmi, N., & Malone, T. W. (2010). Evidence for a collective intelligence factor in the performance of human groups. *Science, 330,* 686–688.

12

Integration of Frameworks and Theories Across Disciplines for Effective Cross-Disciplinary Communication

◆ Wayde C. Morse

Independent disciplines have developed explicit frameworks and theories that conceptualize taxonomies of components and fundamental underlying assumptions about the nature of the world regarding their subject matter. Frameworks and theories are tools used as guiding principles for understanding, explaining, and making predictions about classes of phenomena. However, independent disciplines in isolation are not sufficient to solve many complex problems whose subject matter is not circumscribed by traditional disciplinary boundaries. This has led to collaboration of individual specialists across disciplines in an effort to address these issues. Teams vary in the interaction of participants and in the degree of integration of insights sought from disciplines. Both inter- and transdisciplinary researchers seek to integrate by developing conceptual frameworks that synthesize discipline-specific frameworks and theories in an attempt to build novel means to understand and address complex problems. This chapter presents a method that uses concept mapping to direct a dialogue process that will result in an interdisciplinary metatheoretical framework to guide research.

_____ Communication and Cross-Disciplinary Research

Complex Problems Require New Approaches

Academic disciplines are social communities institutionalized within universities, scholarly associations, and disciplinary journals (Weingart, 2010). "The essence of discipline formation . . . is self-referential communication" regarding "the delineation of a subject matter, a common set of problems and theories, concepts and specific methods to study it, the criteria of quality of achievement which are the basis for the evaluation and attribution of reputation by peer review" (p. 8). Disciplinary specialization has and will continue to produce significant advancements in science. However, independent disciplines alone are not sufficient to solve many complex problems whose subject matter is not circumscribed by traditional disciplinary boundaries (Bammer, 2005; Klein, 2004; National Academy of Sciences, 2005). Complex issues such as climate change, cancer, AIDS, sustainable development, and biological conservation cannot be sufficiently addressed by a single discipline (Ewel, 2001; Ostrom, 2009; Stokols, Hall, Taylor, & Moser, 2008). A form of systems thinking that examines the interrelationships of multiple variables within complex systems is required to address multidimensional complex issues (Hirsch Hadorn, Pohl, & Bammer, 2010; Mathews & Jones, 2008; Repko, 2012). Following Mathews and Jones (2008), Repko (2012) describes systems thinking in the following way: "It breaks down complex problems into their constituent parts, identifies which parts different disciplines address, evaluates the relative importance of different casual linkages, and recognizes that a system of linkages is much more than the sum of its parts" (p. 152). Accordingly, to address complex cross-disciplinary issues, there is a widely acknowledged need for increased collaboration and integration of research across disciplines. The first half of this chapter provides a background to interdisciplinary research and discussion of communication as it is applied to integrating insights from multiple disciplines. The second half of the chapter presents a combined conceptual mapping and dialogue method developed to enhance communication and facilitate research integration during interdisciplinary project framing. Several examples of integrated conceptual frameworks are provided at the end of the chapter to demonstrate the usefulness of the method.

Degrees of Integration

Integration has been defined as "the cognitive process of critically evaluating disciplinary insights and creating common ground among them to construct a more comprehensive understanding" (Repko, 2012, p. 263).

Disciplinary research is often considered one end of a spectrum of integration with the categories of multi-, inter-, and then transdisciplinarity research working across the spectrum to the other end. The degree of integration of insights from disciplines and interaction of participants often distinguishes where on the spectrum they fall (Klein, 2010). The degree of integration can vary across multiple aspects of research, including the problem definition, epistemology, research design and methods, framework and theories, and through to the final product (Morse, Nielsen-Pincus, Wulfhorst, & Force, 2007). In multidisciplinary research, problems are often defined by a lead discipline and disciplines work independently or sequentially (Stokols et al., 2010). Multidisciplinary researchers each apply their own frameworks, theories, designs, and methods to address the common problem (Golde & Gallagher, 1999; Rosenfield, 1992). Interdisciplinary research is

> a mode of research by teams or individuals that integrates information, data, techniques, tools, perspectives, concepts, and/or theories from two or more disciplines or bodies of specialized knowledge to advance fundamental understanding or to solve problems whose solutions are beyond the scope of a single discipline or area of research practice. (National Academy of Sciences, 2005, p. 26)

Importantly, the numerous insights accumulated through disciplines are the foundation and starting point for doing interdisciplinary research (Repko, 2012). At the far end of the spectrum is transdisciplinary research, which can be defined as where researchers from multiple disciplines come together with a specific goal to synthesize and extend theories and concepts from different disciplines to develop shared conceptual frameworks (Stokols, Hall, et al., 2008) with the intent to be holistic and restructure knowledge, synthesizing and transcending insights from individual disciplines (Klein, 2010). Beginning in the 1980s in Europe, transdisciplinary research has emphasized a focus on real-world application and problem solving, and the incorporation of insights and perspectives has been extended beyond academia to include those of other stakeholders and/or the general public (Klein, 2012; Lawrence, 2004).

Frameworks and Theories

When addressing a complex problem, there are likely to be a number of frameworks or theories from a variety of disciplines that provide at least a partial explanation of the concepts involved and how they influence the problem. *Concept*, as defined here, is a technical term used to represent an abstract idea or phenomenon (Repko, 2012). Disciplinary frameworks and theories represent taxonomies of concepts and outline relationships among them, providing organization and explanation of how and why the concepts are related (Repko, 2012). Frameworks and theories are tools used as guiding principles for understanding, explaining, and making predictions about classes of phenomena. While the terms *framework* and *theory* are often used interchangeably, they can be conceptualized as nested concepts, each representing a different level of specificity (Ostrom, 2005). Theories provide specificity regarding specific concepts and the strengths of relationships: "Theories make assumptions that are necessary for an analyst to diagnose a specific phenomenon, explain its processes, and predict outcomes" (Ostrom, 2011, p. 8). Theories are generally subjected to rigorous empirical evaluation over time before they are widely accepted within a discipline. Significant knowledge about the attributes, functions, and interactions of concepts within numerous disciplines has been accumulated through use and application of disciplinary theories. Frameworks are more general, identifying a broad set of concepts and general relationships among them, providing a metatheoretical language—that is, a language for talking about multiple theories (Ostrom, 2011). Frameworks, defined in this way, "attempt to identify the universal elements that any theory relevant to the same kind of phenomena needs to include" (p. 8). As a metatheoretical construct, frameworks provide a useful tool for organizing insights from multiple theories and concepts from different disciplines.

Disciplinary frameworks and theories can offer significant insight into research problems; however, the concepts, relationships between the concepts, and underlying assumptions of the disciplinary theories can lead to significant misunderstanding and conflict (Repko, 2012). The underlying assumptions of a discipline include the epistemology (i.e., concepts that frame the pursuit of knowledge), metaphysics (i.e., concepts that represent the nature of the world), and axiology (i.e., how values are represented) (Eigenbrode et al., 2007). These assumptions are often embodied within the discipline's frameworks and theories and are not made explicit outside of disciplinary forums (if then). These underlying assumptions lead to what has been called *trained incapacities* (Rosa & Machlis, 2002) leading researchers to view the world through a particular lens (Boix Mansilla, 2010). However, the depth and detail of work realized within a discipline is exactly what can be used to make productive contributions to integrated research. A specific goal of much interdisciplinary and transdisciplinary research is to develop new interdisciplinary frameworks and theories (Bammer, 2005; Klein, 2010; Stokols, Misra, Moser, Hall, & Taylor, 2008). Much of the training of inter- and transdisciplinary scientists is based on enhancing the ability to synthesize frameworks and theories, and evaluations of successful integrated research are based in part on these synthetic products (Nash, 2008; Stokols et al., 2010).

Communication Fosters Learning

Effective communication is the foundation for learning in inter- and transdisciplinary research (National Academy of Sciences, 2005). "The purpose of performing integration is to develop collaborative communication across disciplines and reconcile different or conflicting insights" (Repko, 2012, p. 328). Conflicts, differences, and gaps in knowledge are to be expected when examining a complex problem through the lenses of different disciplines (Newell, 2007; Repko, 2012). Developing common ground regarding concepts, their relationships, the frameworks or theories that explain the system, and the underlying assumptions of the theories is done through the process of communication. The cognitive processes that lead to learning and subsequent understanding are the result of communications during the integrative process (McDonald, Bammer, & Deane, 2009; Repko, 2012). Effective communication has been described variously as resulting in interdisciplinary learning, social and collaborative learning, and macrocognition (Boix Mansilla, 2010; Fiore et al., 2010; Keyton, Beck, & Asbury, 2010).

Boix Mansilla (2010) defines interdisciplinary learning as the process where insights or ways of thinking from multiple disciplines are integrated to advance understanding beyond a single discipline. In presenting a pragmatic, constructionist epistemology of interdisciplinary learning, Boix Mansilla highlights the importance of a collaborative team member's knowledge base in a disciplinary background: "Prior knowledge sets the stage for the insights to come, by informing questions, affording hypotheses, and providing an initial representation of the problem under study" (p. 295). The author proposes that it is necessary to actively learn about, identify, and reflect on the contributions of each discipline to the understanding of the whole.

Research focused on collaborative learning and cognition within interdisciplinary teams has defined macrocognition within teams as "the process of transforming internalized knowledge into externalized team knowledge through individual and team knowledge-building processes" (Fiore et al., 2010, p. 205). Communication is the primary means used to develop understanding, and the study of macrocognition focuses on how teams exchange information and how they develop a shared understanding. Particular emphasis is given to a recursive process of knowledge construction around a problem with individuals communicating their knowledge to the team, learning within the team environment, presenting new internalized ideas (i.e., individual interpretations or meanings gleaned from team discussions) to the team based on what was learned from team interactions, and continuing this process until the knowledge "is essentially the team's shared understanding of the problem and its parameters" (p. 215). Importantly, if team members have the ability to clarify meanings, to interact, and to ask questions with explicit feedback, it will "create the opportunity for the social construction of knowledge" (Keyton et al., 2010, p. 277). However, from a strict communication perspective, a more nuanced understanding of macrocognition would be labeled *meaning coherence* or *cognitive similarity*, as not every thought, interpretation, or individual meaning can be shared (Keyton et al., 2010).

Each of the descriptions of learning presents communication as the critical factor that fosters learning. They are all process oriented, interactive, and present learning as a cyclic or recursive task. They all present learning as the achievement of consensus, shared meanings, mental models, or macrocognition regarding an integrated team goal, or a shared view of the problem (Stokols et al., 2010). In essence, communication is the process through which learning and therefore integration happens.

Identifying the Problem

Inter- and transdisciplinary research are frequently designed to answer fundamental questions and address specific, complex problems identified in the field (Hirsch Hadorn et al., 2010; Klein, 1990). Therefore, discussions usually begin by identifying a problem and determining (at least roughly at first) the range of knowledge needs (Klein, 1990). Incorporating diverse perspectives at the initial stages of problem framing is a key element for successful synthesis and integration in inter- and transdisciplinary research (Stokols et al., 2010). Diverse disciplinary insights provide the first guidelines for defining a problem. "To ensure integrative problem framing, managers of interdisciplinary research projects have to make sure that this is accompanied by careful reflection on the disciplinary way of structuring the world and on the disciplinary contributions to the solution of the problem by the members of the team" (Stokols et al., 2010, p. 484). However, it is likely that the team will not initially agree on the problem or the main drivers or outcomes or how best to address the research (Hirsch Hadorn et al., 2010), and some conflict is to be expected (Repko, 2012). In fact, these differences are why we work together:

> The whole point of working with someone else is that he or she has an alternative perspective, skills, or some other attribute that contributes something relevant to addressing the issue either in improving understanding about it or in implementing that understanding in decisions and action. (Hirsch Hadorn et al., 2010, p. 446)

Nonetheless, "many projects fail in their efforts at collaborative problem framing, and, consequently, in developing integrated results" (Stokols et al., 2010, p. 482).

Methods to Facilitate Communication and Integration of Frameworks

There is currently no widely accepted systematic or standard approach to integration (Hirsch Hadorn et al., 2010). However, several authors have offered guidelines or methods for conducting interdisciplinary research.

Szostak (2002) presented a 12-step process, Newell (2007) developed a two-part process with 14 steps, while Repko (2012) has a two-part integrated model with 10 steps. Each method builds on previous versions and presents two overriding components: the use of disciplinary insights and the integration of those insights. Each of the authors indicates that the steps are not simply sequential but iterative, with a return to earlier steps as warranted when new insights or problems develop. Repko (2012) provides an extensive review of previous models and a detailed guide for how to do each of the steps on his list.

The process I propose is a dialogue method designed around the construction of a collaborative interdisciplinary concept map of complex systems. *Conceptual mapping* is a generic term used for any technique that visually represents multiple variables and their relationships (Kane & Trochim, 2007). The development of an interdisciplinary team concept map can be used as a platform to facilitate communication and understanding across disciplines. Visual organization through concept mapping can help individuals (or groups) explain and share their understanding of a topic (Hay & Kinchin, 2006). It is a method that helps groups manage complexity and "think more effectively as a group, but without losing the uniqueness of their individual contributions" (Kane & Trochim, 2007, p. 4). Concept maps are networks where the nodes are main concepts, lines connecting nodes represent relationships, and labels on the lines describe the relationship (van Boxtel, van der Linden, Roelofs, & Erkens, 2002). It has been shown that through the process of making collaborative concept maps, participants are more engaged, actively apply prior knowledge, articulate thoughts and elaborate on meanings of concepts, actively explore relationships between constructs, and coconstruct meaning and conceptual understanding (Kinchin, Streatfield, & Hay, 2010; Nesbit & Adesope, 2006; van Boxtel et al., 2002). As these shared meanings are discussed and added to the concept map, they become externalized team collaborative cognition (Fiore et al., 2010). Concept maps also facilitate negotiation or communication processes that allow for coconstructing meaning (van Boxtel et al., 2002). A powerful feature of concept maps is that they explicitly require the elaboration of organization and structure (Hay & Kinchin, 2006).

Repko (2012) promotes the use of concept mapping as a method to identify relevant disciplines and "identify the constituent parts of the problem, understand how these relate to each other and to the problem as a whole, and view the problem as a system" (p. 149). He provides guidelines for developing descriptive sheets with useful comparison questions for outlining the research purpose, concepts or principles, and theory (and refers to them as maps—though the questions could simply be listed on a sheet). Repko then draws heavily on Mathews and Jones's (2008) application of systems thinking to develop a systems concept map. "Systems thinking is an inquiry-based method of learning that uses the technique of perspective-taking, fosters holistic thinking, and engages in belief-testing" (p. 73). The examples of systems concept maps that Mathews and Jones provide include a casual loop diagram and a stock and flow diagram with descriptions of what the different symbols and formats represent (Mathews & Jones, 2008). A similar systems concept-mapping method used formalized symbols from ecology to describe the relationship between variables (Heemskerk, Wilson, & Pavo-Zuckerman, 2003). It is recommended here to use simple node shapes and textual descriptors in the concept map, in contrast to the more formalized symbols, as they tend to add another layer of interpretation and disciplinary bias that is unnecessary and detracts from the dialogue process. Different-shaped nodes may be used to identify the theoretical origins of a concept if desired. If simple order and direction between nodes are needed, then arrows may suffice. However, if descriptions of the links are needed, textual descriptors make conversation easy and more informative by identifying linkages with terms such as *influences, drives, provides, supplies, uses, includes, goes through, increases/ decreases, is modified by, offers, receives, impacts, regulates,* and *organizes.* Conceptual mapping done in this manner is simple to explain and can be easily done in small groups on whiteboards or paper where everyone can see. The development of this type of conceptual map across disciplines provides an ideal tool for inter- and transdisciplinary training in communication focused on collaborative learning with the goal of integrating frameworks from multiple theories (Nash, 2008).

Method: Using Systems Concept Mapping to Drive an Interdisciplinary Dialogue Process

What is offered here is a brief outline of the use of collaborative concept mapping of complex systems as a guide for a dialogue method for interdisciplinary project theme definition and metatheoretical framework development. It is intended to supplement the literature above and to add to the short dialogue methods used for research integration provided in McDonald et al. (2009). A systems perspective allows individual disciplinarians to include their traditional representations of the problem while also freeing them to explore the perspectives of others. Collaborative concept map development is then used to facilitate the dialogue about concepts, relationships, and theories to develop common ground as part of the interdisciplinary group learning process and to facilitate collaborative communication. An integrative metatheoretical framework (i.e., the final collaborative concept map) is developed from the understanding of common ground on concepts, relationships among concepts, and the theories that explain the relationships within the system. The metatheoretical framework can then be used to guide development of specific interdisciplinary research questions.

Developing an Interdisciplinary Project Theme

The first step of each of the previously mentioned methods began with an interdisciplinary question or problem definition. At times, even the development of initial research questions or problem definitions can inhibit integrated work, because researchers are accustomed to forming these from their own disciplinary perspectives. If this is the case, developing an interdisciplinary project theme may be a helpful alternative and is explained here. It should be noted that developing an interdisciplinary project theme here (in place of a problem definition) is both a beginning and outcome for this method, as the final systems concept map is necessary to ensure that the project has been sufficiently defined. The transition to the use of the word *theme* here is purposeful in that it is designated to indicate the main point, central message, or a unifying idea in contrast to a specific research question or problem statement that may give little indication of how the problem might be addressed in an integrated manner. It is useful to be as inclusive as possible at the outset when defining an interdisciplinary project theme; however, the scope must still be narrow enough to be manageable with the given time and resources available. The project theme will help determine which components and processes are emphasized and which are excluded (Hirsch Hadorn et al., 2010).

The example provided here is outlined for a collaborative team of disciplinary specialists (see Figure 12.1). A researcher (specialist) may begin with a topic or general problem he or she wishes to address, or, alternatively, a problem may be brought to the researcher. The general problem identification and team formation may occur in any number of different ways. (How a team forms and selects a problem is not inconsequential, but it is not addressed here.)

The first iterative position in the concept map dialogue process is with the initial team working to build an initial interdisciplinary project theme. A theme provides perspective and a central message that helps team participants (and other readers) understand what type of information will be required and what phenomena will or won't need to be studied, and helps define the scope of the project. A project theme should be clear and concise, reveal the overall purpose of the study, delimit the scope of the study, and be written as a complete sentence (Ham, 1992). The theme should also be written in everyday language and be free of disciplinary bias and jargon (Repko, 2012). The team development of a research theme is intended to focus the individual specialists on the big systems picture and away from individual disciplinary research questions.

A straightforward fill-in-the-blank exercise was designed to build thematic interpretative messages and has been modified to fit the purposes here (see Table 12.1; Ham, 1992). Interpretation "involves translating the technical language of natural science or related field into terms and ideas that people who aren't scientists can readily understand" (p. 3), a useful perspective for working across disciplinary languages as well. The result, then, is an interdisciplinary project theme that will be readily accessible by all disciplines and can also facilitate communication of the research with other stakeholders and the general public.

Figure 12.1 Concept Mapping as a Dialogue Process

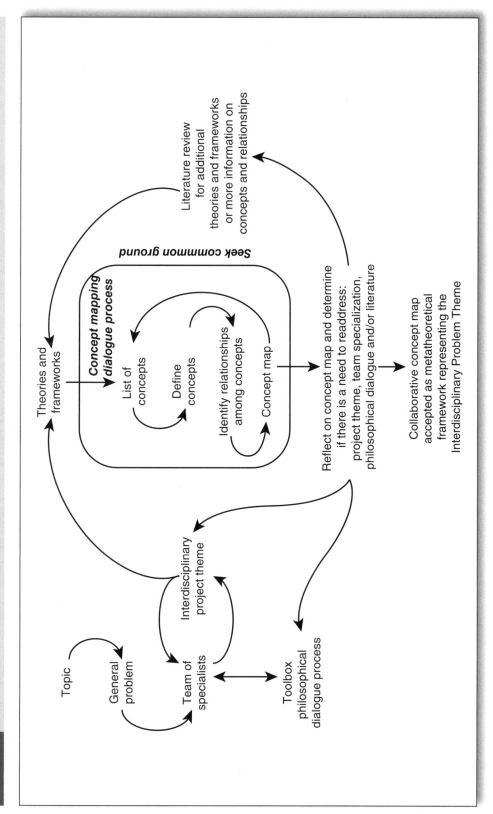

Two examples of initial interdisciplinary project themes are as follows:

- How we address dam removal on the Salmon River will impact salmon populations and the tribal peoples who depend on them for their livelihood and cultural heritage.
- There are important trade-offs between biodiversity conservation and rural development in anthropogenically fragmented landscapes in the Pacific Northwest.

The exercise is intended to initiate an interdisciplinary problem theme at a very general level. Both disciplinary and interdisciplinary research questions that fit under the research theme will begin to emerge almost immediately—and keeping track of these is a good idea—but they should not be the focus of discussion at this point.

If there is difficulty developing an interdisciplinary project theme because the underlying disciplinary assumptions of the various team specialists seem incompatible (e.g., there is little agreement on the nature of reality and/or how to study it), then the team should conduct the Toolbox method outlined in Chapter 11 of this book. This is more likely to be the case when addressing issues of wide interdisciplinarity that draws on epistemologically distant disciplines, such as biology and philosophy (Repko, 2012). The Toolbox is a "set of questions for self-examination that cross-disciplinary collaborators can use to identify and address their philosophical disparities and commonalities" (Eigenbrode et al., 2007, p. 55). Once these underlying assumptions have been addressed, the team can return to project theme development and then move on to developing a team systems concept map. The team may return to the Toolbox method if further exploration of concepts, relationships, and theories in the concept mapping portion of this method uncovers more philosophical issues (see Figure 12.1).

Table 12.1 Problem Definition Worksheet

Please complete the following sentences:

1. Generally, this research project is about [general topic] in [general location]. *Ex.: Ecosystem services in Costa Rica.*

2. Specifically, through this research project we will learn about [more specific topic] in [more specific location]. *Ex.: The effectiveness of Costa Rica's policy of payments for ecosystem services in the Sarapiquí region of Costa Rica.*

3. After this research project is complete, we will understand that . . .
   Es.: The effectiveness of Costa Rica's policy of payments for ecosystem services in the Sarapiquí region of Costa Rica is dependent on how the payments influence landowner decisions about landcover and how those landcover changes scale-up across the landscape.

Developing a Team Systems Concept Map

The first pass through the concept mapping dialogue process box in Figure 12.1 is done independently by each member of the team so each can develop his or her own disciplinary project concept map to be shared later with the group. Team members are considered disciplinary specialists and are not expected to reflect the perspectives of an entire discipline, only their own specialty within that discipline. Each team member identified so far should develop a concept map (as described previously) that outlines the project using theories within his or her specialty. I use the term *theories* here because "it is virtually impossible to conduct research in any discipline on any topic and not have to deal at some level with theory" (Repko, 2012, p. 198). Team members should also develop a concept definition sheet that provides working definitions (also written in everyday language without jargon) of the concepts they use in their maps and descriptions of how they are linked to one another from their perspective. The linkage words or phrases written on the concept map should reflect the more elaborate descriptions on the concept definition sheet. Once team members have completed their concept maps and concept definition sheets, they should reflect on their own maps and the team interdisciplinary project theme to identify their next step. Team members may decide to collect more literature and information on the project to revise their own concept maps. They may also decide that they need to go to the Toolbox (though this is more likely after they have seen other specialists present their conceptual frameworks). The next step might also be reconvening as a team to discuss the interdisciplinary project theme to see if it needs adjusting or if other disciplinary specialists should be added to the team.

If new team members (disciplinary specialists) need to be added, they should be invited for the next round of project theme definition. After a (revised) project theme is agreed on, the team should again go to the concept mapping dialogue process. This time, however, they should take turns presenting their specialist concept map to the others. Concept definition sheets should be shared. The theoretical understanding that provides the overall understanding of the concepts and their relationships should be explained as each team member guides the rest of the team through his or her concept map. As each team member presents, a larger collaborative concept map (i.e., a metatheoretical framework) should be constructed that identifies all the concepts and their linkages. At this point, the map should be all inclusive and like items simply placed near one another. A key reason for each specialist presenting his or her concept map is to develop team interdisciplinary adequacy. Adequacy, in this context, implies that each specialist does not need to be a master of all disciplinary specialties but that the other specialties defining elements must be understood, including the theories, concepts, and assumptions relevant to the problem (Klein, 1996; Repko, 2012). The process of listing and defining concepts, identifying relationships between them, placing them visually in relationship, and explaining the theory will fuel dialogue, helping develop adequacy among all team members.

Once adequacy has been established with individual specialist concept maps, it is possible to move toward establishing common ground regarding the concepts, relationships among them, and theories explaining the systems interactions. Frequently, concepts presented by different specialists will use different terms to describe similar ideas, use the same term to describe different ideas, have related ideas, and also have concepts that are not included in the theories of different disciplines (Newell, 2007). Common ground can be created through dialogue during the process of listing and defining concepts. Four techniques for harnessing commonalities of insights from different disciplinary specialties through conceptual modification are redefinition, extension, transformation, and organization (Newell, 2007). Redefinition involves "modifying or redefining concepts in different texts and contexts to bring out common meaning" (Repko, 2012, p. 258). Examination of comparable concept sheets should help identify concepts with different labels but overlapping meanings, or concepts with meanings so similar that slight redefinition could bring them into congruence. Extension differs from redefinition in that it involves extending the meaning of a concept until it can encompass the domains of both disciplinary insights (Newell, 2007). More creativity is involved in extension of concepts, and understanding the definitions from the various concept sheets (i.e., those you are trying to "extend"), their relationships to other variables, and their place within the concept map will aid this endeavor. Transformation is for situations where the concepts are opposites, such as war and peace, and for transforming them into a new continuous concept, such as the "amount of violence." Organization identifies the common meaning of a concept (using any of the three previous techniques) and then arranges the concepts spatially on a concept map within the system to reveal relationships among them (Newell, 2007). The specific emphasis on describing relationships among concepts on the concept definition sheets and developing a collaborative concept map (metatheoretical framework) to demonstrate organization is particularly useful for visually representing the relationships.

The concept mapping activities of Repko (2012) are also particularly relevant. The collaborative team concept map will help identify like items, as they should have been positioned near one another and have similar relationship terminology. It should also be noted that the same kind of redefinition, extension, and transformation techniques applied to concepts should be used on the descriptions of the relationships among concepts. Modifying relationships where necessary should be an equal part of the process for seeking common ground. Last, there are bound to be some concepts that are represented in some individual concept maps but not others. In this case, the relationships from the concept definition sheets containing these concepts and the theoretical insights as to how they fit into the system can be used to address their relationships with the more commonly used concepts; it could be that conceptual modification of one sort or another could be used to absorb them into existing concepts, or it might be deemed necessary to add them to the all-inclusive team concept map. As a new concept is added, there should be some reflection on how other concepts in the concept map may interact with it, and those relationships should be added to those particular concept sheets. Once a collaborative team concept map has been developed from the common ground established during the last round of presentations and dialogue, time should be taken to reflect on the map and associated modified concepts, relationships, and theoretical understanding. Points of clarification and new insights into meanings should be shared at this time. To facilitate this discussion, it is sometimes useful to have everyone identify something that surprised them in the model and explain why it surprised them. It may also be useful at this point to trim the concept map to those nodes and connections that are most relevant. Working back up from the new common-ground concepts and relationships among those concepts, theoretical implications of the way the new interdisciplinary system is expected to operate should be discussed. In this way the metatheory of the new collaborative conceptual map can be developed. Individual specialist theoretical foundations will likely be apparent and may even drive the explanation of the system, but the metatheory should emerge from and adhere to the integrated understanding developed by the team.

Next, the team should decide if they need to research additional literature, head to the Toolbox for philosophical discussion, return to the project theme and team composition, or accept the map and associated concept definitions and relationship definitions as their metatheoretical framework for conducting research. The process continues until the collaborative concept map is accepted. If the collaborative concept map (i.e., the metatheoretical framework) is accepted, the team will then start formulating interdisciplinary questions with a better understanding of the complete system they are investigating.

Examples of Three Integrated Frameworks

This section outlines three examples of framework and theory integration across insights from two or more disciplines through the use of concept maps.

Case 1

Interdisciplinary problem theme: The planning frameworks for recreation and for other natural resources on U.S. National Forest Service lands are not spatially compatible, and this leads to suboptimal management (Morse, Hall, & Kruger, 2009).

To explore this issue, we first looked at the planning frameworks the Forest Service used in natural resources management and those used in recreation. We found that much of the planning was spatially explicit and becoming increasingly so (Bettinger & Sessions, 2003). The primary theories used by forest managers, landscape ecologists, and conservation biologists for managing other natural resources were hierarchy theory and the theory of patch dynamics (Baskent & Jordan, 1995; Turner, Gardner, & O'Neill, 2001). Hierarchy theory is a perspective used to simplify research on scale effects in complex ecological systems (Ahl & Allen, 1996). A critical tool from this perspective is that for any focus level within a system (say, a patch of forest), it is essential to look both at the scale above that level (the whole forest) and the scale below that level (a tree-fall gap within the forest patch) in a process called "enveloping" (O'Neill & King, 1998). The theory of patch dynamics posits that ecologic systems are dynamic patch mosaics (Pickett, Wu, & Cadenasso, 1999), where patches are relatively homogeneous areas of vegetative cover or assembly that are situated spatially within the context of other patches, forming a mosaic. Hierarchy theory has been incorporated into patch dynamics to suggest that each patch is also composed of its own patch mosaic (Wu & Loucks, 1995). The concept map in Figure 12.2 demonstrates the focal-level vegetative patch (riparian area) as a nested component of the vegetative mosaic (forest, pasture, riparian area, recent harvest) across an entire forest (level above) and the riparian area as its own mosaic formed of riparian forest openings or subset of patches (level below).

The key recreation planning framework examined was the Recreation Opportunity Spectrum (ROS). The ROS is also a spatially explicit approach used to develop to a relatively broad extent an inventory of unique recreation settings (McCool, Clark, & Stankey, 2007). The guidelines for identifying those places as unique included (1) remoteness, (2) size of area, (3) evidence of humans, (4) social setting, and (5) managerial setting (More, Bulmer, Henzel, & Mates, 2003). Six classes of recreation opportunity settings have been operationalized using these guidelines: primitive, semiprimitive nonmotorized, semiprimitive motorized, roaded natural, rural, and urban.

The first integration point between natural resource management planning and recreation planning was to use the extension technique to conceptually consider each ROS setting category area as a patch within the patch mosaic of recreation opportunities across the forest (see Figure 12.2). Next, we identified the omission (i.e., the missing variable) of natural features, such as vegetative cover in the definition of recreation patches, and addressed that with a simple overlay of those on the ROS patches. Finally, we framed the new ROS with vegetation cover under the perspective of hierarchy theory (borrowing from another discipline) to identify nested patch mosaics of vegetative cover within ROS patches or, conversely, nested patch mosaics of ROS patches within vegetative cover patches (see Figure 12.2).

> The addition of the new level of recreation analysis based on vegetative associations and application of the concepts of "nested patch mosaics" and "enveloping" from theories in ecology provides additional detail on recreation opportunities and impacts and facilitates spatial integration in a way that improves analysis of trade-offs with the management of other resources at multiple scales. (Morse et al., 2009, p. 378)

Figure 12.2 Spatial Integration of Recreation and Resource Management

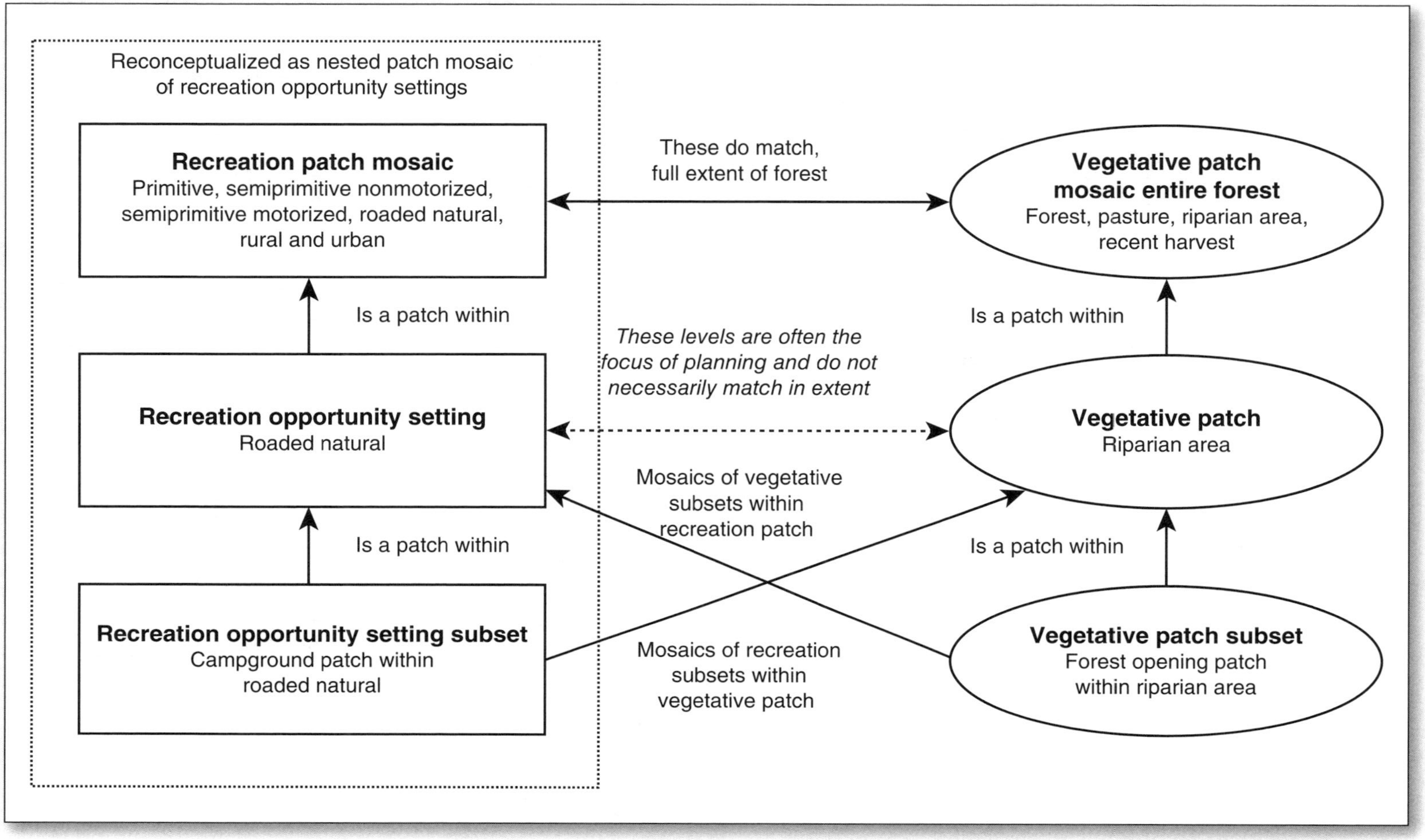

Case 2

Interdisciplinary problem theme: It is difficult to simultaneously manage for recreation and ecosystem services on U.S. National Forest Service lands because neither concept accurately portrays the other (Morse, Hall, & Kruger, 2012).

Ecosystem services is a new paradigm that links human welfare with functioning ecosystems (Fisher, Turner, & Morling, 2009); it is a concept used to describe the benefits that ecosystems contribute to human well-being. The most common categorization of ecosystem services comes from the Millennium Ecosystem Assessment (2005) and includes supporting, provisioning, regulating, and cultural services. Recent discussions of these categorizations argue that cultural services should not be considered ecosystem services because they are not ecological phenomenon (Boyd & Banzhaf, 2007; Fisher et al., 2009). In this literature, recreation is used as an example of the inappropriate categorization. However, the examples they use do not consider recreation theories and frameworks and therefore miss how benefits to human well-being have been defined and tested regarding the recreation experience. Through the integration of recreation theory and the ecosystem services framework, we clarify how ecosystem services contribute to the recreation experience. Additionally, we show that the ecosystem service framework is in need of a transformation construct that will help clarify the "difficult and unsatisfying" category labeled "cultural services," of which recreation is a part (Boyd & Banzhaf, 2007; Wallace, 2007). According to the authors, "final ecosystems services are components of nature, directly enjoyed, consumed, or used to yield human well-being" (Boyd & Banzhaf, 2007, p. 619). They have developed a simple sequential concept map of ecosystems services where intermediate services provide the foundation for final ecosystems services that then provide benefits (see Figure 12.3a). Fisher at al. (2009) build on this definition but note that the final services "typically require other forms of capital" (p. 646; e.g., pipes to get clean water to your house) to transform the final service into a benefit. In their examples, the fish population, the water body, and the landscape are final ecosystem services that lead to the benefit of recreation.

Recreation theory, however, has an experiential framework of recreation behavior that states that individuals participate in outdoor recreation with the expectation that the recreation activity, done in a particular setting, will result in certain beneficial psychological and physiological outcomes (Manfredo & Driver, 1996; Moore & Driver, 2005). The setting is further differentiated into social (i.e., who you recreate with and how crowded it is), managerial (i.e., level of management restrictions and facilities), and physical setting (i.e., level of remoteness) as demonstrated in the concept map in Figure 12.3b (Driver, Brown, Stankey, & Gregoire, 1987). The first and obvious point of integration is linking final ecosystem services to the recreation model through the physical setting, a simple redefinition. It is this ecological portion of the physical recreation setting that includes the final services (e.g., the landscape, the water body, and the fish) recognized by the other authors (Boyd & Banzhaf, 2007; Fisher et al., 2009). Other human inputs such as social and managerial conditions and infrastructure (e.g., facilities, roads) contribute to and transform the biophysical recreation setting (e.g., the final ecosystem services) and its potential as an opportunity setting for different types of beneficial recreational outcomes. Additional recreation skills and equipment are brought to the recreation experience by the individual recreationist. Therefore, it is relatively straightforward to integrate ecosystems services into recreation theory (see Figure 12.3b).

Figure 12.3   Recreation Theory and Ecosystem Services

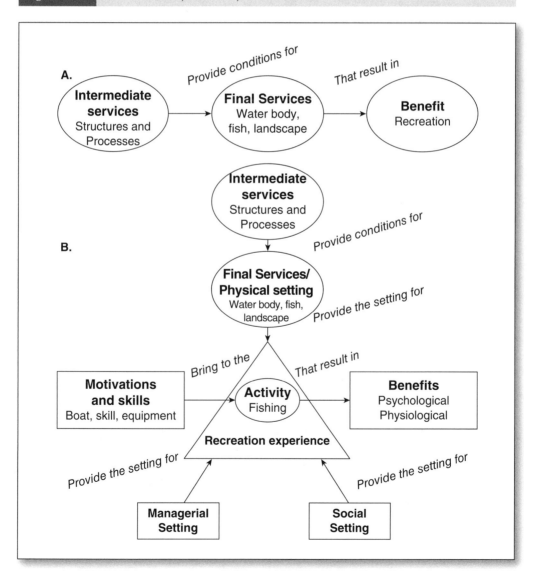

Alternatively, the first change resulting from integrating recreation theory into the ecosystem services framework is difference in the meaning of the terms *recreation* and *benefit*. Recreation in itself is not a benefit as framed in the ecosystem service literature but an experience that yields personal, psychological, and physiological benefits. This involves a redefinition of these terms. Integration of the full theory of the recreation experience provides insight into how experiences and social and cultural transformations can create benefits from final ecosystem services. Additionally, it is expected that differentiating the types of benefits achieved (i.e., physiological, psychological, economic) will help clarify the "cultural services" category of ecosystem services; some of them are transformative experiences (e.g., recreation), while others are final benefits of the experiences (e.g., aesthetic appreciation; see Figure 12.3b). This example demonstrates how commensurate concepts were defined slightly differently, but through redefinition a coherent conceptual framework was obtained.

Case 3

Emergent interdisciplinary project theme: Costa Rica's national program that pays landowners to maintain their forest is designed to influence landowner land-use decisions and increase forest cover and subsequent ecosystem services.

Ecosystems provide such benefits as carbon sequestration, drinking water, aesthetics, and biodiversity habitat. However, the lack of markets for these services means that landowners will not have an incentive to provide a socially optimal amount (Brown, Bergstrom, & Loomis, 2007). This has led to an interest in alternative markets to help incentivize the maintenance of ecosystem services (Wunder, 2007). In 1996, Costa Rica established a program of payments for ecosystem services that is designed to pay landowners for the services their land provides (Pagiola, 2008). The simple logic of the policy is that payments to individual landowners will influence their land-use decisions and subsequent actions to maintain or improve those services and have a positive impact on the provision of ecosystem services at the landscape scale. Frameworks that link social policies such as the ecosystem service payment program to the ecological provision of ecosystem services do not exist.

Several fundamental assumptions were applied as the basis for developing a framework to assess this policy within the larger social ecological system. First, social and ecological systems are dynamic and change over time, they are inextricably linked, and they co-evolve over time, exhibiting characteristics of what have been called complex adaptive systems (Berkes, Colding, & Folke, 2003). Structuration from the social sciences (Giddens, 1984; Stones, 2005) was integrated with theories detailing complex adaptive ecologic systems (Gunderson & Holling, 2002; Levin, 1998) to develop a framework of social ecological complex adaptive systems (SECAS; Morse, McLaughlin,

Wulfhorst, & Harvey, 2013). Through the recognition of how the theories explained the process of current conditions changing future contexts, it was possible to extend both theories to explain how the joint systems operated. Complex adaptive ecologic systems are represented as multiscale systems where lower-level components interact (through action or disturbance) to result in emergent patterns at higher levels, and the higher-level patterns from that period then feed back to influence lower-level patterns during interactions for the next period (Levin, 1998) The right-hand side of the concept map in Figure 12.4 demonstrates complex adaptive ecologic systems with disturbance as the driver of change in the system. Similarly, in structuration theory, social systems (structures) enable or constrain individual actions (which can have ecological implications such as deforestation or afforestation) during one time period, while those same actions produce, transform, or change those social structures for the next time period, continually producing and reproducing society (Giddens, 1984; Stones, 2005). The left-hand side of the concept map in Figure 12.4 outlines the process of social structuration with human actions driving change. For this analysis using the SECAS framework, individual land-use decisions by landowners provided the action/disturbance link between the social and ecological system. "A primary contribution of this framework is the application of social theory to social ecological complex adaptive systems to better explain human intent, learning and adaptation within and across the systems and, importantly, scales" (Morse et al., 2013, p. 56). The third example recognized similarities in theoretical models in both systems that through extension could find common ground. The other key integration point was recognizing that the actions of humans were driven in part by policy influences and a direct cause of disturbance and environmental change, thus linking the systems (see Figure 12.4).

Conclusion

This chapter outlines the rationale, proposes a method, and then provides some examples of framework integration and theory integration for inter- and transdisciplinary research. This method uses many of the same features and is guided by those found in Repko (2012) and Newell (2007). However, it diverges from other concept mapping techniques in the following ways: (1) the specialist concept maps that serve as the foundation for the collaborative map, (2) the more structured and iterative presentation of specialist theoretical concept maps used to build adequacy across the team, (3) pulling any philosophical discussion out of the concept mapping process and focusing it with a Toolbox workshop as foundational understanding that should be discussed prior to specific theoretical discussions, (4) the focus on the definitions of interactions among concepts (and modification of interaction definitions), (5) the dialogue instead of symbol-based concept mapping technique, and

Figure 12.4   Social Ecological Complex Adaptive System

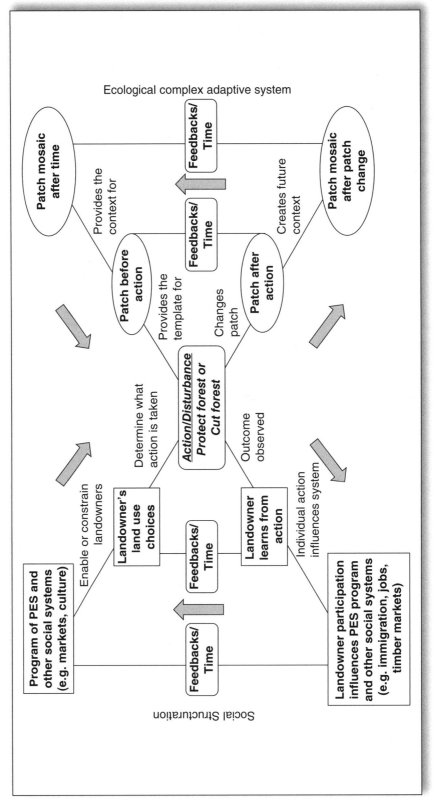

SOURCE: Morse, W. D., McLaughlin, W. J., Wulfhorst, J, D., Harvey, C. (2011). Social ecological complex adaptive systems: A framework for research on payments for ecosystem services. *Urban Ecosystems*. DOI 10.1007/s11252-011-0178-3

(6) less deference to a "lead" theory. This method is designed to be iterative and flow through disciplinary sharing to develop adequacy and collaborative team conceptual mapping and negotiation of common ground. It is designed to encourage reflection and facilitate communication specifically around frameworks and theories. It is suggested that through this, "intellectual integration is leveraged socially through mutual learning and joint activities that foster common conceptions of a project or program and common assessments. Mutual knowledge emerges as novel insights are generated, disciplinary relationships redefined, and integrative frameworks built" (Klein, 2008, p. S119).

Take-Home Messages

- Focused disciplinary research and self-referential communication has led to detailed and useful frameworks and theories.
- Inter- and transdisciplinary research should take advantage of these existing frameworks and theories in dialogue designed to develop shared meanings integrating them.
- A simple and iterative exercise developing an interdisciplinary project theme can help focus research.
- A group dialogue method built around developing a collaborative concept map will

  o develop team adequacy across disciplines by sharing specialist theoretical concept maps,
  o facilitate negotiation of common ground regarding concepts and relationships among concepts, and
  o result in a collaborative concept map that represents an interdisciplinary metatheoretical framework useful as a guide to developing interdisciplinary research questions.

- If success of inter- and transdisciplinary research can be identified by the development of integrated frameworks and theories, this should be a central focus of a research project.

References

Ahl, V., & Allen, T. F. H. (1996). *Hierarchy theory: A vision, vocabulary, and epistemology.* New York: Columbia University Press.

Bammer, G. (2005). Integration and implementation sciences: Building a new specialization. *Ecology and Society, 10*(2), 6.

Baskent, E. Z., & Jordan, G. A. (1995). Characterizing spatial structure of forest landscapes. *Canadian Journal of Forest Resources, 25*, 1830–1849.

Berkes, F., Colding, J., & Folke, C. (2003). *Navigating social-ecological systems: Building resilience for complexity and change.* Cambridge, UK: Cambridge University Press.

Bettinger, P., & Sessions, J. (2003). Spatial forest planning: To adopt or not to adopt? *Journal of Forestry, 101*(2), 24–29.

Boix Mansilla, V. (2010). Learning to synthesize: The development of interdisciplinary understanding. In R. Frodeman, J. T. Klein, & C. Mitcham (Eds.), *The Oxford handbook of interdisciplinarity* (pp. 288–306). New York: Oxford University Press.

Boyd, J., & Banzhaf, S. (2007). What are ecosystem services? The need for standardized environmental accounting units. *Ecological Economics, 63*, 616–626.

Brown, T. C., Bergstrom, J. C., & Loomis, J. B. (2007). Defining, valuing, and providing ecosystem goods and services. *Natural Resources Journal, 47*(2), 329–376.

Driver, B. L., Brown, P. J., Stankey, G. H., & Gregoire, T. G. (1987). The ROS planning system: Evolution, basic concepts, and research needed. *Leisure Sciences, 9*, 201–212.

Eigenbrode, S. D., O'Rourke, M., Wulfhorst, J. D., Althoff, D. M., Goldberg, C. S., Merrill, K., et al. (2007). Employing philosophical dialogue in collaborative science. *BioScience, 57*(1), 55–64.

Ewel, K. C. (2001). Natural resource management: The need for interdisciplinary collaboration. *Ecosystems, 4*, 716–722.

Fiore, S. M., Rosen, M. A., Smith-Jentsch, K. A., Salas, E., Letsky, M., & Warner, N. (2010). Toward an understanding of macrocognition in teams: Predicting processes in complex collaborative contexts. *Human Factors, 52*(2), 203–224.

Fisher, B., Turner, R. K., & Morling, P. (2009). Defining and classifying ecosystem services for decision making. *Ecological Economics, 68*(3), 643–653.

Giddens, A. (1984). *The constitution of society: Outline of the theory of structuration.* Cambridge, UK: Polity Press.

Golde, C. M., & Gallagher, H. A. (1999). The challenges of conducting interdisciplinary research in traditional doctoral programs. *Ecosystems, 2*, 281–285.

Gunderson, L. H., & Holling, C. S. (2002). *Panarchy: Understanding transformations in human and natural systems.* Washington, DC: Island Press.

Hirsch Hadorn, G., Pohl, C., & Bammer, G. (2010). Solving problems through transdisciplinary research. In R. Frodeman, J. T. Klein, & C. Mitcham (Eds.), *The Oxford handbook of interdisciplinarity* (pp. 431–452). New York: Oxford University Press.

Ham, S. (1992). *Environmental interpretation: A practical guide for people with big ideas and small budgets.* Golden, CO: Fulcrum.

Hay, D. B., & Kinchin, I. M. (2006). Using concept maps to reveal conceptual typologies. *Education + Training, 48*(2–3), 127–142.

Heemskerk, M., Wilson, K., & Pavo-Zuckerman, M. (2003). Conceptual models as tools for communication across disciplines. *Conservation Ecology, 7*(3), 8.

Kane, M., & Trochim, W. M. K. (2007). *Concept mapping for planning and evaluation.* Thousand Oaks, CA: Sage.

Keyton, J., Beck, S. J., & Asbury, M. B. (2010). Macrocognition: A communication perspective. *Theoretical Issues in Ergonomics Science, 11*(4), 272–286.

Kinchin, I. M., Streatfield, D., & Hay, D. B. (2010). Using concept mapping to enhance the research interview. *International Journal of Qualitative Methods, 9*(1), 52–68.

Klein, J. T. (1990). *Interdisciplinarity: History, theory, and practice.* Detroit, MI: Wayne State University Press.

Klein, J. T. (1996). *Crossing boundaries: Knowledge, disciplinarities, and interdisciplinarities*. Charlottesville: University Press of Virginia.

Klein, J. T. (2004). Interdisciplinarity and complexity: An evolving relationship. *E:CO, 6*(1–2), 2–10.

Klein, J. T. (2008). Evaluation of interdisciplinary and transdisciplinary research: A literature review. *American Journal of Preventative Medicine, 35*(2S), S116–S123.

Klein, J. T. (2010). A taxonomy of interdisciplinarity. In R. Frodeman, J. T. Klein, & C. Mitcham (Eds.), *The Oxford handbook of interdisciplinarity* (pp. 15–30). New York: Oxford University Press.

Klein, J. T. (2012). Research integration: A comparative knowledge base. In A. F. Repko, W. H. Newell, & R. Szostak (Eds.), *Case studies in interdisciplinary research* (pp. 283–298). Los Angeles: Sage.

Lawrence, R. J. (2004). Housing and health: From interdisciplinary principals to transdisciplinary research and practice. *Futures, 36*, 487–502.

Levin, S. A. (1998). Ecosystems and the biosphere as complex adaptive systems. *Ecosystems, 1*, 431–436.

Manfredo, M. J., & Driver, B. L. (1996). Measuring leisure motivation: A meta-analysis of the recreation preference scales. *Journal of Leisure Research, 28*(3), 188–213.

Mathews, L. G., & Jones, A. (2008). Using systems thinking to improve interdisciplinary learning outcomes: Reflections on a pilot study in land economics. *Issues in Integrative Studies, 26*, 73–104.

McCool, S. F., Clark, R. N., & Stankey, G. H. (2007). *Recreation and tourism initiative: An assessment of frameworks useful for public land recreation planning*. Pacific Northwest Research Station: U.S. Department of Agriculture Forest Service.

McDonald, D., Bammer, G., & Deane, P. (2009). *Research integration using dialogue methods*. Canberra: Australian National University E Press.

Millennium Ecosystem Assessment. (2005). *Ecosystems and human well-being: Current state and trends* (Vol. 1). Washington, DC: Island Press.

Moore, R. L., & Driver, B. L. (2005). *Introduction to outdoor recreation: Providing and managing resource-based opportunities*. State College, PA: Venture Publishing.

More, T. A., Bulmer, S., Henzel, L., & Mates, A. E. (2003). *Extending the recreation opportunity spectrum to nonfederal lands in the Northeast: An implementation guide*. Northeastern Research Station: U.S. Department of Agriculture Forest Service.

Morse, W. C., Hall, T. E., & Kruger, L. E. (2009). Improving the integration of recreation management with management of other natural resources by applying concepts of scale from ecology. *Environmental Management, 43*(3), 369–380.

Morse, W. C., Hall, T. E., & Kruger, L. E. (2012). *The integration of recreation theory with frameworks for ecosystem services*. Unpublished manuscript.

Morse, W. C., McLaughlin, W. J., Wulfhorst, J. D., & Harvey, C. (2013). Social ecological complex adaptive systems: A framework for research on payments for ecosystem services. *Urban Ecosystems, 16*(1), 53–77.

Morse, W. C., Nielsen-Pincus, M., Wulfhorst, J. D., & Force, J. E. (2007). Bridges and barriers to developing and conducting interdisciplinary graduate-student team research. *Ecology and Society, 12*(2), 8.

Nash, J. M. (2008). Transdisciplinary training: Key components and prerequisites for success. *American Journal of Preventative Medicine, 35*(2S), S133–S140.

National Academy of Sciences and Institute of Medicine of the National Academies. (2005). *Facilitating interdisciplinary research*. Washington DC: National Academies Press.

Nesbit, J. C., & Adesope, O. O. (2006). Learning with concept and knowledge maps: A meta-analysis. *Review of Educational Research, 76*(3), 413–448.

Newell, W. H. (2007). Decision making in interdisciplinary studies. In G. Morcol (Ed.), *Handbook of decision making* (pp. 245–264). Boca Raton: Taylor & Francis.

O'Neill, R. V., & King, A. W. (1998). Homage to St. Michael; or, Why are there so many books on scale? In D. L. Peterson & V. T. Parker (Eds.), *Ecological scale: Theory and applications* (pp. 3–15). New York: Columbia University Press.

Ostrom, E. (2005). *Understanding institutional diversity*. Princeton, NJ: Princeton University Press.

Ostrom, E. (2009). A general framework for analyzing sustainability of social-ecological systems. *Science, 325,* 419–422.

Ostrom, E. (2011). Background on the institutional analysis and development framework. *Policy Studies Journal, 39*(1), 7–27.

Pagiola, S. (2008). Payments for environmental services in Costa Rica. *Ecological Economics, 65,* 721–724.

Pickett, S. T. A., Wu, J., & Cadenasso, M. L. (1999). Patch dynamics and the ecology of disturbed ground. In L. R. Walker (Ed.), *Ecosystems of disturbed ground: Ecosystems of the world* (Vol. 16, pp. 707–722). Amsterdam: Elsevier.

Repko, A. F. (2012). *Interdisciplinary research process and theory* (2nd ed.). Los Angeles: Sage.

Rosa, E. A., & Machlis, G. E. (2002). It's a bad thing to make one thing into two: Disciplinary distinctions as trained incapacities. *Society and Natural Resources, 15,* 251–261.

Rosenfield, P. L. (1992). The potential of transdisciplinary research for sustaining and extending linkages between the health and social sciences. *Social Science Medicine, 35*(11), 1343–1357.

Stokols, D., Hall, K. L., Moser, R. P., Feng, A., Misra, S., & Taylor, B. K. (2010). Cross-disciplinary team science initiatives: Research, training, and translation. In R. Frodeman, J. T. Klein, & C. Mitcham (Eds.), *The Oxford handbook of interdisciplinarity* (pp. 471–493). New York: Oxford University Press.

Stokols, D., Hall, K. L., Taylor, B. K., & Moser, R. P. (2008). The science of team science: Overview of the field and introduction to the supplement. *American Journal of Preventative Medicine, 35*(2S), S77–S89.

Stokols, D., Misra, S., Moser, R. P., Hall, K. L., & Taylor, B. K. (2008). The ecology of team science: Understanding contextual influences on transdisciplinary collaboration. *American Journal of Preventative Medicine, 35*(2S), S96–S115.

Stones, R. (2005). *Structuration theory*. New York: Palgrave Macmillan.

Szostak, R. (2002). How to do interdisciplinarity: Integrating the debate. *Issues in Integrative Studies, 20,* 103–122.

Turner, M. G., Gardner, R. H., & O'Neill, R. V. (2001). *Landscape ecology in theory and practice*. New York: Springer.

van Boxtel, C., van der Linden, J., Roelofs, E., & Erkens, G. (2002). Collaborative concept mapping: Provoking and supporting meaningful discourse. *Theory Into Practice, 41*(1), 40–46.

Wallace, K. (2007). Classification of ecosystem services: Problems and solutions. *Biological Conservation, 139*, 235–246.

Weingart, P. (2010). A short history of knowledge formations. In R. Frodeman, J. T. Klein, & C. Mitcham (Eds.), *The Oxford handbook of interdisciplinarity* (pp. 3–14). New York: Oxford University Press.

Wu, J., & Loucks, O. L. (1995). From balance of nature to hierarchical patch dynamics: A paradigm shift in ecology. *Quarterly Review of Biology, 70*(4), 439–466.

Wunder, S. (2007). The efficiency of payments for environmental services in tropical conservation. *Conservation Biology, 21*(1), 48–58.

13

Modeling as a Tool for Cross-Disciplinary Communication in Solving Environmental Problems

◆ Laura Schmitt Olabisi, Stuart Blythe, Arika Ligmann-Zielinska, and Sandra Marquart-Pyatt

Interdisciplinary teams of academics are being challenged to take on ever more complex environmental problems, with implications for decision making that reach decades or centuries into the future. Models are important tools for representing the future states of complex environmental systems and how management or policy decisions might affect these states. Easy access to high-speed computing power and sophisticated model-building software have made quantitative, data-intensive computer models central to research that informs policy or management outcomes. Yet the potential of these models to facilitate interdisciplinary communication and understanding of the research problem within and outside of the research team remains underdeveloped. In this chapter, we explore the types of communicative benefits that quantitative models can promote, describe challenges to communication that can arise in research teams using models, and propose best practices for overcoming these challenges.

Introduction: The Benefits and Challenges of Modeling

In interdisciplinary teams studying environmental problems, quantitative computer models are widely used. These models depict hypothesized relations between theoretical constructs and are subject to rigorous testing of proposed relations through a variety of analytical techniques. Examples of these types of models include process-based models that depict water run-off, soil erosion, or climate change; system dynamics models that describe the interactive feedbacks between predator and prey species; agent-based models that describe the cumulative effects of individual developer decisions on landscape patterns; and so on.[1] Quantitative, computer-based models are used for environmental research because they can represent feedbacks between human and environmental systems (Hall & Day, 1977; Ligmann-Zielinska & Sun, 2010); portray potential future states of these systems and explore options for managing them (Costanza & Ruth, 1998); integrate different types of information from multiple sources (Schmitt Olabisi et al., 2010); and generate hypotheses for future research (McIntosh, Seaton, & Jeffrey, 2007).

Increasingly, models are not confined to one disciplinary tradition, as multiple correlated environmental impacts must be modeled in any given decision context (Milne, Aspinall, & Veldkamp, 2009). This means that researchers from diverse disciplinary backgrounds, with different perspectives on the system being modeled, are frequently collaborating in cross-disciplinary research teams. A team using a model will often have a particular member with expertise in the kind of modeling the team is using. This individual (the modeler) has special responsibilities and challenges to guide the process of building and using the model. Quantitative models have the potential to be powerful communicative tools for facilitating communication within research teams and between these teams and other scientists and decision makers. Yet their potential remains largely unexplored compared with other process tools such as mind mapping, causal loop diagrams, scenario development, and facilitated dialogue (Checkland & Poulter, 2006; Eigenbrode et al., 2007; Schmitt Olabisi et al., 2010; Swart, Raskin, & Robinson, 2004).

In contrast to these other techniques, quantitative models are viewed by research teams primarily as scientific tools rather than communicative tools, and they have been designed by scientists, not group process experts. As a result, the communicative aspect of these models—their ability to provide a platform for dialogue around the philosophical and practical aspects of the research project—is often glossed over when these models and their

---

[1]For an excellent guide to the most commonly used types of quantitative simulation models and other modeling methods, see Badham (2010).

findings are discussed. Unfortunately, this impedes the ability of the research team and their professional colleagues to achieve a highly in-depth and nuanced understanding of the science represented in the model. For example, one of the authors recently attended a scientific symposium on the effects of climate change on human health, whose audience included both scientists and public health decision makers. Over the course of the 2-day symposium, out of about 20 talks that referenced or explicitly discussed quantitative computer-based models, only two speakers explained the assumptions behind the model they used, described the limitations of the model, or spoke about the uncertainty represented in the model and how this uncertainty might affect scientific understanding and policy or management implications. Audience members were consequently left without a clear understanding of how the researchers represented the system under study, and why they represented it in the way they did. Critical aspects of the scientific issues raised by the presentations were therefore neither communicated nor discussed.

We propose that quantitative, computer-based modeling can contribute to three communicative tasks any collaborative team doing research on environmental issues must undertake and that these tasks should be taken as seriously as the model's scientific purpose (i.e., testing a hypothesis). These tasks are exploring individual perceptions regarding problem formulation (i.e., worldviews or disciplinary background), achieving a degree of consensus or shared understanding of the complex system being investigated, and determining how to use this understanding to inform practical policy or management decisions[2] (Klein, 2012). Teams rarely move through these three activities in a linear fashion. The process is iterative, with teams having to revisit each activity from time to time to achieve shared understanding of the system (see Figure 13.1). For example, a disagreement about the model's conceptual foundations or the validity of a model's output might prompt a return to shared assumptions. We discuss each of these activities in more detail below and conclude with practical suggestions for managing dialogue in the context of an interdisciplinary modeling project.

One final note is warranted about the context in which quantitative computer-based models are typically used in a research group context. It is highly unusual for research teams to use an "off-the-shelf" model to address a particular research focus without rebuilding portions of the model. Even if there is a preexisting modeling framework that fits the research topic, usually the model must be calibrated and adapted for the specific circumstances in which the research takes place. Therefore, there is little distinction

---

[2]Participants in a modeling research project also will engage in individual activities during such a process, but we are interested here in the work team members must do together; in this regard, we draw from interdisciplinary models where researchers continually translate global questions in disciplinary languages and the reverse in an iterative fashion to achieve consensus.

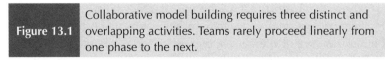

Figure 13.1   Collaborative model building requires three distinct and overlapping activities. Teams rarely proceed linearly from one phase to the next.

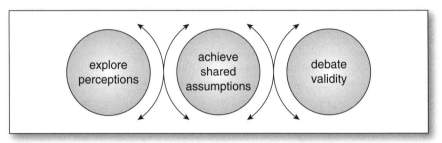

between "building" and "using" a quantitative computer model in a group research environment. We use these terms interchangeably throughout the chapter to refer to the entire process of conceptualizing, developing, calibrating, and validating the modeling approach associated with a scientific research problem.

Exploring Participants' Perceptions of an Environmental System

Quantitative, computer-based models have unique properties that can contribute to research team building through the cocreation of meaning unique to the research project (Keyton & Beck, 2010) and through facilitating shared cognition (Fiore & Schooler, 2010). These types of models can be extremely powerful tools for group sharing and reflection because they are able to make explicit and then test the assumptions and heuristics that are usually held implicitly by individuals on a team (Hall & Day, 1977; Morgan & Morrison, 1999; see also Kahneman & Tversky, 1974). Other types of group process and group reflection tools—such as mind mapping, causal loop diagramming, and scenario development—allow group members to share and discuss their assumptions and perspectives on the research problem. However, these tools do not typically allow research team members to treat their assumptions or perspectives as hypotheses, and test them using a data-driven model. This is a unique service that a quantitative, computer-based model can perform. Moreover, quantitative models are replicable in a way that other group process tools are not, due to the unequivocal representation and testing of assumptions in these models (Epstein, 2008). Quantitative models can point out to team members assumptions they hold that are logically flawed or inconsistent with other data, and systemic feedbacks they have not considered (Schmitt Olabisi et al., 2010). Of course, quantitative models contain their own assumptions, and it is important for a research team to achieve a working consensus around how these assumptions are represented. This can be the most challenging aspect of a research project involving a quantitative, computer-based model.

As an example, one of the authors was involved in a study commissioned by a legislative body in Minnesota whose aim was to examine the sustainability of Minnesota water resources under different future scenarios of population growth, energy production, and climate change. The author and fellow members of her modeling team met with key water experts around the state before beginning the project to gain some context for the model and to establish key assumptions. These water experts represented the project's stakeholders, as they would be using the information generated by the modeling project. The modeling team quickly found that these water experts disagreed dramatically about the definition of "sustainability." Ecologists and some hydrologists felt that a sustainable water management regime must leave room for water consumed by nonhuman ecological systems; however, most engineers and hydrologists responsible for monitoring water permits in Minnesota were trained to consider sustainable water use to be any use that did not draw down aquifers or surface water bodies by a noticeable amount. These different definitions of the term *sustainability* reflected the different worldviews and responsibilities of the various stakeholders. Because choosing which definition to adopt would determine the assumptions, structure, and approach of the model, the modeling team had to achieve a consensus on a working definition of sustainability in the context of the project. The existence of the research project itself brought to light these important disagreements about what constitutes water sustainability in Minnesota and facilitated dialogue among individuals critically involved with water management in the state. A discussion about the meaning of sustainability in the context of Minnesota's water resources could have taken place through group discussion or other nonmodeling tools. However, by quantifying and testing a definition of "water sustainability" with a simulation model, the author and her colleagues were able to treat this definition as a hypothesis and examine the implications for water management within a variety of future contexts. This brought a level of scientific rigor to the discussion that might not have been achieved through the use of other tools (Suh, Chiu, & Schmitt Olabisi, 2010).

Models also have utility as storytelling devices, and some researchers have proposed that this is, or should be, their primary function (Couclelis, 2005; Guhathakurta, 2002). Stories need not be only verbal. Kok (2009) argues that stories "can be told in both words and numbers, offering an internally consistent and plausible explanation of how events unfold over time" (p. 122). According to Kok,

> There is a high degree of potential complementarity between stories that involved stake-holders and stimulated creative thinking, and models that are quantitative and rigorous. In fact, this is the very reason that the Story-and-Simulation approach has been suggested and successfully adopted. (pp. 122–123)

Thus, it is possible to develop stories using models, or linked to model data. Doing so can bring unique perspective to a scientific or management problem, because it is not common to see imaginative stories and scientific data coexisting and informing one another.

For example, one author was a member of a team that developed quantitative simulation models around imaginative scenarios proposed by groups of community partners in various locations in Minnesota (Johnson et al., 2012). The participants developed narratives of the state of critical natural resources in Minnesota in the year 2050. The author, as a modeler, started from the assumptions used by the participants and then used available data, projected trends, and dynamic relations between variables to describe the same scenarios quantitatively. The dialogue between the modeled and imaginative scenarios produced fascinating results. In one region of the state, participants were surprised at how much land would be required to grow biofuels to meet their transportation and electricity needs; they hadn't considered some key feedbacks that affected energy consumption in their region, which were pointed out by the model. In an agricultural region, participants questioned assumptions behind model projections of land requirements to feed regional populations, pointing out the limitations of available data. The "stories" told by the imaginative scenarios and the model were different but complementary. Like conflicting narratives of an historical event, much can be learned by studying and discussing these differences! Therefore, a model may be used as a storytelling device to deepen scientific understanding of the research problem.

Many modeling approaches use special symbols or objects to represent variables and the relations between them—examples include the stock-and-flow structure of system dynamics models, the Odum symbology adopted by systems ecologists, or path analysis (Meadows, 2008; Odum, 1983; Wright, 1960). These symbols may serve as communication tools, allowing research team members to discuss interconnections between different components of a system. Modeling symbology can therefore create shared meaning and symbolic convergence (Bormann, 1996).

As discussed earlier, models can stimulate productive dialogue around differing views of a research problem in three ways: by making assumptions and heuristics of a problem explicit; by telling a story about the problem; and by providing symbols for a group to define, discuss, and manipulate.

Achieving Shared Understanding of an Environmental System

Many modelers and researchers have written about the utility of quantitative simulation models for shedding light on the operation of complex systems (Epstein, 2008; Hall & Day, 1977; Meadows, 2008). Indeed, this is one of the strengths of using modeling for interdisciplinary environmental research (Odum & Odum, 2000). Models can illuminate interactions, feedbacks, emergent behavior, and reciprocal relations between human and environmental systems that are not immediately apparent to individual researchers. For instance, a classic example of a three-variable feedback loop is found in climate science. That is, a warmer climate leads to less snow and ice on the surface of the earth, which leads to less reflection of heat, which makes the climate warmer (a positive, or reinforcing, feedback loop). Social scientists might introduce the role of human behavior, societies, and/or policies into the model as potentially mitigating factors, thereby creating an important negative, or balancing, feedback loop. This adds complexity to the model as the individual researcher is often in unfamiliar territory in describing relations among variables that span both the natural and social sciences.

In many types of models (like system dynamics and agent-based models), different types of information, including both qualitative and quantitative information, may be integrated—something that is not possible with diagramming tools (Schmitt Olabisi, 2010). This is true not only of differences between qualitative and quantitative but between scientific data (that is, hypothesis-driven, statistical data) and nonscientific data (Mackinson & Nøttestad, 1998). For example, key informant interviews or focus groups can be used to collect information about how variables in the models relate to one another. Interviewees would typically describe these relations in qualitative terms (e.g., "When people understand health risks from extreme heat, they are more likely to take action during a heat event by going to a cooling center"). Quantitative information from other data sources may then be used to parameterize these relations. This allows researchers to access local experts' perceptions of the way the system works and combine this knowledge with empirically derived information.

Models may also be used to challenge prevailing beliefs and theories about the nature of a system by examining the boundary conditions of model inputs. Such "stress testing" involves studying extreme values and outliers within the distribution of inputs and analyzing the consequences of input conditions, which are evaluated singly and in combinations with a varying level of dimensionality. Stress testing generates surprise and novelty that illuminate aspects of the underlying system and its representation. As a result, teams using models are exposed to unanticipated outcomes, resulting from their lack of knowledge about the system structure and function (system-model mismatch) or to logical inconsistencies in the model (model-implementation mismatch). In both cases, research teams gain insight into the collectively shared flaws in systemic thinking about the modeled problem. A model can therefore be a means of creating a research product that is greater than the sum of its diverse disciplinary parts.

Challenges to Achieving Shared Understanding Through Modeling

In addition to enhancing cognitive understanding of an environmental problem through facilitating communicative dialogue, models can create a group learning experience as research team members discover aspects of system behavior together (Kolb, 1984). However, there are several challenges to designing a modeling project for achieving enhanced understanding of an environmental system.

First, a research team must avoid mismatches between model conceptualization and development and the underlying science. In their thought-provoking dialogue, Seppelt, Müller, Schröder, and Volk (2009) argue that complex systems modeling is generally too abstract and intricate, which stands in sharp contrast to the "concealed-yet-concrete" problems that gave rise to environmental science. Too often, mathematical complexity (that is, the number of variables in the model and the relations between them) is inappropriately equated with the complexity of the system under study. This model-science incongruity is further exacerbated by the inability to "sell" the simulation results to practitioners, who perceive modelers more as mathematicians than environmental science experts. Consequently, empirically grounded models require modelers to be conversant with the disciplinary theories describing the systems they model (such as landscape ecology or political science); the manner in which empirical data are collected in these systems and the limitations of these data; and the theory and practice of modeling itself. This can represent a daunting challenge, which is why many modelers tend to develop expertise in one type of system or field of study.

Second, a model that is an effective tool for achieving systemic understanding must be formulated at a level of detail or aggregation that appropriately represents the system under study without becoming too complex. This tension is the classic trade-off between achieving model comprehensiveness while simultaneously achieving model parsimony. The more elaborate and detailed the model, the more incomprehensible it may be to nonmodeling members of a research team, or to scientists outside of the modelers' field of study. Models with too many parameters or components can become a "black box," which diminishes their utility as tools for group thinking and learning about a system (Bankes, 1993). Some modelers have argued that significant, formal models are almost always understood only by a select few (Richardson & Andersen, 1995). Other modelers have argued that a simpler model is almost always better than a detailed one for achieving clarity about key drivers in the system of interest. Most systems have only a few strongly significant drivers; the challenge for the modeler is to find them (Saltelli, Ratto, Tarantola, & Campolongo, 2006). Modelers, and teams using models, must therefore find a balance between detail and comprehensibility. This might be done by isolating particular relations in the model to investigate them in more depth.

A final challenge to using models as tools for shared understanding of human/environmental systems involves the articulation of uncertainty, which embodies the incompleteness of the model as a representation of the real world. Scientists from different disciplinary backgrounds have vastly different expectations and conventions for managing and communicating uncertainty (Climate Change Science Program, 2009). Furthermore, a modeling project may require the representation of many different types of uncertainty. For example, parametric uncertainty, which represents the appropriateness of parameter estimates within a model, must be discussed and managed differently from structural uncertainty, which indicates how appropriate a model is for addressing a given problem (Draper, 1995; Wintle, McCarthy, Volinsky, & Kavanagh, 2003). Other conceptualizations of uncertainty pertain to the *context of the model* (how the model is represented within the larger-scale system), *inputs and structure* (data and formulae have uncertainty associated with their collection and representation), and *technical aspects* (how algorithms are used to represent key model concepts; Warmink, Janssen, Booij, & Krol, 2010). Research teams using models must understand that some uncertainty lies outside the realm of scientific inquiry altogether—for example, uncertainty over which values or heuristics are appropriate for understanding an environmental problem (Sarewitz, 2004). Other types of uncertainty cannot be quantified, because they represent the "unknown unknowns," or the limits of our understanding about a system (Helton & Burmaster, 1996). Lempert, Popper, and Bankes (2003) argue that such *deep uncertainty* occurs when the probability distributions of key model variables are ill defined or when the stakeholders have little knowledge of or consensus on the descriptions of the key system drivers. For example, in land use and land cover change (LULC) modeling, the variability of inputs often comes from the distributions of socioeconomic characteristics of individual farmers that operate on land. In such models, the quantifiable uncertainty, referred to as the "known unknowns," is implemented in the form of probability distributions of socioeconomic variables such as land tenure, off-farm income, and family size. A more challenging aspect, however, is to incorporate intangible model variables that significantly affect land-related decision making, such as subjective values and beliefs, the magnitude of proximal and distal social interactions that influence farmer's behavior, or their choice heuristics. Even more challenging is the conceptualization and implementation of the indirect drivers of LULC systems, including the extent of impact of the applied herbicide on aquatic organisms in a remote lake, the nutritional value of food produced from crops treated with such herbicides, or the influence of the toxic byproducts of these herbicides on the surrounding forests.

Different understandings of how uncertainty affects the formulation of a model and interpretation of model results are common in interdisciplinary research teams and must be resolved through ongoing communication. At the same time, building a model together can facilitate discussions of uncertainty in the context of the research project.

Using Model Outcomes to Inform Decisions_____

Many models are developed as tools to inform policy or management decisions. They are uniquely suited to this challenge, because an appropriately developed model has some predictive power and can therefore provide insight into the future of human and environmental systems under different management or policy options (Von Bertalanffy, 1968). Models allow scientists and decision makers to experiment with a representation of a system before committing to a given policy or course of action, thereby generating policy alternatives (Ligmann-Zielinska & Jankowski, 2007). In some cases—particularly through participatory modeling approaches—models can also be used to generate consensus among stakeholders about which policy or decision to adopt (Van den Belt, 2004).

Some of the challenges of using models to inform decision making are practical. Building a model and developing policies based on model output tends to be far more time-consuming and expensive than a "top-down" decision-making paradigm (Hodges, 1991; North & Macal, 2007). Taking the extra time and expense to incorporate a modeling approach may be worth it if there is a need for dialogue around the cognitive, substantive, and informative dimensions of the decision to be made. Studies have indicated that when participants collaborate on building a quantitative model of a system to inform a policy decision, more concepts are discussed in greater depth compared with groups that engage in a facilitated discussion around the decision (Dwyer & Stave, 2008).

Another challenge involved in using models to inform decision making is the potential mismatch between the temporal and spatial scale of important model drivers and the scale of human decisions (Agarwal, Green, Grove, Evans, & Schweik, 2002). To cite a commonly used example, models of climate change suggest that policy decisions on carbon emissions have biophysical ramifications decades or even centuries into the future, but politicians making those decisions are typically judged on a reelection cycle of only 2 to 6 years. This can create a "scale-of-action" mismatch between models and the decisions they are meant to inform (Hare, Letcher, & Jakeman, 2003).

Finally, using a model to represent alternative futures for informing decision making can present a challenge, as different members of a research team frequently hold different disciplinary and personal attitudes toward "predicting," "forecasting," or depicting the future in any way. For example, some researchers—particularly those trained in statistical methods—often want to associate a probability distribution with any future state depicted by a model, while researchers who work with complex systems are often resistant to doing this, preferring a scenario approach so model users can understand the variety of plausible future states given initial conditions of a system. Representing the future state of a complex system at all is fraught with uncertainty, and some researchers argue that it shouldn't even be attempted (Edwards, 1999). In defense of the attempt, neglecting to build a formal model of the future typically means a deference to commonly held mental models of the future, which are often deeply flawed (Sterman & Sweeney, 2007).

A common aphorism invoked about the problems with using models to portray the future is George Box's famous quotation, "All models are wrong, but some models are useful" (Epstein, 2008; Hodges, 1991). Modelers point to this saying to explain that their portrayals of a system's future state are not predictions but representations of plausible futures (Bawden & Packham, 1993; Couclelis, 2005; Schmitt Olabisi et al., 2010). A model's primary value may therefore be as an exploratory tool to guide further study and to generate robust decision paradigms, not as a predictive tool that describes what the future will be (Epstein, 2008; Oreskes, Shrader-Frechette, & Belitz, 1994; Van Der Leeuw, 2004). However, the value of a model for informing policy and management decisions depends on that model's ability to persuade those responsible for making these decisions that the model can accurately represent causal connections between current decisions and future impacts on human or environmental systems. Aristotle said that rhetoric was necessary whenever absolute certainty was impossible to achieve; a model is inevitably rhetorical when it comes to its ability to inform policy. It has to be designed in a way that persuades others that its outcomes have enough validity to warrant action. Participatory modelers address the challenge of persuading decision makers of model validity by including their voices, perspectives, and concerns in the modeling process (Van den Belt, 2004). In fact, the very effort to develop a model through participatory means is an effort to ensure that an account of a system is persuasive for stakeholders. An effort to develop "shared problem perspectives" between disparate stakeholders is essentially an effort to persuade them to adopt a new perspective.

The tension between the need for models to convince decision makers of their ability to represent causal outcomes and the impossibility of accurately predicting future states of complex systems is both unresolved in the modeling world and one of the biggest misunderstandings of modeling work by nonmodelers (Bankes, 1993; Moss, 2008; Thompson & Derr, 2009). It is imperative that cross-disciplinary research teams discuss how the future will be represented in their modeling work and what kind of forecasting accuracy will be expected from the model.

Suggestions for Model-Building Best Practices

We conclude with some practical suggestions for harnessing the power of quantitative, computer-based models for facilitating interdisciplinary team communication, while acknowledging that relatively little attention has been paid in the literature to "best practices" that address the communication and team science involved in environmental model building (Martinez & Richardson, 2001). These best practices are standard in the literature on communication and group process, but they may be relatively more novel to quantitative modelers and model-building teams, who (as discussed earlier) tend to focus on developing their models as scientific rather than communicative tools. More research should document the process of model conceptualization, construction, and use by interdisciplinary teams and associated communication and learning outcomes (Oreskes, Shrader-Frechette, et al., 1994). This would allow modelers and other members of research teams to achieve both the best communicative process and the best science through model building (see Figure 13.2).

Best Practices for Teams Building a Model

Modelers and models can contribute optimally to a group research project when they are involved in the project from the beginning stages, as the research question is first being defined (Becu, Neef, Schreinemachers, & Sangkapitux, 2008). This allows the model to be a tool for the initial assumption- and boundary-setting discussions that are crucial to defining the research question in an interdisciplinary team setting. For example, participatory system dynamics modeling typically involves group codevelopment of variables and relations between variables depicted in the model, through causal loop diagramming.[3] Members of an interdisciplinary team could use this technique to frame a research question at the beginning of a project, as opposed to developing a scientific question and then "handing it over" to a modeler. Modelers could also learn from social science and communication research on how to incorporate group input and facilitate dialogue (Luna-Reyes & Andersen, 2003).

Modelers should ensure a minimal degree of modeling transparency for all members of the research team to work effectively when constructing and using a model. This transparency may be realized by using well-defined ontologies and well-structured description protocols, which allow for potentially replicating the reported modeling experiments by other research groups (Grimm et al., 2006; Polhill & Gotts, 2009). Modeling ontologies are formal conceptualizations of the simulated structures and relationships, in which the intricacies of the implementation algorithms are eliminated. By applying such ontologies, modelers learn how to decouple the programmed procedures (the syntax) from the modeled processes (the meaning). Description protocols offer a standard device for reporting different model aspects, thereby ensuring methodological and technical clarity. As discussed earlier, model comprehensibility may also be improved by developing the simplest possible model that addresses the research question adequately (Martinez & Richardson, 2001), and by articulating model uncertainties.

---

[3]Causal loop diagramming is a method for conceptualizing the dynamics of a system with feedback and circular causality. System dynamics modelers commonly use it as a first step in model development, or as a communications tool. For more on this technique, see Lane (2008).

Figure 13.2 Best practices for cross-disciplinary research teams working with models, compiled from the modeling literature and authors' experience.

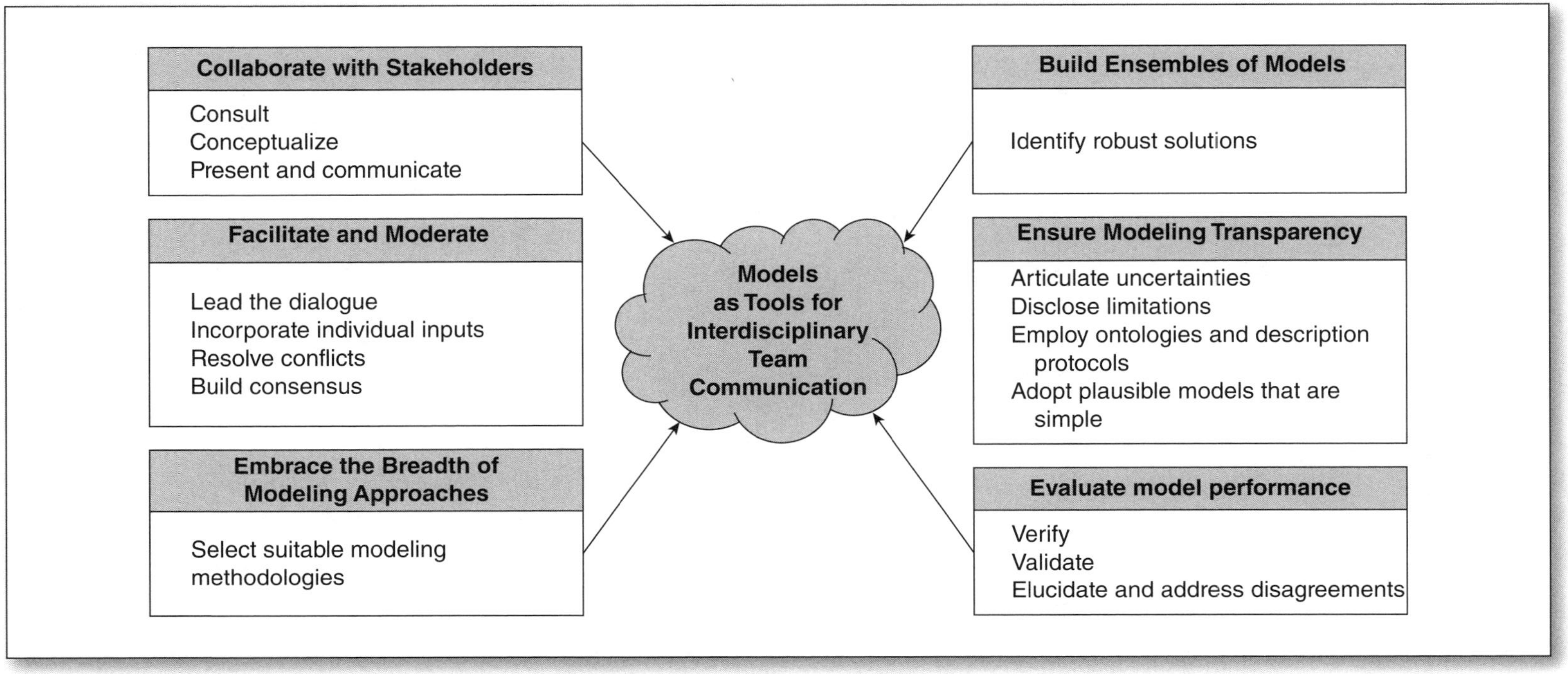

Collaborate with Stakeholders

Consult
Conceptualize
Present and communicate

Facilitate and Moderate

Lead the dialogue
Incorporate individual inputs
Resolve conflicts
Build consensus

Embrace the Breadth of Modeling Approaches

Select suitable modeling methodologies

Models as Tools for Interdisciplinary Team Communication

Build Ensembles of Models

Identify robust solutions

Ensure Modeling Transparency

Articulate uncertainties
Disclose limitations
Employ ontologies and description protocols
Adopt plausible models that are simple

Evaluate model performance

Verify
Validate
Elucidate and address disagreements

Finally, research teams using models must agree that the model is performing adequately in order to use the model as a communicative tool and to "believe" the model results. Evidence of model adequacy is sometimes called *validation*, although this term is controversial and sometimes replaced with *verification* (Oreskes, Shrader-Frechette, et al., 1994). Many different forms of validation may be appropriate or acceptable, depending on the model's intended use and the availability of data with which to compare model results (Richardson & Andersen, 1995). Ideally, teams should discuss the validation process, and what constitutes acceptable evidence of model performance, at the beginning of the modeling project. This discussion should include group consensus on how to handle a disagreement of the model with other data (Brugnach, Dewulf, Pahl-Wostl, & Taillieu, 2008).

Best Practices for Institutions Training Modelers

For effective communication to take place, quantitative modelers must be able to develop and facilitate the group process around model building (Fiore & Schooler, 2010; Keyton & Beck, 2010; Oreskes, Belitz, & Shrader-Frechette, 1994). Modelers almost always work in interdisciplinary teams in which they are the team member primarily responsible for integrating perspectives and information from multiple disciplines, so it is especially important that they recognize and promote the use of the model as a communicative tool in addition to its use for testing a scientific hypothesis. Unfortunately, modeling classes and programs tend to be heavily goal oriented and not self-reflective around the process of constructing and using models. Most quantitative modelers, like most other scientists, are therefore not trained in facilitation and group process. Some excellent examples of quantitative models being used as communicative tools may be found in the participatory modeling literature; these examples should become more widely known among modelers who do not work directly with stakeholders, because the techniques used by participatory modelers are applicable in interdisciplinary team settings as well (Beall & Zeoli, 2008; Stave, 2002; Van den Belt, 2004).

In addition, power dynamics are inherent in model building as they are in any group process (Becu et al., 2008). Modelers should be trained to recognize and mediate these power dynamics, just as any skilled facilitator would. Modelers trained as group facilitators would be able to lead research teams more effectively through a group discussion of model assumptions and limitations at the beginning of a research project. Achieving consensus on these critical aspects of model development would increase the likelihood of a positive team experience and enhance the quality of scientific output (Brugnach et al., 2008). A short course or workshop on facilitation and group process would be helpful to all scientists who work in teams, but modelers would especially benefit from this training.

Modelers should also be aware of a range of modeling techniques. In our experience, researchers and modelers are often not aware of the spectrum of modeling techniques that might be available to address a research question.

In many graduate programs, PhD students tend to learn only one quantitative methodology—statistics—when the variety of quantitative modeling approaches that may be brought to bear on environmental problems is becoming increasingly diverse. A list of these approaches (by no means comprehensive) would include system dynamics modeling (Martinez & Richardson, 2001); structural equation modeling (Bollen, 1989); agent-based modeling (Richiardi, Leombruni, Saam, & Sonnessa, 2006); social network analysis (Scott & Carrington, 2011); evolutionary algorithms (DeJong, 2006); Bayesian modeling (Ando, 2010); and discrete event simulation (Fishman, 2001). Most modelers and scientists are trained in only one type of modeling, and collaborations among modelers to integrate different types of modeling approaches remain the exception. We suggest that more graduate programs in the environmental sciences should educate students on at least a handful of modeling approaches and their appropriate applications. A modeling "typology" could be useful for this type of education, and more such publications should be developed (Badham, 2010).

Best Practices for Modeling Teams Interacting With Stakeholders

Although participatory modeling approaches are beyond the scope of this chapter, we recommend that modelers and environmental researchers become familiar with these approaches and know when to use them. Involving stakeholders and decision makers in the model-building process can have positive outcomes for consensus building and improving systemic understanding around solutions to environmental problems (Antunes, Santos, & Videira, 2006; Dwyer & Stave, 2008; Van den Belt, 2004). At least, model-building teams should understand which stakeholders will be using the model output and should consult these groups as needed when developing the model and communicating model results (Checkland & Poulter, 2006; Costanza & Ruth, 1998). If stakeholders are involved in commissioning and funding the project, time and budget limitations for model building should also be clearly discussed and understood between researchers and stakeholders (Martinez & Richardson, 2001). The best possible techniques for communicating model output to the stakeholders should be employed, and modelers would do well to reach out to scholars with expertise in this area. For example, researchers in the field of technical and scientific communication devote significant time and research to studying how lay people make sense of concepts and technologies, and how scientific information may be made more accessible. In addition, the new subdiscipline of visual analytics employs interactive graphical interfaces that allow users to sweep through a large number of options (like modeling scenarios). These techniques can graphically represent patterns that emerge from large amounts of information (Wong & Thomas, 2004). This allows researchers and stakeholders to identify points where intervention in the system would have the maximum desired effect, as well as "thresholds" where a system shifts suddenly from one relatively stable state to another in response to a slow-moving driver. Bankes (2002) provides an example of generating diagrams of "policy landscapes," in which the whole parameter space of model inputs is mapped into a graphical matrix of outcome scenarios that can be directly retrieved and manipulated by the stakeholder. This allows for a dynamic examination of outcome patterns in a multidimensional input space, extending the set of acceptable solutions from one "optimal" scenario to an ensemble of satisfactory scenarios that hold true under a variety of input conditions.

Model-building groups should also consider using ensembles of models to inform robust rather than optimal policies (Lempert & Collins, 2007; Lempert et al., 2003). Model ensembles comprise a large number of differing yet plausible environmental scenarios, which are evaluated against benchmark measures representing many value systems, to select blueprints that would hold under variable future conditions. In this respect, the selected scenarios may not be optimal given a particular research or policy objective but are good enough to succeed when both baseline futures and low-probability high-consequence events occur. In our experience, many research teams are unaware of how scenario analysis may be used to explore uncertain future conditions, and how it differs from sensitivity analysis. Modelers can introduce these methodologies to research teams, and they should be taught in graduate programs.

Conclusion

We propose that nonmodelers interested in facilitating cross-disciplinary communication may wish to acquaint themselves with quantitative simulation models as a tool for guiding and informing this communication. Conversely, quantitative modelers would do well to understand their models' capabilities and limitations for communication in the context of cross-disciplinary research projects, and to prepare themselves to occupy a facilitative, communicative, and translational role on a research team, in addition to performing their duties as a modeler and scientist.

Take-Home Messages

- Interdisciplinary teams working on complex environmental problems frequently use models as communication tools

  o to explore individual perceptions about a problem,
  o to achieve shared understanding, and
  o to debate the validity of proposed courses of action.

- Team communication and scientific results can be improved through careful and deliberate use of models.
- There are various important challenges to using models for this purpose, including the articulation of uncertainty.

- There exist "best practices" for dealing with these challenges, available to research institutions and individual research teams.

References

Agarwal, C., Green, G. M., Grove, J. M., Evans, T. P., & Schweik, C. M. (2002, November). *A review and assessment of land-use change models: Dynamics of space, time, and human choice*. Newtown Square, PA: USDA Forest Service.

Ando, T. (2010). *Bayesian model selection and statistical modeling*. Boca Raton, FL: Taylor & Francis Group.

Antunes, P., Santos, R., & Videira, N. (2006). Participatory decision making for sustainable development: The use of mediated modeling techniques. *Land Use Policy, 23*, 44–52.

Badham, J. (2010). *A compendium of modeling techniques*. Canberra: Australian National University.

Bankes, S. (1993). Exploratory modeling for policy analysis. *Operations Research, 41*(3), 435–449.

Bankes, S. C. (2002). Tools and techniques for developing policies for complex and uncertain systems. *Proceedings of the National Academy of Sciences, 99*(Suppl. 3), 7263–7266.

Bawden, R. J., & Packham, R. G. (1993). Systemic praxis in the education of the agricultural systems practitioner. *Systems Practice, 6*(1), 7–19.

Beall, A., & Zeoli, L. (2008). Participatory modeling of endangered wildlife systems: Simulating the sage-grouse and land use in Central Washington. *Ecological Economics, 68*, 24–33.

Becu, N., Neef, A., Schreinemachers, P., & Sangkapitux, C. (2008). Participatory computer simulation to support collective decision-making: Potential and limits of stakeholder involvement. *Land Use Policy, 25*(4), 498–509.

Bollen, K. A. (1989). *Structural equations with latent variables*. Hoboken, NJ: John Wiley.

Bormann, E. G. (1996). Symbolic convergence theory and communication in group decision making. In R. Y. Hirokawa & M. S. Poole (Eds.), *Communication and group decision making* (pp. 81–113). Thousand Oaks, CA: Sage.

Brugnach, M., Dewulf, A., Pahl-Wostl, C., & Taillieu, T. (2008). Toward a relational concept of uncertainty: About knowing too little, knowing too differently, and accepting not to know. *Ecology and Society, 13*(2), 30.

Checkland, P., & Poulter, J. (2006). *Learning for action: A short definitive account of soft systems methodology, and its use for practitioners, teachers and students*. Chichester, UK: John Wiley.

Costanza, R., & Ruth, M. (1998). Using dynamic modeling to scope environmental problems and build consensus. *Environmental Management, 22*(2), 183–195.

Couclelis, H. (2005). "Where has the future gone?'" Rethinking the role of integrated land-use models in spatial planning. *Environment and Planning A, 37*(8), 1353–1371.

DeJong, K. A. (2006). *Evolutionary computation: A unified approach*. Cambridge: MIT Press.

Draper, D. (1995). Assessment and propagation of model uncertainty. *Journal of the Royal Statistical Society B, 57*(1), 45–97.

Dwyer, M., & Stave, K. A. (2008). *Group model building wins: The results of a comparative analysis*. Paper presented at the 2008 International Conference of the System Dynamics Society, Athens, Greece.

Edwards, P. N. (1999). Global climate science, uncertainty and politics: Data-laden models, model-filtered data. *Science as Culture, 8*(4), 437–472.

Eigenbrode, S. D., O'Rourke, M., Wulfhorst, J. D., Althoff, D. M., Goldberg, C. S., Merrill, K., et al. (2007). Employing philosophical dialogue in collaborative science. *Bioscience, 57*(1), 55–64.

Epstein, J. M. (2008). Why model? *Journal of Artificial Societies and Social Simulation, 11*(4), 12.

Fiore, S. M., & Schooler, J. W. (2010). Process mapping and shared cognition: Teamwork and the development of shared problem models. In E. Salas & S. M. Fiore (Eds.), *Team cognition: Understanding the factors that drive process and performance* (pp. 133–152). Washington, DC: American Psychological Association.

Fishman, G. S. (2001). *Discrete-event simulation: Modeling, programming, and analysis*. New York: Springer.

Grimm, V., Berger, U., Bastiansen, F., Eliassen, S., Ginot, V., Giske, J., et al. (2006). A standard protocol for describing individual-based and agent-based models. *Ecological Modelling, 198*(1–2), 115–126.

Guhathakurta, S. (2002). Urban modeling as storytelling: Using simulation models as a narrative. *Environment and Planning B: Planning and Design, 29*(6), 895–911.

Hall, C. A. S., & Day, J. W. (Eds.). (1977). *Ecosystem modeling in theory and practice*. Niwot: University Press of Colorado.

Hare, M., Letcher, R. A., & Jakeman, A. J. (2003). Participatory modelling in natural resource management: A comparison of four case studies. *Integrated Assessment, 4*(2), 62–72.

Helton, J. C., & Burmaster, D. E. (1996). Guest editorial: Treatment of aleatory and epistemic uncertainty in performance assessments for complex systems. *Reliability Engineering & System Safety, 54*(2–3), 91–94.

Hodges, J. S. (1991). Six (or so) things you can do with a bad model. *Operations Research, 39*(3), 355.

Johnson, K. A., Dana, G., Jordan, N. R., Draeger, K. J., Kapuscinski, A. R., Olabisi, L. K. S., et al. (2012). Participatory scenarios and social learning for sustainability. *Ecology & Society, 17*(2), 9.

Kahneman, D., & Tversky, A. (1974). Judgment under uncertainty: Heuristics and biases. *Science, 185*(4157), 1124–1131.

Keyton, J., & Beck, S. J. (2010). Perspective: Examining communication as macro-cognition in STS. *Human Factors, 52*(2), 335–339.

Klein, J. T. (2012). Research integration: A comparative knowledge base. In A. Repko, W. Newell, & R. Szostak (Eds.), *Case studies in interdisciplinary research* (pp. 283–298). Thousand Oaks, CA: Sage.

Kok, K. (2009). The potential of Fuzzy Cognitive Maps for semi-quantitative scenario development, with an example from Brazil. *Global Environmental Change, 19*, 122–133.

Kolb, D. A. (1984). *Experiential learning: Experience as the source of learning and development*. Englewood Cliffs, NJ: Prentice Hall.

Lane, D. C. (2008). The emergence and use of diagramming in system dynamics: A critical account. *Systems Research and Behavioral Science, 25*, 3–23.

Lempert, R. J., & Collins, M. T. (2007). Managing the risk of uncertain threshold responses: Comparison of robust, optimum, and precautionary approaches. *Risk Analysis, 27*(4), 1009–1026.

Lempert, R. J., Popper, S. W., & Bankes, S. C. (2003). *Shaping the next one hundred years: New methods for quantitative, long-term policy analysis* (No. MR-1626-RPC). Santa Monica, CA: RAND.

Ligmann-Zielinska, A., & Jankowski, P. (2007). Agent-based models as laboratories for spatially explicit planning policies. *Environment and Planning B, 34*(2), 316–335.

Ligmann-Zielinska, A., & Sun, L. (2010). Applying time-dependent variance-based global sensitivity analysis to represent the dynamics of an agent-based model of land use change. *International Journal of Geographic Information Science, 24*(12), 1829–1850.

Luna-Reyes, L. F., & Andersen, D. L. (2003). Collecting and analyzing qualitative data for system dynamics: Methods and models. *System Dynamics Review, 19*(4), 271–296.

Mackinson, D., & Nøttestad, L. (1998). Combining local and scientific knowledge. *Reviews in Fish Biology and Fisheries, 8*(4), 481–490.

Martinez, I. J., & Richardson, G. P. (2001). *Best practices in system dynamics modeling.* Paper presented at the 19th International Conference of the System Dynamics Society, Atlanta, GA.

McIntosh, B. S., Seaton, R. A. F., & Jeffrey, P. (2007). Tools to think with? Towards understanding the use of computer-based support tools in policy relevant research. *Environmental Modelling & Software, 22*, 640–648.

Meadows, D. (2008). *Thinking in systems: A primer.* White River Junction, VT: Chelsea Green.

Milne, E., Aspinall, R., & Veldkamp, T. (2009). Integrated modelling of natural and social systems in land change science. *Landscape Ecology, 24*(9), 1145–1147. doi:10.1007/s10980-009-9392-2

Morgan, M. S., & Morrison, M. (1999). *Models as mediators: Perspectives on natural and social science.* Cambridge, UK: Cambridge University Press.

Moss, S. (2008). Alternative approaches to the empirical validation of agent-based models. *Journal of Artificial Societies and Social Simulation, 11*(1).

North, M. J., & Macal, C. M. (2007). *Managing business complexity: Discovering strategic solutions with agent-based modeling and simulation.* Oxford, UK: Oxford University Press.

Odum, H. T. (1983). *Systems ecology: An introduction.* New York: Wiley.

Odum, H. T., & Odum, E. C. (2000). *Modeling for all scales: An introduction to system simulation.* San Diego: Academic Press.

Oreskes, N., Belitz, K., & Shrader-Frechette, K. (1994). Response. *Science, 264*(5157), 331.

Oreskes, N., Shrader-Frechette, K., & Belitz, K. (1994). Verification, validation, and confirmation of numerical models in the Earth sciences. *Science, 263*(5147), 641–646.

Polhill, J., & Gotts, N. (2009). Ontologies for transparent integrated human-natural system modelling. *Landscape Ecology, 24*(9), 1255–1267. doi:10.1007/s10980-009-9381-5

Richardson, G. P., & Andersen, D. F. (1995). Teamwork in group model building. *System Dynamics Review, 11*(2), 113–137.

Richiardi, M., Leombruni, R., Saam, N. J., & Sonnessa, M. (2006). A common protocol for agent-based social simulation. *Journal of Artificial Societies and Social Simulation, 9*(1), 15.

Saltelli, A., Ratto, M., Tarantola, S., & Campolongo, F. (2006). Sensitivity analysis practices: Strategies for model-based inference. *Reliability Engineering & System Safety, 91*(10–11), 1109–1125. doi:10.1016/j.ress.2005.11.014

Sarewitz, D. (2004). How science makes environmental controversies worse. *Environmental Science & Policy, 7*, 385–403.

Schmitt Olabisi, L. (2010). The system dynamics of forest cover in the developing world: Researcher vs. community perspectives. *Sustainability, 2*(6), 1523–1535.

Schmitt Olabisi, L., Kapuscinski, A. R., Johnson, K. A., Reich, P. B., Stenquist, B., & Draeger, K. J. (2010). Using scenario visioning and participatory system dynamics modeling to investigate the future: Lessons from Minnesota 2050. *Sustainability, 2*(8), 2686–2706.

Scott, J., & Carrington, P. J. (Eds.). (2011). *The SAGE handbook of social network analysis*. London: Sage.

Seppelt, R., Müller, F., Schröder, B., & Volk, M. (2009). Challenges of simulating complex environmental systems at the landscape scale: A controversial dialogue between two cups of espresso. *Ecological Modelling, 220*(24), 3481–3489.

Stave, K. A. (2002). Using system dynamics to improve public participation in environmental decisions. *System Dynamics Review, 18*(2), 139–167.

Sterman, J. D., & Sweeney, L. B. (2007). Understanding public complacency about climate change: Adults' mental models of climate change violate conservation of matter. *Climatic Change, 80*(3–4), 213–238.

Suh, S., Chiu, Y., & Schmitt Olabisi, L. (2010). *The future of energy and Minnesota's water resources*. Saint Paul: Legislative Citizen's Commission on Minnesota Resources

Swart, R. J., Raskin, P., & Robinson, J. (2004). The problem of the future: Sustainability science and scenario analysis. *Global Environmental Change, 14*, 137–146.

Thompson, N. S., & Derr, P. (2009). Contra Epstein, good explanations predict. *Journal of Artificial Societies and Social Simulation, 12*(1), 9.

U.S. Climate Change Science Program and the Subcommittee on Global Change Research. (2009). *Best practice approaches for characterizing, communicating, and incorporating scientific uncertainty in climate decision making*. Washington, DC: UNT Digital Library.

Van den Belt, M. (2004). *Mediated modeling: A system dynamics approach to environmental consensus building*. Washington, DC: Island Press.

Van Der Leeuw, S. E. (2004). WHY MODEL? *Cybernetics and Systems: An International Journal, 35*(2), 117–128.

Von Bertalanffy, L. (1968). *General system theory: Foundations, development, applications* (Rev. ed.). New York: George Braziller.

Warmink, J. J., Janssen, J. A. E. B., Booij, M. J., & Krol, M. S. (2010). Identification and classification of uncertainties in the application of environmental models. *Environmental Modelling & Software, 25*(12), 1518–1527.

Wintle, B. A., McCarthy, M. A., Volinsky, C. T., & Kavanagh, R. P. (2003). The use of Bayesian model averaging to better represent uncertainty in ecological models. *Conservation Biology, 17*(6), 1579–1590.

Wong, C., & Thomas, J. (2004). Visual analytics. *IEEE Computer Graphics and Applications, 24*(5), 20–21.

Wright, S. (1960). Path coefficients and path regressions: Alternative or complementary concepts? *Biometrics, 16*, 189–202.

PART IV

Contexts

Interdisciplinary research is not conducted in a vacuum—it is always located in a particular context that has considerable influence on how the research unfolds. This suggests that adequate coverage of communication issues relevant to interdisciplinary research must address the *context* of that research—that is, its physical, cultural, and intellectual location. Perhaps this seems out of place in a book that concerns communication and collaboration in interdisciplinary research, but it is not; in fact, the relationship between a collaborative, interdisciplinary research project and its context is a key determinant to project success. Contemporary efforts to address complex, wicked problems such as climate change and sustainability typically involve teams that draw from multiple units in a single institution and often from multiple institutions. Communication among collaborators about their science is clearly central to such an effort, but there will also be a need to communicate effectively with departmental administrators, deans, research vice presidents, grant administrators, provosts, and others who provide logistical, infrastructural, and administrative support for the research effort. Beyond the organization, there are representatives of funding agencies, editors, managers, policymakers, stakeholders, and others on whom the successful dissemination and implementation of the project depends. These lists highlight the fact that communication in collaborative; interdisciplinary research projects have both an *intrinsic* dimension that is team internal and an *extrinsic* dimension that involves the team in context. Both of these are crucial to the success of any project, and while the former has been emphasized in the first three parts of this volume, this part shifts the emphasis to the latter.

A typical interdisciplinary research project will reside in multiple, over-lapping contexts, including the physical and virtual spaces in which the research is conducted; the organizational locations that are home to offices, laboratories, and meeting rooms; the social and cultural spaces in which data are collected, disseminated, and implemented; and the economic contexts that include funders and their programs. A critically important context is the *institutional* context, understood as comprising the colleges, universities, national laboratories, or other organizations that are the professional homes of the researchers. This context provides the policies and local cultures that shape professional activities and careers, and it is the focus of Part IV. The first two chapters include university presidents among their authors, and they address the question of how to structure academic institutions to enhance their ability to support interdisciplinary research. Chapter 16 addresses the impact of a long-running agency program that aims to "catalyze" institutional changes that facilitate integration in education and research. The final chapter focuses on the challenges that make communication between researchers and their institutions difficult. Together, these chapters supply a detailed picture of the institutional complexities that are both part of the problem, at times hindering the communication necessary for successful research, and part of the solution, providing the infrastructure and other resources without which contemporary interdisciplinary research would not be possible.

In the first of these chapters, "Interdisciplinarity as a Design Problem: Toward Mutual Intelligibility Among Academic Disciplines in the American Research University," Michael M. Crow and William B. Dabars focus on the institutional context of university-based interdisciplinary efforts. Noting that disciplines are "social constructs," Crow and Dabars maintain that we must attend to the sociocultural character of interdisciplinary efforts if we are to understand and foster them. Specifically, they argue that we must work to design universities and related institutions to support interdisciplinary efforts—the epistemic research enterprise is essentially dependent on the social context and structure in which it takes place. In developing this argument, they consider a range of theoretical perspectives on the social character of the interdisciplinary "knowledge enterprise." These perspectives supply "models of . . . interdisciplinary collaboration" (p. 304). After discussing these models, they illustrate them and the larger project of institutional design for interdisciplinarity with detail drawn from Arizona State University, where Crow has served as president since 2002.

Land-grant universities in the United States, created to "democratize" education and "advance the agricultural and technological fields essential to our country's success," have taken up a leading role in developing the culture and capacity for interdisciplinary research in institutions of higher education (p. 324). In Chapter 15, "Defining 21st Century Land-Grant Universities Through Cross-Disciplinary Research," M. Duane Nellis, former president of the University of Idaho, describes this role and articulates a number of opportunities and challenges that mark the future of interdisciplinary research in land-grant systems. He argues that these systems will need to implement more effective and inclusive communication strategies to foster integrative activity that takes advantage of the opportunities while meeting the attendant challenges. Acknowledging the existence of "traditional barriers" to interdisciplinary approaches in the three tiers of the land-grant system—learning, research, and outreach—he describes novel and "robust" integrative strategies at land-grant universities that represent "exciting transitions" into the future. Nellis concludes the chapter with a detailed illustration of this vision of the 21st century land-grant institution that focuses on integrative learning, research, and outreach programs developed at the University of Idaho.

Chapter 16 provides another examination of the university as an institutional context for interdisciplinary research but, in this case, from the perspective of integrative education and research projects funded by the National Science Foundation. In "Institutionalizing Interdisciplinary Graduate Education," Maura Borrego, Daniel Boden, David Pietrocola, Carol F. Stoel, Richard D. Boone, and Melur K. Ramasubramanian describe aspects of the institutionalization of several Integrative Graduate Education and Research Traineeship (IGERT) projects at two institutions, each of which had received at least four IGERT awards. The IGERT program aims to "catalyze cultural change in institutions to support interdisciplinary collaboration," and this chapter evaluates the degree to which IGERT-related changes have been taken up by their institutional homes. Interviews with faculty, students, support staff, and administrators associated with the two actively funded IGERT projects at each of the two institutions yield insight into structural and policy changes, as well as communication and culture changes that are critical to organizational change. IGERT has been a catalyst for organizational change in U.S. universities, and this chapter illuminates many of the reasons behind its success.

The institutional context of interdisciplinary research is also the focus of the final chapter in this part, "Supporting Interdisciplinary Collaboration: The Role of the Institution." Specifically, L. Michelle Bennett and Howard Gadlin examine communicative aspects of the relationship between interdisciplinary research teams and their institutional and organizational contexts. These contexts can facilitate or obstruct interdisciplinary research teams, depending on whether there are mechanisms in place that support their efforts. This chapter analyzes five areas where institutional practice can negatively affect collaborative, interdisciplinary research: "institutional self-awareness, organizational trust, leadership, management of difference, and handling of conflict and disagreement" (p. 000). Bennett and Gadlin's analysis and several "case study" illustrations generate concrete suggestions for improving communication between interdisciplinary teams and the organizations in which they are embedded.

14

Interdisciplinarity as a Design Problem

Toward Mutual Intelligibility Among Academic Disciplines in the American Research University

◆ Michael M. Crow and William B. Dabars

The relationship between institutional design and the advancement of knowledge in the American research university may appear to be a perfunctory administrative matter. Despite broad consensus regarding the imperative for inter- or transdisciplinary approaches to inquiry and scholarship, the traditional correlation between academic disciplines and departments remains the basis for academic organization and administration. As simultaneously epistemological, administrative, and sociocultural categories, disciplines continue to dominate the reflexive relationship between knowledge and its organizational context. This chapter contends that the design of our knowledge enterprises is not merely adventitious to discovery, creativity, and innovation, and that a critique of institutional design is no mere quibbling over the arbitrary disposition of the bureaucratic substratum that supports epistemological superstructures. The prerequisite for successful implementation is mutual intelligibility between and among academic disciplines and interdisciplinary fields. The concept of institutional design and various "design limitations" in the American research university that impede interdisciplinary collaboration and communication are considered, as well as paradigms for inquiry and organizational and institutional models generally regarded as extraneous in this context. Prototypes for interdisciplinary collaboration examined include "invisible colleges," "communities of practice," "epistemic communities," and knowledge-based theories of the firm. The chapter concludes with a brief case study of the implementation of interdisciplinarity within the broader context of the comprehensive reconceptualization of Arizona State University.

> For science is not often the sudden blossoming of the flower of genius, even in the soil of freedom. It is a group activity carried on by limited and fallible men, and much of their effectiveness stems from their organization and the continuity and flexibility of their institutional arrangements.
>
> —A. Hunter Dupree (1957, p. 9)

Introduction

The relationship between institutional design and the advancement of knowledge in the American research university may appear at first glance to be a perfunctory administrative consideration, both self-evident and obvious: "All arts and sciences faculties contain more or less the same list of departments," observes the sociologist Andrew Abbott (2001, p. 126), remarking on the traditional correlation between academic disciplines and departments. While disciplines are now increasingly interrelated or conjoined with rapidly speciating interdisciplinary fields, their identification with academic departments, or, as the case may be, units such as centers, institutes, schools, or colleges, nevertheless often persists. Because of their "extraordinary ability to organize individual careers, faculty hiring, and undergraduate education," Abbott observes, disciplinary departments appear to be the "essential and irreplaceable building blocks" of American academia (p. 128). Similarly, "Americans seem unable to conceive of an undergraduate curriculum without majors. And of course, there are no majors without disciplines" (p. 127). Once consolidated into their present configuration during the final decades of the 19th century, which witnessed the emergence of the American research university, the department-based "American system of disciplines" would remain "uniquely powerful and powerfully unique" (p. 128).

The political scientist Mattei Dogan (1997) offers a corresponding synopsis of the administrative correlate to disciplinary knowledge: "In all universities, teaching, recruitment, promotion, peer review, and administration are organized along disciplinary lines" (p. 429). And from his perspective as president emeritus of the University of Michigan, James Duderstadt (2000) similarly perceives the "deification of the disciplines," which through departmental structures "continue to dominate the modern university, developing curriculum, marshaling resources, administering programs, and doling out rewards" (pp. 120–121).

The sociologist Immanuel Wallerstein (2003) points out that academic disciplines are "three things simultaneously:

> The so-called disciplines . . . are, of course, intellectual categories— modes of asserting that there exists a defined field of study with some kind of boundaries, however disputed or fuzzy, and some agreed-upon modes of legitimate research. . . . The disciplines are in addition institutional structures that since the late nineteenth century have taken on ever more elaborate forms. . . . Finally, the disciplines are cultures. (p. 453)

While the disciplines and interdisciplinary fields that constitute our academic culture thus first and foremost represent epistemological categories— referring here in the most general sense to the stock of knowledge in any given area—they may be construed secondarily in their administrative contexts, and it is primarily to this organizational substratum of knowledge that in the following we recur. The important sociocultural context of disciplinarity undergirds the epistemological and administrative dimensions, variously construed in terms of the disciplinary cultures—or more equivocally, "social constructs"—that represent the outcome of "disciplinary socialization." Abbott (2001) cautions that assessments of the epistemological "flux" of disciplines must be counterbalanced by an understanding of what he terms the "extraordinary stasis of disciplinary social structure" (pp. 122–125).

Of all that has been said about the reflexive relationship between knowledge and its organizational context, insufficient focus has been devoted to an appreciation of the role of institutional design in the advancement of interdisciplinarity. This reflexive relationship is nowhere more critically instantiated than in the institutionalization of the disciplines and interdisciplinary configurations in the American research university. Any institutional platform constructed to support the growth of knowledge—in other words, any knowledge-producing organization or "knowledge enterprise"—is the product of a sequence of decisions that determine its structure and functions, which may be termed the "design process." While the various strains of interdisciplinarity have been subject to sophisticated explication from any number of perspectives, the concept of "design" in the present context—the advancement of interdisciplinary collaboration in knowledge enterprises, and especially the American research university—is itself often taken for granted or only perfunctorily considered. Whether one focuses on disciplinary genealogies or interdisciplinary confluence, an understanding of the dynamics that determine their institutionalization and dissemination requires an appreciation of their institutional determination.[1] Inasmuch as the design of our knowledge enterprises is not merely adventitious to the advancement of knowledge, administrators and academicians alike do well to analyze fundamental determinants in the structure and operations of an academic institution that when optimally designed facilitate teaching and research across the disciplines (Crow, 2010).

If by "optimal knowledge production" we assume interdisciplinary teaching and research unfettered by conventional design limitations, the success of the outcome is intrinsically interrelated with an appropriate institutional platform.[2] The prerequisite for the implementation of interdisciplinarity, we argue, is mutual intelligibility between and among academic disciplines and interdisciplinary fields. Within the context of advancing interdisciplinary inquiry, the outcome of optimal institutional design aligned with the various purposes of the university is aptly characterized by Jonathan Cole (2009): "Almost all truly distinguished universities create a seamless web of cognitive influence among the individual disciplines that affects the quality of the whole" (p. 5).

Many academicians, we suspect, would dismiss a critique of conventional academic organization, epitomized by the congruence of disciplines and departments, as mere quibbling over the disposition of the requisite bureaucratic substratum that supports epistemological superstructures. We thus concur with the assessment of John Seely Brown and Paul Duguid (1991): "In a society that attaches particular value to 'abstract knowledge,' the details of practice have come to be seen as nonessential, unimportant, and easily developed once the relevant abstractions have been grasped" (p. 40). But while abstract knowledge is *prima facie* generally perceived as distinct from organizational structure and attendant social relations, which are deemed nonessential or ancillary, following Anthony Giddens (1984), we contend that to an extent often insufficiently appreciated, knowledge, organizational structure, and social relations are intrinsically interrelated. His theory of "structuration" assesses the "situated activities of human agents" (p. 25). As Scott Cook and John Seeley Brown (1999) explain, structuration treats "praxis as constitutive of social structure, while social structure informs praxis" (p. 399).

It is precisely with the "details of practice" of institutional design that we are here concerned, and in the following we canvass a selection of relevant

---

[1]For an extended discussion of the trajectory of the institutionalization of interdisciplinarity in the American research university, see Dabars (2008).

[2]Our usage of "interdisciplinarity" is taken generally to convey the various subtypes that have elsewhere been elucidated specifically, including multidisciplinarity, pluridisciplinarity, transdisciplinarity, and postdisciplinarity. Where distinctions between disciplinarity and interdisciplinarity appear superfluous, we conflate discussion of the categories, consistent with the justification provided by Robert Frodeman and Carl Mitcham (2007): "Both science and society now recognize that disciplinarity and interdisciplinarity are not mutually exclusive but complementary" (pp. 506–507).

theoretical approaches and models applicable to interdisciplinary collaboration in teaching and research. The survey is intended to suggest the range of paradigms for interdisciplinary collaboration and the variety of possible approaches to organizational and institutional structure to provide a foundation for an appreciation of their mutual interrelatedness and relevance to knowledge organizations. As a case study in the large-scale institutional implementation of interdisciplinarity, we conclude with a brief overview of the reconceptualization of Arizona State University during the past decade.

Organizing for Interdisciplinary Collaboration: Transcending the Design Limitations of Our Knowledge Enterprises

The intrinsic impetus to advance new knowledge distinguishes the American research university from other institutional platforms in higher education, but entrenched design limitations restrict their potential to advance discovery, creativity, and innovation. Ubiquitous generalized calls for enhanced interdisciplinary collaboration notwithstanding, we tend to assume that our academic institutions have as a matter of course been optimally structured and moreover inherently calibrated not only to promote effective teaching and research but also to seek knowledge with purpose and link useful knowledge with action for the common good. Leaving aside important considerations of equity and access, the persistence of disciplinary partitioning in our estimation represents one of the most critical design limitations to the further evolution of this set of transformative institutions.

The American research university retains structural characteristics it assumed during its emergence in the late 19th century. During that period, no more than 15 institutions, both public and private, grafted programs of specialized graduate study, modeled on the practices of German scientific research institutes, onto their undergraduate curricula, derived from the British model exemplified by the "ancient universities" of Oxford and Cambridge (Geiger, 1986, pp. 2–3). To this day, the academic organization and practices of the American research university remain to a remarkable extent based on this prototype.

However we conceive the purposes and functions of our colleges and universities, we tend to assume that their organizational structure inherently facilitates the advancement of knowledge. But if the structure of an organization is inimical to its purposes and functions, the design of the institution must be radically reconsidered. Leaving aside academic organization that retains irreducible foundational disciplines such as physics or chemistry, we contend that the entrenchment of universities in conventional discipline-based academic organization often represents the triumph of inertia and bureaucratization. The policy scholar Anthony Downs (1967) specifies that bureaucracies tend toward routine, standardization, and inertia. "Once the users of the bureau's services have become convinced of their gains from it, and have developed routinized relations with it," Downs explains, "the bureau can rely upon a certain amount of inertia to keep on generating the external support it needs." Moreover, bureaus "tend to develop more formalized rule systems covering more and more of the possible situations they are likely to encounter," which

> divert the attention of officials from achieving the social functions of the bureau to conforming to its rules. . . . They increase the bureau's structural complexity, which in turn strengthens its inertia because of greater sunken costs in current procedures. The resulting resistance to change further reduces the bureau's ability to adjust to new circumstances. (pp. 8, 18–19)

Our academic culture not only perpetuates traditional disciplinary thinking but also assigns inordinate significance to distinctions in an implicit hierarchy. The "gulf of mutual incomprehension" C. P. Snow (1960) observed between what he termed "literary intellectuals" and "natural scientists" more than half a century ago persists. Avowals of parity between the various disciplinary cultures notwithstanding, the prestige and preeminence accorded science in the academy remains undiminished just as disciplines trump other disciplines based on their quantitative capacities. Each disciplinary culture must overcome its ambivalence toward different orientations and approaches to solving problems that may have arisen through more than a millennium of institutional evolution (Crow, 2007).

A corollary to the assumption that the disciplinary configuration of the research university has once and for all been suitably disposed is that research or scholarship is an individual endeavor and that optimal outcomes will inevitably emerge from the amalgamation of the results of individual efforts. Our competitive nature values the individual over the group, and while we valorize the discovery of the unknown by individual scientists, less prestige attaches to collaborative endeavors that target real-world problems and team participation in projects that accomplish assessment, assimilation, synthesis, implementation, and application. Without sufficient coordination and strategic collaboration, however, the ad hoc aggregation of individual endeavors does not necessarily transcend the inevitable limitations of an isolated investigator (Crow, 2007). As Cook and Brown (1999) frame the dilemma: "Not every action by a human collective can be meaningfully or usefully reduced to an account of actions taken by the individuals in them" (p. 399).

Recognizing that such entrenched and arbitrary organizational constructs more likely obstruct rather than facilitate the advancement of useful knowledge, it becomes incumbent on faculties and administrators to remediate the design limitations of their respective knowledge enterprises. We must organize for collaboration across disciplines to establish the preconditions essential to effective teaching and research, as well as constructive social and economic outcomes. Mutual intelligibility between academic disciplines and robust interdisciplinary collaboration are foundational to all aspects of the academic enterprise. But the persistence of disciplinary entrenchment interrelates with other shortcomings and so must be understood in the broader context of critical societal goals. This, then, is to reiterate the contention that the academy must seek knowledge with purpose and link useful knowledge with action for the common good.

The maintenance of strict disciplinary boundaries undermines the impetus to establish mutual intelligibility with other disciplines. We cannot expect biologists alone to solve the loss of biodiversity, nor chemists in isolation to negotiate the transition to renewable energy. Because each academic discipline has over time developed its own vernacular, the impetus may be lacking to cultivate "interlanguages" intelligible to other disciplines—the "pidgins" or "creoles," which in the metaphor enlisted by Peter Galison (1997) are the mutually comprehensible languages of different subcultures found in "trading zones." The exchanges of knowledge between "theoretical subcultures" thus represent the "movement of ideas, objects, and practices as . . . local coordination through the establishment of pidgins and creoles" (p. 48). But chemists have not sufficiently developed a *lingua franca* to communicate with either philosophers or engineers. The debate must engage a broad community of disciplines and advance not only on the basis of the understanding found within the academy but also the wisdom and expertise developed in commerce, industry, and government (Crow, 2007).

Insufficiently robust interdisciplinary collaboration restricts negotiation of emergent, nonlinear, and unpredictable new complexities and impedes progress in efforts to mount responses to intractable global problems. This lack of adaptive capacity is nowhere more evident than in the institutional posture of our research universities when confronted by the need to address the "grand challenges" of our epoch—one need only think in terms of global climate change, air and water pollution, overpopulation, hunger and poverty, extinction of species, exhaustion of natural resources, and destruction of ecosystems. As the National Academies report on interdisciplinarity considered in the following section explains, such challenges require interdisciplinary collaboration, which facilitates applied research initiatives that often engage large-scale team efforts to address complex and intractable problems (Committee on Facilitating Interdisciplinary Research [CFIR] & Committee on Science, Engineering, and Public Policy [COSEPUP], 2005). Moreover, such collaboration must take place transinstitutionally and transnationally. Only an amalgamation of transdisciplinary, transinstitutional, and transnational frameworks has the potential to advance knowledge and innovation on the requisite scale in real time, as well as desired social and economic outcomes on a global scale.

Applied research initiatives are inherently "use-inspired," which is a concept that informs the critique of the American research university posited in this chapter. The *locus classicus* formulation of use-inspired research comes from the policy scholar Donald Stokes. In an effort to reveal the limitations of the standard binary opposition between basic and applied research,

Stokes constructed a table to represent types of research ("Quadrant Model of Scientific Research"), which may be inspired by the quest for fundamental understanding or considerations of use. In this conceptualization, "Bohr's quadrant" (so called, he explains, for the quest of a model atomic structure by Niels Bohr) represents pure basic research. "Pasteur's quadrant," however, represents "basic research that seeks to extend the frontiers of understanding but is also inspired by considerations of use." The designation memorializes the research of the eminent chemist and microbiologist whose late career was devoted to the development of vaccines that have protected millions from disease: "Pasteur's drive toward understanding and use illustrates this combination of goals" (Stokes, 1997, pp. 72–75).

Consistent with recent discussions of learning or knowledge networks, we contend that conceptualizations of the "flow" of knowledge—as opposed to its accumulation or maintenance within "stocks of knowledge"—represents a fundamental metaphor for enhanced interdisciplinary communication and collaboration facilitated through interpersonal and group dynamics. The inverse correlation between the proverbial "silo mentality" of disciplinary knowledge and the potential for synergies during interdisciplinary exchange is patently evident. Organizational theorists John Hagel, John Seely Brown, and Lang Davison (2010) observe that in the past "we could rely on 'stocks' of knowledge—what we know at any point in time—but these stocks are diminishing in value more rapidly than ever before" (p. 11). Instead, we must "continually refresh our stocks of knowledge by participating in relevant 'flows' of knowledge—interactions that create knowledge or transfer it across individuals" (p. 11). They envisage institutional change thus derived driven not by an administrative elite but rather by "passionate individuals distributed throughout and even outside the institution, supported by institutional leaders who . . . realize that this wave of change cannot be imposed from the top down" (p. 7).

While institutional design is fraught with the potential for unforeseen misalignments between disciplinary factions and may require individuals and groups to transcend entrenched sociocultural barriers, reorganization to enhance interdisciplinary collaboration offers new ways of shaping and examining problems and advancing questions through interaction between heterogeneous groups, programs, and initiatives. Novel interdisciplinary configurations—what are in a sense institutional "experiments"—possess the potential to alter the course of inquiry, discourse, and the application of research, and even to reveal new paradigms for knowledge production, organization, and application. An overarching principle shaping the implementation process could be expressed as follows: If academic units commensurate to the resolution of a given challenge or problem do not already exist, appropriate new units must be configured. In its inception, the new aggregation may simply comprise a best-guess strategic amalgamation of researchers representing different disciplines and interdisciplines or particular specializations. The amalgamation may even begin or remain resolutely multidisciplinary. Such novel organizational configurations may lead to unexpected discovery through serendipity, the role of which in scientific research has been comprehensively assessed by Robert K. Merton and Elinor Barber (2004). But any such arrangement offers at the very least new potential to address critical challenges or resolve intractable problems—or even evolve into differentiated new interdisciplines. An overarching objective in institutional design is thus to engender an ecosystem of innovation.

New Structural Models for Interdisciplinarity: Practical Advice From the National Academies

Rather than exploring new paradigms for inquiry, academia too often restricts its focus to existing organizational models. The well-known call to action issued by the National Academies regarding the imperative for interdisciplinary collaboration and problem-driven research, *Facilitating Interdisciplinary Research* (CFIR & COSEPUP, 2005), offers an approach that represents a fundamental prototype for institutional efforts to remediate institutional design limitations in this context. The report envisions "scientists, engineers, social scientists, and humanists . . . addressing complex problems that must be attacked simultaneously with deep knowledge from different perspectives," and serves here broadly as proxy for our general recommendations (p. 17). The committee called for new "structural models" to "stimulate new modes of inquiry and break down the conceptual and institutional barriers to interdisciplinary research that could yield significant benefits to science and society" and experimentation with "substantial alteration of the traditional academic structures or even replacement with new structures and models to reduce barriers" to interdisciplinary research (pp. ix, xi).

Recommendations for new institutional structures that support the implementation of interdisciplinarity are based on the "matrix model." In contrast to existing configurations of disciplinary-based "silos," the committees recommend structures long evident in industry and government laboratories:

> a matrix, in which people move freely among disciplinary departments that are bridged and linked by interdisciplinary centers, offices, programs, courses, and curricula. There are many possible forms of coupling between departments and centers, including appointments, salary lines, distribution of indirect-cost returns, teaching assignments, . . . curricula, and degree-granting. (CFIR & COSEPUP, 2005, p. 172)

The report similarly stresses the imperative for "institutional policies that govern faculty appointments and salary lines, faculty recruitment, responsibility for tenure and promotion decisions, allocations of indirect-cost returns on grants, development of new course and curricular materials, and so on" (p. 172).

With economic growth increasingly tied to knowledge-intensive innovation, interactions between universities, industry, and government have been critically important during the past half-century. These interrelationships constitute what the economist Henry Etzkowitz (2008, p. 1) terms the "triple helix" of university-industry-government innovation. The National Academies report stresses that interdisciplinary research in industrial and government laboratories should serve as a prototype for academia: "Industrial and national laboratories have long experience in supporting IDR. Unlike universities, industry and national laboratories organize by the problems they wish their research enterprise to address. As problems come and go, so does the design of the organization" (CFIR & COSEPUP, 2005, p. 3). Moreover, "collaborative interdisciplinary research partnerships among universities, industry, and government have increased and diversified rapidly. Although such partnerships still face significant barriers, well-documented studies provide strong evidence of both their research benefits and their effectiveness in bringing together diverse cultures" (p. 3).

New structural models are moreover required because

> prevailing academic cultures and structures tend to replicate existing areas of expertise, reward individual effort rather than collaborative work, limit hiring input to a single department in a single school or college, and limit incentives and rewards for interdisciplinary and collaborative work. (CFIR & COSEPUP, 2005, p. 100)

The implementation of institutional policies conducive to interdisciplinarity is critical for two reasons: (1) Academic careers have historically been forged within strictly demarcated disciplinary delimitations, and (2) disciplinary affiliation defines the social organization of American higher education to such an extent that recipients of interdisciplinary training or practitioners of interdisciplinary scholarship often find recognition among peers and advancement difficult. Such policies must moreover advance recognition of interdisciplinary research by professional associations, business and industry, and, most important, within federal agencies, which in the estimation of this report remain resistant to interdisciplinary categorization (CFIR & COSEPUP, 2005, pp. x, 6).

Communication is intrinsic to the vision for interdisciplinary collaboration of the National Academies committees that produced the report: "At the heart of interdisciplinarity is communication—the conversations, connections, and combinations that bring new insights to virtually every kind of scientist and engineer" (CFIR & COSEPUP, 2005, p. 19). While focused on science and engineering, the report recapitulates the imperative for interdisciplinarity relevant across the spectrum of disciplines. Consistent with its call for new structural models, the report underscores the importance of concordant and supportive institutional policies: "Whatever their structure, interdisciplinary projects flourish in an environment that allows researchers to communicate, share ideas, and collaborate across disciplines" (p. 172).

Institutional Design and the Context for Interdisciplinarity

Institutional design, in our usage, refers broadly to both the process of design and its product, the organizational structure of a knowledge-producing institution and the attendant social formations and networks its disciplinary configuration engenders. The flux that underlies the interrelated and interdependent relationship between organizational form and knowledge is well expressed by Cook and Brown (1999): "It is our contention that there are, in fact, a number of distinct forms of knowledge, and that their differences are relevant, both theoretically and practically, to an effective understanding of organizations" (p. 381). While our approach draws from various perspectives relevant to the design of knowledge enterprises, in this section we consider a number of conceptualizations regarding the role of communication in the enhancement of interdisciplinary collaboration, which we construe as requisite not only for the growth of knowledge but also for the diffusion of innovation.

We begin to conceptualize the basis for an approach to the optimal design of knowledge enterprises using the fundamental distinction between the natural and the artificial explored by the polymath Herbert A. Simon in *The Sciences of the Artificial,* first published in 1969. In his usage of these concepts, "artificial" refers to objects and phenomena—artifacts—that are man-made as opposed to natural. He terms knowledge of such products and processes "artificial science" or the "science of design" and suggests that the most obvious "designers" of artifacts are engineers. But he broadly extends the sphere of the artificial even to our use of symbols—the "artifacts" of written and spoken language. In his expansive usage, everyone is a designer who "devises courses of action aimed at changing existing situations into preferred ones." The natural sciences are concerned with how things are, as he puts it, while the artificial sciences are concerned with how things ought to be. Artificial science—or design science—determines the form of that which we build—tools, farms, and urban agglomerations alike—but also our institutional and organizational structures. Implicit within Simon's conceptualization is an affirmation of the potential for evolution and differentiation in the structure and organization of knowledge enterprises. There is thus no reason why the redesign of an institution or organization cannot represent a process as focused and deliberate and precise as the work undertaken by scientists and engineers. We may thus begin to assess the design limitations inherent in existing knowledge enterprises and posit new models that better address the complex challenges that confront global society (Simon, 1996, pp. 1–24).

To argue that the advancement of interdisciplinarity may be construed as a "design problem" suggests that the concept of "design" itself in this context may require further assessment. In his collection of essays on the "design process," the computer scientist Frederick P. Brooks (2010) paraphrases the definition of the verb *design* provided by the editors of the *Oxford English*

Dictionary: "To form a plan or scheme of, to arrange or conceive in the mind for subsequent execution" (p. 4). His point is to emphasize the imperative for planning prior to execution, but Brooks overlooks one of the senses of the noun, which in this context seems especially pertinent: "That which is aimed at; an end in view; an ultimate goal or purpose" (*Oxford English Dictionary*, 2012). Inasmuch as the goals or purposes of academic inquiry in a world of emerging complexity might justifiably be characterized as critical to our survival as a species—setting aside for the moment skepticism regarding "weighty metaphysics" and even "truth" claims, as the philosopher Philip Kitcher (2001, p. 11) suggests—we contend that deliberation regarding the design of our knowledge enterprises should become integral to the discourse of our academic culture, if not an aspect of a larger public debate. Further, we maintain that the design of our knowledge enterprises depends on fundamental determinants in the structure and operations of an academic institution that when optimally designed facilitates teaching and research construed across the disciplines.

Brooks (2010) reminds us that the design process both expresses a vision and facilitates its accomplishment. Plato, he informs us, articulated this correlation when in a dialogue he spoke of "corresponding ideas and forms"—for example, the idea of a bed or table facilitating its construction "for our use, in accordance with the idea" (Plato, *The Republic,* Book X, as quoted in Brooks, 2010, p. 6). The execution of the design thus instantiates the idea. While the value of a "design concept" serving to guide the implementation of a plan or execution of an object or construction has been obvious since antiquity—Brooks adduces Vitruvius as an exemplar in the lineage of design—the value for our understanding of interdisciplinary collaboration comes with his point that beyond "conceptual integrity" ("unity, economy, clarity"), a design concept "vastly aids communication within a design team." Adducing as an example the use of storyboards by filmmakers, which facilitate focus on concept rather than details of implementation, Brooks writes: "Unity of concept is the goal; it is achieved only by much conversation." Moreover, "The conversation is much more direct if the design concept per se, rather than derivative representations or partial details, is the focus" (pp. 8–9).[3]

As an epigraph to the first chapter of his book, Brooks (2010) quotes Herbert Simon to underscore the centrality of communication to the design process: "Few engineers and composers . . . can carry on a mutually rewarding conversation about the content of the other's professional work. What I am suggesting is that they can carry on such a conversation about design." Such mutual intelligibility regarding what Simon (1996) terms "common creative activity" is one of the signal characteristics of interdisciplinary collaboration (as quoted in Brooks, 2010, p. 3). With reference to engineering design, Brooks makes the broadly applicable point that because increased

---

[3]The allusion to Vitruvius is germane to the discussion inasmuch as one may appropriately term the designer of knowledge enterprises a "knowledge architect."

technological sophistication inevitably demands ever more specialization, team design has become the contemporary standard: "The designer of today's state-of-the-art artifact needs help from masters of various crafts" (pp. 66–67).

The exhaustive reconceptualization of an institution undertaken to remediate its design limitations requires "massive change," a concept we adapt from the designer and design theorist Bruce Mau, who together with his colleague Jennifer Leonard conceive of change in terms of "designing systems, designing organizations, designing organisms" to "meet human needs the world over" (Mau & Leonard, 2004). We concur with Mau and Leonard in their assessment that change at this scale requires the exploration of "design economies" wherein the "patterns that emerge reveal complexity, integrated thinking across disciplines, and unprecedented interconnectivity" (pp. 16–17).

Paradigms for Inquiry: A Survey of Theoretical Approaches and Organizational and Institutional Models of Interdisciplinary Collaboration

An appreciation of the implications of the organizational context for knowledge may derive from reference to more than a half-century of empirical study and theoretical analysis, beginning with pioneering work by Thomas S. Kuhn (1970). One account traces the lineage of the "awareness that science is a social formation amenable to sociological investigation" to Kuhn, as well as such figures as Ludwig Wittgenstein, Jean-François Lyotard, and Richard Rorty (Miller & Fox, 2001, pp. 668–669). The foundational work in the sociology of science of Robert K. Merton (1973) similarly provides a conceptualization of "socio-cognitive networks" that underscores the importance of a researcher's milieu in understanding and contextualizing discovery. Derek J. de Solla Price brought historical perspective to assessments of social networks associated with research frontiers as well as quantitative approaches to the proliferation of scientific publications (see Price, 1965b, pp. 510–515; 1986, pp. 103–135).

Approaches including the sociology of science, organizational theory, and social network analysis model interrelationships in scientific and scholarly collaboration and their social institutionalization in a number of organizational types. Analysis of such patterns of collaboration underscores (1) the reflexive relationship between knowledge and its organizational context and social situatedness and (2) the patterns' innate tendency toward interdisciplinary configuration and the imperative role of informal communication in their establishment and maintenance. Economic and organizational theorists have advanced knowledge-based conceptualizations of organizational types and social formations both permanent and transient. Social network analysis and organizational theory continue to evolve in the wake of our increasingly nuanced conceptions of knowledge. In the following, we briefly canvass a number of models of the organizational or social contexts of interdisciplinary collaboration, beginning with "invisible colleges," "communities of practice," "epistemic communities," and various knowledge-based conceptualizations of the firm. A more expanded analysis of relevant concepts often regarded as extraneous in this context would include "tacit knowledge," elucidated by Michael Polanyi (1983); the "stickiness" of information, as assessed by Eric von Hippel (1994); and the "strength of weak ties," articulated by Mark Granovetter (1973). Following in this tack, the assessment would consider concepts such as clustering, agglomeration, and knowledge spillovers, and would survey the literature on knowledge management, the scientific collaboration networks M. E. J. Newman (2001, p. 404) terms "small worlds," the "interpretive communities" of Stanley Fish, and complexity and patterns of interaction. From a list compiled by Cook and Brown (1999, pp. 381–382), additional themes associated with organizational knowledge and knowledge-based organization would include organizational learning, organizational memory, collective mind, management of intellectual capital, core competencies, patterns of communication, and cognitive systems.

Invisible Colleges: A Prototype for Interdisciplinary Collaboration

An important historical model for interdisciplinary collaboration is found in the knowledge networks known as "invisible colleges," a concept that derives from the early modern period and refers to any informal collaborative engagement of scholars and scientists focused on similar or related problems. Merton attributes the metaphor to the pioneering 17th century chemist and "natural philosopher" Robert Boyle, who coined the term with reference to his peers in the Royal Society of London (Price, 1986, pp. viii–ix). Price explains that these early scientists "communicated by letter to gain an appreciative audience for their work, to secure priority, and to keep informed of work being done elsewhere by others" (p. 119). With reference to the "knowledge revolution" of this period, Joel Mokyr (2002) explains the relevance of the concept thus: "The blossoming of open science and the emergence of invisible colleges—that is, informal scholarly communities spanning different countries, within which seventeenth-century scholars and scientists kept close and detailed correspondences with each other—compounded these advances" (p. 56).

While his objective is to offer perspective on the historical origins of the knowledge economy, Mokyr (2002) offers an assessment of the proliferation of knowledge since the Scientific Revolution that both establishes its grounding within organizations and institutions and traces its circulation through social networks. "The central phenomenon of the modern age is that as an aggregate we know more" (p. 2), he observes, and his analysis underscores that the era was determined not only by the codification of disciplinary

knowledge within universities and scientific institutes but also by its dissemination through social networks and professional societies such as invisible
colleges. Only through access to the epistemic base does knowledge become
"useful" in the present and for future generations: "Much of the likelihood
that knowledge will be transmitted depends on the social organization of
knowledge . . . and who controls access to it," Mokyr explains (p. 8).[4]

Much like their historic counterparts, contemporary invisible colleges,
which form the "in group" in any given research frontier, serve to advance
communication and collaboration (Price, 1986, p. 119). Price (1965a) suggested the scope of a hypothetical invisible college active in contemporary
research when he estimated that it would

> correspond with the work of something like the order of one hundred
> scientists who probably constitute the peer group of a typical new
> invisible college of all the people who really do the work at that par-
> ticular segment of the research front. (p. 557)

Such an assemblage represents the vanguard of scientific research in a given
arena, for "whenever we see invisible colleges we have research-front science" (p. 567). Price underscored the significance of informal communication in advancing knowledge in such groups: "In fields that are cumulating
strongly," he explained, "the news of research flows by personal contact and
verbal report through the invisible college and the surrounding peer group"
(p. 562) While the process has become "blatantly obvious" only recently,
Price deemed it to have been operative since the convention of scientific
publication became standard practice in the mid-17th century.[5]

Diana Crane (1969, 1972) characterized the invisible college as a "network of influence and communication" constituted by scientists, sometimes
"widely separated geographically," whose "productivity is sufficient to make
them visible to most of those who enter the field." Formal collaboration is
facilitated through informal communication, which may be "fleeting" or
"relatively unstructured." She underscored the extent to which the growth of
knowledge and innovation is a "diffusion process" that is at once cognitive
and social. Through sociometric data, she demonstrated that social interaction with colleagues despite geographic dispersion—what she termed "relat-
edness" and "connectivity"—produces cumulative and even "exponential"
growth in scientific knowledge through a "contagion process in which early
adopters influence later adopters." (See Crane, 1969, p. 349; 1972, pp. 3–5,
22–23, 41–42, 52.) A recent case study of an interdisciplinary research group
corroborates her sociometric analysis and finds that in the collaborative

---

[4]The invention of the printing press and, more recently, proliferation of ubiquitous
information technologies provide unparalleled examples of increased access at
reduced costs.

[5]In this context, Price cites the discussion by Hagstrom (1964).

milieu certain individuals inevitably emerge as "interdisciplinary linchpins" (White, Wellman, & Nazer, 2004). Karim Lakhani, Lars Bo Jeppesen, Peter Lohse, and Jill Panetta (2006) present a compelling argument for collaboration in such knowledge networks, drawing the following conclusion: "Lack of openness and transparency means that scientific problem solving is constrained to a few scientists who work in secret and who typically fail to leverage the entire accumulation of scientific knowledge available" (p. 2).

Communities of Practice: Learning as Social Participation

A correlate to institutional design that encourages social interactions conducive to interdisciplinary collaboration is to be found in the concept of "communities of practice" elucidated by Etienne Wenger (1998), which is predicated on the assumption that learning is a process of "social participation." Wenger thus argues that whether one is a mechanic or poet or scientist, knowledge is not only a "matter of competence" but also of active and meaningful engagement. He specifies that whether on the playground or in the office or laboratory, "participation shapes not only what we do, but also who we are and how we interpret what we do" (p. 4). Communication is fundamental to the four interrelated components of his social theory of learning: meaning, practice, community, and identity, each of which he defines as "a way of talking about" the respective aspects of learning. Thus, "community" itself is defined as "a way of talking about the social configurations in which our enterprises are defined" (p. 5).

Wenger (1998) explains that from playground to classroom to workplace to cyberspace, communities of practice are ubiquitous and sometimes "so informal and so pervasive that they rarely come into explicit focus" (p. 7). His examples range from garage bands to the academic research environment: "In laboratories, scientists correspond with colleagues, near and far, in order to advance their inquiries" (p. 6). In this context and relevant to our assessment of the collaborative research environment, Wenger considers the analytical framework of the concept of communities of practice as derivative from theories of both social structure and "situated experience." While theories of social structure underscore the "primacy" of institutions, norms, and rules, theories of situated experience accord primacy to the "dynamics of everyday existence," which include "improvisation, coordination, and interactional choreography" (pp. 12–13).

Paul Duguid (2005) points out the "interdependent tension and dynamism" of such communities, noting that the concept is frequently applied to "transient, cross-functional teams and miscellaneous work groups," which would be typical in academic research. Other social constructs include apprenticeship, which Duguid contends should be construed as "not merely the preferred method of 'manual' trades, but also of the higher reaches of academic disciplines." When dispersed globally, Duguid recommends their conceptualization as "networks of practice" (pp. 112–113, 115).

Participation in communities of practice emphasizes "learning by doing," and Wenger (1998) identifies three conceptual dimensions by which practice becomes a "source of cohesion" for a community: mutual engagement, joint enterprise, and shared repertoire. Through mutual engagement, a community of practitioners negotiates a joint enterprise, which engenders a "communal regime of mutual accountability" that sometimes transcends "reified rules, policies, standards, and goals" (p. 81). Such accountability develops "specialized sensitivities, an aesthetic sense, and refined perceptions" that may become integral to the joint enterprise (p. 81). Wenger identifies the shared repertoire of a community of practice as comprising all facets of the "participative" dimension of the enterprise, including routines, gestures, symbols, narratives, and discourse that in their totality secure the meaning and identity of the enterprise (pp. 72–83).

Of particular relevance to interdisciplinary collaboration, which by some accounts advances on the margins of disciplines,[6] is the conceptualization of marginality and peripherality in learning communities offered by Wenger (1998). On the margins of "regimes of competence" one may find the "wisdom of peripherality," which includes "paths not taken, connections overlooked, choices taken for granted" by core participants (p. 216). Wenger explains that such "legitimate peripheral participation" (p. 100) correlates with the practice of apprenticeship, as disclosed in a number of ethnographic studies (pp. 11, 100–101, 216–217).

"Learning happens, design or no design," Wenger (1998) observes, yet he underscores the imperative for appropriate institutional accommodation because there are "few more urgent tasks than to design social infrastructures that foster learning." According to Wenger, "a learning community must be given opportunities to become involved in the institutional arrangements in the context of which it defines its enterprise." Consistent with the oft-quoted maxim attributed variously to the computer scientist Alan Kay and management consultant Peter Drucker that "the best way to predict the future is to invent it," Wenger writes: "Those who understand the informal yet structured, experiential yet social, character of learning—and can translate their insight into designs in the service of learning—will be the architects of our tomorrow" (pp. 225, 274).

Epistemic Communities: Inquiry as "Cognitive Socialization"

The sociocultural foundation of interdisciplinary collaboration is well represented in the concept of the epistemic community, which has been

---

[6]For discussion of a model of interdisciplinary formation that focuses on the fragmentation of disciplines into subfields followed by their strategic recombination or hybridization, see Dogan and Pahre (1990); for contextualization of the model, see Dabars (2008, pp. 45–60).

defined by Hugh Miller and Charles Fox (2001) as a "group of inquirers who have knowledge problems to solve." Any such community shares "norms of inquiry," and while these "vary from community to community," they are determined by tradition, which through "long apprenticeships socialize members of any particular epistemic community" and shape "our institutions and attitudes, our scholarly practices, and our standards of evidence" (pp. 669, 681, 683). While the concept, first introduced by Burkart Holzner in 1968, identifies a type of social formation broadly consistent with communities of practice and other knowledge-based conceptualizations of social organization, it privileges the dynamics of knowledge creation, which Holzner equated with "cognitive socialization" (p. 28).

Epistemic communities are variously conceived, and while the concept is often applied to scientific research, Peter M. Haas (1992) explains, members may come from varied disciplinary backgrounds. He defines an epistemic community as a "network of professionals with recognized expertise and competence in a particular domain and an authoritative claim to policy-relevant knowledge within that domain or issue-area." Members of epistemic communities share "set[s] of normative and principled beliefs" that include "notions of validity"—that is, beliefs about what counts as intellectual adequacy within the community. Haas points out that the concept "somewhat resembles Kuhn's broader sociological definition of a paradigm" ("an entire constellation of beliefs, values, techniques, and so on shared by members of a given community"). The community may be interdisciplinary since in this sense the paradigm "governs not a subject matter but a group of practitioners" (p. 3).

Irma Bogenrieder and Bart Nooteboom (2004) contend that epistemic communities tend to be interdisciplinary and problem focused: "Epistemic communities engage in transdisciplinary and/or transfunctional activities, at the interstices between the various disciplines. In contrast with communities of practice, they are not organized around a common discipline but around a common topic or problem" (p. 49). Consistent with knowledge-based theories of the firm, considered in the following section, Lars Håkanson (2010) thus recommends that epistemic communities be "premised on a contextual conceptualization of knowledge" to "denote groups of people mastering the theories, codes, and tools of a common practice regardless of their geographical location" (pp. 1804, 1809).

Knowledge-Based Theories of the Firm: Enterprise as Knowledge Network

American research universities, both public and private, are the primary source of the discovery and innovation that fosters economic and social development at all levels of analysis in the global knowledge economy. Institutional design that engenders interdisciplinary collaboration inevitably advances the basic and applied research that constitutes a critical national asset. Further critical leverage is attained when we reach out beyond the walls of the academy and engage transinstitutionally. The "triple helix" of university-industry-government innovation described by Etzkowitz (2008, p. 1) represents a series of knowledge networks that inevitably interconnect and leverage respective knowledge bases from diverse and, given the multiplicity of actors, inherently multidisciplinary perspectives. The literature on economic development derived from science-based technological innovation thus offers concepts relevant to our understanding of interdisciplinary collaboration within the research environment (Crow & Dabars, 2012).

In particular, an appreciation of the organizational correlates to interdisciplinary collaboration may be derived from an emerging literature on knowledge-based theories of the firm. David J. Teece (2003) has characterized the firm, referring to a business enterprise either small or large, as a "repository for knowledge," which is "embedded in routines and processes." Competitive advantage derives from the communication of knowledge ("intellectual capital"): "The essence of the firm is its ability to create, transfer, assemble, integrate, and exploit knowledge assets" (p. 149). In a knowledge-based conceptualization of the firm, the enterprise has moreover been construed as a communication network, albeit concerned primarily with variables of specialization and the exploitation of efficiencies: "The internal organization of firms is seen as a communication network that is designed to minimize both the costs of processing new information and the costs of communicating this information among its agents" (Bolton & Dewatripont, 1994, p. 809). Håkanson (2010) even proposes that because "firms offer superior governance structures primarily for knowledge processes, which involve exchanges of tacit, poorly articulated knowledge across epistemic boundaries," they can "meaningfully be seen as epistemic communities in their own right" (p. 1806).

Another analysis proposes that a firm be understood as a "social community specializing in speed and efficiency in the creation and transfer of knowledge" (Kogut & Zander, 1996, p. 503). Bruce Kogut and Udo Zander (1992) invoke Polanyi to underscore the extent to which both explicit and tacit knowledge informs this process: While the "central competitive dimension of what firms know how to do is to create and transfer knowledge efficiently within an organizational context," the capacity to do so derives from the "combinative capability to synthesize and apply current and acquired knowledge" (p. 384). Other scholars, following Pierre Bourdieu, construe "organizational advantage" as derivative of social capital, which is said to engender the creation of intellectual capital. Social capital has been variously interpreted but in general usage refers to the significance of networks of relationships that define individuals or groups, while intellectual capital refers broadly to possession by an individual or collective of various types of knowledge. In one such analysis, social capital produces intellectual capital within a "framework of combination and exchange" (Nahapiet & Ghoshal, 1998, p. 251).

The recognition that firms may be understood as knowledge-centric is confirmed by their correlation with academic, and especially scientific, research groups by Etzkowitz (2003, 2008), whose work both delineates the dynamic interrelationships between academia, industry, and government, and elucidates the broader parallel between academic research and economic development. Indeed, Etzkowitz terms the "entrepreneurial academic model" of the contemporary research university a "teaching, research, and economic development enterprise." He observes that academic research groups have "firm-like qualities, especially under conditions in which research funding is awarded on a competitive basis." Moreover, the "research university shares homologous qualities with a start-up firm even before it directly engages in entrepreneurial activities" (Etzkowitz, 2003, pp. 109–110; 2008). Indeed, along with firms and corporations, universities are key institutional actors in national systems of innovation because of their crucial role in discovery as well as the commercialization of university-based research (Niosi, Saviotti, Bellon, & Crow, 1993, pp. 207–208).

The knowledge-centric social formations considered in this section of the chapter—invisible colleges, communities of practice, epistemic communities, and firms construed as knowledge-centric—represent prototypes for the organization of teaching and research not generally associated with the advancement of interdisciplinarity. Interdisciplinary collaboration may not be strictly required for their operation, but as we have seen in the foregoing assessment, it is generally implicit to their success even if sometimes perceived as merely adventitious. Theoretical discussions of interdisciplinarity tend to overlook such formations, which would probably be deemed extraneous to the repertoire of favoured models. Yet each is relevant to university design because any research enterprise is essentially dependent on its social context and organizational or institutional structure. Recognition of their potential to enhance interdisciplinary collaboration along the epistemological, administrative, and sociocultural dimensions of knowledge described by Wallerstein (2003) may be especially relevant for research universities because these institutions operate on the frontiers of discovery.

The Institutional Implementation of Interdisciplinarity: A Case Study

With simultaneous pressures impelling scholarship toward increasing specialization on the one hand, and greater synthesis, integration, or convergence on the other, the implications of the organizational context of knowledge within the complex matrix of a comprehensive research university are not always readily apparent. Yet the reconfiguration of disciplinary knowledge has the potential to profoundly affect learning outcomes and leverage research transinstitutionally. While chronicles of institutional efforts to implement interdisciplinarity have contributed to a considerable body of analysis, its conceptualization and implementation at Arizona State University has proceeded largely unencumbered by extraneous rationalization or theoretical justification. In some cases, models of interdisciplinarity—perhaps even including those surveyed in the preceding section—may have served loosely as broad prototypes for new organizational configurations. But in practice, the process—interchangeably referenced as inter- or transdisciplinarity, or even "intellectual fusion"—has been shaped through exhaustive trial and error, a number of course corrections, and the best efforts of administration and faculty at the application of common sense.

During the past decade, the institutional implementation of interdisciplinarity has been one of eight explicit "design aspirations" of Arizona State University (ASU), the nation's youngest major research institution and—with an enrollment surpassing 73,000 undergraduate, graduate, and professional students—the largest university governed by a single administration. ASU seeks to advance knowledge and human well-being through teaching and research conducted within a flexible organizational framework that maximizes collaboration and communication between the core disciplines—some of which remain departmentally based, while others are construed across departments, centers, institutes, schools, and colleges—and new explicitly transdisciplinary configurations. These new academic entities ("new schools") have been established to advance teaching and foster both fundamental and applied research, which possesses the interdisciplinary breadth to address the large-scale "grand challenges."

Because academic organization historically reflected the conventional correlation between discipline and department, the design process from the outset sought to clarify the relationships between core academic disciplines and the new interdisciplinary configurations that emerged (i.e., identity), their disposition within the university (i.e., configuration), and their anticipated evolution (i.e., trajectory). A comprehensive unit-level assessment of the institutional status of disciplines and interdisciplines sought to articulate disciplinary identities and examine their interrelationships, including analysis of each in terms of optimal alignment with fundamental and irreducible disciplines. Assessments of positional embeddedness within institutional coordinates further clarified their interactions and interrelationships. Finally, consideration of trajectory sought to establish the status of an entity within its disciplinary continuum, its role in the emergence of associated interdisciplinary formations, and its relationship to emerging peer entities. These same considerations continue to inform analysis of subsequent proposed organizational reconfigurations.

The implementation of interdisciplinarity at ASU, however, must be understood within the broader and interrelated context of the comprehensive, decade-long institutional reconceptualization launched in 2002, which was conceived with the objective of establishing a foundational model for a "New American University," an institution predicated on the pursuit of academic excellence, inclusiveness to a broad demographic, and maximum societal impact.[7] While the interplay between the various design aspirations, which include local embeddedness, societal transformation, academic enterprise, and "use-inspired" research, informed the reconceptualization of academic organization and operations, transdisciplinarity is foundational to each and to the entire conception. Rather than extrapolate from existing structure or replicate historical models perceived to represent a putative "gold standard," ASU sought to produce a federation of unique transdisciplinary departments, centers, institutes, schools, and colleges ("schools") and a deliberate and complementary clustering of programs arrayed across four differentiated campuses. In this "school-centric" conception, academic units compete for status not intramurally but with peer entities globally. In the process, ASU has advanced interdisciplinarity through the consolidation of a number of traditional academic departments—including anthropology, geology, sociology, and several areas of biology—which henceforth no longer serve as the sole institutional locus of a given discipline. While more than two dozen new transdisciplinary schools were conceptualized and operationalized, some have been subsequently further reconfigured or merged (Capaldi, 2009).

The differentiation of knowledge enterprises through their interdisciplinary configuration facilitates their integration into coordinated and synergistic networks, thus expanding their potential to offer multiple solutions and exert greater impact across broader swathes of knowledge. Inasmuch as knowledge and innovation flourish when embedded in and interrelated through transinstitutional and transnational networks, the reconceptualized institution has proactively sought to advance connectivity, engaging other academic and research institutions, business and industry, and governments around the world in collaborative teaching and research. Transnational endeavor to lend direction and purpose to the artistic and humanistic insight, social scientific understanding, scientific discoveries, and technological adaptations that are the product of academic culture represents our best hope in surmounting the challenges ahead.

The impetus to rethink discipline-based academic departments began with an ambitious reorganization of the biological faculties to overcome disciplinary entrenchment. In July 2003, the departments of biology, microbiology, plant biology, and the program in molecular and cellular biology merged to form the new School of Life Sciences. While administrative efficiency was cited as an objective, the motivation was largely to advance interdisciplinarity:

> to facilitate collaboration across the range of disciplines covered by the School; . . . [and] to exploit the fact that the key research challenges in the life sciences lie at the interface of sub-disciplines, often involving integration of knowledge from different levels of biological organization and across different kinds of organisms. (ASU School of Life Sciences, 2010, p. 1)

---

[7]Michael M. Crow articulated the vision for a New American University when he became the 16th president of ASU in July 2002. See, for example, Crow (2010).

The school was conceived "without internal disciplinary barriers, allowing it to plan strategically at the seams of intersecting disciplines" (p. 2). Faculty groups include biomedicine and biotechnology; cellular and molecular biosciences; genomics, evolution, and bioinformatics; ecology, evolution, and environmental science; and organismal, integrative, and systems biology. Consistent with the prototypes of an invisible college or epistemic community, the arrangement promotes self-organization among life scientists, engineers, philosophers, and social scientists.

Among the new transdisciplinary schools conceptualized and operationalized during the past decade are the School of Earth and Space Exploration; School of Human Evolution and Social Change; School of Politics and Global Studies; School of Social and Family Dynamics; School of Social Transformation; and School of Historical, Philosophical, and Religious Studies. These complement initiatives such as the Global Institute of Sustainability (GIOS), which incorporates the first-of-its-kind School of Sustainability, and the Biodesign Institute, the premier transdisciplinary research center dedicated exclusively to advancing biologically inspired design to address global challenges in health care, sustainability, and national security. The research of this large-scale array of labs and centers working in the broad domains of biological, nanoscale, cognitive, and sustainable systems is aimed at improving human health and the environment through interdisciplinary efforts in such areas as personalized diagnostics and treatment, infectious diseases and pandemics, and renewable sources of energy.

Other transdisciplinary configurations include the Complex Adaptive Systems Initiative, a collaborative effort to address global challenges in health, sustainability, and national security through the creation of new technologies and novel solutions; Security and Defense Systems Initiative, which addresses national and global security and defense challenges through an integrative approach to technology solutions, legal and policy issues, and the root social causes in areas of emerging threats; Flexible Display Center, a cooperative agreement with the U.S. Army to advance the emerging flexible electronics industry; LightWorks, a collaborative effort to advance research in renewable energy fields, including artificial photosynthesis, biofuels, and next-generation photovoltaics; and initiatives in the humanities and social sciences, including the Institute for Social Science Research and Center for the Study of Religion and Conflict.

The School of Earth and Space Exploration (SESE) represents a transdisciplinary conceptualization of the quest to discover the origins of the universe and expand our understanding of space, matter, and time. SESE combines the conventional disciplines of astronomy and astrophysics, cosmology, Earth systems sciences, planetary sciences, and systems engineering. Strategic research initiatives include the emergence of planetary bodies; the origin, evolution, and distribution of life; and the coevolution of Earth's surface environment and human societies. While the conventional disciplines of the Earth and space sciences are predominantly historical, according to planetary geologist Ronald Greeley and his colleagues (2010), transdisciplinarity offers the potential to "elevate both to predictive sciences" to address such questions as the ultimate fate of the universe (p. 2). Established in July 2006 through amalgamation of the former Department of Geological Sciences and the astronomy, astrophysics, and cosmology faculties of the former Department of Physics and Astronomy—thereafter, the Department of Physics—SESE boasts a faculty roster that includes theoretical physicists, systems biologists, biogeochemists, and engineers who bring technological expertise that advances the development and deployment of critical scientific instrumentation on Earth and in space.

The School of Human Evolution and Social Change (SHESC) combines the major areas of anthropological enquiry, including archaeology, bioarchaeology, physical anthropology, cultural anthropology, and linguistics, with such areas as mathematics and computer science, geography, political science, museum studies, epidemiology, economics, and sociology. The new school boasts such transdisciplinary research centers as the Archaeological Research Institute, Center for Digital Antiquity, and Institute of Human Origins. The allied Consortium for Biosocial Complex Systems engages the Complex Adaptive Systems Initiative. Transdisciplinary collaboration allows SHESC scientists and scholars to address complex problems from comparative and holistic perspectives, whether the challenge is epidemics of infectious disease, sustainable management of natural resources, or adaptation to climate change. The quest to understand human origins, evolution, and diversity engages research in such areas as societies and their natural environments; biocultural dimensions of global health, culture, heritage, and identity; and global dynamics and cultural interactions. The school thus offers an integrated curriculum in the social, behavioral, and natural sciences focused on the evolution of our species and trajectories of human societies.[8]

The design aspirations are intrinsically interrelated, and the interplay between interdisciplinarity and efforts to advance sustainability as a core value is representative of their dynamic. With the establishment of the GIOS in 2004 and School of Sustainability 3 years later, ASU has positioned itself in the vanguard of interdisciplinary research on environmental, economic, and social sustainability. In a social network reminiscent of an invisible college or epistemic community, the institute brings together scientists and engineers with government policymakers and industry leaders to conduct research in areas as diverse as agriculture, air quality, marine ecology, materials design, nanotechnology, policy and governance, renewable energy, risk assessment, transportation, and urban infrastructure. Sustainability is thus representative of the interdisciplinary theme-based approaches that epitomize the reconceptualization of the university.

---

[8]See ASU School of Human Evolution and Social Change, *Seven-Year Program Review (2005–2011)*, http://shesc.asu.edu/, and http://casi.asu.edu/.

Each institution must advance a differentiated profile, determined by its mission and setting; the character of its academic community; the scope of its constituent colleges, schools, and departments; and the extent of its commitment to public service and community engagement. Any comprehensive reconceptualization of an organization or institution must thus proceed according to its own intrinsic logic, especially in the case of an institution as complex as a major research university. The purposes of this chapter, therefore, do not include the articulation of a set of design prescriptions applicable in all contexts. Rather, our intent has been to call attention to the focus and deliberation that must be expended on institutional design in general, including the problem of how to structure institutions to foster more meaningful interdisciplinarity.

Toward Interdisciplinary Knowledge Enterprises _____

Even before the advent of organized science and the formation of the modern research university, our intellectual progenitors understood the need to think at scale and across disciplines. Four centuries of scientific focus on the ever smaller and more fundamental secrets of nature have seemingly impaired our ability to frame inquiry standpoints commensurate to the challenges that confront us. During this same time frame, through our increasingly sophisticated manipulation of limited knowledge coupled with brute force and an astonishing measure of hubris, we have shaped a world that in all likelihood cannot sustain our collective standard of living. Although disciplinary specialization has been key to scientific success, such specialization can diminish holistic understanding. It has also diminished our ability to construe teaching and research between and among the disciplines. Our academic culture, and science in particular, uses disciplinary organization to recognize and focus on questions that *can* be answered while there is absolutely no a priori reason to assume that what we *can* know is what we most *need* to know.[9]

Concern with institutional design and optimal organization for research may well be subsumed in more epistemologically grounded discussion; indeed, the question, "How should inquiry be organized so as to fulfill its proper function?" has been crucial to modern science, as we are reminded by the philosopher Philip Kitcher (2001), beginning with the quest of Bacon and Descartes for suitable methods of discovery and justification. The quest for a "community well-designed for the attainment of epistemic goals" elucidated by Kitcher—balancing consideration of social institutions with abstract knowledge—requires no further justification (pp. 109, 113).

_____

[9]An analysis of human limitation in this context is to be found in Crow (2007). See also Frodeman, Chapter 6, this volume.

The well-known observation by University of California president emeritus Clark Kerr (1982) that universities dominate the list of institutions established before 1500 that still exist "in recognizable forms, with similar functions, and with unbroken histories" expresses the intergenerational sweep of great teaching and research. Against the present backdrop of encroaching complexity, it is obvious that we need new ways to conceive the pursuit of discovery, creativity, and innovation, to understand and build our knowledge enterprises, and to endow academic culture with meaning for people other than academicians. Our collective survival as a species may depend on our capacity to adapt and innovate, which assumes mutual intelligibility between and among academic disciplines and interdisciplinary fields, and knowledge enterprises designed to engender interdisciplinary collaboration.

Take-Home Messages

- The relationship between institutional design and the advancement of knowledge in the American research university is no mere perfunctory administrative matter.
- Despite broad consensus regarding the imperative for inter- or transdisciplinary scholarship, academic disciplines continue to dominate academic structures and practices at both the institutional level and transinstitutionally, in their relationships with other institutions, industry, and government.
- Institutional design has the potential to remediate design limitations inherent within the American research university, including those that impede interdisciplinary inquiry and collaboration.
- An appreciation for the reflexive relationship between knowledge and its organizational context may be derived from theoretical approaches and organizational models generally regarded as extraneous to interdisciplinary analysis.
- Inasmuch as the design of our knowledge enterprises is not merely adventitious to the advancement of knowledge, administrators and academicians alike do well to advance their understanding of and appreciation for institutional design.

References

Abbott, A. (2001). *Chaos of disciplines*. Chicago: University of Chicago Press.

Arizona State University School of Life Sciences. (2010, April 15). *Strategic plan*. Retrieved from http://www.sols.asu.edu/publications/pdf/strategic_plan_april_2010.pdf

Bogenrieder, I., & Nooteboom, B. (2004). The emergence of learning communities: A theoretical analysis. In H. T. Tsoukas & N. Mylonopoulos (Eds.), *Organizations as knowledge systems: Knowledge, learning, and dynamic capabilities* (pp. 46–66). Hampshire, UK: Palgrave MacMillan.

Bolton, P., & Dewatripont, M. (1994). The firm as a communication network. *Quarterly Journal of Economics, 109*(4), 809–839.

Brooks, F. P. (2010). *The design of design: Essays from a computer scientist.* Boston: Addison-Wesley.

Brown, J. S., & Duguid, P. (1991). Organizational learning and communities-of-practice: Toward a unified view of working, learning, and innovation. *Organization Science, 2*(1), 40–57.

Capaldi, E. D. (2009, July–August). Intellectual transformation and budgetary savings through academic reorganization. *Change,* 19–27. Retrieved from http://www.changemag.org/Archives/Back%20Issues/July-August%202009/full-intellectual-budgetary.html

Cole, J. R. (2009). *The great American university: Its rise to preeminence, its indispensable national role, and why it must be protected.* New York: Public Affairs.

Committee on Facilitating Interdisciplinary Research and Committee on Science, Engineering, and Public Policy. (2005). *Facilitating interdisciplinary research.* Washington, DC: National Academies Press.

Cook, S. D. N., & Brown, J. S. (1999). Bridging epistemologies: The generative dance between organizational knowledge and organizational knowing. *Organization Science, 10*(4), 381–400.

Crane, D. (1969). Social structure in a group of scientists: A test of the "invisible college" hypothesis. *American Sociological Review, 34*(3), 335–352.

Crane, D. (1972). *Invisible colleges: Diffusion of knowledge in scientific communities.* Chicago: University of Chicago Press.

Crow, M. M. (2007). None dare call it hubris: The limits of knowledge. *Issues in Science and Technology, 23*(2), 29–32.

Crow, M. M. (2010). The research university as comprehensive knowledge enterprise: A prototype for a New American University. In L. E. Weber & J. J. Duderstadt (Eds.), *Glion Colloquium 6: University Research for Innovation* (pp. 211–225). London: Economica.

Crow, M. M., & Dabars, W. B. (2012). University-based research and economic development: The Morrill Act and the emergence of the American research university. In D. M. Fogel & E. Malson-Huddle (Eds.), *Precipice or crossroads: Where America's great public universities stand and where they are going midway through their second century* (pp. 119–158). Albany: State University of New York Press.

Dabars, W. B. (2008). *Disciplinarity and interdisciplinarity: Rhetoric and context in the American research university.* Doctoral dissertation, University of California, Los Angeles. Retrieved from University Microfilms International (3347020).

Price, D. J. de S. (1965a). Is technology historically independent of science? A study in statistical historiography. *Technology and Culture, 6*(4), 553–568.

Price, D. J. de S. (1965b). Networks of scientific papers. *Science, 149,* 510–515.

Price, D. J. de S. (1986). *Little science, big science, and beyond* (2nd ed.). New York: Columbia University Press.

Dogan, M. (1997). The new social sciences: Cracks in the disciplinary walls. *International Social Sciences Journal, 153,* 429–443.

Dogan, M., & Pahre, R. (1990). *Creative marginality: Innovation at the intersections of social sciences.* Boulder, CO: Westview Press.

Downs, A. (1967). *Inside bureaucracy.* Boston: Little, Brown.

Duderstadt, J. J. (2000). *A university for the twenty-first century.* Ann Arbor: University of Michigan Press.

Duguid, P. (2005). The art of knowing: Social and tacit dimensions of knowledge and the limits of the community of practice. *Information Society, 21*, 109–118.

Dupree, A. H. (1957). *Science in the federal government: A history of policies and activities to 1940.* Cambridge, MA: Belknap Press of Harvard University.

Etzkowitz, H. (2003). Research groups as quasi-firms: The invention of the entrepreneurial university. *Research Policy, 32*, 109–121.

Etzkowitz, H. (2008). *The triple helix: University-industry-government innovation in action.* New York: Routledge.

Frodeman, R., & Mitcham, C. (2007, December). New directions in interdisciplinarity: Broad, deep, and critical. *Bulletin of Science, Technology, and Society, 27*, 506–514.

Galison, P. (1997). *Image and logic: A material culture of microphysics.* Chicago: University of Chicago Press.

Geiger, R. L. (1986). *To advance knowledge: The growth of American research universities, 1900–1940.* Oxford, UK: Oxford University Press.

Giddens, A. (1984). *The constitution of society: Outline of the theory of structuration.* Berkeley: University of California Press.

Granovetter, M. S. (1973). The strength of weak ties. *American Journal of Sociology, 78*(6), 1360–1380.

Greeley, R., Anbar, A., Arrowsmith, R., Garnero, E., Rhoads, J., & Hodges, K. (2010, November). *Academic program review for the School of Earth and Space Exploration (SESE), Arizona State University.* Retrieved from http://graduate.asu.edu/sites/default/files/SESESelf-StudyReport_0.pdf

Haas, P. M. (1992). Epistemic communities and international policy coordination. *International Organization, 46*(1), 1–35.

Hagel, J., Brown, J. S., & Davison, L. (2010). *The power of pull: How small moves, smartly made, can set big things in motion.* New York: Basic Books.

Hagstrom, W. O. (1964). Traditional and modern forms of scientific teamwork. *Administrative Science Quarterly, 9*(3), 241–263.

Håkanson, L. (2010). The firm as an epistemic community: The knowledge-based view revisited. *Industrial and Corporate Change, 19*(6), 1801–1828.

Holzner, B. (1968). *Reality construction in society.* Cambridge, MA: Schenkman.

Kerr, C. (1982). The uses of the university two decades later: Postscript 1982. *Change, 14*, 23–31.

Kitcher, P. (2001). *Science, truth, and democracy.* Oxford, UK: Oxford University Press.

Kogut, B., & Zander, U. (1992). Knowledge of the firm, combinative capabilities, and the replication of knowledge. *Organization Science, 3*(3), 383–397.

Kogut, B., & Zander, U. (1996). What firms do: Coordination, identity, and learning. *Organization Science, 7*(5), 502–518.

Kuhn, T. (1970). *The structure of scientific revolutions.* Chicago: University of Chicago Press.

Lakhani, K. R., Jeppesen, L. B., Lohse, P. A., & Panetta, J. A. (2006, October). *The value of openness in scientific problem solving* (Harvard Business School Working Paper 07-050). Retrieved from http://www.hbs.edu/faculty/Publication%20Files/07-050.pdf

Mau, B., & Leonard, J. (2004). *Massive change.* London: Phaidon Press.

Merton, R. K. (1973). *The sociology of science: Theoretical and empirical investigations.* Chicago: University of Chicago Press.

Merton, R. K., & Barber, E. (2004). *The travels and adventures of serendipity: A study in sociological semantics and the sociology of science.* Princeton, NJ: Princeton University Press.

Miller, H. T., & Fox, C. J. (2001). The epistemic community. *Administration and Society, 32*(6), 668–685.

Mokyr, J. (2002). *The gifts of Athena: Historical origins of the knowledge economy.* Princeton, NJ: Princeton University Press.

Nahapiet, J., & Ghoshal, S. (1998). Social capital, intellectual capital, and organizational advantage. *Academy of Management Review, 23*(2), 242–266.

Newman, M. E. J. (2001). The structure of scientific collaboration networks. *Proceedings of the National Academy of Sciences, 98*(32), 404–409.

Niosi, J., Saviotti, P., Bellon, B., & Crow, M. M. (1993). National systems of innovation: In search of a workable concept. *Technology in Society, 15,* 207–227.

Oxford English Dictionary (3rd ed.). (2012). Oxford, UK: Oxford University Press. Retrieved March 2012 from http://www.oed.com/

Polanyi, M. (1983). *The tacit dimension* (2nd ed.). Gloucester, MA: Peter Smith.

Simon, H. A. (1996). *The sciences of the artificial* (3rd ed.). Cambridge: MIT Press.

Snow, C. P. (1960). *The two cultures and the scientific revolution.* Cambridge, UK: Cambridge University Press.

Stokes, D. E. (1997). *Pasteur's quadrant: Basic science and technological innovation.* Washington, DC: Brookings Institution Press.

Teece, D. J. (2003). Knowledge and competence as strategic assets. In C. W. Holsapple (Ed.), *Handbook on knowledge management* (Vol. 1, pp. 129–152). Berlin: Springer Verlag.

von Hippel, E. (1994). Sticky information and the locus of problem solving: Implications for innovation. *Management Science, 40,* 429–439.

Wallerstein, I. (2003, August–October). Anthropology, sociology, and other dubious disciplines. *Current Anthropology, 44,* 453–465.

Wenger, E. (1998). *Communities of practice: Learning, meaning, and identity.* Cambridge, UK: Cambridge University Press.

White, H. D., Wellman, B., & Nazer, N. (2004). Does citation reflect social structure? Longitudinal evidence from an interdisciplinary research group. *Journal of the American Society for Information Science and Technology, 55*(2), 111–126.

15

Defining 21st Century Land-Grant Universities Through Cross-Disciplinary Research

◆ M. Duane Nellis

U.S. land-grant universities have a 150-year history of providing world-class public education, research, and outreach to their respective states, regions, the nation, and the world. At the same time, the 21st century has brought new challenges as well as emerging opportunities to land-grant systems. Some of the opportunities relate to the growing emergence of approaches to the three tiers of land-grant activity—learning, research, and outreach—that involve a greater degree of integration and creative communication. Although there are traditional barriers to interdisciplinary learning, research, and outreach, new collaborative initiatives and structures are facilitating exciting transitions, allowing for more robust integrative efforts. This chapter provides an illustration of one such land-grant university, the University of Idaho, where emerging efforts are creating national prototypes toward more effective trends linked to the strategic land-grant mission areas in learning, research, and outreach.

Introduction

This past year, our nation commemorated the 150th anniversary of what the National Archives describes as one of the 100 most important pieces of legislation in American history: the Morrill Act of 1862. Signed into law by President Abraham Lincoln during the Civil War, the act gifted federal land to each state for the purpose of creating colleges to educate "the masses" and advance the agricultural and technological fields essential to our country's success. The law was nothing short of revolutionary at the time: From the Morrill Act's passage, the democratization of higher education was born. Until then, higher education was available principally to America's wealthy, influential, and mostly urban citizens who could pay handsomely for access to private universities and colleges. Today, every American citizen has access to world-class public higher education through the land-grant university system. Such institutions share a common mission and distinction, and in many cases, collaborations involving faculty, staff, and students take place across this system. Universities such as Cornell; Penn State University; Michigan State University; The Ohio State University; University of California, Davis; Oregon State University; and the University of Idaho are among 76 land-grant institutions in the nation.

Together, land-grant universities address a broad range of research questions and issues. They find new ways to grow more and safer crops and build stronger buildings, materials, and infrastructure. They develop innovations to manage water and sustain both the environment and its resources. They prevent and fight disease and create healthier people and communities. They expand and deepen our connection to the humanities and bring its beauty to our statewide communities.

Land-grant institutions also share a direct bond with our home states, a partnership and a promise to bring the strength of our research and teaching—and our graduates—to bear on local and regional issues. As a result, every state can trace a significant aspect of its economic success to the innovations fueled through its partnership with its land-grant university. At the same time, the 21st century has brought new challenges to land-grant universities. In addition, there has been an evolution in the way some land-grant universities, and faculties within such institutions, are approaching key research questions, learning environments, and outreach efforts. In this context, in this chapter I (1) convey some of the challenges we are facing at land-grant higher education research universities and (2) outline relatively new and emerging opportunities associated with new approaches to research, learning, and outreach at such institutions, with a focus on the University of Idaho, including more integrative approaches to address our strategic land-grant mission.

Challenges and Opportunities at Land-Grants

The U.S. great recession, major budget cuts, and overall global economic turmoil have brought stress to most of academia, including land-grant universities. We, in Idaho, are down in our state appropriations just over 20% in the past 3 years. Idaho is certainly not alone in this downturn, as a vast majority of U.S. states struggle with significant deficits in their state budgets. From 2011 to 2012 fiscal years alone, total state support to higher education nationally declined 7.6%, and 29 states appropriated less for colleges in 2012 than they did 5 years ago (Kelderman, 2012).

A proliferation of federal regulations has also been impacting higher education. There have been new efforts, for example, by the U.S. Department of Education to standardize the definition of *credit* to regulate online learning opportunities where universities and colleges offer such courses outside their state boundaries. Federal agencies also provide significant oversight of research projects and research facilities using federal dollars on university campuses. In addition, the federal government has made significant efforts to strengthen regional accreditation processes at universities in an effort to ensure "appropriate" assessment of student learning, with clearly measured outcomes of educational experiences at our respective institutions. And with the federal government struggling with trillion-dollar deficits, it has focused in part on cuts in the Federal Pell Grant program that provides funds to the most financially needy students, a program that gives them the opportunity to attend colleges and universities. Further exacerbating the stress on our U.S. land-grant and public universities in general is elimination of federal earmarks (i.e., directed funding from a federal agency to a university that doesn't go through a competitive review process) and the potential for reduced funding to the national-level research funding agencies (e.g., National Science Foundation [NSF], National Endowment for the Humanities) that help fund faculty innovation and graduate and undergraduate educational programs that contribute in multiple ways to America's economic competitiveness and quality of life.

At the same time, today's land-grant and other research universities are at a crossroads in creating a new dynamic that will allow them to address key research questions and create new learning paradigms in the 21st century. Although research in the past has used integrative approaches, the scale of key research questions today now requires more integrative or cross-disciplinary approaches to research discovery. Issues such as global climate change and its implications require complex teams of researchers to understand all the dimensions of the human–environmental system. Coupled with the need to be more cross-disciplinary is the need to think differently about our structures and be more energized across our campuses and in our states and regions. The National Academies report *Facilitating Interdisciplinary Research* (Committee on Facilitating Interdisciplinary Research, 2004) was produced to help institutions understand how to systematically encourage interdisciplinary research by changing academic organizations and cultures (Kezar & Elrod, 2012). In addition to pointing out barriers, such as reward systems that failed to incentivize collaboration, it also identified a vision for fostering interdisciplinary work that involves adequate start-up resources, cross-campus dialogues, collaborative research facilities, and other incentives. Each of these strategies requires effective and constructive communication. Land-grants of the past in many cases were siloed in their college and disciplinary structures, and a broader and more effective campus dialogue can help universities produce a more interdisciplinary culture that is consistent with the democratizing idea behind the Morrill Act, bringing us back to our pragmatic roots (Burkhardt, 2000).

Twenty-first century universities must also be more globally connected, scaling discoveries at the local and regional level to broader contexts. And 21st century universities need to be more entrepreneurial and sustainable, building new partnerships that generate new perspectives, resources, and a greater potential for new discoveries. Each of these themes (such as being more entrepreneurial) has implications for the development of new learning paradigms as we educate students and new faculty to meet the needs of our 21st century world. By addressing these themes, we can help meet the needs of an increasingly complex world.

Interdisciplinary Communication and Collaboration in the Land-Grant University

I would like to focus on key aspects of interdisciplinarity and how I believe such efforts will be one of the key catalysts for positive change in the 21st century land-grant university. In traditional universities (including land-grants), interdisciplinary research can be more difficult even though such approaches are extremely worthwhile. Even given the difficulties in communication across different methods and epistemologies and conflicting opinions about interdisciplinary approaches, many university leaders and faculty feel supportive of the opportunities afforded through interdisciplinarity (Paletz, Smith-Doerr, & Vardi, 2010). Although many early land-grant universities focused on applied research, particularly in agriculture and engineering, a broader sweep of discovery and creativity is crucial to today's land-grants and sets the stage for greater interdisciplinary work.

Like in Lincoln's time, we are living in a country facing profound challenges of identity, security, and equality. Addressing these substantial challenges requires us to think creatively as we strive for understanding. Einstein once said that imagination is more important than knowledge. And some argue that the humanities do the most to tap and expand the imagination (Leach, 2009). Yet, during budget contraction, the humanities are sometimes targeted as less important than science and engineering. Clearly, future research initiatives and structures must recognize the importance of breadth in addressing some of the most pressing issues confronting the nation and the world. Human factors of science and engineering research require closer attention in these transdisciplinary efforts. Such efforts must be led both from administrators at the top and from a broad spectrum of faculty at the base.

At the same time, recent effort to promote interdisciplinary scholarship in the United States is coming from numerous sources, including federal agencies, private foundations, and universities. These efforts have taken several forms, including dedicated grant support, competition for seed projects, interdisciplinary training programs, programs targeted to enhance campus communication, and hiring initiatives targeted at faculty where expertise spans traditional academic boundaries (Frickel & Jacobs, 2009). Specifically as an example, in 1998, the NSF set aside funds for an interdisciplinary training program for graduate research fellows called the Integrative Graduate Education and Research Traineeship (IGERT) Program (http://www .igert.org). Universities have benefited tremendously from these grants in ways that extend graduate education but also strengthen faculty perspectives in interdisciplinarity as they develop appropriate graduate training projects. There have been 215 IGERT projects funded since the program's inception. Similarly, the National Institutes of Health have funded interdisciplinary research consortia as a means of incentivizing integrating aspects of key disciplines to address health challenges that have been resistant to traditional research approaches (e.g., see http://www.nih.gov).

As one of the most important funding agencies for the land-grant institutions historically and currently, the U.S. Department of Agriculture (USDA) is also working toward more program integration. The requirement for transdisciplinary dimensions in large cooperative agricultural projects funded by USDA's National Institute for Food and Agriculture (NIFA) is a case in point. Traditionally, the USDA's internally funded research efforts through the Agricultural Research Service are science driven and disciplinary, often lacking explicit social dimensions and funding for outreach. The NIFA-funded cooperative agricultural projects represent an effort to facilitate more cross-disciplinary research in an era of transdisciplinary, actionable science.

While these efforts are occurring at the federal level, there are challenges to them at universities. There are many opportunities for creative discovery in universities, but there are also a number of barriers and disincentives toward implementing the most effective forms of cross-disciplinary research. As articulated by Klein (2010), these include challenges in the organizational structure and administration; institutional procedures and processes; resources and infrastructure; and recognition, reward, and incentives. Universities need to create a more robust structural approach that allows faculty the latitude to participate outside of traditional disciplinary and related college or multidisciplinary organizations; this more robust approach should facilitate interdisciplinary interactions and provide appropriate reward structures. Too often, there are issues of territoriality and turf battles over ownership of the research budget and associated research overhead.

In addition, there are often inadequate guidelines governing faculty rewards at universities for those who participate in cross-university, cross-disciplinary projects. Even when procedures and policies are set at the university level, traditional department and disciplinary boundaries make implementation uneven. And there is often inadequate funding at the university and college level for those willing to reach out beyond historic boundaries to find resources—for example, for research assistantships to support graduate students as participants in such projects.

The 21st century land-grant university must be positioned to better address complex issues outside traditional, discipline-based inquiry. To do so, we must determine "what type of academic forum or structure creates the greatest sensitivities to facilitate progress toward such possibilities" (Bammer, 2013). The traditional American university structure of colleges and academic units will be challenged to facilitate integrative, cross-disciplinary approaches. How can a land-grant research university meet this challenge?

One key structural dimension for future-looking land-grant institutions is dual evaluation and reward organizations for faculty and staff that recognize and encourage transdisciplinary research. Faculty members at all levels need to feel encouraged rather than discouraged, as is often the case, from pursuing interdisciplinary efforts. In this context, universities must reward multi-authored efforts, including coauthored proposals and published papers with faculty members from multiple departments. Dual or higher order appointments for faculty in a home discipline and interdisciplinary units should help facilitate such changes. I will elaborate on this concept later in this paper.

Another key dimension is partnership with individuals and groups that are committed to the land-grant mission but have a base that extends beyond the university. For example, many U.S. universities have departmental advisory boards or oversight structures representing a wide range of interests that could add to the understanding required for tackling complex problems. At the same time, however, such structures and entities can be impediments to integration. Departments, for example, can create territorial boundaries for their faculty members that reduce incentives for interdisciplinary work.

Effective communication channels constitute a third key dimension, one that is a central theme of this volume. At many universities, the infrastructure does not support networking channels that extend communication and interactions beyond traditional boundaries. Land-grant universities have traditional college boundaries in areas such as engineering, agriculture, business, and the liberal arts and sciences, and college traditions and territorial protection practices may limit full support for universitywide networking and collaborations.

As was stated earlier, significant state disinvestment of public higher education across the United States has created major new challenges for such institutions. But these challenges have also created new opportunities and incentives for structural and cultural changes that bring more efficiency and, if implemented appropriately, can facilitate cross-disciplinary, integrative efforts. Although some public universities are slow to adjust to needed changes, some are aggressively pursuing new models designed to produce a more fertile environment for cross-disciplinary communication and action. Michael Crow, for example, president of Arizona State University (ASU), has led an aggressive restructuring of academic colleges at ASU, creating common themes that span new disciplinary associations (see Chap. 14, this volume). He has also advocated a more entrepreneurial university, with incentives to faculty and staff who are willing to work outside traditional boundaries. Lou Anna Simon (2009), president of Michigan State University, paints a vision of a "world grant ideal" that is "a way of understanding how a research-intensive university can adapt to a changing world while helping shape changes that will be hallmarks of our future" (p. 5). She advocates fostering new linkages across university campuses to address global challenges, as well as new linkages with global partners.

Universities must look creatively at approaches such as these and others as we build the 21st century land-grant university. The requisite cultural changes must be pursued and embraced at all levels, from department chair to dean to provost to president. The cultural transformation must be palpable to individual faculty through reward and recognition structures and tenure criteria at the level of the academic unit.

The University of Idaho as an Illustration

Like other land-grant research universities, the University of Idaho (UI) has long had a tradition of outreach and engagement across our state. As we have worked to support Idaho, we have addressed key research questions related to natural resources, agricultural production, infrastructure, economy, and quality of life, including health research and community sustainability.

In recent years, it has become apparent that addressing the key questions concerning complex issues facing human populations in Idaho, our region, and the world requires a more robust interdisciplinary effort. I am pleased that at UI, there is generally strong advocacy at all levels for interdisciplinary research, learning environments, and outreach. As president of the university, it has been a key priority for me, and one I speak to within and outside the university on a regular basis. Creating such an environment at the university has taken on varied forms. At the institutional level, many of our policies and procedures have been changed in ways that allow for appropriate reward structures for faculty who participate in such activities. At the learning and outreach level, the university has created an Office of Community Partnerships. This office works closely with our dean of students as well as with our academic affairs office to offer a broad range of Idaho, U.S., and global opportunities for our students to participate in service learning activities. These student interdisciplinary teams work on projects that assist communities in various dimensions of economic development, sustainability, and quality of life. Such activities lead students to work firsthand in interdisciplinary teams to solve problems, and those that go on for graduate work are better prepared to contribute to their cross-disciplinary efforts.

A powerful example of a successful community engagement project involving an interdisciplinary team of students is our partnership with the

Coeur d'Alene Reservation communities, a cluster of small towns about 60 miles from UI's main campus. This partnership has produced tangible outcomes—more than $2 million in Housing and Urban Development grants for affordable housing, a new nonprofit, and a reservation arts council. This partnership contributes to the understanding of community engagement along four dimensions. First, universities can support community engagement by creating interdisciplinary, cross-college structures and rewarding faculty members who mentor students and use outreach to strengthen teaching and research. Second, local UI Extension faculty members are critical to success because they help teaching and research faculty members build local relationships and access local knowledge. Third, community engagement strengthens academic programs by attracting high-quality, motivated students who want to ground theory in community settings. And fourth, capacity and leadership programs build "community readiness" that in turn contributes to productive university–community partnerships.

Within this environment, a number of key research and education initiatives have emerged as examples of significant interdisciplinary success at the university, regional, and national levels. These projects include the Institute for Bioinformatics and Evolutionary Studies (IBEST), the Sustainable Agriculture IGERT project, and the Regional Approaches to Climate Change–Pacific Northwest Agriculture (REACCH) cooperative agricultural project, as well as efforts and approaches linked to the Toolbox Project and universitywide forums for cross-disciplinary discussion. These efforts, too, are reflected in the interdisciplinary/integrative themes throughout our university strategic plan.

IBEST is a "grassroots" interdisciplinary faculty group at UI focused on understanding the pattern and processes of evolution that occur over comparatively short periods of time (http://www.ibest.uidaho.edu). IBEST places high value on interdisciplinary collaborations that blend the expertise of biologists, biochemists, ecologists, evolutionary biologists, mathematicians, statisticians, computer scientists, and other related disciplines to examine the underpinnings of evolutionary biology. The institute facilitates productive interdisciplinary dialogue across the university through seminars and common and open luncheon discussions with those involved in associated projects (including faculty and staff), plus others who may have an interest in dimensions of these projects. In the continuum of this research effort, extensive data sets collected by biologists in contemporary studies of natural and experimentally evolved populations enable mathematicians, statisticians, and computer scientists to quantify the problems of various evolutionary events and develop models that can then be empirically evaluated and refined by biologists.

The NSF-funded Toolbox Project, initiated at UI with partners at Michigan State University, Boise State University, and the University of Alaska–Anchorage, has provided a philosophical yet practical enhancement to cross-disciplinary collaborative science (http://www.cals.uidaho.edu/toolbox/). Rooted in philosophical analysis, Toolbox workshops enable cross-disciplinary collaborators to engage in structural dialogue about their research assumptions (see Chap. 11, this volume). This process yields both self-awareness and mutual understanding, creating a strong foundation for effective collaborative research. The approach has been integrated into many of our interdisciplinary efforts at UI, including the Waters of the West Program, the NSF-IGERT projects, REACCH, the Legume Virus Project, and others.

Using principles linked to the Toolbox approach, UI received its largest grant in university history, $20 million (USD), in spring 2011, led by faculty member Sanford Eigenbrode and involving a team of 22 principal investigators and key collaborators in partnership with other land-grant universities Oregon State University and Washington State University, as well as USDA's Agricultural Research Service. This grant focuses on the development of a comprehensive and extensive infrastructure to support research, outreach, and education that will support sustainable agriculture in the Pacific Northwest region. This interdisciplinary project, REACCH, is a 5-year effort. To succeed, the project must communicate effectively with farmers, industry personnel, and other stakeholders and partners. Because of the land-grant structure and extension networks of UI and our partners in REACCH, communication and other forms of engagement with stakeholders are being facilitated.

UI is also one of the few institutions nationally to receive a renewal for an NSF-approved IGERT project. The project focuses on evaluating resilience of ecological and social systems in changing landscapes, with a focus on doctoral research and education programs in Idaho and Costa Rica. It is implemented jointly with the tropical agricultural research and Higher Education Center (CATIE) in Costa Rica. Doctoral students involved in this project are expected to work in interdisciplinary teams, and their dissertation will include a multiauthored chapter that reflects the results of integrative research. The program is made possible by a joint doctoral program, which formalizes the partnership between UI and CATIE in research and education aimed at improving the sustainability of agriculture and forestry and the well-being of resource-dependent communities.

The interdisciplinary culture of our university is reflected in the highly successful weekly Malcolm M. Renfrew Interdisciplinary Colloquium, which facilitates cross-disciplinary dialogue across the institution. This colloquium has been ongoing for more than 12 years and is well attended by faculty from across the university. In addition, a year and a half ago I instituted a Friday-afternoon faculty gathering once a month to foster informal dialogue among faculty from across the university. Each month, this gathering is sponsored by a different college. The gathering has resulted in new communication and connections among faculty from across the university, stimulating discovery of new opportunities for cross-disciplinary research, new learning paradigms, and outreach efforts.

Although significant progress has been made in creating an environment that would recognize interdisciplinary research and appreciate integrative research, learning, and outreach at UI, there remain challenges that must be addressed. These include the lack of central and college-level resources to invest in such initiatives, additional policy changes that facilitate more robust implementation of these important cultural changes within the university, and cultural changes in some units that want to hold on to traditional approaches. To address these challenges, additional steps are required. One such step could involve the creation of an interdisciplinary entity, cluster, or institute. Such an institute might serve as a college-level incubator for interdisciplinary programming and help permeate traditional college boundaries. One or more such institutes could be created with input from faculty, students, and advisors to the university to respond to widely recognized issues, whether these be complex problems or opportunities for new types of synthesis and creativity. This institute could include joint appointments with traditional colleges, and faculty commitment would need to be recognized and rewarded. The concept should appeal to faculty who want to spend quality time with others who share their belief in the value of interdisciplinary research. Implementation will likely be challenged by departments and colleges that feel threatened by new and nontraditional assignments of faculty and the loss of control over traditional resources. At the same time, new constructs could facilitate new revenue that would generate new grant successes and greater universitywide dialogue while retaining many of our "rising star" faculty.

Conclusions

As noted earlier, land-grants have historically played a significant role in engagement and outreach activities. Although most of the learning and research environments have been discipline based, land-grant universities are gradually developing new initiatives to overcome traditional barriers that enhance interdisciplinary communication and collaboration across campuses. These include such strategies as ensuring that interdisciplinary programs have the same rights and responsibilities as disciplinary programs, ensuring that interdisciplinary faculty have input on strategic university budgeting and planning, creating transparent financial policies that allow interdisciplinary teams to have the same rewards as disciplinary faculty, and creating visible support through resources to incentivize interdisciplinary work (Kezar & Elrod, 2012).

Like other land-grants who support such interdisciplinary efforts, UI has a tremendous opportunity to be among the national leaders in interdisciplinary work.

- We have well-established interdisciplinary programs and broad campuswide interest and support for such work.
- Our university strategic plan is focused in learning, research, and outreach linked to integrative approaches.

- There has been progress in more supportive culture and more open dialogue beyond department and college boundaries.
- The university has fostered major projects that facilitate the multidimensional successes of interdisciplinary work as we redefine the current and further role of our land-grant university.

Clearly, land-grant universities must continue to refine themselves and interdisciplinarity must be a key part of our dynamic future. Through such efforts, we can be the most important partner our states have—in economic development, in community building, and in educating the next generation of state leadership. If we aren't clear about that—both with ourselves and the public, whose trust we earn—then the audacious spirit brought to life by President Lincoln and developed during our first 150 years could very well be in peril. If we are clear and open to new structures through integrative discovery, then many of the issues we face become easier to address as we strengthen our universities and those we serve in the 21st century.

Take-Home Messages

- The scale of research questions today requires more integrative approaches that break down the more traditional, siloed approach to problem solving.
- Land-grant universities are well placed to take a leadership role in integrative learning, outreach, and research given their commitment to broad, democratic higher education and their well-developed extension mission.
- Although traditional barriers still exist at many land-grant universities, new collaborative strategies are facilitating exciting transitions toward more robust integrative approaches to learning, outreach, and research.
- National and state-level budget challenges have created incentives at land-grant universities to accelerate more integrative approaches to better serve society and through such efforts turn fiscal challenges into opportunities.
- The University of Idaho is one institution dedicated to creating national prototypes in integrative approaches that serves as a model for 21st century land-grant universities.

References

Bammer, G. (2013). *Disciplining interdisciplinarity: Integration and Implementation Sciences for researching complex real-world problems.* Canberra: Australian National University E Press. Retrieved from http://epress.anu.edu.au/titles/disciplining-interdisciplinarity

Burkhardt, J. (2000). Coming full circle? Agrarian ideals and pragmatist ethics in the modern land-grant university. In P. B. Thompson & T. C. Hilde (Eds.), *The agrarian roots of pragmatism* (pp. 279–303). Nashville, TN: Vanderbilt University Press.

Committee on Facilitating Interdisciplinary Research, National Academy of Sciences, National Academy of Engineering, and Institute of Medicine. (2004). *Facilitating interdisciplinary research*. Washington, DC: National Academies Press.

Frickel, S., & Jacobs, J. A. (2009). Interdisciplinarity: A critical assessment. *Annual Review of Sociology, 35*, 43–65.

Kelderman, E. (2012, January 23). State support for colleges falls 7.6% in 2012 fiscal year. *Chronicle of Higher Education*. Retrieved from http://chronicle.com/article/article-content/130414/

Kezar, A., & Elrod, S. (2012, February). Facilitating interdisciplinary learning: Lessons from Project Kaleidoscope. *Change*. Retrieved from http://www.changemag.org/Archives/Back%20Issues/2012/January-February%202012/Facilitating-learning-full.html

Klein, J. T. (2010). *Creating interdisciplinary campus cultures: A model for strength and sustainability*. San Francisco: Jossey-Bass.

Leach, J. A. (2009). *Lincoln's unfinished work: The Morrill Act and the future of higher education*. Retrieved from http://www.neh.gov/about/chairman/speeches/lincolns-unfinished-work-the-morrill-act-and-the-future-higher-education

Paletz, S., Smith-Doerr, L., & Vardi, I. (2010). National Science Foundation workshop report: *Interdisciplinary collaboration in innovative science and engineering fields*. Retrieved from http://csid.unt.edu/nsf/nsf-workshop-report.pdf

Simon, L. A. (2009). *Embracing the world grant ideal: Affirming the Morrill Act for twenty-first-century global society*. East Lansing: Michigan State University. Retrieved October 24, 2012, from http://www.worldgrantideal.msu.edu/_files/documents/monograph.pdf

16

Institutionalizing Interdisciplinary Graduate Education

Maura Borrego, Daniel Boden, David
Pietrocola, Carol F. Stoel, Richard
D. Boone, and Melur K. Ramasubramanian

Since 1998, the U.S. National Science Foundation (NSF) has been funding Integrative Graduate Education and Research Traineeship (IGERT) grants to institutions to create graduate traineeships around an interdisciplinary theme. One goal of this program has been to catalyze cultural change in institutions to support interdisciplinary collaboration. In this chapter, we describe analysis of interviews with faculty members and administrators at two institutions with at least four IGERT grants. A number of structural and policy changes were reported to support interdisciplinary research and graduate education, including new courses and changes to university-level graduate student policies. Multiple IGERT grants to a single institution particularly helped create a community of advocates for interdisciplinary education and research that effected institution-level policy changes through communication with administrators. In sum, IGERT has been an influential model for interdisciplinary education and research at U.S. universities, particularly as a driver for organizational changes to foster interdisciplinary collaboration. Additionally, interdisciplinary graduate traineeship funding initiatives have been effective at changing faculty attitudes and policies related to hiring, workload, and promotion and tenure.

Introduction

Interdisciplinary approaches are necessary for attacking the most critical societal challenges facing the nation and the world today, such as energy and environmental sustainability, globalization, health care, and poverty (Brown, Harris, & Russell, 2010; Committee on Facilitating Interdisciplinary Research, 2004; Metzger & Zare, 1999; National Institutes of Health, 2006; NSF, 2011a). Despite the widely touted importance of interdisciplinary research, colleges and universities remain largely organized by traditional disciplines and thus ill equipped to foster interdisciplinary research, teaching, and learning (Boardman & Bozeman, 2007). The disciplinary departmental structure of institutions is frequently identified as the most significant barrier to interdisciplinary collaboration in higher education settings (Amey & Brown, 2004; Bozeman & Boardman, 2003; Committee on Facilitating Interdisciplinary Research, 2004; Sa, 2008). As Holley (2009) states, "The organizational culture of the university is one divided by disciplinary ways of thinking and behaving" (p. 242). Resources, rewards, and accountability are directed via a hierarchical organizational structure of departments, schools, and colleges. Although novel organizational structures such as research centers and institutes can direct resources such as research assistantship funding to new interdisciplinary endeavors (Sa, 2008), departmental alignment remains the norm.

Established disciplines—some more than others—have reached a degree of consensus regarding what constitutes quality work (Pfeffer, 1993) that is absent in most interdisciplinary domains. Since so few referees are sufficiently knowledgeable about multiple foundational disciplines and their synergistic integration, interdisciplinary work is far more challenging to evaluate (Committee on Facilitating Interdisciplinary Research, 2004; Oberg, 2009; Payton & Zoback, 2007; Pfirman, Collins, Lowes, & Michaels, 2005). Administrative concerns over efficient use of budgeted funds, difficulties evaluating interdisciplinary work, and the additional time it takes to sufficiently integrate perspectives all stand as strong disincentives for junior researchers to pursue interdisciplinary scholarly work (Pfirman et al., 2005).

More recent literature has explored the impacts of higher education structures and policies on graduate students pursuing interdisciplinary research. Disciplinary departments support socialization of graduate students in disciplinary programs relatively well through interaction with peers, faculty members, and practicing professionals (Boden, Borrego, & Newswander, 2011; Golde & Gallagher, 1999). However, students pursuing interdisciplinary research topics, especially those seeking degrees in traditional disciplines, are at risk for feeling isolated and misunderstood (Golde & Gallagher, 1999; Graybill et al., 2006; McKenzie & Galar, 2004; Tress, Tress, & Fry, 2009), which can result in attrition from graduate study. Advisors wield significant power over students' professional development (Golde & Gallagher, 1999), and if they are unaccustomed to interdisciplinary approaches, advisors can (and do) discourage interdisciplinary dissertation topics (Boden et al., 2011; Tress et al., 2009). Recommendations emphasize building a supportive community or network of students and faculty members enthusiastic, knowledgeable, and successful in interdisciplinary research (Boden et al., 2011; Graybill et al., 2006; Holley, 2009; Newswander & Borrego, 2009a). However, if the institution does not foster interdisciplinary research success among its faculty members, then supportive mentors will not be available to graduate students (Boden et al., 2011; Golde & Gallagher, 1999). Even when these welcoming environments exist, students can feel torn between allegiance to disciplinary and interdisciplinary communities (Boden et al., 2011; Graybill et al., 2006; Newswander & Borrego, 2009a).

Given that the basic organizational structure of most higher education institutions is all but incompatible with interdisciplinary education and research, we posit that organizational change is necessary to create an environment in which interdisciplinary collaboration can survive and thrive. Institutions cannot simply add new degree programs and research centers without considering existing policies and attitudes. U.S. approaches to interdisciplinary graduate education in science, technology, engineering, and math (STEM) disciplines over the past 15 years have been strongly influenced by NSF's IGERT funding program. Since 1998, 5-year IGERT grants of $2.8 million to $3.4 million each have been awarded to groups of faculty members at more than 100 institutions across the United States to develop graduate traineeships around an interdisciplinary theme. A primary goal of the program, as stated in its 2000-to-2011 solicitations, has been to "catalyze a cultural change in graduate education, for students, faculty, and institutions, by establishing innovative new models for graduate education and training in a fertile environment for collaborative research that transcends traditional disciplinary boundaries" (NSF, 2010, p. 4). The description of cultural change and transcendent new models suggests that changes made by IGERT projects will extend beyond the 5-year funding period and perhaps beyond the students and faculty directly involved in the grant. Thus, the implicit theory of change for this funding program culminates in institutionalization. IGERT's long history, implicit goal of institutional change, and emphasis on interdisciplinary education and research provide a unique opportunity to study the types of institutional changes that support interdisciplinary collaboration.

The purpose of the analysis presented in this chapter is to understand *how* interdisciplinary research and traineeship projects are institutionalized at higher education institutions with NSF IGERT awards. The research question that guided the study was, "After funding was awarded, what strategies (intentional or unintentional) helped institutionalize interdisciplinary graduate education?" For the purposes of this study, interdisciplinary graduate education is defined as projects intended to integrate traditional academic departments and disciplines.

We begin with a review of existing literature on interdisciplinarity in graduate education and institutions of higher education, including a summary of prior studies of the IGERT program. Then, we describe the methods and results of an interview-based study of the institutional changes in support of interdisciplinarity at two public universities that had each received four IGERT grants. The discussion and conclusion clarify the communication processes involved in institutionalization and tie the findings to broader efforts at the NSF and beyond.

Literature Review

Institutionalization

It is common for changes in higher education to be prompted or supported by external sources of funding (Colbeck, 2002). Unfortunately, after grants end, new projects are often left with the responsibility of finding new donors or becoming financially self-sustainable (Curry, 1992). As a result, many are forced to scale back or are abandoned altogether (Conklin, 1978). No matter how well funded an initiative is from the outset, for it to have a lasting effect at a university, focus must eventually shift to long-term institutionalization.

Institutionalization involves not only funding and policies but also convincing others of the value of the effort (in this case, interdisciplinarity) through various communication channels, a process that can be arduous and politically charged (Bleiklie & Byrkjeflot, 2002; Conrad, 1978). Organizational structures can also act as roadblocks for institutionalizing change (Kezar, 2006; Marshak & Grant, 2008). Institutionalization, then, requires broader consideration of the cultural and organizational contexts of colleges and universities (Bess & Dee, 2008). The literature suggests that "cultural innovations," or changes to the way a group thinks or acts, are necessary (Schofer, 2003) and that innovations that are institutionalized through culture, policies, or practical reform have higher rates of success (Kezar & Eckel, 2002). Institutionalization, however, is just one part of a larger change process (Kezar, 2001). Curry (1992) describes institutionalization as the final phase in a change process, "when an innovation or program is fully integrated into an organization's structure" (p. 8). In many cases, it is neither practical nor wise to attempt to continue certain changes beyond the funding period. In the case of IGERT projects, there are several different elements (e.g., courses, field experiences, research collaborations) that can be considered individually and scaled up or down as necessary.

Prior Studies of IGERT Projects

Several prior studies and evaluations of NSF's IGERT program describe its implementation and success. Evaluations conducted by Abt Associates report on many aspects of implementation and success, including the unique training opportunities afforded to IGERT trainees (Carney, Chawla, Wiley, & Young, 2006) and their graduation and employment rates (Carney, Martinez, Dreier, Neishi, & Parsad, 2011). Similarly, Borrego and Newswander (2010) used successful proposals to clarify the learning outcomes of interdisciplinary graduate education. Many individual IGERT projects have published on different aspects of their projects, including interventions to address the challenges of interdisciplinary research and graduate education (Anthony, Palius, Maher, & Moghe, 2007; Cowan & Gogotsi, 2004; Eigenbrode et al., 2007; Graybill et al., 2006; Martin & Umberger, 2003; Morse, Nielsen-Pincus, Force, & Wulfhorst, 2007; Richards-Kortum, Dailey, & Harris, 2003).

A full understanding of institutionalization requires knowledge of project components eligible to be institutionalized. Typical IGERT project elements have been previously quantified. Borrego and Cutler (2010) found that 80% of successful IGERT proposals described coursework, such as creating new interdisciplinary graduate courses. Carney et al. (2006) reported that 62% of IGERT trainees have taken "courses presenting laboratories or research techniques of multiple disciplines" (p. 22, Exhibit 3.1). Teamwork was also emphasized; 66% of IGERT trainees reported working on a team research project, and 41% of IGERT trainees have reported completing lab rotations (Carney et al., 2006). IGERT projects also frequently develop seminars, workshops, and internships, which are more difficult to define strictly.

An early program evaluation of the IGERT projects funded in 1998, 1999, and 2000 (Carney et al., 2006) explored impacts on institutions, primarily through survey questions related to faculty work, policies, and rewards. IGERT faculty felt well supported in their interdisciplinary research endeavors, but 81% reported no changes to promotion and tenure policies. On the other hand, faculty noted many changes to interdisciplinary teaching policies but little support for it. Control-group participants felt more supported in their interdisciplinary work if their institution had an IGERT grant, even if they had not participated directly. The evaluators also noted that "PIs [principal investigators] at institutions with four or more IGERT grants are also more likely than their counterparts at institutions with three or fewer grants to attribute increased institutional support to the IGERT grant" (Carney et al., 2006, p. 54).

Publications by NSF provide additional detail. The IGERT Impact report (Van Hartesveldt & Giordan, 2009) focuses on challenges and recommendations for universities but cites some specific instances of lasting change, including faculty cluster hire policies and changes to degree programs to accommodate interdisciplinary coursework and dissertation topics. An analysis of 118 IGERT project annual reports to NSF submitted in 2006–2007 indicated that, unprompted, some PIs viewed institutionalization as a challenge (Hrycyshyn, 2008). While most of the challenges cited in the reports focused on cultural and logistical implementation issues, 8% were coded as "Project Sustainability" or "Institutional Issues." While we cannot speculate on why PIs decide to report certain challenges and not others, we note that these PIs were concerned with how elements of their IGERT project would continue beyond NSF funding and had begun exploring alternative funding options.

Proposal analysis confirms this finding that IGERT PIs initially consider institutionalization as a problem of identifying additional funding sources. Only 25% of 114 successful IGERT proposals discussed sustaining the project beyond the funding period, and several of these were renewal proposals for an additional 5 years of funding. The most often cited mechanisms were degree and certificate programs, interdisciplinary courses, tenure-track faculty positions within existing departments, new interdisciplinary research centers, and potential new funding sources. Proposals also included broad vision statements for building interdisciplinary communities, capacity, and appreciation at the host institutions (Newswander & Borrego, 2009b).

Methods

Program Setting

The IGERT program (NSF, 2011b) has been developed to meet the challenges of educating U.S. PhD scientists and engineers with interdisciplinary backgrounds, deep knowledge in chosen disciplines, and technical, professional, and personal skills. The program is intended to establish new models for graduate education and training in a fertile collaborative interdisciplinary environment. It is also intended to facilitate diversity in student participation and preparation, and to contribute to a world-class, broadly inclusive, and globally engaged science and engineering workforce. As described in a recent solicitation (NSF, 2011b), key features of IGERT projects include

- a comprehensive interdisciplinary theme, appropriate for doctoral-level research, that serves as the foundation for traineeship activities and is based on transformative interdisciplinary research in STEM disciplines;
- integration of the interdisciplinary research with novel graduate education and training mechanisms;
- program strategy and plan for recruitment, mentoring, retention, and graduation of U.S. PhD students in NSF-supported STEM fields, including efforts aimed at members of groups underrepresented in science and engineering;
- career development opportunities, provision for developing professional and personal skills, support for developing an international perspective, instruction in ethics and the responsible conduct of research, and training in communication of the substance and importance of research to nonscientist audiences;
- strategy and methodology for formative assessments of the project's effectiveness and program improvements based on these assessments;

- administrative plan and organizational structure that ensures effective management of the project resources and any international cooperative activities;
- institutional commitment to facilitating and furthering the plans and goals of the IGERT project; and
- since 2011, a plan to establish a supportive environment for innovation and for learning and practicing the steps involved in transforming research outcomes and ideas into successfully implemented solutions for societal needs and challenges.

As of 2011, 278 IGERT awards have been made to 122 U.S. institutions, supporting about 6,500 graduate students, and 1,854 IGERT trainees have completed their PhDs at rates that are at or above the national average (Carney et al., 2011, pp. 25–26).

Institutional Setting

Interviews were conducted from 2007 to 2009 at two public U.S. institutions of higher education. Both of the institutions had been recipients of multiple IGERT grants. Each of the two universities in this study had at least four IGERT awards, but only two programs on each campus were actively funded by NSF at the time of the site visits. Due to the availability of current faculty member and student participants, we relied heavily in this study on the programs that were currently funded at the time of the site visits. To ensure confidentiality, the institutions and interdisciplinary programs are referred to by pseudonyms. The disciplinary backgrounds of students and faculty members from the programs that were actively funded at the time of data collection are summarized in Table 16.1.

Table 16.1 Summary of Active IGERT Sites Included in This Study

Institution	Pseudonym	IGERT Theme	Disciplines (included but not limited to)
Eastern State University	ESU-A	Materials science and engineering	Agriculture, chemical and biological sciences, medicine, engineering and natural resources
Eastern State University	ESU-B	Sustainability: ecology and the environment	Physical sciences, engineering, and social science
Western State University	WSU-A	Computational science and engineering	Social sciences, engineering and computer science, arts (dance, music, theater, film), design, and life sciences
Western State University	WSU-B	Sustainability: ecology and the environment	Social sciences, life sciences, planning and public affairs, and engineering

Participants and Data Collection

Permission to observe participants from these programs was approved through human subjects (institutional review board) review at both site visit institutions and that of the interviewers. Data collection took place during multiple visits to each institution between fall of 2007 and spring of 2009. As part of this study, 43 interviews were conducted with faculty, students, support staff, and administrators at both institutions. Those interviewed included all the current and former graduate deans, current and former IGERT PIs, and current IGERT faculty and students who agreed to participate. At least one graduate dean and one PI from each IGERT were interviewed. Table 16.2 offers a summary of the individuals interviewed at the two institutions. PIs were asked questions such as what kinds of information (if any) are transferrable across IGERT grants in different research domains, how early they began considering extending IGERT program components beyond the funding period, and whether they would have done anything differently. Administrators were asked about the role of IGERT in advancing interdisciplinary work at the institution, future plans for interdisciplinary graduate education, and best practices for sustaining interdisciplinary training after a grant has ended. The interviews resulted in more than 30 hours of recordings. Following the interviews, the recordings were transcribed by one researcher, and all identifying information was removed from the transcripts prior to analysis.

Data Analysis

In case study research, analysis focuses on describing the case and building explanations for why various outcomes were observed (Creswell, 2007;

Table 16.2 Summary of Interviewees

Pseudonym	Students	Faculty	Staff	Administrators	Female	Male
WSU-A	6	7	2	—	8	7
WSU-B	5	2	1	—	4	4
WSU	—	3	—	2	3	2
ESU-A	4	2	—	—	2	4
ESU-B	4	2	—	—	2	4
ESU	—	2	—	1	1	2
Totals	19	18	3	3	20	23

NOTE: PIs and Co-PIs of the IGERT grants are listed as faculty members.

Stake, 1995; Yin, 2009). First, separate fact-based case descriptions (Stake, 1995) of the institutionalization and change processes at each institution were developed. Second, techniques drawn from the constant comparative method (Bogdan & Biklen, 2003) were employed to compare the two institutions and the different IGERT projects at each. In this method, the data are initially broken down into categories (e.g., specific types of policies, cultural changes) and then built up into relationships by comparing sites (i.e., institutions and projects) and testing theoretical propositions. Consistent with institutionalization theory cited earlier (e.g., Bess & Dee, 2008; Kezar & Eckel, 2002), we found that successful strategies of institutionalization addressed both written policies and cultural innovations in the way institutional faculty think and act. The results are presented as four examples of successful strategies that addressed policies and culture in concert.

Limitations

Like any in-depth investigation of one or two cases, our findings are specific only to those settings. We intentionally selected institutions with at least four IGERT grants to increase the chances of gathering high-quality data, which limits the applicability of findings to institutions with fewer grants. To mitigate this, we include additional detail from prior evaluations, the IGERT resource center,[1] PI meetings, site visits, annual reports, and informal conversations with IGERT PIs to triangulate findings. Additionally, we link our findings to organizational change and communication theory (Yin, 2009). Finally, we shared the institutional case descriptions with participants and integrated their comments into the analysis (Creswell, 2007; Lincoln & Guba, 1985).

IGERT is only one model of interdisciplinary research and graduate education. We have provided as much detail as possible for readers to judge transferability to other settings. To the extent that IGERT projects have many elements in common, this makes the program easy to study. However, there are other ways for universities to support interdisciplinary research and graduate education, particularly in the humanities and social sciences. These need to be studied to understand the complete range of successful approaches to supporting interdisciplinary research and graduate education.

This analysis is based on the assumption that at least some IGERT projects are effecting positive changes to support interdisciplinary collaboration. The effectiveness of these approaches is validated by consistency between the literature, the data, the coauthors' consensus interpretation of the data, and readers' critical interpretation of this evidence.

---

[1]The IGERT Resource Center (http://www.IGERT.org) provides comprehensive information about IGERT and each of its actively funded projects. It is also an e-community for current IGERT students and faculty to share resources, research, presentations, challenges, and best practices.

Results

In the interviews, faculty and administrators emphasized the relationship between written policies and cultural norms, which the literature explains can be mutually reinforcing of institutionalization (Bess & Dee, 2008; Kezar & Eckel, 2002). One PI explained that Western State University (WSU) "was still a very different university. The idea of the IGERTs really helped to get the change going. Now interdisciplinary thinking is a bigger thing across campus. Everything is being reorganized. Right now it's pervasive." In other words, the very practice of interdisciplinary graduate education on campus became part of the institutional culture. Once policies and organizational barriers to it were identified, the cultural process of removing them became possible.

Courses

There are several examples of specific policy changes that were enabled by the multiple IGERT projects at both institutions. The first concerns interdisciplinary graduate courses, which were discussed extensively by several participants at Eastern State University (ESU). It is common for IGERT projects to create a few new interdisciplinary graduate courses to introduce the domain to students (Borrego & Cutler, 2010). However, since scheduling, curricula, and teaching assignments are made through departments, many struggled with appropriate listing and teaching credit for the courses. The graduate dean[2] at ESU described the solution of a designated number for a course in interdisciplinary research in science and engineering, listing these courses in the graduate school rather than in academic departments, which "allows students from other disciplines to come and take the course[s]." The idea is that in the future, other groups of faculty can offer sections in other research areas. One of the PIs continued that with the graduate school's course designation, "[our course is] definitely set to continue on into the future. And I certainly hope it does."

WSU was also planning a similar mechanism at the time of our site visit. The WSU graduate dean explained,

> [We're] putting together a couple of grants to create what we call the [Program Title], which will in essence be a format and a forum for university-wide seminars, workshops, and synergy to cross-cut the interdisciplinary programs. . . . [This] could really elevate again the importance of interdisciplinary [work] and provide a place for students, a virtual place as well as a physical space, for them to engage with faculty and do bigger things.

---

[2]"Graduate school" and "graduate dean" are not necessarily the exact titles used at these institutions, but we use them for clarity and to protect participant identities.

The graduate school at WSU also administers a small number of interdisciplinary graduate programs (with courses and faculty members still housed in traditional departments) to address some of the same issues of ownership and administrative support.

We know from previous studies of IGERT projects that coursework is a common focus of IGERT training. In the 1998-to-2000 cohort survey, 68% of participating departments[3] reported that new courses were created (Carney et al., 2006). We also see similar issues related to interdisciplinary teaching credit reported by many IGERT PIs. An additional challenge related to coursework that was not prominent in these interviews was curriculum changes to accommodate interdisciplinary training. The survey of the 1998-to-2000 cohorts of IGERT projects reported that 49% of projects and 27% of participating departments reported changes to degree requirements (Carney et al., 2006).

Advisor Eligibility

A second policy change that was adopted quickly because of cultural norms was an extended graduate faculty of eligible advisors for graduate students in every degree program at WSU. This system, adopted at WSU a few months before the site visit, "required in essence, that no program be allowed to only have committee members from its own department, that it had to be open." Each graduate program was required to identify qualifications for advising a student in the program that are broader than a faculty appointment in that department. This has clear implications for facilitating interdisciplinary research, as students can more readily work with projects and faculty members across campus.

Several WSU administrators and faculty members commented on the timing of this new policy in relation to changing culture and expectations. One PI said that "even though people resisted at the beginning," it has been "a very positive step." Another commented that the graduate administration "decided not to use a sledgehammer to make it happen." The graduate dean explained that although there was "some pushback . . . generally it's worked well . . . because I think there was a readiness at [WSU]." In other words, the policy was accepted because it was introduced at a time when the culture of expectations had evolved to accept it.

The system at ESU still relied on primary advisors from the department, but many faculty members noted an overall willingness to collaborate across disciplinary boundaries. Specific to dissertation committees, one PI said,

> Anybody on campus can call someone in another department and start chatting and start working with them, but one thing in particular that

---

[3]IGERT projects are typically collaborations of faculty members and students from several departments.

makes it easy here is that graduate students can be advised very readily by people in various departments. At least in this department, we have virtually no rules in terms of who can be on your advisory committee. . . . So [students will have on their dissertation committees] people from other departments on this campus and other departments on other campuses and government agencies in all kinds of things in this department listening away . . . , which is very important for soliciting interdisciplinary research.

Similar policy changes have taken place at other IGERT institutions, as evidenced by informal communications from IGERT.org, PI meetings, site visits, annual reports, and personal conversations with PIs. Types of policy changes have included advisor eligibility, faculty credit for interdisciplinary graduate advising, coauthored dissertation chapters, and eligibility for funding.

IGERT PI Groups

Instrumental in these policy changes was communication among the various groups running interdisciplinary graduate programs. At both institutions, the four IGERT awards were staggered over about a decade, which allowed for wisdom gained from one to be shared with the next. Given the broad diversity of interdisciplinary domains represented, it wasn't always clear to PIs what they could learn from each other (even in retrospect), but a recognition of the need for specific policy changes regarding graduate education at the institutional level was an important outcome of these interactions.

There were conflicting reports of exactly when or how the group of IGERT PIs at WSU was formalized, but it was coordinated by the Graduate Division and met multiple times a year for at least a few years to discuss issues around interdisciplinary graduate education. In explaining how this group developed organically from requests to help with subsequent IGERT proposals, an early PI explained the rationale as, "Why not link IGERT resources and impact to actually expand the impact of IGERT to develop more of an interdisciplinary program and change the structure and change the culture [of the university]?" A later PI explained the focus in this way:

What barriers [do] students and faculty face, and what can we do as a group to facilitate that? . . . You want to take the knowledge about the IGERT and make it work in the specific structure and setting [of this institution]. That's a very important catalyst, and I think bringing in that type of money and that type of student is important to getting change going.

In recent years, membership in this group has grown beyond IGERT to a "federation of different pockets of people who are crosscutting disciplines and are participating on multiple interdisciplinary initiatives," as described by WSU's graduate dean.

Along similar lines, ESU hosted a summit of students, faculty, and administrators to discuss the challenges of interdisciplinary research and graduate education. The dean explained,

> I think it's important to identify what the barriers are and say them out loud and think of what we might do to change them . . . especially with the deans and directors [present]; these are the people who can effect some kind of a change. [The purpose was] to talk about how we're going to change that because we need to know where they are coming from, the faculty's perspective or the students' perspective.

One of ESU's PIs described a less formal network:

> We have developed our own community, although we don't get together often. But we encounter each other at meetings, and we have a recognition and immediate comfort because we know that you are going through the same kinds of experiences or at least somewhat have a clue or equivalence of what we are doing.

This type of networking and sharing among IGERT PIs at the same institution is fairly common, in our experience. PIs have explained to us how they banded together to advocate for the changes they needed to be successful. Examples of issues they have tackled include graduate student policies, coordinated diversity recruiting efforts, and evaluation capacity. A few have also reported being asked to serve on formal interdisciplinary advisory committees to provosts and presidents, or being appointed to administrative positions that would allow them to expand their educational efforts to more students.

General Awareness of Interdisciplinarity

On both campuses, interdisciplinary efforts moved beyond IGERT to include interdisciplinary programs, centers, and institutes. However, many participants acknowledged the important role of IGERT grants in raising awareness of interdisciplinary research and graduate education. WSU deans explained IGERT "was the only formal representation of interdisciplinary activity in the research and education area" and "it was the representation of interdisciplinary activity" and "one of the first real manifestations of interdisciplinar[it]y." Faculty emphasized the "importan[ce] in bringing the outside recognition" through multimillion-dollar grants that "show that the NSF is willing to put money behind it." Another PI reflected,

> The conclusion I came to from the IGERT is that it was a great beginning. And we were able to do some really interesting stuff with the students and the students have benefited greatly from it. . . . There's no question that the IGERT, it's played a big role in focusing on thinking about how interdisciplinary science on campus should be.

Faculty and administrators also had enough time to reflect on the process of interdisciplinary research and graduate education becoming normal. The graduate dean at ESU lamented,

> I wish there would have been more faculty buy-in earlier, that it would be easier. It would have been easier to have more of the faculty members had pitched in earlier on this . . . because what we had to do was prove that it worked and get students committed to it and then the faculty are going, "Oh okay."

A PI from ESU explained that once her IGERT students had built successful interdisciplinary professional networks across campus, "the motivations are improved" and "faculty have embraced the idea, too." Similarly, a WSU PI explained an evolutionary process whereby small successes allow faculty to "see that it's possible to work, and then they start to loosen up enough. If we tried to do this five or ten years ago, people just would have refused it wouldn't have worked." A third PI, from WSU, said: "The support and the success of some of the IGERTs made the faculty think about being more collaborative."

These types of comments are also common from other IGERT PIs. Many have described how being awarded an IGERT grant raised the profile for interdisciplinary research at the institution, resulting in an increase in the number of IGERT proposals being submitted by the institution.

Promotion and Tenure

As a final example of how interdisciplinary graduate education grants impacted interdisciplinary activity across these two campuses, we include some participant comments related to promotion and tenure. In general, promotion and tenure processes are a good example of the interplay of policy and culture, as expectations for research, teaching, and service can be codified in policies, procedures, and dossier formatting, but cultural expectations often influence final votes as procedures are applied and interpreted by senior faculty members and administrators. One of the graduate deans noted this when she said,

> Our P&T guidelines I think have already opened [to interdisciplinarity]. It's the people who sit on the committees that are holding things back. It's not the tenure-track faculty that need P&T workshops so much as the senior faculty—they are the ones that need to go to the workshops and understand what the guidelines are, in my opinion.

One of the early PIs at ESU related a story that attests to the cultural changes of accepting interdisciplinary research:

> I remember being on the college P&T committee one year and there was a case of someone that came up, who's very clearly doing

multidisciplinary work, not as part of an IGERT or anything else, but he worked with people outside of the department in publishing in different places than people in that discipline normally published. And one guy sort of stood up and said negative things about that, and I actually took a shot at it and said, [regarding the possibility of this candidate being denied tenure], "No I'm not going to allow this to happen." And it was lots of people. It wasn't just me saying, "No, [this criticism of the candidate] is not valid." We can recognize where things are going through. And just about everybody except for that person seemed to be on board. And these are the sort of . . . people that are on P&T committees.

In fact, in claiming that all but one person in the meeting agreed that interdisciplinary research was worthy of tenure, this PI is suggesting that this change is becoming part of the cultural expectations at the institution. Faculty members at both ESU and WSU who had been involved in multiple programs explained how they can use interdisciplinary graduate programs to bring new faculty to interdisciplinary research from the beginning.

[We] really tried to bring in new faculty to that IGERT which meant that relatively younger faculty or newer faculty to campus, trying to get them on board quickly. . . . When new professors come . . . how are we judged? "Oh, you need to have your own individual investigator award. Where is your individual CAREER award?" If you said, "No, I participated in an interdisciplinary grant with professors X, Y and Z," they'd be like, "Oh man, you really need to get your individual—." So to a certain extent I think the university culture promotes more of an individualistic type of strategy for research and education because we need to get tenure when in reality I think interdisciplinary research is certainly equal and in my opinion probably exceeds the potential for impact at the university. . . . IGERT will help to change that. It will help for younger scientists that we bring in to recognize the value of interdisciplinary work.

Similarly, a PI from WSU explained that the programs "help some of the young faculty, settle down and get into the new interdisciplinary research."

While promotion and tenure is not necessarily a common topic in IGERT circles, many institutions have reported to us that new interdisciplinary faculty lines resulted from IGERT success. IGERT PIs have described their leadership in helping develop hiring and support structures to ensure the success of new interdisciplinary faculty members.

Discussion

The communication processes underlying institutionalization of interdisciplinary research and graduate education are broader and more diffuse than those described in most other chapters in this volume. For organizational change to happen across the entire institution, a significant proportion of administrators, faculty members, and students must be engaged in a social learning process through which they openly discuss the value of interdisciplinarity and the barriers (e.g., policies and practices) that need to be removed to foster it. Daniels and Walker (1996) describe this process in public policy initiatives that engage the public, environmental experts, and legislators. They argue that the outcome is of higher quality and the participants are more satisfied if the focus shifts to collective learning about a complex phenomenon, as opposed to compromise among special interests. Among their key learning assumptions are that "learning is improved by systems thinking" (p. 77). When IGERT PIs and other faculty members attempt to work across departments and colleges, this helps them develop a perspective on the system (and the many obstacles it creates for interdisciplinarity). At its best, an institution of higher education is an organization that values learning and may be more open to taking a social learning approach. Finally, in emphasizing graduate education and what is best for students, stakeholders may be able to find common ground and deflect discussion from other special interests (e.g., protecting territory).

IGERT is one of few long-standing, federally funded programs with such an explicit goal of institutional change. As such, it is in a unique position to inform our understanding of the role of communication in institutionalizing interdisciplinary research and graduate education. This work provides insight into the process through which faculty members raise the profile for interdisciplinary research and advocate for policy changes necessary to sustain interdisciplinary graduate education. The communication perspective on this process is social learning, through which administrators and faculty members seek to understand the complex system of interdisciplinary education and research at an institution organized by traditional disciplines. Specifically, IGERT grants are large enough to draw attention to interdisciplinary research on campus as soon as the award is announced. IGERT PIs and other directors of interdisciplinary programs come together, perhaps initially to commiserate about the challenges of interdisciplinary work at disciplinary institutions. They begin to share best practices and form a community that supports interdisciplinarity at the institution. They communicate within their programs about the value of interdisciplinary research, and to others beyond their program about their program successes. Together, these leaders advocate for university-level policy changes. When leaders from multiple units (e.g., colleges) present a united front to administrators, they can convince them of the need for policy changes. At the same time, these interdisciplinary leaders have been building coalitions of supportive students and faculty who are willing to approve or enforce these new policies. The data retrospectively cover nearly a decade of a long-running program, giving a glimpse of the time, effort, and money that it takes to effect lasting change in support of interdisciplinary collaboration and education at research universities.

One additional mechanism that was not prominent in these data is that of IGERT graduates moving into faculty positions. IGERT graduates hired as assistant professors are teaching interdisciplinary courses, conducting interdisciplinary research, and are now training the next generation of inter-disciplinary STEM professionals. As the number of IGERT alumni in the professoriate continues to grow, the purposes and goals of IGERT will become institutionalized more broadly across the nation. Interdisciplinary STEM research cannot thrive without graduate students who are trained to employ interdisciplinary approaches. Learning on the job post-PhD is simply not efficient enough, and successful models for interdisciplinary graduate training clearly exist.

Conclusion

Skeptical readers may argue that it cannot be proven that the changes at ESU and WSU were the direct result of IGERT funding. Nonetheless, it is difficult to deny that research has become more interdisciplinary over the 12-year life span of IGERT, and the data clearly show that IGERT has played a significant role in advancing these goals. The close relationship between research and graduate education has allowed this traineeship program to impact institutional policies and structures—including those directly related to faculty members—to better foster interdisciplinary collaboration.

NSF is increasingly promoting interdisciplinary research. New programs such as the cross-directorate Science, Engineering and Education in Sustainability (SEES) program, a $900 million effort to promote sustainability science, has garnered a large proportion of IGERT funding with 13 new sustainability-themed IGERT awards in the past 3 years. NSF recently announced the new Integrated NSF Support Promoting Interdisciplinary Research and Education (INSPIRE) initiative. These projects integrate multiple disciplines and by design will encourage institutional changes that support interdisciplinary STEM research and training. They continue the interdisciplinary legacy of IGERT.

Take-Home Messages

- A number of structural and policy changes were reported by IGERT PIs and administrators that supported interdisciplinary research and graduate education, including new courses and changes to university-level graduate student policies.
- Although structural policy changes are easier to measure and report, communication and culture change are critical components of any successful organizational change effort.

- Multiple IGERT grants to a single institution particularly helped create a community of advocates for interdisciplinary education and research that effected institution-level policy changes.
- IGERT is an influential model for interdisciplinary education and research at U.S. universities, particularly as a driver for organizational changes to foster interdisciplinary collaboration.
- Additionally, interdisciplinary graduate traineeship funding initiatives can be effective at changing faculty attitudes and policies related to hiring, workload, and promotion and tenure.

Acknowledgments

The interview portion of this research was funded by NSF through grant number EEC-0643107. Views expressed in this paper are those of the authors and do not necessarily represent those of NSF. The authors wish to thank Dr. Lynita Newswander for assistance with data collection and Dr. Kate Stoll for assistance with data analysis.

References

Amey, M. J., & Brown, D. F. (2004). *Breaking out of the box: Interdisciplinary collaboration and faculty work*: Greenwich, CT: Information Age.

Anthony, L. J., Palius, M. F., Maher, C. A., & Moghe, P. V. (2007). Using discourse analysis to study a cross-disciplinary learning community: Insights from an IGERT training program. *Journal of Engineering Education, 96*(2), 141–156.

Bess, J. L., & Dee, J. R. (2008). *Understanding college and university organization: Theories for effective policy and practice*. Sterling, VA: Stylus.

Bleiklie, I., & Byrkjeflot, H. (2002). Changing knowledge regimes: Universities in a new research environment. *Higher Education, 44*, 519–532.

Boardman, C., & Bozeman, B. (2007). Role strain in university research centers. *Journal of Higher Education, 78*(4), 430–463.

Boden, D., Borrego, M., & Newswander, L. K. (2011). Student socialization in interdisciplinary doctoral education. *Higher Education, 62*(6), 741–755.

Bogdan, R. C., & Biklen, S. K. (2003). *Qualitative research for education: An introduction to theories and methods*. New York: Allyn & Bacon.

Borrego, M., & Cutler, S. (2010). Constructive alignment of interdisciplinary graduate curriculum in engineering and science: An analysis of successful IGERT proposals. *Journal of Engineering Education, 99*(4), 355–369.

Borrego, M., & Newswander, L. K. (2010). Definitions of interdisciplinary research: Toward graduate-level interdisciplinary learning outcomes. *Review of Higher Education, 34*(1), 61–84.

Bozeman, B., & Boardman, C. (2003). *Managing the new multipurpose, multidiscipline university research centers: Institutional innovation in the academic community* (Transforming Organizations Series). Arlington, VA: IBM Center for the

Business of Government. Retrieved from http://www.cspo.org/rvm/reports/reports_docs/IBM_Centers.pdf

Brown, V. A., Harris, J. A., & Russell, J. Y. (2010). *Tackling wicked problems: Through the transdisciplinary imagination.* New York: Routledge.

Carney, J., Chawla, D., Wiley, A., & Young, D. (2006). *Evaluation of the initial impacts of the national science foundation's integrative graduate education and research traineeship program.* Bethesda, MD: Abt Associates.

Carney, J., Martinez, A., Dreier, J., Neishi, K., & Parsad, A. (2011). *Evaluation of the National Science Foundation's Integrative Graduate Education and Research Traineeship Program (IGERT): Follow-up study of IGERT graduates final report.* Bethesda, MD: Abt Associates.

Colbeck, C. L. (2002). Assessing institutionalization of curricular and pedagogical reforms. *Research in Higher Education, 43*(4), 397–421.

Committee on Facilitating Interdisciplinary Research. (2004). *Facilitating interdisciplinary research.* Washington, DC: National Academies Press.

Conklin, G. H. (1978). The frustration of academic innovation. *Teaching Sociology, 5*(2), 125–140.

Conrad, C. F. (1978). A grounded theory of academic change. *Sociology of Education, 51*(2), 110–112.

Cowan, K., & Gogotsi, Y. (2004). The Drexel/UPenn IGERT: Creating a new model for graduate education in nanotechnology. *Journal of Materials Education, 26*(1–2), 147–152.

Creswell, J. W. (2007). *Qualitative inquiry and research design: Choosing among five approaches.* Thousand Oaks, CA: Sage.

Curry, B. K. (1992). *Instituting enduring innovations: Achieving continuity of change in higher education* (ASHE-ERIC Higher Education Report No. 7). Washington, DC: George Washington University, School of Education and Human Development.

Daniels, S. E., & Walker, G. B. (1996). Collaborative learning: Improving public deliberation in ecosystem-based management. *Environmental Impact Assessment Review, 16,* 71–102.

Eigenbrode, S. D., O'Rourke, M., Wulfhorst, J. D., Althoff, D. M., Goldberg, C. S., Merrill, K., et al. (2007). Employing philosophical dialogue in collaborative science. *BioScience, 57*(1), 55.

Golde, C. M., & Gallagher, H. A. (1999). The challenges of conducting interdisciplinary research in traditional doctoral programs. *Ecosystems, 2,* 281–285.

Graybill, J. K., Dooling, S., Shandas, V., Withey, J., Greve, A., & Simon, G. L. (2006). A rough guide to interdisciplinarity: Graduate student perspectives. *BioScience, 56*(9), 757–763.

Holley, K. (2009). The challenge of an interdisciplinary curriculum: A cultural analysis of a doctoral-degree program in neuroscience. *Higher Education, 58,* 241–255.

Hrycyshyn, G. (2008). *Challenges to implementation and how they were overcome: 2006–2007 IGERT annual report.* Arlington, VA: National Science Foundation.

Kezar, A. (2001). Understanding and facilitating organizational change in the 21st century: Recent research and conceptualizations. *ASHE-ERIC Higher Education Report, 28*(4).

Kezar, A. (2006). Redesigning for collaboration in learning initiatives: An examination of four highly collaborative campuses. *Journal of Higher Education, 77*(5), 804–838.

Kezar, A., & Eckel, P. (2002). The effect of institutional culture on change strategies in higher education: Universal principles or culturally repsonsive concepts? *Journal of Higher Education, 73,* 435–460.

Lincoln, Y. S., & Guba, E. G. (1985). *Naturalistic inquiry.* Beverly Hills, CA: Sage.

Marshak, R. J., & Grant, D. (2008). Transforming talk: The interplay of discourse, power, and change. *Organization Development Journal, 26*(3), 33–40.

Martin, P. E., & Umberger, B. R. (2003). Trends in interdisciplinary and integrative graduate training: An NSF IGERT example. *Quest, 55,* 86–94.

McKenzie, R. B., & Galar, R. (2004). The importance of deviance in intellectual development. *American Journal of Economics and Sociology, 63*(1), 19–49.

Metzger, N., & Zare, R. N. (1999). Interdisciplinary research: From belief to reality. *Science, 283*(5402), 642–643.

Morse, W. C., Nielsen-Pincus, M., Force, J. E., & Wulfhorst, J. D. (2007). Bridges and barriers to developing and conducting interdisciplinary graduate-student team research. *Ecology and Society, 12*(2), 8–21.

National Institutes of Health. (2006). *NIH roadmap for medical research.* Bethesda, MD: Author.

National Science Foundation. (2010). *Integrative Graduate Education and Research Traineeship Program (IGERT).* Arlington, VA: Author.

National Science Foundation. (2011a). *Empowering the nation through discovery and innovation: NSF strategic plan for fiscal years (FY) 2011–2016.* Arlington, VA: Author. Retrieved from http://www.nsf.gov/news/strategicplan/nsfstrategic plan_2011_2016.pdf

National Science Foundation. (2011b). *Integrative Graduate Education and Research Traineeship Program, NSF 11-533.* Arlington, VA: Author.

Newswander, L. K., & Borrego, M. (2009a). Engagement in two interdisciplinary graduate programs. *Higher Education, 58*(4), 551–562.

Newswander, L. K., & Borrego, M. (2009b). *IGERT funding and the institutionalization of interdisciplinary graduate education.* Paper presented at the American Society for Engineering Education Annual Conference, Austin, TX.

Oberg, G. (2009). Facilitating interdisciplinary work: Using quality assessment to create common ground. *Higher Education, 57,* 405–415.

Payton, A., & Zoback, M. L. (2007). The inside track from academia and industry: Crossing boundaries, hitting barriers. *Nature, 445*(22), 950.

Pfeffer, J. (1993). Barriers to the advance of organizational science: Paradigm development as a dependent variable. *Academy of Management Review, 18*(4), 599–620.

Pfirman, S. L., Collins, J. P., Lowes, S., & Michaels, A. F. (2005). *To thrive and prosper: Hiring, supporting, and tenuring interdisciplinary scholars.* Retrieved from http://www.pkal.org/documents/Pfirman_et-al_To-thrive-and-prosper.pdf

Richards-Kortum, R., Dailey, M., & Harris, C. (2003). Educational brief: Formative and summative assessment of the IGERT program in optical molecular bioengineering at UT Austin. *Journal of Engineering Education, 92*(4), 345–350.

Sa, C. M. (2008). 'Interdisciplinary strategies' in U.S. research universities. *Higher Education, 55,* 537–552.

Schofer, E. (2003, October). The global institutionalization of geological science, 1800 to 1990. *American Sociological Review, 68,* 730–759.

Stake, R. E. (1995). *The art of case study research.* Thousand Oaks, CA: Sage.

Tress, B., Tress, G., & Fry, G. (2009). Integrative research on environmental and landscape change: PhD students' motivations and challenges. *Journal of Environmental Management, 90,* 2921–2929.

Van Hartesveldt, C., & Giordan, J. (2009). *Impact of transformative interdisciplinary research and graduate education on academic institutions.* Arlington, VA: National Science Foundation.

Yin, R. K. (2009). *Case study research: Designs and methods* (4th ed.). Thousand Oaks, CA: Sage.

Supporting Interdisciplinary Collaboration

The Role of the Institution

◆ L. Michelle Bennett and Howard Gadlin

The recent growth of interest in and funding for interdisciplinary research programs has not been matched by a parallel development of institutional mechanisms for preparing and supporting researchers to participate in such programs. Drawing from our own work and relevant empirical and theoretical approaches, this chapter analyzes five areas where current institutional practices undermine interdisciplinary research teams and collaborations: institutional self-awareness, organizational trust, leadership, management of difference, and handling of conflict and disagreement. Consideration of communication approaches highlights how researchers find themselves in a "double bind" between opposing messages conveyed by leadership. After discussing the ways extant organizational policies and practices create obstacles for the full development of successful collaborative research activities, we offer concrete suggestions for creating an organizational climate more compatible with the direction in which biomedical research is moving.

Introduction

Anyone who has worked within a larger organization knows how complicated it is to lead change. While most organizations have processes for developing and implementing new programs and initiatives, it often takes considerable time before the policies and culture of the organization have caught up and are compatible with new directions and initiatives, even when there is no overt resistance. Although recent years have seen a proliferation of collaborative research ventures within and across institutions, such ventures still sit on shaky foundations. The lure of research funds and the publicity-garnering successes of some collaborative scientific efforts (e.g., The Human Genome Project) have led many academic institutions to actively promote the formation of scientific teams and collaborative ventures. However, we repeatedly hear from researchers that the norms, values, policies, and procedures in their field, their department, or their university are misaligned with the messages being sent.

It is ironic that collaborative, interdisciplinary scientific research has struggled to find support in universities and medical research institutions, which are themselves multidisciplinary institutions designed to pursue cooperative efforts to achieve individual and common goals. Yet the policies, procedures, and values of these institutions are for the most part structured to maintain boundaries between the various departments and disciplines that both cooperate and compete for resources, power, influence, and status. In some ways, it could be said that the very emergence of interdisciplinary collaborative research stands as an implicit critique of segregated disciplinary studies even while research results within those disciplines have provided the motivation for crossing disciplinary boundaries (Fiore, 2008).

In this chapter, we will focus on the institutional context within which teams and collaborations operate, paying particular attention to the strategies, policies, and procedures necessary for sustaining research teams over time. We demonstrate the importance of several factors as they relate to institutional support. We make the case for the importance of institutional trust and we provide strategies for assessing, building, and maintaining it. A similar approach is taken for other factors that contribute to organizational support of interdisciplinary work, including vision, difference, and power. We conclude the chapter with a discussion of leadership and the critical role organizational self-awareness has on overall support of interdisciplinary work. Pivotal to the entire chapter is the crosscutting role interdisciplinary communication plays in bringing all these pieces together. By default, communication across institutions is interdisciplinary.

Integrating personal, conceptual, technical, and disciplinary differences to construct an effective and productive interdisciplinary team is a complicated task in its own right, requiring strong leadership and cooperation among collaborators. A recent paper (Salazar, Lant, Fiore, & Salas, 2012) details the complex social, psychological, and cognitive processes that must interact synergistically to develop "effective communication practices, a shared identity, and a shared conceptualization of a problem." Salazar et al. refer to this as the team's "integrative capacity." This capacity is the measure of the team's ability to exploit the diversity of methodologies, techniques, conceptual frameworks, and epistemologies that characterize interdisciplinary collaborations. However, no amount of team building and training by itself can provide the institutional foundation for such work. Just as trust, communication, leadership, power, and the management of difference play an important role within research collaborations, these same factors have to be understood as they operate at the organizational and interorganizational level, because support at this level is critical (Stokols, 2006).

Much is now known about how people's relationships with organizations affect the way they "think and feel about themselves" in relation to the larger collective (i.e., their social identity). It is clear that social identity (where group membership is an important component of the sense of self) strongly affects motivation and participation in work and the larger organization (Blader & Tyler, 2009).

> An individual's behavioral effort on behalf of a collective to which he or she belongs . . . is influenced by the role the group plays in how the individual thinks and feels about themself around the group. . . . Group members with strong social identities vis-à-vis a group are intrinsically motivated to facilitate the viability and success of their group. (pp. 445–446)

Research on procedural justice in organizations—the perception that the procedures by which decisions are made are fair—reveals four dimensions to procedural justice: the fairness of an organization's formal decision-making rules, the quality of treatment people receive under those rules, the fairness of decision making by each person's supervisor, and the quality of treatment by that supervisor. In turn, there are four criteria by which people judge fairness: consistency (i.e., like cases are treated alike); lack of bias (i.e., those implementing procedures should be impartial and objective); participation (i.e., those affected by a decision should have a voice in the process by providing information and having representation); and transparency (i.e., open procedures, without secrecy or deception, and clear unbiased criteria are employed) (Tyler & De Cremer, 2005).

Tyler's research is a useful complement to the recent scholarship about interdisciplinarity. Julie Thompson Klein (2010), from another perspective, has written extensively about features of the academy—its structure, culture, and policies—that impede the development and maintenance of the cross-disciplinary research and collaborations called for by the academy. Collectively, such studies provide a useful framework within which we can explore the challenges faced by interdisciplinary research teams and collaborations as they strive to function effectively within academic research institutions.

In our own investigation into research teams and collaborations at the National Institutes of Health (NIH) a few years ago, we were surprised to learn that despite formal institutional pronouncements of support for research collaborations, most scientists interviewed felt they were going against the grain of the larger organization (Bennett & Gadlin, 2012; Bennett, Gadlin, & Levine-Finley, 2010). To understand why members of scientific teams might feel that they do not have the support of the institutions in which they are housed, even when those institutions issue statements supporting interdisciplinary research and have been actively seeking funds to support such research, we need to examine many aspects of the experience of research collaborators as they interact and communicate with their home institutions

Organizational Communication

One of the great clichés of critical self-analysis in relationships, groups, and organizations is to attribute problems and conflicts to "problems in communication." The implication is usually that there hasn't been enough communication when, in fact, the very problems or conflicts are most often grounded, in part, in the communications that have already occurred. We must be very clear that when we refer to communications we are pointing to more than spoken or written exchanges between parties who are in dialogue with one another, exchanging information or expressing attitudes or feelings. Here we follow Burbules and Bruce (2001):

> What people say and how they are heard is wrapped up with other kinds of relations and interactions among them, which might range from specific practices . . . to very general institutional norms or structures. . . .
>
> [A]ny particular pattern of speech acts . . . must be seen as situated in a complex net of interactions that govern how those speech acts are expressed, heard, interpreted and responded to. In such a net of interactions the full meaning and effects of discourse will be impossible to read off the surface meanings of the words themselves. The nature of the relations fostered by particular forms of verbal interaction may be utterly unpredictable from the actual intentions and purposes of the agents concerned.

From this framework, we can observe the problematic location of scientific teams and collaborations within the institutions that house them when even the institutions that "support" scientific teams and collaborations work against the success of those teams. Institutions may issue statements supporting interdisciplinary research and may initiate programs soliciting collaborations, yet in many ways the policies and norms of these institutions communicate just the opposite and send very different and often contradictory messages. One of the most damaging consequences of communications where there is a conflict between the stated message and the message that is actually conveyed by actions (policies, procedures, etc.) is the erosion of trust. We believe that trust not only is the cornerstone to effective group functioning but also plays a pivotal role between the organization and any interdisciplinary team.

Trust

As practitioners who work with scientific collaborations we are constantly reminded that successful scientific collaboration hinges on trust. This is underscored when we observe the impact of betrayal and lost trust on team dynamics. These encounters along with many published reports on the significance of trust in group functioning lead us to expand our examination of the role of trust and to explore trust in the context of the system in which an interdisciplinary team is operating (Cohen & Cohen, 2005; Kramer & Lewicki, 2010; Tamm & Lyuet, 2005). Paul Rabinow's (1999) brilliant *French DNA: Trouble in Purgatory* provides an in-depth study of the loss of trust and the collapse of a collaboration.

Establishing organizational trust provides a platform for direct communication and the foundation on which vision can be articulated, change implemented, and conflict managed. It is very difficult to provide a structured road map for developing organizational trust since the needs, context, and experiences of every institution are distinct. The factors that support successful working relationships between such teams and the leaders of the organizations that house them are not so different from those that support successful collaborations.

While trust may extend from the individual to the institution (Tamm & Lyuet, 2005), it is critical to recognize that organizational trust encompasses more than interactions with specific persons. It is tied tightly to policies, procedures, and their implementation. Consequently, even when people from interdisciplinary teams have good, trusting personal relationships with individuals in positions of power and responsibility within the administrative hierarchy of the organization, it is often the case that they do not trust the institutions within which they are employed to support and advance the interdisciplinary nature of their work. Indeed, in some situations it appeared that solidarity and cohesiveness within the team were strengthened by the team members' lack of trust for the larger organization. In our work, we noticed that even when members of scientific teams had, on the whole, positive views of the larger organization, they were notably sensitive to what they saw as a serious misalignment between the institutional promotion of collaboration and the teams' perception that such approaches are not truly supported by their organization.

Kramer and Lewicki have introduced the concept of presumptive trust in the context of organizations (Kramer & Lewicki, 2010; Lewicki, 2006; Reina & Reina, 2006). Just as trust can be categorized in several ways among individuals, extending from trust based on procedures to a deeper intimate type of trust that is relatively rare (Bennett & Gadlin, 2012), trust can be subcategorized at the organizational level. Presumptive trust includes identity-based trust characterized by shared organizational identity, in the sense that members with a shared social identity will often trust one another based on that shared experience of belonging and attribute other positive characteristics such as honesty; role-based trust focused on the roles people occupy within organizations and how the role itself is trusted as opposed to the individual in that role; and rule-based trust, which codifies norms of conduct and sets expectations for behavior based on shared understanding (Kramer & Lewicki, 2010; Reina & Reina, 2006). The violation of these trust elements in organizations can result from communication issues, incongruence, structural issues, or perceptions of unfairness, all of which are relevant to our discussion (Kramer & Lewicki, 2010).

While studies of scientific collaborations have examined issues of trust between collaborating organizations, it seems less attention has been paid to the issue of trust between scientific teams and the organizations of which they are a part. In their extensive study of collaborations among physicists, Shrum, Genuth, and Chompalov (2007) distinguish between trust based on an interpersonal bond between collaborators and trust grounded in interorganizational relationships. They observe that "a basic level of trust is necessary for collaboration in general, within science and without" and that scientists who seriously doubt each other's "scruples or competence" simply cannot collaborate (Shrum et al., 2007). However, they assert that trust based on structures put in place by the organization (for example, standard operating procedures) is distinct and can often be established even when identity-based trust is not strong. Overall, many studies demonstrate a strong relationship between trust in an organization and identification with it. To the extent people identify with an organization, they are also more committed to its goals and cooperative in their dealings with it (Blader & Tyler, 2009).

The following hypothetical case study, drawn from stories we have heard from scientists across the country, illustrates the sort of experiences that lead many participants in cross-disciplinary research teams to conclude that they do not really have support for the very activities their institution calls for and thus leads to distrust of the institution or its leaders.

Case Study 1

Dr. X was a highly talented junior investigator and recruited in part because of the creative contributions he had made in highly integrated research collaborations. He was told repeatedly during the recruitment process from several levels of the organization that team science and collaboration were highly valued. After about 4 years of what many in the organization considered stellar performance, he went through a formal pre-review to evaluate his progress toward tenure. Institutional criteria for tenure stated explicitly that participation in team science was considered by the tenure committee, and he knew he had made the most of his natural abilities both to lead and to integrate with highly complex research initiatives, bringing his expertise to advance projects.

When he received the results from the evaluation committee, he felt completely betrayed by the organization. He had been raked over the coals for spending too much time in collaborative efforts, failing to demonstrate progress on individual projects, and not having enough first- and last-author papers that demonstrated independence. The committee agreed he held great promise as a researcher in their organization but stated that he was spending too much time on collaborative efforts. They recommended that he focus on individual projects and publishing them for the next 2 years before submitting his case to the promotions committee.

When Dr. X approached the committee chair, with whom he had established a good relationship and whom he had considered one of his mentors, for more information about how the committee came to their decision—especially in light of the existing tenure criteria—the chair indicated that the committee discussions were confidential. He suggested following the review committee's recommendations for his case if he wanted to be positively reviewed by the tenure committee. When the leader from one of the most productive integrated research teams on which Dr. X was participating tried talking to the dean about the inconsistencies between the pre-review and the published tenure criteria, he was told that the pre-review committee had been in existence for many years and always did a good job in advising junior investigators, as evidenced by the high tenure success rate of their organization.

This case study provides an example of a situation where the official communications are negated or at least diluted by other "communications" within the organization. In this case, the espoused norms and values are not those applied when assessing performance. Often, even when "revised" tenure criteria valorize collaborative research, personnel committees continue to apply older notions of "independent contribution" to scientists who are functioning under a newer model of scientific practice structured around collaboration across disciplines and institutions. This is the classic "double bind"—whichever command one follows, one is automatically violating the other command (Bateson, Jackson, Haley, & Weakland, 1956). In this case, scientists working in these circumstances are essentially given two contradictory commands—"work collaboratively" and "be independent," which are especially problematic for junior investigators (Curtin, 2008; Hackett, 2005).

The consequences of institutionally embedded mixed messages include a significant demoralization and uncertainty on the part of the individual scientists and decrease in organizational trust (Cohen & Cohen, 2005; Curtin, 2008; Hackett, 2005; Rhoten, 2004).

The misalignment of messages and actions of the institution violates both role- and rule-based trust. The role of the committee as fair judge of scientific contributions and the supposedly unbiased rules by which decisions are made are both called into question here. Also, it is highly unlikely that researchers who believe they have not been given a fair shake will identify positively with the organization that treats them this way. We hear stories like this all the time—policies are either not in place or are in place but not honored in practice.

We also repeatedly hear stories about the consequences of the loss of organizational trust. Sometimes it results in lost talent—people leaving the organization or science altogether. But even if people stay, some withdraw from team-based efforts, frustrated and unwilling to engage without the prospect of career growth and reward, and concerned about the risks associated with collaborative research.

Assessing, Building, and Maintaining Trust

The establishment and maintenance of trust between research teams and the institutions that house them are of pivotal institutional importance. It begins with an organizational leader's willingness to evaluate the current level of institutional trust and the recognition that organizational trust is not primarily personal. It requires a commitment from leadership to establish a trust that is grounded in more than strong interpersonal relationships. A number of tools and approaches exist and are summarized in Table 17.1.

Table 17.1	List of Tools, Resources, and Approaches for Facilitating Communication at the Institutional Level

Framework	Tool, Approach, Strategy	Reference
Assessing trust	Organizational Trust Inventory	Cummings and Bromiley (1996), Nyhan and Marlowe (1997)
	Mixed-methods approach for assessing trust	Bachmann (2010)
	Repertory grid	Bachmann (2010), Jankowicz (2003), Kelly (1955)
	Assessing patient trust	Pearson and Raeke (2000)

(Continued)

Table 17.1   (Continued)

Framework	Tool, Approach, Strategy	Reference
Assessing power	Assessing power dynamics	Hill (1994)
	Approach for assessing power dynamic	French and Raven (1959)
Assessing the environment	Assessing the academic work environment for science and engineering faculty	University of Michigan (2010b)
Shared vision	Organizational visioning	O'Connell, Hickerson, and Pillutla (2011)
	Inspirational communication of a vision	Frese, Beimel, and Schoenborn (2003), Thoms and Greenberger (1998)
	Reflexivity to generate shared vision	Barry, Britten, Barber, Bradley, and Stevenson (1999)
Building teams	Intervention approaches	Shuffler, DiazGranados, and Salas (2011)
	Collaboration Success Wizard	Olson and Olson (2012)
Setting expectations	Collaborative agreement	Bennett and Gadlin (2012), Bennett et al. (2010), Berndt (2011)
	Criteria for tenure at NIH	Garcia-Perez, Wyatt, and Gottesman (2010)
	Policy for interdisciplinary teams	University of Southern California (2011)
	Criteria and evaluation	Feder and Madara (2008), Rikakis (2009)
	Mutual understanding	Eigenbrode et al. (2007)
	Organizational support	University of Michigan (2010a)
	Association of American Medical Colleges contracts for graduate students and postdoctoral fellows	Association of American Medical Colleges (2013)
Trust repair	Apology assessment	Kellerman (2006)
Science of team science	Team Science Toolkit	National Cancer Institute (2012)

NOTE: This list, which is not exhaustive, was compiled from literature reviews, materials gathered from colleagues, and our own practical experiences working with research teams/collaborations in an academic setting. The exclusion of other relevant materials is not a reflection of their merit.

The Organizational Trust Inventory, or OTI, introduced in 1997, was based on research and has been validated as a reliable measure of trust (Cummings & Bromiley, 1996; Nyhan & Marlowe Jr, 1997). The OTI uses a 7-point scale to assess 12 different elements that rate various aspects of confidence, trust, and behavior as they relate to one's supervisor as well as the organization as a whole. The assessment has the advantage of being simple to administer and score while having a strong theoretical foundation.

Reinhard Bachmann (2010) has proposed two more complex approaches. One is a mixed-methods approach, and its use is encouraged on the premise that the populations from which information about trust is collected will have their own contextual backgrounds and foundations. Each approach should be tailored to the population, and by using a variety of tools including surveys, interviews, and a mixture of open-ended and closed-ended questions, the information collected will be rich in depth and texture, providing a robust view of the overall sentiment as it relates to organizational trust. The other is a repertory grid approach[1] that has its origins in Personal Construct Theory (Jankowicz, 2003; Kelly, 1955), which takes into account how a person interprets his or her experiences through a series of interview sessions. This approach permits in-depth and insightful research into what a group means by trust, honors different interpretations of trust, and remains constant with a high dependency on local responsiveness of the individual administering the assessment.

Trust is always being tested and fairness evaluated in every administrative action and during every interaction with leadership. It is not simply a matter of what policies and procedures are in place but whether and how they are implemented and whether they truly align with the messages from leadership (Tyler & De Cremer, 2005).

Imagine in the first case study if an institutional leader had briefed the pre-review committee members on the new criteria and expectations were established for how to implement them prior to conducting any reviews with them in place. Many people report to us that their trust is violated when previous standards are used even after new criteria are disseminated. The implementation of clear procedures or training programs ensures that reviewers are knowledgeable about their responsibilities during evaluations, and when reviews align with messages, trust will build. These elements can

---

[1]In the traditional interview approach, the categories of comparison are selected by the interviewer, while in the repertory grid approach the categories are elicited from those interviewed. Specifically, the repertory grid approach discerns the distinct elements by which people structure their experience of others. Imagine interviewing participants in a collaboration. In a traditional interview approach, each participant might be asked to talk about how reliable or honest the other participants are. In the repertory grid approach, the dimensions of comparison are not preselected by the interviewer. Instead, the interviewee may be given the names of three of the participants and asked to describe how he or she is working with two of them differently than with the third. One interviewee might say that Persons A and B are more enjoyable to work with than Person C. Another interviewee might say that Persons A and B are more reliable than Person C. Through a series of comparisons, the dimensions of interaction most important for each of the people interviewed are elucidated.

contribute to positive organizational identity and alignment of individual values with organizational values, which contributes to identity-based trust (Kramer & Lewicki, 2010).

Rebuilding Trust

In our interviews with successful research teams at NIH (Bennett & Gadlin, 2012; Bennett et al., 2010), it became evident that while most teams had created a climate in which differences of opinion could surface and be explored, there was no clear avenue or forum for discussing differences of opinion between a research team and the organization. Frustrations resulting from this absence do indeed exist, as the examples in this chapter illustrate. Yet, typically, mechanisms for being heard and exchanging ideas and effecting change in institutional policy, procedure, and/or interpretation of criteria are lacking, and attempts to address such differences are often experienced as a personal rather than an institutional matter. Overt conflict is masked behind committee decisions (by "the organization") without opportunities for open discussion and dialogue about whether committee decisions are appropriate in the context of current messages being communicated by the leadership. The areas of frustration are illustrated in the first case study, which also demonstrates that individual relationships do not often serve to raise the systemic issues of which individual conflicts are an example. The following case study focuses on rebuilding organizational trust, which is when all parties, especially the leadership, are involved and committed. The case illustrates well that for a group to get back on track after trust has been betrayed, it is important to spend time disentangling and understanding what led to the loss of trust, and then to work together to slowly rebuild it. Rebuilding benefits from the establishment of some structures or scaffolds that everyone can adhere to as they learn to work together again. Organizational support is critical for success.

Case Study 2

At the invitation of leaders from three separate departments within an organization, we were given the opportunity to work with an interdisciplinary team that had derailed. While the team was more than ready to disband, the leadership still believed there was value in having such a team. As a first step to understanding what had caused this particular group to derail, we had conversations with the leaders and with the team, with and without the leaders present. All the facets discussed in this chapter were at play and were considered as the dynamics both within the team and between the team and leadership were evaluated. When the information from the interviews was compiled, it was clear that interactions of the team with the larger organization's leadership had direct and indirect impacts on both team function and the relationships within the team. Several significant factors were exposed.

While there was a very clear mission for the umbrella organization, the vision for the team lacked clarity. There was no consensus about team vision, either within or among the three organizational units. This lack of clarity about vision resulted in the erosion of trust in large part because roles and responsibilities of the team members, in the context of their work together, had not been clarified. Although individual team members understood their own role, there was great confusion of how their roles were meant to be interrelated. People were unclear about when and who they could ask for help, when they were expected to exercise autonomy, and when they were expected to work conjointly. In addition, because the positions of the individuals were not equivalent, resentment had built around perceptions of how people were spending their time. Reporting structures were clear in the context of the organization, but reporting, resource allocation, and team structure were not. Finally, power contributed to the dysfunction in that one of the organizational leaders who supported the team's development was what we describe as "absent but present." While hesitant, and even resistant, to engage directly with the team, he sent a representative to every meeting who was not fully a team member. This individual would speak on behalf of the leader at meetings and then report back to the leader, putting himself in a powerful position with both sides and helping the absent leader maintain control while stating that the team was acting independently. This was an organizational leader who provided surveillance but not guidance, hardly an approach likely to engender the trust of or provide autonomy to the team.

The first step in rebuilding trust involved bringing the team together to deconstruct how they arrived at the current state. It is difficult for a team to move forward and rebuild trust if they are not given the opportunity to explain from their own vantage points how it was lost. This is especially the case when the group's past failure has been understood in terms of expressions of mutual blame. They need to reconstruct the history of the group in such a way that they could understand what had gone wrong. Blaming, as anyone who has experienced morbidity and mortality rounds knows quite well, never results in understanding the cause of a failure. This process allowed team members to realize how, in the past, members of each department had been operating under different unspoken expectations while assuming that their expectations were the same. Consequently, each department had been consistently disappointed in the performance of and relationships with the other departments. Not having established a process for ongoing assessment of team functioning, the different departments alternated between quiet resentment and open blame.

Once the group had come to consensus about where they were as a team and made a joint commitment to work together to rebuild the team, the next steps were to openly discuss the value of and need for trust and then to develop a shared vision. To begin repairing trust between the team and the organization, the leadership was engaged in discussions since absolute alignment of the team's activities with organizational vision was critical. Once the vision was determined and clear to all involved, the group could begin developing goals and objectives for implementation. In parallel, the group worked to define and agree on the logistical aspects related to group functioning, including governance, rules for working together, and processes and procedures for securing needed resources, roles, and responsibilities. Another critical activity of the group was to perform an assessment of the existing strengths among the group members, followed by asking what additional expertise was needed to make their work more effective and productive. Once these different elements were assembled, the appointed representatives met with the leadership to present their approach for moving forward. One of the lessons they took from this examination was that it was imperative for the team to incorporate processes for ongoing self-assessment into their practice.

Organizational Vision

Leaders create and support the organizational vision. This is critical because vision drives the direction of the organization and is responsible for establishing the values by which goals are obtained. If the organizational goal is to encourage, catalyze, and support interdisciplinary research teams, approaches must be put in place for achieving that vision. Without a plan for achieving the goals, a vision statement is just words and is likely to elicit cynicism from within the organization. There are particular points in time when the establishment of a vision may be more important, such as when a new leader is appointed, organizational priorities change, an unexpected scientific challenge emerges, or even a novel funding opportunity presents itself.

Visioning can take place either through a top-down approach or via participatory processes. In the top-down approach, the vision is developed at the leadership level and then disseminated and "sold" to the individuals and departments in the organization. In the participatory processes, those who will be asked to embrace the vision and play a role in implementing it are also involved in the various stages of formulating the vision (O'Connell et al., 2011). While unusually charismatic leaders can often elicit deep commitment and trust, the participatory approach allows the leader to share ownership of the vision with others in the organization and ensures that the commitment is to the vision itself and not just to the particular leader. Willingness by the leadership to share control of the process almost always leads to a community whose participants believe that they are trusted and in turn trust those who lead them (reviewed in Frese et al., 2003; O'Connell et al., 2011). Studies have shown that training leaders in message delivery can be effective and results in the perception of the leader as charismatic (Awamleh & Gardner, 1999; Frese et al., 2003; Thoms & Greenberger,

1998). Awareness of the importance of vision delivery from an organizational perspective should not go unrecognized.

In our experience working with teams, if the organizational vision is clear and clearly communicated to those expected to implement it, people who are excited by its promise are eager to participate. Setting expectations for the group, either in a top-down fashion or in a participatory manner, is critical so the group will not derail. While the vision is a good first step, a team charter or team mission statement is crucial, as it is where policies, processes, and organizational approaches are aligned with messages about vision (Bennett & Gadlin, 2012; Berndt, 2011; Hackett & Martin, 1993).

Supporting the Vision and Setting Expectations

Interdisciplinary teams undergoing formation often find themselves looking for guidance. It is not unusual for them to discover that the practical aspects of putting a team together, improving group functioning, and setting expectations are not as clearly defined as are the practices required for successful functioning of discrete organizational components (e.g., departments). While any given team can work with its host organization to establish expectations and parameters for its functioning, organizations can establish systematic approaches to provide guidance and support to interdisciplinary teams and collaborations.

Several universities have put into place programs that provide training, resources, and support mechanisms for those involved or interested in cross-disciplinary and/or cross-institutional collaborative ventures (e.g, National Cancer Institute, 2012; Northwestern University, 2012; Stanford University, 2012; University of Southern California, 2011). In addition to training programs, there are many resources and approaches at the disposal of the institution and the team (see Table 17.1). The advantage of these is that they force the institution to move from stating ideals to creating realities. It is up to the organization to decide whether there will be a commitment by the institution to encourage their use broadly.

In our experience, many difficulties within scientific collaborations and between scientific teams and their institutions arise because of a lack of clarity about expectations—expectations about who will do what, how communication will occur and how often, how data will be shared, etc. The use of simple approaches to clearly stipulate expectations can help reinforce rule- and role-based trust, which in turn can serve as a scaffold for the establishment of deeper identity trust. One example of an approach for setting expectations that works extremely well is the development of a document that is given to all new team members stating explicitly how the team works, what is expected of them in their role, and what they can expect from the leader and the organization in return. Even aspects of the hiring process can be designed to clarify expectations and set the ground for a relationship of trust between new researchers, their colleagues, and the organization. For example, the inclusion of language in offer letters or in other documents early in the probationary period, providing expectations about the individual's conduct in interdisciplinary research as well as expectations for the institution, have been suggested by us in the form of an agreement at the time of an offer for a position or soon after hire (see Table 17.2). Such

Table 17.2	Guidance for crafting an agreement for a junior faculty member to be involved in highly collaborative work, to be included in the offer letter or during the probationary period

Roles, Responsibilities, Expectations

- What will be the role of the individual?
- What will be expected of the early career scientist?
- How will success be defined for those participating in interdisciplinary research? Leading an interdisciplinary team?
- What will be the role of the department? Chair?
- What will be expected of the department? Chair?

Review and Reward

- Success: What criteria will be used to assess the progress and success of the scientist for interdisciplinary work?
- Sharing credit and data: How will data sharing, processes for access to data, authorship decisions be reviewed and assessed?

Mentoring

- How will the early career scientist be mentored in interdisciplinary research (individual mentor, mentoring committee, etc.)?
- What will be expected of the scientist in mentoring his or her own lab/team members?
- What training is expected and/or required of those participating in or leading interdisciplinary efforts?

Joint Appointments

For researchers appointed in more than one department, the agreement will clearly

- identify the departments/organizations involved in supporting the scientist,
- state that the departments/organizations are committed to the tenure-track scientist,
- state who will be responsible for the administration of the scientist (performance reviews, human resources, budget tracking, etc.) and define administrative home,
- determine which resources will be provided by which department/organization,
- commit to annual review and define who will participate,
- establish a procedure to follow in case of disagreement,
- establish a procedure to follow should any party decide to withdraw or significantly alter the agreement.

documents can contain any elements of importance, such as how individuals will be reviewed in the team context, what the responsibilities of the organization are, and what processes are in place to address conflict early before problems arise.

One resource that deserves note is the explicit interdisciplinary review criteria for promotion and tenure at the University of Southern California (2011). The criteria document describes organizational commitment through competitive funding support, implementation of structural changes, and education and training in research collaboration. In addition, University of Chicago and Arizona State University have implemented evidence-based appointment and promotion systems that provide not only clear criteria but also a systematic approach to the tenure review process (Feder & Madara, 2008; Rikakis, 2009). The practice of requiring CVs to be annotated is another approach implemented by several of our colleagues in senior leadership positions at their academic institutions. In this way, the accomplishments of the individual on multiauthored papers are made clear. When requesting letters for promotion, review referees (noncollaborators and collaborators) can be asked to provide explicit feedback on the individual contributions and recognized expertise in the context of collaborative work being performed. We have been told that these approaches provide robust mechanisms for determining if the individual is making outstanding, novel, significant, and independent intellectual contributions to his or her field. It enables the evaluation of the individual in the context of a team. In short, teams can fail as teams when reward structures are based on individual performance without consideration of the overall performance of the team.

Some research institutions are reformulating the criteria for assessing the importance of individual contributions to collaborative endeavors and modifying their decision-making procedures for tenure and advancement (Feder & Madara, 2008; Garcia-Perez et al., 2010; Rikakis, 2009). Almost always, these organizations want to ensure that these new approaches are compatible with their traditional standards for evaluating excellence and with their organizational structure. Consequently, some degree of conflict about these issues will be part of the organizational context within which team science and collaborative research operate in the foreseeable future. The manner in which these differences are negotiated will play a significant role in advancing or hindering the growth of interdisciplinary research.

Difference

In their book *Cultures and Organizations*, the anthropologist Geert Hofstede and her colleagues Gert Jan Hofstede and Michael Minkov (2010) have a chapter titled "What Is Different Is Dangerous." This sums up well the challenge of interdisciplinary ventures—managing differences knowing that they are potentially enriching and potentially dangerous. Especially dangerous are differences that are not recognized as differences. Typically, within interdisciplinary teams, many differences are easily spotted and include different disciplines, vocabularies, techniques, and methodologies, as well as varied ways of thinking about science, conducting research, and sharing credit. In addition, there are differences in the nationality, language, and race of participants. When attention is turned to the relationship between a scientific team and its larger organization, it is much easier to overlook some of the most significant differences and therefore to misunderstand some of the communications between the team and the larger organization or its executives (Hofstede et al., 2010).

One of the most basic differences is between scientists and administrators. In their excellent book *Lab Dynamics*, Cohen and Cohen (2005) state:

> Science organizations are often led by executives who have little or no science training. In fact it is not uncommon to find individuals with financial, legal, and business development backgrounds heading such organizations. Such leaders suffer from definite disadvantages if they do not understand the nature of the scientific process, and especially if they believe that research and discovery can be managed by conventional "command and control" approaches. (p. 138)

These differences can be more profound and difficult to overcome than differences that result from bringing together researchers from different scientific disciplines or different cultures. While different scientific disciplines can vary significantly, they are alike in their basic acceptance of the values and culture of research, and even when researchers have different interpretations of what constitutes "real" science, they share the identity of being scientists. For the most part, they understand one another. However, when confronted with nonscientists who wield power over them and whose approaches to decision making and resource allocation have a direct impact on their ability to pursue their work, the significance of these differences can escalate.

In fact, even executives who were originally scientists are often mistrusted and disrespected because they have left the world of science and gone over to the "dark side" of administration. In essence, this means that scientists and administrators/executives often differ in two significant ways—by discipline and by role. It is almost as if a certain amount of distrust is built into their organizational relationships even if the head of a particular scientific team and the chancellor of the university have a trusting relationship as individuals. If anything, recognizing and managing differences is even more important in structuring interactions between people in administrative roles and people in research positions than it is within a team. It is also more difficult. Because both researchers and administrators agree about the ultimate value of "supporting team science and interdisciplinary collaborations," they can easily overlook how differently they interpret those words. Of course, recognizing differences does not imply that those differences can be negotiated away or reconciled. Consider, for example, the unsuccessful appeal made by the team leader to the dean in the case of Dr. X, where the dean stood by the pre-review committee despite the contradiction between the written tenure criteria and those employed in the committee's recommendation.

All interdisciplinary interactions, whether within or across institutions, involve the negotiation of differences: differences in meaning, in norms and values, in technique and methodology, in roles and status. But differences need not create incommensurability. Addressing issues of communication between identity groups that vary in social and political power, Burbules and Rice (1991) wrote:

> There is no reason to assume that dialogue across differences involves either eliminating those differences or imposing one group's views on others; dialogue that leads to understanding, cooperation and accommodation can sustain differences within a broader compact of toleration and respect. (p. 402)

Their observations are equally apt when considering the handling of differences in interdisciplinary and interinstitutional collaborations. This is especially important because every collaboration entails the loss of some degree of autonomy and is therefore somewhat threatening to the identity of the collaborating partners, especially when it comes to sharing power (Rock, 2008). The recognition of differences is the first step toward establishing relationships in which negotiation and cooperation facilitate the pursuit of common interests (see Figure 17.1). And it is around these common interests that partners can construct a new identity that helps compensate for the loss of some degree of autonomy.

Power

One dimension of difference demands particular attention—power. Linda Hill (1994), an expert in understanding the power dynamics in organizations, defines power as "the potential of an individual (or group) to influence another individual or group. Influence, in turn, is the exercise of power to change the behavior, attitudes, and/or values of that individual or group."

Power dynamics play a significant role in interactions at many levels, including between organizations that support the teams that are involved in interdisciplinary, cross-institutional collaborations. When there are vast differences in power, the more powerful party can dominate the processes by which vision is formulated, decisions are made, methodologies chosen, and data analyzed and interpreted. Typically, the institutions are more powerful than the teams they support, and those institutions can constrain or shape the sorts of collaborations entered into by those teams. While perhaps obvious, it is important to note that power dynamics are especially apparent during conflicts and disagreements.

Figure 17.1 Steps for Building Awareness and Managing Key Differences

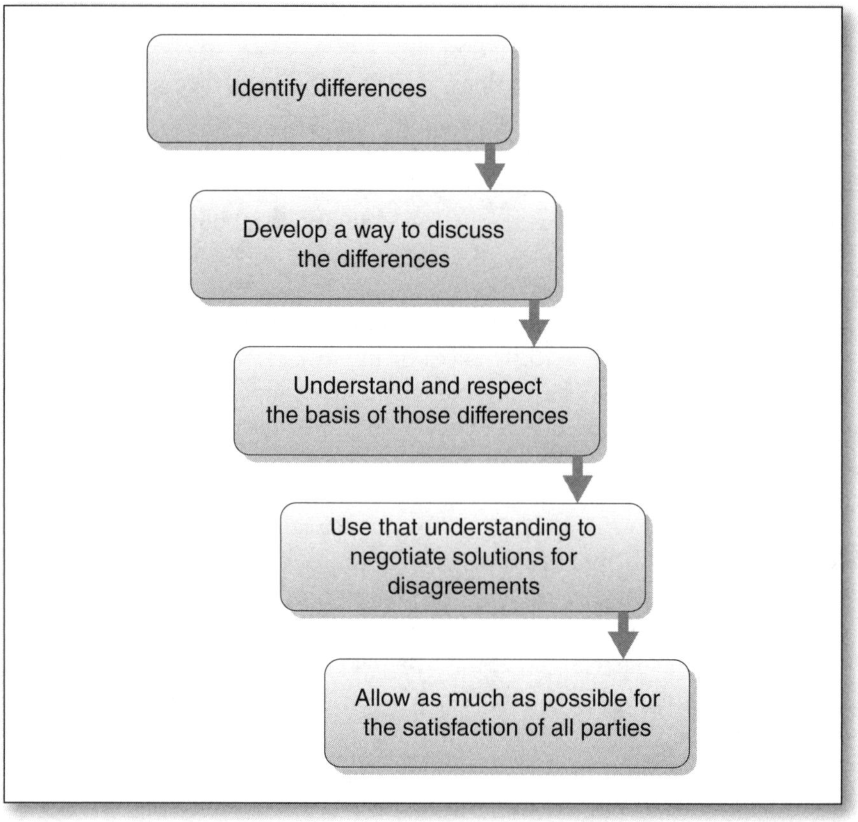

It is unrealistic to imagine a situation in which power is perfectly balanced among all parties to a project. Each party should have enough power to effectively participate in disagreements and come to mutual solutions. This requires recognition of imbalances of power, willing acceptance of all views by those with the most power (Mayer, 1987), and the organizational leadership to create an environment where this is possible. When people identify with a group, that identification becomes more important than maintaining their individual status/title; group cohesion can diminish the need for exercising power (Edmondson, 2003; Keyton, 1999).

Power ought not to be thought of only in quantitative terms. It is rarely the case that power can be assessed only in terms of who has more. There are many sources of power within organizations and many ways those sources of power can be applied. Just about everyone who writes about power has his or her own list of the sources of power, and these lists vary considerably (French & Raven, 1959). Linda Hill (1994) provides a framework for thinking about power that seems relevant to the dynamics in scientific teams and collaborations. She distinguishes between positional and personal power. Included under positional power are formal authority, relevance of work in relationship to organizational goals, positions with multiple others dependent on them, freedom to make decisions, and recognition or visibility to powerful people in the organization. Personal power exhibits itself in the forms of expertise, record of accomplishment, having attributes others find desirable, and putting forth large effort (Hill, 1994).

Of course sources of power are not, in and of themselves, good or bad. It is how power is used that matters. There are three primary ways that power can be used to influence others: the normative approach, in which influence is built around the attempt to convince others that an idea is the "right" way to do things; the utilitarian approach, in which persuasive efforts are grounded in the beneficial outcomes that will follow from pursuing an idea; and the coercive approach, in which the more powerful party asserts his or her preference and is able to back up that assertion with a threat of sanctions or punishments. Mayer (1987) has stated that neither the coercive nor the utilitarian approach will succeed for inducing teamwork.

One other manifestation of power needs to be considered in thinking about the power dynamics involved in interdisciplinary collaboration. This form of power is neither personal nor positional and has been defined as "infrastructural." It originates in the work of the sociologist Michael Mann (1984), who was researching the ways the modern bureaucratic state wields power without resorting to despotism and force. He referred to the structures and services provided by the state that in and of themselves become a manifestation of power because they form the basis of civil society. Large, complex academic institutions are analogous to the state in that they wield considerable power merely by virtue of providing and controlling the organization's infrastructure. Some examples include information technology departments, the budget office, and facilities management services.

Infrastructural power is particularly noteworthy because it plays a significant role in determining the degree of institutional trust between scientific research groups and the institutions within which they function. Research groups, like all other departments and administrative units of a university, are dependent on the rules, policies, procedures, and processes of the larger organization that serve many of their needs while also defining the limits of their autonomy. Necessarily, such an arrangement is a breeding ground for distrust. The first case study illustrates how the institution's oversight mechanisms can sometimes be experienced as intrusive and insensitive to the very specific needs and aims of an individual in the context of an interdisciplinary research program.

It is critical to recognize the positive side to infrastructural power, which does allow for trust building and is explored more in the second case study. It follows from the very same uniform rules and procedures that sometimes elicit distrust. Simply put, rules and policies can create a predictable environment (Bachmann, 2010). Although this is obviously true for group members from within an institution, this clarity of rules and standards can also have implications for establishing interorganizational trust. Material transfer agreements, for example, have long been the norm in interorganizational sharing of biomedical materials and service-level agreements between information technology departments and other parts of an organization. So while some aspects of bureaucracy can create obstacles for collaborations that cross the boundaries of organizational units, in other ways those same features of bureaucracy can bolster or even take the place of trust. This observation is supported by Shrum et al. (2007) when they discuss the "paradox of trust," wherein rules and regulations substitute for trust in collaborative efforts, and is further buttressed by Bachmann (2010), who adds that individual power does not contribute to trust building in these situations. When it comes to collaborations, the structures put in place by leadership will have a profound effect on the outcomes of that group work (Shrum et al., 2007).

In many ways, there is a symbiotic relationship between power and trust; they can amplify or substitute for each other (Bachmann, 2010). In circumstances in which there is mistrust between research teams involved in cross-institutional collaborations, strong leaders in positions of power can serve as honest brokers between wary participants and can bridge that distrust. Even before trust is firmly established, strong leaders can encourage others to believe that some future state will be achieved.

Assessing and Managing Power

Linda Hill (1994), who eloquently stated, "People in power can shape their environment, whereas the powerless are destined to be molded and constrained by theirs," has put forward an approach that has similarities to one introduced earlier by French and Raven (1959). The approach is designed to be situation dependent and lends itself well to assessing the power dynamic between an interdisciplinary team and the organization. This five-step approach starts with evaluating the interdependencies among the relevant parties, answering such questions as what dependencies exist in the relationship and why cooperation is needed, and determining the sources of power that each possesses and follows. Once that is established, the parties can analyze the relevant differences and dig deeper to understand what factors may reinforce the extant differences and incite conflict. Following such an analysis, Hill suggests reflecting on the broader organizational political environment, where alliances and rivalries exist, to identify preventive measures that could be put into place, determine if predictions could be made about how conflict would be handled, and anticipate interventions that would enable more effective management of such conflicts. Finally, she strongly encourages periodic reevaluation since the power dynamics within an organization often shift.

An assessment of the forms and distribution of power at the organizational level can enable the leadership and the organization to decide which types of power to encourage and shape how they are deployed. For example, if the organization encourages collaboration and team science, it should facilitate interactions among researchers from different parts of the organization with supportive policies and processes. Power can be used to facilitate interaction and cooperation in organizations, or it can be abused, with the end result of damaging trust and creating frustration. While both leaders of and participants in an interdisciplinary team may have relationships with members of the institutional leadership, the relationship of the team to the organization takes on a different dynamic. Leaders sometimes avoid discussing areas of potential disagreement by ceding to "the committee" or "the organization" as the responsible party for decision making, as illustrated in the first case study. But yielding to the larger organization without addressing areas of disagreement can have a demoralizing effect on a team. Leaders benefit from and build trust through promoting and addressing areas of disagreement while managing personal conflicts.

Organizational Leadership

Institutional leaders constitute a critical base of support for team science and research collaborations. Just as leadership is a pivotal element in the success of an interdisciplinary team, organizational leadership holds critical keys to success in creating an environment where teams can thrive. There are two aspects of leadership that warrant attention. The first has to do with how the power discussed in the previous section is deployed. As we move away from command-and-control notions of leadership toward more collaborative interpretations, the role of the leader within the institution becomes more important, not less. Sharing power increases a manager's influence, and stability across organizations can be enhanced with multiple leaders (Gray, 2008a, 2008b; Hill, 1994).

This stance toward power is well illustrated in an interview with John Donovan, the chief technology officer at AT&T.

> I started to engage in deliberate deflection of credit in an environment where it was all about credits. . . . I started realizing that people appreciated you when you played for the result, and not for your role on the team. . . . I learned that giving credit away was effective. (Bryant, 2011)

The second aspect has to do with self-awareness. As important as self-awareness is among leaders of collaborations, it is even more important among institutional executive leadership. Increasing self-awareness among institutional executives can be challenging. Certainly, leaders can learn a lot from self-reflection and attending to feedback. However, executives must choose to become aware of the impact the organization's policies, procedures, culture, and norms have on those functioning within the organization. This expanded organizational self-awareness is a lubricant that facilitates the interactions on which everything else depends—communication, trust, power, conflict management, reconciliation of differences, and collaboration.

Organizational Self-Awareness and Assessment_____

Vast amounts have been written about the nature and importance of leadership in organizations. In addition to their individual attributes, leaders serve as the focal point of organizational self-awareness. Effective leaders recognize the importance of self-awareness, are willing to make strategic decisions about the kind of organization they want to lead, and, most important, are willing to set in motion the changes required to achieve that goal. When such leaders have the respect of their employees and there is a strong foundation of trust, employees will model their behavior after the leader. In turn, leaders need to understand that their behavior is being modeled (Cohen & Cohen, 2005; French & Raven, 1959).

Organizational self-awareness does not emerge automatically from a leader's personal self-reflections; it has to be structured around the results of consciously directed assessments of an organization's culture, policies, power dynamics, and work relationships. Just as assessments can be a valuable tool in developing personal self-awareness, as evidenced by their use in many leadership training courses, approaches exist that can help organizations assess their environments and determine where work may be required to achieve the desired outcomes. As one example, the University of Michigan began assessing its environment for science, engineering, and social sciences faculty in 2001 as part of an ADVANCE award from the National Science Foundation. The value of taking a broad and sweeping approach to an organizational assessment is that it can provide the big picture with respect to individual perceptions of the climate in which they work and enables the institutional leadership to determine where the most critical attention needs to be focused. The assessment tool used at the University of Michigan was designed to assess a number of climate indicators, including service, mentoring, gender discrimination, positive climate, fairness of the leader, and ability of the leader to create a positive environment. Their approach enabled them to make assessments at different organizational levels and then develop approaches for addressing the deficiencies and problem areas (University of Michigan, 2010a). Of course organizational self-awareness is no guarantor of organizational change, recognizing that academic institutions are notoriously slow to change even when they become aware of the necessity to do so.

Conclusion_____

Earlier we mentioned that many organizations lack mechanisms whereby those who believe that the organization's policies are not being fairly implemented or evaluation criteria are being misapplied can address these concerns without bringing formal charges or without making accusations. Systems can be put in place at the leadership level to explicitly address this need and thereby support interdisciplinary efforts. Of course, it may also be possible to leverage or expand existing efforts to meet such a need. The NIH Center for Cooperative Resolution headed by the ombudsman is an example of a community resource that has expanded its repertoire in this way. Specifically, it has moved beyond managing conflict situations to become fully engaged in executing a more preemptive approach to minimizing unproductive or harmful conflict while creating opportunities for the open discussion and productive disagreement that are most often at the heart of any collaborative venture. In addition, the ombudsman's office plays a dynamic role in assisting organizational entities in repairing damaged trust or perceptions of betrayal.

With institutional support, such an office can encourage the use of assessments, approaches, and resources to set expectations and develop mutual understanding through collaborative agreements and philosophical dialogue; it can also aid in the development of language to include in offer letters and/or pre-tenure agreements (Bennett & Gadlin, 2012; Berndt, 2011; Eigenbrode et al., 2007; see Table 17.1). Tools such as these provide scaffolds for intervening at an early point if tensions start to emerge within the group context, and they also provide guidance for rebuilding lost or damaged trust.

Another demonstration of institutional support for interdisciplinary work is to provide the community with the opportunity to build skills and abilities that align with organizational vision. Among those things that were perceived to be most lacking in our examination of successful research teams was training in interdisciplinary research, collaboration, and/or team science. This sentiment has been communicated to us numerous times by others at research institutions nationally. The overwhelming frustration expressed is that if the institution wants to encourage team science and collaboration, it should provide instruction so people learn what characteristics contribute to successful team functioning and should articulate its active support of team science.

Can change really be effected through a training program? Training alone is not likely to be sufficient for leading and managing change. However, if organizational commitment is coupled with a holistic approach, supporting activities that improve interdisciplinary communication can occur, as illustrated in Case Study 3.

Case Study 3

This is a compelling example of the formation of an interdisciplinary team by university leadership with the clear vision of addressing the gender disparity among its faculty. Trust in the organization had faltered with respect to its support for recruiting and hiring talented women. Not all the individuals in decision-making positions and with role-based power recognized there was a problem that needed to be addressed, and the recruiting procedures were affected by the tacit assumption that the best way to recruit was the way it had always been done.

The effort, spearheaded at the University of Michigan under the leadership of Dr. Abby Stewart, is demonstrating a shift in the culture after 8 years of implementation. Taking on the challenge of changing a culture with respect to recruitment and hiring practices required a multipronged approach. A number of factors are contributing to the early success of this effort.

First, the University of Michigan leadership clearly and articulately delivered messages of support for the initiative. They backed up their words with action by participating heavily in the early stages of the project, and they continue to be involved. They engaged the community through discussions, information collection about search practices, and substantive training sessions for faculty and administrators focused on elements that contribute to bias in the hiring process. They engaged well-respected academic leaders from across the organization to serve on the first iteration of the committee and to facilitate the discussions and group training. This required substantial dedication and commitment from all involved.

The coursework and training program developed are evidence based and focus on the multiple aspects of the hiring process. This participatory approach employed by the university provided a way for the vision to be disseminated through conversation and word of mouth from those participating to those not yet engaged. People serving on the search committees, through the training process, became more aware of their unconscious biases and were able to apply principles learned in order to change entrenched recruiting and hiring practices.

Clear guidance and criteria were developed and provided to assist the overall process. The criteria are accompanied by a series of uniform and standardized tools made available through a website that also provides a "toolkit" for chairs, deans, and other administrative leaders (University of Michigan, 2010a).

Over time, best practices were developed for the search process and this work became visible with a demonstrated increase in women hired.

Over the past several years, institutions and associations have been sponsoring meetings and workshops focused on developing best practices for supporting interdisciplinary research. Sharing information gained from these events can inform practices and approaches at the organizational level. Admittedly, there is not a complete collection of evidence-based approaches for developing the skills, attitudes, and sensibilities that are most important for collaborative work, but this is an exciting area of current focus at the National Cancer Institute, which is working to develop and disseminate such information (see the National Cancer Institute toolkit listed in Table 17.1).

Organizational leaders can communicate support for their messages about the value of interdisciplinary research by developing a shared vision. They can ask whether the institutional policies, approaches, and procedures in place support the institutional messages being shared. In addition, they can instruct committee members to routinely evaluate how well the existing criteria they are using or the charters that formed them align with institutional messages. If there are gaps or inconsistencies, they should have the power to revise them or recommend revisions when needed and should develop clear guidance for their implementation. In this way, the organization and its leaders can be assured that the vision being communicated from those at the highest levels is being carried out at all management and operational levels.

Take-Home Messages

Successful interdisciplinary collaboration is not possible without effective interdisciplinary communication. Effective interdisciplinary communication is inextricably linked to establishing institutional trust, which in turn is foundational for the following:

- *Establishing an institutional vision.* This can be done in a way that engages members of the organization through the creation of a shared vision, or it can alienate them.
- *Creating an environment where difference is an integral element of the organizational culture.* This requires making explicit not only that differences can and should be discussed but also that the knowledge gained from those discussions should be used as the foundation for developing solutions.
- *Attending to how power is used within an organization and recognizing its ties to trust.* Infrastructural power can play a significant role in contributing to the degree of institutional trust.
- *Taking responsibility as leaders for providing the organization with the information and tools it needs to achieve the organizational vision and goals.* One of those goals for many academic environments, currently, is the support of interdisciplinary research.

References

Association of American Medical Colleges. (2013). *Graduate Research, Education, and Training (GREAT) Group.* Retrieved from https://www.aamc.org/members/great/

Awamleh, R., & Gardner, W. L. (1999). Perceptions of leader charisma and effectiveness: The effects of vision content, delivery, and organizational performance. *Ledership Quarterly, 10,* 345–373.

Bachmann, R. (2010). Towards a context-sensitive approach to researching trust in inter-organizational relationships. In M. N. K. Saunders, D. Skinner, G. Dietz, N. Gillespie, & R. J Lewicki (Eds.), *Organizational trust: A cultural perspective* (pp. 87–106). Cambridge, UK: Cambridge University Press.

Barry, C. A., Britten, N., Barber, N., Bradley, C., & Stevenson, F. (1999). Using reflexivity to optimize teamwork in qualitative research. *Qualitative Health Research, 9*(1), 26–44.

Bateson, G., Jackson, D. D., Haley, J., & Weakland, J. (1956). Towards a theory of schizophrenia. *Behavioral Science, 1*, 251–263.

Bennett, L. M., & Gadlin, H. (2012). Collaboration and team science: From theory to practice. *Journal of Investigative Medicine, 60*(5), 768–775.

Bennett, L. M., Gadlin, H., & Levine-Finley, S. (2010, August). *Team science and collaboration: A field guide*. Bethesda, MD: National Institutes of Health. Retrieved from http://teamscience.nih.gov

Berndt, A. E. (2011). Developing collaborative research agreements. *Journal of Emergency Nursing, 37*(5), 497–498.

Blader, S. L., & Tyler, T. R. (2009). Testing and extending the group engagement model: Linkages between social identity, prodedural justice, economic outcomes, and extrarole behavior. *Journal of Applied Psychology, 94*, 445–464.

Bryant, A. (2011, December 31). Strive for results but never accolades. *New York Times*. Retrieved from http://www.nytimes.com/2012/01/01/business/john-donovan-of-att-on-seeking-results-instead-of-praise.html?pagewanted=all

Burbules, N. C., & Bruce, B. C. (2001). Theory and research on teaching as dialogue. In V. Richardson (Ed.), *Handbook of research on teaching* (4th ed.). Washington, DC: American Educational Resarch Association. Retrieved from http://faculty.education.illinois.edu/burbules/papers/dialogue.html

Burbules, N. C., & Rice, S. (1991). Dialogue across differences: Continuing the conversation. *Harvard Educational Review, 61*, 393–416.

Cohen, C. C., & Cohen, S. L. (2005). *Lab dynamics*. Woodbury, NY: Cold Spring Harbor Press.

Cummings, L. L., & Bromiley, P. (1996). The Organizational Trust Inventory (OTI): Development and validation. In R. M. Kramer & T. R. Tyler (Eds.), *Trust in organizations: Frontiers of theory and research* (pp. 68–89). Thousand Oaks, CA: Sage.

Curtin, C. (2008, March). Works well with others. *Genome Technology*, 36–42. Retrieved from http://www.genomeweb.com/works-well-others

Edmondson, A. C. (2003). Speaking up in the operating room: How team leaders promote learning in interdisciplinary action teams. *Journal of Management Studies, 40*(6), 1419–1452.

Eigenbrode, S. D., O'Rourke, M., Wulfhorst, J. D., Althoff, D. M., Goldberg, C. S., Merrill, K., et al. (2007). Employing philosophical dialogue in collaborative science. *Bioscience, 57*(1), 55–64.

Feder, M. E., & Madara, J. L. (2008). Evidence-based appointment and promotion of academic faculty at the University of Chicago. *Academic Medicine, 83*(1), 85–95.

Fiore, S. M. (2008). Interdisciplinarity as teamwork: How the science of teams can inform team science. *Small Group Research, 39*, 251–277.

French, J. P. R., Jr., & Raven, B. (1959). The bases of social power. In D. Cartwright (Ed.), *Studies in social power* (pp. 150–167). Ann Arbor: University of Michigan Press.

Frese, M., Beimel, S., & Schoenborn, S. (2003). Action training for charismatic leadership: Two evaluations of studies of a commercial training module on inspirational communication of a vision. *Personal Psychology, 56*, 671–697.

Garcia-Perez, A., Wyatt, R. G., & Gottesman, M. M. (2010). Changes in NIH criteria for tenure to reward clinical/translational teams. *Clinical and Translational Science, 3*(1), 4–5.

Gray, B. (2008a). Enhancing transdisciplinary research through collaborative leadership. *American Journal of Preventive Medicine, 35*(2), S124–S132.

Gray, B. (2008b). Intervening to improve interdisciplinary partnerships. In C. Huxham, S. Cropper, M. Ebers, & P. Ring (Eds.), *Handbook of interorganizational relations*. Thousand Oaks, CA: Sage.

Hackett, D., & Martin, C. L. (1993). *Facilitation skills for team leaders: Leading organized teams to greater productivity*: Menlo Park, CA: Crisp.

Hackett, E. J. (2005). Identity, control, and risk in research. *Social Studies of Science, 35*, 787–826.

Hill, L. (1994). Power dynamics in organizations. *Harvard Business School Note, 9-494-083*, 1–13.

Hofstede, G., Hofstede, G. J., & Minkov, M. (2010). *Cultures and organizations: Software of the mind*. New York: McGraw-Hill.

Jankowicz, A. D. (2003). *The easy guide to repertory grids*. Chichester, UK: Wiley.

Kellerman, B. (2006). When should a leader apologize—and when not? *Harvard Business Review, 84*, 72–81.

Kelly, G. A. (1955). *The psychology of personal constructs*. New York: Norton.

Keyton, J. (1999). Relational communication in groups. In L. R. Frey, D. Gouran, & M. S. Poole (Eds.), *The handbook of group communication theory and research* (pp. 192–222). Thousand Oaks, CA: Sage.

Klein, J. T. (2010). *Creating interdisciplinary campus cultures: A model for strength and sustainability*. San Francisco: Jossey-Bass.

Kramer, R. M., & Lewicki, R. J. (2010). Repairing and enhancing trust: Approaches to reducing organizational trust deficits. *Academy of Management Annals, 4*, 245–277.

Lewicki, R. J. (2006). Trust and distrust. In A. K. Schneider & C. Honeyman (Eds.), *The Negotiator's Fieldbook* (pp. 191–202). Washington, DC: American Bar Association.

Mann, M. (1984). The autonomous power of the state: Its origins, mechanisms and results. *Archives Européennes de Sociologie, 25*, 185–213.

Mayer, B. (1987, Summer). The dynamics of power in mediation and negotiation. *Mediation Quarterly, 16*, 75–86.

National Cancer Institute. (2012). *Team Science Toolkit*. Retrieved from https://www.teamsciencetoolkit.cancer.gov/public/home.aspx?js=1

Northwestern University. (2012). *TeamScience training modules*. Retrieved September 15, 2012, from http://www.teamscience.net/

Nyhan, R. C., & Marlowe, H. A., Jr. (1997). Development and psychometric properties of the Organizational Trust Inventory. *Evaluation Review, 21*, 614–635.

O'Connell, D., Hickerson, K., & Pillutla, A. (2011). Organizational visioning: An integrative review. *Group and Organizational Management, 36*, 102–125.

Olson, G., & Olson, J. (2012). *Collaboration Success Wizard*. Retrieved March 26, 2012, from http://hana.ics.uci.edu/wizard/

Pearson, S. D., & Raeke, L. H. (2000). Patients' trust in physicians: Many theories, few measures, and little data. *Journal of General Internal Medicine, 15*(7), 509–513.

Rabinow, P. (1999). *French DNA: Trouble in purgatory*. Chicago: University of Chicago Press.

Reina, D. S., & Reina, M. L. (2006). *Trust and betrayal in the workplace* (2nd ed.). San Francisco: Berrett-Koehler.

Rhoten, D. (2004, Spring). Interdisciplinary research: Trend or transition. *Social Science Research*, 6–11.

Rikakis, T. (2009, October 18–21). *Innovative faculty evaluation criteria for incentivizing high-impact interdisciplinary collaboration.* Paper presented at the Frontiers in Education Conference, 39th IEEE, Tempe, AZ.

Rock, D. (2008). SCARF: A brain-based model for collaborating with and influencing others. *NeuroLeadership Journal, 1,* 1–9.

Salazar, M. R., Lant, T. K., Fiore, S. M., & Salas, E. (2012). Facilitating innovation in diverse science teams through integrative capacity. *Small Group Research, 43,* 527–558. doi:10.1177/1046496412453622

Shrum, W., Genuth, J., & Chompalov, I. (2007). *Structures of scientific collaboration.* Boston: MIT Press.

Shuffler, M. L., DiazGranados, D., & Salas, E. (2011). There's a science for that: Team development interventions in organizations. *Current Directions in Psychological Science, 20*(6), 365–372.

Stanford University. (2012). *Bio-X: Supports interdisciplinary research.* Retrieved from http://biox.stanford.edu/

Stokols, D. (2006). Toward a science of transdisciplinary action research. *American Journal of Community Psychology, 38*(1–2), 63–77. doi:10.1007/s10464-006-9060-5

Tamm, J. W., & Lyuet, R. J. (2005). *Radical collaboration: Five essential skills to overcome defensiveness and build successful relationships.* New York: HarperCollins.

Thoms, P., & Greenberger, D. B. (1998). A test of vision training and potential antecedents to leaders' visioning ability. *Human Resource Development Quarterly, 9,* 3–19.

Tyler, T. R., & De Cremer, D. (2005). Process-based leadership: Fair procedures and reactions to organizational change. *Leadership Quarterly, 16*(4), 529–545.

University of Michigan. (2010a). *ADVANCE "toolkit" for deans, chairs, and other administrative leaders.* Retrieved March 15, 2012, from http://sitemaker.umich.edu/advance/_toolkit_

University of Michigan. (2010b). *Campus-wide climate reports for faculty.* Retrieved September 15, 2012, from http://sitemaker.umich.edu/advance/campus-wide_climate_for_faculty

University of Southern California, University Committee on Appointments, Promotions and Tenure. (2011, January). *UCAPT manual.* Los Angeles: Author. Retrieved September 15, 2012, from http://www.usc.edu/academe/faculty/private/1011/UCAPT_Manual_Jan_2011_for_posting.pdf

PART V

Conclusion

18

From Toolbox to Big Science Project

A Bold Proposal

◆ Gabriele Bammer

Those involved in interdisciplinary research and education are, by and large, not well versed in the insights available from the communications field, so enhancing links can be a win-win situation for all. Indeed, this disconnect is typical of the fragmentation that characterises interdisciplinarity. Interdisciplinary research and education is not only poorly connected with relevant aspects of communication, such as dialogue and practice-research engagement, but is also not able to effectively transmit insights between different projects or education programs. The fragmentation is compounded by the unorganized diversity of interdisciplinarity. There are different kinds of interdisciplinary research and education, which require different forms of communication. For example, one interdisciplinary researcher bringing together insights from several disciplines engages in different processes from a large, diverse team of disciplinary experts and stakeholders. The chapter begins by describing these problems of fragmentation and unorganized diversity.

Overcoming these challenges requires bringing together comprehensive collections of concepts and methods useful for interdisciplinary investigations, as well as case studies to illustrate them. This chapter describes the development of a compilation of dialogue methods and the issues this raised. In particular, compilations need to be solidly anchored in theory and practice, and the chapter describes how this could be aided by developing a new discipline—Integration and Implementation Sciences, or I2S. Three core domains and a five-question framework that define the discipline and provide the scaffold for the compilations of concepts, methods, and case studies are outlined. Building a new discipline is a bold proposal requiring an effort on the scale of a Big Science project.

Introduction

Two objectives motivate this chapter. The first is to argue that enhancing interdisciplinarity, including the essential ingredient of interdisciplinary communication, requires ready access to everything relevant that we have learned from theory and practice—in other words, comprehensive compilations of concepts, methods, and case studies. The second is to stimulate discussion about how best to organize these compilations. Specifically, I argue that disciplines are the best way we currently have for systematizing knowledge and that, therefore, a new discipline is warranted, which I propose to call Integration and Implementation Sciences (I2S).

My starting point is as someone with a long interest in interdisciplinarity who has been frustrated by the fragmentation of the knowledge needed to undertake such research and education. For example, links between groups interested in various aspects of communication, such as dialogue, practice-research engagement, advocacy, conflict resolution, negotiation, and consensus development remain weak. Further, practice-based groups often have little knowledge about theoretical developments that could improve their activities. The opposite also holds in that those conducting experiments or building theory in other ways often have little insight into the complexities of real-world interdisciplinary communication issues.

This chapter is written from the perspective of an outsider to the communications field and aims both to stimulate interest in promoting linkages between diverse, related groups and to provide a mechanism by which this can occur. The goal is to replace the current fragmentation and unorganized diversity with a new discipline built by a systematic combination of forces. In the next section of this chapter I spell out the challenges that we face currently, when there is limited cross-fertilization between bodies of knowledge relevant to interdisciplinarity. The remaining sections of the chapter deal with the proposed way forward.

The Problems of Fragmentation and Unorganized Diversity

One of the substantial challenges for interdisciplinary research and education is that there is currently no established way to capture the wealth of experience so it can be transmitted and built on. Instead, lessons from previous interdisciplinary investigations and insights gained in teaching languish undocumented in people's heads or scattered in the published and grey literatures. As a consequence, it has not been possible to institute a substantial, internationally accepted methodology for interdisciplinary communication or other aspects of interdisciplinary research and teaching.

An important manifestation of fragmentation is that concepts and methods developed in one area of endeavor—say, in tackling environmental problems—are rarely picked up by those researching and teaching in a different field, such as population health or policing. For example, the idea of "adaptive management"[1] is well known in the environmental field but has hardly been acknowledged elsewhere. Fragmentation has two important consequences. One is that there is often "reinvention of the wheel," with individual research groups independently developing concepts and methods similar to ones already used by others. The other consequence is that those using substandard methods struggle on, oblivious to improvements that could markedly enhance their research or teaching practice.

It is heartening to see those developing new methodologies starting to pay conscious attention to this problem. The Toolbox method for sharing worldviews about research (see Chap. 11, this volume) was developed in the context of an environmental investigation, but its originators are now actively fostering its use in other areas, with particular advances in the health domain (Schnapp, Rotschy, Hall, Crowley, & O'Rourke, 2012).

The fragmentation issues are exacerbated by the multiple forms of teaching and research practice encompassed by the word *interdisciplinarity* (Bammer, 2012). Let us take three examples from research. For instance, *interdisciplinarity* can refer to one researcher drawing on ideas and methods from two or more disciplines to address a specific problem, such as bringing together insights from sociology, anthropology, and psychology to study crime victimisation. In addition, it is the term used when researchers and business partners collaborate to invent a new commercial product or process, such as a new blood pressure drug or a mineral extraction technique that can be used in mining. It also covers major team efforts on complex problems (such as global warming or obesity) with implications for

---

[1]Adaptive management involves learning by doing, but "adds an explicit, deliberate, and formal dimension to framing questions and problems, undertaking experimentation and testing, critically processing the results, and reassessing the policy context that originally triggered the investigation in light of the newly acquired knowledge" (Stankey, Clark, & Bormann, 2005, p. 7).

government policy and how we live, and where experts from multiple disciplines, stakeholders, and end users are brought together. These three kinds of research require different skills with obvious ramifications for undergraduate and graduate teaching. Yet recognition of these important variations and their consequences for capacity building is lacking in both the research and education spheres. A significant consequence is that there is a diverse range of research and educational practice that is not clearly specified and defined. This, in turn, results in confusion about the concepts and methods required to underpin different kinds of research practice, as well as about what it is most useful to teach in various "interdisciplinary" courses. I refer to this as "unorganized diversity." Of particular relevance here is that the key communication issues vary with different types of interdisciplinarity. Key parameters include the number of people involved and how different their perspectives are; hence, communication issues are different for small groups versus large ones and for groups where perspectives are similar versus those where they vary, and perhaps even conflict.

So far, I have laid out two key problems—fragmentation and unorganized diversity—that hinder progress in interdisciplinary research and teaching and impede the widespread application of the sterling research in the communications field. Let us now turn to possible ways forward.

Comprehensive Compilations of Concepts, Methods, and Case Studies

One way to overcome fragmentation is to develop comprehensive compilations that bring together concepts and methods useful for interdisciplinary investigations, as well as case studies to illustrate them.[2] For a compilation to be more than a list, the material needs to be organized, and deciding on an agreed way to do this involves confronting all the challenges of fragmentation and unorganized diversity head-on.

Let me illustrate these points using a book that gathered 14 dialogue methods and illustrative case studies (McDonald, Bammer, & Deane, 2009). We were interested in dialogue methods to combine insights about a problem from different disciplines and stakeholders—in other words, using conversation to "jointly create meaning and shared understanding" (Franco, 2006, p. 814). The first thing to say is that formal methods are not required in every interdisciplinary situation. They are not necessary for the types of interdisciplinarity that involve only one person or a small group with similar perspectives. Structured methods come into their own when

---

[2]As I will argue below, it will be important that these compilations are systematic in their organization. To that end, reflection on the nature of concepts and methods will be useful, and that is modelled for concepts in Chapters 3 and 10 of this volume.

the interdisciplinary team is large and/or has diverse outlooks, as they help ensure that all perspectives are appropriately heard and included.

To assemble the book, we searched the literature, from which we identified the 14 methods suitable for interdisciplinary dialogue. Some methods are broadly useful, bringing together different people's judgments about an issue. They include consensus conference,[3] Delphi technique,[4] and nominal group technique.[5] For example, the Delphi technique was used to develop an implementation plan for sustainability policies at a Canadian university, drawing on the judgments of knowledgeable representatives of students, staff, faculty, and administrators (Wright, 2006).

Other dialogue methods are useful for specific tasks, such as combining different visions about an issue (appreciative enquiry[6]) or reconciling various interests (principled negotiation[7]). For instance, a U.K. research team used appreciative inquiry to engage older people's groups, the hospital trust, voluntary agencies, and others to figure out how better to meet the needs of the elderly in transition from hospital back to their own homes. There were diverse visions for improved post-hospital experiences—for example, regarding flexible care, individual carer responsibility, and process coordination—all of which were drawn together using the method (Reed, Pearson, Douglas, Swinburne, & Wilding, 2002).

Reviewing all the methods together demonstrated that they could accommodate different requirements and preferences for engagement of disciplinary and stakeholder expertise. For instance, some methods, such as the consensus development panel,[8] are most suitable for tasks requiring discipline-based

---

[3]A consensus conference involves a representative sample of "non-expert, nonpartisan" citizens, and they are provided with written evidence and access to experts to deliberate on "important (and typically complex) social, technological, planning and/or policy issues" (McDonald et al., 2009, p. 29).

[4]The Delphi technique involves "the systematic solicitation and collation of judgments on a particular topic through a set of carefully designed sequential questionnaires interspersed with summarized information and feedback of opinions derived from earlier responses" (Delbecq et al., 1975, p. 10; as cited in McDonald et al., 2009, p. 41).

[5]Nominal group technique involves generating, recording, discussing, and voting on ideas. The structure aims to give everyone an equal say (McDonald et al., 2009).

[6]Appreciative enquiry focuses "on what has worked well within a team or organisation, in contrast to the more common approach of identifying problems (what has not worked well) and analysing these" (McDonald et al., 2009, p. 93).

[7]Principled negotiation is the underpinning of "getting to yes" (Fisher, Ury, & Patton, 1991). It has four steps: (1) separate the people from the problem; (2) focus on interests, not positions; (3) generate a variety of possibilities before deciding what to do; and (4) insist that the results be based on some objective standard.

[8]A consensus development panel involves scoping, exploring, assessing, and synthesizing scientific evidence, especially in areas where there is controversy (McDonald et al., 2009).

experts only. An example of its use was bringing together discipline-based experts to develop a "state-of-the-science" statement on prevention, cessation, and control of tobacco smoking (National Institutes of Health State-of-the-Science Panel, 2006). Other techniques, such as the citizens' jury,[9] work best for bringing together stakeholder views. An illustration is its application in formulating a community decision on the future of a former local wetland by assisting 16 representative citizen stakeholders to come to a judgment based on the best available evidence (Aldred & Jacobs, 2000). Still others are designed to combine discipline-based and stakeholder knowledge. This is demonstrated by open space technology,[10] which has been used for a range of problems, including putting participants from various organizations on an equal footing in generating ideas and plans for the development of the public health workforce in the United Kingdom (Brocklehurst, Hook, Bond, & Goodwin, 2005).

Some methods, such as consensus conference and nominal group technique, are designed for small numbers (12–25), while others, such as future search conferences[11] and most significant change technique,[12] can accommodate scores to hundreds. Some require significant preparation; others do not. And each has particular strengths and limitations (McDonald et al., 2009).

We looked for examples of how these techniques had been applied in four areas: environment, public health, security, and technological innovation. It is worth noting that finding good case examples was difficult. Most came from public health (seven examples), followed by environment (five examples), technological innovation (three examples), and security (two examples). For 10 of the methods, we found only one example of application in any of these topic areas. The Delphi technique alone had examples in each of the four areas.

Producing this book illustrated that searching out techniques was relatively straightforward, although finding cases from a range of different areas was not. This provides a further example of the problem of fragmentation, as many dialogue methods seem to be used in only limited areas of application.

------

[9]A citizens' jury involves "providing the citizens with information from subject-matter experts, advocates and other stakeholders and then bringing together the range of judgments of the citizens into a single judgment" (McDonald et al., 2009, p. 20).

[10]Open space technology assists groups of people to self-organise to "identify and explore issues, identify opportunities for change and identify and set priorities among action steps to achieve desired goals" (McDonald et al., 2009, p. 70).

[11]Future search conferences are "large-group planning conferences, using face-to-face dialogue to develop plans, including the identification of action steps. They begin with a focus on visions and use these to guide the proposals for action" (McDonald et al., 2009, p. 51).

[12]Most significant change technique focuses on program improvement through "the generation, analysis and use of stories" (McDonald et al., 2009, p. 57).

Even more instructive were the challenges we faced when we sought to group the methods. We were unable to find a ready-made classification of dialogue methods that was applicable to knowledge synthesis. As our reading of the literature progressed, we toggled between induction and deduction to develop a list of the different kinds of knowledge relevant in interdisciplinary projects—namely, "facts, judgments, visions, values, interests, epistemologies, time scales, geographical scales and world views" (McDonald et al., 2009, p. 3). Similarly, we invented our own way of characterising dialogue methods, reflected in the structure of the above discussion.

We then started to consider how we could test and improve our classification. What we have done so far is to see if there is an identifiable college of peers experienced in dialogue methods who could be called on to further develop the classification. We thought they might also be a source of additional techniques and case examples. We began by contacting authors of the case studies used in the book (and people they referred us to), interviewing 29 by telephone. An important discovery was that most tended to be familiar with, and deploy, only one dialogue method (although caution is needed because the sample is small). Nevertheless, it is useful to draw an analogy. If we had contacted a similar group of researchers who do quantitative research, we would not have expected them to be proficient in, and employ, only one statistical method, such as a t-test or even something more sophisticated such as structural equation modelling. A narrow repertoire of methods has two possible consequences: Either the research is constrained to questions that can be addressed with the one analysis method, or at times the method is used in a less optimum way or inappropriately. Let me hasten to add that the point here is not to be critical of researchers who use dialogue methods. Instead, this provides another illustration of the consequences of fragmentation. Before our book, there was no readily available resource that would make it easy for them to access other methods. Interestingly, in developing a compilation of modelling methods that is currently under way, colleague Jen Badham and I are finding similar narrow sets of expertise among modellers.[13]

It certainly seems that there is much to be gained from putting effort into developing comprehensive compilations of concepts, methods, and case studies relevant to interdisciplinary communication, as well as other aspects of interdisciplinary research. The challenge is to make them more than lists, which involves also developing useful classifications. If we want to see interdisciplinary research thrive and prosper, we need to move in this direction.[14]

---

[13]For more on dialogue and dialogue methods in this volume, see Chapters 2, 5, 11, and 12.

[14]Examples of case studies that address aspects of interdisciplinary communication and collaboration are included in Part II of this volume. These include chapters that address "big-program" interdisciplinary scientific research (Chap. 7) and transdisciplinary research involving stakeholders (Chaps. 8 and 9). In Part I, Chapter 4 supplies a rich discussion of training programs for those who wish to engage in transdisciplinary research.

A New Discipline of Integration and Implementation Sciences (I2S)

The challenge of how to improve interdisciplinary research systemically has exercised my thinking for several years. I propose that developing compilations is not enough; they need to be solidly anchored in theory and practice, which is exactly what a discipline provides (Bammer, 2013). My focus has been on interdisciplinary research rather than teaching, especially the type of research that involves large diverse teams tackling complex, real-world problems. The framework provided here aims to help such research teams undertake their investigations more efficiently and effectively, by helping them think about all aspects of their project and providing easy access to all the tools they need (e.g., concepts, methods, and case studies).

Before moving on to describe the proposed structure for the discipline, it is important to acknowledge that for some the idea of building a discipline to underpin interdisciplinarity will seem counterintuitive, even bizarre. Nevertheless, the exercise of thinking through how the knowledge of interest here could be structured in a discipline is instructive whether or not the idea of a discipline is supported. The aim is to overcome the problem that, currently, thinking about interdisciplinarity is often unsystematic, unclear, and very limited. The exercise of thinking through an underpinning discipline can be tackled in various ways—for example, developing a consensus on what every interdisciplinary researcher should know (analogous to thinking about what every sociologist or chemist should know). This book provides a useful starting point in working through what every interdisciplinary researcher and educator should know about collaboration and communication. It is also useful to ask what every communication scholar should know about interdisciplinarity. The point here is that thought experiments and exercises along these lines will help each of us clarify our approaches to interdisciplinary research and education and expose the similarities and differences between us.

I propose that a discipline to support this type of research has three domains, each of which is structured around five questions. Let us deal with the domains first.

Domain 1 is the one most commonly associated with interdisciplinarity—namely, bringing together knowledge from different disciplines.[15] I expand this to also include relevant stakeholder perspectives, where stakeholders include two broad groups: those affected by the problem of interest and those in a position to act on the problem. For example, the World Commission on Dams (2000) worked with people who had been displaced because of dams and those whose livelihoods had been impacted (such interaction

---

[15]This "bringing together," or *integration*, of knowledge is typically taken to require common ground; for an alternative perspective on the role common ground can play in this domain, see Chapter 5, this volume.

usually occurred through relevant nongovernmental organizations), as well as "government agencies, ... the dam construction industry, the export credit agencies and private investors, and the international development community" who were in a position to act on dams (p. viii). Interdisciplinary communication is critical to understanding and accommodating this range of perspectives.[16]

While few would argue with the necessity of bringing together what is known about a problem, the need to understand and manage what we don't know is less well recognised. This second domain of I2S is the most challenging, because thinking about unknowns is not well developed. Most researchers and higher education teachers have received a discipline-based education, the hallmark of which is to carve out a specific, productive unknown to work on and to banish the rest from consideration. In other words, unknowns are seen as the substrate for knowledge production. While this has been outstandingly productive, it has also led to a blind spot when it comes to considering unknowns more comprehensively. In particular, not all unknowns are tractable, new unknowns arise all the time, unknowns can be beneficial, and, significantly, there can never be enough researchers to investigate all the researchable unknowns. From the perspective of acting on a problem, therefore, there may be critical gaps resulting from issues that do not come into the domain of a discipline or have been banished in the various disciplinary approaches. Furthermore, there are disciplinary and stakeholder differences in dealing with unknowns, and these also have to be synthesized. The relevance for interdisciplinary communication is profound. Ways of discussing the unknown are still in their infancy, as is recognition that different disciplines and stakeholder groups deal with unknowns differently and that this can be a block to communication (Bammer & Smithson, 2008). The default position of researchers and educators tends to be to get rid of unknowns, either by studying them (to turn them into knowledge) or by classifying them as irrelevant or unimportant. Helping interdisciplinarians move to a more nuanced understanding of unknowns and different ways of dealing with them is a major communications challenge.

The third I2S domain is to support policy and practice change with a combination of the best available knowledge plus the most advanced ways of understanding and managing the remaining unknowns.[17] The focus in this domain is identifying who is in a position to take action, what support they need (in terms of knowledge and appreciation of unknowns), and how best to make that information available. Assessment is needed, for example, about whether action is required from government, business, or civil society, or perhaps from a combination of these. Further appraisal is then of the

---

[16]For additional examples of collaborations involving stakeholder perspectives, see Chapters 8 and 9 in this volume.

[17]Current notions of evidence-based policy, commercialization, and practice-research engagement tend to focus only on knowledge and ignore unknowns.

level inside, say, government, at which decisions are taken, and within those levels where individuals or committees or other units will be influential. Having some appreciation of the administrative processes under which these individuals, committees, and others operate is also helpful. Providing them with the best possible understanding of the situation involves not only being responsive to what they *want* to know but also figuring out if there are things they are unaware of that they *need* to know. In addition, consideration has to be given to the best ways of getting information to them, such as a personal briefing, seminar invitation, or via the media. These are all critical interdisciplinary communication issues.

In summary, therefore, I2S comprises three domains:

1. Synthesising disciplinary and stakeholder knowledge

2. Understanding and managing diverse unknowns

3. Providing integrated research support (i.e., combining synthesized knowledge with a solid appreciation of remaining unknowns) for policy and practice change

The aim is to ensure that large, diverse research teams tackling complex real-world problems consider different relevant types of knowledge, the likely importance and impact of remaining unknowns, and how they can use their research to support policy and practice change.

The second part of the disciplinary structure is a framework that can be applied in each domain (described next) and that provides a systematic way for teams to plan and report research on complex real-world problems. It also provides the scaffold for compilations of concepts, methods, and case studies, which is relevant to building the discipline of I2S. Developing the discipline, especially populating it with the full array of concepts and methods that interdisciplinary research has developed, along with an extensive range of illustrative case studies, requires a major commitment, analogous to that given to Big Science projects such as developing the atomic bomb or unraveling the human genome. In describing the framework, I also outline the magnitude of the task required to populate it with all the available concepts, methods, and case studies.

A Five-Question Framework

As outlined earlier, there is currently no agreed, systematic way to capture the wealth of experience gained in interdisciplinary research and teaching so it can be transmitted and built on. I propose that five questions provide a useful framework for this purpose, and describe them here as applied to the first domain—namely, synthesizing disciplinary and stakeholder knowledge. (The five-question framework can also be adapted to the other two domains of I2S, allowing them to be covered systematically.) The questions are as follows:

1. What is the synthesis of disciplinary and stakeholder knowledge aiming to achieve, and who is intended to benefit?

2. Which disciplinary and stakeholder knowledge is synthesized?

3. How is the disciplinary and stakeholder knowledge synthesized, by whom, and when?

4. What circumstances might influence the synthesis of disciplinary and stakeholder knowledge?

5. What is the result of the synthesis of disciplinary and stakeholder knowledge?

While these questions look simple, they encompass considerable methodological depth, which is fleshed out below. As a set, the questions can be used to plan new research or to describe ongoing or completed research. The order of the questions is not fixed. Sometimes it may be useful, for example, to describe the context first or to consider Questions 2 and 3 together. Let us now deal with each question in turn and consider the concepts, methods, and case studies to be collected in a Big Science–type undertaking.

Question 1: What is the synthesis of disciplinary and stakeholder knowledge aiming to achieve, and who is intended to benefit?

From the perspective of research teams, the purpose of this question is to help them think specifically about their objectives and beneficiaries so they can target their efforts most effectively. This is important for two reasons. First, teams have often not thought clearly about what they are trying to achieve and find it very helpful to be pushed to do so. Second, for teams to choose the most appropriate options in terms of concepts, methods, and case examples, they need to have well-formulated goals.

What the synthesis of disciplinary and stakeholder knowledge is aiming to achieve is more comprehensive insight into the problem by bringing together what is already known, as well as what can be readily ascertained through new research. It sets out to draw on a diverse range of relevant disciplines and stakeholders. For this question, "who is intended to benefit" is defined as those whose knowledge is included in the synthesis.

From the perspective of developing compilations to provide tools for these research teams and to develop the discipline of I2S, the primary task motivated by this question is to gather case examples demonstrating different ways of describing the knowledge synthesis purpose, and the beneficiaries (i.e., which perspectives were included).

Question 2: Which disciplinary and stakeholder knowledge is synthesized?

For this question, I suggest that there are six key, interrelated categories of concepts and methods: taking a systems view, scoping, boundary setting, framing, dealing with values, and harnessing or managing differences. Again, these can help the research team think systematically about its investigations, as well as providing the categories under which to collect concepts, methods, and case studies. Let us deal with each in turn.

Taking a Systems View

Systems thinking allows the real-world problem to be placed center stage and makes it feasible to examine a range of discipline-based and stakeholder perspectives in a coherent and systematic way. It involves looking at the inter-relationships between various aspects of the problem, as well as the broader issues the problem relates to and those interconnections. A systems view about heroin use, for example, involves examining the interactions between users, their families, treatment providers, police, and the community at large, with different foci on crime, social functioning, health, and so on. It also means examining the broader context of the heroin supply system—the drug cartels, supply lines, and international law enforcement. It is important to note, however, that it is impossible to focus on the *whole* problem at once. Instead, different systems approaches emphasise different aspects of the whole. For instance, some are useful for seeing the big picture (e.g., general systems approaches; Mesarovic, 1964), others can clarify driving forces (e.g., causal loop diagrams and system dynamics modelling; Sterman, 2000), and still others look at combining different worldviews (e.g., soft systems thinking; Checkland, 1984). From the perspective of compilations, the task is to collect case examples illustrating how different systems approaches are useful for describing a complex problem and for bringing together discipline-based and stakeholder knowledge (see Badham, 2010, for a first attempt).

Scoping

From the perspective of researchers looking to better understand a problem, scoping is a process to determine the full range of those who have something relevant to contribute. It is a critical step in deciding which systems approach to take, as well as which disciplines and stakeholders to involve. Scoping moves those planning the investigation beyond focusing only on what they know (based on their own interests and expertise) to considering the problem more broadly. If scoping does not occur, critical issues may be ignored. If we consider the 1940s project of building the atomic bomb, for example, the domination of physical scientists, engineers, and the military meant that significant environmental, social, and health aspects were not considered, leading to ongoing difficulties in those areas.

The compilation task is to gather together literature and undocumented practical experience providing concepts for knowledge scoping, methods for undertaking it, and illustrative case examples.

Boundary Setting

The point of scoping is to illuminate a range of options for developing a better understanding of a problem. Practicalities, however, dictate that everything cannot be included in the investigation, so boundaries must be set. This requires systematic thinking about what can best be done with the available time, money, and person power. Boundaries define not only what is included and excluded but also which issues are more central and which are marginal (Midgley, 2000). Both inclusion/exclusion and centrality are relevant to which disciplines and stakeholders are involved in the knowledge synthesis, what they are invited to contribute, and how. This translates into allocation of resources, with the lion's share going to the disciplines and stakeholders deemed to be most central. The point of linking scoping and boundary setting is that it allows the most critical issues to be identified and addressed.

To illustrate this, let us imagine a research project about the factors leading to heroin use. Scoping involves considering all the different ways of tackling this problem, such as looking at genetic predispositions, individual character traits, family influences, peer-group pressure, drug availability, and societal norms. It is immediately apparent that covering all these would be a massive undertaking. Decisions will have to be made about what can be done with the available funding, time, and personnel. But let us also imagine (to take an extreme example) that one of the research team is interested in parenting and sport. While the resource is available to address that aspect of the problem, it is unlikely to be central, and the research team will make a better contribution to understanding the problem by choosing an aspect identified through the scoping process. The needs of the problem, not just the available resources, should drive what is undertaken.

Elements of scoping and boundary setting occur in all research, usually intuitively. This framework makes the decision process explicit, allowing it to be evaluated and improved in the future. The compilation task is to collate published and unpublished concepts and methods for boundary setting, along with case examples that emphasise how and why decisions were made.

Framing

The frame is the way the problem is presented and is a key communication issue. The language used to describe the problem is powerful. For example, people who inject illicit drugs can be referred to as "dirty junkies," "cool nonconformists," or "sons and daughters who have lost their way." Critically, the problem will be framed by the way it is described, regardless of whether conscious attention is paid to this process. The idea here is to raise awareness of the importance of framing so the research team can accurately convey what it is setting out to do. The compilation task is to draw together useful concepts and practical methods for framing, along with case examples of when it has worked well and when it has failed.

Dealing With Values

The values brought to the research will both determine and reflect the systems approach used, the way the problem is scoped, and the boundaries set, as well as how the problem is framed. In addition, there are likely to be several sets of values in play at the same time: values about the problem, about research, and even about the approach that should be taken to values. The task here is to examine interactions between values and knowledge synthesis. For example, are the team's values generating important blind spots about incorporating some kinds of knowledge, or leading to disproportionate emphasis on the perspectives of some stakeholders at the expense of others? The compilation task is to gather case examples that illustrate different experiences in bringing values into play and their consequences for the knowledge synthesis.

Harnessing and Managing Differences

Bringing together different disciplinary and stakeholder perspectives is about more than combining different relevant "facts." Among those involved, there will also be differences in, for example, visions for addressing the problem, worldviews about the problem, epistemological approaches to research, working habits, career goals, and so on. The challenge is to identify and deal separately with two types of differences:

1. Those relevant to developing a rich appreciation of the problem, which need to be harnessed as part of the knowledge synthesis

2. Those that may get in the way, which need to be managed so that they do not negatively impact the knowledge synthesis (Bammer, 2008)

For example, bringing together two dissimilar worldviews is often a difference to be harnessed, whereas personality clashes involve differences to be managed. The compilation task involves gathering together concepts and methods for understanding differences, as well as for harnessing and managing them, along with illustrative case examples.

Before moving on to the next question, it is important to note that in practice the implementation of the six categories of concepts and methods is not linear. Instead, the categories must be considered together and iteratively, as each influences the others. Research is messy, and it is difficult to have clear definitions, aims, and processes up front. The reality of iteration and messiness does not, however, contradict the need for a systematic approach. Indeed, the framework provides a way through.

Question 3: How is disciplinary and stakeholder knowledge synthesized, by whom, and when?

There have been surprisingly few attempts to identify, let alone classify, methods for addressing this question. I propose three classes:

- Dialogue based
- Model, product, or vision based
- Common metric based

Dialogue-based methods were discussed earlier, so the presentation here will focus on the other two categories, followed by a brief overview of who undertakes the synthesis and when in the research process it occurs.

Model-, product-, and vision-based methods are related, as they use a specific goal as the focus for synthesis. Model-based methods use the development of a conceptual or mathematical representation of a problem as the "device" for bringing together disciplinary and stakeholder knowledge. In other words, building the model is used to stimulate communication and capture the shared understandings.[18] Building a product and implementing a vision both rely on the same principle in that the focused task brings different understandings together. The development of the atomic bomb is an exemplar of product-based synthesis. This effort combined knowledge from physical scientists, engineers, the military, and private industry (Rhodes, 1986). The World Commission on Dams framework for decision making about future dams is an example of vision-based synthesis. A guiding ideal was proposed for bringing together different perspectives and for deciding on action—namely, a globally accepted framework of norms about human rights and economic cooperation, as well as social development and environment. These were derived from U.N. declarations and principles (World Commission on Dams, 2000).

Common metric–based methods rely on single measures that can be employed to encapsulate the range of relevant disciplinary and stakeholder knowledge about the problem. The best-known and most widely used common metric is monetary value. Synthesis can then be based on simple arithmetic or more complex manipulations, such as cost-benefit analysis. Other common metrics that have been developed and used for environmental problems include the area of land necessary to sustain a given level of resource consumption and waste assimilation (i.e., ecological footprint;

---

[18]For a relevant case study, see Chapter 7, this volume; for more on modelling methods, see Chapter 13.

Wackernagel & Rees, 1996) and measures of carbon dioxide equivalent (Michaelowa & Koch, 2001). For health problems, common metrics include disability-adjusted life-years and quality-adjusted life-years (Murray, Salomon, & Mathers, 2000). An example of the use of the ecological footprint for knowledge synthesis is a collaboration between university-based researchers and the Cardiff Council in the United Kingdom to develop local government policies and practice on sustainability (Cardiff Council, 2005; Collins & Flynn, 2005, 2007; Collins, Flynn, Wiedmann, & Barrett, 2006).

Let us move on now to the question of who undertakes the synthesis.[19] It is often assumed that the synthesis should be a group process. However, even though perspectives are drawn from researchers representing a number of different disciplines and from various stakeholder groups, each contributor does not necessarily have to be involved in bringing the knowledge together. The options for undertaking the synthesis are to involve the whole group or a subgroup or for it to be the task of an individual. In the last case, the synthesizer is often the research leader. Each of these options has advantages and disadvantages. For example, a disadvantage of involving the whole team is that the time it takes can be very demanding. A disadvantage of the synthesis being undertaken by the team leader is that one person is likely to have only a limited grasp of some aspects of the project.

An additional consideration for undertaking knowledge synthesis is when it will be carried out. Just as there is often an assumption that synthesis will be a whole group process, some people presume that it will occur at the end of the research, while others suppose that it must be established right from the beginning. But again there is a range of options, each with advantages and disadvantages.

The compilation tasks are to identify and catalogue the full range of methods that have been used for knowledge synthesis, as well as their conceptual bases and case examples of their application. Collected case examples should reflect the full range of options for who conducts the knowledge synthesis and when in the research process this occurred.

Question 4: What circumstances might influence the synthesis of disciplinary and stakeholder knowledge?

There are at least three areas to be considered here:

1. The overall context of the problem, which comprises the circumstances that led to the research and that may be influential during its conduct, such as the problem's history, the geographical locations in which it occurs, and cultural differences between those affected and those charged with responding to the problem

---

[19]For a relevant case study, see Chapter 7, this volume.

2. The sources of authorization or legitimacy for the knowledge synthesis and how they affect what is investigated

3. The organizational facilitators of, and barriers to, undertaking the synthesis of disciplinary and stakeholder knowledge[20]

Let us begin with overall context and return to the building of the atomic bomb. The important contextual factor was World War II (1939–1945), which explains why, in scoping the problem, there was minimal attention to social, environmental, and health impacts. In the circumstances of a major war, including these aspects in the synthesis was not a high priority. The general challenge is to find useful starting points for taking context into account in planning knowledge synthesis—in other words, figuring out which circumstances are likely to be most pertinent and how to address them.

Moving on to authorization, the sources of legitimacy are usually closely tied to the finances. For most research, receiving support from a recognised funding source is all that is needed for an investigation to be seen as legitimate and to go ahead. However, in certain cases, such as when projects are large scale or politically sensitive, authorization may be more complex. In particular, obtaining backing from influential organizations or individuals may be critical for the research to proceed. However, as well as providing legitimacy, both funding and backing can also impose limitations. Funding success may be patchy, so that only some aspects of a research program may eventuate. Organizations that auspice research or boards that oversee it can impose constraints on what is undertaken or how it is pursued.[21]

The third contextual issue is organizational facilitators and barriers that can impact synthesis of disciplinary and stakeholder knowledge. Here the focus is on the research organizations. It may be useful to think about structure and culture separately. For example, structural issues can include the disciplinary mix in an organization, the availability of seed funding to encourage cross-disciplinary collaboration, and organizational financial mechanisms. If a center established to examine global climate change does not include any social scientists, for instance, it is probably less likely that good social science research will be part of the knowledge synthesis. In contrast, seed funding to encourage collaborations between researchers who have not worked together before may increase the numbers of disciplines included in the knowledge synthesis. Similarly, barriers to sharing money across different parts of an organization may work against joint funding applications and reduce disciplinary scope. Cultural factors can include organizational attitudes toward stakeholders and norms regarding idea

---

[20]For relevant discussion, see Part IV in this volume.

[21]For discussion of the benefits and limitations associated with funding from a particular program, see the discussion of the U.S. National Science Foundation's Integrative Graduate Education and Traineeship Program in Chapter 16, this volume.

exchange. If the organization's leaders are antagonistic toward particular stakeholders, such as big business or particular nongovernment organizations, it is less likely that their perspectives will be included in the knowledge synthesis. If it is "the done thing" that everyone attends morning or afternoon tea breaks or annual retreats, this may facilitate cross-fertilisation of ideas between disciplines.[22]

Compilation tasks associated with this question include collecting case examples

- dealing with overall context relevant to the knowledge synthesis;
- describing funding, endorsement, and other forms of authorization, along with any restrictions on knowledge synthesis; and
- describing the diversity and impact of organizational barriers and facilitators.

Question 5: What is the result of the synthesis of disciplinary and stakeholder knowledge?

One advantage of the structured approach resulting from the five-question framework is that it also provides a systematic process for evaluation, ensuring that each of the issues raised above is covered. Some of the relevant questions include the following:

- Was the systems view taken suitable? Would a different systems view have been more useful?
- Within the necessary limitations of the research, were the most worthwhile disciplines and stakeholders included? Was the balance between different disciplines and stakeholders fitting? Did any of those excluded turn out to be critical?
- Was the problem framed accurately?
- Was sufficient flexibility and iteration built into the processes of deciding on a systems view, scoping, boundary setting, framing, considering values, and harnessing and managing differences?
- Were applicable synthesis methods used? Would other methods have made better contributions? Were justifiable decisions made in choosing by whom and when the synthesis was undertaken?
- Did the host organizational structure or culture provide barriers to the knowledge synthesis? If so, were these effectually recognized and managed? Were facilitators beneficially mobilized?

---

[22]Chapters 14, 15, and 17 in this volume address different aspects of the organizational context of interdisciplinary research, with special emphasis in Chapters 14 and 15 on the research university. For a different take on the future of the interdisciplinary research enterprise in these contexts, see Chapter 6.

Conclusion

If we want to maximize the benefits of the initiatives described in this book, we need to ensure that, following the example of the Toolbox (Chap. 11, this volume), major advances can be accessed and implemented across a wide range of problem areas, not only in environmental science and policy but also in population health, national security, education, and so on. This may require the bold proposal, on the scale of a Big Science project, to construct a new discipline and populate it with the extensive array of concepts, methods, and case studies that interdisciplinary research, education, and communication have produced and continue to provide.

Take-Home Messages

- Getting serious about improving interdisciplinary communication—and through it, interdisciplinary research and education—involves overcoming the structural problems of fragmentation and unorganized diversity.
- Developing comprehensive compilations of relevant concepts and methods, along with illustrative case studies, is a good start.
- But compilations need to be solidly anchored in theory and practice, which a new discipline of Integration and Implementation Sciences (I2S) could provide.
- I2S has three major domains: (1) synthesising disciplinary and stakeholder knowledge, (2) understanding and managing diverse unknowns, and (3) providing integrated research support (combining the synthesized knowledge with a solid appreciation of remaining unknowns) for policy and practice change.
- Each domain is structured using a five-question framework, which for the first domain comprises these questions: (1) What is the synthesis of disciplinary and stakeholder knowledge aiming to achieve, and who is intended to benefit? (2) Which disciplinary and stakeholder knowledge is synthesized? (3) How is the disciplinary and stakeholder knowledge synthesized, by whom, and when? (4) What circumstances might influence the synthesis of disciplinary and stakeholder knowledge? (5) What is the result of the synthesis of disciplinary and stakeholder knowledge?
- These questions provide the scaffold for organizing the compilations of concepts, methods, and case studies.

References

Aldred, J., & Jacobs, M. (2000). Citizens and wetlands: Evaluating the Ely citizens' jury. *Ecological Economics, 34*(2), 217–232.

Badham, J. (2010, May). A compendium of modelling techniques. *Integration Insights, 12.* Retrieved from http://i2s.anu.edu.au/sites/default/files/integration-insights/integration-insight_12.pdf

Bammer, G. (2008). Enhancing research collaboration: Three key management challenges. *Research Policy, 37*, 875–887.

Bammer, G. (2012, February). *Strengthening interdisciplinary research: What it is, what it does, how it does it and how it is supported* (Report for the Australian Council of Learned Academies). Retrieved from http://i2s.anu.edu.au/sites/default/files/alcoa-report/bammer_2012.pdf

Bammer, G. (2013). *Disciplining interdisciplinarity: Integration and Implementation Sciences for researching complex real-world problems*. Canberra: Australian National University E Press. Retrieved from http://epress.anu.edu.au/titles/disciplining-interdisciplinarity

Bammer, G., & Smithson, M. (2008). The nature of uncertainty. In G. Bammer & M. Smithson (Eds.), *Uncertainty and risk: Multidisciplinary perspectives* (pp. 289–304). London: Earthscan.

Brocklehurst, N. J., Hook, G., Bond, M., & Goodwin, S. (2005). Developing the public health practitioner work force in England: Lessons from theory and practice. *Public Health, 119*(11), 995–1002.

Cardiff Council. (2005). *Reducing Cardiff's ecological footprint: A resource accounting tool for sustainable consumption*. Cardiff, Wales, UK: Author.

Checkland, P. (1984). *Systems thinking, systems practice*. Chichester, UK: John Wiley.

Collins, A., & Flynn, A. (2005). A new perspective on the environmental impacts of planning: A case study of Cardiff's International Sports Village. *Journal of Environmental Policy and Planning, 7*(4), 277–302.

Collins, A., & Flynn, A. (2007). Engaging with the ecological footprint as a decision-making tool: Process and responses. *Local Environment: The International Journal of Justice and Sustainability, 12*(3), 295–312.

Collins, A., Flynn, A., Wiedmann, T., & Barrett, J. (2006). The environmental impacts of consumption at a subnational level: The ecological footprint of Cardiff. *Journal of Industrial Ecology, 10*(3), 9–24.

Fisher, R., Ury, W., & Patton, B. (1991). *Getting to yes: Negotiating an agreement without giving in* (2nd ed.). London: Random House.

Franco, L. A. (2006). Forms of conversation and problem structuring methods: A conceptual development. *Journal of the Operational Research Society, 57*, 813–821.

McDonald, D., Bammer, G., & Deane, P. (2009). *Research integration using dialogue methods*. Canberra: Australian National University E-Press. Retrieved from http://epress.anu.edu.au/dialogue_methods_citation

Mesarovic, M. D. (Ed.). (1964). *Views on general systems theory: Proceedings of the Second Systems Symposium at Case Institute of Technology*. New York: John Wiley.

Michaelowa, A., & Koch, T. (2001). *Glossary of international climate policy terms* (Marrakesh Accords ed.). Hamburg, Germany: Hamburgisches Welt-Wirtschafts-Archiv.

Midgley, G. (2000). *Systemic intervention: Philosophy, methodology, and practice*. New York: Kluwer Academic/Plenum.

Murray, C. J. L., Salomon, J. A., & Mathers, C. (2000). A critical examination of summary measures of population health. *Bulletin of the World Health Organization, 78*(8), 981–994.

National Institutes of Health State-of-the-Science Panel. (2006). National Institutes of Health State-of-the-Science Conference statement: Tobacco use: Prevention, cessation, and control. *Annals of Internal Medicine, 145*(11), 839–844.

Reed, J., Pearson, P., Douglas, B., Swinburne, S., & Wilding, H. (2002). Going home from hospital—an appreciative inquiry study. *Health and Social Care in the Community, 10*(1), 36–45.

Rhodes, R. (1986). *The making of the atomic bomb.* London: Simon & Schuster.

Schnapp, L. M., Rotschy, L., Hall, T. E., Crowley, S., & O'Rourke, M. (2012). How to talk to strangers: Facilitating knowledge sharing within translational health teams with the Toolbox dialogue method. *Translational Behavioral Medicine, 2,* 469–479. doi:10.1007/s13142-012-0171-2

Stankey, G. H., Clark, R. N., & Bormann, B. T. (2005, August). *Adaptive management of natural resources: Theory, concepts, and management institutions.* Portland, OR: U.S. Department of Agriculture, Forest Service, Pacific Northwest Research Station. Retrieved from http://www.fs.fed.us/pnw/pubs/pnw_gtr654 .pdf

Sterman, J. D. (2000). *Business dynamics: Systems thinking and modeling for a complex world.* Boston: Irwin/McGraw-Hill.

Wackernagel, M., & Rees, W. E. (1996). *Our ecological footprint: Reducing human impact on the earth.* Gabriola Island, British Columbia, Canada: New Society.

World Commission on Dams. (2000). *Dams and development: A new framework for decision-making.* London: Earthscan.

Wright, T. S. A. (2006). Giving "teeth" to an environmental policy: A Delphi study at Dalhousie University. *Journal of Cleaner Production, 14*(9–11), 761–768.

Author Index

Subject Index

⑤SAGE research**methods**

The essential online tool for researchers from the world's leading methods publisher

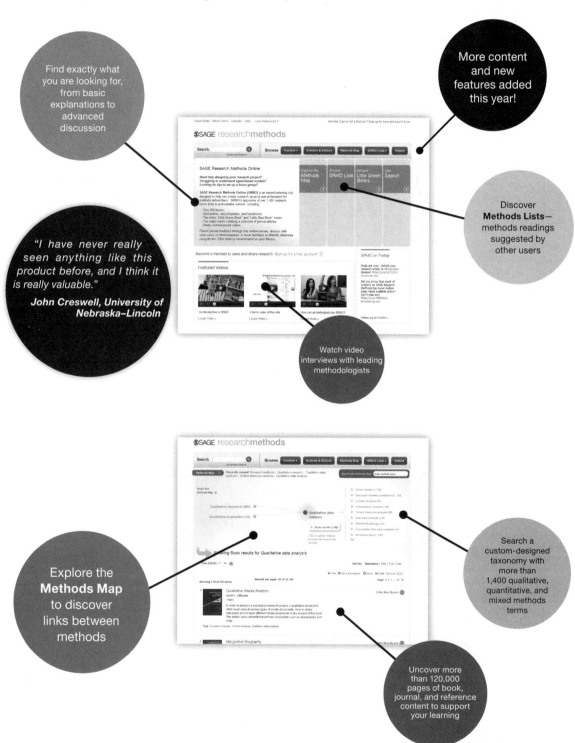

Find exactly what you are looking for, from basic explanations to advanced discussion

More content and new features added this year!

"I have never really seen anything like this product before, and I think it is really valuable."

John Creswell, University of Nebraska–Lincoln

Discover **Methods Lists**— methods readings suggested by other users

Watch video interviews with leading methodologists

Explore the **Methods Map** to discover links between methods

Search a custom-designed taxonomy with more than 1,400 qualitative, quantitative, and mixed methods terms

Uncover more than 120,000 pages of book, journal, and reference content to support your learning

Find out more at
www.sageresearchmethods.com